INTRODUCTION TO
Social Work

The People's Profession (5th Edition)

RELATED BOOKS OF INTEREST

Getting Your MSW: How to Survive and Thrive in a Social Work Program, **Second Edition**
Karen M. Sowers and Bruce A. Thyer

Food for Thought: A Two-Year Cooking Guide for Social Work Students
Kevin Corcoran

Women in Social Work Who Have Changed the World
Alice Lieberman

Introduction to Competence-Based Social Work: The Profession of Caring, Knowing, and Serving
Michael E. Sherr and Johnny M. Jones

The Practice of Social Work in North America: Culture, Context, and Competency Development
Kip Coggins

Essential Skills of Social Work Practice: Assessment, Intervention, and Evaluation, **Second Edition**
Thomas O'Hare

Navigating Human Service Organizations, **Third Edition**
Rich Furman and Margaret Gibelman

Straight Talk About Professional Ethics, **Second Edition**
Kim Strom-Gottfried

Modern Social Work Theory, **Fourth Edition**
Malcolm Payne

INTRODUCTION TO SOCIAL WORK
The People's Profession

Sophia F. Dziegielewski
University of Central Florida

Debra Nelson-Gardell
The University of Alabama

Ira Colby
University of Houston

Oxford University Press is a department of the University of Oxford.
It furthers the University's objective of excellence in research, scholarship,
and education by publishing worldwide. Oxford is a registered trade mark
of Oxford University Press in the UK and in certain other countries.

Published in the United States of America by Oxford University Press
198 Madison Avenue, New York, NY 10016, United States of America.

© 2025 by Oxford University Press

For titles covered by Section 112 of the US Higher Education Opportunity
Act, please visit www.oup.com/us/he for the latest information about
pricing and alternate formats.

All rights reserved. No part of this publication may be reproduced,
stored in a retrieval system, or transmitted, in any form or by any means,
without the prior permission in writing of Oxford University Press,
or as expressly permitted by law, by license, or under terms agreed with
the appropriate reprographics rights organization. Inquiries concerning
reproduction outside the scope of the above should be sent to the Rights
Department, Oxford University Press, at the address above.

You must not circulate this work in any other form
and you must impose this same condition on any acquirer

CIP data is on file at the Library of Congress.
Library of Congress Control Number: 2023049401
ISBN 978-0-19-763769-2

Printed by Marquis, Canada

About the Authors

Sophia F. Dziegielewski, PhD, LCSW, referred to as "Dr. D.," is a professor emerita with the School of Social Work at the University of Central Florida. Throughout her academic, administrative, and practice career she has been active in health and mental health practice and research, maintaining her license and serving as an expert witness in the courts. For over seventeen years she chaired the institutional review board at two major universities, providing oversight for the protection of human subjects in all the universities' research studies and clinical trials. Her scholarly productivity ranks  among the highest in her profession, with a Google Scholar H index of 36. To her credit, she is the recipient of numerous awards supporting her research and practice activity, and has authored over 165 publications, including 8 textbooks in health and mental health, 110 articles, 31 book chapters, and hundreds of workshops and community presentations.

For the past fifteen years, Dr. Dziegielewski has served as editor in chief of the *Journal of Social Service Research*. She has received seven federal- and state-level funded grants. In 2016, she received the Educator of the Year Award from the National Association of Social Workers, Florida Chapter. One of her most popular textbooks, *DSM-5 in Action*, outlines many of the most common mental health disorders along with assessment and treatment strategy. She also has two textbooks in psychopharmacology designed for non-medically trained individuals. Considered an expert in social worker licensure, she created and implements a highly acclaimed social work license exam preparation course that has helped over twenty thousand social workers across the United States to successfully pass their exams.

Debra Nelson-Gardell, PhD, LICSW, serves as an associate professor, PhD program director, and coordinator of international programs in the School of Social Work at the University of Alabama in Tuscaloosa, Alabama. Trained in clinical social work at the master's and doctoral levels, she has presented at local, regional, state, national, and international conferences. With the career goal of joining social work practice with social work research, Dr. Nelson-Gardell has worked as a social work treatment provider,

supervisor, program evaluator, consultant, presenter, educator, researcher, and administrator. Her clinical expertise focuses on intervening with the mental health aftereffects of interpersonal victimization using cognitive behavioral interventions, along with trauma systems therapy and eye movement desensitization and reprocessing. Her teaching focuses on micro-level social work practice, along with research methods with an emphasis in qualitative and mixed methods at the doctoral level. She is proud of her record of teaching and mentoring, with a history of over thirty years of social work education instruction at all three levels of social work education, including completed mentorship of fifteen doctoral graduates, with five more underway. She has worked extensively with scholars from outside the United States in both teaching and research. Her leadership of students to engage in international social work learning experiences includes the creation and oversight of an international professional social work placement program and the mentoring of over fifty social work students who completed their professional social work internships outside the United States.

Dr. Nelson-Gardell's areas of research and scholarship include childhood emotional trauma with a focus on sexual victimization, sexual victimization disclosure across the life span, family social work, and program evaluation. With a solid history of publication, her vision for social work education is to harness the power of information in service of the values of our social work profession. Dr. Nelson-Gardell believes information serves as currency in the practice and educational landscape. She desires social workers to have the resources they need to enact the changes needed to improve all our lives. Self-care matters to Dr. Nelson-Gardell, and she relies on her husband, her cat, and her paper-crafting hobby for that purpose.

Ira Colby had an exciting and storied five-decade career in social work. His work allowed him to travel throughout the United States and around the world, where he learned from and worked with leading scholars and social work practitioners, passionate advocates, governmental officials, and Nobel peace laurates. His work in social work education began in the early 1970s and over time he held a variety of administrative positions in social work and criminal justice programs in public and private settings; his work culminated in a fifteen-year tenure as dean of the University of Houston Graduate College of Social Work. He was elected or appointed to numerous national and international leadership positions, such as president of the Council on Social Work Education; co-chair of the National Association of Social Workers (NASW) Advocacy Network for Social Work Education and Research; chair of the CSWE–NASW Congressional Fellows Committee; a member of the Hong Kong, China Social Work Registration Board; and a member of the International Association of Schools of Social Work Board of Directors. His public policy work in Virginia, Florida, Texas, and Washington, DC, included advocacy for expanding services to at-risk youth, in particular runaways, throwaways, and pushouts. His public policy work in Texas led to the creation of the state-funded initiative STAR Program (Services to At-Risk Youth).

Dr. Colby authored more than 79 articles, book chapters, and books while presenting 110 papers or invited speeches worldwide. Dr. Colby has been recognized by several universities, honorary societies, and state legislatures. These include honorary professorships in China and Wales and an honorary doctorate of humanics from Springfield College, the Distinguished Alumni Award from the VCU School of Social Work, emeritus status granted by the University of Houston Board of Regents, and recognition by the NASW as a pioneer. Today, with his wife and best friend of fifty-fhree years (and still counting), he lives in southern Vermont.

Table of Contents

PREFACE XXI

PART ONE: THE CONTEXT OF SOCIAL WORK 1

1 Social Work: The Profession 3

    1.1 Toward a Definition of Social Work 8
        Formal Education Defines the Basis of Professional Social Work 15

    1.2 Social Work Defined 16

    1.3 Becoming a Social Worker 19

    1.4 The Professional Social Worker 25

    1.5 The Importance of Professional Membership 27

    <u>BOXES</u>
        1.1. MISSION AND VARIOUS DEFINITIONS OF SOCIAL WORK 17
        1.2. EXAMPLES OF SOCIAL WORK MEMBERSHIP ORGANIZATIONS 30
        Summary 31
        Questions to Think About 32
        References 32

2 Social Welfare: A System's Response to Personal Issues, Social Justice, and Public Problems 35

    2.1 Welfare Quiz 36

    2.2 Toward a Definition of Social Welfare 38
        Respect and Dignity: A Social Worker's Premise 38
        Social Services for Social and Economic Justice 40

    2.3 Social Welfare Defined 45

    2.4 Residual and Institutional Social Welfare 46
        Residual Social Welfare 47
        Institutional Social Welfare 49

    2.5 Is Everyone Really on Welfare? 51

    2.6 Public Social Welfare 53
        Federal Welfare 53
        State Welfare 55
        Local Welfare 55

2.7 Private Social Welfare 55
2.8 Social Work in the Social Welfare System 56
    The Fading Distinction between Public and Private 58
    Cost Containment versus Quality 59

TABLES AND BOXES
    2.1. EXAMPLES OF RESIDUAL AND INSTITUTIONAL PROGRAMS 46
    2.2. TEN LARGEST TAX EXPENDITURES FOR FISCAL YEAR 2019 52
    2.3. EXAMPLES OF SOCIAL WELFARE PROFESSIONALS BY PRIMARY OR SECONDARY CLASSIFICATION 57
    2.1. EACH DAY IN AMERICA FOR ALL CHILDREN 41
    2.2. WELFARE: CRITICS OF WELFARE ACROSS THIRTY-EIGHT YEARS; NOTHING REALLY CHANGES 48
    2.3. FEDERAL SOCIAL WELFARE PROGRAMS 54
    Summary 60
    Quiz Answers 60
    References 61

3 How Did We Get Here from There? 64

3.1 Time for a Brief History Quiz 65
3.2 The Elizabethan Poor Law of 1601 67
3.3 Colonial America 68
3.4 Nineteenth-Century Reform Efforts 72
    Almshouses and Asylums 72
    Charity Organization Societies 74
    Settlement House Movement 75
3.5 The Twentieth Century 76
    Social Reform in the 1960s 78
    The 1980s and 1990s: A Return to the Work Ethic 79
3.6 Compassionate Conservatism and the New Millennium 80

BOX
    3.1. SELECTED DATES IN AMERICAN SOCIAL WELFARE HISTORY 70
    Summary 85
    Movies to See 86
    Quiz Answers 88
    References 88

4 So, You Want to Be a Social Worker! 90

4.1 The Education of a Social Worker 91
4.2 Accreditation and Why It Matters 97
    Council on Social Work Education 97
    Commission on Accreditation 99
    Commission on Educational Policy 100

4.3 Social Workers Today **112**
    What Are Social Workers Paid? 113
    Where Do Social Workers Work? 114

4.4 Getting a Social Work Job after Graduation **115**
    Prepare Your Resume Carefully 116
    Licensing Requirements 116
    Networking with Social Work Professionals 117
    Use Your Field Placement Experience 117
    Use the Internet, of Course! 118
    Get to Know Your Social Work Faculty Advisors and Instructors 119
    Explore Your Social Work Student Association or Club 120
    Last Thoughts About Your Job Search 120
    Self-Care 120

<u>TABLES AND BOX</u>
    4.1. NUMBER OF ACCREDITED BSW AND MSW PROGRAMS AND NUMBER OF PHD/DSW PROGRAMS 95
    4.2. NUMBER OF BSW, MSW, AND PHD/DSW STUDENTS AND GRADUATES OF ACCREDITED PROGRAMS 98
    4.3. 2022 EDUCATIONAL POLICY AND ACCREDITATION STANDARDS: NINE CORE COMPETENCIES FOR SOCIAL WORK EDUCATION 103
    4.4. SOCIAL WORK POSITIONS BY COMMON WORK ROLES, AUSPICES, SETTING, AND PRACTICE AREA 114
    4.5. A SALARY OF $63,000 IN HOUSTON, TEXAS, IN OCTOBER 2022 IS THE SAME AS... 121
    4.1. SPECIALIZATION MODELS 109
    Summary 121
    References 122

PART TWO: THE PRACTICE OF SOCIAL WORK 125

5 Social Work Practice 127

5.1 Understanding Diversity **130**
5.2 Cultural Responsiveness and Cultural Humility **131**
5.3 Technology, Societal Lag, and Changing Times **132**
5.4 Cultural Influences in the Assessment Process **134**
5.5 The Basics of Practice **136**
5.6 Concepts Essential to Social Work Practice **137**
    Skills 137
    Knowledge Base 139
    Values and Ethics 140

- 5.7 Importance of Anti-oppressive Social Work **143**
- 5.8 Trauma and Recovery **144**
- 5.9 Differentiating between Generalist and Specialist Practice **145**
  - Generalist Practice 145
  - Specialist Practice 146
- 5.10 The Emergence of Evidence-Based Social Work Practice **147**
- 5.11 The Steps in Professional Helping **148**
  - Social Work Process 149
  - Evaluation and Follow-Up 152
- 5.12 Practice Application: The Role of the Medical Social Worker **152**
  - Case Example Discussion 154

  BOX
  - 5.1. DYNAMIC INTERPLAY OF KNOWLEDGE, VALUES AND ETHICS, AND SKILLS 138
  - Summary 154
  - References 155

6 Recognizing Diversity and Applying It to Generalist Practice **159**

- 6.1 Diversity and Social Work Practice **162**
- 6.2 Measurement of Diverse People—the U.S. Census **167**
- 6.3 Diversity by Race and Ethnicity in the United States **169**
- 6.4 The Generalist Social Worker and Diversity **171**
  - Taking an Empowering Approach to Practice 171
  - Recognizing Clients and Client Systems through a Systems Perspective 173
- 6.5 Person-in-Situation: Guiding the Practice Framework **177**
- 6.6 Cultural Awareness and Selecting a Practice Method **179**
  - Micropractice 181
  - Mezzopractice 182
  - Macropractice 183
- 6.7 Recognizing Diversity and Short-Term, Evidence-Based Intervention Approaches **185**
- 6.8 We Will Never Have All the Answers! **189**
- 6.9 Cultural Awareness, Sensitivity, and Inclusion in Practice **190**

  BOXES
  - 6.1. THE CASE OF DON: CONSIDERING THE CLIENT AND THE CLIENT SYSTEM 174
  - 6.2. THE CASE OF MARIA: MICROPRACTICE 181
  - 6.3. THE CASE OF A DRUG-FREE COMMUNITY: MACROPRACTICE 184
  - Summary 192
  - References 195

Table of Contents | XV

PART THREE: SETTINGS FOR SOCIAL WORK PRACTICE 201

7 Poverty and Income Maintenance 203

7.1 Poverty Defined **208**
 Measuring Poverty 208
 Other Considerations in Measuring Poverty 211
 Number in Poverty versus Poverty Rate 212

7.2 Who Are the Poor? **213**
 Poverty and Location 215
 Poverty and Race 216
 Poverty and Gender 217
 Poverty and Age 218

7.3 Why Is There Poverty in a Wealthy Nation? **222**

7.4 Programs to Aid the Poor **223**
 Temporary Assistance for Needy Families 224
 Food Programs (SNAP, School, WIC) 228
 Supplemental Security Income 232
 Immigrants 232
 Earned Income Tax Credit 234

TABLES
 7.1. PROFILE OF PERSONS IN POVERTY, 2020 207
 7.2. 2021 DEPARTMENT OF HEALTH AND HUMAN SERVICES POVERTY GUIDELINES 209
 7.3. POVERTY STATUS 2000–2020 213
 7.4. POVERTY STATUS BY RACE AND HISPANIC ORIGIN (POPULATION IN THOUSANDS) 214
 7.5. POVERTY RATES BY AGE, GROUP, AND ETHNICITY, 2020 218
 7.6. POVERTY STATUS OF PEOPLE BY AGE 219
 7.7. NAMES OF STATE TEMPORARY ASSISTANCE FOR NEEDY FAMILIES (TANF) PROGRAMS 224

Summary 234
Further Readings on Theories About Poverty 236
References 237

8 Child Welfare Services 241

8.1 The Child Welfare System Defined **245**

8.2 America's Diverse Children and Their Families **247**

8.3 The Rights of Children **251**

8.4 The Design of the American Child Welfare System **254**
 Child Protective Services 254
 Family Preservation Services 257
 Out-of-Home Services 258

8.5 Children with Special Needs **264**
　　Other Services 266
8.6 Child Sexual Abuse and Trauma **267**
　　Mandatory Reporting: Who Is Expected to Report? 268
TABLE AND BOXES
　　8.1. AMERICA'S MOST VULNERABLE CHILDREN: A SNAPSHOT 255
　　8.1. CHILD FACT SHEET 251
　　8.2. THE BEGINNINGS OF CHILD PROTECTIVE SERVICES: THE CASE OF MARY ELLEN 256
　　8.3. MYTHS AND FACTS ABOUT OUT-OF-HOME PLACEMENTS 259
　　Summary 272
　　References 273

9 Health Care 279

9.1 Efforts toward Inclusive Health Care Access **284**
9.2 Defining Health Care Social Work **288**
9.3 The Practice of Health Care Social Work **291**
9.4 A Brief History of Health Care Social Work **292**
9.5 Understanding the Current Health Care Environment **297**
9.6 Roles and Tasks of the Health Care Social Worker **301**
9.7 Direct Practice **301**
　　Focus on the Interprofessional Approach 304
9.8 Support Services **305**
　　Direct Supervision 306
　　Health Education and Health Counseling 307
　　Administration 308
　　Acute and Long-Term Care Settings 309
　　Hospital Emergency Room Social Work 311
　　Home Care Services 313
　　Hospice Social Work 314
9.9 Why Do It? **315**
TABLE AND BOX
　　9.1. TYPES OF COLLABORATIVE TEAMS 290
　　9.1. AFFORDABLE CARE ACT (PATIENT'S BILL OF RIGHTS) 285
　　Summary 319
　　References 321

10 Mental Health 328

- 10.1 Multidimensional Psychosocial Assessment 332
- 10.2 Placing a Diagnosis and Use of the *DSM* 340
- 10.3 The Behavioral Biopsychosocial Approach 341
- 10.4 When Medical and Mental Health Conditions Coexist 343
  - When There Is More Than One Mental Health Diagnosis: The Dual Diagnosis 345
- 10.5 Mental Health and Working with the Family in Acute Care Settings 349
- 10.6 Telemental Health and the Electronic Age 354
- 10.7 The Mentally Ill in the Criminal Justice System 356

TABLES AND BOXES

- 10.1. BIOMEDICAL OR BIOLOGICAL FACTORS TO BE CONSIDERED IN MENTAL HEALTH ASSESSMENT 345
- 10.2. SOCIAL FACTORS TO BE CONSIDERED IN THE MENTAL HEALTH ASSESSMENT 345
- 10.3. PSYCHOLOGICAL FACTORS TO BE CONSIDERED IN MENTAL HEALTH ASSESSMENT 350
- 10.4. FUNCTIONAL/SITUATIONAL FACTORS TO BE CONSIDERED IN A MENTAL HEALTH ASSESSMENT 359
- 10.1. MENTAL ILLNESS CAN STRIKE ANYONE AND THE CONSEQUENCES CAN BE DEVASTATING: A TRUE CASE STORY 333
- 10.2. MENTAL HEALTH SOCIAL WORK PRACTICE IN THE NEW MILLENNIUM 348
- 10.3. PROFESSIONAL CONTACT INFORMATION AND EMAIL ADDRESSES 348

Summary 359
Questions to Consider 361
References 361

11 Older Adults 367

- 11.1 Defining the Older Adult and Avoiding Ageism 373
- 11.2 Aging: What Can Be Expected 374
- 11.3 Theoretical Frameworks for Practice with Older Adults 377
- 11.4 Health, Mental Health, and the Older Adult 380
  - The Affordable Care Act 383
  - Physical Health Conditions and the Older Adult 385
  - Mental Health and the Older Adult 386
  - Continued Care Options and the Need for Extended Care 389
- 11.5 Community Care and Case Management 390
- 11.6 Employment and Older Adults 391
  - Living Longer, Working Longer 391
  - Retirement Life Changes 393

11.7 Abuse, Neglect, Risk of Exploitation, and Aging **398**
11.8 Assessing Suicide Risk and Planning for Death **399**
  BOXES
    11.1. ERIKSON'S STAGES OF HUMAN DEVELOPMENT 377
    11.2. DISENGAGEMENT THEORY 378
    11.3. ACTIVITY THEORY 379
    11.4. THE PAIN IN MY ELBOW 381
    11.5. SOCIAL SECURITY RETIREMENT BENEFITS 393
    11.6. GETTING COMMITMENT AND FORMULATING A SAFETY PLAN 401
    Summary 403
    References 404

12 Intimate Partner Violence **411**

12.1 Intimate Partner Violence Defined **413**
12.2 Risk Factors for Perpetrating IPV **415**
12.3 Barriers to Escaping IPV **416**
12.4 Helping Survivors of Abuse **420**
   Children: The Forgotten Victims 421
   The Legal System 422
   The Role of the Social Worker 423
12.5 Practice Application: The Role of the Women's Shelter Social Worker **428**
  TABLES
    12.1. TYPES OF ABUSE 415
    12.2. RISK IDENTIFICATION 417
    Summary 430
    References 431

13 Social Work Advocacy in the Political Arena: Economic and Environmental Justice **437**

13.1 What Is Meant by Politics? **440**
13.2 Why Politics and Social Work? **441**
13.3 Social Work Values and Political Activity **443**
13.4 A Historical Overview of Political Activity by Social Workers **444**
13.5 Electoral and Legislative Politics **449**
13.6 Social Work Organizations and Electoral Politics **450**
   Education Legislative Network 451
   Political Action for Candidate Election 452
   Social Workers and Political Campaigns 457
   Lobbying for Social Work Legislation 459

13.7 Community Organization: Linking the Political to the Community 463

TABLE AND BOXES

    13.1. VOTING: WHAT CAN A SOCIAL WORKER DO IN A POLITICAL CAMPAIGN? 458

    13.1. TERMS AND DEFINITIONS USED BY POLITICAL ACTION FOR CANDIDATE ELECTION (PACE), 2014 452

    13.2. EXAMPLE OF A CANDIDATE SURVEY 455

    13.3. SALUTATIONS FOR LETTER WRITING 461

    Summary 464

    References 466

PART FOUR: EXPANDING HORIZONS FOR SOCIAL WORK 469

14 Global Social Welfare 471

14.1 Social Work Is Expanding Globally 476

14.2 How Do We Compare Different Nations? 477

14.3 How Do We Look at International Social Welfare? 482

14.4 International Social Welfare Associations 484

    UN Structures 484

    U.S. Government Agencies 486

    Private Voluntary Bodies 487

14.5 International Professional Social Welfare Organizations 487

    International Federation of Social Workers 487

    International Association of Schools of Social Work 494

    International Council on Social Welfare 495

14.6 International Initiatives of the NASW and CSWE 498

    National Association of Social Workers 498

    Council on Social Work Education 499

    Other Programs 500

TABLES AND BOXES

    14.1. WELFARE TRENDS ON SELECTED ISSUES IN THE THREE WORLDS 481

    14.2. COMPARISON OF ELEVEN WELFARE STATE VARIABLES 482

    14.1. THE WORLD SYSTEM 479

    14.2. REGIONS OF THE WORLD AS DEFINED BY THE WORLD BANK 479

    14.3. MEMBERS OF THE INTERNATIONAL FEDERATION OF SOCIAL WORKERS, 2014 488

    14.4. GLOBAL DEFINITION OF SOCIAL WORK AS POSTED IN VARIOUS LANGUAGES BY THE INTERNATIONAL FEDERATION OF SOCIAL WORKERS, 2014 490

    14.5. MEETINGS SPONSORED BY THE INTERNATIONAL FEDERATION OF SOCIAL WORKERS 493

Summary 500
References 504

15 **Conclusion** 509

15.1 The Time to Decide Is Approaching **514**
   The Non–Social Work Major 515
   The Social Work Major 517

15.2 The Future and You **522**
   Social Work as a Profession: Future Considerations 523
   The American Social Welfare System: The Future 526

15.3 Social Work Practice **529**

15.4 Special Topic: Regulation of Social Work Practice **531**
   Why Do We Regulate Occupations and Why Is Credentialing Important? 531

   TABLE
   15.1. PARTIAL LIST OF OCCUPATIONS REGULATED BY THE STATE OF FLORIDA 532

   Summary and Final Thoughts 534
   References 535

Appendix A: Selected National and International Social Work Associations and Related Web Pages 539

Glossary 541

Index 547

Preface

We understand that your career activities will comprise much of your day-to-day life and provide income for you and your family, but they should also be personally rewarding. In social work, your work activities can result in not only helping clients and client systems but also reaching beyond the intended targets, thereby creating a life legacy. Feeling a sense of accomplishment when you make a difference in someone else's life provides a natural high that is both uplifting and fulfilling. Social work provides ample opportunities to make positive differences in others' lives and to help make our communities better and safer for all people.

In the pages that follow, you will be introduced to the social work profession—its obvious strengths as well as its limitations. You will see how social work started and has grown from those early sixteenth- and seventeenth-century beginnings, working with poor and underserved populations, to the global profession of the early twenty-first century. In addition to the information about the field, each chapter introduces aspiring professionals to the context, explaining the variety of roles and associated tasks these social workers perform. Although social work is an old profession, rich in tradition, it remains dynamic, flexible, nimble, and open to change. Indeed, with the field's focus on the client and the client system, taking the perspective of person-in-situation and person-in-environment remains at its core. People, problems, situations, and the environmental context are never static, and all successful change strategy must be continuous and ongoing. To facilitate this process, in addition to examining the field of social work in its present form, we make suggestions for future exploration and expansion. A review of the past and the present and a look toward the future provides fertile ground for social workers to develop new services, allowing the best possible support and work with clients, be they individuals, a family, a neighborhood group, or even elected officials and advocacy groups.

By presenting the many facets of social work, we attempt to provide a realistic and varied overview to help you develop a more authentic understanding and appreciation of the profession. At a minimum, you will be exposed to what social workers do and the importance of considering the environmental context that surrounds all decisions. Throughout the book are bios of social workers who are doing some amazing things while clearly reflecting the heart and soul of the profession. You will discover they come from all walks of life, enjoy working with and being with others, and, to be very honest, make us proud of the profession. As you read their statements, you will see many similarities in their work: they believe strongly in allowing ethical principles and a respect for cultural diversity to guide their practice; they recognize that differences in individuals are acknowledged and that concepts such as dignity, worth, and respect, along with a nonjudgmental attitude, provide the cornerstone for their work. Their work is being done on a global stage as well as in local neighborhoods, literally down the street from us.

In this fifth edition of the book, it remains our hope that its success will be measured in part by whether it can help answer the following question: Is social work really the profession for me? If so, the book will introduce you to the field and the rewards and challenges that lie ahead. If not, we hope that you will gain increased awareness of the needs and struggles people face and the knowledge that most of these problems and issues are not self-perpetuated. And although you may not decide to become a social worker, what you learn in the chapters of this text will help to enrich your life and enhance your contributions to society no matter the career you choose.

Part One provides a broad overview of the profession, in which we introduce professional terminology and acronyms. This is followed by a discussion of social workers' typical employment settings, responsibilities, and salaries. After that, we explore, albeit briefly, the rich traditions within the field of social work, highlighting how the past clearly relates to the present and predicting what the future has in store.

In Part Two, you will be introduced to the practice of social work at the micro, mezzo, and macro levels. We discuss concepts such as the client system and the notion that this system almost always involves more than one person. Although it is possible to view clients as individuals, they are most often addressed in terms of context or systems. This can involve individuals, families, groups, communities, or policies that either directly or indirectly affect client system well-being.

The chapters in Part Three present several examples of the various practice settings where social workers are employed, along with suggestions for expanding current activities and exploring further development of new areas.

Part four discusses the expanding horizons for social work from global international connections to seeking economic and social justice through macro system level efforts and advocacy. Lastly, the conclusions chapter discusses important areas for social workers to consider and the importance of being proactive in all we do.

This book is unique in that it will challenge you to synthesize information about successes and events in the field. Activities are included to give beginning professionals a sense of hands-on learning. These activities will help you develop a more in-depth understanding of the profession. There is also an emphasis on the use of the internet, a tool that is part of all our lives. Case examples are used throughout to help you see the interface between what is written in the text and actual practice.

On a personal note, we would like to say that putting together this fifth edition, selecting and updating the topics most germane to the social work field, was not an easy task—nor should it have been. This book represents over 125 years of combined direct practice and teaching experience by the authors. All authors and contributors of this text committed to using our passion for the profession to introduce others to this exciting and challenging field. As practitioners, we believe that much can be learned from the clients we serve. In fact, many of the examples we present have been drawn from our own practical, administrative, or academic experience. Using our actual experiences in direct practice and as educators helped us decide how best to present information in a practical and informative way, one that is sensitive to students' interests and concerns while considering the important concepts central to a beginning social work course.

This book would not be complete if we did not acknowledge the individuals in our own support systems who have made this effort possible. Sophia Dziegielewski thanks her family, friends, and colleagues, who respect and support her passion for the field and tolerate her workaholic ways. Debra Nelson-Gardell offers gratitude for this opportunity to contribute and recognizes her extraordinary life partner, who offers consistent encouragement. Ira Colby thanks his wife and best friend of more than fifty years, Deborah, who has honestly critiqued his teaching, writing, and thinking.

Foremost, however, we would like to thank all the social workers who graciously allowed us to use their biographical sketches. Special thanks to our publisher, Oxford University Press, and to Sarah Jacobs and Aswini Ashokkumar for leading the editorial review as well as Hayden Merrick for his earlier contributions.

Now, with all of that said, we invite you to begin this adventure in learning about one of the oldest and most honorable helping professions ever developed. May this book and its description of the social work profession ignite a fire in you, as those we have helped throughout our careers in social work have done for us.

PART ONE
The Context of Social Work

Social Work
The Profession

CHAPTER 1: EPAS COMPETENCIES

Social work programs at the bachelor's and the master's level are accredited by the Council of Social Work Education (CSWE). CSWE's Educational Policy and Accreditation Standards (EPAS) describe the processes and criteria that social work courses should cover. In 2022, CSWE updated its EPAS standards. The following competencies are addressed in this chapter.

Competency 1: Demonstrate Ethical and Professional Behavior

Social workers understand the value base of the profession and its **ethical** standards, as well as relevant laws and regulations that may affect practice with individuals, families, groups, organizations, and communities.

Competency 3: Engage in Anti-racism, Diversity, Equity, and Inclusion in Practice

Social workers understand how racism and oppression shape human experiences and how these two constructs influence practice at the individual, family, group, organizational, and community levels and in policy and research.

Competency 5: Engage in Policy Practice

Social workers identify social policy at the local, state, federal, and global level that affects wellbeing, human rights and justice, service delivery, and access to social services. Social workers recognize the historical, social, racial, cultural, economic, organizational, environmental, and global influences that affect social policy.

Competency 6: Engage with Individuals, Families, Groups, Organizations, and Communities

Social workers understand that engagement is an ongoing component of the dynamic and interactive process of social work practice with, and on behalf of, individuals, families, groups, organizations, and communities.

Competency 8: Intervene with Individuals, Families, Groups, Organizations, and Communities

Social workers understand that **intervention** is an ongoing component of the dynamic and interactive process of social work practice.

When writing his classic work *Moby Dick* in 1851, Herman Melville began his work with a simple statement, "Call me Ishmael" (Melville, 1993, p. 3), followed by an incredible story depicting the quest of a sea-sailing captain to hunt down a great white whale. But what if Melville, sitting at his desk in his summer home in Pittsfield, Massachusetts, in 2023 started a new novel and began his work with the unpretentious words "Call me a social worker," as he detailed the life of a social worker trying to help people and their communities? Melville would describe the social worker's life as rewarding and exciting, with no two days alike. The worker's cases, Melville would write, run the gamut from simple to complex; whereas many are successfully resolved, some do not reach a positive outcome. Throughout the novel, Melville would repeatedly intimately describe the many challenges facing new and experienced social workers.

Herman Melville's social work novel might not make the *New York Times* bestseller list or be referenced centuries later, but it would be an honest attempt to portray the life and commitment necessary for social workers in the early twenty-first century. The profession of social work is an old one whose story began in the mid-1880s, when professional helping and assistance, often referred to as *social casework*, was first introduced. At this time, social workers were active with all types of people, regardless of age, color, or creed, and this helping activity involved individuals, families, groups, and communities in both public and private social service settings. In social work, the emphasis is placed on realizing that **client** helping efforts do not occur in silos. Therefore, professional helping efforts are embedded in addressing the client's needs as part of a system considering the *person-in-situation* or the *person-in-environment*.

• • •

Today, helping efforts focus on three areas of practice: **micro**, **mezzo**, and **macro**. These terms will be explained in further detail throughout this chapter and the book, but most social workers focus their helping efforts at the micro level, sometimes referred to as the **micro system** level. The micro level is best suited to individual practice efforts because this level focuses primarily on the needs of individuals, families, and groups. A mezzo perspective (sometimes referred to as the **mezzo system level**) consists of schools, communities, and neighborhoods, and in some cases professionals who work in administrative **roles**. The **macro** (a.k.a. **macro system level**) consists of large systems such as the health care system, the legislative system, and international organizations (Kelly, Schroeder, & Leighton, 2022). As you can see from the profession's initial roots, the comprehensiveness of serving clients and recognizing the importance of starting where the client is with a person-in-environment or person-in-situation approach at all levels of practice (micro, mezzo, and macro) has come a long way.

Social work is now a global profession and is reported to be one of the fastest growing professions internationally, with approximately 3 million social workers worldwide (International Federation of Social Workers [IFSW], 2022a). In the United States alone, there are approximately 700,000 social workers with the task of serving individuals, families, communities, and the society (National Association of Social Workers, 2022a). With more than 120,000 individual members, the **National Association of Social Workers (NASW)** is the world's largest professional membership organization for the profession (NASW, 2022b). For example, in October 2022, the NASW launched its first chapter in the central district of Kamenets, Podolsk, in Ukraine (IFSW, 2022b).

In addition to the NASW, there are at least eleven professional social work specialty practice settings in the United States that support specific interests or fields of practice, such as child welfare; children, adolescents, and young adults; health; mental health; private practice; school social work; research; gerontology; health care; and clinical social work. The memberships of these various associations comprise professional social workers in all occupations, from those who work with the elderly to those who work with infants. With approximately 20 percent of social workers serving clients in rural and underserved communities, collectively they help to address the needs of over sixty million Americans (Hogue & Huntington, 2019).

It would be incorrect to suggest that simply totaling the members of different social work membership groups or educational programs around the world would give us an accurate number. This is simply not the case. Put another way, counting the membership lists results in duplicate or double counting. Let us take the United States as an example. In 2022, the NASW, according to its website, totaled 120,000 members, yet the Department of Labor identified approximately 708,100 social work jobs in the

United States. Where were the other 588,100 social workers? Maybe some belonged to other social work groups. We cannot just count the membership rolls of each association, because social workers typically belong to multiple groups. Or maybe those positions posted did not require a professional degree in the field of social work to practice. Finally, some social workers are employed in positions that are not called social work, but that certainly require specific social work skills. Employee assistance programs in corporations are an example.

Since the field of social work comprises more than just trying to be helpful, another way of estimating the number of social workers is by addressing those who have professional education and training. To provide professional education to social workers in the United States, in 2022 there were 851 baccalaureate (n = 538) and master-level social work (n = 313) education programs accredited by the **Council on Social Work Education (CSWE)**, with 16 additional programs in **candidacy (pre-accreditation)** and 29 master's programs in candidacy (CSWE, 2022a).

In 2021, CSWE and its **Commission on Accreditation (COA)** launched a pilot program for the accreditation of professional practice for doctoral programs. These pilot programs will focus on advanced practice at the micro, mezzo, and macro levels and most will be titled with granting a doctorate in social work (**DSW**) (CSWE, 2022b). The Group for the Advancement of Doctoral Education in Social Work (2022) notes that they have over ninety programs worldwide that represent local universities in both PhD programs in social work and DSW programs. Historically, colleges and universities offering academic programs leading to a doctoral degree, either a doctorate in philosophy (**PhD**) or a DSW, were not accredited by the CSWE, so doctoral education varies from school to school, with a program's focus being influenced by the values and beliefs of its faculty. Individuals pursuing doctoral degrees in social work will often become employed in academic settings, although some will work in agency settings, primarily in education, administration, supervisory positions, or research.

As social work continues to grow globally, no precise figure or estimate of the number of social work educational programs worldwide exists. The **International Association of Schools of Social Work (IASSW)** reports that as of June 29, 2022, the "global census" of social work education member programs consisted of 416 entities worldwide (IASSW, 2022). Although looking at education numbers may be helpful, we must recognize that no one organization or group really knows the exact number of degreed (i.e., bachelor of social work [**BSW**], master of social work [**MSW**], DSW, or PhD) social workers in the world.

So, what can we conclude about the United States? If simply looking at membership in professional organizations or the number of educational programs won't work, what is next? We might simply have to accept that there may not be a way to count the exact number of social workers in our country—and recognize that this ambiguity is also common to other nations around the world. What we can agree on in 2023, however, is that there are more than 700,000 social workers nationwide. In addition, 250,000 are licensed in the United States and can practice independently (NASW, 2022a, 2023). Education-wise, a master's degree is considered the terminal degree for professional practice. The BSW and the first year of a two-year MSW program relate to the generalist practitioner with strict accreditation guidelines. The second year or the specialization of the MSW program and the DSW and PhD social work degree programs have flexibility in terms of scope of practice and requirements. The profession is female dominated, with approximately 90 percent of the graduates identifying as female. The social work profession also includes a diverse group of professionals, both racially and socioeconomically (Salsberg et al., 2020).

Let us forget the numbers for a moment and look at what we do know. Social work professionals are employed in more than 90 percent of the nations of the world. Schools of social work can be found all regions of the world—in the north, south, east, and west.

Social work is not unique to the United States or to the United Kingdom. We can conclude that social work is growing around the world based on both the number of social work educational programs and the number of nation-based professional membership associations (see Figure 1.1). This worldwide activity is primarily represented by three global associations: the IASSW, the International Consortium for Social Development, and the IFSW. In addition, social workers throughout the world can join social work membership associations like those in the United States in their own countries. In Canada, for example, social workers may join the Association canadienne des travailleuses et travailleurs sociaux (Canadian Association of Social Workers); the British Association of Social Workers is a large professional social work group in the United Kingdom; and the National Association of Social Workers in South Africa is a nongovernmental organization that supports social workers and the development of the profession in South Africa.

As global expansion of the profession continues, China, for example, is currently amid an expansion in social work (Niu & Haugen, 2019). After the profession was abolished during the so-called Cultural Revolution, social work is once again growing with the support of the Chinese central government. The Ministry of Civil Affairs reported that there were 669,000 certified social workers nationwide in 2020, an increase of approximately 534,000 from the 135,000 listed in 2019 (Ministry of Civil Affairs of the People's Republic of China, 2020). Although the applicability of Western models of practice may cause some social and political conflicts, social work as a profession in China continues to grow (Niu & Haugen, 2019). Interest in the profession continues to grow globally as well. Looking at the increasing number of social workers in China, as well as the newly established chapter of the NASW in Ukraine, we can easily deduce that the social work profession is being recognized and is growing in all regions of the world.

FIGURE 1.1
Social work is expanding, with advancing international ties.

1.1 TOWARD A DEFINITION OF SOCIAL WORK

Now that we have discussed the profession of social work and how the numbers are increasing through membership, employment, education, and globally, the question remains, What exactly is social work? Interestingly, although it is a well-established profession, any ten people will give you ten different answers. One weekend morning at a doughnut shop in Orlando, Florida, we asked ten people to describe what social workers do. We received the following responses:

- Social workers give out **food stamps, administer food stamp programs** and give money to freeloaders.
- I do not know.
- Do they work at the welfare office?
- They help abused kids.
- My mom had one while in the hospital and really liked that young gal!
- They work in mental hospitals.
- One helped my wife and I when we adopted our baby. He helped prepare us for parenting and has stayed in touch ever since. Now, some four years later, he still stays in touch.
- It is helping poor individuals to get services.
- Social workers are liberal thinkers that support programs for the poor.
- Help private and public agencies to help individuals in need.

One of the more interesting answers, however, was one from an older gentleman who said, "A social worker? I do not really know. Maybe they work at social events like the Wednesday night bingo game at the recreation center." See the activity below and try this yourself.

Activity
Select a few family members, or if you're really feeling ambitious, approach ten people at a local mall or any other shopping area and ask them, "What is social work?" Write down their answers. Also take notes on their nonverbal reactions to the question.

The variety of responses you will receive illustrates two major points. First, the profession is a diverse one, and this diversity means that the roles and tasks that social workers perform are varied and client or client-system relevant, so the tasks may often be poorly defined. Second, our neighbors, members of the public, are often confused about the profession. Many people simply do not understand the mission of this diverse profession. This confusion is deepened when social work professionals themselves define what they do based on their scope of practice, using job-specific descriptions such as health care social worker, working in **community organization**, adoptions worker, or health or mental health counselor. The profession of social work remains flexible because the tasks to be completed can vary depending on the individual needs of the client, the client system, and any greater system changes that are needed. The diversity and broad purview of social work practice make it difficult to reach a simple, all-inclusive definition of social work.

Social work is not the only profession that is difficult to define; however, professions whose tasks are easier to specify are received more positively by the community. For example, most people can describe accurately what a dentist, nurse, or physician does, or they can quickly describe the role of a stockbroker or a lawyer. Defining exactly what a social worker does and is expected to do is much more complex. Think about a dentist for a moment. What picture comes to mind? What do you see the dentist doing? Can you describe what the dentist's office looks like? When you think of health care profession, what does the nurse do? Again, what do you picture in your mind? Finally, think about a social worker. Can you visualize a social worker in the workplace? What are the typical duties? Do others share the same image?

Name: Joanne Terrell, MSW LICSW-S PIP
Place of Residence: Tuscaloosa, Alabama
College/university degrees: BA in psychology, State University of New York, and MSW, University of Alabama
Present position: I am a retired social work professor, having taught at the University of Alabama for twenty years. My area of expertise is forensic social work. Currently, I maintain a full-time private practice in forensic social work. As a forensic social worker, I work in both the family court and criminal  court systems. In the family court system, I work as a therapeutic divorce mediator. So at least four days per week I am working with families in high-conflict divorce and/or custody cases. I assist these families in reducing conflict between the parents and improving their co-parenting relationships. I also work with children who are victims of parental alienation, helping to improve their relationships with one or both their parents.

In the criminal justice system/courts, I have been qualified as a mitigation specialist and provide mitigation in a variety of cases, but mostly in death penalty cases. I usually provide services for those cases when their trials come up. But I am busy interviewing defendants and their family members and writing reports about two days per week.

What do you do in your spare time? I spend my spare time with my family and my dogs.
Why did you choose social work as a career? I chose social work as a profession because I saw how varied and enriching this profession can be. It is the only helping profession that allows you to work with clients in a variety of settings and work as an advocate for social

continues

continued

and economic justice. So, we work for the well-being of both the client and the community.

What is your favorite social work story? I have many stories. But the most touching story is this one. I went to interview a death penalty defendant in prison. He was already on death row, and we were working to overturn his death sentence. He came from a poor and abusive background. He was intellectually disabled and had been taken advantage of by much smarter co-defendants. After I was finished with his interview, he asked me if he could sing a religious hymn for me because he had a good singing voice. I said yes, of course, I would love to hear him sing.

So, he stood up in the middle of a bleak interview room, in his prison jumpsuit. He cleared his throat and began singing "Amazing Grace." The guards all stopped in their tracks. They were stunned (as was I) by the quality of and poignancy in his voice. Suddenly none of us was in a prison—we were in a church listening to the voice of an angel...

I believe it was his way of telling me: "I am more than the worst thing I did in my life."

What is one thing you would change in the community if you had the power to do so? The one thing I would change in our community is the unfair advantage privileged people have over the less fortunate, especially in the criminal justice system.

There is so much confusion about what social workers do that you might have had an experience like that of a former student who is now an accomplished social worker: A person at a holiday party asked what they studied in college. The social worker proudly announced "Social work." A disquieting hush spread over the room, and the party seemed to grind to a halt. Some of the social worker's relatives looked shocked and glanced around at other family members in astonishment. When the social worker's parent noted the reaction, the parent simply shrugged their shoulders and said, "That's nice," noting that this career choice was "just a youthful phase" and that the adult child's major could change before year's end. Although this young social worker has now become a successful university professor of social work, the parent and other relatives still refer to the college-educated adult as a psychologist! When asked why they keep making this mistake, they reply that they can usually explain to others what a psychologist does, but defining social work takes a lot more time and effort. "Besides," the parent still asks, "is there really that much of a difference?" Although this question may at first seem alarming, it is a question those in the profession must face daily. What further complicates this distinction is the fact that several professions do perform many of the same functions, making it difficult to formulate an exact role for social workers, particularly those in what is referred to as *direct practice* (Dziegielewski & Holliman, 2020).

Did You Know . . .

The member countries of the United Nations (UN) maintain missions in cities throughout the United States. You can learn from them about customs and cultural nuances that may affect your work with clients. Also, many international laws that affect practice pertain to individual visitors. If you are not sure about a particular situation, contact the relevant UN mission. Finally, a UN mission can provide you with a great deal of information about the welfare system of its home country.

Most social workers, old and new alike, have at least one or two related stories about how their families reacted when they announced that they had selected social work as a career, and many of the stories will parallel the one above. The confusion surrounding what social workers do, as well as the image of them working primarily with the poor and disenfranchised in our communities, complicates efforts to define what social work is—or, indeed, what people perceive it to be. Now, despite the difficulties in making a simple definition, can we define social work?

To reach a more inclusive definition of social work, let us start by considering some of the key factors that affect the provision of social work. Most people will agree that social work services include working with vulnerable populations; helping individuals, families, groups, and communities to adjust to role changes; and providing direct and indirect services to clients. To implement these services, a comprehensive professional education is required. First, most people would agree that the profession involves addressing the needs of **at-risk populations** in a community, and when looking at problem-solving activities, this often starts by concentrating on working directly with the individual-in-situation or the client in the environment. From this perspective, the professional helping activities performed by the social worker can be seen as the bridge between the person and the environment or the person and the situation.

Second, in our society most people would agree that the traditional definitions of family structure are changing, and societal resistance and trouble accepting and adjusting to these changes can lead to discriminatory practices and hate crimes. For example, the traditional family structure has changed. According to the 2021 U.S. Census, there were 1.2 million same-sex couple households, and it was estimated that 710,000 of the heads of these same-sex households were married (Scherer, 2022). This makes social workers important contributors in implementing helping activities designed to assist individuals, families, groups, communities, and the society to adjust to these basic societal changes.

Third, in the past, most of the helping activities and problem-solving assistance provided to people in the community were given face to face and within an agency-based setting. This traditional format for service delivery has been challenged with the increase in internet technology and the increased availability and expectation for utilizing telemedicine and teletherapy services. For many, this gift of convenience is also linked clearly to ableism for use and access to these services. Beyond teletherapy and telemedicine, just having access and a general understanding of what is included along with interpretation of a person's electronic record can be a daunting task. Ableism and the use of these services must always be considered, especially for older adults, who may not be able to use the technology as easily as younger adults (Lepkowsky, 2020, 2022). This lack of ability to access these services may connote unintentional **ageism** that results in **discrimination** against older adults who might be more familiar with accessing care through face-to-face or telephone-related contact (Lepkowsky & Arndt, 2019).

Fourth, social work is a profession and therefore requires a professional education, as well as clearly defined ethical standards for practice. Becoming aware professionally and helping others such as family and friends to understand what professional helping can entail is a crucial step to educating the public about what social workers do. Social workers practice under the guidelines of a strong professional ethical code. These practice standards are embodied in a professional code of **ethics**, where awareness and application remain crucial to approaching professional practice regardless of the employment setting (NASW, 2018).

In moving further toward a definition of social work, now let us explore these ideas more fully to develop an understanding of the breadth and depth of the profession. Thinking about helping people focuses our attention on what social workers do. Through programs and intervention services, social workers help people—individuals, families, groups, communities, and organizations—in their day-to-day life situations. A hallmark of social work helping is its focus on the interaction between person and social environment. Whereas a psychologist, for example, would consider primarily an individual's psychological state in trying to help, social workers go beyond this to provide a bridge that includes the interplay between the individual's life situation and social environment.

In the provision of social work services, at-risk populations comprise those people who, for any number of reasons, are vulnerable to any or all societal threats. Children and older adults are often viewed as at-risk populations. Other people considered at risk are those who may be victimized by a person or group through a series of life events that leaves them susceptible to unwarranted pain and resulting problems. Certainly, the larger context affects how we define at-risk populations. For example, the 2009 economic crisis led to home foreclosures and increased unemployment rates in all workforce sectors. Many middle-class individuals and families who had been financially secure found themselves, for reasons beyond their control, in significant at-risk situations. It is interesting how history repeats itself; in 2024, there is talk of another recession like the one that occurred in 2009. We need to recognize that any individual, at any time, may unexpectedly become at risk. Being at risk is not limited to one or two population groups, but crosses all ages, racial and ethnic groups, and socioeconomic statuses.

> ### Did You Know . . .
> **In social work, words matter.** Social workers worldwide are bound together by a simple ethical principle: All people are treated with respect and dignity. This basic ideal is written in the various codes of ethics of social work organizations, from the U.S.-based NASW to the global IFSW. The words we use to describe people and situations are a clear indicator of how one perceives others. Some words are clearly and tenaciously hateful, while others are less obvious.

Think for a moment about what an "illegal alien" is. What image does the word *illegal* conjure up for you? Criminals, drug dealers, hustlers . . . the list goes on. And *alien*: for many, the mind's eye sees a terrestrial from another planet who is invading our planet to destroy our way of living and take over our communities. In other words, an alien is "different from me" and cannot be trusted in any form or manner. A simple question for you, the reader, is, How would you feel being called an illegal or an alien or an illegal alien?

Let's consider the term *developmental disability*, which reflects a broad and diverse group of chronic disorders, both mental and physical. Dyslexia, Tourette's syndrome, Down syndrome, autism spectrum disorder (including Asperger's syndrome and autism), and attention deficit hyperactivity disorder are some of the more common developmental conditions. We are pretty sure that you have heard people who face any of these challenges referred to as *disabled* or a *disabled person*. But let's step back for a moment. What comes to mind when you hear the phrase "disabled person" or "person with a disability?" For some, there is the notion that a disabled person is unable to fully participate in their community, or they just need help most of the time. So, here is a question: Do you know someone who wears glasses or uses a hearing aid? Do you think that person is a disabled person? Most folks would say no. Yet, without glasses or hearing aids, these people would not be able to fully participate in their community and would need special assistance. Just as these individuals have *adaptive equipment* (glasses and hearing aids) at their disposal, so, too, do individuals with developmental disabilities. Visit the International Paralympic Committee web page and look at the various global sports that so-called disabled persons are engaged in worldwide. Here's another quick question: Can you do any of these sports at an international level with the skills these individuals demonstrate? A more inclusive description of people with developmental or physical challenges, in fact, for all of us, is "people with differing abilities." This is not a demeaning phrase, but one that shows respect for all people. This phrase also accepts all people for who they are.

As you read the following chapters, you will see the purposeful use of words in social work that demonstrate respect for others. This is not a "woke" mentality, but reflects that we, as social workers, firmly believe in respecting others no matter who they are, their politics, their gender identity, or any attribute that we or others feel are "wrong" or uncomfortable. People in the social work profession try to be careful with terminology because we believe that the words to describe the conditions people experience can inadvertently **stigmatize** and **label** them inaccurately and unfairly. As professionals, we do indeed believe that words matter.

Like other disciplines such as business and law, the social work profession is *sanctioned* to provide certain services. **Sanction** refers to the official, formal blessing or recognition of the need for a service or program. Professional sanctioning of services comes in many forms, but state licensing or state registration and professional certification are among the more common types. Community funding agents, such as the United Way or private foundations, also sanction an activity by supporting it financially. When a funding entity such as the United Way supports a social service agency, it is indicating its belief that the services provided are important to the community good. This type of support is often called having *the gold stamp of approval*. Having the legitimacy that comes from such support is essential in gaining community approval. Formalized public (or community) sanctioning of the provision of social services can also protect the public by distinguishing between authorized and unauthorized service delivery.

Agency-based practice consists of social work services conducted by or delivered under the auspices of **social welfare** agencies. A social service agency can be public (funded by federal, state, or local tax dollars) or it can be private (funded by donations or foundations and commonly referred to as a nonprofit or, in the international community, a **nonprofit and nongovernmental agency**). Most practicing social workers are agency based; that is, they are employed by either a public or a nongovernmental social services agency. In addition to social service agencies, this can include other type of agencies and organizations such as hospitals, physicians' offices, rehabilitation facilities, and other types of for-profit or nonprofit agencies. In addition, a smaller percentage of social workers provide professional practice in group counseling practices or full-time independent private practice. Independent practitioners are educated at the master's degree level or beyond; some states allow bachelor-level social workers to engage in independent practice, but only in limited situations and under direct supervision. For independent decision-making and billing in any of these settings, a license is usually required. More information about licensure and how it relates to professional practice will be presented later in this book.

It is common for social workers, both students and practitioners alike, to want to become private practitioners in mental health and other health-related settings. As will be discussed later, launching a successful private practice is difficult. When setting up a sole practitioner in clinical practice, being an educated provider is essential. This will require knowledge of a variety of potential barriers, such as restricted and reduced insurance reimbursements, the growth and resulting competitiveness of other helping professions, the significant costs of establishing and maintaining a private practice, and the difficulty and ethical expectations when soliciting new clients. Even if one wishes to pursue a private clinical practice, the social worker must be cognizant, as acknowledged by most professionals working in this area, that the old notion of long-term clinical therapy is rare. Outcomes-focused intervention strategies where mutually negotiated treatment gains are desired in the fastest, most efficient means possible predominate (Dziegielewski & Holliman, 2020).

Formal Education Defines the Basis of Professional Social Work

Earlier in this chapter, we talked about educational programs to identify the profession. Now we will focus briefly on the advanced education that provides the beginning skills for defining what a social worker can do. But we want to be careful not to put the cart before the horse and continue adding to this information by further identifying the basic requirements to be a professional social worker. To start the educational process, being a professional requires, at a minimum, a formal four-year baccalaureate degree or a graduate degree in social work. College- or university-based professional education provides the basic preparation for social work practice. Professional social work education takes place in baccalaureate and graduate-level degree programs at colleges and universities. Such programs are accredited by the CSWE. Simply stated, a social worker must have a degree in social work from an academic program accredited by the CSWE. Do not worry; we will go into more detail about the council and its sanctioning authority. The bottom line to remember is that a degree in sociology, psychology, or any other course of study does not qualify a person to be a social worker.

Professional social work education begins in the classroom setting. This is expanded and strengthened by practice-based experiences through what is commonly called field education, field practicum, or internships involving **field practicum placements**. In an internship, students work in a specific field agency or setting, where they practice the skills, apply the theories taught in school, and begin the integration of the entire educational experience, both classroom and field, into the so-called professional self. To further advance their professional education, social workers, following graduation, typically begin working in a social work setting under the direct supervision of an experienced professional social worker while completing **continuing education** programs each year. The ongoing continuing education requirement recognizes the profession's long-standing belief that a professional social worker's education is never-ending, because new ways of knowing and doing are discovered through research and practice.

All accredited educational programs have ethical standards of practice among the key components of social work education. Social work, like other helping professions, has an established and coordinated professional set of standards. This is often referred to as a code of ethics, which is designed to govern the moral behavior of those in the field (NASW, 2018). In social work, the professional is bound to the code of a particular membership organization or state licensing board. For example, if you are a member of the NASW or the IFSW or the National Association of Black Social Workers (NABSW), you are bound to follow that organization's specified ethical standards. The Association of Social Work Boards, like professional membership organizations, promotes its own version of an ethical code, although the state licensing boards are not required to subscribe to this model. And, as you might have already guessed, the codes of the various state licensing boards differ from each other.

In addition, when licensed to practice in a state, the social worker must also abide by the state licensing board's code of conduct. What makes this complicated for the profession and the individual is that there are fifty different state licensing or regulatory boards, which may have modified ethical codes that are state specific.

In summary, recognize that there is no one legal unified code of ethics in social work. Even with the variety of ethical codes among social work member organizations and state licensing boards, however, there is a consensus among social workers that the NASW Code of Ethics is the most referenced set of standards (NASW, 2018). Remember, however, that only NASW members are held responsible and could face professional discipline. Regardless, in the United States, when you graduate from a CSWE-accredited program, the NASW Code of Ethics is embedded in the coursework, and all social workers are expected to abide by this code.

In general, ethical and moral issues should always be evaluated in the definition of social work practice (Reamer, 2020, 2022). Social workers use the guidelines for professional practice given in the code of ethics to understand their moral and legal obligations in assisting their clients. Social workers entering the field must not only be aware of this document, but also agree to adhere to the standards it sets forth. Any questions about moral and ethical practice should be addressed using the guidelines it provides. Therefore, the centrality of the code of ethics to all practice decisions is crucial to formulating a moral vision within our field that will help to determine all professional helping activities (Reamer, 2022).

Did You Know . . .

In August 1996, the NASW delegate assembly met in Washington, DC, and updated social work's code of ethics to bring it more in line with social work practice. This was the first major revision since 1979. This updated and revised code of ethics went into effect on January 1, 1997. The current code of ethics was revised by the 2018 NASW Delegate Assembly, again to reflect the changes in practice.

1.2 SOCIAL WORK DEFINED

We hope the information provided thus far has stimulated your interest in the professional, situational, and educational factors that are essential in defining a field of practice. As you can see, a simple definition of social work is not easy to formulate or apply. As a broad field, the expansiveness of the service provided in the micro, mezzo, and macro areas makes professional identity difficult (Forenza & Eckert, 2018).

Most professionals would agree, however, that the field of social work involves working actively to change the social, cultural, psychological, and larger societal conditions that most individuals, families, groups, and communities face (O'Hare, 2009). According to NASW (2023, (2022a), it is the professional activity of helping individuals, groups, or communities to enhance or restore their capacity for social functioning and creating societal conditions favorable to this goal. In defining social work, the helping process emphasizes the use of **advocacy** to create societal conditions that lead to a stronger sense of person-in-situation or person-in-environment; this promotes the community good, which benefits all individuals. According to this perspective, social work is directed to two ends: first, to help resolve the micro (individual) and mezzo (group) issues that clients face, and second, to create societal macro (community) changes that prevent or ameliorate such problems for all individuals, families, groups, or communities. See Box 1.1 for a list of mission statements for social work by selected key leadership groups.

BOX 1.1

MISSION AND VARIOUS DEFINITIONS OF SOCIAL WORK

National Association of Social Workers

The primary mission of the social work profession is to enhance human well-being and help meet the basic human needs of all people, with particular attention to the needs and empowerment of people who are vulnerable, oppressed, and living in poverty.

Source: https://www.socialworkers.org/About/Ethics/Code-of-Ethics/Code-of-Ethics-English.

Council of Social Work Education

To advance excellence and innovation in social work education and research by providing leadership, ensuring quality in teaching and learning, and strengthening the capacity of our member institutions.

Source: https://www.cswe.org/about-cswe/#:~:text=Mission,capacity%20of%20our%20member%20institutions.

International Federation of Social Workers and the International Association of Schools of Social Work

The primary mission of the social work profession is to enhance human well-being and help meet the basic human needs of all people, with particular attention to the needs and empowerment of people who are vulnerable, oppressed, and living in poverty.

Source: https://www.ifsw.org/what-is-social-work/.

To initiate the helping process, a social worker may begin by working with an individual or family on an issue. This micro-level work will continue until the issue is resolved; however, the task of the social worker does not end there. This is especially true when the social worker recognizes that the causes of the client's problems are not unique to that client. Many individual problems have deep roots in the policies and procedures of larger institutions. When these problems have the potential to affect others in the community, the social work practitioner must take a macro perspective. If current policies or programs may harm others unless certain changes take place, the social worker is called to action. The worker begins macro intervention and moves to promote changes in the larger system.

For example, Ellen, a social worker employed in a family agency, learned that a newly assigned client had been evicted and was homeless. After helping the client to find a new apartment, Ellen discovered that the evicting property owner had not followed the procedures outlined in the city's ordinances. Ellen had to decide what to do next. For most social workers, the task of helping the client would not be considered complete, even though the client had a safe place to stay. The social worker might feel the need to continue helping this client and future potential clients who might also fall victim to this failed system enforcement. In this case, Ellen could begin working on macro issues by contacting city officials to ensure that local ordinances are enforced and to make them aware of the problems that can occur when ordinances are not enforced. Her advocacy efforts could prevent other people in similar circumstances from becoming homeless (see Figure 1.2).

In sum, a social worker's immediate focus is usually on a particular client population, providing service to individuals, couples, or families. These immediate efforts take a micro or mezzo perspective; however, the macro perspective should never be ignored.

FIGURE 1.2
For so many, social work is more than a profession; it is a calling.

Service provision in the field of social work cannot be defined simply—to be successful, it often must go beyond the identified client and include the larger system. Social work, like many professions, is both science and art. A skilled social worker must be knowledgeable about all aspects and perspectives of client helping and flexible in their application. The best-prepared social workers are those who recognize the science, with **evidence-based practice** efforts that identify the needs of the client and client system, as well as the art, where professional helping goes beyond the simple application of the science and becomes a multifaceted process. From this perspective, the social worker can easily move between microsystems, mezzosystems, and macrosystems with and on behalf of the client populations they serve.

1.3 BECOMING A SOCIAL WORKER

People sometimes call themselves social workers even when they do not possess the required professional qualification (i.e., a social work degree from a CSWE-accredited undergraduate or graduate social work program). Often newspaper articles, television news broadcasts, and talk radio hosts reference a social worker whose mishandling of a case led to negative consequences for an individual or family. The two following case examples are typical.

In the first case, a child abuse report was made to the state child protective services agency, but the child was not removed from the home. Later, the child died following a severe beating by the caretaker. The media reported that the social worker responsible for the case did not follow through with a proper investigation and ignored a variety of information and signals. The community was given the impression that, if the job was properly done by the social worker, the child would still be alive. Unfortunately, there is no simple formula for managing such situations or for avoiding them in the first place—even though we want there to be one. The glaring fact is that a child died, and no one was able to help. This is disturbing to everyone, and it is difficult to look beyond the initial fact. However, if the event is not examined more deeply, other children may be placed in harm's way.

It is also important to look beyond the media's simplified portrayal of the situation: Because of cutbacks and limited funding, or for other reasons, the person responsible for the investigation may not be a social work professional at all. If you look closely, this person's formal title may be caseworker or child protective services worker, but not social worker. This may be puzzling given that the work is typically associated with a social worker. Thus, it is fair to ask, Why is this person called a social worker? In most states, the term social work is a *protected title* through state licensing; a protected title means that only a person licensed by the state may be called a social worker. This so-called title protection is a consumer safeguard to inform the client that the practitioner meets standards set by the state and, in effect, is sanctioned to provide the service. In the case around the child's death, the college degree and professional training of the alleged social worker were not in social work. Instead, this individual's college education and training were in the liberal arts, with no formal coursework in the problem assessment and intervention methods essential to social work practice. Similarly, their professional education included no content on the theories and practice frameworks necessary to understand and integrate the micro, mezzo, and macro perspectives. A convincing argument could be made that knowledge of these perspectives was required to address this client and client system's situation and problems.

The second case involves a young family with a reported case of child neglect. The mother had been sending her children to school without their coats, and the weather was too cold for their attire. A state social service worker, a nondegreed worker, visited the house and agreed that the mother seemed unfit to handle the children's needs. The state worker reported that the mother's responses to questions were extremely basic and brief, and the parent did not appear to understand the seriousness of what the child was allowed to do. The worker was preparing to recommend that all the children be removed from the home before any harm came to them.

This case gets a bit complicated, but stay with us. One of the authors of this text participated in an unexpected request by a client who wanted to be discharged from the hospital against medical advice. The author met with the client, who had recently suffered a small stroke and had been immediately admitted to the hospital; the client was the partner of the mother who was facing child neglect charges and at risk of having her children removed. The client feared their children were not being cared for properly and wanted to go home immediately. According to the client, the children's mother had a mild to moderate intellectual disability and needed assistance with child care. After meeting with the client, the author placed several phone calls to help secure child care coverage and, as a result, the client agreed to stay in the hospital for the remainder of his treatment.

Although you might think this was a successful resolution, this was not the end of the case.

Later that day, the client became terribly upset when a family friend, who stopped by the hospital for a visit, told the client that the children were going to be removed from the home. The facility floor staff again called the author. In collaborating with the client, who was clearly angry and upset, the author received permission to release information about the situation (remember, the author's work was with the inpatient client only); the author contacted the state social services worker who had recommended removing the children from their home. The author shared with the state worker the plan that had been developed to care for the children. The state social services worker reconsidered the pending removal decision, and because support was in place, decided to only do a follow-up visit to make sure the plan remained in place until the hospitalized parent came home.

In debriefing the case with the state social services worker, the author learned that the worker was justifiably frustrated because the large caseload did not allow time to explore disposition options. The worker was also concerned that a child had died several weeks prior in a remarkably similar case. Because of the attention paid to that case, the worker felt it was best not to take a chance on this one. The worker did not realize that the mother had a partner in the hospital and suffered from a moderate developmental disability. Initially, the state worker thought the mother might be on drugs or merely resistant to intervention. Also, how with intellectual functioning limitations would the mother interpret having the children removed. In addition, not having partner assistance or support could be extremely traumatic for her. In trying to explain why such a limited assessment was made, the state social service stated, "Child safety is the priority." The level of frustration was obvious in talking with the state worker, and it became apparent that on-the-job training and in-service provision opportunities were often used to catch up on overdue paperwork. Moreover, although the state worker had a four-year professional degree, as required by the state, the degree was in physical education.

Cases like these are all too common. For whatever reason—be it a desire to cut costs or a lack of recognition for professional intervention—there is a widespread but false impression that anyone can be a social worker and that anyone can manage the tasks and responsibilities expected of people in the profession. It is common for state governments to redefine or reclassify a position that was once titled social worker I or social worker II under a different title, such as child protective services worker I or mental health worker II. This is called *declassification*; it allows the public agency to hire an individual without a social work degree at a much lower salary and, as a result, to realize a cost savings for the state (but often at a cost to the vulnerable individuals meant to be served).

Sadly, there are even people who believe that they can be their own social workers. For example, a plumber working for one of the authors asked what the author did for a living. The plumber smiled when he heard the author was a social worker and said, "Oh, never needed one of them before; always do my own social work." When asked what the plumber meant by that statement, he said, "Don't need somebody else to solve my problems. I can solve them for my family and myself. I had additional training on how to deal with people with life experiences and that helped." Such comments are disturbing because they show that people do not know what social workers do. It was very tempting when viewing the leaking toilet to reply, "Yes, I know—I used my life experience to do my own plumbing and you can see how that worked and your expertise is why you are here now." When people assume that social work is simply everyday problem-solving, they conclude that anyone can do it, no matter what education or training exists. The irony in this statement is as pronounced as believing that everyone can do their own plumbing, but what happens when you try to fix your sink drain and you end up breaking the garbage disposal? You thought you knew what you were doing, but, in fact, you only made the problem worse. Just as plumbing requires a specific set of skills and knowledge, so too does social work. Simply *thinking* you can do it does not mean that you can.

Confusion also exists among helping and counseling professionals about who can be a qualified social worker. For example, at a public hearing held by the Florida Board of

Clinical Social Work, Marriage & Family Therapy and Mental Health Counseling a board member opposed the licensing of BSW and MSW social workers who do not do direct practice sometimes referred to as clinical social work. A marriage and family therapist added, "Anyone can do social work. There is such a thing as social work with a small *s* and *w*."

On the surface, this statement makes sense, but it only reflects the idea around "anyone can do plumbing." Yes, all social workers must have good hearts, be compassionate, and willing to help others. But do these qualities alone make someone a professional social worker?

Let us make a comparison. Suppose you have a sore throat, feel congested, and have hot and cold sweats. Your roommate says, "You may be coming down with the flu. Why don't you take brand X over-the-counter cold pills, use some brand Y throat lozenges, and stay home and rest?" This could be particularly good and helpful advice, but does this mean that your roommate is a medical doctor, albeit with a small *m* and *d*? Of course not—it seems crazy to even suggest that. Everyone knows that a medical doctor must have a formal education and supervised experience in a medical setting. You cannot hang out a shingle that says MD (or md) just because you think you can diagnose select physical ailments.

So, what are the requirements for becoming a social worker? Certainly, there are personal attributes that a social worker must have; many of these characteristics are common among people, no matter their education or chosen career. First, a social worker must like collaborating with people. A social worker is involved with people from all levels of society. These people, who come from widely varying backgrounds, can have ideas and expectations that are quite different from those of the social worker. Being aware of and sensitive to the beliefs of others is not always a simple task. In dealing with different people, a social worker must really want to understand the troubles others face. So a good social worker must genuinely like working with diverse individuals.

Second, a social worker must want to help people. A professional social worker encounters all sorts of client problems, ranging from abuse and neglect to homelessness and from mental health issues to community-based substance abuse problems. A good social worker wants to help his or her clients in their efforts to figure out what is going on and how best to resolve their problems.

Third, a social worker wants the community to be a better place for all people. Through his or her professional activities, a social worker helps a specific client while at the same time trying to better the community for *all* people. For example, ideally social workers want to end **poverty** and its debilitating effects on people and communities. Social workers envision communities where all people have access to decent housing and health care. They also strive to end unfair treatment of individuals, the isms that face millions of people today—**racism**, **sexism**, and ageism. The personal traits that foster the desire to work with and help individuals, families, and communities are critical ingredients in creating a social worker. To finish the mix, however, these personal traits must be complemented by professional education and training. In the United States, the core of professional social work education takes place in baccalaureate or graduate-level degree programs at specific colleges and universities.

> ### Did You Know . . .
> The CSWE is the only national standard-setting and accrediting body for social work education in the United States. It was organized in 1952 through the merger of two professional educational associations that coordinated baccalaureate and graduate programs, respectively.

For any US college or university to offer a recognized social work educational program, it must meet the **accreditation** standards of the CSWE. The accreditation standards build on CSWE's **Educational Policy and Accreditation Standards**, which were updated in 2022 (CSWE, 2022c). The CSWE is authorized by the Council for Higher Education Accreditation to set and oversee educational standards for social work programs across the United States and is the sole social work accreditation authority in the United States. The CSWE was first established in 1952; at its inception, there were 59 graduate schools (i.e., MSW programs) and 19 undergraduate (i.e., BSW) programs (Watkins & Holmes, 2008). As stated earlier in the chapter, by 2022 there were 851 baccalaureate ($n = 538$) and master-level social work ($n = 313$) education programs accredited by the CSWE (CSWE, 2022a). As can be seen by the sheer number of programs, social work education is an exceptionally large enterprise in the United States.

Other countries have their own accrediting bodies for social work education. For example, the Joint University Council for Social and Public Administration oversees social work educational programs in the United Kingdom, Brazilian schools of social work are members of the National Association of Schools of Social Work, and Indian social work educational programs are members of the Association of Schools of Social Work. International accreditation associations can be found in different nations; as might be expected, the accreditation standards vary by country because they reflect the unique cultural, historical, and regional differences of a particular nation-state. Although accrediting associations throughout the world can vary, the IASSW is the worldwide association for schools of social work, other tertiary-level social work educational programs, and social work educators (IASSW, 2022). These standards attempt to develop consistency among social work educational programs around the world. The global standards, however, do not hold any authority from a particular nation or university. They are simply basic guidelines that are extremely useful for programs in nations that do not have an accrediting association such as the CSWE.

Regardless of where a professional social work program is located, following specific standards consistent with the mission of the profession is essential. Curriculum format and delivery, which are the heart of the educational experience, must be coherent, built on a series of specific behavioral competencies and a supervised field placement or internship experience; through an internship, a social work professional learns to apply in the field environment what has been taught in the classroom. Standards require that the faculty members who instruct students possess certain types of degrees, as well as professional work experience that can facilitate the education process. Accreditation standards also specify that a variety of institutional (e.g., college or university) resources be available. Finally, an accredited program must identify specific behavioral outcomes that all graduates are expected to demonstrate at the end of their course of study (see the activity below and look at the accreditation document from your own program).

Activity

Ask to review your social work program's latest self-study for accreditation. Compare this self-study to the CSWE's Educational Policy and Accreditation Standards and the *Education Policy and Accreditation Standards Handbook*. To be accredited, your program must conform to these standards. Being part of an accredited program is important for your future development.

Attending and graduating from an accredited social work program is crucial for future social work professionals. Remember that only a graduate of an accredited social work program is recognized as a professional social worker. Because CSWE accreditation standards apply nationally, the public recognizes that a graduate of a BSW program in California has completed the same minimum educational requirements as a graduate of a BSW program in New Hampshire or Georgia. Uniformity of foundation content throughout the country means that social workers can be hired in any state and meet specific educational requirements for employment and subsequent licensing in the field. This is particularly important for employers and supervisors of social work professionals because they can assume that a particular educational background implies familiarity with certain content. Employers report that this standardization of course content across social work programs makes social workers predictable employees regarding what they have and have not been educated to do.

A BSW education prepares individuals for entry or beginning-level social work practice, commonly referred to as *generalist practice*. Baccalaureate studies occur in the junior and senior years of study. An MSW education prepares individuals for advanced practice, also called *specialization* or *concentration practice*. (We will explore advanced practice in more detail in several of the application chapters: Chapters 5 through 10). Although an MSW program typically requires two years of full-time study, a person with a BSW degree may be eligible for advanced standing in a graduate program, thus bypassing up to half of the graduate coursework through proficiency in foundation competencies. The number of courses waived or exempted for BSW study is different for each graduate program; the waived courses range from a maximum of one full year of full-time study to no courses waived. The decision on how to implement an advanced-standing program and what courses to waive is made by the faculty of a particular social work program, not by the CSWE.

> ### Did You Know . . .
> The abbreviation BSW stands for baccalaureate social worker and MSW stands for master social worker. The abbreviations BSSW and MSSW also signify degrees in social work: bachelor of science in social work and master of science in social work. The most advanced degrees in social work are the DSW and the PhD. In most circles, the MSW or the MSSW is considered the highest level needed to practice in the field.

1.4 THE PROFESSIONAL SOCIAL WORKER

Considering the enduring popularity of the social work profession, you may ask how and why this interest began and why it continues to grow in scope within the global community. The answer is simple: People across the world and in our own neighborhoods face similar problems and need the assistance that social workers provide. When these problems are in the micro area and remain client or individual client system focused, they are referred to as microsystem problems. The responsibility for finding solutions to microsystem problems often rests squarely on the shoulders of the individual client or the relevant family system.

For example, when a single older adult falls at home and fractures a hip, the person will need to be admitted to a local hospital for treatment. Often, after admission, the emergency room physician refers the case to the **hospital social worker**, who is tasked with assessing the client's situation and preparedness for discharge. Suppose that, during the assessment process, the social worker learns that the client has no immediate family and lives alone. Considering the needs of the client, the social worker helps develop a plan with the client that ensures provision of the appropriate support and services. In many cases, this includes arranging home health care so that the client can receive medical services in the home (Dziegielewski & Holliman, 2020). It can also include ensuring that the client has access to nutritious meals by arranging contact with a **Meals on Wheels** program. Once the immediate medical rehabilitation needs have been addressed, to increase socialization and provide mealtime activity, the client can be referred to a local neighborhood center's senior citizens' program. Arrangement of transportation will be a priority for medical check-ups or socialization events. Further, individual or group supportive counseling can be provided directly or by referral within the community. From a micro perspective, one-on-one attention to a client's situation is crucial, and the person-in-situation, person-in environment perspective will also include assessing the client system. The client system, which can include partners, immediate family members, and others involved in the client's care, will also be considered. The role of the social worker through the micro perspective is essential because this role stresses the individual client's personal and social needs designed to ensure independence in as many activities of daily living as possible. These factors must be considered to complete a comprehensive problem-solving strategy for the assessment and intervention processes.

> ### Did You Know . . .
> Over 90 percent of the workers trained by the American Red Cross are volunteers and respond to sixty thousand disasters a year, most of which are home and apartment fires (American Red Cross, 2022).

A second system often addressed in social work is the mezzosystem. Through the mezzo perspective, the social worker highlights the needs of the client by focusing primarily on achieving **environmental justice** and **social justice** and working with the systems that can provide aid. The client is linked directly to support systems that enhance and maximize individual functioning. The focus could be on working with schools or community services. From a mezzo perspective, family and friends are paramount. This perspective also incorporates those social workers who work in administration as an **agency's** director or chief executive officer, a unit director, or a program supervisor. In both governmental and nonprofit social service agencies, we find that social workers lead many of the programs that a client will need and that they can either initiate or oversee service delivery.

Unfortunately, many problems have much wider roots in broader community or social institutions. Social workers must be well versed in multiple roles, "from adding a few lines to a policy and procedures manual to altering the laws that guide how nations interact" (Ellis, 2008, p. 131). When addressing these problems on a much larger scale, which is often referred to as macropractice, involving the larger macrosystem may also be referred to as a macrosystem approach. From the macro perspective, solutions to the problems that clients face must be tied directly to larger systems. As a result, macropractice often starts with social and political advocacy and ranges from working in politics to influence policy formulation to helping neighborhoods organize activities to directly address a local social issue.

For example, providing decent and safe places to sleep for people who are homeless requires more than a "hot (meal) and a cot." To truly address the problem and avoid the situation from occurring again and with others, it often requires advocacy with local and state governments. The social worker may need to initiate and organize a citywide movement to open a shelter or advocate for more system-level changes that will help the client with development and, once available, location of the resources and services they need. Indeed, macro intervention for this population is not as easy to accomplish as an inexperienced observer may think. At a minimum, to initiate macro change, the social worker must understand housing policy as it affects the homeless. Even the term *homeless* must be clearly understood—there are many ways people can experience housing insecurity. The social worker must also be knowledgeable about housing options and shelter alternatives used elsewhere. In addition to this basic knowledge, the social worker must be aware of and anticipate resistance from the community to avoid these changes. It is important to work with the larger community to get everyone to understand why a homeless shelter is needed and to mobilize agreement. However, caution must always be exercised when one is working within the macro area of practice; providing a homeless shelter is much more complicated than simply securing the site and the funds to construct a building. In implementing this type of change, the social worker must be sensitive to current community concerns and political issues that can enhance or impede service assistance and progression. The social worker may also need to advocate for overall law and **policy** changes that could assist with this problem in the future.

This list of some of the most serious macrosystem social problems—homelessness, living in a rural community with chronic health conditions, physical and emotional **abuse**, mental health, substance abuse, addressing poverty and the **poverty threshold**, immigration, health care, and community development—touches on only some of the areas that make up the domain of social work practice. Specht and Courtney (1994) stated, and the CSWE (2022a,c) continues to support, that the goal of the profession is to seek full and complete equality and social justice in all communities. From this perspective, all people are given the opportunity to live their lives to the fullest and to achieve their own potential. At first sight, the concept of full and total equality without any form of prejudice or discrimination appears to represent a utopian goal that is unattainable. Evaluated more closely, however, the aim of such a community is not that unusual. Helping clients to improve their life situations and their capacity to achieve their full potential has been one of the central forces driving the profession since its modest mid-nineteenth-century beginnings. Stressing the importance of building trust, acceptance, transparency, and accountability. such groups as Black Lives Matter (2022) and the Gay and Lesbian Alliance against Defamation (2022) continue the focused movements of today.

1.5 THE IMPORTANCE OF PROFESSIONAL MEMBERSHIP

All professionals can belong to membership organizations or associations that represent their interests (see the activity below and consider attending an NASW meeting to see what it is like). Attending a meeting can be helpful because an association provides professional self-identity and an opportunity to meet colleagues to discuss ideas and share innovations in practice.

> ## Activity
> Gather information about your local unit of the NASW. Ask one of your instructors or a social worker in the community when your local unit of NASW will be meeting. These days, those meetings might take place online. Try to attend the next meeting. Also, find out when the state board of directors of the NASW meets next. These meetings occur several times each year and are held somewhere in the state. Try to attend one of these meetings to see the process firsthand.

The NASW is the largest membership organization for social workers. As stated earlier, according to the NASW's website, its membership in 2022 totaled 120,000 persons, making it the largest social work membership organization in the world. One crucial point to recognize is that membership is voluntary. Indeed, in the most recent edition of its annual publication, the *Occupational Outlook Handbook*, the U.S. Department of Labor (2022) reported that in 2021 there were about 708,100 professional social work positions in the United States, which means that only slightly more than one-fifth (17 percent) of all social work professionals are members of the NASW.

The NASW is not the sole professional organization, however, and as its membership numbers indicate, it does not represent most social workers in the United States. Nevertheless, it remains the largest social work membership organization in the world; consequently, social workers should understand its role and function. The NASW was first organized in 1955, with the merger of five special-interest organizations: the American Association of Group Workers, the American Association of Medical Social Workers, the American Association of Psychiatric Social Workers, the American Association of Social Workers, and the National Association of School Social Workers. In addition, two study groups joined the new organization: the Association for the Study of Community Organization and the Social Work Research Group. The ideas of all these groups were merged to unify the profession (Alexander, 1995). Today, the national offices of the NASW are in Washington, DC, only a few blocks from the U.S. Capitol.

The NASW regards itself as a bottom-up members' organization. What this means is that governance and direction are established from below, and responsibility lies with the units and chapters in each state. Each state has its own NASW chapter, and each chapter is further subdivided into regional units. Each local unit covers a geographical area small enough to allow members to attend meetings and programs together.

After joining the NASW, each member is assigned to a state chapter and then to a local unit that reflects his or her home location. Many local units conduct quarterly or monthly meetings. These gatherings run the gamut of formality, from very formal meetings with an invited speaker to informal after-work get-togethers. Unit meetings offer social workers from the same geographical area an opportunity to meet on a regular basis and strengthen their professional networks.

The state chapter coordinates activities between the local units and offers ongoing educational opportunities, known as continuing education, around the state. A significant function of the state chapter is its political activity with state and local governments. The state chapter brings to the attention of its membership issues in the state legislature that could affect the profession or clients being served. Most state chapters provide their members with a monthly newsletter, as well as professional and social activities such as an annual or biannual convention. The state chapter is staffed by a paid employee, a social worker, and is governed by a board of directors elected by the membership of the state and serving for a prescribed term.

The national office of the NASW comprises divisions ranging from membership services to political advocacy to publications. The national office's focus is on issues that affect the profession, thus leaving state-specific matters to the state chapters. The national office is responsible for carrying out the policy of the national board of directors, which is made up of elected social work members from across the country. The national office also publishes a monthly newspaper that provides an exhaustive overview of social work around the country. Other member benefits include opportunities to purchase life and malpractice insurance and reduced registration fees for national meetings.

Through local units, state chapters, and the national office of the NASW, individual social workers have numerous opportunities to affect the profession. Individual social workers mold the profession and give direction to future activities by holding leadership positions; serving on various committees; and attending local, state, and national meetings. Social workers belong to groups to support specific interests. Such groups give the individual practitioner a connection with others who share similar professional interests and concerns while broadening the sphere of professional influence and encouraging the ongoing development of research in practice.

In addition to the NASW, there are more than fifty other national membership or professional social work associations in the United States. It is not certain how many different professional social work membership groups exist in the United States, but the various groups are based on a variety of attributes, ranging from race and ethnicity to practice interests (see Box 1.2 for examples of professional associations). The total membership of these groups ranges from a few hundred to a few thousand individuals. Yearly and joint conferences among these organizations can help all the diverse groups to have a better understanding of other such groups, their issues, and potential collaborations. Therefore, most special-interest groups sponsor an annual meeting, and some publish a journal or newsletter. The membership rolls of these organizations are much smaller than that of the NASW, and they may not have state or local units or paid staff to run the organization.

One would think that the substantial number of social work membership groups, combined with the low membership for the NASW, would send a clear message that the profession needs to reorganize its efforts on behalf of individual practitioners and clients. Since there is no one organization that can claim that it represents all social work, developing more unified ties between these specialty groups is important. Since these organizations represent the best interest of the profession, more activities to unify these groups are encouraged. The question remains as to whether it is necessary and possible for the various social work professional associations to come together as one professional association like those formed by professions such as law, medicine, and psychology. Sadly, because some associations have complex organizational structures, folding into one group is not likely. So the profession remains disjointed, splintered into selective special-interest groups and membership associations, with some working together better than others.

BOX 1.2

EXAMPLES OF SOCIAL WORK MEMBERSHIP ORGANIZATIONS

American Association for Psychoanalysis in Clinical Social Work, https://www.aapcsw.org/

Association for Community Organization & Social Action, https://acosa.clubexpress.com/

Association of Oncology Social Workers, https://aosw.org/

Association of Veterans Affairs Social Workers, https://www.vasocialworkers.org/

Clinical Social Work Association, https://www.clinicalsocialworkassociation.org/About-CSWA

Council on Social Work Education, https://www.cswe.org/

International Federation of Social Workers, https://www.ifsw.org/

Latino Social Workers Organization, https://lswo.org/

National Association of Black Social Workers, https://www.nabsw.org/

National Association of Puerto Rican Hispanic Social Workers, https://www.naprhsw.com/

North American Association of Christians in Social Work, https://www.nacsw.org/

Professional Association of Social Workers in HIV & AIDS, https://paswha.org/

Social Welfare Action Alliance, https://www.socialwelfareactionalliance.org/

Society for Social Work Leadership in Health Care, https://sswlhc.org/

SUMMARY

Social work is a diverse profession that is not easily defined and, as a result, is often misunderstood by the public and the greater community. One thing remains evident: social work is a profession of people helping people. Despite confusion about the daily activities of social workers, there is growing recognition that social work plays a key role today. Children, seniors, families, communities, and rich, poor, and middle-class people are all represented among the many clients who benefit directly from social work. Social work clients are found in all parts of the country. Social work is a global profession, with many of its efforts designed to assist and stimulate an informed practice strategy rich with methods designed to incorporate helping activities at the grassroots level.

Today, thousands of people studying in colleges and universities are striving to become professional social workers. It is these new social work professionals who will steer the profession and support the mission of micro, mezzo, and macro intervention well into the twenty-first century. The Grand Challenges for Social Work (2022), supported by NASW (2022c), has put forth thirteen grand challenges for the social work profession. These challenges are in the general areas of individual health and well-being, stronger social fabric, and a just society. It is our hope that views and ideas on how to achieve each of these grand challenges for the profession will be addressed in the chapters of this book. The thirteen Grand Challenges for Social Work include:

Individual Family Well-Being

1. Ensuring healthy development for youth
2. Closing the health gap
3. Building healthy relationships to end violence
4. Advancing long and productive lives

Stronger Social Fabric

1. Eradicating social isolation
2. Ending homelessness
3. Creating social responses to a changing environment
4. Harnessing technology for social good

Just Society

1. Promoting smart decarceration
2. Reducing extreme economic inequality
3. Building financial capabilities and assets for all
4. Achieving equal opportunity and justice
5. Eliminating racism

Sources: Grand Challenges of Social Work (2022); NASW (2022c).

QUESTIONS TO THINK ABOUT

1. What do you say to a friend who, after learning that you want to be a social worker, states, "You won't make any money doing that"?
2. What do you think a meeting of professional social workers, such as a local NASW unit meeting, would be like?
3. Do you know any professional social workers? What personal qualities do they have that you think might be useful for a social worker?
4. Do you think there should be one professional membership association that all social workers belong to, or does the variety of special-interest groups, as discussed in this chapter, create better opportunities for members?
5. Why do you think there is a general misunderstanding of social work?
6. What are some ways in which social workers could help to educate family and friends about what they do?
7. To what extent, if any, is social work different in other nations such as South Africa, India, or Vietnam compared to the United States?
8. How will the growth of the social work profession affect social work in the United States and other countries in the world?
9. What are some efforts that social workers can do to help address the thirteen challenges put forth by the NASW in 2022?

REFERENCES

Alexander, C. (1995). Distinctive dates in social welfare history. In R. Edwards & J. G. Hopps (Eds.), *Encyclopedia of social work* (19th ed., pp. 2631–2647). Washington, DC: NASW Press.

American Red Cross. (2022). *Disaster volunteers.* Retrieved November 18, 2022, from https://www.redcross.org/volunteer/volunteer-opportunities/disaster-volunteer.html

Black Lives Matter. (2022). *BLM: Welcome.* Retrieved November 18, 2022, from https://blacklivesmatter.com/transparency/#welcome

Council on Social Work Education. (2022a). *Accreditation.* Retrieved from http://www.cswe.org

Council on Social Work Education. (2022b). *Professional practice doctoral educational program accreditation.* Retrieved from https://www.cswe.org/accreditation/accreditation-process/professional-practice-doctoral-program-accreditation/

Council on Social Work Education. (2022c). *2022 EPAS—Educational Policy, and Accreditation Standards for baccalaureate and master's social work programs.* Alexandria, VA: Author. Retrieved from https://www.cswe.org/getmedia/bb5d8afe-7680-42dc-a332-a6e6103f4998/2022-EPAS.pdf

Dziegielewski, S. F., & Holliman, D. (2020). *The changing face of health care social work: Opportunities and challenges for professional practice* (4th ed.). New York, NY: Springer.

Ellis, R. A. (2008). Policy practice. In K. M. Sowers & C. N. Dulmus (Series Eds.) & I. C. Colby (Vol. Ed.), *Comprehensive handbook of social work and social welfare: Social policy and policy practice* (Vol. 4, pp. 129–143). Hoboken, NJ: Wiley.

Forenza, B., & Eckert, C. (2018). Social worker identity: A profession in context. *Social Work*, *63*(1), 17–26.

Gay and Lesbian Alliance against Defamation. (2022). *History*. Retrieved November 18, 2022, from https://www.glaad.org/about/history

Grand Challenges for Social Work. (2022). *The challenges*. Baltimore, MD: University of Maryland, School of Social Work. Retrieved from https://grandchallengesforsocialwork.org/#the-challenges

Group for the Advancement of Doctoral Education in Social Work. (2022). *About us*. Retrieved from https://www.gadesocialwork.org/

Hogue, A., & Huntington, M. K. (2019). Family physician burnout rates in rural versus metropolitan areas: A pilot study. *South Dakota Medicine*, *72*(7), 306–308.

International Association of Schools of Social Work. (2022). *Our members*. Retrieved from https://www.iassw-aiets.org/our-members/#1580474749191-922e5540-25f2

International Federation of Social Workers. (2022a). *About IFSW*. Retrieved from https://www.ifsw.org/about-ifsw/

International Federation of Social Workers. (2022b). *National Association of Social Workers launched in Ukraine*. Retrieved from https://www.ifsw.org/national-association-of-social-workers-launched-in-ukraine/

Kelly, D., Schroeder, S., & Leighton, K. (2022). Anxiety, depression, stress, burnout, and professional quality of life among the hospital workforce during a global health pandemic. *The Journal of Rural Health*, *38*(4), 795.804. https://doi.org/10.1111/jrh.12659

Lepkowsky, C. M. (2020). Telehealth reimbursement allows access to mental health care during COVID-19. *The American Journal of Geriatric Psychiatry*, *28*(8), 898–899.

Lepkowsky, C. M. (2022). Ageism, mentalism, and ableism shape telehealth policy. *American Journal of Geriatric Psychiatry*, *31*(3), 235–236.

Lepkowsky, C. M., & Arndt, S. (2019). The internet barrier to healthcare for older adults? *Practice Innovation*, *4*(2), 124–132.

Melville, H. (1993). *Moby Dick*. Hertfordshire, UK: Wordsworth Editions.

Ministry of Civil Affairs of the People's Republic of China. (2020). *Statistical bulletin on civil affairs development in 2020*. Retrieved April 20, 2022, from http://www.mca.gov.cn/article/sj/tjgb/202109/20210900036577.shtml

National Association of Social Workers. (2018). *Code of ethics of the National Association of Social Workers*. Washington, DC: Author. Retrieved December 27, 2022, from https://socialwork.sdsu.edu/wp-content/uploads/2011/09/NASW-Code-of-Ethics2017.pdf

National Association of Social Workers. (2022a). *Social Work Month 2022*. Retrieved September 10, 2022, from https://www.naswnc.org/page/287

National Association of Social Workers. (2022b). *Social Workers Interstate Compact public comment*. Retrieved November 6, 2022, from https://www.socialworkers.org/LinkClick.aspx?fileticket=fSvAwJFwleg%3d&portalid=0

National Association of Social Workers. (2022c). *Grand challenges for social work: Eliminating racism becomes the 13th challenge as initiative evolves*. Retrieved from https://www.socialworkers.org/News/Social-Work-Advocates/October-November-2022-Issue/Grand-Challenges-for-Social-Work-Eliminating-Racism-Becomes-13th-Challenge

National Association of Social Workers. (2023). *Social Work Month 2023.* Retrieved September 10, 2022, from https://www.naswnc.org/page/287

Niu, D., & Haugen, H. O. (2019). Social workers in China: Professional identity in the making. *The British Journal of Social Work, 49*(7), 1932–1949.

O'Hare, T. (2009). *Essential skills of social work practice: Assessment, intervention, and education.* Chicago, IL: Lyceum Books.

Reamer, F. G. (2020). *Ethics and risk management in online and distance behavioral health.* San Diego, CA: Cognella Academic Publishing.

Reamer, F. G. (2022). *The philosophical foundations of social work* (2nd ed.). New York, NY: Columbia University Press.

Salsberg, E., Quigley, L., Richwine, C., Sliwa, S., Acquaviva, K., & Wyche, K. (2020, August). *The social work profession: Findings from three years of surveys of new social workers.* National Association of Social Workers. Retrieved from https://www.socialworkers.org/LinkClick.aspx?fileticket=1_j2EXVNspY%3d&portalid=0

Scherer, Z. (2022) *Key demographic and economic characteristics of same-sex and opposite sex couples differed.* U.S. Census Bureau. Retrieved from https://www.census.gov/library/stories/2022/11/same-sex-couple-households-exceeded-one-million.html?utm_campaign=20221122msacos1ccstors&utm_medium=email&utm_source=govdelivery

Specht, H., & Courtney, M. (1994). *Unfaithful angels.* New York, NY: Free Press.

U.S. Department of Labor. (2022). *Occupational outlook handbook.* Retrieved from https://www.bls.gov/ooh/community-and-social-service/social-workers.htm

Watkins, J. M., & Holmes, J. (2008). Educating for social work. In K. M. Sowers & C. N. Dulmus (Series Eds.) & B. W. White (Vol. Ed.), *Comprehensive handbook of social work and social welfare: The profession of social work* (Vol. 1, pp. 25–36). Hoboken, NJ: Wiley.

Social Welfare

A System's Response to Personal Issues, Social Justice, and Public Problems

CHAPTER 2: EPAS COMPETENCIES

Social work programs at the bachelor's and the master's level are accredited by the Council of Social Work Education (CSWE). CSWE's Educational Policy and Accreditation Standards (EPAS) describe the processes and criteria that social work courses should cover. In 2022, CSWE updated its EPAS standards. The following competencies are addressed in this chapter.

Competency 1: Demonstrate Ethical and Professional Behavior

Social workers understand the value base of the profession and its ethical standards, as well as relevant policies, laws, and regulations that may affect practice with individuals, families, groups, organizations, and communities.

Competency 5: Engage in Policy Practice

Social workers identify social policy at the local, state, federal, and global level that affects wellbeing, human rights and justice, service delivery, and access to social services.

Competency 8: Intervene with Individuals, Families, Groups, Organizations, and Communities

Social workers understand that intervention is an ongoing component of the dynamic and interactive process of social work practice.

• • •

When you hear the words *social welfare,* what comes to mind? Many people think of cash assistance to the poor, child protective services, food stamps (note that the food stamp program no longer exists, having been replaced by the Supplemental Nutritional Assistance Program [SNAP] in 2008; see Figure 2.1), or low-income housing. Before we begin to delve into social welfare, its meaning, and whether these examples are accurate, let's first test your knowledge of welfare with the following quiz. We expect that, as a beginning professional interested in this field, some of your answers will be right and others will be wrong; just give it your best guess.

2.1 WELFARE QUIZ

1. What is the Supplemental Nutrition Assistance Program?
    a. The former Food Stamp Program
    b. Primarily a prenatal food program
    c. Federal government support for a food program limited to older adults
    d. Faith-based food programs

FIGURE 2.1
The Supplemental Nutrition Assistance Program serves as the U.S. social welfare benefit that provides for food benefits for low-income qualifying families.

CHAPTER 2: SOCIAL WELFARE: A SYSTEM'S RESPONSE TO PERSONAL ISSUES

2. Who makes up the majority (more than 50 percent) of people receiving public assistance?
   a. Mothers and their children
   b. Unemployed adults
   c. Older adults
   d. Single females
3. In the United States, more than fifty million people live in poverty.
   a. True
   b. False
4. Many individuals who receive welfare benefits have children just to get more money from the government.
   a. True
   b. False
5. When we talk about the unemployment rate, we are referring to those people who are not working at the present time.
   a. True
   b. False
6. The amount given to poor people in a welfare subsidy check is the same in all states.
   a. True
   b. True, but prorated for family size
   c. False
7. More than half of the people who receive welfare could be working, but choose not to.
   a. True
   b. False
8. Which of the following groups are not considered welfare recipients by the U.S. government (circle all that apply)?
   a. Schoolchildren
   b. Older adults receiving Social Security
   c. Armed forces veterans
   d. Supplemental Nutritional Assistance Program recipients
   e. College students receiving Pell grants
   f. Medicare recipients
9. Temporary Assistance to Needy Families is the only federal program that provides cash assistance to poor families.
   a. True
   b. False
10. In your own words, define *social welfare*.

Now, turn to the back of this chapter to find the correct answers and see how you did. You'll find no answer to question 10. After you read this chapter, come back and answer the questions again, especially question 10. Be sure to compare your two responses to see if your first response is different from your second.

Are you surprised by some of the answers? Think about which questions you got wrong and what you learned from this brief quiz. Clearly, social welfare is a very complicated system that is often misunderstood.

In this chapter, we will discuss the dimensions of social welfare—in particular, what is meant by the term. We will also direct attention to the role of the social work profession, as well as that of each individual social worker within our current social welfare system.

2.2 TOWARD A DEFINITION OF SOCIAL WELFARE

To begin our discussion of the current social welfare system, we would like you to try this exercise. To prepare, take a piece of paper and a pencil and get ready to write down some of your ideas. First, think of your hometown or the community where you were raised. Second, imagine that you could transform it into what you consider the ideal place to live. What kinds of services would be needed to improve this neighborhood or community, bringing it to the perfection that you believe would benefit the community served and reflect the social work profession's goal?

Respect and Dignity: A Social Worker's Premise

Use the following list of questions to suggest possible ideas and guide your thinking on this topic:

Housing and employment
1. Would everyone have safe and affordable housing?
2. Would everyone be able to find employment?
3. Would employment pay enough to provide for adequate housing, food, and clothing and include social and health benefits?

Education and services
1. Would the education of the young be given top priority?
2. Would the community help all schools to get the services and supplies they need (e.g., fully equipped classrooms and state-of-the-art technology), public and private alike?
3. Would a safe learning environment be provided?
4. Would the curriculum covered be factual, yet in agreement with parents and other constituencies related to what needs to be taught in the classroom?

Community safety and security
1. Would older adults be protected from abuse and neglect?
2. Would older adults have access to the services they need to complete their activities of daily living?

3. Would children be protected from exploitation and abuse?
4. Would domestic violence and intimate partner violence be tolerated, and what options would be available to those who are victimized and those who victimize?
5. Would discrimination based on race, skin color, age, gender expression, sexual orientation, and the like be tolerated?
6. Would food be provided to those who cannot afford to buy their own?
7. Are there any drug- or substance-related problems that could disturb community security or safety?

Your own list probably includes many more considerations that you believe are essential to address. Nevertheless, we believe that if you compared your list with someone else's, you'd be surprised at how similar the two lists are. Most people agree that, in an ideal community, all people are treated with respect and dignity. Further, most people agree that, for a community to be responsive, it must be a place where members are valued for who they are and what they can offer to their community. For those who struggle, services to assist those in need remain essential for the success of community change efforts.

> ### Did You Know . . .
> According to the federal agency Substance Abuse and Mental Health Services Administration, in 2018, 20.3 million people aged twelve or older in the United States had experienced substance use disorder and 47.6 million adults had experienced mental illness; 9.2 million adults experienced both.

Identifying what a community needs may seem simple. Once the needs are identified, however, it becomes clear that some issues are going to be much more difficult to address. When you discussed the factors you identified with other students, it becomes obvious that most people cannot agree on what services are needed in a community, who deserves these services, and how many services need to be provided. To further complicate things, communities are not static entities. A community needs to shift and change in response to current social, political, and economic conditions.

Changing times can create and worsen social problems. The **COVID-19** pandemic serves as a vivid example. For example, in 2019, the U.S. Bureau of the Census reported that 34 million people, about 10.5 percent of the U.S. population, were in poverty, and of those living in poverty, many were women, children, and elderly individuals. The World Bank (2020) reported that between 2000 and 2017 the number of people living in poverty worldwide dropped from 741 million to 689 million, but COVID-19 increased the number of persons living in poverty by approximately 70 million, to 719 million people.

The World Bank Group calculated this number by using the World Bank definition of extreme poverty, which includes individuals living on less than $2.15 per day. Of course, the decline in global poverty was good news (although the decline began slowing after 2017 and COVID-19 reversed the downward trend), but 689 million is a considerable number of humans, especially when you consider that around half were children. For a moment, think about what your life would be like if all you had in your pocket was $65, the World Bank metric for extreme poverty per month to buy food, pay for your transportation, purchase medicines, and pay your rent and utilities. Would you be able to afford to live in a dorm? Would you be sleeping in your car? In fact, could you afford a car? Would you be "couch surfing"? How would you purchase your textbooks? Think about your basic needs of food, shelter, adequate clothing, and safety—how would you meet them? It is not surprising that living in poverty raises susceptibility to other social issues such as poor health, low school attendance and graduation rates, increased crime rates, and, sadly, an increase in the risk of abuse and neglect, both physical and emotional.

Did You Know . . .

Intimate partner violence results in 741 million days of lost productivity (work or school) because of victimization. That's $730 per victim across their lifetimes, or $110 billion in lost economic value across the U.S. population (Peterson et al., 2018).

Did You Know . . .

According to the federal Administration for Children and Families, nationally in 2018, 678,000 children were determined to be victims of child maltreatment, with the highest rates among babies and young children.

Social Services for Social and Economic Justice

The United States is among the wealthiest countries in the world. It has abundant natural resources and technology, yet many American citizens battle daily with poverty, as well as emotional and psychological difficulties that can impede their ability to function at home and in their communities. In 2021, the National Center for Children in Poverty (NCCP, 2021) reported that 17 percent of all children (almost twelve million children) lived in poverty, defined as a family with an income below the federal poverty level. *The State of America's Children 2021* (Children's Defense Fund, 2021) concluded that "our youngest Americans are being hit hardest during their years of greatest development. Nearly 1 in 6 children under six were poor in 2019 and almost half of them lived in extreme poverty." Every day, millions of children are ill fed, live in

> **BOX 2.1**
>
> **EACH DAY IN AMERICA FOR ALL CHILDREN**
>
> - A baby is born into poverty every minute
> - A baby is born at low birth weight every 2 minutes
> - A baby dies before their first birthday every 25 minutes
> - A child is arrested for a drug offense every 6.5 minutes
> - A child is arrested for a violent offense every 12 minutes
> - A child or teen dies from an accident every hour and 11 minutes
> - A child or teen dies by suicide every 3 hours and 11 minutes
> - A child is killed by abuse or neglect every 5 hours
>
> *Source*: This material was sourced from the Children's Defense Fund, https://www.childrensdefense.org/state-of-americas-children/soac-2021-moments/.

unsafe environments, and have no access to high-quality health care services. And just who are these young people? The Children's Defense Fund describes child poverty in the United States as a "national disgrace" and offers a portrait of each day in the life of America's children in 2021 (see Box 2.1). Of course, poverty does not just affect children. In fact, most Americans will confront poverty during their lives (Rank & Hirschl, 2021).

Did You Know . . .
In 2019, there were thirty-four million people in poverty in the United States.

Did You Know . . .
According to the Children's Defense Fund, in 2019, approximately 423,997 children were in foster care. On average, more than 20,445 youth each year age out of the foster care system at age eighteen or older and are left on their own, without ever finding a caring, permanent family connection. Homelessness, unemployment, and incarceration await many of these fledgling adults.

In 2000, former surgeon general David Satcher (2000) reported that one of the greatest challenges for the U.S. health care system is to respond to both the physical and the mental health of our children, and quite clearly this challenge remains decades later. Yet, children seemed to have slipped further off the nation's political and social agenda, even in the face of these overwhelming problems.

Poverty is defined in several ways—situational poverty, generational poverty, **relative poverty**, rural poverty, and urban poverty. Poverty generally, however, is defined using an *absolute* definition: when income falls below an exact number. For example, in 2019, the poverty threshold was set at $13,300 for a single person under age sixty-five and $20,335 for a three-person family (U.S. Census Bureau, 2023. With this threshold figure, the U.S. Census Bureau reported that in 2019, 10.5 percent of the U.S. population, or approximately thirty-four million people, lived in poverty (Semega et al., 2020). The website Poverty USA (povertyusa.org) described how poverty affects distinct groups: women (12.9 percent), men (10.6 percent), children (16.2 percent), older adults (9.7 percent), Native Americans (25.4 percent), Blacks (20.8 percent), Hispanics (17.6 percent), and Whites (10.1 percent) and Asians (10.1 percent). Let's think about that for a second. What does this mean for thirty-four million people who had an income below the poverty threshold? The poverty threshold is a dollar amount set by the U.S. government to give a cutoff for the least amount of income a person or family needs to meet basic needs. This means that in 2021 an individual in poverty had an annual income below $12,880, or a little above $1,000 per month—at a time when the median rent cost per month in the United States was $1,228 and even a "low-cost plan" (Center for Nutrition Policy and Promotion, 2021) for home-prepared food would run about $230 monthly.

Did You Know . . .

The poverty rate for children under the age of eighteen fell from 21.8 percent in 2012 to 16.2 percent in 2018. Even so, approximately 11.9 million children (under age eighteen) were in poverty in 2018.

The list of social issues facing America today goes on and on. Education, health care, employment, and the environment are just a few, but also think of our global relations and obligations. The economic crisis that hit America with a vengeance in 2008 reverberated around the world. In the United States alone, some 8.4 million jobs were lost and nearly 3 million homes were foreclosed (American Land Title Association, 2010). More recently, the social and economic consequences and the ripple effects of business closures and recommendations by the Centers for Disease Control and Prevention resulting from increasing rates of COVID-19 infection will continue to be felt for years to come.

Did You Know . . .

In 2019, the poverty rate for families with a female head of house was 24.9 percent, whereas the poverty rate for families with a male head of house was 12.7 percent.

Thus, we are left with a daunting question and task—How do we determine who should get service priority? Different people have different ideas about what is needed. With each member of a community who is asked for input, the list of suggestions will grow.

For social workers, whose primary mission is to help individuals in need, challenging social injustice is critical. Their goals for helping vulnerable populations include (1) assessing and enhancing social resources, (2) acquiring and increasing economic resources, (3) increasing self-determined behavior, and (4) influencing the social policies and organizational and community practices that affect the lives of vulnerable groups (Eamon, 2008). The role of the social worker is crucial in challenging systems that do not treat all individuals fairly. If social justice equates to *fairness* in terms of human relationships within the society, then conditions such as unemployment, poverty, starvation, and inadequate health care and education are only a few of the problems that will need to be addressed. Furthermore, what remains central is that the conditions that exist are often beyond the control of the individual. Frequently, circumstances develop because of often-unrealized coercion imposed by outside political and economic influences and the social order of systems—people sometimes dismiss this concern with the phrase, "That is just the way it is." Starting with the core belief in advocacy for social justice, social workers cannot agree with this statement.

Addressing social justice and encouraging social change are so important to the field of social work that the Ethical Principles of the National Association of Social Workers' Code of Ethics (NASW, 2021) clearly states that "social workers' social change efforts are focused primarily on issues of poverty, unemployment, discrimination, and other forms of social injustice. These activities seek to promote sensitivity to and knowledge about oppression and cultural and ethnic diversity." Our purpose in this chapter is not merely to develop a laundry list of society's ills and social injustices; rather, it is to identify how individuals within a community can begin to address these issues.

Social welfare may be best thought of as public and private programs and services that address social needs while promoting social justice. Our perceptions of social welfare vary. Social welfare conjures an array of images ranging from a homeless person walking to a shelter to a tornado victim receiving assistance from the Red Cross. From the varied perceptions of social welfare, two common but opposing threads emerge.

Many people believe that social welfare recipients are those who cannot make it on their own and need society's help and intervention. Some people also believe that most recipients are responsible for the misfortunes they are experiencing and, in some cases, have created their own problems. This misperception contributes to the view that welfare recipients are not worthy or lack the motivation to help themselves. It is important to note, however, that not everyone feels this way. Many people believe that some of the problems facing welfare recipients are not of their own making. They think that these problems should be regarded like unexpected crises or traumas. In times of crisis, almost everyone expects victims to seek government assistance; such help is considered a right of citizenship.

The varying opinions that people can hold about government assistance and the wide range of social welfare services that can be provided make an accurate definition of social welfare essential. If the concept is defined too narrowly, people may focus on a few programs that account for only a small portion of welfare spending and decide that welfare policy is too specialized. If social welfare is defined too broadly, people may decide that entitlements are being given too freely and that society's limited resources cannot sustain the policy.

Name: Terry Werner
Place of residence: Lincoln, Nebraska
College/university degrees: University of Nebraska, BSW, magna cum laude
Present position and title: Executive director of the Nebraska chapter of the National Association of Social Workers
Previous work experience:
2001–2005: At-large member of the Lincoln City Council and city council chairperson from May 2004 to May 2005
1977–1991: Vice president, Baker Hardware Co., Lincoln, Nebraska
1991–present: President/owner, Werner Family Business, Inc. In 1991, opened a Dairy Queen and later expanded to a second fast-food restaurant. In 1995, opened and operated Nebraska Discount Travel. In 1997, sold the restaurants and concentrated on the travel business.

Why did you choose social work as a career? When I discovered what social work is about, it was an "aha!" moment. I was drawn to the profession because it was a way to contribute by advocating for people less fortunate than me. My orientation was business and much of my career was in business, but my social work degree allowed me to succeed because all careers are about human relationships. I can think of no better college education for nearly any profession. This career has allowed me to continue my life's work of serving the public in a capacity that reflects my personal philosophies and beliefs. What I learned in social work school has enhanced my ability to be a public servant, a personnel manager, a volunteer, an executive director, a political advocate, and a business manager.

What is your favorite social work story? While serving on the Lincoln City Council I was able to pass an initiative called Ride for Five. This program allowed people living in poverty to have unlimited rides on the bus for $5.00 per month. When I was running for re-election, I received a campaign contribution in the mail from a man with mental illness and living on disability. In the envelope were three $1 bills and a note. The note simply said that he wanted to support the person who started the Ride for Five. I was extremely moved by his contribution, knowing that he was truly giving until it hurt.

> *What is one thing you would change in the community if you had the power to do so?* There are so many, but I'll limit it to one. Nebraska has more than sixty-three thousand children living in poverty, equivalent to the population of our third largest city. We consistently rate in the top five states with children in poverty with at least one parent working full-time. I would love to see living wage legislation pass in our state so that parents can raise their families with dignity.

2.3 SOCIAL WELFARE DEFINED

Let's approach the concept of social welfare by examining several existing definitions. Later, we will formulate a definition of our own.

Social welfare is . . .

- "A system of social services and institutions, designed to aid individuals and groups to attain satisfying standards of life and health and personal social relationships which permit them to develop their full capacities and promote their well-being in harmony with the needs of their families and community" (Friedlander, 1955, p. 140).
- "Collective interventions to meet certain needs of the individual and/or to serve the wider interests of society" (Titmus, 1959, p. 42).
- "The assignment of claims from one set of people who are said to produce or earn the national product to another set of people who may merit compassion and charity but not economic rewards for productive service" (Titmus, 1965).
- "Society's organized way to provide for the persistent needs of all people—for health, education, socioeconomic support, personal rights, and political freedom" (Bloom, 1990, p. 6).
- "A concept that encompasses people's health, economic condition, happiness, and quality of life" (W. Segal & Brzuzy, 1998, p. 8).
- "An encompassing and imprecise term but most often it is defined in terms of organizational activities, interventions, or some other element that suggests policy and programs to respond to recognized social problems or to improve the well-being of those at risk" (Reid, 1995, p. 2206).
- "A nation's system of programs, benefits, and services that help people meet those social, economic, educational, and health needs that are fundamental to the maintenance of society" (Barker, 2003, p. 221).
- "Social welfare policy is the collective response to social problems" (E. Segal, 2015, p. 3).
- "The term 'social welfare' does not have a precise definition. Currently, social welfare refers to a wide range of activities and services by volunteers, non-profit organizations and governmental agencies providing help to needy persons

unable to care for themselves; activities and resources designed to enhance or promote the well-being of individuals, families, and the larger society; and efforts to eliminate or reduce the incidence of social problems" (Hansan, 2017).

Close examination of these definitions throughout the years shows that, while the phrasing differs, the content and focus are similar. Let's identify the common themes in these statements as we develop a comprehensive definition of social welfare. First, social welfare includes a variety of programs and services that yield some type of benefit to their consumers. People participating in any type of welfare-based program benefit because they receive some form of assistance. Many times, the assistance, or social provision, is given in cash. At other times, a social provision is given **in kind**, for example, as clothes, food, shelter, or counseling.

Second, social welfare, as a system of programs and services, is designed to meet the needs of people. The needs to be addressed can be all-encompassing, including economic and social well-being, health, education, and overall quality of life.

Third, the result of social welfare is to improve the well-being of individuals, groups, and communities. Helping those systems in time of need will later benefit society at large.

2.4 RESIDUAL AND INSTITUTIONAL SOCIAL WELFARE

In their classic work *Industrial Society and Social Welfare*, Harold Wilensky and Charles Lebeaux (1965) attempted to answer a basic question: Is social welfare a matter of giving assistance only in emergencies, or is it a front-line service that society must provide? As part of their discussion, Wilensky and Lebeaux (1958) developed two important concepts that continue to frame and influence our understanding and discussions of social welfare: **residual social welfare** and **institutional social welfare** (see Table 2.1 for examples). They defined the terms as follows:

- *Residual social welfare* institutions come into play only when the normal structures of supply, the family, and the market break down.
- *Institutional social welfare* services are normal, front-line functions of modern industrial society.

Table 2.1 Examples of Residual and Institutional Programs

Residual	Institutional
Supplemental Nutrition Assistance Program	Social Security
Medicaid	Medicare
Head Start	Libraries
Temporary Assistance for Needy Families	Health departments
Homeless shelters	Veteran's benefits

Residual Social Welfare

The residual conception of social welfare rests on the individualistic notion that people should take care of themselves and rely on government support only in times of crisis or emergency. People are not considered eligible for help until all their own private resources have been exhausted, which may include assistance from the church, family wealth and inheritance, friends, and employers. Only then do public welfare efforts at assistance come into play. To access residual social welfare services, people must first prove their inability to provide for themselves and their families. As a result, the help received often carries the stigma of failure.

Qualifying for this type of service is often referred to as selective eligibility. When eligibility is selective, social services are delivered only to people who meet certain defined criteria, those considered "worthy." When a person needs cash assistance as a service, the eligibility determination procedure is commonly called **means testing**. To access means-tested programs, people must demonstrate that they do not have the financial ability to meet their specific needs. When a residual type of program provides cash assistance, clients must recertify their eligibility every few months. The recertification process is designed primarily to document that clients are still unable to meet their needs through private or personal sources.

People who receive residual services are generally viewed as being different from people who receive other kinds of services. They are often regarded as failures because people think they do not show the "rugged individualism" that many assume serves as a cornerstone ideal of our society. Many times, beneficiaries of residual programs are labeled lazy, immoral, and dishonest. They are often accused of making bad decisions and of needing constant monitoring because of their untrustworthiness. In short, people in residual programs carry a stigma.

Imagine for a moment that you are standing in the checkout line of your local grocery store. The person in front of you is paying for some items with their Electronic Benefits Transfer (EBT) card. Noting this, would you feel compelled to look more closely at what is being purchased? In the grocery cart are potato chips, soda, some candy, and beer, as well as other food items. You have comparable items in your own cart. On a piece of paper, write down your first thoughts about this; is it okay for the person with the EBT card to purchase beer or liquor and potato chips, or should the money be spent on fruits and vegetables? Be honest and allow yourself to express any thoughts and feelings you might have. One response to this kind of situation is shown in Box 2.2.

The response illustrated in Box 2.2 is not unusual. In fact, it is typical of the way many people view and react to beneficiaries of residual programs, and it raises some interesting questions. Do people receiving assistance have a right to entertainment? Or when they accept public assistance, do they give up their right to the luxuries that are available to people who are not dependent on this social welfare service? Look at it another way: Should the person on food stamps be treated any differently from you, your friends, or members of your family? As we will see in Chapter 3, the history of social

> **BOX 2.2**
>
> ## WELFARE: CRITICS OF WELFARE ACROSS THIRTY-EIGHT YEARS; NOTHING REALLY CHANGES
>
> ### Example 1: January 1, 1983, *Dallas* (TX) *Morning News*, Letters to the Editor
>
> Last week I was passing through the checking line at a supermarket. In front of me was a young woman with two children about 5 and 6. She paid for her groceries with food stamps. On their way out they stopped by the store's video game machines. All three played the game, once each. In other words, the woman squandered 75 cents while letting taxpayers pay for the groceries. That money would have bought a dozen eggs for that "poor" family. I wonder if their color TV and stereo are working? I never have objected to my tax dollars being spent to help the truly poor, but I protest vehemently the idea of helping them pay for their entertainment or luxuries.
>
> (Name Withheld)
> Dallas, Texas
>
> ### Example 2: September 23, 2014, *Modesto* (CA) *Bee*, Letters to the Editor
>
> We constantly hear about how Social Security is going to run out of money. How come we never hear about welfare running out of money? What is interesting is the first group "worked for" their money; the second didn't. The Food Stamp Program, administered by the U.S. Department of Agriculture, is proud to be distributing this year the greatest amount of free meals and food stamps ever to 47 million people, according to the most recent figures in 2013. Meanwhile, the National Park Service asks us: "Please do not feed the animals." The stated reason is because "animals will grow dependent on handouts and will not learn to take care of themselves."
>
> (Name Withheld)
> Ceres, California
>
> ### Example 3: August 17, 2021, Facebook comment on a story about a "raise to food stamps."
>
> Yea right. There [sic] talking about 30 plus percent increase in food stamps and [the current president's administration] is bragging about a whooping 5 per cent increase for Social Security. That my friend is just Plain BULLS***. They are giving money from people who worked all their life and paid into SSI [sic]. and giving it too Lazy A** People who REFUSE to work. It is time for CHANGE.
>
> (Name Withheld)
> Unverified location

welfare is marred by a reluctance to help others in need. Residual programs and services are stigmatized, and those who need these types of services are constantly scrutinized. Many people believe that such services, although necessary as temporary forms of assistance or as last-resort charity, reinforce negative behaviors rather than promoting rugged individualism and a strong work ethic. In 2024, social media comments certainly come across as less filtered than letters to the editor from past years, but the sentiment remains constant.

In summary, residual programs highlight narrow views of helping. Assistance is minimal and temporary and designed only to help people survive immediate problems or crises. These types of programs provide support only when no other options are available. In other words, a residual program is a program of last resort. In the 1980s, American public welfare programs were categorized as essentially residual in nature. Collectively referred to as *the safety net*, these programs could be accessed only after all other avenues of assistance had been exhausted.

There are three important points to keep in mind regarding residual programs. First, these programs are all means tested. To be eligible for benefits, people must document their inability to care financially for themselves and their families. In a typical residual program, clients are routinely means tested or recertified for continued eligibility every few months.

Second, residual programs can create barriers for those who seek assistance. The numerous eligibility criteria, which often force clients to produce a variety of supporting documents and evidence, can be disheartening. Continual recertification processes can thus encourage clients to give up, forgoing assistance even when their needs persist.

Third, residual programs carry a stigma, and recipients are not proud to receive services. SNAP, more commonly referred to as the food stamp program, is a typical residual program (see Table 2.1). Recipients must qualify to receive program services, they must be recertified every few months by the state, and they are not viewed positively in the greater community.

Recall the SNAP recipient in our hypothetical grocery checkout line. How often do we look at what the person ahead of us is buying? Do we spend more time scrutinizing the purchases of those who pay with a "food stamp" EBT card? If another person had been purchasing the same items and paying with cash, would our reactions have been the same? Probably not. Why? Because both individuals have similar buying habits, why is there a difference in how these two people are viewed? The sad reality is that the person receiving food assistance from the government carries a stigma. Some people believe that beneficiaries of residual programs such as food stamps cannot be trusted, are morally weak, and do not make good decisions. They are often thought to be different from people who do not receive public aid.

Institutional Social Welfare

The second conception of social welfare described by Wilensky and Lebeaux (1965) is institutional social welfare. This definition of social welfare gives it much broader scope and function than the residual definition. In the institutional conception, the community is expected to assist individual members because problems are viewed not as failures, but as part of life in modern society. This broader community responsibility allows members in need to be provided with services that go beyond immediate response to emergencies. Help is often provided before people exhaust all their own resources, and preventive and rehabilitative services are stressed.

Therefore, an institutional program, as opposed to a residual program, is designed to meet the needs of all people. Eligibility is universal. Institutional programs have no stigma attached and are viewed as regular front-line programs in society. In fact, institutional programs are so widely accepted in society that many are not viewed as social welfare programs at all (see examples in Table 2.1). Institutional programs are often called entitlement programs, meaning that services and benefits are available because of a person's earned status (see activities in this chapter). Many laypersons do not understand the term *entitlement*, and people have begun to connote the term pejoratively. One legislator declared Social Security to be an insurance program, not an entitlement program (Larson, 2018), saying calling Social Security an entitlement is simply wrong and that it is the insurance Americans have paid to fund retirement, disability, and survivor benefits based on previous work history over a lifetime.

In concluding our discussion of residual and institutional provision of social welfare as outlined by Wilensky and Lebeaux, we must note the primary weakness of this framework. Specifically, not all programs and services are easily classified as institutional or residual; some programs have both institutional and residual attributes. The Head Start program, for example, is institutional in nature, but it is means tested and restricted to a particular segment of the population. One solution is to expand the traditional dichotomy and classify social programs on a residual–institutional continuum. A program's position on the continuum reflects whether it is more residual or more institutional in design. Some questions to help guide the classification process, include the following:

1. Is the program short or long term?
2. Is the program open to all people or a selected group of people?
3. Do program participants carry a stigma?
4. Does the public embrace the program?
5. Is the program controversial?
6. How would you feel if you were a program participant?

For all social programs, whether institutional or residual, the importance of ensuring social justice by addressing social stigma and misperception cannot be underestimated. The public does appear to openly support some forms of social welfare, but these feelings and expectations seem to vary based on individual perception and the service that is being received.

> **Activity**
>
> Ask fifteen to twenty people to define the term social welfare. Then ask them to list five social welfare programs of which they are aware. Review these responses considering the work of Wilensky and Lebeaux. Do you notice any patterns? How many of the programs would you identify as residual, institutional, or a mix of both types? In analyzing these responses, do you find that people have a narrow or a broad view of social welfare? How do you feel about the responses you received? Do you think your respondents' views are accurate?

2.5 IS EVERYONE REALLY ON WELFARE?

Famed British social scientist Richard Titmus (1965) argued that social welfare was much more than aid to the poor and in fact represented a broad system of support to the middle and upper classes. In his model, social welfare has three branches:

1. Fiscal welfare: tax benefits and supports for the middle and upper classes.
2. Corporate welfare: tax benefits and supports for businesses.
3. Public welfare: assistance to the poor.

Abramowitz (1983) applied the Titmus model to American social welfare. She identified a *shadow welfare state* for the wealthy that parallels the social service system available to poor people. She concluded that poor and nonpoor individuals alike benefit from government programs and tax laws that raise their disposable income. In other words, were it not for direct government support—whether through SNAP food assistance or through a child care tax exemption—people would have fewer dollars to spend and to support themselves and their families.

So, is everyone really on welfare? To address this question, let's focus first on college students. Did you know that college students are probably one of the largest groups of welfare recipients in the United States today? Most college students first attended public school, which was provided at no direct cost to them. Why? Because our government subsidizes the public school system. It is important for all children to have nutritious meals, and the daily school lunch is relatively inexpensive. In fact, try to buy the same meal in a restaurant and compare costs—the school lunch is much cheaper. Why? Because the government subsidies given to public schools lower the cost of these meals for all students. Okay, that's what happens in public school. Now consider the role of government in a public college. Compare tuition fees at a private college or university with those at a state- or community-supported institution. Why are tuition costs at the public college lower? Once again, the answer is simple: because of government subsidies. The government is involved in subsidizing the educational needs of students at the elementary, secondary, and college levels. Students are very dependent on these subsidies to complete their education.

With all the support provided and the need for continuing support, don't these educational subsidies sound like welfare? Why then is there no stigma attached to this form of social provision? Some people may say, "I paid for my *welfare* through taxes on my earnings, which makes me different from those people who did not." There is no easy response to this statement, and such attitudes continue to disturb social work professionals who do not agree with the distinction between worthy and unworthy people that is often applied to recipients of social services. Is there really a difference in the welfare service provided? Could most individuals and families afford to pay the full tuition for college that include the costs, such as but not limited to heating and cooling, building maintenance, and campus security? Government subsidies are important to the maintenance of society and are used by all people.

Mettler (2011) wrote that a system of social programs for wealthy individuals is consuming the federal budget, although most of those who receive these benefits do not see themselves as welfare recipients. From this perspective, it was stated that the most affluent Americans receive the largest benefits on social tax expenditures. For example, 64 percent of veterans reported in 2008 that they had not participated in a government program even though they were directly receiving benefits from the tax-advantaged 529 savings account for education. By 2017, some believed the average amount of dollars returned to people through so-called tax loopholes reached $1.4 trillion per year; see Table 2.2 for the top ten largest tax expenditures (so-called loopholes). The examples go on and on. The bottom line is that *everyone is on welfare.*

Table 2.2 Ten Largest Tax Expenditures for Fiscal Year 2019

Rank	Tax expenditure	Billions ($)
1	Exclusion of employer contributions for health care, health insurance premiums, and long-term care insurance	164.1
2	Reduced rates of tax on dividends and long-term capital gains	127.0
3	Credit for children and other dependents	121.2
4	Tax benefits for employer-defined contributions plans	120.8
5	Tax benefits for defined benefit plans	90.2
6	Earned income credit	71.4
7	Depreciation of equipment in excess of the alternative depreciation system	71.2
8	Reduced tax rate on active income of controlled foreign corporations	68.0
9	Subsidies for insurance purchased through health benefit exchanges	53.2
10	20 percent deduction for qualified business income	48.6

Source: Joint Committee on Taxation (2018).

2.6 PUBLIC SOCIAL WELFARE

Social welfare is found in both public and private settings. *Public* refers to programs within the purview of state, federal, or local (city or county) government. Examples of public welfare include state agencies that deal with child protective services, adult protective services, housing services, SNAP, some mental health agencies, social security, and employment. *Private* refers to services provided for nonprofit agencies, voluntary services, and international nongovernmental organizations (NGOs). Agencies funded by the United Way and faith-based programs are types of private, nonprofit agencies. Increasingly, the difference between the two has blurred as government has "outsourced" what had been public welfare programs to private providers (e.g., in some states, child protective services are implemented via private social service agencies or nongovernmental agencies). Additionally, social welfare services also get delivered via for-profit organizations.

Federal Welfare

One would think it would be easy to find out how much money the government spends each year on social welfare. That is not the case, however, and to make matters even more difficult, the published information is often badly out of date.

Why is it difficult to determine the government's welfare expenditures? The answer rests with how you define welfare and what programs you count as social welfare (see Figure 2.2). For example, do you consider the reduced school meals program, veterans' affairs, and Section 8 housing social welfare? The budgets for these three programs are in three different federal agencies; they are not part of one major federal welfare budget. What about Medicare and unemployment insurance? What about a library, a police or fire department, or a local waste management control agency—are they social welfare programs? As you can see, trying to identify all welfare programs and their budgets is problematic.

The federal government classifies social welfare into seven broad areas: social insurance, education, public aid, health and medical programs, veterans' programs, housing, and other social welfare (see Box 2.3). Social insurance has been and continues to be the costliest area of federal welfare, followed by education. The federal government, at the time of writing this chapter, expected to spend upward of $6.011 trillion in 2022, with more than 65% of that amount paying for mandated services, including Social Security, Medicare, and Medicaid (Amaedo, 2022). It is interesting to note, however, that when welfare cuts are discussed, the emphasis is on public aid. But what would happen, for example, if the federal appropriation for

FIGURE 2.2
The U.S. Social Security Administration serves as a hub for administering many public social welfare benefits.

> **BOX 2.3**
>
> ## FEDERAL SOCIAL WELFARE PROGRAMS
>
> In 2022, there were eighty-plus means-tested federal programs. Examples include:
>
> - *Social insurance*: retirement for older adults (a.k.a. Social Security), workers' compensation, disability, unemployment assistance, railroad retirement, public employee retirement, and Supplemental Social Security
> - *Education*: Elementary, secondary, and higher education; vocational education
> - *Public aid*: Cash payments under Temporary Assistance to Needy Families including pass-through child support, general assistance, and emergency assistance
> - *Veterans' programs*: Assistance to veterans and their families, burial, health and medical programs, education, life insurance
> - *Housing*: Public housing, Section 8 housing vouchers
> - *Health and medical programs*: Medicare, Medicaid, **Affordable Health Care Act**, maternal and child health programs, medical research, school health, other public health, medical facilities construction
> - Other social welfare: vocational rehabilitation, institutional care, child nutrition, child welfare, ACTION programs, social welfare not classified elsewhere, food and nutrition through Supplemental Nutrition Assistance Program and Women, Infants, and Children

the basic welfare programs, such as housing assistance, health, and SNAP, were to aggressively cut this allocation by $500 billion? The savings would be huge, right? Yet, this $500 billion would reduce the total federal budget by approximately 0.075757 percent, or approximately three quarters of one percent.

Any number of people and groups will advocate for the government to cut welfare to balance the budget. Yet, the numbers just do not add up and would do more harm to those in poverty by exacerbating the fragility of their day-to-day living circumstances. That harm extends to the larger society through an increase in the micro- and macro-level ills that accompany poverty, ultimately manifesting in a less healthy and less productive population.

Activity

For a moment, pretend to be a U.S. senator or a member of the U.S. House of Representatives. Your assignment is simple: balance the federal budget and eliminate the projected 2022 $1.2 trillion deficit. Search for the website Federal Budget Challenge and follow the directions. You will be asked to increase, decrease, or maintain expenditures and revenues for the federal government.

State Welfare

State welfare programs differ across the country. Each state develops its own set of social programs to augment the federal government's initiatives. Typically, a state establishes rules and provides funds for statewide social agencies. State social welfare agencies include protective services for children and vulnerable adults and juvenile justice. Funding for state services comes from two sources: block grants from the federal government and state tax revenues. A block grant is a lump sum of funds given to a state, which then has the authority to determine how best to spend the dollars. The federal government imposes few rules on block grants, allowing each state to determine how programs will be structured. A state can also supplement block grant funding to expand services.

Local Welfare

City and county welfare programs depend on local taxes for funding. Such funds are primarily used for community protection and support, such as police, fire, and other basic local services. Funding and provision of most of these types of local social services are considered mandatory. By contrast, many government officials and community leaders see social welfare provision as a minimal, *fill the gap* measure. Those in power are usually reluctant to develop and sponsor costly local services. As with state government programs, the types and levels of local welfare programs vary by municipality. Because of their gap-filling status, local programs are generally residual in nature. Typical local programs include emergency food relief and housing and clothing vouchers.

2.7 PRIVATE SOCIAL WELFARE

Private social welfare consists of for-profit and not-for-profit agencies, also called voluntary agencies, nonprofits, or NGOs. Examples of nonprofits include the United Way, Red Cross, Salvation Army, Boys & Girls Clubs, Girl Scouts, YMCA, YWCA, Jewish Community Centers, Catholic Charities, and Family Services. Whereas in the United States such social service agencies are commonly referred to as nonprofits, internationally they are called NGOs.

Karger and Stoesz (2010) wrote that confusion exists around the role of private social welfare and characterize it as "the forgotten sector" (p. 150). For the most part, American social welfare rested within the public domain since the 1930s, when the government implemented a series of welfare programs to combat the effects of the Great Depression. As the government took on greater welfare responsibility, the voluntary sector's activities lessened (Karger & Stoesz, 2010, p. 4). With financial cuts in federal welfare funding beginning in the early 1980s and continuing well into the twenty-first century, private welfare has taken on new importance. This forgotten sector is now recognized as a crucial player in the delivery of social services.

The nonprofit sector relies on donations from public foundations and federal, state, and local governments. For nonprofits to provide services, their fundraising efforts, including grant writing, must be successful. The success of fundraising depends on three factors: (1) the agency's ability to provide a high-quality program, (2) the agency's ability to communicate its successes, and (3) the community's financial ability to support the program. Karger and Stoesz (2010) suggested that the voluntary sector, although well received by the public, faces many challenges, including commercialization, an increase in faith-based services, and the growth of private independent practice (pp. 159–163). Therefore, in most instances, the level of private social welfare programming available depends directly on the financial well-being of the surrounding community. This dependence on private funding is particularly problematic during periods of economic turmoil, such as recession and rising unemployment. During these periods, people have less money and time to donate to private charities, which in turn forces these organizations to make critical choices about which programs to close or cut.

According to the Social Security Administration, the role of the private sector in financing social welfare continues to grow, and this growth is needed to complement public social welfare expenditures and programs. Hoeffer and Colby (1998) referred to the private sector as the "mirror welfare state," a system of services that reflect public programs but are more supportive of the middle and upper classes than of the poor population.

2.8 SOCIAL WORK IN THE SOCIAL WELFARE SYSTEM

Social workers make up a primary professional group in the social welfare system. But social work is not the sole social welfare profession. Given the broad definition of social welfare used here and in the social work literature, many other professional groups are welfare providers as well. Although it is possible to lump the various professionals together and classify them all as welfare workers, it is more accurate to recognize that some professions are more concerned than others with people's social, health, wellness, and economic welfare needs. A useful way to differentiate among professions is to classify their level of involvement as either primary or secondary.

The primary category consists of professions whose principal efforts are in the provision of social, health, or economic services. The principal activities of professions in the secondary category are not directed toward welfare, but their work does at times involve social, health, or economic service provision (see Table 2.3).

Look at the professionals listed in Table 2.3. What is your opinion of who is included and where they have been placed? Do you think the professionals listed would agree with their classification? For example, how would an elementary school teacher react to being described as a welfare worker? We believe that many of the professionals listed would openly disagree that they are welfare providers. It is possible that the stigma attached to programs and services offered under the rubric of welfare might influence

Table 2.3 Examples of Social Welfare Professionals by Primary or Secondary Classification

Primary	Secondary
Social workers	Police officers
Mental health counselors	Librarians
Schoolteachers	Recreational specialists
Marriage and family therapists	Road crews
Psychologists	Government officials
Psychiatrists	Military personnel
Nurses	Sanitation workers

their reactions. To explore this possibility, how do you think these professionals would reply to the following question: Do you as a professional provide a program, benefit, or service that helps people meet those social, economic, educational, health, and wellness needs that are fundamental to the maintenance of society?

We believe that, as this question is framed—without openly addressing the concept of social welfare provision—most of the professionals listed in Table 2.3, whether classified as primary or secondary service providers, would answer yes. The simple truth is that, although few professionals think of their activities in this way, providing welfare services is an integral part of their jobs.

Our broad definition of social welfare also suggests some rethinking and challenging of the narrow, rigid ideas about social work. Social work began as a profession that primarily worked with the poor and disenfranchised (Hepworth, Rooney, & Larsen, 2002); sadly, in the twenty-first century, these groups of people are negatively stereotyped by the general public, and there are increased calls to reduce and eliminate services.

Although social work may have started out working with poor populations and those generally cast off by society, the profession broadened its scope of work. Services and interventions were created to reach into new practice arenas such as mental health and health care. Both the 2008 and the 2018 revisions of the NASW Code of Ethics reflected this dynamic expanding purpose:

> The primary mission of the social work profession is to enhance human well-being and help meet the basic human needs of all people, with particular attention to the needs and empowerment of people who are vulnerable, oppressed, and living in poverty. A historic and defining feature of social work is the profession's focus on individual well-being in a social context and the well-being of society. Fundamental to social work is the attention to the environmental forces that create, contribute to, and address problems in living. . . . These activities may be in the form of direct practice, community organizing, supervision,

consultation, administration, advocacy, social and political action, policy development and implementation, education, and research and evaluation. (NASW, 2008, 2018)

So today we find that the social welfare system and the social work profession address an array of diverse populations—such as people who are situationally and chronically homeless; victims of child and adult abuse and neglect; couples dealing with marital stress, unemployment, or underemployment; persons with behavioral health issues; individuals facing medical crises or addicted to a variety of substances; or juveniles in conflict with the law—with a variety of public and private programs and services.

We also find that the term *client* is now used inclusively and can mean individuals, groups, families, organizations, and communities. Adopting, in essence, the institutional perspective, the social worker strives to restore and enhance client wellness and to provide preventive as well as basic services (Dziegielewski & Holliman, 2020). Strategies to assist clients must address all these areas because often the factors involved are intertwined and interdependent.

The Fading Distinction between Public and Private

Changes in the social welfare environment have blurred once-clear distinctions in social work—for example, whether an agency that employs a social worker is public or private. For simplicity, public agencies are understood to be primarily, if not totally, funded through tax-supported dollars. It is the public agency that is regarded as most representative of social welfare services and programs (see activity below). Most people believe that these agencies have the primary responsibility for residual or means-tested social welfare programs. Private agencies, however, are believed (although that belief may not be entirely true) to be voluntarily supported and to rarely have tax-supported dollars as part of their basic budgets.

If public and private agencies were distinctly different, these straightforward definitions would suffice. However, in today's political world, nothing could be further from the truth. There is no longer any clear distinction between public and private agencies because their funding and the services they deliver so often overlap. Many private agencies now actively seek public or tax-supported funds, and many public agencies now contract with private agencies and individual providers to serve their clients. Because private agencies can specialize in a way that public agencies with their broad

Activity

Go to your local (county or city) welfare or public assistance office. Look around and try to get a feel for the setting. What messages does the physical structure send to the clients? Does this environment seem like a typical business setting? Do the setting and staff

> suggest an interest in serving the clients, and are the clients made to feel important? How does this facility differ from a physician's office? What sorts of informational brochures are available to read? How long do clients wait before a worker sees them?
>
> After you have visited a public agency, visit a private social service agency. What differences, if any, do you see between the two agencies? Why do you think they exist? Should there be any physical differences between public and private agencies?

responsibilities cannot, such contracts allow public agencies to secure services that they do not have the budget or the skilled personnel to offer on their own.

In addition to this blurring of public and private agencies, a dispersion of social workers across both the public and the private sectors has placed social work practitioners in new roles. Traditionally, social workers found jobs in public agencies because these agencies and programs assumed the primary responsibility for poor and underserved individuals. Today, however, social workers practice in diverse agency settings that have many different goals and allegiances.

Cost Containment versus Quality

For all social workers, the current state of social work practice mirrors the turbulence in the general social welfare environment. There is little consistency in the delivery of social welfare services because a primary emphasis has been placed on cost containment, with each state designing and creating its unique services' structures. Social welfare program administrators, forced to justify each dollar billed for services, may reduce the provision of what some see as *expendable services*, designed to promote the mental health and well-being of clients. They may be tempted to regard the role of social workers as adjunct to the delivery of care and to cut back on professional staff or replace them with nonprofessionals simply to lower costs. These substitute professionals, or more appropriately *paraprofessionals*, have neither the depth nor the breadth of training of social work professionals, often resulting in substandard professional services.

The employment of these kinds of paraprofessionals, though cost-effective, is not quality driven. When social services are rushed or minimized, issues such as the individual client's sense of well-being, ability to self-care, and family and environmental support may not be considered. The involvement of social work professionals is thus essential to ensuring that personal, social, and environmental issues are addressed and clients are not put at risk of harm.

For social workers, a client who is discharged home to a family that does not want them is at risk of abuse and neglect. A client who has a negative view of themselves and a hopeless and hapless view of their condition is more likely to attempt suicide or come to some other harm. Many paraprofessionals and members of other professional disciplines differ from social work professionals in that they do not recognize the paramount importance of culture and environmental factors to efficient and effective practice.

Their outlook may enable the delivery of cheap service at the cost of substandard care that has a direct negative impact on the client.

As social service administrators strive to cut costs by eliminating professional social work services, the overall philosophy of wellness may be sacrificed. It is important to note, however, that staff reorganizations and reductions in social welfare services are rarely personal attacks on social work professionals. The changes and cutbacks in services and those who provide them are responses to an immediate need to provide cost reduction. Fluctuating employment and downsizing of a social work professional workforce, like other allied health professionals, simply reflects the varied support of the public, and the ensuing political implications, for general and shared social well-being (Dziegielewski & Holliman, 2020; Falck, 1990).

SUMMARY

So, what is social welfare? The residual view suggests that welfare support should be temporary, only for poor individuals, and as little as possible. If we look at actual public welfare spending, however, it seems that social welfare as practiced is much broader. In fact, everyone in society is a welfare recipient of one type or another, including corporations.

The role of the social work professional is broader than many people expect. Originally, social workers served poor and disenfranchised populations; however, over the years, the role of the social worker has expanded tremendously. Many social work professionals now provide services outside the traditional social welfare realm. This diversity of style, task, and approach makes it difficult to define exactly what social workers do. Clarity of definition has been further complicated by changes in scope of practice, roles served, and expectations within the client–professional relationship. Recent portrayals of social workers in the media as "action heroes" who, in their frustration, turn vigilante further serve to show the frustration that can be experienced when caught between advocating for social justice and being trapped within the rigid rules of the social welfare system (see the 2021 film *The Gateway*).

In today's turbulent social welfare environment, social work professionals face a constant battle of system restrictions and quality-of-care issues for clients versus cost containment measures (Dziegielewski & Holliman, 2020). In addition, in a profession rich in ethical standards and expectations, they must strive to maintain a secure place as professional providers in the delivery of social welfare services.

QUIZ ANSWERS

1. a. The former Food Stamp Program.
2. a. Mothers and their children. Approximately 60 percent of all welfare recipients, according to the U.S. Census Bureau, are mothers and their children.
3. a. True. More than fifty million people in the United States lived in poverty in 2021.
4. b. False. Under federal welfare rules, a family on welfare that has another baby will not receive any additional benefits.

CHAPTER 2: SOCIAL WELFARE: A SYSTEM'S RESPONSE TO PERSONAL ISSUES

5. b. False. The unemployment rate identifies only those people not working who actively looked for a job within the past thirty days.
6. c. False. Each state determines the amount a family receives on public assistance. As a result, the amount received by a person in Florida is a different amount from the amount received by someone in Alabama.
7. b. False. According to reports by the U.S. Bureau of Labor Statistics, more than 70 percent of public assistance recipients are women with children, children, and older adults.
8. All groups listed are participants in programs the federal government defines as "social welfare." As a result, people in all these groups are welfare recipients.
9. b. False. This is a trick question—Aid to Families with Dependent Children was replaced by Temporary Assistance to Needy Families in 1996.
10. Revise your original answer to this question using the information presented in this chapter.

REFERENCES

Abramowitz, M. (1983). Everyone is on welfare: "The role of redistribution in social policy" revisited. *Social Work, 28,* 440–445.

Amaedo, K. (2022, June 24). U.S. federal budget breakdown. Retrieved December 26, 2022, from https://www.thebalancemoney.com/u-s-federal-budget-breakdown-3305789

American Land Title Association. (2010, April 15). *Study: 1.2 million households were lost during recession.* TitleNews Online Archive. Retrieved from https://www.mba.org/news-and-research/research-and-economics/research-institute-for-housing-america

Barker, R. L. (2003). *The social work dictionary* (5th ed.). Washington, DC: NASW Press.

Bloom, M. (1990). *Introduction to the social work drama.* Itasca, IL: Peacock.

Center for Nutrition Policy and Promotion (2021). *USDA Food Plans: Cost of Food Reports (monthly reports). USDA Food and Nutrition Service.* https://www.fns.usda.gov/cnpp/usda-food-plans-cost-food-reports-monthly-reports

Children's Defense Fund. (2021). *The State of America's Children® 2021.* https://www.childrensdefense.org/state-of-americas-children-2021/soac-2021-child-poverty/

Dziegielewski, S. F., & Holliman, D. (2020). *The changing face of health care social work: Opportunities and challenges for professional practice* (4th ed.). New York, NY: Springer.

Eamon, M. K. (2008). *Empowering vulnerable populations.* Chicago, IL: Lyceum Books.

Falck, H. S. (1990). Maintaining social work standards in for-profit hospitals: Reasons for doubt. *Health & Social Work, 15,* 76–77.

Friedlander, W. (1955). *Introduction to social welfare.* Englewood Cliffs, NJ: Prentice Hall.

Hansan, J. E. (2017). *What is social welfare history?* Social Welfare History Project. Retrieved from http://socialwelfare.library.vcu.edu/recollections/social-welfare-history/

Hepworth, D. H., Rooney, R. H., & Larsen, J. (2002). *Direct social work practice: Theory and skills.* Pacific Grove, CA: Brooks/Cole.

Hoeffer, R., & Colby, I. (1998). Private social welfare expenditures. In I. C. Colby, A. Garcia, R. G. McRoy, L. Videka-Sherman, & R. L. Edwards (Eds.), *Encyclopedia of social work: 1997 supplement*. Washington, DC: NASW Press.

Joint Committee on Taxation. (2019). *Estimates of Federal Tax Expenditures for Fiscal Years 2019–2023 (JCX-55-19)*, December 18, 2019. Retrieved September 3, 2021 from https://www.jct.gov/CMSPages/GetFile.aspx?guid=71b5ac20-f36a-46fb-9def-f7194212e849.

Karger, H. J., & Stoesz, D. (2010). *American social welfare policy: A pluralist approach* (6th ed.). Boston, MA: Pearson Education/Allyn Bacon.

Larson, J. P. (2018, March 14). *Larson: Social security is not an entitlement* [press release]. Retrieved from https://larson.house.gov/media-center/press-releases/larson-social-security-not-entitlement

Mettler, S. (2011, July/August). 20,000 leagues under the state. *Washington Monthly*. Retrieved from https://washingtonmonthly.com/2011/06/24/20000-leagues-under-the-state/

National Association of Social Workers. (2008). *Code of ethics of the National Association of Social Workers*. Washington, DC: Author.

National Association of Social Workers. (2018). *Code of ethics of the National Association of Social Workers*. Washington, DC: Author. Retrieved December 27, 2022, from https://socialwork.sdsu.edu/wp-content/uploads/2011/09/NASW-Code-of-Ethics2017.pdf

National Association of Social Workers. (2021). *Highlighted Revisions to the Code of Ethics*. https://www.socialworkers.org/About/Ethics/Code-of-Ethics/Highlighted-Revisions-to-the-Code-of-Ethics

National Center for Children in Poverty. (2021). Child poverty. Retrieved from https://www.nccp.org/data-table/?data=per&unit=Children&age=18&inc=Poor&cat=income&denom=char&state=US

Peterson, C., Liu, Y., Kresnow, M., Florence, C., Merrick, M. T., DeGue, S., & Lokey, C. N. (2018). Short-term lost productivity per victim: Intimate partner violence, sexual violence, or stalking. *American Journal of Preventive Medicine*, 55(1), 106–110. https://doi.org/10.1016/j.amepre.2018.03.007

Rank, M., & Hirschl, T. (2021). Poverty Facts and Myths. Confronting Poverty. https://confrontingpoverty.org/poverty-facts-and-myths/

Reid, P. N. (1995). Social welfare history. In R. Edwards & J. G. Hopps (Eds.), *Encyclopedia of social work* (19th ed.). Washington, DC: NASW Press.

Satcher, D. (2000). Foreword. In U.S. Public Health Service, *Report of the surgeon general's conference on children's mental health: A national action agenda* (pp. 1–2). Washington, DC: U.S. Department of Health and Human Services.

Segal, E. (2015). *Social Welfare Policy and Social Programs: A Values Perspective* (4th ed.). Belmont, CA: Brooks/Cole, Cengage Learning.

Segal, W., & Brzuzy, S. (1998). *Social welfare policy, programs, and practice*. Itasca, IL: Peacock.

Semega, J., Kollar, M., Shrider, E., & Creamer, J. (2020). *Income and Poverty in the United States: 2019*. United States Census Bureau. https://www.census.gov/library/publications/2020/demo/p60-270.html

Titmus, R. (1959). *Essays on the welfare state*. New Haven, CT: Yale University Press.

Titmus, R. (1965). The role of redistribution in social policy. *Social Security Bulletin*, 28(6), 34–55.

U. S. Census Bureau. (2023, September 12). *Poverty Thresholds*. https://www.census.gov/data/tables/time-series/demo/income-poverty/historical-poverty-thresholds.html

Wilensky, H., & Lebeaux, C. (1958). *Industrial society and social welfare*. New York, NY: Russell Sage Foundation.

Wilensky, H., & Lebeaux, C. (1965). *Industrial society and social welfare*. New York, NY: Free Press.

World Bank. (2022). *Poverty and shared prosperity 2022: Correcting the course*. Washington, DC: World Bank Group (https://www.worldbank.org/en/home). Retrieved from: https://openknowledge.worldbank.org/server/api/core/bitstreams/b96b361a-a806-5567-8e8a-b14392e11fa0/content

World Bank. (2020). *Poverty and shared prosperity 2020: Reversals of fortune* -Frequently asked questions. Washington, DC: World Bank Group (https://www.worldbank.org/en/home). Retrieved from: https://www.worldbank.org/en/research/brief/poverty-and-shared-prosperity-2020-reversals-of-fortune-frequently-asked-questions

3

How Did We Get Here from There?

CHAPTER 3: EPAS COMPETENCIES

Social work programs at the bachelor's and the master's level are accredited by the Council of Social Work Education (CSWE). CSWE's Educational Policy and Accreditation Standards (EPAS) describe the processes and criteria that social work courses should cover. In 2022, CSWE updated its EPAS standards. The following competencies are addressed in this chapter.

Competency 1: Demonstrate Ethical and Professional Behavior

Social workers understand the value base of the profession and its ethical standards, as well as relevant policies, laws, and regulations that may affect practice with individuals, families, groups, organizations, and communities.

Competency 2: Advance Human Rights and Social, Racial, Economic, and Environmental Justice

Social workers understand that every person regardless of position in society has fundamental human rights.

Competency 5: Engage in Policy Practice

Social workers identify social policy at the local, state, federal, and global levels that affects well-being, human rights and justice, service delivery, and access to social services.

3.1 TIME FOR A BRIEF HISTORY QUIZ

1. Why is the year 1492 important in American history?
2. The **New Deal** was the name given to what set of programs?
3. What did the Emancipation Proclamation address?
4. What important event took place in Seneca Falls, New York, in 1848?
5. Where was an immigrant arriving at Ellis Island (see Figure 3.1) most likely to be from?
6. What is Salem, Massachusetts, perhaps best known for?
7. The United States acquired California, Nevada, Utah, and parts of Texas, Colorado, New Mexico, and Wyoming as part of what act or event?
8. What document preceded the U.S. Constitution?
9. What does the term Seward's Folly refer to?
10. What was at issue in the Dred Scott case?

FIGURE 3.1
Ellis Island served as the first contact with the U.S. government for immigrants arriving to the United States from 1892 to 1924.

So, how did you do? (The answers are at the end of the chapter.) For most people taking this quiz, the results are mixed. A few of the questions seem easy, whereas others are complete mysteries. Yet each of these questions addresses a meaningful part of American history. The importance of being familiar with such events is twofold: (1) as informed citizens, we need to know about our history; and (2) knowledge of the past forms a crucial basis to help us understand and attempt to influence both present and future societal developments.

In the field of social work, as in other disciplines, knowing the history of the profession is essential to understanding its past, present, and future (Alexander, 1995). Social work has come a long way from its early beginnings, transcending its origins within religious orders to be adopted by public/private benefactors (Leighninger, 2008; Stern & Axinn, 2018). Unfortunately, however, studying history and looking at what happened in the past may not seem as exciting as learning about direct social work practice, policy, or social action (see the activity below). When history is discussed in the classroom or in less formal situations, it is frequently met with an air of indifference and reluctance. As one student remarked, "It's over and done with, so why should I be concerned about it? I want to learn how to help people. What happened two hundred years ago won't help me today."

Is this statement valid? It is true that in social work practice, regardless of the model or technique employed, the emphasis is on the here and now. Nevertheless, most social workers recognize the importance of history in their practice. For example, when first meeting a client, the social worker asks probing, thoughtful questions about the client's past. This systematic accumulation of information is referred to as gathering a social history or a **psychosocial history**. A social work practitioner would never consider the social history that they complete for each client to be useless information. In particular, the social history is important to understand and explore a client's growth and development process, as well as to identify possible effects of events and relations with others in the client's past.

The past offers valuable clues to interpreting the present and anticipating the future. History is essential to helping all of us better understand who we are and how we got here. It also influences our future decisions. Indeed, some people take the extreme position that we are so profoundly influenced by the past that it determines the future. This theory is called *determinism*.

Activity

Think about three people from social welfare or social work history who you would like to meet and invite to dinner. Maybe Nobel Peace Prize recipient Jane Addams or Queen Elizabeth I. How about Frederick Douglass, an activist and social reformer who opposed the denial of Black exclusion from citizenship? What about Mary Richmond, who was a leader of the Charity Organization Society in the late nineteenth and early twentieth centuries, or Frances Perkins, the first woman to hold a president's cabinet position? You decide. What would you want to ask them and what do you think they would say?

Whatever degree of importance we place on history, it is obvious that people—sometimes intentionally, sometimes unintentionally—use past experiences as a frame of reference for current and future experiences. For example, a person must burn his or her hand only once before learning not to put it on a hot stove. History can teach us if we allow it to do so—we do not put our hand on a hot stove because at some time in the past we learned that it hurt. Clearly, the importance of history cannot be underestimated. We hope we have sparked your interest in history to understand the roots of social welfare and general aspects of social work practice. In many cases, considering the experiences of the past can teach us valuable lessons worth remembering.

Did You Know . . .

Harry Hopkins, a social worker, was one of President Franklin D. Roosevelt's closest friends and the administrator of a Great Depression program called the Federal Emergency Relief Administration.

This chapter will make a brief foray into social welfare history. Other researchers have undertaken comprehensive examinations of social welfare history (Axinn & Levin, 1982; Chambers, 1967; Jansson, 2004; Katz, 1986; Lubove, 1965; Stern & Axinn, 2018; Trattner, 1989), and this area is well worth the effort of further investigation. For an online interactive experience with social welfare history, visit the Virginia Commonwealth University Libraries' Social Welfare History Project. We will briefly examine significant events and trends that influenced the emergence of our current American social welfare system.

3.2 THE ELIZABETHAN POOR LAW OF 1601

Most social work historians would agree that the watershed year for social welfare was 1601, when English **poor laws** were *codified*, or brought together under one law. This codification is commonly called the Elizabethan Poor Law of 1601. Colonial America adopted the central tenets of this law, and perhaps surprisingly, many of its principles continue to underpin the design and implementation of our current social services.

As an important note of caution, welfare did not begin with the Elizabethan Poor Law of 1601. Karger and Stoesz (2017) tracked the development of the English poor laws back through a series of events to the mid-fourteenth century. Gilbert and Specht (1981, p. 17) noted that modern-day social welfare has roots in the Reformation period and the Middle Ages. And Trattner (1989), in his classic work *From Poor Law to Welfare State*, traced the roots of American welfare efforts to the ancient Greeks and Romans. In advanced social policy courses, you'll learn more about the rise of social welfare as a system, but for our purposes, we will begin with the Elizabethan Poor Law.

Before 1601 in Europe, welfare attempts to assist people in need were generally viewed as the province of the church. With the advent of the industrial era, great changes occurred in society. Many new and better-paying jobs arose, and men and women of all ages were encouraged to apply. Rural communities began to decrease in population as people left the limited and shrinking opportunities of farm life for what the industrialized cities offered. Unfortunately, the promise of more jobs and a better way of life was not fulfilled for everyone, and many became unemployed and homeless. People who were newly destitute turned to the churches, the traditional providers of assistance to poor people. With the ranks of poor individuals growing to unprecedented levels, however, these urban churches did not have the resources or the expertise to cope with the swelling numbers of rural migrants and their assorted needs.

Faced with a growing population of urban poor people, the English government implemented a series of sweeping reforms to gain control of this problem. The result, the 1601 Poor Law, radically changed the form, function, and scope of welfare assistance. First, it redefined welfare as a public responsibility rather than a private affair. Second, it identified local government as the public entity responsible for poor individuals. Third, it denied relief if family resources were available (Katz, 1986, pp. 13–14).

In addition to setting the parameters for public aid, the 1601 Poor Law divided potential recipients into two groups, the *worthy poor* and the *unworthy poor*. On the one hand, the worthy poor included people who were ill, disabled, orphans, and elders. These people were viewed as having no control over their life circumstances. A second group of the worthy poor consisted of people who were involuntarily unemployed. Although they were seen as bearing some responsibility for their own situation, due consideration was given to the fact that their misfortunes were beyond their control. The unworthy poor, on the other hand, included the vagrant or able-bodied individuals who, although able to work, did not seek employment (Cole, 1973, p. 5).

Overall, assistance was first given to the worthy poor, who were considered helpless to control their situations. Some assistance was provided to those who were involuntarily unemployed. No assistance was given to the unworthy poor, who were treated with public disdain.

3.3 COLONIAL AMERICA

The provision of public assistance in colonial America was tenuous at best. Influenced by strong Puritan and Calvinist views, most citizens regarded both the worthy and the unworthy poor as morally flawed. They believed that individuals who had been stricken by poverty had somehow caused their own distress. This belief released society from any obligation to lend assistance and implied that it was the impoverished individual who was responsible for finding and providing a remedy. Aid or charity assistance, in any form, was thought to lead to an "erosion of independence and self-respect; the spread of idleness and the loss of the will to work; the promotion of immorality in all its ugly forms; and the increase in public costs through the growth of poorhouses and jails" (Katz, 1986, p. 40). Benjamin Franklin, for example, strongly opposed public aid: "[The] 'natural state' of working persons was one of sloth, wastefulness, and dissipation. The Common people do not work for pleasure, but for necessity" (Williams, 1944, p. 83). Relief, Franklin felt, simply provided an opportunity for people to return to their natural state of laziness at the expense of others.

> ### Did You Know . . .
> In 1931, Jane Addams, social worker and founder of Hull House, was the first American woman to win the Nobel Peace Prize. The Jane Addams Hull-House Museum in Chicago offers a virtual tour and is an excellent source for more information.

Based on a weak commitment to a public welfare system, American colonists developed a dual system of relief that was modeled on the English Poor Law of 1601. The resulting programs provided aid to the worthy poor, who in this case comprised people who were ill, older adults, orphans, widows, and veteran soldiers. The unworthy or able-bodied poor, including individuals who were involuntarily unemployed, were provided little, if any, assistance.

Support to the worthy poor was given primarily in the form of **outdoor relief**, which was aid to a person or a family in the home; the assistance may have been cash based, but generally consisted of in-kind provisions such as food and clothing. Conversely, the unworthy poor were not provided aid in their homes and were typically moved to the local poor house, commonly referred to as indoor relief. It was also commonplace for a community to encourage the unworthy poor to move on to another county. Further, an individual deemed unworthy would be required to return to his or her county or town of origin to receive any help.

Funds to support the worthy and unworthy poor were collected at the town or county level through a special tax assessed by the local **overseer of poor** populations. In many ways, this overseer was a colonial version of a social worker. The overseer's responsibilities included identifying local poor people, determining if they were in fact residents of the jurisdiction, determining what their specific needs were, classifying the individual or family as worthy or unworthy poor, and determining how the community would respond to the individual or family.

In general, the availability and accessibility of colonial public services reflected Franklin's negative view of relief. These programs were often designed with a punitive intent to shame people out of their poverty (see Box 3.1). Typical of this approach was the practice of forcing poor people into apprenticeships and indentured service offered by the lowest bidder—that is, the person who would charge the community the least for taking a pauper off its hands. Another example of this reluctant attitude toward helping poor individuals is the treatment of a widow in Hadley, Massachusetts. In 1687, a woman who had no resources of her own was forced to live for two-week periods with those families who were "able to receive her" (Trattner, 1989, p. 18).

Further, in Pennsylvania those receiving aid were required to wear a scarlet letter *P* sewn on their right sleeves, "with the first letter of the county, city, or place of his or her residence underneath" (Heffner, 1913, p. 11). Even more extreme was a 1754 North Carolina law that allowed vagrants (in 2015 they would be called homeless) to be whipped in the public square simply because of their impoverished state (Rothman, 1971, p. 25).

Not all potential recipients of social welfare services were viewed negatively in colonial America. For example, veteran soldiers who had fought for the colonies and later became impoverished were given a more honored status because they were generally considered to be among the worthy poor (Axinn & Levin, 1982, p. 31). As early as 1624, veterans could expect to receive social welfare benefits as a right earned because of the service they had provided. It was believed that, because veteran soldiers had shown their willingness to risk life and limb in defense of their nation, they deserved public aid if they needed it. Providing relief to veterans was not considered the responsibility of the town; rather, it was the obligation of the colony. In addition, veterans did not have to satisfy residency requirements to receive aid (Axinn & Levin, 1982, p. 31).

BOX 3.1
SELECTED DATES IN AMERICAN SOCIAL WELFARE HISTORY

1601	Elizabethan Poor Law enacted by the English Parliament
1642	Plymouth Colony enacts first poor law in the colonies
1657	Scots Charitable Society, first nonprofit organization focused on the provision of welfare, founded in Boston
1773	First public mental asylum opens in Williamsburg, Virginia
1790	First public orphanage opens in Charleston, South Carolina
1798	U.S. Public Health Department established
1817	Gallaudet School, a school for the deaf, founded in Hartford, Connecticut
1822	Kentucky opens first public asylum for deaf people
1829	First asylum for the blind opens in Massachusetts
1841	Dorothea Dix begins investigations into mental institutions in the United States
1851	The YMCA is founded in North America (Montreal)
1853	The Reverend Charles Loring Brace organizes the Children's Aid Society
1854	President Pierce vetoes federal legislation designed to use federal land for state asylums
1865	Freedmen's Bureau is organized
1869	The first permanent state board of health and vital statistics is founded in Massachusetts
1880	The Salvation Army is organized in the United States, although it was founded in London in 1878
1889	Hull House is opened in Chicago, Illinois, by Jane Addams and Ellen Gates Starr
1905	Medical social work is initiated at Massachusetts General Hospital in Boston
1912	The Children's Bureau is organized by the federal government
1917	*Social Diagnosis*, the first textbook on social casework, is written by Mary Richmond
1923	The first course on group work is offered at Western Reserve University in Cleveland, Ohio
1934	The first social work licensing law is passed in Puerto Rico and becomes the precursor for other state licensing and registration laws

For other dates and events, see *Distinctive Dates in Social Welfare History* by Chauncey Alexander (1995).

In summary, two of the primary components of colonial poor relief legislation—local responsibility and residency—did not apply to veterans because they enjoyed the status of the worthy poor.

What events in social welfare history strike you or surprise you? What do you think is the most important social welfare event on the list? Why? How do you see the history of social welfare echoed in today's social welfare policies and practices?

> ## Did You Know . . .
>
> Jeannette Rankin, a social worker, was the first woman elected to the U.S. Congress, representing Montana, in 1916. And she was elected prior to the passage of the Nineteenth Amendment, which granted women the right to vote!

> **Name:** Jan Ricks, LCSW, ACSW
> **Place of residence:** Central Florida
> **College/university degrees:** MSW, University of Central Florida; and BSW, University of Central Florida
> **Present position and title:** Retired instructor, Online MSW School of Social Work, University of Central Florida Retired associate professor, University of Cincinnati, School of Social Work, emeritus professor
> **Present work:** Working as a child protective investigator for several years and with individuals with developmental disabilities, I later became licensed in four states in social work and worked as a mental health therapist. With my passion for the field, I felt that teaching would be the most effective way to help share my experience and knowledge with future social workers. After almost twenty years, I have recently retired from full-time academia and plan to devote my time working with the transgender population. As an out lesbian I have found my place in this world, and I would like to be able to help others do the same.
>
>
>
> *Why did you choose social work as a career?* I didn't choose social work. I have spent my whole life helping, inspiring, and believing; it wasn't until someone said "You should be a social worker" that I realized that was who I was and I wanted to learn everything I could, so I could move forward and change the world. I always wanted to make the world a better place (on a macro level) and I realized that the most effective way to do that was teaching. I have been an educator on the university level for over twenty years and have had the honor of teaching hundreds (if not thousands) of social work students. I am proud to have been a part of every student's educational journey. I believe that social workers change the world, and that is how I have created change!

continues

> *continued*
>
> *What is your favorite social work story or volunteer experience?* When I was thirteen, I volunteered at the YWCA summer program teaching swimming to individuals with Down syndrome. It was the first time I had ever volunteered. The first day I was in the pool with seven people and there was one young girl standing on the edge crying. She was very fearful and refused to get in the water and participate. I tried everything to make her feel more comfortable, but nothing worked. The second day she got in the water but froze and did not move. One of the other girls, who was also disabled, reached out her hand to the girl and said something in Spanish, and together they floated across the water, hand in hand. I learned that day that people are unique, and human kindness is powerful; collectively we are a force that can create change. Instilling hope and trust can move mountains! That was a long time ago, but it lit a fire in me that has only grown brighter over the years. I did not choose social work; I am social work.
>
> *What is one thing in the community you would change?* People's perception and reaction to difference.

3.4 NINETEENTH-CENTURY REFORM EFFORTS

Throughout American history, immorality and pauperism have been tightly linked by the idea that poverty is a direct result of an individual's flawed character. Nineteenth-century programs intended to help poor individuals sought to do so by changing their behavior and making them overcome their personal failings. At the same time, public opinion turned hostile toward all those living in poverty. As Benjamin Disraeli lamented following passage of the punitive 1834 British poor law reform, it was "a crime to be poor" (Trattner, 1989, p. 49).

Despite the strong resistance to helping poor people, poverty was widespread enough that some form of relief was necessary. Welfare organizations became more formalized and commonplace, particularly in large urban areas. The most prominent agencies for the delivery of social welfare services and programs for poor individuals were **almshouses** and asylums, charity organization societies, and settlement houses.

Almshouses and Asylums

The roots of service provision for poor and disabled populations can be traced back as far as the 1700s, to the first almshouses. Almshouses, also called poorhouses, were intended to be places of refuge for individuals of all ages who were poor, medically ill, or mentally ill. In colonial times, however, caring for the family and its members was considered a private matter, and people who had any kind of family support were kept at home. Therefore, the almshouse was an option of last resort, providing shelter and relief for society's outcasts—those who were poor, incapacitated, or suffering from contagious disease. Because they were severely underfunded, almshouses were dirty and disease filled, and the workers who staffed them, who can be regarded among the earliest practical social workers and health care providers, often became ill (Dziegielewski & Holliman, 2020).

> ### Did You Know . . .
> In 1713, William Penn founded the first almshouse in Philadelphia. In 1736, a second almshouse was founded at Bellevue Hospital in New York. The almshouse in Bellevue usually housed mentally ill individuals and later became one of the most famous mental health hospitals in the country.

At one point, almshouses housed all poor individuals. However, children were eventually removed from almshouses by the efforts of the Children's Aid Society and placed in orphanages. In 1851, individuals who were mentally ill were also removed and sent to improved facilities and asylums, primarily through the crusading efforts of Dorothea Lynde Dix. Basically, the almshouse as *holding tank* was replaced with more segregated forms of institutionalized care, such as orphanages and other residential facilities, referred to as asylums.

Asylums, the most common human service organizations in the 1800s, became the homes for people who were lumped and labeled in the parlance of the times as "blind, deaf and dumb, and insane." These institutions developed regimented programs formed by a guiding trinity of work, religion, and education. Tightly regulating an inmate's life with scheduled activities throughout each day, according to Rothman (1971, p. 145), reflected belief in the "therapeutic value of a rigid schedule." For example, in the Pennsylvania Hospital, patients were awakened at 5:00 a.m. They "received their medicines at six, and breakfast at 6:30; at eight o'clock, they went for a physical examination, and then to work or to some other form of exercise. At 12:30 they ate their main meal and then resumed work or other activities until six, when everyone joined for tea" (Rothman, 1971, p. 145).

As can been seen from this detailed and rigid daily schedule, labor was a central component of asylum life. Inmates, as they were being taught jobs, supposedly learned the value and importance of work. This training, coupled with the regimented schedule, in theory imparted "habits . . . necessary for patients' recovery" (Rothman, 1971, p. 146). A portion of the poem attributed to Thomas Hood Esq., titled "The Song of the Shirt" and referenced in the Library of Congress, reveals the negative side of work as the cornerstone of welfare programming:

> Work, work, work
> till the brain begins to swim;
> work, work, work
> till the eyes are heavy and dim;
> seam, gusset, and bond,

bond, gusset, and seam
till over the buttons I fall asleep
and sew them on in dream.

> ### Did You Know . . .
> The first American charity organization society was established in Buffalo, New York, in 1877.

Charity Organization Societies

A second innovative approach to combating poverty was the **charity organization society (COS)**, founded in London, England, in the mid-1800s. Besides its significance as a social welfare development, the COS is important to the history of social work because some social work historians view its founding as the profession's birth event. The first American COS, modeled after the British program, was founded in Buffalo, New York, in 1877 by the Reverend Humphrey Gurteen.

In the mid-1800s, private charitable efforts proliferated in American cities, resulting in many duplicated and uncoordinated programs. Following the British model of coordination, the COS movement made its way to the United States, first in Buffalo, New York, to organize the various charities within a city to reduce program duplication and to certify the needs and claims of clients in a systematic investigative fashion. Only those individuals or families certified as eligible by the COS were able to receive services from the various charities. Finally, the COS sought to change the lives of poor people through home visits by volunteers; these so-called **friendly visitors** are generally considered the forerunners to American social workers. The friendly visitors by and large were females from middle- to upper-middle-class families; the local COS was characteristically headed by a male, who was the only paid staff person in the organization.

These COS subscribed to the philosophy that poverty was a consequence of moral decay, and the eradication of slums depended on poor people recognizing and correcting their personal deficiencies (Boyer, 1978, p. 144). The friendly visitor, a key volunteer in the COS movement, was to establish a personal relationship with each client through home visits and by serving as a role model to help poor individuals change their behavior. The 1889 *Buffalo Charity Organization Society Handbook* declared that the friendly visitor soon would be a power in the home: "In a very short time, the houses would be clean and kept clean for her reception. Her advice would be sought. . . . In a word, all avoidable pauperism would soon be a thing of the past when the poor would regard the rich as their natural friends" (Gurteen, 1882, p. 117).

Women volunteers, particularly those from middle- and upper-class families, were preferred for the role of friendly visitor. These women would be able to demonstrate and foster the values of the successful family to less fortunate individuals and families. In essence, by psychological and social osmosis, poverty and its companion evils would be uprooted through the kind works of middle-class ladies. Specifically, Gurteen wrote, "[All that is] needed to make our work a grand success . . . is hundreds of women from the educated and well-to-do classes, especially women of our city, who as mothers and daughters, coming from bright and happy homes—homes adorned by virtue and radiant with love, can impart to the cheerless tenement or the wretched hovel, a little of their own happiness" (1882, p. 116).

The COS movement also relied on female volunteers to staff the various organizations. As these societies became more accepted and formalized, the role of women changed. For example, by the end of the nineteenth century, the COS women were paid for their work, and COS became a primary employment arena for women. It is interesting to note, however, that the first COS administrators were men; the first female administrator, Mary Richmond, was not appointed until late 1891.

In summary, the COS were an important development in the history of social work because they provided the basis for the modern social service agencies of today. The workers they employed were some of the first to deliver social services in the home setting to poor and disenfranchised people. The COS provided an opportunity for systematic investigation of people who were in poverty and need. Home visitation, which today remains a highly valued social work intervention technique, allowed volunteers to learn more about individuals and their environments.

Did You Know . . .

The first social work educational program started in 1898 as a summer training course at the New York Charity Organization Society. It later became the Columbia University School of Social Work.

Settlement House Movement

Another major British innovation also crossed the Atlantic during the mid-1800s and made a significant impact in the American social service arena. Known as the settlement house movement, its philosophy was remarkably different from that of the COS. The settlement house movement sought the causes of poverty in macrosystems rather than microsystems. For example, poor education, lack of health care, and inadequate housing were considered the primary reasons for poverty. The settlement house was an actual house in a neighborhood where the workers lived year-round, coordinating and providing programs, activities, and services directed to the needs of their neighbors.

FIGURE 3.2
This stamp depicts Jane Addams, Nobel Peace Prize winner, champion of women's rights, and one of the foremothers of social work.

The most famous nineteenth-century settlement house was Hull House, founded by Jane Addams (see Figure 3.2) and Ellen Gates Starr in 1889. Located in a poor West Side Chicago neighborhood, Hull House forged a strong bond between neighborhood immigrants and social workers with its efforts to bridge the gulf between rich and poor (Leighninger, 2008). By the beginning of the twentieth century, there were more than one hundred settlement houses located in the United States.

The settlement house movement initiated the macro model for social work practice, more commonly referred today as *community organization* and *group practice*. Problems were seen as resting not with the individual, but at the larger organizational or community level. Poverty was the result not of an individual's lack of morality, but of a system that kept wages low, did not enforce housing or health codes, and maintained a marginalized working class. Through client empowerment, problems could be confronted and social resources redistributed.

Did You Know . . .

W. Gertrude Brown was among a very small group of women, aside from her identity as a person of color, able to obtain higher education in her time. Brown was hired as "head resident" of the Phyllis Wheatley Settlement House in Minneapolis, Minnesota, in 1924. Her innovative leadership focused on advocacy for her community when most settlement houses were focused on immigrant assimilation.

3.5 THE TWENTIETH CENTURY

At the dawn of the twentieth century, the United States was poised to become a world economic leader. By the 1920s, economic prosperity seemed within reach of a growing number of Americans. Yet for Blacks and immigrants, economic gains were elusive. Blacks continued to suffer racism and discrimination, especially under nineteenth-century Jim Crow laws that were commonplace in the South and were enacted in White supremacists' response to the Fourteenth Amendment to the U.S. Constitution. As immigration increased, laws inspired by xenophobia (fear of foreigners) also framed social policy initiatives.

The prosperity of the first quarter century quickly unraveled in the worldwide depression of the 1930s. By 1929, 1.6 million people were unemployed, and by the mid-1930s, nearly 1 in 4 Americans was unemployed.

Everyone knew someone—a brother, sister, father, mother, aunt, uncle, grandparent, or friend—who was out of work. Poverty was no longer a distant concept reserved for Blacks, immigrants, and those seen as "others" by the White majority population. Very quickly, the philosophy that poor individuals were morally depraved and had no work ethic became unacceptable because more people had become poor who were never poor before. The new poor people were friends and family and did not fit the image of the lazy, immoral poor population.

With the presidential election of Franklin Roosevelt, relief measures were immediately put in place, followed by the ambitious New Deal programs. These programs were funded and coordinated at the federal level and dramatically changed government's ambivalent role in social welfare (see the activity below).

The most important New Deal initiative was the Social Security Act of 1935, which established the Social Security system to provide cash assistance to retired workers. This act—which also established the precursors of today's **Temporary Assistance to Needy Families (TANF)** program and unemployment insurance—became the organizing framework for the federal social service system. By the end of the twentieth century, the 1935 act had been amended on numerous occasions to include cash assistance, health benefits, and services for people who were disabled, blind, heads of single-parent families, children, and seniors.

Did You Know . . .

Frances Perkins, a social worker, was the first woman appointed to the U.S. cabinet when she was named secretary of labor in 1933. She played a very significant role in the creation of the Social Security Act of 1935.

The New Deal, which was the nation's first national welfare program, included initiatives directed toward a variety of people. The Federal Emergency Relief Act, the Civilian Conservation Corps, and the Works Progress Administration formed the backbone of the New Deal. All these programs were unprecedented in that they were developed and coordinated by the federal government, but like local relief efforts of the nineteenth century, they made work a condition of relief. The New Deal essentially affirmed the federal government's role in social welfare. The national effort was unparalleled in American history until the massive social movement of the 1960s.

> ### Activity
> Go to a library or look online and read newspapers from the 1930s. Try to get a feel for life during the Depression. Then visit a local nursing home or senior center to meet people who lived during the Depression. Ask them how the Depression affected their families and neighbors and how it influenced the rest of their lives.

Social Reform in the 1960s

By 1960, slightly more than one in five Americans lived in poverty. In 1962, Michael Harrington's classic work *The Other America: Poverty in the United States* (1962) helped the nation to rediscover the poverty in its backyard. This short book had a profound impact within the halls of Congress and reawakened nationwide debate on the role of government in combating poverty.

In the early part of his administration, President Lyndon Johnson declared a War on Poverty that intended to make full use of the nation's resources. The resulting initiative—later referred to as the Great Society programs—brought a new federal presence into local communities that was far different from previous welfare program efforts. Guided by the phrase "maximum feasible participation" of poor people, welfare programs involved poor populations in local decision-making in their neighborhoods and communities.

The coordinating agency for the Great Society was the Office of Economic Opportunity. Typical new welfare strategies included assistance to newborn babies and their mothers (Women, Infants, and Children), preschool education (Head Start), health care for seniors (Medicare) and poor people (Medicaid), employment programs for young adults (Job Corps), community action programs that encouraged neighbors to marshal resources, legal services for poor individuals, food stamps, and model city projects that were designed to provide assistance to the poorest neighborhoods.

> ### Did You Know . . .
> Social worker and civil rights trailblazer Whitney M. Young Jr. became the executive director of the National Urban League while serving as dean for the Atlanta School of Social Work. He also served as president of the National Association of Social Workers in the late 1960s.

The Great Society was spurred by a newfound belief that the nation could fight and win any battle it chose, and the War on Poverty had no borders. The Peace Corps, developed in 1965, sent volunteers to nations around the world to work in poor communities. Volunteers in Service to America was a domestic version of the Peace Corps, with volunteers working in low-income American neighborhoods.

By the end of the 1960s, the Great Society was under growing attack for being too costly, with too few benefits to the larger society. During the presidential administration of Richard Nixon, the influence of the Office of Economic Opportunity was minimized, and numerous programs were scrapped. In their place, Nixon proposed an innovative guaranteed annual income for poor people—a *negative income tax*. Known as the Family Assistance Program, Nixon's plan would have subsidized a poor family by $2,400 a year. This plan required work or job training, with the states eventually having full responsibility for program operation. This controversial proposal was ultimately rejected by Congress, but it was nevertheless a dramatic attempt to establish a minimum income based on work requirements.

The 1980s and 1990s: A Return to the Work Ethic

With the election of Ronald Reagan to the presidency and a more politically conservative Congress, the attacks on public service relief programs became more numerous and boisterous. Numerous federal public assistance programs were eliminated, while others had their funding cut and their eligibility requirements tightened to weed out "**unworthy**" **poor** people. The results of this realignment were dramatic. Palmer and Sawhill (1984, pp. 363–379) found that five hundred thousand families were removed from **Aid to Families with Dependent Children** and an additional three hundred thousand families received reduced benefits. One million people were eliminated from food stamp rolls. In 1985, the National Anti-Hunger Coalition charged that the federal government was not spending allocated funds for the Women, Infants, and Children nutrition program, depriving thousands of pregnant women and newborn infants of health and nutrition services.

Children, women, seniors, and racial and ethnic minorities were the primary victims of the Reagan welfare reforms. The message of the 1980s was clear: First, public assistance was contributing to the national debt. Second, only truly needy individuals, the poorest of the poor, would be helped with a safety net to ensure survival. Third, welfare was a state and local, not federal, concern.

The safety net approach places responsibility for helping poor, vulnerable, and **disadvantaged** populations on the doorstep of local government and private sources; the federal government becomes a resource of last resort. To achieve this purpose, the Reagan administration adopted three overriding goals about income security programs: (1) reduce short-term spending by implementing changes in **entitlement programs**, (2) turn over welfare responsibility to the states, and (3) promote reliance on individual resources rather than create and maintain dependence on governmental benefits (Storey, 1982). According to the American Assembly at Columbia University, the result was "a patchwork of programs at the federal, state, and local level that results in gross inadequacies in education.... We have developed too few resources to prevention and maintenance, and too many to picking up pieces after the damage is done.

On the other hand, the United States has established a broad welfare system for the non-poor while the middle and upper classes and corporate America are able to take advantage of many benefits and, to a large extent, have become dependent on government support" (American Assembly, 1989, p. 34).

Welfare reform continued in the 1990s with the 1992 presidential election of Bill Clinton, who promised to "end welfare as we know it." His ambition came within reach with later developments in Congress. The midterm congressional election in 1994 brought a Republican sweep, and in their "Contract with America," conservative congressional Republicans made welfare reform a top priority.

In 1996, Congress essentially ended federal relief programs with the passage of the Personal Responsibility and Work Opportunity Reconciliation Act. In other words, Clinton's pledge to end welfare as we know it became reality. The new law abolished specific categorical programs and provided federal block grants to the states. Today, the federal government is no longer responsible for operating public welfare programs. No longer does the country have a national welfare program. Rather, each state operates its own public welfare services, each with its own set of eligibility criteria, program rules, and benefits. Another way of looking at public welfare is to recognize that the nation has fifty different welfare programs, each operating under a different set of rules with varying levels of financial resources. Commonalities come from conditions placed on federal block grants: a lifetime limit of five years of relief, a work requirement, and participation in job-training programs.

According to the federal Welfare Reform Act of 1996, all adult welfare recipients are required to work, be registered for work, or be participating in job-training or educational programs. The food stamp program—now run by the states—has similar eligibility criteria; failure to follow these work guidelines results in program disqualification. This welfare reform act also ended the Aid to Families with Dependent Children program, in place since the New Deal. It was replaced by TANF, a short-term program that incorporates lifetime limitations and work requirements.

The Clinton administration can claim a number of achievements: the lowest number of people receiving public welfare; an 80 percent increase in child support payments; increased availability of housing vouchers; the creation of incentives to save, such as individual development accounts; increased minimum wage; protected Medicare and modest health care reform; immunization rates raised to an all-time high; and the enactment of the largest health care act for children (Children's Health Insurance Program).

3.6 COMPASSIONATE CONSERVATISM AND THE NEW MILLENNIUM

Moving into the twenty-first century, President George W. Bush pledged a new approach to social welfare, which he referred to as *compassionate conservatism*. Essentially, this philosophy relies on the private, voluntary sector to provide assistance. Through volunteerism and private, nonprofit, and faith-based organizations, people in need of help are provided with locally developed programs. At the same time, the compassionate conservative philosophy seeks out programs and policies that support the traditional two-parent family; strategies that encourage a rewards-based public education system; public assistance programs that are temporary in nature and support individual responsibility; and, when appropriate, assistance, both monetary and humanitarian aid, to Third and Fourth World nations. What emerged was a federal welfare program that was almost 180 degrees from the 1930s New Deal program or the 1960s War on Poverty. President Reagan's stance that "government is not the solution but the problem" was almost completely realized under compassionate conservatism.

Yet, when looking at the Bush years, one must recognize that slightly less than eight months after Bush took office, the United States was attacked. Eighteen months after 9/11, in March 2003, the United States invaded Iraq, and this war became the singular focus of the Bush administration, ultimately becoming the nation's longest war. Some might argue that the Bush presidency was not preoccupied with Iraq, but we will leave that analysis to the historians.

Allard (2007, p. 305) noted that the Bush presidency significantly changed public welfare from direct cash benefits to "a system that provides most assistance through social services programs supporting work activity." The Bush years also saw further reliance on faith-based charities, blurring what had been a distinct line between church and state. Other significant changes revolved around increasing the TANF work requirement from twenty to thirty hours per week. At the same time, TANF moved away from direct cash payments to providing more services, such as day care, job search, mental health services, and substance abuse programs. By the mid-2000s, the earned income tax credit program became the largest means-tested program with work as the key criterion for entry, thus reinforcing the Bush administration goal of independence with less reliance on the government (Allard, 2007).

By the time President Barack Obama took office in 2009, the nation's economy was in dire straits—unemployment was rising, along with home foreclosures, and businesses were collapsing. The pressures felt in the United States were reverberating around the world. People understood that Main Street and Wall Street were connected.

The first term of the Obama administration was filled with congressional gridlock. Little was accomplished because the art of political compromise seemed to be a memory of the distant past. The most significant act passed during Obama's first term dealt with health care. A Democrat-controlled Congress passed the Patient Protection and Affordable Care Act, also referred to as the Affordable Care Act (ACA) and sarcastically called Obamacare, which was signed into law on March 23, 2010. From the day the law was passed and then signed into law, the Republican Party and many state governments challenged its legality. More than half of the states, as well as several faith-based organizations and nonprofit agencies, challenged the legality of the law while the U.S. House of Representatives voted more than fifty times to defund the ACA. The U.S.

Supreme Court, somewhat surprisingly, upheld the key parts of the law on two separate occasions, first in 2012 and again in 2015. The latter Supreme Court decision basically ended the major legal tests to the veracity of the ACA, although legal challenges continued to plague it, just as there were ongoing legal battles over the Social Security Act following its passage in 1936 and the Medicare Act in 1965. As with Social Security and Medicare, the ACA has remained the law of the land and a major front-line social welfare program, with a ruling by the Supreme Court in 2021 throwing out a lawsuit filed by eighteen Republican state attorneys general and the Trump administration.

This health insurance law created important access to the health care system for many who were unable to receive health services prior to its enactment. Other important features include provisions that individuals with preexisting conditions could not be denied health insurance, younger adults could remain on their parent's insurance program, and states were to create exchanges whereby insurance companies competed, by offering lower prices, to enroll individuals.

In 2012, as Obama headed into his second term as president, he set forth a progressive agenda that clearly addressed social justice issues, including women's rights, Black rights, and gay rights. As the Twitterverse noted the day following his inaugural address, "no other president has even mentioned gay rights in an inaugural speech, let alone mentioned it alongside other movements that forged a more equal America." And on June 26, 2015, the U.S. Supreme Court legalized same-sex marriage; that night, the White House was lit up in rainbow colors to celebrate the broadening of rights to all people.

President Donald Trump real estate developer turned politician, during his presidency (January 20, 2017–January 20, 2021), took up the issues of tightening border security and championed building a wall in service of this goal. The detainment of migrant families at the southern borders inadvertently resulted in the separation of children from their parents, which caused major controversy. In contrast to popular assumptions about the delivery of social welfare services, under Trump's conservative administration, many people no longer appeared to embrace the compassionate part of compassionate conservativism touted by leaders at the end of the twentieth century. Two examples of that trend include tightened eligibility for food stamps and federal support of states implementing more stringent work requirements for Medicaid eligibility. Eligibility requirements were tightened for Medicaid, and under the Trump administration, concerted efforts were made to undermine and roll back the health benefits of the ACA, true to Trump's stated campaign promise to repeal the act.

Issues regarding immigration and so-called border control came to the forefront by 2014 and became central to the national discussion around citizenship. The political right called for tightening border security by building walls on the country's southern border with Mexico while sending National Guard and federal troops to guard the border. It is interesting to juxtapose this conservative call for building a wall to keep people out of the United States with conservative President Ronald Regan's 1987 speech in Berlin, demanding that Russian leader Mikhail Gorbachev "tear down this wall." It is curious to contemplate how, over thirty years, the United States changed its position from tearing down barriers to freedom to building both legal and physical hurdles to citizenship.

A strong political statement was made by an activist group called Black Lives Matter (also referred to as BLM). This group made its first appearance in 2013 as part of widespread concern and outrage regarding the shooting of Trayvon Martin, a young Black man shot by George Zimmerman, a White/Hispanic neighborhood watch captain. The Black Lives Matter movement focuses on the violence suffered by people of color, specifically Black communities, and the issue of U.S. and global White supremacy took on an elevated focus in the wider world and especially in social media, perhaps especially on the X platform (formerly called Twitter), where the hashtag has seen more general use focused on social injustices beyond those affecting the Black community. The conservative presidency of Donald Trump coincided with an increase in hate crimes directed at minority populations and increased outspokenness among racist hate groups. The phrase *White supremacy* entered the popular lexicon, along with an awareness of critical race theory. Critical race theory represented a movement of civil rights leaders who wanted to examine the intersection of race, society, and the law. From this perspective, race is viewed as a social construct and its long-standing influence is not just an individual bias or prejudice, but rather a form of American racism that shapes public policy (Sawchuk, 2021). This increased public awareness has caused a divide among the American people with regard to the government's role and how the wrongs of the past can be identified, acknowledged, and addressed. Regardless of one's political views, contention about these ideas and their meaning affects the work of social workers, and continued focus on all ideas related to social and racial justice among social workers remains an ethical imperative.

In April 2021, President Joe Biden announced a major thrust in the social welfare arena of the 2020s, on the heels of the COVID-19-related American Rescue Plan. The American Families Plan sought to do more than "rescue." The new legislation focused, among other things, on higher education and child care support, paid family leave, nutrition, and tax cuts for lower- and middle-income families.

The political world of the twenty-first century is fraught with emotion and gridlock. The idea to seek common ground and negotiate on differences seems lost in today's bitter political discourse. Social issues are complex and interwoven with the ever-changing global environment. We do not know how social media will continue to affect or change how we work with and on behalf of others. We do know, however, that as social workers we must stay informed about the present while recognizing and understanding the successes and failures of the past. The social work profession has much to offer, but without a doubt you must watch to see what unfolds over these next critical years and, most important, become an engaged partner in the process of change. And as you participate in the molding of our collective future, be sure that your debate is fair and accurate, no matter what your position.

Name: Sarah Young

Place of residence: Binghamton, New York

College/university degrees: BSW, Syracuse University; MSW, University of Michigan; PhD in social work, University of Alabama

Present position: Associate professor and BSW program director at Binghamton University

Previous work/volunteer experience: I started my career in social work, convinced I would work with my BSW degree and not go to graduate school. My first job was in London, England, doing child protective work. When my work visa expired, I returned to the United States and worked in preventive services for youth for several years. Soon, I realized that the types of social work I was most interested in required a master's degree. I enrolled at the University of Michigan because they had a focus on community organizing. One of my internships—in Jackson, Mississippi—changed my life. I ended up working with the American Civil Liberties Union in Mississippi for several years as a community organizer. I helped build coalitions to protect the rights of LGBTQ+ people, people living with HIV/AIDS, people who were incarcerated with mental health challenges. Much of my work has been macro, and many of the organizing and research projects I've worked on are with interdisciplinary teams (such as with attorneys, physicians, etc.). It's another part of social work I am passionate about—interdisciplinary work.

What does a typical day at work look like for you? What tasks do you generally complete as a social worker in your area of expertise? When I was a community organizer, much of my day was spent planning events, connecting with potential coalition members, and being in community, building relationships. As a BSW program director, my days look quite different. I get to mentor up-and-coming social work students, which is very rewarding.

What do you do in your spare time? I'm a relationships person and love spending time with friends and family. I enjoy cooking and reading recipes, listening to music, and walking.

Why did you choose social work as a career? I've always been passionate about injustices and speaking up for the "underdog," even as a child. When I was in high school I had a serious head injury while playing sports, and I almost died. It was a dark and confusing time for me and my family, and we were supported by many people, including a social worker. The accident changed the course of my life and I learned that there was a profession that could combine my passion for supporting people alongside skills related to promoting social change.

What is your favorite social work story? There are so many stories that are dear to me. One pivotal moment was in my very first social work internship. I worked at an agency that served people living with or impacted by HIV/AIDS. One of my clients, a single father,

> wanted support to disclose his HIV diagnosis to his daughter who was about six or seven years old. He invited me to be present when he disclosed to her, and I was so honored that he invited me into that important moment in his family.
>
> *What would be the one thing you would change in our community if you had the power to do so?* I would end poverty and redistribute wealth equitably. Absent that power, I'd work to help build trust and connection between groups of people where there is mistrust.

SUMMARY

The fabric of American social welfare history is marked by a deep mistrust of poor people. The pattern is so ingrained that many individuals may have trouble recognizing it in themselves—our own unexamined assumptions can stand in our way of clear thinking without our awareness. Persistent beliefs that poor individuals are immoral and lacking either the ability or the desire to work have inspired repeated attempts to condition relief on work and improved behavior—and, above all, to make relief as difficult to obtain as possible. Social welfare and ensuring social justice are much bigger than programs to support poor and disadvantaged populations, such as Section 8 housing and the Supplemental Nutritional Assistance Program. The federal government provides support to a variety of groups; banks requiring bailouts, farmers needing subsidies, and cities requiring federal loans to make payroll are just some of the many acceptable forms of welfare. In these circumstances, however, bankers, farmers, and mayors do not consider themselves welfare recipients; rather, these federal supports are viewed as necessary subsidies that benefit the community.

Workfare, training programs, and stringent program eligibility requirements, coupled with ongoing recertification required to continue receiving even minimal assistance, are the punitive features of today's federal and state **social welfare** systems. When it comes to poverty, Americans are inclined to continue to **blame the victim**. Rather than maintaining a dignified helping system that is accessible to poor people, American welfare policy is designed to exclude people and to discourage clients by constantly setting hurdles to eligibility.

The philosophy that undergirds today's welfare system meant to help poor people reflects some of Benjamin Franklin's admonitions. The reluctance to acknowledge government responsibility continues, and with a lifetime limit on years of eligibility for welfare, so do deep concerns about dependence. Recipients are meant to be forced into a completely independent and self-reliant mode of existence.

Throughout its history, finding the appropriate balance between public and private responsibility has plagued American social welfare. There is a clear record of national ambivalence and resistance toward welfare services and the poor. The current debate on welfare is an extension of a discussion that extends back to colonial times. The lack of national consensus on who is to receive what type of social provisions for what period and on how these services will be funded means that the debate will continue well into the twenty-first century. Social workers are among the leaders promoting social justice by advocating for increased and improved services for all groups. This challenge supports the notion that social justice is a human issue and much more than just a legal or moral issue (Monroe, 2003). Primary emphasis needs to be placed on: (1) understanding the current social, political, and economic environment; (2) realizing it is never static and changes that can have major implications can occur rapidly; and (3) using this knowledge to educate and mobilize the community and other stakeholders to work together to identify and address social problems and to develop effective programs designed to address these needs.

MOVIES TO SEE

Movies on social welfare history rarely receive Academy Award consideration or excite producers. The following movies, while not specifically detailing social welfare history, help us to better understand people and their conditions in the past. Many of these films can be found through digital content providers.

Across the Sea of Time: 1920s New York City as seen through the eyes of Russian immigrants.

All Mine to Give: Orphaned children in nineteenth-century Wisconsin are put in different homes to survive.

Amend: The Fight for America: This six-part, well-produced documentary hosted by Hollywood star Will Smith focuses on the role of the Fourteenth Amendment in bettering the lives of people of color, immigrants, women, and LGBTQI+ individuals.

America, America: In the 1890s, a Greek youth immigrates to New York City; the film is an emotional presentation of an immigrant's challenges.

April Morning: A solid portrayal of a teenager's life in the American colonies immediately before the American Revolution.

Attacks on Culture: A brief (forty-nine minute) examination of the U.S. government's legislative attacks on Native Americans.

Autobiography of Miss Jane Pittman: An examination of life from the Civil War through the 1950s as remembered by a 110-year-old former slave.

Avalon: A Russian Jewish immigrant family moves to New York City.

Black West: An examination of African American cowboys, the unsung heroes of the West.

Cyberbully: A teenager finds herself the target of bullying on a popular social media website.

Freedom Writers: A young teacher has her students keep journals about their troubled lives, hoping they will apply history's lesson from *The Diary of Anne Frank* to break the cycle of violence and despair.

Gandhi: A 1982 film about a young attorney who leads change in India and becomes a global symbol of nonviolence and understanding.

Grapes of Wrath: A classic John Steinbeck story of a family's search for a better life than that in 1930s Depression Oklahoma.

The Hate U Give: Released in 2018, the film is about a girl's experiences in two worlds, the poor, mostly Black neighborhood in which she lives and the school she attends, a mostly White prep school.

I Am Sam: After fathering a child with a homeless woman, Sam—who is developmentally delayed—raises the baby until Child Protective Services steps in.

If Beale Street Could Talk: Produced in 2018, this romantic drama is an adaptation of James Baldwin's 1974 novel of the same name about a love story within the context of racial injustice.

Jasper, Texas: Film on the horrific 1998 murder of African American James Byrd in Jasper, Texas.

Just Mercy: A 2019 production detailing a wrongful conviction for murder and the efforts to free the accused from unjust imprisonment.

Lean on Me: A tough-talking high school principal uses everything in his power to turn around an inner-city, drug-infested, violence-ridden school.

The Molly Maguires: Interesting film set in the 1870s Pennsylvania coal country, as the Irish try to organize a union.

Philadelphia: An attorney sues his law firm after being fired because he is gay and HIV-positive.

Precious: Viciously abused by her mother and impregnated by her father, a Harlem teen has an unexpected chance at a different life when she enrolls in an alternative school while continuing to face barriers and struggles.

Roll of Thunder Hear My Cry: A Black teen copes with depression, poverty, and racism in 1930s Mississippi.

Separate but Equal: An examination of Thurgood Marshall as the attorney for the National Association for the Advancement of Colored People, whose U.S. Supreme Court case led to the end of segregation.

Sounder: A sharecropper is forced to steal to feed his family while the family deals with poverty and racism in the 1930s.

To Kill a Mockingbird: A White southern attorney defends an innocent Black man against rape charges and ends up in a maelstrom of hate and prejudice.

We Were Here: The AIDS health crisis changed the culture in San Francisco; this documentary explores the lives of five individuals affected by this disease.

Wild Women of the Old West: The stereotype of the quiet housewife is broken with this analysis of women in the 1800s.

A Woman Called Moses: An examination of the life of Harriet Ross Tubman, a fugitive slave, founder of the Underground Railroad, and leader in the abolitionist movement.

QUIZ ANSWERS

1. In October 1492, Christopher Columbus reached the Bahamas, marking Europe's first documented contact with the Americas.
2. The New Deal was the name given to a set of social and economic programs established under the leadership of President Franklin D. Roosevelt in the 1930s to combat the Depression.
3. The Emancipation Proclamation freed slaves in areas (rebellion states) no longer loyal to the union.
4. In Seneca Falls, New York, in 1848, women's rights advocate Elizabeth Cady Stanton organized a convention that generated a declaration of women's rights.
5. Earlier immigrants arrived from northern and western Europe. By 1900, there was a significant rise in people from eastern and southern Europe.
6. In the late seventeenth century, nineteen people were executed for witchcraft in Salem, Massachusetts.
7. In 1845, the United States annexed most of what is now Texas. Mexico ceded the remaining land in 1848 following the Mexican–American War.
8. The Articles of Confederation, adopted in 1777, united the colonies; it created a one-house Congress.
9. In 1867, William Seward negotiated the purchase of land, now Alaska, from Russia for $7.2 million. This transaction was called Seward's Folly because, until the discovery of gold, people saw little value in this distant purchase.
10. Dred Scott, a Missouri slave, sued for his freedom in 1847. The 1857 Supreme Court decision held that slaves were property and had no claim to the rights of citizenship.

REFERENCES

Alexander, C. (1995). Distinctive dates in social welfare history. In R. Edwards et al. (Eds.), *Encyclopedia of social work* (19th ed., pp. 2631–2647). Washington, DC: NASW Press.

Allard, S. (2007). The changing face of welfare during the Bush administration. *Publius: The Journal of Federalism, 37,* 304–332.

American Assembly. (1989, November). *The future of social welfare in America.* Harriman, NY: Arden House.

Axinn, J., & Levin, H. (1982). *Social welfare: A history of the American response to need* (2nd ed.). New York, NY: Harper & Row.

Boyer, P. (1978). *Urban classes and moral order in America, 1820–1990.* Cambridge, MA: Harvard University Press.

Chambers, C. A. (1967). *Seedtime of reform: American social service and social action, 1918–1933.* Ann Arbor: University of Michigan Press.

Cole, B. (1973). *Perspectives in public welfare: A history* (3rd ed.). Washington, DC: U.S. Government Printing Office.

Dziegielewski, S. F., & Holliman, D. (2020). *The changing face of health care social work: Opportunities and challenges for professional practice* (4th ed.). New York, NY: Springer.

Gilbert, N., & Specht, H. (1981). *The emergence of social welfare and social work* (2nd ed.). Itasca, IL: Peacock.

Gurteen, H. (1882). *A handbook of charity organization*. Buffalo, NY: Charity Organization Society.

Harrington, M. (1962). *The other America: Poverty in the United States*. New York, NY: Macmillan.

Heffner, W. (1913). *History of poor relief legislation in Pennsylvania, 1682–1913*. Cleona, PA: Holzapfel.

Jansson, B. S. (2004). *The reluctant welfare state: American social welfare policies past, present, and future* (5th ed.). Pacific Grove, CA: Brooks/Cole.

Karger, H. J., & Stoesz, D. (2017). *American social welfare policy: A pluralist approach* (8th ed.). Boston, MA: Pearson Education/Allyn & Bacon.

Katz, M. B. (1986). *In the shadow of the poorhouse: A social history of welfare in America*. New York, NY: Basic Books.

Leighninger, L. (2008). The history of social work and social welfare. In K. M. Sowers & C. N. Dulmus (Series Eds.) & B. W. White (Vol. Ed.), *Comprehensive handbook of social work and social welfare: The profession of social work* (Vol. 1, pp. 1–24). Hoboken, NJ: Wiley.

Lubove, C. (1965). *The professional altruist*. Cambridge, MA: Harvard University Press.

Monroe, I. (2003). Becoming what we ought to be: We cannot separate our efforts to heal the world from the difficult work of healing ourselves. *The Other Side, 39*, 43–45.

Palmer, J., & Sawhill, I. (1984). *The Reagan record*. Cambridge, MA: Ballinger.

Rothman, D. (1971). *The discovery of the asylum social order and disorder in the new republic*. Boston, MA: Little, Brown.

Sawchuk, S. (2021). *What is critical race theory, and why is it under attack?* EducationWeek. Retrieved from https://www.edweek.org/leadership/what-is-critical-race-theory-and-why-is-it-under-attack/2021/05

Stern, M. J., & Axinn, J. (2018). *Social welfare: A history of the American response to need* (9th ed.). New York, NY: Pearson.

Storey, J. R. (1982). Income security. In J. Palmer & I. Sawhill (Eds.), *The Reagan experiment* (Vol. 5, pp. 361–392). Washington, DC: Urban Institute Press.

Trattner, W. (1989). *From poor law to welfare state: A history of social welfare in America* (4th ed.). New York, NY: Free Press.

Williams, H. (1944). Benjamin Franklin and poor laws. *Social Service Review, 18*, 77–84.

4

So, You Want to Be a Social Worker!

CHAPTER 4: EPAS COMPETENCIES

Social work programs at the bachelor's and the master's level are accredited by the Council of Social Work Education (CSWE). CSWE's Educational Policy and Accreditation Standards (EPAS) describe the processes and criteria that social work courses should cover. In 2022, CSWE updated its EPAS standards. The following competencies are addressed in this chapter.

Competency 1: Demonstrate Ethical and Professional Behavior

Social workers understand the value base of the profession and its ethical standards, as well as relevant policies, laws, and regulations that may affect practice with individuals, families, groups, organizations, and communities.

Competency 6: Engage with Individuals, Families, Groups, Organizations, and Communities

Social workers understand that engagement is an ongoing component of the dynamic and interactive process of social work practice with and on behalf of individuals, families, groups, organizations, and communities.

There are numerous jobs for social workers throughout the country in cities, suburbs, and rural communities. Through 2030, the increase in employment opportunities for social workers will be "faster than average," with a 12 percent projected increase in opportunities (U.S. Department of Labor [DOL], 2022). The growth in positions will be in both public and private agencies, large and small alike. Mental health clinics, schools, child welfare and human service agencies, hospitals, settlement houses, community development corporations, and private practices are all cited in the DOL's *Occupational Outlook Handbook* as opportunities for social workers. On any given day, social work job opportunities across the country are listed by a variety of sources, including the national and state offices of the National Association of Social Workers (NASW), schools of social work, university career placement offices, online platforms such as LinkedIn, and national magazines such as *Social Work Today*. For example, on January 11, 2022, there were 2,375 jobs listed on the NASW JobLink site available via the NASW Career Center. The U.S. Council on Social Work Education Kendall Institute offers links to international career options, for example, the International Federation of the Red Cross or United Nations jobs.

FIGURE 4.1
Social work can be practiced at the micro, mezzo, and macro levels. This picture depicts a micro-level social worker talking to her client.

Suffice it to say, there is an array of employment opportunities for BSW, MSW, and DSW or PhD practitioners in every state and throughout the world. What is most exciting to the job seeker is that social work positions offer a variety of challenges working with individuals, groups, families, organizations, and communities (see Figure 4.1).

This chapter will explore the nature of employment opportunities in the field of social work. We will first discuss the educational requirements to become a social worker and the role that accreditation standards play. Then we will look at an overview of prospects for social workers today, presenting salary and employment projections into the twenty-first century. We will conclude with tips on finding that first social work job.

4.1 THE EDUCATION OF A SOCIAL WORKER

What educational criteria are needed to make a person a social worker? The answer is simple: a baccalaureate or master's degree in social work—that is, a BSW, BSSW, or BA or BS in social work or an MSW, MSSW, or MA or MS in social work—from a program accredited by the Council on Social Work Education, more commonly referred to as the CSWE. When students graduate from these kinds of degree programs in social work, they are considered to have professional practice degrees. CSWE maintains a directory of accredited programs that can be accessed online.

A degree in sociology, psychology, anthropology, or any other -ology does not make a person a social worker. The major difference between a degree in social work and these other degrees is that sociology, psychology, and anthropology have to do with focus. Social workers focus on the person within their environment and help people make the changes they want to make. The value base of the social work profession differs from that of those other disciplines. Social work defines itself with paying special attention to the empowerment of humans who are vulnerable, oppressed, and living in poverty. It is a value-based profession. People who major in these other fields may specialize in practice or complete practice-based courses, but they are not based in practice as social work graduates are.

It is also important to note that working in a social agency for ten years, even under the tutelage of a degreed social worker, does not alone make a person a qualified social worker. Further, a doctoral degree or PhD in social work is not recognized as a practice degree. Since the early 2000s, a number of graduate social work programs have begun to offer the doctorate in social work, or DSW, as a practice doctorate, and some states will license an individual with a DSW for practice even if they do not have a BSW or MSW (or equivalent, e.g., MPhil or MSSW) degree. A move to accreditation of DSW degrees by CSWE is under way at the time of this edition's writing, and their graduates are considered researchers, administrators, educators, or scientific practitioners. As a result, entry into the social work profession is currently limited, and those interested in becoming social workers must pass through at least one of the two degree doors, BSW or MSW.

Not to muddy the waters, but in some states, it is possible to be licensed to practice social work without having a degree in social work. For example, some states may choose to "grandfather in"—or make exceptions for—certain individuals to practice or sit for a qualifying exam. Each state sets its own criteria and deadlines for this type of exception, so it is best to contact respective state licensing boards directly to find out if and how these exemptions are made. For example, in Alabama, certain client protection workers for the state have been grandfathered in and are therefore eligible to be licensed as baccalaureate-level social workers; these individuals do not have BSWs, a standard requirement in most states. West Virginia has also used a similar practice. Caution should be exercised, however, because people who use this nontraditional door into social work may be disappointed if they move out of the granting state. Other states may not honor their designated status, and appeal based on reciprocity may not be possible.

The best way to ensure entry into the field of social work is the traditional way: by earning a baccalaureate or master's degree in social work from a program accredited by the CSWE. As of February 2022, the CSWE had accredited 842 BSW and MSW social work programs across the country (Council on Social Work Education, 2022a).

The difference between someone who simply wants to help and someone who is professionally educated in the knowledge and skills to give help is pronounced. Nevertheless, some professionals from other disciplines feel that the demanding requirements that must be satisfied to qualify as a social worker are unfair. That most states require a professional social worker to have either a bachelor or a graduate college degree in social work strikes them as elitist. In fact, they may say, a lot of good people carry out important activities on behalf of individuals in need, and these helping workers should also be considered social workers. Most professional social workers would disagree because they believe that social work is indeed a profession and, as such, must have clear rules and requirements for entry. Social workers believe that, within the field, professionals are expected to confront the full range of human problems and to do so in multiple practice settings (Burger & Youkeles, 2004); this requires professional education as a generalist.

To support this position, let's look at the entry requirements for several professions:

- *Law*: Completion of a baccalaureate degree in any discipline, graduation from a law program accredited by the American Bar Association, and successful completion of a state bar examination. At one time, a person could sit for the bar exam without graduating from a law program. In such cases, individuals were required to have worked in a law office under the mentorship of a board-certified lawyer, that is, one who had passed the bar exam, for a number of years. This practice is no longer allowed. In February 2022, the American Bar Association accredited 199 programs.
- *Medicine*: Completion of a baccalaureate degree, preferably in the natural or physical sciences, such as chemistry, biology, physics, or astronomy; graduation from a medical school accredited by the American Medical Association; and successful completion of a state medical examination. In the past, as with law school graduation, medical school graduation was not a requirement for practice, but that is no longer the case. The accreditation standards of the Accreditation Commission on Colleges of Medicine (2014) require both "didactic and practical" educational experiences, as does social work.
- *Nursing*: Education in the scientific basis of nursing under defined standards of education and concern with the **diagnosis** and treatment of human responses to actual or potential health problems (*PDR Medical Dictionary*, 2005). Most nurses have completed their education in accredited programs and can practice at the level appropriate to their educational qualifications. Degrees include an associate degree in nursing, bachelor of science in nursing, master of science in nursing, and doctorate of nursing practice. In addition, there are several specializations, such as midwifery and nurse practitioner. For example, a licensed practical nurse has graduated from an accredited school of practical (vocational) nursing (one year of training), passed the state exam for licensure, and is licensed to practice by the state authority. Similar requirements with varying education exist at the associate, baccalaureate, and graduate levels. An individual without a degree in nursing may assist a nurse in daily routines; often, this individual is called a nurse's aide or assistant. Regardless of education, nurse's aides are not nurses and cannot perform the traditional duties of nurses licensed at distinct levels of skill acquisition.

- *Physical therapy*: Completion of a baccalaureate degree, with emphasis in biology, chemistry, physics, and social sciences, or graduation from a graduate physical therapy program accredited by the Commission on Accreditation in Physical Therapy Education. In February 2022, there were 271 accredited physical therapist programs, and an additional 389 physical therapist assistant programs were accredited nationwide.

Law, medicine, nursing, and physical therapy are only a few of the professions that require professional education regulated by a professional accrediting body and usually successful completion of a state examination to practice. Until the nineteenth century, people were not required to complete any formal education to enter a particular profession. Instead, someone hoping to enter a profession studied and worked as an apprentice under a practicing member of that profession who was recognized as experienced. This mentoring model was acceptable for three main reasons. First, at that time, the existing few colleges and universities were geographically inaccessible to many. Second, because there were fewer schools, the number of people who could participate in higher education was limited by the availability of educators and seats. Third, few families could afford the costs of a college education. Higher education was reserved for the elite and, for the most part, White males. With these limits on access to formal education, most aspiring professionals found it productive to learn under the watchful eye and guidance of a successful practitioner.

With the spread of the public state college system and the democratization of all higher education, the historical barriers were slowly chipped away. As formal education became more accessible, many professionals moved their courses of study from the practical to the academic setting. Social work was no exception.

Did You Know . . .

In 2023, Texas had more accredited BSW and MSW programs (fifty-nine) than any other state. Following Texas were New York (fifty-five) and Pennsylvania (-fifty-three). Delaware (two) and Wyoming (two) were the two states that had the fewest BSW and MSW programs. Visit CSWE.org for more information about accreditation and updated statistics.

The first documented educational training program in social work was a six-week-long summer institute offered in 1898. Sponsored by the New York Charity Organization Society, this program is credited with contributing to the founding of the Columbia University School of Social Work. Before this summer institute was held, almost all social work training took place within agencies and was provided by agency staff.

In the years that followed, social work education became a fixture of higher education. Following the June 2020 meeting of the CSWE's Commission on Accreditation

Table 4.1 Number of Accredited BSW and MSW Programs and Number of PhD/DSW Programs

Year	BSW	MSW	PhD/DSW
2020	549	311	98
2015	504	235	76
2013	482	219	73
2011	472	213	71
2009	470	195	NA
2007	462	186	NA
2005	450	174	NA
2003	437	159	NA
2000	420	139	67

Source: Council on Social Work Education, 2020 *Annual Statistics on Social Work Education in the United States*. Table updated using most recent numbers retrieved from https://www.cswe.org/getattachment/726b15ce-6e63-4dcd-abd1-35d2ea9d9d40/2020-Annual-Statistics-On-Social-Work-Education-in-the-United-States.pdf?lang=en-US.

(CSWE, 2022b), there were a total of 558 accredited baccalaureate-level and 348 master-level programs; there were also 36 BSW and MSW programs in candidacy (that is, working to meet the CSWE accreditation standards). Table 4.1 shows the increasing numbers of degreed programs in social work from 2000 until 2020.

Social work education also prepares individuals in doctoral education. The national organization for social work doctoral education is called the Group for the Advancement of Doctoral Education in Social Work and had a membership in 2022 of over ninety social work doctoral program directors representing their respective academic institutions.

Thousands of social work educational programs are found in all regions of the world. There is no reliable estimate of the total number of social work programs worldwide, but the conservative consensus of the International Association of Schools of Social Work is that there are a minimum of 2,500 programs.

Did You Know . . .

In 2020, the Association of Social Work Boards reported that the national pass rate was 68.5 percent for the bachelor's licensing exam and 75.4 percent for the master's exam.

The twentieth century was critical for the developing field of social work. During this time, social work was transformed from a volunteer activity into an established profession requiring an intentionally designed education. When apprenticeship occurs now, it is intertwined with or follows a competency-based educational process provided within the rigorous setting of baccalaureate or graduate study.

Name: Lai Kwan (Denise), KAN
Place of residence: Vancouver, Canada
College/university degrees: University of Alabama, MSW with mental health concentration
Present position: Mental health and addictions intake clinician/PhD student at University of Alabama School of Social Work

What does a typical day at work look like for you? What tasks do you generally complete as a social worker in your area of expertise? As a mental health and addictions intake clinician working in an outpatient mental health clinic, I am expected to work a twelve-hour shift between 7:00 a.m. and 7:00 p.m. My work schedule is laid on a rotational roster—three days on and three days off. Due to increasing service needs, social workers who work in clinical settings are expected to accommodate and to collaborate with multidisciplinary teams, which follow rotational schedules. My typical workday starts with reviewing my daily to-do list, answering voice messages and emails, and attending regular administrative and clinical meetings. Afterward, I am expected to attend four intake appointments; each one-hour intake appointment I will conduct bio-psycho-social-spiritual assessment; simultaneously I will discuss and formulate a treatment plan together with my patient (and family). Psychoeducation, crisis intervention, and triage services are also parts of the job responsibility. Before making any in-house or community patient referrals, with my patient's consent, I will also need to collect collateral information, follow by assessment report writing and documentation gathering. Additionally, I am required to deliver in-house and general public phone/in-person mental health consultation and education. Occasionally, I also act as a cultural broker or mediator who provides interpretation to patients (and their families) of diverse cultural and linguistic backgrounds.

As a PhD in social work student, since I am still in the phase of finishing my two-year coursework, my typical day starts with attending course(s), following by reading articles and books, writing proposals and manuscripts, working on assigned assistantship, and attending meetings, etc. I spend around seventy hours weekly for my PhD studies.

What do you do in your spare time? Both ballroom and Zumba dancing allow me to immerse myself in music and movements so that I can completely forget my stress and worries. They are vital to my bio-psycho-social health and to maintain my work–life balance. Archery helps to train my attention and to calm and ground myself. Moreover, I love animals and nature; I enjoy walking, arts, traveling, listening to music, and watching imaginary action movies in my spare time.

Why did you choose social work as a career? Growing up in a family of immigrants, we have experienced discrimination, inequity, racism, sexism, and being marginalized. Along our journeys of adjustment and settlement, we are thankful to people who have kindly offered us guidance and support. Because of their extended love and care, we have seen light and hope and have created better lives and promising future through opportunities. Because I have witnessed and encountered hope and positive changes, I would like to create and bring forward encouragement and inspiration to people who are in need. The social work profession is where I can make my desire come true, where people who are in need will be able to connect to hope and positive changes.

What is your favorite social work story or inspiration? Mr. Shing Nam Hung, a candid social worker, a gifted instructor, and a dedicated caregiver, has committed to and has contributed his life to the social work profession, his students, and his family. His teaching philosophy and life experience have not only demonstrated an unconditional love and passion, but also an excellent model of critical thinking, empathy, and justice.

What would be the one thing you would change in our community if you had the power to do so? A society of humanity, equity, justice, integrity, and freedom where everyone takes part to enjoy and to maintain the harmony of our ecosystem, where human–animal–nature bonding can be generated and nurtured creatively and safely.

4.2 ACCREDITATION AND WHY IT MATTERS

As an aspiring social work professional, you should be aware of the accreditation standards your social work program must meet. By meeting these standards, your program assures you and society that when you complete its requirements you will be well prepared for your future career, including eligibility for licensure. Because of the importance of this information, we will present an overview of accreditation and explain how it relates directly to your development as a professional in the field of social work.

Council on Social Work Education

The CSWE is the primary national organization that oversees and provides guidelines for social work education in the United States. The council was organized in 1952 with the merger of the National Association of Schools of Social Administration, which had coordinated baccalaureate education, and the American Association of Schools of Social Work, the membership body for graduate programs (Beless, 1995). Today, social work education is a big enterprise, with programs found at more than five hundred

Table 4.2 Number of BSW, MSW, and PhD/DSW Students and Graduates of Accredited Programs

	2020	2013	2011	2006	2000
BSW students*	61,907	58,087	40,369	32,457	35,255
BSW degrees awarded	19,474	17,221	14,662	12,845	11,773
MSW students	75,851	54,188	49,236	39,566	33,815
MSW degrees awarded	31,750	22,677	20,573	17,209	15,016
PhD/DSW students	3,783	2,545	2,575	2,554	1,953
PhD/DSW degrees awarded	582	339	321	293	229

*Includes both full-time and part-time students.
Sources: Council on Social Work Education, *Social Work Program Data*, 2015. Retrieved from http://www.cswe.org/CentersInitiatives/DataStatistics/ProgramData.aspx. Council on Social Work Education, *Annual Statistics on Social Work Education in the United States*, 2020. Alexandria, VA: Council on Social Work Education.

colleges and universities nationwide. There are 128,744 full-time and part-time students enrolled in BSW, MSW, and doctoral programs (see Table 4.2). In total, 48,852 social work degrees were awarded in 2019.

Activity

Visit the CSWE website and look for the listing of schools, colleges, departments, and programs of social work under the accreditation link. Compare and contrast programs from around the country, urban and rural programs, and large and small colleges/universities. What differences, if any, do you find? What kinds of electives do programs offer? How do BSW and MSW programs differ? What patterns of interesting educational activities do you find?

Although the CSWE was formed by the merger of two organizations that concentrated on baccalaureate and graduate education, respectively, undergraduate education over time appeared to take a back seat to graduate studies (Leighninger, 1987). It was not until 1974 that the CSWE implemented accreditation standards for baccalaureate programs. As Gardellia (1997) noted, BSW and MSW educational programs have never been fully integrated—that is, they have never viewed each other as equal partners—which has created tension between the groups. Moreover, the CSWE board of directors initially included ten seats for BSW educators and twenty seats for MSW educators (Gardellia, 1997, p. 39). But over time, the disproportional number of board seats changed to increase the number of BSW educators on the board. In 2009, the

CSWE board undertook significant structural revisions that included equal representation of baccalaureate and graduate educators. Even so, there are some social work faculty, both undergraduate and graduate educators alike, who may continue to foster unnecessary tensions between the program levels, perhaps because of competition for limited resources.

For social work students, knowing how CSWE conducts its business can clarify why its educational programs are organized as they are. The CSWE is governed by six commissions: Accreditation; Diversity and Social and Economic Justice; Educational Policy; Global Social Work Education; Membership and Professional Development; and Research. Working with the commissions are councils that focus on specific interest areas. For example, four councils work with the Commission for Diversity and Social and Economic Justice: (1) the Council on Disability and Persons with Disabilities; (2) the Council on Racial, Ethnic, and Cultural Diversity; (3) the Council on the Role and Status of Women in Social Work Education; and (4) the Council on Sexual Orientation and Gender Identity & Expression. Explore the various councils and commissions on the CSWE website. Look at the important work each one is doing to promote, enhance, and strengthen social work education. You will discover that social work educators are tackling a variety of issues and that they do this for free! That's right, social work educators volunteer countless hours serving on the board of directors, commissions, and councils. They do this because as social workers they understand the importance of working on behalf of the entire professional community.

Did You Know . . .
The U.S. Department of Labor reported that in 2020 the most frequent employers of social workers were individual and family services (18 percent), local government, excluding education and hospitals (14 percent), ambulatory health care services (14 percent), and state government, excluding education and hospitals (14 percent). For more information, see the *Occupational Outlook Handbook*.

Now let's explore two of these commissions in detail to learn more about their work and significance to you: the CSWE Commission on Accreditation and the CSWE Commission on Educational Policy.

Commission on Accreditation
One of the principal functions of the CSWE is the accreditation of baccalaureate and master's degree programs. Why is accreditation important? States require an individual to graduate from a CSWE-accredited program to be eligible for licensure/registration to practice social work. In general, this is a fixed requirement (e.g., state rule) that is in place throughout the United States.

Social work accreditation is coordinated by the Commission on Accreditation, a thirty-member committee that includes social work educators representing both BSW and MSW faculties, BSW and MSW students, and social work practitioners. Referred to as commissioners, these individuals are volunteers appointed by the president of the CSWE for three-year terms; a commissioner may serve no more than two consecutive terms or a total of six years. A professional CSWE staff supports the commission. The commission influences the direction of social work education through such activities as maintaining and updating accreditation standards; conducting commissioner **site visits** to programs in candidacy; voting on candidacy status, initial accreditation, and **reaffirmation**; and ensuring the quality of social work education and of the commission's functions.

Commission on Educational Policy

This commission sets CSWE's educational direction through its work around educational policy and accreditation standards. The commission is responsible for thinking through current and future practice needs while considering differing ways to build social work educational programs. This commission includes eighteen volunteers who represent all levels and sectors of social work education.

EDUCATIONAL POLICY AND ACCREDITATION STANDARDS

The Educational Policy (EP) and Accreditation Standards (AS) are written by the CSWE's Commission on Educational Policy and are the central and critical document to social work educators and program developers. As part of its compliance with the CSWE's bylaws, which require that EP and AS be reviewed at least once every seven years, the board of directors approved the current EP in 2022 (CSWE, Commission on Educational Policy, and Commission on Accreditation, 2022, p. 6). The CSWE Commission on Educational Policy is responsible for drafting the EP, whereas the CSWE Commission on Accreditation establishes the AS.

The EP serves a threefold purpose. First, it describes in broad terms the essence of social work education at the bachelor and master levels of education. Second, the EP sets forth core practice competencies, that is, measurable practice skills expected for beginning-level BSW and MSW practitioners. And third, the EP establishes the basic educational principles from which the AS are developed.

These documents are critical to social work education and your program. You may wonder why certain courses are required whereas others are electives; you just need to read the EP and AS to gain a beginning understanding of your program's structure (see CSWE, Commission on Educational Policy, and Commission on Accreditation, 2022). Your faculty crafted the curriculum based on the EP for what they believe meets the program's mission and broader practice community needs. You should also know that students are expected to be familiar with the EP and AS. Just as important to remember is that, if your program is being accredited or reviewed for reaccreditation, you may be asked by the site visit team to share your reactions to and observations about the policy.

> **Did You Know . . .**
> Social workers can be found anywhere, from libraries, to public and private social service organizations, to Capitol Hill. The CSWE web page includes information about these and other aspects of trends in social work.

As you read through the EPAS, you will find that it addresses several different subjects, including curricular design and educational context to prepare students for professional social work practice. The EP and resulting AS focuses on nine specific practice competencies and related demonstrable behaviors that a social work student must exhibit in their course of study. All students, BSW and MSW alike, must master and demonstrate these nine competencies and their related practice behaviors, but we will discuss more on that later. Certain EPAS standards are identified at the beginning of each chapter in this book. They are also listed at the beginning of many of your textbooks to verify that the course information being provided relates to the accreditation standards.

According to the EP, the BSW is the entry-level degree, and a BSW practitioner's interventions are developed within a *generalist practice* framework (CSWE, Commission on Educational Policy, and Commission on Accreditation, 2022, p. 17). The MSW is the advanced practice degree, and an MSW practitioner's interventions are developed within a **specialist practice** framework.

Generalist and specialist social workers can be characterized as follows:

- *Generalist*: A social work practitioner whose knowledge and skills encompass a broad spectrum and who assesses problems and their solutions comprehensively. A generalist often coordinates the efforts of specialists by facilitating communication between them, thereby fostering continuity of care.
- *Specialist*: A social work practitioner whose orientation and knowledge are focused on a specific problem or goal or whose technical expertise and skill in specific activities are highly developed and refined (Barker, 2003).

ACCREDITATION STANDARDS FOR SOCIAL WORK PROGRAMS

The EPAS requires all social work educational programs to be grounded in the liberal arts from which the professional education grows (CSWE, Commission on Educational Policy, and Commission on Accreditation, 2022). According to the Commission on Accreditation, the liberal arts perspective "enriches understanding of the person–environment context of professional social work practice and is integrally related to the mastery of social work content. . . . It provides an understanding of one's cultural heritage in the context of other cultures; the methods and limitations of systems of inquiry; and the knowledge, attitudes, ways of thinking, and means of communication that are characteristic of a broadly educated person" (CSWE, 1994, pp. 99–100, 138).

That is why you may have been required to complete several courses in liberal arts before you were allowed to enroll in social work classes. The completion of these courses satisfies part of the social work program's liberal arts educational requirement. Content areas most often completed are English, additional electives in the arts and humanities, science, history, political science, sociology, anthropology, and psychology. A point to remember is that accreditation standards do not specify liberal arts courses that must be completed; instead, your program faculty identifies courses that they feel will prepare you for the social work program's course of study.

> ### Did You Know . . .
> The median annual salary for a social worker was $50,390 nationwide in 2022.
> According to the 2022 EPAS,
>
> > The explicit curriculum is the program's design and delivery of formal education to students, and it includes the curriculum design, courses, course content, and field education curriculum used for each of its program options. Social work education is grounded in the liberal arts and a commitment to anti-racism, diversity, equity, and inclusion, which together provide the intellectual basis for the professional curriculum and inform its design. The integration of anti-racism, diversity, equity, and inclusion principles across the explicit curriculum includes anti-oppression and global positionality, interdisciplinary perspectives, and comparative analysis regarding policy, practice, and research. Using a competency-based education framework, the explicit curriculum prepares students for professional social work practice at the baccalaureate and master's levels. Baccalaureate programs provide students with strong generalist practice knowledge, values, skills, and cognitive and affective processes that prepare them for professional practice with individuals, families, groups, organizations, and communities. Master's programs provide students with knowledge, values, skills, and cognitive and affective processes at both generalist and specialized levels that prepare them for professional practice with individuals, families, groups, organizations, and communities. (CSWE, Commission on Educational Policy, and Commission on Accreditation, 2022, p. 17)

The key requirement according to the 2022 EPAS is the mastery of the nine core competencies, though a program may add additional competencies. Table 4.3 offers a complete rundown of those competencies. We know that sometimes it is tempting to overlook tables in a textbook, but we encourage you to examine the competencies closely. They can help you determine if social work is the career for you.

All programs, BSW and MSW alike, must ensure that students address and are able to demonstrate the nine competencies. As a result of this mandate, a BSW student in

Table 4.3 2022 Educational Policy and Accreditation Standards: Nine Core Competencies for Social Work Education

Specific competency	Educational policy explanation of competency	Social workers
Competency 1: Demonstrate ethical and professional behavior	Social workers understand the value base of the profession and its ethical standards, as well as relevant policies, laws, and regulations that may affect practice with individuals, families, groups, organizations, and communities. Social workers understand that ethics are informed by principles of human rights and apply them toward realizing social, racial, economic, and environmental justice in their practice. Social workers understand frameworks of ethical decision-making and apply principles of critical thinking to those frameworks in practice, research, and policy arenas. Social workers recognize and manage personal values and the distinction between personal and professional values. Social workers understand how their evolving worldview, personal experiences, and affective reactions influence their professional judgment and behavior. Social workers take measures to care for themselves professionally and personally, understanding that self-care is paramount for competent and ethical social work practice. Social workers use rights-based, anti-racist, and anti-oppressive lenses to understand and critique the profession's history, mission, roles, and responsibilities and recognize historical and current contexts of oppression in shaping institutions and social work. Social workers understand the role of other professionals when engaged in interprofessional practice. Social workers recognize the importance of lifelong learning and are committed to continually updating their skills to ensure relevant and effective practice. Social workers understand digital technology and the ethical use of technology in social work practice.	a. Make ethical decisions by applying the standards of the National Association of Social Workers Code of Ethics, relevant laws and regulations, models for ethical decision-making, ethical conduct of research, and additional codes of ethics within the profession as appropriate to the context; b. Demonstrate professional behavior; appearance; and oral, written, and electronic communication; c. Use technology ethically and appropriately to facilitate practice outcomes; and d. Use supervision and consultation to guide professional judgment and behavior.
Competency 2: Advance human rights and social, racial, economic, and environmental justice	Social workers understand that every person, regardless of position in society, has fundamental human rights. Social workers are knowledgeable about the global intersecting and ongoing injustices throughout history that result in oppression and racism, including social work's role and response. Social workers critically evaluate the distribution of power and privilege in society in order to promote social, racial, economic, and environmental justice by reducing inequities and ensuring dignity and respect for all. Social workers advocate for and engage in strategies to eliminate oppressive structural barriers to ensure that social resources, rights, and responsibilities are distributed equitably, and that civil, political, economic, social, and cultural human rights are protected.	a. Advocate for human rights at the individual, family, group, organizational, and community system levels; and b. Engage in practices that advance human rights to promote social, racial, economic, and environmental justice.

continues

Part 1: The Context of Social Work

Table 4.3 (continued)

Specific competency	Educational policy explanation of competency	Social workers
Competency 3: Engage anti-racism, diversity, equity, and inclusion (ADEI) in practice	Social workers understand how racism and oppression shape human experiences and how these two constructs influence practice at the individual, family, group, organizational, and community levels and in policy and research. Social workers understand the pervasive impact of White supremacy and privilege and use their knowledge, awareness, and skills to engage in anti-racist practice. Social workers understand how diversity and intersectionality shape human experiences and identity development and affect equity and inclusion. The dimensions of diversity are understood as the intersectionality of factors including but not limited to age, caste, class, color, culture, disability and ability, ethnicity, gender, gender identity and expression, generational status, immigration status, legal status, marital status, political ideology, race, nationality, religion and spirituality, sex, sexual orientation, and tribal sovereign status. Social workers understand that this intersectionality means that a person's life experiences may include oppression, poverty, marginalization, and alienation as well as privilege and power. Social workers understand the societal and historical roots of social and racial injustices and the forms and mechanisms of oppression and discrimination. Social workers understand cultural humility and recognize the extent to which a culture's structures and values, including social, economic, political, racial, technological, and cultural exclusions, may create privilege and power resulting in systemic oppression.	a. Demonstrate anti-racist and anti-oppressive social work practice at the individual, family, group, organizational, community, research, and policy levels; and b. Demonstrate cultural humility by applying critical reflection, self-awareness, and self-regulation to manage the influence of bias, power, privilege, and values in working with clients and constituencies, acknowledging them as experts of their own lived experiences.

Competency 4: Engage in practice-informed research and research-informed practice	Social workers use ethical, culturally informed, anti-racist, and anti-oppressive approaches in conducting research and building knowledge. Social workers use research to inform their practice decision-making and articulate how their practice experience informs research and evaluation decisions. Social workers critically evaluate and critique current, empirically sound research to inform decisions pertaining to practice, policy, and programs. Social workers understand the inherent bias in research and evaluate design, analysis, and interpretation using an anti-racist and anti-oppressive perspective. Social workers know how to access, critique, and synthesize the current literature to develop appropriate research questions and hypotheses. Social workers demonstrate knowledge and skills regarding qualitative and quantitative research methods and analysis, and they interpret data derived from these methods. Social workers demonstrate knowledge about methods to assess reliability and validity in social work research. Social workers can articulate and share research findings in ways that are usable to a variety of clients and constituencies. Social workers understand the value of evidence derived from interprofessional and diverse research methods, approaches, and sources.	a. Apply research findings to inform and improve practice, policy, and programs; and b. Identify ethical, culturally informed, anti-racist, and anti-oppressive strategies that address inherent biases for use in quantitative and qualitative research methods to advance the purposes of social work.
Competency 5: Engage in policy practice	Social workers identify social policy at the local, state, federal, and global level that affects well-being, human rights and justice, service delivery, and access to social services. Social workers recognize the historical, social, racial, cultural, economic, organizational, environmental, and global influences that affect social policy. Social workers understand and critique the history and current structures of social policies and services and the role of policy in service delivery through rights-based, anti-oppressive, and anti-racist lenses. Social workers influence policy formulation, analysis, implementation, and evaluation within their practice settings with individuals, families, groups, organizations, and communities. Social workers actively engage in and advocate for anti-racist and anti-oppressive policy practice to effect change in those settings.	a. Use social justice, anti-racist, and anti-oppressive lenses to assess how social welfare policies affect the delivery of and access to social services; and b. Apply critical thinking to analyze, formulate, and advocate for policies that advance human rights and social, racial, economic, and environmental justice.

continues

Table 4.3 (continued)

Specific competency	Educational policy explanation of competency	Social workers
Competency 6: Engage with individuals, families, groups, organizations, and communities	Social workers understand that engagement is an ongoing component of the dynamic and interactive process of social work practice with and on behalf of individuals, families, groups, organizations, and communities. Social workers value the importance of human relationships. Social workers understand theories of human behavior and person-in-environment, and critically evaluate and apply this knowledge to facilitate engagement with clients and constituencies, including individuals, families, groups, organizations, and communities. Social workers are self-reflective and understand how bias, power, and privilege as well as their personal values and personal experiences may affect their ability to engage effectively with diverse clients and constituencies. Social workers use the principles of interprofessional collaboration to facilitate engagement with clients, constituencies, and other professionals as appropriate.	a. Apply knowledge of human behavior and person-in-environment, as well as interprofessional conceptual frameworks, to engage with clients and constituencies; and b. Use empathy, reflection, and interpersonal skills to engage in culturally responsive practice with clients and constituencies.
Competency 7: Assess individuals, families, groups, organizations, and communities	Social workers understand that assessment is an ongoing component of the dynamic and interactive process of social work practice. Social workers understand theories of human behavior and person-in-environment, as well as interprofessional conceptual frameworks, and they critically evaluate and apply this knowledge in culturally responsive assessment with clients and constituencies, including individuals, families, groups, organizations, and communities. Assessment involves a collaborative process of defining presenting challenges and identifying strengths with individuals, families, groups, organizations, and communities to develop a mutually agreed-upon plan. Social workers recognize the implications of the larger practice context in the assessment process and use interprofessional collaboration in this process. Social workers are self-reflective and understand how bias, power, privilege, and their personal values and experiences may affect their assessment and decision-making.	a. Apply theories of human behavior and person-in-environment, as well as other culturally responsive and interprofessional conceptual frameworks, when assessing clients and constituencies; and b. Demonstrate respect for client self-determination during the assessment process by collaborating with clients and constituencies in developing a mutually agreed-upon plan.

Competency 8: Intervene with individuals, families, groups, organizations, and communities	Social workers understand that intervention is an ongoing component of the dynamic and interactive process of social work practice. Social workers understand theories of human behavior, person-in-environment, and other interprofessional conceptual frameworks, and they critically evaluate and apply this knowledge in selecting culturally responsive interventions with clients and constituencies, including individuals, families, groups, organizations, and communities. Social workers understand methods of identifying, analyzing, and implementing evidence-informed interventions and participate in interprofessional collaboration to achieve client and constituency goals. Social workers facilitate effective transitions and endings.	a. Engage with clients and constituencies to critically choose and implement culturally responsive, evidence-informed interventions to achieve client and constituency goals; and b. Incorporate culturally responsive methods to negotiate, mediate, and advocate with and on behalf of clients and constituencies.
Competency 9: Evaluate practice with individuals, families, groups, organizations, and communities	Social workers understand that evaluation is an ongoing component of the dynamic and interactive process of social work practice with and on behalf of diverse individuals, families, groups, organizations, and communities. Social workers evaluate processes and outcomes to increase practice, policy, and service delivery effectiveness. Social workers apply anti-racist and anti-oppressive perspectives in evaluating outcomes. Social workers understand theories of human behavior and person-in-environment, as well as interprofessional conceptual frameworks, and critically evaluate and apply this knowledge in evaluating outcomes. Social workers use qualitative and quantitative methods for evaluating outcomes and practice effectiveness.	a. Select and use culturally responsive methods for evaluation of outcomes; and b. Critically analyze outcomes and apply evaluation findings to improve practice effectiveness with individuals, families, groups, organizations, and communities.

Source: Council on Social Work Education, Commission on Educational Policy, and Commission on Accreditation (2022), pp. 8–13.

New York, New York, addresses the same core competencies as a BSW student in Missoula, Montana. This results in a common ground for all social workers whatever their individual agency settings, client populations, practice functions, or practice methods. This common educational content is a real asset. This competency model helps supervisors and coworkers know what new social workers can complete because of their formal professional education. There is limited uniformity in educational content for some related disciplines, such as the various counseling specialties.

> ### Activity
> Meet with a social work advisor to discuss your program's admission process. Is the program a limited-access program? What is the application process? Are all applicants accepted into the program? What are some of the reasons that people are denied admission to the program? Explore with the advisor the program's liberal arts requirements. Why are these specific courses required? Are you surprised by some of the required courses?

Baccalaureate in Social Work (Educational Model). The typical baccalaureate social work program begins in the sophomore year of college and requires four to five semesters of study. Accreditation standards require some form of admission process into the BSW program, and these standards are established by the program's faculty. Limited-access programs require a formal application and review process for admission. There are no set national admission standards for a program; faculty determines the admission criteria for their program, set within the policies of the home college or university. Admission may depend on such criteria as cumulative grade point average, successful completion of the liberal arts requirements, reference letters, and a narrative statement. In programs that are not limited access, admission depends on successful completion of the liberal arts requirements. Whether access to a program is limited or not depends on school policy.

Accreditation standards require that, while enrolled in the program as a major, the student receive at least four hundred hours of field education, although some programs may require more than this minimum. These requirements are not etched in stone, however, and during a crisis period, realistic modifications can be made. For example, during the COVID-19 pandemic, some modifications were made to the number of in-person hours and how they could be completed. CSWE published a survey titled *CSWE COVID-19 Member "Pulse" Survey*, which was utilized to make changes to how social work classes were delivered and the field placement requirements during this period to ensure student and public safety while maintaining academic integrity (CSWE, 2020).

Programs currently use several models to address the field placement requirement. One option is *block placement,* in which the student is assigned to an agency full-time, up to forty hours a week, for an entire semester. A second approach, *concurrent placement*, assigns the student to an agency one to three days a week while the student takes courses, usually for two semesters. A third approach combines concurrent and block placements; concurrent placement is used in the student's junior year of study and block placement in the senior year. This approach allows the student to be assigned to different agencies. What is more important to remember is that whatever field model your program uses, you must complete at least four hundred hours in the field practicum. This is nonnegotiable, and previous work experience cannot be substituted for your practicum requirement. Because this requirement is set forth in the accreditation standards, your program is very unlikely to allow modifications or exceptions.

Master of Social Work (Educational Model). Professional education at the master's level requires the equivalent of two academic years of full-time study and combines two components, foundation, and specialization in a particular area of study.

The professional foundation content is the same as for baccalaureate programs. Traditionally, the foundation content was most often studied in the first year, with specialization taking place during the equivalent of the second year of full-time study. A number of graduate programs are moving away from this so-called 50–50 model by emphasizing specialization with the advanced studies beginning during the first year of study (Colby, 2013). According to the social work educational model, specialization must be firmly rooted in the foundation content. A specialization can be designed around different areas of social work practice (see Box 4.1); second-year courses and field education should reflect this specialization area. Accreditation standards require that MSW students complete at least nine hundred field hours. Like BSW field experiences, some programs may require more hours than the minimum required by CSWE. Students complete two placements, one in the foundation year and another in the specialization year, and together these must total a minimum of nine hundred hours.

BOX 4.1

SPECIALIZATION MODELS

Methodology: Specialization by intervention, such as critical social work, community organization, or group work.

Setting: Specialization by agency setting or type, such as child welfare, mental health, criminal justice, rural practice, or gerontology.

Population group: Specialization by a specific client population, such as children, families, women, and seniors.

Problem area: Specialization by a focused problem, such as alcohol, tobacco, and other substances; mental illness; family violence; and poverty.

Combination: A combination of specializations, such as methodology and population growth, for example, or clinical social work with children.

A common complaint among newly enrolled graduate students is that their field placements are not in their intended areas of specialization. Students need to remember, however, that the first field placement is intended to be generalist in nature to allow them to demonstrate the acquisition of the core competencies. Competencies for specializations are developed in the equivalent of the specialization or advanced study; it is at this point that specialization placements occur.

> ### Did You Know . . .
> The Department of Veterans Affairs—the largest employer of social workers in the country—employs more than 17,300 master's-prepared social workers to assist veterans and their families with individual and family counseling, client education, end-of-life planning, substance abuse treatment, crisis intervention, and other services.

Students choosing a graduate program should know that not all programs offer the same choices of specialization and some limit the advanced study to one specialization. A colleague has remarked that, when reviewing admission folders for graduate program admission, students often know little about the program to which they are applying. One student, for example, wanted to study administration, but the school offered only a clinical specialization. The student had a grade point average of 3.8 and a Graduate Record Exam score of 1,175. Nevertheless, the admission committee rejected the application because the student's career interests did not match the school's mission and curriculum. The applicant was incredibly angry and complained about the rejection. Even when the committee's rationale was explained, the student did not accept the decision, saying, "What I want to do professionally has nothing to do with the type of program I want to apply to." The moral of this story: Be sure that your career goals match the school's mission and educational program.

> ### Did You Know . . .
> Social workers can be found doing military social work, international social work, forensic social work, and veterinary social work, among other unexpected settings, in addition to the more commonly expected practice areas of child and family social work, mental health/clinical social work, or health care social work.

Advanced Standing (Educational Program). Some graduate programs offer advanced standing. Advanced standing, which is limited to graduates of CSWE baccalaureate programs, allows these students to have certain graduate courses waived because they mastered the content in their baccalaureate studies. Advanced standing reflects the long-standing accreditation standard that a graduate program does not require coursework to be repeated once it has been mastered; this is detailed in the EPAS under the student admission protocols (CSWE, Commission on Educational Policy, and Commission on Accreditation, 2022, p. 26).

Social work is the only profession that offers an advanced standing option in its educational model. Even within social work, advanced standing is very controversial in both theory and practice. The profession's ambivalence toward advanced standing is seen in its inconsistent application. Some programs waive the entire foundation year of study, whereas others limit the exemption to one or two courses. Some require successful completion of content-specific examinations, and some programs do not offer an advanced standing option at all. Some programs require BSW practitioners to enroll in the graduate program within a specific period from the time of their BSW graduation, typically ranging from four to seven years; otherwise, they are not eligible for advanced standing and are required to complete the regular two-year curriculum.

PhD/DSW (Educational Program). The CSWE does not currently regulate doctoral study, although at the time of this edition's publication, the organization was exploring the possibility of accrediting DSW, but not PhD, programs. As a result, doctoral programs differ in required courses, program structure, and specialization. Generally, a doctorate is required for people who teach in BSW or MSW programs. Although it is not required for agency practice, there is a small but growing trend in agencies to hire upper-level administrators who hold doctoral degrees.

Two types of doctoral degrees are associated with social work, the PhD and the DSW. The PhD is the familiar research-focused doctor of philosophy of social work; the DSW designates a practice-focused doctoral course of study allowing for depth and breadth not available in the MSW. When doctoral programs first originated in the field of social work, the DSW was the most-offered doctoral degree. As time passed and social workers were hired as educators and research became increasingly valued by our discipline, schools often changed the doctorate they offered to a PhD. Both degrees require the equivalent of two years of full-time coursework and some sort of culminating project. Those pursuing a PhD with the focus on preparation as a researcher complete a dissertation in either monograph or multiple article formats. Those pursuing DSWs follow various paths delineated by their specific programs, but those programs also commonly include some sort of capstone project. It is important to remember, however, that because of the differences between the types of doctoral degrees, along with the greater variability, careful exploration to find the right match between student and program remains essential.

Name: Ariel Champaloux Ford
College/university degrees: BSW and MSW, University of Central Florida, Orlando, Florida
Credentials: LCSW, MCAP, QS, EMDR trained
Employment history:
- Director of Social Work, Circles of Care, Inc.
- Clinical Therapist, St. Johns Recovery Place, PHP/IOP
- Director of clinical services and director of Christian programming, the Blackberry Center
- Lead social worker, LCSW for Inpatient Baker Act Psychiatric Unit, Lawnwood Regional Medical Center (HCA) Psychiatric Unit, Fort Pierce, Florida
- Clinical Therapist, U.S. Air Force, Patrick Air Force Base, Florida
- Hospital/emergency room social worker, Holmes Regional Medical Center

What do you do in your spare time? The most important thing in my life is my relationship with God, my husband, and family/friends. I spend my spare time obtaining strength from my daily devotions. I just got EMDR trained and have been spending my spare time learning new techniques and practicing EMDR.

Why did you choose social work as a career? I have always had a passion and big heart and wanted to help everyone. My mother is a LCSW and I have seen the amazing things she has done with her clients. Another facet of social work that was important in my choice is that there are so many different avenues that you can pursue with this degree.

What is your favorite social work story? I have over twenty years of amazing stories I can share from being a social worker. My favorite stories share one common factor and that is helping people during the worst point in their lives. This is a priceless feeling knowing that you made a difference in someone's life. It doesn't matter where I have ended up in my career, I have always had the opportunity to help someone and this has fulfilled me professionally, personally, and spiritually.

What would be the one thing you would change in our community if you had the power to do so? I truly believe God equips me to help people even if it's one person at a time.

4.3 SOCIAL WORKERS TODAY

Here is some good news for you. According to the DOL, social work is expected to be among the fastest-growing professions through the year 2031. The DOL identified 708,100 social work jobs in 2022, with most positions in children and family settings, health care, and schools (U.S. Department of Labor, 2022). The DOL also noted that mental health and substance abuse intervention social work specializations will grow as more people seek treatment (U.S. Department of Labor, 2022). A much earlier study (Gibelman & Schervish, 1997, p. 5) estimated that the number of people employed in social work and holding social work degrees ranged from 645,000 to 693,000. The DOL (2022) expects the overall employment of social workers to grow at a rate of 9 percent from 2021 to 2031, faster than average for all occupations, with an average of 74,700 openings per year.

The bottom line is that no single information source provides a detailed overview of social work employment. We know that social workers are employed in a variety of settings, both public and private, and employment prospects continue to be sound.

> ## Activity
> Contact your state's department of labor. The agency is usually located in the state capital and will have a website. Does your state offer data about social worker employment in your state? If they do, do the data match national trends?

What Are Social Workers Paid?

Of significant interest to people considering social work as a career is salary: How much can I make? Well, you won't be poor, and you'll be able to live a comfortable life. According to the DOL (2022), the median salary (that means half the salaries reported are lower than the median and half are higher) was $50,390 in May 2021. Trying to identify average salaries or answer the question "What can I expect to earn?" is difficult. A social worker in New York City will, on average, earn more than a social worker in Reno, Nevada. The point is not that there is salary discrimination in Reno, but that the cost of living is much less. So be careful when comparing salaries.

A useful source on salaries is right in your own city or town. Go to a local NASW meeting and ask the social workers what the salaries are in your community. Some social work programs have their own career services office and collect salary information. Check around and see what you find. Salary information will also, of course, be available on online job listings. The U.S. Bureau of Labor Statistics (2022) offers data on a state-by-state basis for various specialization areas. Remember that these figures combine all salaries and do not consider the differences based on degree (e.g., BSW or MSW) or specialization area.

> ## Activity
> Check out the Career Center of the NASW. There, you can find social work jobs, learn about career development, access resources for students, and even sign up to get new job notifications in your inbox.

Where Do Social Workers Work?

To better understand where job opportunities might be, let's look at social work practice from four interrelated perspectives: job function, auspices, setting, and practice area (see Table 4.4).

Table 4.4 Social Work Positions by Common Work Roles, Auspices, Setting, and Practice Area

Common work roles: What do I do?	
Direct service	Supervision
Management/administration	Policy development/analysis
Consultant	Research
Planning	Education/training
Auspices: Where do I work?	
Public, local	Private nonprofit, sectarian
Public, state	Private nonprofit, nonsectarian
Public, federal	Private for profit, proprietary
Public, military	
Setting: What type of agency do I work in?	
Social services agency	Nursing home
Private practice, self-employed	Criminal justice system
Private practice, partnership	College/university
Membership organization	Elementary/secondary schools
Hospital	Non–social service organization
Outpatient facility	Group home
Practice area: What is my practice area?	
Children and youth	School social work
Community organization/planning	Services to the aged
Family services	Alcohol and other substance abuse
Criminal justice	Developmental disabilities
Group services	Occupational social work
Mental health	Public assistance

Any set of choices, one from each list, defines a social work position. For example, you can be a supervisor (function) in a private nonprofit sectarian (auspices) nursing home (setting), providing services to aged individuals (practice area). Or you may provide direct service (function) in a public local (auspices) outpatient facility (setting) as an alcohol and substance abuse counselor (practice area). The thousands of potential combinations demonstrate the versatility of social work employment opportunities (see Figure 4.2).

FIGURE 4.2
Social workers can be called on to share their expertise in many venues, including government, legal, and other places in which people gather looking for information or for societal change.

Did You Know . . .
There are hundreds of social workers in national, state, and local elected office, including two U.S. senators and three U.S. representatives in 2022.

Another way to discover the breadth of the social work profession is to examine CSWE studies of social work education programs. Each year, the council collects these data to track the state of the profession and to detect trends in education. In the council's Directory of Accredited Programs, over thirty different practice area concentrations were offered in graduate social work schools, although the offerings in each program are limited to three or four concentrations. Visit the directory yourself and see which programs offer which specializations/concentrations.

4.4 GETTING A SOCIAL WORK JOB AFTER GRADUATION

There is no secret to finding a job, whether in social work, law, nursing, or any other profession. It takes a great deal of arduous work and a lot of patience on the part of the job seeker. Although jobs in general are available, it takes time to find the one that is right for you. A rule of thumb is that it takes three to four months to find a job from the time you begin your search in earnest. So, if you want to have a job by June, you will need to have your résumé prepared and your search strategy developed and implemented no later than the preceding February.

A note of caution: Be prepared not to get the one job you have always wanted right out of the gate. Even for the most experienced social worker, a job rejection letter hurts. Great jobs are waiting for competent social workers—the key is finding a position in which you can make full use of your knowledge, skills, and potential.

Prepare Your Resume Carefully

Be sure your résumé is up to date. You can get an easy-to-use résumé software program at the college bookstore or computer store. There are also any number of books on résumé writing that you can review. Ask your academic advisor or another social worker for tips and ideas about what to highlight. (Your field internship supervisor is always a good person to talk to about what to put on a résumé.) Consider taking advantage of your school's job placement office by attending a résumé-writing workshop, but recognize that most helpers in the résumé-writing process are not well versed in social work; their work is geared to a general audience and does not reflect the nuances of social work. The key is to ask social workers in the field what they did and what they listed on their résumés.

Be sure your résumé is clean and error free—no spelling errors, no photocopied hard copies with wrinkled edges, and so on. Your résumé is your introduction to a potential employer, and you want to make the best impression possible. Consider writing an initial goal or objective for the type of work you want to do in the field. Be sure to link the contents of this statement with the job you are applying for. As a new social worker, you may not have much paid clinical or administrative experience, so be sure to highlight volunteer experiences and start with your most recent field placement. For other tips and suggestions, present a draft of your résumé to a favorite social work instructor or a social worker in the field. Your university career service professionals may also provide valuable assistance. Listen to their suggestions carefully because they have been through the employment process; hearing their words of wisdom first may save you a great deal of time and effort later. To accompany your careful work on your résumé, practice interviewing using technology or social workers you know or even friends. Pay attention to professional attire and demeanor—these details may be the ones that make you stand out from a group of also-qualified applicants.

Licensing Requirements

All states have some sort of regulation on social work practice; some regulate BSW and MSW practice, whereas others regulate only advanced (e.g., MSW/DSW/PhD) practice. As you begin your job search, you must become familiar with the state's requirements as well as the employing agency's expectations. Check to see if your state provides a temporary license; this license allows you to be licensed for a brief period, generally six months, without having to take an exam. Some states allow you to sit for the exam in your last semester of study. The bottom line is to become familiar with your state's licensing/registration requirements. Go to the website for your state, get a recent application, and look at the requirements carefully. You can learn a great deal and you can be linked to other states' licensing/registration information through the national organization Association of Social Work Boards (ASWB).

In 2022, the ASWB published the results of its analysis of its own licensure exam. The analysis showed worrying disparities in the pass rates based on race, age, and native language. The ASWB reported in that 2022 publication that 45 percent of Black test-takers passed the clinical exam on the first try, compared with 84 percent of White test-takers. Responses to this circumstance were emerging slowly at the time of publication of this text. You should check with your state's licensing authority to see what the implications may be for you when you are ready to seek licensure. Because rules and regulations change regularly and can vary from state to state, stay aware of the latest changes and check the website regularly for updated information. Getting a license in your profession is your responsibility, so take a proactive role in learning what is needed and stay aware of the state's licensing/registration requirements.

Networking with Social Work Professionals

To facilitate your job search, attend NASW and other social work professional meetings (local, state, and national) as often as you can. Networking works! You can begin to network by checking out NASW's social media pages, attending meetings, and becoming active with this group as soon as you declare your major. Dues for a student are a real bargain! Go online to apply.

While getting to know other NASW members, whether online, at face-to-face meetings, or at conferences, you'll make new friends, begin to develop a professional network, and keep abreast of issues within your new social work community. Most people would be surprised at how much information about job openings and availability is spread by word of mouth and social media networks and through other types of informal networks. For example, you may even get firsthand information on a position that has just become available from the contact person within the agency.

> ### Activity
> Check out social media pages for the National Association of Social Workers. Check the internet and see what kind of jobs you can find in at least five different states. Try looking in large cities as well as small towns. A first step is to see if a social work program offers a career services program/web page. Read several job announcements and look for qualifications that are minimum requirements versus those that are preferences.

Visit your school's job placement office. See what the staff recommends about putting together a job search packet. Remember, it's never too early to begin collecting material for your résumé. Put together a draft résumé and pass it around, asking for suggestions on how to make it better.

Use Your Field Placement Experience

Each student must complete a field placement. Don't be surprised if your field agency offers you a position following graduation. The field site has the luxury of assessing your work; if you do an excellent job, the agency may ask you to consider moving into a regular position. An agency benefits from hiring a field placement student who has already worked in the agency because this new employee can be moved into a regular position more quickly and with less orientation time. Furthermore, there is little need for an initial skill and knowledge assessment period because the agency, through the internship experience, is aware of the student's practice abilities and thus the level of supervision needed.

Employment in a field placement agency also has advantages for the student accepting the job. The student already knows the agency and how they will fit into the overall organization. Based on direct experience, the student knows that it is the setting in which they want to start a social work career.

Look closely at the words used in the announcement. Words such as *must have* or *minimum* or *required* signal baseline qualifications that the successful candidate must possess. For example, if the announcement requires an MSW degree and five years of post-MSW experience, don't apply if you are a newly graduated BSW or an MSW with three years of experience. Words such as *should have* or *preferred*, however, signal not minimum criteria, but preferences. These words introduce the agency's wish list for the desired candidate, and employers understand that they often don't get everything on their wish lists. If you find an interesting job for which you meet the minimum requirements but not the preferences, go ahead and apply.

Use the Internet, of Course!

The internet has been become the most common avenue of information access in our everyday lives, and finding a job is no different. Online search engines provide many options—but remember and use your savvy digital literacy skills! Through the web, you can locate job search engines (e.g., Indeed.com), state NASW offices, career service web pages on various social work educational programs sites, and other employment services across the country. Federal jobs can be searched at . State governments post jobs on their state government web pages or respective departmental web pages. Look for websites that allow you to post your résumé. Social media are a growing source of help in finding a job. Individuals and employers often post information on their Facebook or Instagram pages and other comparable sites; and, of course, LinkedIn is an excellent avenue for creating a professional pathway to employment.

Do your homework. Take the time and energy to learn how to use the various online job resources and investigate how to drill down to the details about people, employing organizations, and job postings. Develop skill with the social media platforms you intend to use for job searching—for example, Twitter and LinkedIn both offer connections, but they need to be used very differently. For job hunting, who you follow is more important than who follows you on the various social media platforms. Be aware in all your postings of your presentation style, your grammar, your professionalism, and your headshot. Managing your online presence is more important than ever.

Interviews in the online environment using, for example, Zoom or Skype or similar platforms are commonplace. Digital interviewing has become a go-to resource, an easy-to-use and cost-effective technique for employers to screen in and screen out applications. Be careful if you are interviewing online. When interviewing online, remember your background discloses information about you. Be sure that your background is clean, there are no distracting noises, and what you wear is appropriate. A colleague reported that a job candidate in one Skype interview had clothes dangling over the chair in the background with a beer can on the windowsill. Another colleague noted that a dog continually ran in and out of the interviewee's room barking while the candidate repeatedly told it to "shush!" Suffice it to say, neither candidate was asked to interview at the agency.

We know you've probably heard this already, but a word of caution about posting personal information on the internet: Be careful about what pictures and comments you post. Employers typically search an applicant's background on social media. The old saying that a picture is worth a thousand words is so true; one college picture of a what seemed to be a fun time may stop your application dead in its tracks. Keep your privacy settings up to date. Keep your personal and professional social media separate. Although we're suggesting you maintain this separation for your own well-being in terms of your professional future, we'd be remiss if we didn't also mention that this separation holds importance for your practice. Staying aware of how your online presence today might affect your future professional social work functioning with clients and other professionals matters.

Get to Know Your Social Work Faculty Advisors and Instructors

One of your best sources of employment information and strategies is your program faculty, both full-time and part-time faculty. They are interested in your success, they have years of experience, and they know people in the field in the surrounding community who can help you. Your social work teachers have had contact with most local agencies. A good word, phone call, or reference letter from a faculty member can be one of your greatest aids in getting your first job. Adjunct faculty members who are employed full-time in the community can help you in your job search because they are tied into the local informal social work network.

Did You Know . . .

All states have some form of licensing or regulation of social work practice, but in many states, such regulation is limited to MSW or advanced practice and does not apply to BSW practice. The ASWB web page is a good place for information about licensure.

The NASW also credentials social workers for specific practice specializations. These specializations include leadership, military, clinical, gerontology, hospice and palliative care, youth and families, health care, addictions, case management, and education.

Explore Your Social Work Student Association or Club

Your program's social work student association or club can help in your job search. The association can invite area agency directors to provide workshops or panels on finding a job. The club can also sponsor a job fair on campus at which area agencies set up booths, distribute agency information, and recruit potential employees. The fair can be coordinated with the program's field office and the local NASW chapter.

A job fair is a win–win–win situation. Students win because they have immediate access to potential employers. Agencies win because the fair is a cost-effective recruiting mechanism that reaches a large pool of potential job applicants. The social work program and university win because the job fair is a positive public relations tool that strengthens ties between the university and the community. Sometimes universities themselves sponsor these kinds of events—keep your ears and eyes open.

Last Thoughts About Your Job Search

We often get caught up in salary and look for the best-paying jobs. Yes, salary is important, but consider other aspects of the job as well. Who works at the agency? What kind of colleagues will you have, and can you learn from them? Who will supervise you? Your first job will be a major source of knowledge and experience. Will the job be exciting and offer you a variety of learning opportunities? What kinds of benefits are in place? These can range from health care and vacation time to time with pets—one organization allows staff members to bring their pets to work each Friday. (Now what does that say about the organization?)

A few years ago, a student came into the office extremely excited about a job offer in New York City as a child care worker. The individual said, "I'm getting a great salary. They're going to pay me $65,000!"

But what does $65,000 mean to a new, twenty-one-year-old social worker? It sounds like a great deal, but is it really? Use the internet to find salaries for comparison purposes; the easiest way is to search for *salary converters*. For example, as you can see in Table 4.5, $63,000 in one city means something quite different somewhere else.

Remember that you need to be happy with what you find. Be sure the setting offers you an opportunity for continued professional growth and self-fulfillment. Don't focus only on the salary—there is much more to a job than money! Fulfillment from work can be gained via multiple paths (Willner, Lipshits-Braziler, & Gati, 2020), including salary, status, calling, belongingness, and plain-out busyness. Many social workers who consider themselves happy report that fulfillment of their calling results in satisfaction with their career lives. We spend at least a third of our lives working, and only you can decide what will be best for you, but these five things drive each of us in unique ways.

Self-Care

We would be remiss if we did not bring up the issue of self-care. Your education as a social worker will include much more information about this topic than can be included here. The COVID-19 pandemic heightened awareness of the need for self-care, but focus on

Table 4.5 A Salary of $63,000 in Houston, Texas, in October 2022 Is the Same As . . .

City	Salary
Hartford, Connecticut	$58,502
New York City (Manhattan)	$134,697
Orlando, Florida	$53,082
Fairbanks, Alaska	$67,269
Burlington, Vermont	$62,540
Chicago, Illinois	$66,419
Los Angeles, California	$80,128
Portland, Oregon	$69,182

Source: CNN Money, *Cost of living: How far will my salary go in another city?* Retrieved October 13, 2022, from https://money.cnn.com/calculator/pf/cost-of-living.

this critical issue began long before that crisis. Social work can be a demanding profession. The rewards are great, but the emotional cost can also be real (van Dernoot Lipsky & Burk, 2009). For that reason, the issue of self-care holds major importance, personal importance, social importance to you as a family member and friend, and importance to the profession. As the saying goes, you cannot fill the cup of others if your cup is empty. Self-care is an ethically responsible professional duty. Your preparation as a social worker will take resources, your personal resources and resources from those around you, including societal resources. You must take care of yourself to make that kind of investment worthwhile and to keep the skills you work hard to attain available to the clients and causes that underpin the reason for the existence of our profession. Self-care is more than a piece of jargon. It entails intentionally paying attention to your reactions to what you are learning and what you experience and responding to manage potential distress. You can do this using personally relevant activities (e.g., seeking balance with work/life commitments, using supervision, building and nurturing personal relationships, focusing on your spirituality, and so on) (Diebold, Kim, & Elze, 2018). As such, self-care in social work begins during your social work education—perhaps even today! Some of the information we have shared in this textbook could be a source of anxiety and stress for you. Jackson (2014) urged workers to create self-care plans. If you have not already, we encourage you to begin focusing on building your self-care competency starting now.

SUMMARY

Students entering social work will find the field rich in opportunities. The profession's future is bright. When you embark on a professional career in social work, the selection of an educational program is important. A social work career should begin with either a baccalaureate or a master's degree, and this degree must come from a CSWE-accredited program. Request admission information directly from the programs you are interested in attending. Programs are in every state in the United States and throughout the world, and accredited programs via the internet provide another convenient option. Gather information early so you have plenty of time to prepare what is required. Some baccalaureate programs have open admission, whereas others use a formal admission process. Admission to graduate programs, in contrast, is usually competitive, and about 30 to 40 percent of applicants are turned down. Also, when selecting a program, think carefully about whether you would do better in a classroom situation or could manage well with a hybrid program or one that is completely online. If the program is accredited, all will be treated equally in the job search process, but you may learn better or experience more satisfaction in one modality compared to others.

Employment possibilities for social workers can be found in both public and private settings. They involve a wide range of activities and tasks and a variety of practice areas. Simply stated, practice opportunities for social work professionals are open and diverse. The key to a successful work experience in social work is planning your education carefully—whether BSW or MSW—and making the most of it. Take advantage of your educational opportunities to develop new knowledge, theories, and skills that will make you more competent, never forgetting the importance of self-care. Remember, before you can help the individuals, groups, families, and communities that you will serve, you must first help yourself to be the best-equipped professional, with the best foundation of education and training possible. For so many of us in the field, social work is more than a profession—it is a calling fueled by passion. If you want to be a social worker, let us leave you with these parting words: Start where the client is and remember, to help others, we must first recognize the importance of taking care of ourselves.

REFERENCES

Accreditation Commission on Colleges of Medicine. (2014). *Standards-elements of accreditation*. Retrieved from https://accredmed.org/standards/

Association of Social Work Boards. (2022). *2022 ASWB exam pass rate analysis*. Culpepper, VA: Author.

Barker, R. L. (2003). *The social work dictionary* (5th ed.). Washington, DC: NASW Press.

Beless, D. W. (1995). Council on social work education. In R. L. Edwards (Ed.), *Encyclopedia of social work* (19th ed., Vol. 1, pp. 632–636). Washington, DC: NASW Press.

Burger, W. R., & Youkeles, M. (2004). *Human services in contemporary America*. Belmont, CA: Brooks/Cole.

Bureau of Labor Statistics. (2022). *State and area data*. Retrieved from https://www.bls.gov/ooh/community-and-social-service/social-workers.htm#tab-7.

Colby, I. (2013). Rethinking the MSW curriculum. *Journal of Social Work Education, 49*, 4–15.

Council on Social Work Education. (1994). *Handbook of accreditation standards and procedures*. Alexandria, VA: Author.

Council on Social Work Education. (2020). *CSWE COVID-19 member "pulse" survey results*. Alexandria, VA: Author.

Council on Social Work Education. (2022a). *Accreditation*. Retrieved from http://www.cswe.org/Accreditation.aspx

Council on Social Work Education. (2022b). *Commission on accreditation*. Retrieved from https://www.cswe.org/Accreditation/Information/COA-Decisions/COA

Council on Social Work Education, Commission on Educational Policy, and Commission on Accreditation. (2022). *2022 Educational Policy and Accreditation Standards for baccalaureate and master's social work programs*. Alexandria, VA: Author.

Diebold, J., Kim, W., & Elze, D. (2018). Perceptions of self-care among MSW students: Implications for social work education. *Journal of Social Work Education*, 54(4), 657–667. https://doi.org/10.1080/10437797.2018.1486255

Gardellia, L. G. (1997). Baccalaureate social workers. In R. Edwards (Ed.), *Encyclopedia of social work, 1997 supplement* (19th ed., pp. 37–46). Washington, DC: NASW Press.

Gibelman, M., & Schervish, P. H. (1997). *Who we are: A second look*. Washington, DC: NASW Press.

Jackson, K. (2014). Social worker self-care: The overlooked competency. *Social Work Today*, 14(3), 14. Retrieved from https://www.socialworktoday.com/archive/051214p14.shtml

Leighninger, L. (1987). *Social work: Search for identity*. Westport, CT: Greenwood.

PDR Medical Dictionary (3rd ed.). (2005). Montvale, NJ: Physician's Desk Reference.

U.S. Department of Labor (2022). *Job outlook. Occupational outlook handbook*. Retrieved from https://www.bls.gov/ooh/

van Dernoot Lipsky, L., & Burk, C. (2009). *Trauma stewardship: An everyday guide to caring for self while caring for others*. San Francisco, CA: Berrett–Koehler.

Willner, T., Lipshits-Braziler, Y., & Gati, I. (2020). Construction and initial validation of the Work Orientation Questionnaire. *Journal of Career Assessment*, 28(1), 109–127. https://doi.org/10.1177/1069072719830293

PART TWO
The Practice of Social Work

Social Work Practice

CHAPTER 5: EPAS COMPETENCIES

Social work programs at the bachelor's and the master's level are accredited by the Council of Social Work Education (CSWE). CSWE's Educational Policy and Accreditation Standards (EPAS) describe the processes and criteria that social work courses should cover. In 2022, CSWE updated its EPAS standards. The following competencies are addressed in this chapter.

Competency 1: Demonstrate Ethical and Professional Behavior

Social workers understand the value base of the profession and its ethical standards, as well as relevant policies, laws, and regulations that may affect practice with individuals, families, groups, organizations, and communities.

Competency 3: Engage in Anti-racism, Diversity, Equity, and Inclusion in Practice

Social workers understand how racism and oppression shape human experiences and how these two constructs influence practice at the individual, family, group, organizational, and community levels and in policy and research.

Competency 7: Assess Individuals, Families, Groups, Organizations, and Communities

Social workers understand that assessment is an ongoing component of the dynamic and interactive process of social work practice.

Competency 8: Intervene with Individuals, Families, Groups, Organizations, and Communities

Social workers understand that intervention is an ongoing component of the dynamic and interactive process of social work practice.

Competency 9: Evaluate Practice with Individuals, Families, Groups, Organizations, and Communities

Social workers understand that evaluation is an ongoing component of the dynamic and interactive process of social work practice with, and on behalf of, diverse individuals, families, groups, organizations, and communities.

Steve, an undergraduate social work student, stopped by a social work professor's office. Steve wanted to tell his professor that he was enjoying his introduction to social work class and that he was learning so much that he had not missed a session. He told the professor that he believed his final grade would be high. Steve was a conscientious student who often asked questions and it was obvious that he enjoyed taking part in class discussions. The professor was surprised, however, when he asked, "So, how do you do it?" The professor, who was not sure what he meant by "it," asked Steve to clarify what he was asking. Very seriously, Steve said, "You know, social work. How do you do social work?" Today, twenty plus years after this visit, Steve remembers that day and laughs. He now has both a BSW and an MSW and is employed in a public mental health facility. Thinking back on his earlier days, he laughs about that question. He says, "I was looking for that magical pill you give a client to make it better or that one specific task we could complete to help a person in pain. Or the standardized protocol that I could follow verbatim to address the problem. I just believed that social workers should have a bag of tricks, and when applied, something instant and magical would happen to solve the client's problem. It certainly is more complicated than that and how wrong I was."

• • •

When they enter the field, social workers often expect specific answers with concrete steps for achieving a desired outcome. Yet, the longer you are in the field, the more you realize there are no simple answers, and as personal and environmental circumstances and technological advances change, so do the answers and the strategies (see Figure 5.1). So even for seasoned practitioners, the quest never ends. The desire for this simplistic approach is complicated further by the fact that this same expectation exists in society. People often want simple answers to complicated problems, and many believe it should be as simple as taking a pill to cure what is ailing.

FIGURE 5.1
Social work is a complex process of helping to find the best fit for the person and situation.

Steve, like so many social workers just starting in the field, consistent with societal beliefs, was unsure what to do in social work practice and hoped for a simple answer. Wouldn't it be wonderful if the unique and ambiguous challenges of human life could be addressed by giving a pat answer, prescribing a simple pill, or using a clearly outlined standard procedure? It is tempting, but unrealistic. If social work practice required nothing more than simple prescriptions and the answers were derived easily, there would be limited need for formal education beyond the basics. Memorization of standardized protocols could be utilized and a "one-size-fits-all" mentality would result in consistent success.

In fact, the practice of social work stems directly from the mission of the profession, which is neither simple nor standardized. Furthermore, market forces, whether academic, governmental, or private in origin, can also affect and transform practice (Dziegielewski & Holliman, 2020; Reardon, 2011; Witkin & Iversen, 2008). If you look at the definition of social work set forth in Chapter 1, you will be looking in the right direction for practice guidance.

Social workers seek to enhance social functioning, promote social justice, and help people to obtain resources. They also support ethical decision-making and empower their clients to make their own choices while respecting self-determination, worth, and dignity (National Association of Social Workers [NASW], 2018).

Did You Know . . .

The number of social work jobs doubled in the 1930s, from forty thousand to eighty thousand, as public sector income maintenance, health, and welfare programs were created in response to the Great Depression (NASW, 1993).

Changes in the detailed definition of social work have occurred over time, yet the basis for social work practice has not changed. Today, there are diversified definitions that outline the profession of social work, but all follow a similar theme highlighting the importance of addressing the person-in-situation or the person-in-environment. According to the NASW (1993), social work is the professional activity of helping individuals, groups, or communities enhance or restore their capacity for social functioning and create societal conditions favorable for achieving their goals.

Furthermore, as outlined in the preamble of the NASW Code of Ethics, social work is engaged in promoting and empowering the individual well-being of all humans within the context and environmental forces that influence problems related to their condition (NASW, 2018). According to Barker (2013), social work is the applied science of helping people achieve increased levels of psychosocial functioning and well-being.

These different interpretations of the profession make it easy to see how the definition has evolved, but remains relevant to the early definition written by Boehm (1959), which defined the profession this way: "Social work seeks to enhance the social functioning of individuals, singly and in groups, by activities focused on their social relationships which constitute the interaction between man [individuals] and his [or their] environment. These activities can be grouped into three functions: restoration of impaired capacity, provision of individual and social resources, and prevention of social dysfunction" (p. 54). Reflective of the revised NASW Code of Ethics (2018), all these definitions highlight the tasks that social workers undertake, the agencies in which they work, and the social policies they support. These helping efforts are all aimed toward three overarching goals: to enhance client social functioning, to remedy client dysfunction, and to promote social justice and environmental justice (Erickson, 2018; Hepworth, Rooney, Rooney, Strom-Gottfried, & Larsen, 2010). Professional education, whether at the BSW or the MSW level, through academic classes and coursework as well as through experiences gained from the field practicum, helps the new social worker to develop the necessary value-driven knowledge and skills to support social work practice.

5.1 UNDERSTANDING DIVERSITY

Although today's definition of social work may seem simple, recognizing the diversity, uniqueness, and complexity in individuals, groups, or communities needs further exploration. As a professor of social work and a practicing clinician, a student asked one of the authors, "In class, why do you rarely give case examples of what might be considered the traditional family?" The response was simple: "If you mean the traditional family as constituting the biological parents with 2.4 children who have never been divorced or separated, I rarely see them in my practice." At first, this statement may seem shocking because the "family" is considered the essential building block for its influence on development, but these changes reflect our current society. In fact, today's traditional family is characterized as yesterday's nontraditional family. Diversity within family systems include multiracial, **blended families**, or stepfamilies and families headed by a single parent, by gay or lesbian partners, or by a grandparent or other relatives. Today, in practice, it has become evident that the basics of what traditionally constituted social structure and societal expectations for individuals, family groups, and communities has changed and will continue to do so with a revived vigor as society embraces biological, medical, societal, and technological advance in an unprecedented way.

When seeking to understand individuals and families, social workers must consider the uniqueness of each situation as well as the worth and dignity of each individual and family system. Social workers need to recognize these differences through a nonjudgmental lens or perspective that embraces rather than discourages diversity. This requires that social workers become familiar with ethical practice and implement practice strategies that highlight client self-determination in the most bias-free, nonjudgmental way possible. From this perspective, individual dignity and worth stand at the forefront of all helping activities. Social workers will be actively engaging with individuals of different social classes, genders, races, ethnicities, and sexual orientations, as well as differing belief systems and spiritual views (see Figure 5.2). This requires awareness of one's own values and beliefs and ensuring that these personal attitudes and expectations do not overshadow developing client awareness and resiliency.

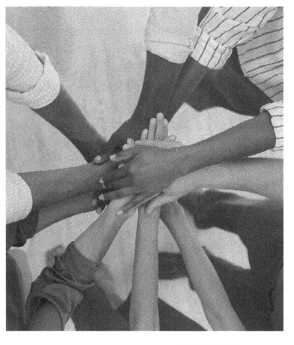

FIGURE 5.2
Recognizing the complexity and uniqueness of individuals is the cornerstone of creating lasting connections.

5.2 CULTURAL RESPONSIVENESS AND CULTURAL HUMILITY

Feelings of marginalization can occur when a client is scrutinized within a system that does not understand the cultural mores and expectations of the client's system. Agencies and providers who practice from a place that is rich with Western scientific values and traditions can create an environment that is counterproductive for the clients served. The NASW Code of Ethics takes a clear stance against racism and oppression of specific groups (NASW Anti-Racism Statement, 2022). For social workers, to escape societal values and traditions, thereby honoring the worth and dignity of clients who are different racially, culturally, or socioeconomically, may not be so easy. Social work educators and practitioners alike often advocate for these clients and set the standard for their conduct high in terms of sensitivity and responsiveness (Dziegielewski, 2015;

Dziegielewski & Holliman, 2020). In cultural humility there is recognition of the difficulty in assuming an expert role in cultures other than your own (Hook, Davis, Owen, Worthington, & Utsey, 2013; Tervalon & Murray-Garcia, 1998). Cultural humility addresses power imbalances. From this perspective, the client is the expert on cultural expectations, not the social worker. In listening to a client's story, the social worker can learn what is important to the client and whether the support system can influence the client's thoughts and actions. Starting where the client is and listening to the client's story is where the social worker's helping activities are derived.

Regardless of the approach used to achieve cultural awareness and responsiveness, a sense of cultural sensitivity and inclusiveness always starts with a social worker's self-awareness. It is this aspect of developing awareness that leads to effective change strategy through developing effective cross-cultural interactions. Furthermore, social workers have an understanding of many personal problems such as health and mental health problems, family issues, and various social problems such as racism, sexism, and the effects of trauma and violence. When additionally coupled with the need for evidence-based practice and the push for more clinical trials that highlight teamwork and the connections between health and mental health, the profession will continue to grow more responsive to the needs of those it serves (Ell, Lee, & Xie, 2010). Therefore, effective individual practice must be transactional. When viewing transactional practice, consider each client or client system as being linked through multiple dimensions and case-specific factors, practice models, ethical principles, and issues of power (Mattaini, 2001).

5.3 TECHNOLOGY, SOCIETAL LAG, AND CHANGING TIMES

As the funding for agencies responsible for assisting clients in need has become more competitive, the emphasis on client outcomes has grown. From this perspective, agencies and thus the services they provide will become increasingly more accountable, with success measured by helping clients to move forward and gain desired outcomes (Poertner & Rapp, 2007). Measurement of client outcomes is shaped by contextual factors such as agency competition for funding, agency practices, natural networks, and social institutions. Social workers must not only be aware of what is changing in the current climate, but also learn how to prepare for what could happen. Being prepared for current and future trends in the surrounding environment enables social workers to help individuals, families, groups, and communities enhance or restore their capability for social functioning.

As genetic testing continues to evolve and usage gains in popularity, people can now easily map out their genetic roots. This ability to explore genetic profiles allows for a greater sense of familial connection, bringing to the forefront past racial and cultural affiliations with the present. It also highlights the importance of the blending of genetic roots and allowing people to see and better understand their ancestral roots. So often, under the guise of diversity, we lump individual or group behavior together and focus on only the similarities, while ignoring differences. From this limited perspective, broad and sweeping assumptions can be made. For example, consider the term *Hispanic*. From the perspective of the U.S. Census, Hispanic includes people of Latin or Mexican descent or origin. As a result, people from Cuba, Mexico, Argentina, Brazil, and Spain would be Hispanic. Yet would you say that the culture, with its traditions, mores, and folkways, is the same for each of these nations? Do you think that a person from Cuba is different from an Argentinean? Of course, Cubans are quite different from Argentineans, as they are from Mexicans, Brazilians, and Spaniards. Or consider the label "of European descent," where cultural expectations can vary dramatically as well. Is a person from Poland the same as one from Germany, England, or Romania in terms of beliefs and expectations? Consideration of human diversity in social work practice requires reflection on and consideration of how such diversity affects the worker–client relationship and the ensuing problem-solving process.

Numerous potential examples highlight the need for the recognition of diversity that expands beyond traditional definitions of family and race. Children learn to use their cultural experiences to interpret their immediate surroundings and interact with others. From this growth and development perspective, interpersonal patterns develop that will shape a child's life. Similarly, culture, with its roots in family roles and expectations, is the first powerful determinant of how children understand, internalize, and act on the expectations of their family, community, and larger society (Morales, Sheafor, & Scott, 2012).

In the United States in 2020, there were 46.9 million Blacks, or African Americans (U.S. Census Bureau, 2022). For African American children specifically, frequent discriminatory experiences provide them with additional information and feelings to decipher and understand. Movements such as **Black Lives Matter** recognize the importance that race and culture can play in societal perceptions and expectations. During times of emotional or psychological turmoil, human nature requires that all children strive for meaning in their lives, and the basis of this derived meaning starts with using their cultural lens, which includes learned values, beliefs, and experiences. In social work practice, these children present a rich and complex biopsychosocial picture requiring examination of the biological, psychological, and social factors within a historical and cultural framework (Austrian, 2009). To address issues of individual diversity and to conduct this task efficiently, culturally responsive social workers must be aware of their own values and the African American child's values, as well as how both relate and integrate with the larger society in which all people must coexist. Therefore, all helping professionals providing services to African American children must be sensitive to the culture of these children (Snowden, 2003). Ridley (1995, p. 10) noted that even the most sincere, caring, and ethical practitioner can be guilty of *"unintentional racism."*

In unintentional racism, the social worker is unaware of what is experienced. Like members of the community, social workers may not be aware of feelings of *internalized racism.* This type of racism is not deliberate or obvious to the social worker and rests in the societal images and beliefs ingrained through the social system. As with *institutional racism*, members of an organization or organizational system may be unaware of how these biases can adversely affect the client served. For social workers, the NASW defines anti-racism as "uplifting the innate humanity and individuality of Black, LatinA/O/X, Indigenous, Asian, Pacific Islander and other People of Color; demonstrating best practices in diversity, equity, and inclusion: and taking conscious and deliberate actions to ensure equal opportunities for all people and all communities. Anti-racism requires active resistance to and dismantling of the system of racism to obtain racial equity" (NASW Anti-Racism Statement, 2022).

The social work profession stands firm in its commitment to racial equity and to addressing personal, professional, and institutional racism, requiring a commitment on the part of the social worker to recognize and participate in efforts to recognize and address such unethical practices, whether personal or institutional. Avoiding bias in assessment and the interventions to follow, regardless of the population served, must rest deeply in cultural awareness, sensitivity, and responsiveness and requires making efforts to promote anti-racism through professional development, education of the public, and other forms of advocacy (NASW Anti-Racism Statement, 2022).

The concepts outlined in 1990 by Gonzalez-Ramos remain applicable today. Specifically, to address diversity and develop cultural awareness, sensitivity, and responsiveness while providing effective services, social work practitioners need to recognize, understand, and appreciate geographic and regional differences among children of color (Gonzalez-Ramos, 1990). Regardless of the child's race, ethnicity, or creed, social workers must also learn to look critically and carefully at their own feelings while confronting their own expectations and cultural biases (Dziegielewski & Holliman, 2020; Sue & Sue, 2008). Although the primary experience of an African American child today may reflect the influence of American society, never minimize the impact of the family's place of origin and sense of connectedness and belonging. The African American family today may have values and traditions from northern states, southern states, or Caribbean areas. Acknowledging differences and not placing judgment is an important first step (Miller & Garran, 2009).

Similarly, family values may reflect differences in urban versus rural expectations and traditions. The first step in combating racism, even if it is unintentional through internalized or institutionalized racism, could be as simple as acknowledging that these differences exist and learning more about them.

5.4 CULTURAL INFLUENCES IN THE ASSESSMENT PROCESS

One big mistake that many individuals make is that they do not clearly differentiate between culture and race. In practice, this distinction is particularly important to make because it allows the helping relationship to become individualized to the client considering the influences of the client's support system. A simple way to differentiate is to think of race as color and think about culture as how a person is raised. In social work, the client-in-situation or client-in-environment resounds clearly as the client cannot be separated from the client-system and its influences. These terms have gained in importance because they highlight how best practice requires considering more than just the client. We could never say that all Latinx people are alike, nor would we say that all Jewish people believe the same things. People of a culture may share some common beliefs and appear like others whose beliefs they share on the outside, yet their inner thoughts and feelings can be truly diverse. Escaping the stereotypes while recognizing the uniqueness of individuals is how cultural responsiveness starts in professional helping. When diversity and culturally aware help-seeking behaviors are recognized and applied to change strategies the helping process becomes comprehensive. Measurement scales that identify cultural responses to helping efforts can provide one way to identify client-system influences that can facilitate or impede the creation of a successful cultural connection.

Congress (2009) and Congress and Gonzalez (2013) recommend that social workers identify appropriate tools to conduct culturally sensitive assessments. One such tool is the *culturagram*, which considers diverse cultural aspects and empowers families to perceive their specific culture as important within the larger society (Congress & Kung, 2013). Congress (2009) believes that creating a culturagram can help a practitioner obtain a better understanding of the family by examining the following areas: "reasons for relocation; legal status; time in community; language spoken at home and in the community; health beliefs; impact of trauma and crisis events; contact with cultural and religious institutions, holidays, food, and clothing; oppression, discrimination, bias, and racism; values about education and work; and values about family structure, power, myths, and rules" (p. 970). Once these factors can be identified and understood, families can become empowered to examine their problems and potential solutions, as well as the role of their culture and that of mainstream society (Parker & Bradley, 2010).

Another measure that has gained increasing importance is outlined in the latest version of the *Diagnostic and Statistical Manual of Mental Disorders* (*DSM*) written by the American Psychiatric Association and often used to complete diagnostic assessment in the United States and Canada. In this edition of the *DSM*, one of these instruments, called the Cultural Formulation Interview, intends to measure culture-related factors than can affect an inclusive and comprehensive diagnostic assessment. Although it is beyond the scope of this chapter to explain the use of this instrument, when utilized, it can help a practitioner consider the possibility of a multifaceted presentation, helping to better assess a wide range of racially minoritized clients who present with varied mental health problems and concerns. The Cultural Formulation Interview can also gather collateral information from someone familiar with the client who can provide information the client is unable to share. In this semistructured interview format, there are no right or wrong answers. All questions are designed purely to better understand the client being served. There is also no fixed format that must be followed, and flexibility in both asking the questions and probing the responses is allowed. To facilitate the assessment, background information is gathered, such as age, gender, racial/ethnic background, marital status, and education. Acquiring this information from the start allows the interviewer the flexibility to better tailor the questions to ask what is most relevant for the client (Dziegielewski, 2015).

5.5 THE BASICS OF PRACTICE

It is important to recognize that Parts Two and Three of this book will introduce the reader to practice only in general terms. You will not be qualified to *do* social work after reading these chapters. Remember that your career in social work is just beginning and numerous courses and field experiences are before you. These studies, combined with your professional learning experiences, will provide you with the foundation for social work practice. This chapter will give you a basic overview of the central concepts related to the delivery of social work services and examine the helping process as it can be applied to the practice of social work.

Before we begin to explore the *doing* of social work, however, we need to remind ourselves that the practice of social work is a professional activity intended to achieve the profession's purpose of helping clients. In examining your own motivation for entering this profession, you must ask yourself why you have decided that this is the profession for you. Be honest with yourself as you explore the areas of social work practice, examining and confronting your own biases and values and using this knowledge to decide which area of practice holds the most interest for you. Do not be surprised if you find that, like many helping professionals, you are initially motivated by wanting to learn more about yourself and your own family. This is not unusual, nor is it particularly problematic. However, when this is your motivation for choosing this field, you must be aware that the professional helping services you provide are not designed to help you—they are for the client. Other typical reasons for choosing a helping profession include the desire to be needed, the desire to give something back to society and humankind, the need to care for others, and the desire for prestige and professional status. As you embark on a helping career, it is essential first to examine what motivated you to select this career and what you want to accomplish. As you explore this motivation, do not be shy about asking for feedback from other professionals who know you, particularly your social work teachers and professionals who are experienced in the field (see the activity below).

Remember that choosing a career path is not simple or quick. Also, staying in the field and flourishing will require work, because the pressures that develop from this kind of work require constant self-examination throughout your educational and professional career. Some students decide early on that social work is not the career for them. This realization should never be considered a personal or professional failure because a career in the helping professions is not for everyone. It is an innovative idea to establish and reaffirm this decision as early as possible, especially before investing a great deal of time, effort, and expense into pursuing it.

> ## Activity
>
> Is social work practice really for me? On a piece of paper, write the following questions and answer them individually. For this exercise you may at first feel more comfortable answering them by yourself. Later, you may choose to discuss your answers with your instructor or academic advisor. Feel free to add questions to this list. You might also want to save your answers and revisit them later in your professional career.
>
> 1. What first attracted you to the profession of social work?
> 2. What needs of your own are likely to be met by serving as a social worker?
> 3. Who in your life has been instrumental in helping you choose this career?
> 4. Have you ever received help from a social worker? What did you like most about this person? What did you like least?
> 5. What do you believe you can contribute to the field of social work?
> 6. In what ways do you believe this profession can help to make you feel like a better person?
> 7. What is evidence-based social work, and how will this trend affect the services you provide?
> 8. How do your values match the values of the profession of social work as outlined in the Council on Social Work Education accreditation standards and the NASW Code of Ethics?

5.6 CONCEPTS ESSENTIAL TO SOCIAL WORK PRACTICE

We have described social work practice as an art and a science. The art of social work involves the sensitive coordination of complex activities to help clients. The science entails selecting, merging, and understanding potentially voluminous amounts of information and applying the conclusions to a specific case situation. Although many are successful in learning the science of the profession, the art is always more difficult to acquire. The interplay of art and science means that effective social work practice grows from the relation among knowledge, skills, values, and ethics (see Box 5.1). Social work practice requires unique skills, either specialized or generalist, derived from specific knowledge areas and guided by a clear, fundamental set of values and ethics.

Skills

Doing social work implies that a social worker has a set of specific skills used in practice. These skills, which are inseparable from the helping process, include the ability to perform critical tasks in working with clients: basic communication, exploration,

> **BOX 5.1**
>
> ## DYNAMIC INTERPLAY OF KNOWLEDGE, VALUES AND ETHICS, AND SKILLS
>
> Often you will hear social workers discuss an empathetic relationship or read in the social work literature about the importance of empathy in the social work process. What is the difference between empathy and sympathy? It was once described by the lead author as the following:
>
> > Sympathy is what you feel when you begin to feel the pain of the client. In a sympathetic relationship the helping professional cannot be objective or render the nonjudgmental intervention required. Say, for example, you wear a size eight shoe, and your client wears a size seven. If you put the client's shoes on your own feet, your feet will be so squeezed that you cannot concentrate on the issues the client is facing.
> >
> > Empathy, on the other hand, is what you feel when you remain in your own shoes while imagining what it is like for the client in his or her situation. The client's situation is assessed based on direct observation and information provided by the client or people from the client's environment. In an empathetic relationship the helping professional utilizes objective and subjective information and professional helping skills to utterly understand the client's situation and the pain that the client is experiencing. In turn, this information is used to empower the client.

assessment and planning, implementation, goal attainment, termination, and evaluation of the services rendered (Hepworth et al., 2010, 2023).

Skill building and the acquisition of knowledge form the bridge between values and all subsequent social service (Trevithick, 2012). Unless knowledge and values underlie skills, the practice of social work is undefined and vague. Social workers must have basic competencies in the following skill areas:

- Cognitive skills related to conducting evidence-based research and practice.
- Administrative skills, including record keeping and report writing.
- Solid assessment and interpersonal skills.

A social worker must be able to balance many critical aspects of the practice relationship with each client. For example, whether in the home or a health care facility, the worker must first work to establish and then maintain a worker–client environment of trust.

In this environment, the client can feel safe revealing emotions and thoughts that might disturb an untrained practitioner; for the skilled worker, the ethical values of client worth, dignity, and self-determination are paramount. When a social worker is providing counseling services to culturally diverse individuals, an awareness and respect for the clients' beliefs, values, and lifestyles is central to creating an atmosphere of sensitivity and trust (Sue & Sue, 2008). The worker also must know how and when to approach those of the client's problems that need further explanation and exploration. The skilled social worker is well versed in empathetic communication and helps the client to clarify and confront what may be difficult issues to address. In short, whether in the home or in a health-related facility, the skilled professional social worker is an expert at establishing a positive worker–client relationship in which problem identification, helping, addressing, and subsequent healing can take place.

Knowledge Base

The practice of social work is based on a specific body of scientifically tested knowledge. Practice evolves from the knowledge base as social work skills that were first developed in the academic curriculum later mature through field experiences and continuing education. Without the appropriate knowledge base and awareness of the theoretical constructs that undergird professional practice, skills would be nothing more than a series of unrelated actions that cannot address the total person-in-situation who is at the heart of professional social work practice. Conversely, knowledge evolves from current practice through practice-based research and evaluation of social work interventions. Without such research and evaluation, social work knowledge would quickly become static, outdated, and unfounded.

In many ways, knowledge drives a professional's daily actions with and on behalf of clients. Knowledge supports practice in its efforts to be client centered and directed to the unique situation of each client. The knowledge base of professional practice premises, skills, and techniques allows social workers to choose the specific set of skills clearly embedded in a theoretical framework that are best applied to a particular client situation. In other words, to achieve client-centered practice, the professional knowledge base must come first. Once this is established, the development of analytical and critical thinking skills will help the new social worker address situations that otherwise might be considered challenging or filled with multiple problems. Utilizing evidence-based practice, the social worker is taught to use skills that clearly identify problem areas and express the probabilities of addressing them (Shlonsky, 2009).

Therefore, to create a consistent and comprehensive knowledge base of professional practice, the Council on Social Work Education (CSWE, 2022), which accredits social work programs, requires that all social work educational programs strive for mastery of foundation content and achieve nine core competencies: (1) demonstrate ethical and professional behavior, (2) advance human rights and social racial and economic justice, (3) engage in anti-racism, diversity, equity, and inclusion in practice, (4) engage in practice-informed research and research-informed practice, (5) engage in policy practice, (6) engage with individuals, families, groups, organizations and communities, (7) assess individuals, families, groups, organizations, and communities, (8) intervene with individuals, families, groups, organizations, and communities, and (9) evaluate practice with individuals, families, groups, organizations, and communities. Be prepared, because the courses you take and the social work program you complete will most assuredly include this information. All the knowledge derived from courses will need to be integrated into competency-based social work practice (Jani, Pierce, Ortiz, & Sowbel, 2011).

Values and Ethics

Values and ethics are the third critical component of social work practice. These humanistic concerns, based on human well-being and justice, help to solidify and provide unification for the field (Hopps & Lowe, 2008, 2012). At the start of your social work education, during the application procedure itself, you were introduced to our professional code of ethics. This document can be called an *ought-to guide* because it specifies how social workers ought to conduct themselves and their helping activities in the professional setting (see the activity below). We cannot emphasize enough the importance of becoming familiar with this code from the very start of your career. As Reamer (2018) stressed, it is essential for social workers to learn ethical expectations and implications and how the code applies to your practice activities.

> ### Activity
> As part of a group or by yourself, download the NASW Code of Ethics and think about how it will shape your practice experiences. Which parts of the code do you find comforting and compatible with your beliefs? Which parts are more difficult for you to understand or support? List the commonalities and differences and note at the end of the educational program whether your views change.

All professionals embrace specific values. All clients embrace specific values. An individual's values, however, may not always be consistent with how he or she behaves (Twohig & Crosby, 2009). Personal values belong to the individual, but professional values are governed by the profession and constitute a professional promise that governs professional conduct and behavior. Although social work values are spelled out in a number of documents, the primary reference for the profession's value base is the NASW Code of Ethics (available online). This code establishes a set of clear beliefs that define ethical social work practice and thus act as a unifying force among all social workers (Reamer, 2009, 2018). The activities we perform on behalf of others—relationship building and maintenance of professional boundaries—as well as our view of social issues and the remedies we consider for individual, group, or community ills are all firmly rooted in our value base. All social workers must be versed in the code and aware of key duties and obligations (Reamer, 2009). Using awareness and knowledge makes ethical decision-making a planned and systematic process. Reamer (2009, 2018) identified the following core values for the social work profession:

- Individual worth and dignity of people
- Respect for people
- A belief in an individual's capacity for change

- A client's right to self-determination
- A client's right to confidentiality and privacy
- A client's right to opportunities that will enable them to realize their own potential
- Belief in social change
- A client's right to adequate resources and services to meet basic needs
- Client empowerment
- Equal opportunity
- Antidiscrimination
- Diversity
- Willingness to transmit professional knowledge and skills to others

As you read the code (NASW, 2018) and consider Reamer's points, several common themes emerge, but let us examine three here. First, all people, no matter who they are or what their circumstances, should be treated with respect, dignity, and civility. Respect and civility are cornerstones of a just society. We show respect in any number of ways: being on time for appointments and apologizing to clients when tardy, using respectful titles (e.g., Mx., Mr. or Ms.) until asked to do otherwise, and listening without interruption and without looking at our watches during interviews. In these sessions, maintaining client confidentiality and privileged communication should always be at the forefront of all helping efforts. When the term *confidentiality* is used, it relates directly to the information shared by clients or those who offer information about them. When the term *privileged communication* is used, it relates to information that will be released only in the context of legal proceedings. Be sure that, as a beginning professional, you discuss this with your supervisor to help make you keenly aware of what information can be shared and how best to do it. Also, as a rule, you should be sure that you have tried to secure written client permission to release information, even if you are ordered to do so by a court.

When given the opportunity, people are often able to participate in solving their own problems in a way of their own choosing. We understand that not all people can participate fully in such processes, but we recognize that everyone should be encouraged to participate as much as possible. We support client self-determination when we help them to figure out ways to identify and deal with their problems; we do not say, "If I were you, I would do this." Clients have strengths, and we must help them to discover and use these strengths as energy sources for change. The only exception to this practice principle involves what has been referred to historically as a *danger to self or others*. In these situations, if a client's action poses an imminent threat or danger to self or others, the social worker may be forced to take action to protect the client or those in danger. Interfering with self-determination when a client is not in imminent danger can block self-determination. Therefore, not allowing clients to make their own decisions and doing so deliberately with the intention to stop them and protect them from self-harm is referred to as *paternalism*. According to Reamer (2009), paternalism refers to a situation in which a social worker decides to withhold information from clients or misleads them. It can also involve lying or coercing clients to do what the social worker, rather than the client, feels is best.

Before you begin your professional practice, topics such as this need to be discussed. It is always best to address a situation before you encounter it. When situations such as this arise and prior to such a discussion, the new social worker should immediately seek guidance on how best to continue and address this type of situation with the intent of protecting all involved.

Although it is not stated explicitly in the code or among Reamer's points, we can infer the basic principle that we do no harm to people. Our work is to help, not harm. We cannot hold back any professional efforts or strategies if we believe they might help our clients. However, we should never work beyond our scope of practice and dabble in areas that we are not yet trained to address. This makes it essential for every social worker to know the intent, limits, and changes in the scope of practice.

As you become more familiar with the NASW Code of Ethics, compare it with other value statements such as that of the International Federation of Social Workers (available online). What similarities do you find? The words and phrases may be different, but the respect for the human condition and the goal of social change are the same.

As professionals, social workers must pursue the art of helping within a context shaped by values and ethics. Practice that is not guided by values or ethics has no meaning because it fails to recognize the unique circumstances of our clients, their individual needs, and appropriate change strategies. Unless we operate within an ethical framework, our clients might just as well be telling their problems to a computer!

Name: Monica M. Adams

Place of residence: Binghamton, New York

College/university degrees: PhD, University of Louisville; MSW, Virginia Commonwealth University; BSW, West Virginia University

Present position: Assistant professor of social work at Binghamton University

What does a typical day at work look like for you? What tasks do you generally complete as a social worker in your area of expertise? A typical day working as a mental health provider was dictated by my work setting. In adolescent residential and group home settings, daily activities included individual, family, and group counselling; precrisis and crisis intervention; milieu counseling; treatment team meetings; attending court; providing transportation to various appointments; and supervising residents' daily activities such as chores, socializing, and meals. In community settings with adults with developmental disabilities my work entailed assisting them with finding and maintaining employment, engaging in activities of daily living, and developing social and independent living skills. In hospitals my typical day involved seeing patients and families to assess their current social, emotional, and material needs and working with them to get these needs met.

What do you do in your spare time? When I was a practicing social worker, I spent my free time socializing with family and friends and engaging in community service work through my sorority. I also was sure to engage in "me time." My favorite "me time" activities included writing spiritually based self-help papers, bike riding, going to the movies, and taking solo trips to recharge.

Why did you choose social work as a career? I feel like social work chose me. I always enjoyed helping others. In sixth grade I was a volunteer helper in the kindergarten class. In junior high I was a candy striper (junior volunteer) at a local hospital. Upon entering college, I majored in education because I always liked to play school as a kid. And honestly, I did not know there was this thing called "social work." But once I discovered it, I changed my major and never looked back!

What is your favorite social work story? It is hard to pick one story as my favorite. But I can say I have a favorite *type* of story. Any time I run into a former client, years after we've worked together, and they run up to me and hug me, and tell me all the wonderful things happening in their life, I'm thrilled. We don't often see the fruits of our labor in real time, when working with clients. Most times we never know what happens after services stop. So, it's always great to see that some seed you planted helped this person to blossom.

What would be the one thing you would change in our community if you had the power to do so? The one thing I would change would be that no one would have trouble accessing any resource that meets their basic needs. Put another way, access to nutritious food, adequate housing, and health care would not be dependent upon a person's ability to pay for these things. Because they are basic human needs, they would be accessible to all.

5.7 IMPORTANCE OF ANTI-OPPRESSIVE SOCIAL WORK

As stated earlier in this chapter, social work remains strong in its commitment to take conscious and deliberate actions to ensure that the clients served are provided with equitable opportunities. This means that best practices are encouraged that help to support and advance anti-racist agendas that can help to close the service availability gaps experienced by people and communities of color, along with vulnerable populations. The CSWE outlines anti-oppressive social work and clearly states the importance of recognizing and supporting practice activities founded in anti-racism, diversity, equity, and inclusion.

From this perspective, social workers are encouraged to advocate at the client (micro), community and client-systems (mezzo), and legislative (macro) levels to ensure services are equitably provided to all. For social workers, anti-oppressive social work starts at a personal level and requires recognizing that internalized racism may not be obvious to the social worker; recognition requires a constant re-examining of ingrained personal bias that could affect the services rendered.

5.8 TRAUMA AND RECOVERY

As helping professionals, assisting clients who are experiencing trauma is central to any practice strategy. Traumatic experiences can exist across all age groups and consist of a wide variety of situations, including domestic violence, sexual abuse, sexual assault, car accidents, being robbed or assaulted, being bullied at school of work, repeated medical interventions from chronic illness, ongoing events of systemic racism, mass shootings, military combat, and law enforcement and firefighter experiences (Gilbert-Elliot, 2021). Trauma-sensitive, trauma-focused, and trauma-informed are terms that are often used interchangeably. When the responses by the client are clinically significant, these extensive symptoms may warrant a diagnosis. Regardless of the trauma experienced, however, all people must recover and rebuild their coping experiences and resources.

According to Colson (2019), in trauma-informed care the social worker internally acknowledges the impact of the trauma on the client, the treatment, and the provider's own feelings and how this can influence practice efforts. Fisher (2021) reminds us that the social worker or helping professional's brain may not experience triggers to this event in the same way the client's does. Therefore, the helper may not see a rational connection for the client's response. Since the trauma victim may have trouble integrating past and present and concepts such as safe versus dangerous, unexpected or extreme responses can be common. The environmental triggers of a traumatic stress response in the client may not be obvious to the helping professional. For example, if a child was victimized by someone who wore a particular cologne, the smell of that cologne when it was worn by someone else, even someone you might judge as safe, could elicit a "fight or flee" behavior on the part of the child—even without their own awareness of why they were "fighting or fleeing."

In addition, the helping professional needs to realize that trauma is often not just an isolated event; rather, a series of events, or in some cases developmental care needs that weren't met, can lead to the reactions experienced. Understanding trauma-informed care can lead to a trauma-responsive approach where the history of the trauma is acknowledged along with the presence of the traumatic stress symptoms. For example, this type of series of events has been linked to a term called posttraumatic stress syndrome (PTSS) symptomology. In this type of syndrome, especially in police-involved PTSS, the risk is higher for low-income or Black youth and youth in general who have been stopped multiple times by police (Gearhart, Bender, Barnhart, Berg, & Courtney, 2022). The symptoms of PTSS are considered less severe. When the symptoms continue and clearly interfere with social and occupational functioning, a more formal diagnosis of posttraumatic stress disorder may be placed. Therefore, when selecting a trauma-specific treatment, responsiveness and questioning need to focus on the frequency, intensity, and duration of the symptoms. The process should begin with questions such as "What happened to you?" instead of "What's wrong with you?" (Winfrey & Perry, 2021).

Once trauma is identified and assessed, helping professionals can agree that efforts toward recovery need to be comprehensive, thereby avoiding circumstances where revictimization may occur. Although recovery is possible for all trauma survivors, what recovery entails can look different for each person (Darsa, 2020). Contrary to previous beliefs that "telling and retelling their story" can resolve these effects, Fisher (2021) warns that just the opposite is possible: that telling and retelling the event could reactivate the trauma response, making it overwhelming. From this perspective, a clear focus on the symptoms that disrupt the daily activities of the individual becomes the focus.

Social workers can provide important services in identifying situations that can lead to traumatic stress and helping to establish a comprehensive strategy to address it. Social workers are uniquely equipped to assist clients experiencing trauma considering the "person-in-situation" and "person-in-environment" stances. Trauma does not occur in a vacuum, and this expansive approach considers the support system that is critical to assist in the recovery process. When addressing trauma, memories are often fragmented, emotional, and contradictory (Herman, 2015). Once clients learn more about what they are experiencing, helping efforts will be the most successful. In addition, trauma and recovery are further complicated when treatment of the trauma has been self-medicated with substances resulting in addiction (Marich, 2020). This makes trauma treatment difficult because neither situation (the trauma or the addiction) stands alone.

5.9 DIFFERENTIATING BETWEEN GENERALIST AND SPECIALIST PRACTICE

Social work practice is organized around two principal service delivery conceptual models: the generalist and the specialist. Generalist social work is more broadly defined and targeted toward a wider variety of client systems and problem areas. Specialist social work is more narrowly defined, with a sharper focus on specific issues or a particular client population.

Generalist Practice

To date, as a profession we continue to struggle with defining what constitutes true generalist practice. First, most professional social workers agree that generalist social work practice is primarily reserved for social workers at the baccalaureate level or the first year in a two-year MSW program, although this view has changed because some graduate programs now offer a specialization reflective of additional coursework in advanced generalist practice. The advanced generalist at the master's level will go into more depth in certain areas of practice. Second, generalist social workers are prepared for entry-level social work practice. Although some programs may have a unique spin on the curriculum, generalist practice social workers consider the environment as the primary focus utilizing some type of systems approach to professional practice and subsequent intervention. According to the *Social Work Dictionary*, a social work generalist is a practitioner with skills and knowledge that encompass a broad spectrum of areas developing comprehensive solutions (Barker, 2013).

The broad-based generalist approach to social work practice integrates clients' needs with those of the environment. In accepting the importance of the person-in-situation, social workers are leaders in understanding and interpreting the interaction among the biological, behavioral, psychological, spiritual, and social factors in the client's condition and the environmental factors that the client faces daily.

Generalist social work follows an integrated approach designed to assist the client on multiple levels, including individuals, families, societies, communities, neighborhoods, and complex organizations. Generalist practice requires understanding how human behavior can affect the environment and how the environment can affect human behavior and make focused change efforts designed to improve system interactions at all levels. Therefore, it is highly possible that the generalist-level social worker may be working directly in a nonclinical setting and that he or she is expected to have developed skills reflective of this type of practice environment (DeAngelis, 2009).

Specialist Practice

The specialist social worker provides a more focused, higher level of intervention. A specialist possesses an MSW degree and is also prepared for advanced social work practice. According to the *Social Work Dictionary*, a specialization is the focus within a profession on the knowledge and skill recognizing a specific objective, a specific type of problem, or a target population (Barker, 2013). Social work specializations have developed in a number of ways over the years. Although each social work program may offer different concentrations of specialist practice, popular specialization areas include health, mental health, substance abuse, corrections, gerontology, children's services, policy, administration, and community-based practice. Alternatively, programs may focus on geographic areas (urban or rural neighborhoods) or social systems (the individual, or microsystem; the family group, or mezzosystem; or the community, or macrosystem). After an extended period of MSW practice, the specialist worker is eligible for independent practice. Through state licensing laws (see Chapter 15 for a more complete discussion of licensing and regulation of social work practice) and professional practice certifications, the master-level practitioner can move into private practice or practice independently within the agency context.

Social work remains one of the most diverse fields of practice imaginable. Specialist- and generalist-level social workers are found in numerous settings: public and private agencies, public and private hospitals, clinics, schools, extended care facilities, private practice, private business, police departments, courts, and countless other workplaces too numerous to name. This diversity of practice can be considered both a blessing and a curse. In one way, it increases visibility and functionality and diversifies the profession. Yet, the diversity of the profession makes it difficult for the broader community to understand what social workers do. It also makes it easier for other disciplines to assume partial roles and specialize in just one or two areas.

In summary, generalist and specialist social workers share similarities because they share a core foundation, including values, although the specialist delves more deeply into a particular concentration. Specializations in social work practice occur as a result of taking advanced graduate courses. Specialist social workers are first trained in the generalist approach to practice and later embark on more specialized career tracks by choosing more concentrated areas in which to apply their skills. It is also in specialization that many professional educators believe real training as counseling professionals and therapists occurs. Master-level social workers, with supervised experience (and certification or licensure), are usually free to engage in full, non–clinically supervised counseling activities or work privately in practice. In the field of social work, the master's degree is considered the terminal practice degree. For those studying at the doctorate (DSW or PhD) level, the focus is often on leadership, advanced practice skills, research, or science and advanced clinical practice.

5.10 THE EMERGENCE OF EVIDENCE-BASED SOCIAL WORK PRACTICE

As technology evolves, so do the expectations of the clients who are served (Dziegielewski & Holliman, 2020). Whether costs for services are covered directly out of pocket or indirectly with our tax dollars, people deserve to receive the best services possible. These expectations extend to social workers, and indeed, the profession itself expects all services and activities performed on behalf of clients to be of the highest quality. Yet, how do we demonstrate to the public that our activities are effective?

Social workers have historically been accused of avoiding the use of empirical techniques to establish practice efficiency and effectiveness. According to Rubin and Babbie (2008), this gap between research and the practice community is so large that the lack of connection extends into the classroom. In this era of professional accountability and client rights, however, the impetus remains high for continued progress toward change, highlighting the importance of assessment, intervention, and evaluation in all activities completed (O'Hare, 2009). The profession continues to be challenged to prove service effectiveness and ensure that interventions are germane to client issues.

The challenge to tie evidence-based research and evaluation to practice is not new. For example, in 1978, Fischer wrote,

> It seems to be difficult to avoid the conclusion that, unless major changes are made in the practice methods—and hence, the effectiveness—of casework, our field, if not the entire profession of social work, cannot long survive. Indeed,

unless such changes are made, it is not clear that as a field, we deserve to survive. On one hand, we have the option of choosing—and building—a new revitalized future for social casework, one rooted in the superordinate principle that our primary if not our sole allegiance is to serve our clients with demonstrable effectiveness. On the other hand, we can continue our outmoded practices, denigrate and resist new approaches to practice, and bury our collective heads in the sand when confronted with the vaguest hint of a threat that we may not be doing all in our power to provide effective services. (p. 310)

The new revitalized casework that Fischer envisioned is today quite closely linked to evidence-based social work practice. All social workers, those trained as generalists and specialists alike, are expected to apply its principles to their activities. In empirically based social work practice, research is used as a practice and problem-solving tool where data are collected and systematically monitored to show whether measurable outcomes have been achieved (Barker, 2013).

Furthermore, with the evolution of terminology, a more common definition was identified, and empirically based changed to evidence based. From this perspective, the use of the best available scientific knowledge, based in controlled outcome studies and meta-analyses, provides the basis for guiding professional interventions and effective therapies (Barker, 2013).

For the beginning social work professional, it is important to understand that in evidence-based social work practice, the application of clear-cut research and evaluation models is guided by four broad ideas. First, research findings must be shown to be relevant to practice by assessing the change in a client's level of effectiveness after a specific intervention directed at a specific problem. Second, applications, practice and evaluation models, and findings are to be drawn from research reports. Third, research findings are to be disseminated so that the results are known in the practice community. Fourth and finally, other social work professionals should be able to interpret, understand, and apply what they read to what they do. CSWE (2022) expects programs to provide competency-based practice principles. This is linked clearly to evidence-based practice mandating that, in developing a practice intervention with a client, the practitioner includes systematic research activities that provide feedback on the intervention's effectiveness, controlling for bias while being potentially replicable (Bronson, 2009; Shlonsky, 2009; Thyer, 2001, 2004, 2022a, 2022b). In addition, the practice intervention may provide additional information on how the client's ability to resolve the problem can be strengthened. A **strengths-based perspective** is often used starting "where the client is" and empowering change based on the positive qualities the client possesses.

5.11 THE STEPS IN PROFESSIONAL HELPING

Work with clients in social work practice has five steps. Note that evaluation is not a distinct step, but takes place throughout all steps of the social work process.

Social Work Process

Remember that evaluation is constant in all steps of the process!

STEP 1: PROBLEM IDENTIFICATION

The first step involves problem identification. The social worker helps the client to identify and concretely define the problem(s) to be addressed by the intervention process. This requires a careful examination of the problem behaviors while establishing a relationship with the client that will foster continued support. Involvement by the client in identifying problem behaviors is crucial to continued engagement.

Once clear, mutually negotiated goals and objectives are identified, the intervention (a.k.a. treatment) plan can be formed (Dziegielewski, 2015). The role of the worker is clear: to apply logical thinking to identify the beginning, end, and dynamics of the problem. Engage the client in the problem identification process because it is central to the developing practice strategy. The client's problems are discussed thoroughly, and the client is made aware of the social worker's serious and dedicated efforts to help. It is during this initial step of the helping process that the **rapport** is established that will characterize the remainder of the practice experience. A working alliance is developed, allowing the client to begin to feel comfortable, yet eager to embark on change. The social worker avoids simply giving advice to the client. Utilizing empathy helps the client see that the social worker understands the client's situation and can relate to the client within the context of the other person's perspective (Koerner & Linehan, 2009).

As the sessions progress, the social worker will remain objective when educating, advocating, facilitating, and intervening on behalf of the client. In establishing rapport and giving feedback validation, the worker often uses active communication that the client's perspective makes sense (Koerner & Linehan, 2009). Moreover, as ironic as it may sound, the social worker always begins early in the encounter to plan for what will happen when the session ends. In fact, plans for what will happen after termination are often outlined in the first session. The client is thus aware of what is coming and what needs to be accomplished by the end of the therapeutic term.

At the end of the first session and each session thereafter, the technique of *summarization* is used. In this technique, the client is asked to state what was most relevant for him or her in the session and whether progress was made regarding the identified goals and objectives. This helps to focus the client on what was covered while helping the social worker to know if the session is following the identified goals and objectives. To ensure that the client is understanding and relating directly to what is covered, the social worker should never summarize the session content for the client. Let the client summarize in his or her own words. Letting the client state what he or she has gotten from the session helps the social worker to determine what really was accomplished and whether both client and social worker are aiming toward the same intervention outcomes. When relevant, the social worker should acknowledge what a client is feeling and validate emotions and change efforts that support the changes desired (Koerner & Linehan, 2009). Clients often need this feedback and reassurance that understanding has occurred and progress is being made.

It is also during this initial step that the social worker decides how accountability or practice effectiveness will be evaluated after the intervention is completed. Exactly what will be measured and how it will be measured varies from case to case. No magic pill ensures evidence-based practice. We hope, however, that knowing its importance piques your interest in the research courses you must take and how to apply this knowledge to increase practice effectiveness.

STEP 2: ASSESSMENT AND GOAL SETTING

The second step involves helping the client set goals and objectives that can be accomplished (Dziegielewski, 2015). Both worker and client assess the client's need for assistance and determine how specifically the problem can be addressed. The *goal* is the overall end that the client wants to accomplish, and the *objectives* are the concrete steps that the client will take to get there and that allow for measurement of the outcome (Dziegielewski, 2008a, 2008b). Setting goals and objectives has the following valuable consequences:

- It ensures agreement between worker and client on intervention focus and purpose.
- It provides the client with knowledge about how to address the problem while establishing a basis for continuity of session content across the intervention process.
- It provides a basis for selecting appropriate treatment strategies.
- It assists the social worker to structure session content and monitor progress of the intervention.
- It yields outcome criteria (the objectives) for measurement of intervention effectiveness.

The following guidelines always apply to setting goals and objectives. First, the goals and objectives must relate to what the client wants to achieve at the end of the intervention. Second, the goals and objectives must be defined in explicit terms so that the client knows what is expected of him or her. Third, the objectives must be feasible. Clients must believe that they can succeed; otherwise, they may become disheartened and drop out of the intervention process. Fourth, the goals and objectives must be consistent with the skills and abilities of the helping professional. Social workers should never try to address medical problems they know little about. For example, if the social worker becomes unsure of his or her abilities, he or she should explore supervision, consultation, and continuing education options before proceeding with the intervention process. Ensuring quality of services in this manner is important for both the client and the social worker. Fifth, whenever possible, goals and objectives should be stated positively rather than negatively. Sixth, although all goals should be mutually negotiated with the client, the social worker must express his or her reservations about these goals. Clients desire input in their decision-making. However, the social worker must be sure that any hesitation reflects concern for the client's good rather than his or her personal bias.

STEP 3: ACTION PLAN DEVELOPMENT

Once goals and objectives have been clearly identified, the social worker helps the client to develop a plan of action. The role of the social worker is paramount in identifying strategies for action and change. The worker may be able to provide the direct supervision or consultation necessary to implement the plan. Often, however, the social worker does not have the required expertise—he or she may be a generalist when a specialist is needed—and will contract with another provider or use work strategies to assist the client in meeting the objectives.

The action plan may include a task or a series of tasks. Each task is specific, clear, and supported by a period monitored by both worker and client. Each task builds on previous efforts, which together lead to the goals and objectives identified. As with goal setting, each task must be understood by both client and worker and, most important, must be within the client's ability to achieve.

Every action plan must have clearly established contingency plans. These plans specify the rewards for completion of the practice strategy agreement and the consequences for noncompliance. Clients participate in this part of the change process because they will accept the consequences of their actions or inactions.

STEP 4: IMPLEMENTATION

Implementation takes place when the client is ready to put the plan into action. During implementation, the worker and client together monitor the progress and determine whether any measurable improvement has occurred. Therefore, practice evaluation is a determination of whether there has been useful improvement with the problem situation. Assessing and evaluating the problem behaviors that have been modified assist both the client and the social worker in measuring progress. Through monitoring, worker and client can assess progress toward the goal and measure the effectiveness of the intervention. Once the goals and tasks have been assessed, the client's reaction to the progress or lack thereof is evaluated. Ongoing monitoring allows worker and client to identify barriers as well as strengths in the process. New strategies can be built to overcome or cope with the barriers. And most important, monitoring provides the client with feedback on positive experiences that in turn reinforce the change efforts.

Implementing an action plan can be intimidating for a beginning social worker. Social work practice knowledge is essential because the social worker will be expected to use multiple practice strategies to assist the client. These can involve the application of strategies such as modeling, behavior rehearsal, role playing, or simple paper-and-pencil exercises in which the client writes down feelings experienced as well as steps to be completed in the action plan. Referrals for additional help and assistance should also be considered and discussed at this time—for example, additional individual therapy, group therapy, couples therapy, or family therapy.

STEP 5: MAINTENANCE AND TERMINATION

The last step in the social work process involves maintenance and termination. In maintenance, it is crucial to identify how change efforts will continue once direct therapeutic measures are no longer the focus. Avoiding relapse or returning to a previous situation need to be clearly recognized and a plan must be established. In termination, the client and social worker end their working relationship and describe how any change strategy developed will be continued in maintenance. Many clients realize at termination that they want additional help. If this happens, the social worker informs the client of options for continued intervention and emotional growth by giving appropriate referrals. Referrals for group therapy, individual growth-directed therapy, couples therapy, and family therapy can be considered.

Evaluation and Follow-Up

Successful practice intervention results in significant changes in a client's levels of functioning and coping. Measures that can substantiate these changes are essential to evidence-based practice. Measuring intervention effectiveness can be as simple as making a follow-up phone call to discuss how things are going, or it can be as structured as scoring the client's behavior on a standardized scale at the beginning and end of treatment and then comparing the two. Scales that measure depression, trauma, and so forth are readily available. If more advanced methods of measuring practice effectiveness are expected, more advanced training and planning are warranted.

Planned practice evaluation and follow-up at the termination of intervention are essential, but these steps are often forgotten. In fact, when you consider the five steps in the social work process, you will see that research and evaluation seem to be missing. And if these steps are missing, how does the process we have outlined lead to empirically based social work practice? In fact, they are not missing—they are simply not separate steps because research and evaluation should be included at each step of the helping process.

5.12 PRACTICE APPLICATION: THE ROLE OF THE MEDICAL SOCIAL WORKER

Ms. Martha Edda had been living with her family for a year. Before that, she had lived independently in her own apartment. Ms. Edda had to leave her apartment after a neighbor found her unconscious. The apartment was unsafe, with rotted food, urine, and feces throughout. Upon discovery, Ms. Edda was immediately admitted to the hospital. Originally, she was believed to have suffered a stroke; later, she was formally diagnosed with a neurological condition called vascular dementia. Doctors believed that she was in the moderate to advanced stage of this condition because, at age sixty-two, she had pronounced movement and memory difficulties.

After discussion with the hospital social worker, it became obvious that Ms. Edda needed a supervised living arrangement. Ms. Edda had a daughter, Joan, who said she would try to help. Once in Joan's home, Ms. Edda received home health care services. However, much to Joan's surprise, all services stopped after just two months because Ms. Edda's physical therapy was discontinued. Joan relied heavily on these services, particularly the nurse's aide who helped to give Ms. Edda a bath. Ms. Edda weighed 170 pounds and could not help herself in or out of the tub. Joan recruited the help of her husband, who reluctantly agreed. Unfortunately, Ms. Edda could not get into the adult day care center in the area because no spaces were available, and she was placed on a waiting list. She required help with all her activities of daily living, and her daughter was afraid to leave her at home alone during the day. Therefore, Joan quit her job to help care for her mother.

On the morning of January 12, Joan found her mother lying face down in her bed. She had become incontinent of bowel and bladder and unable to speak, and the features on the left side of her face appeared distorted. When Joan could not rouse her mother, she panicked and called an ambulance. Ms. Edda was immediately transported to the emergency room.

In the emergency room, the staff began to administer numerous tests to see if Ms. Edda had suffered a stroke. Plans were made to admit her to the hospital, but no beds were available. Because Ms. Edda needed supervised monitoring and a hospital bed could become available in the morning, an agreement was made to keep her overnight. In the morning, she was admitted to the inpatient hospital, where she remained incontinent and refused to eat. She was so confused that the nurses feared she would get out of bed and hurt herself; she was placed in restraints periodically throughout the day.

After two days, most of the medical tests had been performed and determined negative; Ms. Edda's vital signs remained stable. The physician felt that her admission to the hospital could no longer be justified, and the social worker was notified of the pending discharge. On placing the call to prepare Ms. Edda's family for her return home, the social worker was told that the family would not accept her and wanted her placed in a nursing home. The social worker was concerned about this decision because Ms. Edda did not have private insurance to cover a nursing home stay and was too young to be eligible for Medicare. This meant that an application for Medicaid would have to be made. This state-funded program had a lower reimbursement rate, and most privately run nursing homes drastically limited the number of Medicaid clients they accepted. During a search for nursing home services, the social worker was informed of the lack of available beds.

When the social worker explained the problems with the discharge plans to the physician, he simply responded, "I am under pressure to get her out, and there is no medical reason for her to be here. Discharge her home today." Since it was after 4:00 p.m. and the administrative offices were closed, the social worker next attempted to secure an out-of-area placement for the following day.

When the physician returned at 6:00 p.m., he wanted to know why the client had not been discharged. The nurse on duty explained that a nursing home bed could not be found; the physician, who was angry, wrote an order for immediate discharge. The nurse called Ms. Edda's family at 6:30 p.m. and notified them of the discharge. Ms. Edda's family was angry and asked why she had not been placed in a home. The nurse explained to the family that discharge orders had been written and that she was only trying to do her job.

Ms. Edda's daughter, Joan, insisted on speaking to the discharge physician prior to picking up her mother. A message was left for him, and at 8:00 p.m., he returned her call. The physician, sounding frustrated, told Joan that all medical emergencies had been addressed and Ms. Edda would have to leave the hospital immediately. Furious, Joan yelled, "If she is still incontinent and in restraints, how do you expect me to handle her?" Listening to Joan's distress, the physician softened his voice and said, "I will put the nurse on the phone to update you on her condition. In addition, the social worker will call you in the morning to arrange home health care services."

Upon arriving at the hospital, Joan found her mother hooked to an IV, wearing a diaper, and still in restraints. Pleased to see a member of Ms. Edda's family, the nurse sent for a wheelchair, unhooked the intravenous tubing, removed the restraints, and placed Ms. Edda in the wheelchair for transport to the family's car.

Case Example Discussion

Unfortunately, situations like this occur all too often. The social worker was responsible for **discharge planning**, but many other issues needed to be addressed to best serve the client and her family. With perseverance and the help of the hospital social worker, Joan eventually (several months later) placed her mother in a nursing home. However, the strain on Joan was so severe that she requested medication to combat her depression. Joan also began to fight with her husband and children over numerous issues related to the time and care devoted to her mother and the loss of their second family income. Joan's earnings helped to cover necessities such as rent and food, as well as family luxuries (such as movies and eating out).

In this situation, the price of the *cost-effective* **managed care** strategy far exceeded the dollar value placed on it, and the client and her family became silent victims. The role of the social worker—officially labeled a discharge planner—involved more than just finding a place for the client to go. Referrals, counseling, and openness to service flexibility make the social work professional an invaluable member of any **interdisciplinary team**. (This case scenario was adapted from Dziegielewski & Holliman, 2020).

SUMMARY

Social work practice evolved from mid-eighteenth- and nineteenth-century efforts to assist poor people. In those early years, activities were carried out by volunteers, with few organizational supports and limited training. Today, the profession has a well-established knowledge base, a clearly articulated value orientation, and diverse practice methodologies and interventions, which are transmitted to the new practitioner through formal educational processes.

The practice of social work is conducted in one of two major forms: the generalist and the specialist. The generalist works with a wide range of clients and services, whereas the specialist can complete the same duties but also focus more distinctly on groups of clients and provide more individualized therapeutic services. The great variability of what can be done to assist clients and the level at which this can be accomplished are the reasons why social workers are able to practice in diverse types of social agencies and organizational settings.

Social work practice has never been static. It has evolved dramatically since its conception and will continue to change in the future. To grow and adapt, practice must be conducted within a systematic, well-thought-out process that allows the use and production of scientifically tested knowledge and skills, and it must be founded on a clear and coherent set of professional values.

REFERENCES

Austrian, S. G. (2009). Guidelines for conducting a biopsychosocial assessment. In A. R. Roberts (Ed.), *Social workers' desk reference* (2nd ed., pp. 376–380). New York, NY: Oxford University Press.

Barker, R. L. (2013). *The social work dictionary* (6th ed.). Washington, DC: NASW Press.

Boehm, W. (Ed.). (1959). *Social work curriculum study* (Vol. 1). Washington, DC: Council on Social Work Education.

Bronson, D. E. (2009). Critically appraising studies for evidence-based practice. In A. Roberts (Ed.), *Social workers' desk reference* (2nd ed., pp. 1137–1141). New York, NY: Oxford University Press.

Colson, R. D. (2019). *The strategic trauma and abuse recovery system: A Christian-integrated, comprehensive, 3-phase model of individual and group counseling*. McDonough, GA: TraumaEducation.com.

Congress, E. P. (2009). The culturagram. In A. Roberts (Ed.), *Social workers desk reference* (2nd ed., pp. 969–975). New York, NY: Oxford University Press.

Congress, E. P., & Gonzalez, M. J. (Eds.). (2013). *Multicultural perspectives in social work practice with families* (3rd ed.). New York, NY: Springer.

Congress, E. P., & Kung, W. W. (2013). Using the culturagram to assess and empower culturally diverse families. In E. P. Congress & M. J. Gonzalez (Eds.), *Multicultural perspectives in social work practice with families* (3rd ed., pp. 1–20). New York, NY: Springer.

Council on Social Work Education. (2022c). *2022 EPAS—Educational Policy, and Accreditation Standards for baccalaureate and master's social work programs*. Alexandria, VA: Author. Retrieved from https://www.cswe.org/getmedia/bb5d8afe-7680-42dc-a332-a6e6103f4998/2022-EPAS.pdf

Darsa, K. (2020). *The trauma map: Five steps to reconnect with yourself*. Reconnect Center. Pacific Palisades, CA: Reconnect Center.

DeAngelis, D. (2009). Social work licensing examinations in the United States and Canada. In A. Roberts (Ed.), *Social workers desk reference* (2nd ed., pp. 136–147). New York, NY: Oxford University Press.

Dziegielewski, S. F. (2008a). Brief and intermittent approaches to practice: The state of practice. *Journal of Brief Treatment and Crisis Intervention, 8*, 147–163. https://doi.org/10.1093/brief-treatment/mhn005

Dziegielewski, S. F. (2008b). Problem identification, contracting, and case planning. In K. M. Sowers & C. N. Dulmus (Series Eds.) & W. Rowe & L. A. Rapp-Paglicci (Vol. Eds.), *Comprehensive handbook of social work and social welfare: Social work practice* (Vol. 3, pp. 78–97). Hoboken, NJ: Wiley.

Dziegielewski, S. F. (2015). *DSM-5™ in action* (3rd ed.). Hoboken, NJ: Wiley.

Dziegielewski, S. F., & Holliman, D. (2020). *The changing face of health care social work: Opportunities and challenges for professional practice* (4th ed.). New York, NY: Springer.

Ell, K., Lee, P., & Xie, B. (2010). Depression care for low-income, minority, safety net clinic populations with comorbid illness. *Research on Social Work Practice, 20*, 467–475. https://doi.org/10.1177/1049731510361962

Erickson, C. L. (2018). *Environmental justice and social work practice*. New York, NY: Oxford University Press.

Fischer, J. (1978). *Effective casework practice: An eclectic approach*. New York, NY: McGraw-Hill.

Fisher, J. (2021). *Transforming the living legacy of trauma: A workbook for survivors and therapists*. Eau Claire, WI: PESI Publishing and Media.

Gearhart, M. C., Bender, A., Barnhart, S., Berg, K. A., & Courtney, J. (2022). Youth profiles of police-initiated post-traumatic stress symptomatology. *Child Adolescent Social Work, 39*, 525–537. https://doi.org/10.1007/s10560-021-00741-4

Gilbert-Elliot, T. (2021). *Trauma recovery journal: Reflective prompts and evidence-based practices to help you recover, heal, and thrive*. Emeryville, CA: Rockridge Press.

Gonzalez-Ramos, G. (1990). Examining the myth of Hispanic families' resistance to treatment: Using the school as a site for services. *Social Work in Education, 12*, 261–274.

Hepworth, D. H., Rooney, R. H., Rooney, G. D., Strom-Gottfried, K., & Larsen, J. (2010). *Direct social work practice: Theory and skills* (8th ed.). Belmont, CA: Brooks/Cole Cengage Learning.

Hepworth, D. H., Vang, P. D., Blakey, J. M., Schwalbe, C., Evans, C. B., Rooney, R. H., ... Strom, K. (2023). *Direct social work practice: Theory and skills* (11th ed.). Belmont, CA: Brooks/Cole Cengage Learning.

Herman, J. (2015). *Trauma and recovery: The aftermath of violence—from domestic abuse to political terror*. New York, NY: Basic Books.

Hook, J. N., Davis, D. E., Owen, J., Worthington, Jr., E. L., & Utsey, S. O. (2013). Cultural humility: Measuring openness to culturally diverse clients. *Journal of Counseling Psychology, 60*(3), 353–366.

Hopps, J. G., & Lowe, T. B. (2008). The scope of social work practice. In K. M. Sowers & C. N. Dulmus (Series Eds.) & B. W. White (Vol. Ed.), *Comprehensive handbook of social work and social welfare: The profession of social work* (Vol. 1, pp. 37–64). Hoboken, NJ: Wiley.

Hopps, J. G., & Lowe, T. B. (2012). Social work practice in the new millennium. In C. N Dulmus & K. M. Sowers (Eds.), *The profession of social work: Guided by history, led by evidence* (pp. 51–81). Hoboken, NJ: Wiley.

Jani, J. S., Pierce, D., Ortiz, L., & Sowbel, L. (2011). Access to intersectionality, content to competence: Deconstructing social work education diversity standards. *Journal of Social Work Education, 47*, 283–301. https://doi.org/10.5175/JSWE.2011.200900118

Koerner, K., & Linehan, M. M. (2009). Validation principles and strategies. In W. T. O'Donohue & J. E. Fisher (Eds.), *General principles and empirically supported techniques of cognitive behavior therapy* (pp. 674–680). Hoboken, NJ: Wiley.

Marich, J. (2020). *Trauma and the 12 steps*. Berkeley, CA: North Atlantic Books.

Mattaini, M. A. (2001). The foundation of social work practice. In Briggs, H. & Corcoran, K. (Eds.), *Social work practice: Treating common client problems* (pp. 15–35). Chicago, IL: Lyceum Books.

Miller, J., & Garran, A. M. (2009). The legacy of racism for social work practice today and what to do about it. In A. Roberts (Ed.), *Social workers' desk reference* (2nd ed., pp. 928–923). New York, NY: Oxford University Press.

Morales, A. T., Sheafor, B. W., & Scott, M. E. (2012). *Social work: A profession of many faces* (updated 12th ed.). Boston, MA: Allyn and & Bacon.

NASW Anti-Racism Statement. (2022, February 23). *News releases*. NASW. Retrieved from: https://www.socialworkers.org/News/News-Releases/ID/2403/NASW-Anti-Racism-Statement

National Association of Social Workers. (1993). *Choices: Careers in social work*. Washington, DC: Author.

National Association of Social Workers. (2018). *Code of ethics* (Revised by NASW Delegate Assembly, 2018). Washington, DC: Author.

O'Hare, T. (2009). *Essential skills of social work practice: Assessment, intervention, and education*. Chicago, IL: Lyceum Books.

Parker, J., & Bradley, G. (2010). *Social work practice: Assessment, planning, intervention and review* (3rd ed.). England, United Kingdom: Learning Matters.

Poertner, J., & Rapp, C. A. (2007). *The textbook of social administration: The consumer centered approach*. Binghamton, NY: Haworth Press.

Reamer, F. G. (2009). Ethical issues in social work. In A. Roberts (Ed.), *Social workers' desk reference* (2nd ed., pp. 115–120). New York, NY: Oxford University Press.

Reamer, F. G. (2018). *Social work values and ethics* (5th ed.). New York, NY: Columbia University Press.

Reardon, C. (2011, July/August). A decade of *Social Work Today*: 10 trends that transformed social work. *Social Work Today, 11*(4), 10. Retrieved from http://www.socialworktoday.com/archive/071211p10.shtml

Ridley, C. R. (1995). *Overcoming unintentional racism in counseling and therapy*. Thousand Oaks, CA: Sage.

Rubin, A., & Babbie, E. (2008). *Research methods for social work* (6th ed.). Belmont, CA: Brooks/Cole.

Shlonsky, A. (2009). Evidence-based practice in social work education. In A. Roberts (Ed.), *Social workers desk reference* (2nd ed., pp. 1169–1176). New York, NY: Oxford University Press.

Snowden, L. R. (2003). Bias in mental health assessment and intervention: Theory and evidence. *Journal of Public Health, 93*, 239–243

Sue, D. W., & Sue, D. (2008). *Counseling the culturally diverse: Theory and practice*. Hoboken, NJ: Wiley.

Tervalon, M., & Murray-Garcia, J. (1998). Cultural humility versus cultural competence: A critical distinction in defining physician training outcomes in multicultural education. *Journal of Health Care for the Poor and Undeserved, 9,* 117–125.

Thyer, B. (2001). Evidence-based approaches to community practice. In H. E. Briggs & K. Corcoran (Eds.), *Social work practice: Treating common client problems* (pp. 54–65). Chicago, IL: Lyceum Books.

Thyer, B. A. (2004). What is evidence-based practice? *Brief Treatment and Crisis Intervention, 4,* 167–176.

Thyer, B. A. (2022a). What is evidence-based practice? In K. Corcoran & L. Rapp-McCoy (Eds.), *Social workers' desk reference* (4th ed., pp. 693–700). New York, NY: Oxford University Press.

Thyer, B. A. (2022b). Evaluating our effectiveness in carrying out evidence-based practice. In K. Corcoran & L. Rapp-McCoy (Eds.), *Social workers' desk reference* (4th ed., pp. 734–742). New York, NY: Oxford University Press.

Trevithick, P. (2012). *Social work skills and knowledge: A practice handbook* (3rd ed.). London, England: Open University Press/McGraw–Hill Education.

Twohig, M. P., & Crosby, J. M. (2009). Values clarification. In W. T. O'Donohue & J. E. Fisher (Eds.), *General principles and empirically supported techniques of cognitive behavior therapy* (pp. 681–686). Hoboken, NJ: Wiley.

U.S. Census Bureau. (2022). National Black (African American) History Month: February 2022. (Press Release Number CB22-FF.01). Retrieved from https://www.census.gov/newsroom/facts-for-features/2022/black-history-month.html?utm_campaign=20220201msprts1v1pupnl&utm_medium=email&utm_source=govdelivery

Winfrey, O., & Perry, B. (2021). *What happened to you?: Conversations on trauma, resilience, and healing.* New York, NY: Flat Iron Books.

Witkin, S. L., & Iversen, R. R. (2008). Issues in social work. In K. M. Sowers & C. N. Dulmus (Series Eds.) & B. W. White (Vol. Ed.), *Comprehensive handbook of social work and social welfare: The profession of social work* (Vol. 1, pp. 467–496). Hoboken, NJ: Wiley.

6

Recognizing Diversity and Applying It to Generalist Practice

By Sophia F. Dziegielewski, Sarah R. Young, and Debra Nelson-Gardell

CHAPTER 6: EPAS COMPETENCIES

Social work programs at the bachelor's and the master's level are accredited by the Council of Social Work Education (CSWE). CSWE's Educational Policy and Accreditation Standards (EPAS) describe the processes and criteria that social work courses should cover. In 2022, CSWE updated its EPAS standards. The following competencies are addressed in this chapter:

Competency 1: Demonstrate Ethical and Professional Behavior

Social workers understand the value base of the profession and its ethical standards, as well as relevant laws and regulations that may impact practice with individuals, families, groups, organizations, and communities.

Competency 2: Advance Human Rights and Social, Racial, Economic, and Environmental Justice

Social workers understand that every person regardless of position in society has fundamental human rights.

Competency 3: Engage in Anti-Racism, Diversity, Equity, and Inclusion (ADEI) in Practice

Social workers understand how racism and oppression shape human experiences and how these two constructs influence practice at the individual, family, group, organizational, and community levels and in policy and research.

Competency 7: Assess Individuals, Families, Groups, Organizations, and Communities

Social workers understand that assessment is an ongoing component of the dynamic and interactive process of social work practice.

Competency 8: Intervene with Individuals, Families, Groups, Organizations, and Communities

Social workers understand that intervention is an ongoing component of the dynamic and interactive process of social work practice.

In his first field placement, Juan, a social worker working with older adults, often found himself struggling. He joked that he was waiting for the "standardized" single-problem client to come in so that he could carefully choose the best method of helping. Although he wanted to help his clients address their problems and remembered what he had been taught in school, the thought of applying this knowledge was frightening. In school, Juan learned numerous intervention methods that supported a generalist approach to practice, and like most beginning professionals, he was concerned that he would not interpret the client's problems correctly. Misinterpretation or erroneous assumptions could lead to making the wrong decisions when beginning helping activities. Important expectations such as always remembering to respect the individual's worth and the dignity of each client and maximizing self-determination were strong in his memory. He knew that he should never show a lack of respect for the client's culture, values, or beliefs. For Juan, as for many novice social work professionals, it is never easy to discover the best way to recognize, respect, and utilize empowerment to help the client, while being inclusive and mindful of diversity and equity.

CHAPTER 6: RECOGNIZING DIVERSITY AND APPLYING IT TO GENERALIST PRACTICE

Furthermore, Juan questioned where the problems his client was experiencing originated and rested. Was it in the person suffering from the problem? Was it in the family? Was it in the group the person associated with or the community in which the person lived? Was it the policy or legislation leading to the client's problem that required change? Or was it all of the above?

• • •

Juan's experience is quite normal for a beginning social worker. As we have noted before, social work is not purely a science. Many aspects of comprehensive helping may need to move beyond the science and require individualistic helping activities that create the best fit for the client in their situation. The skills required to practice the art and science of social work take time and experience to develop. In fact, the science of social work will always require continual updating as we continue to prove that what we do does indeed make a difference. In this way, we can show that the client situation improves with the intervention, and this is measured through clear goals and guidelines within the practice structure.

For Juan, and for all beginning as well as seasoned social workers, deciding how best to engage with a client's situation is never easy—nor should it be. The best practice interventions require constant assessment, reassessment, evaluation, and collaboration with other professionals (Dziegielewski & Holliman, 2020, O'Hare, 2009). Furthermore, on any professional team, options will vary as to how to interpret, select, and apply the best helping strategies. Remember, even when using basic evidence-supported practice principles, the actual application of the helping skills to problem situations is often an art; and since people and situations vary, options must remain diverse. From an ecological systems perspective, always considering the person-in-environment, practice strategy and intervention must occur on multiple levels to achieve treatment goals and objectives. This comprehensive perspective is a strength within the social work profession, and an important part of the helping process is identifying and supporting alternatives and innovative strategies (Diller, 2011). Therefore, the goal will never be chaotic improvisation. The general practice consensus is that all client-based interventions must take place within a practice framework with clear theoretical foundations (Reamer, 2022). In the practice environment, it remains clear that the expectation is to have good problem identification, contracting, and case planning skills (Dziegielewski, 2008, 2015; Dziegielewski & Holliman, 2020). This approach is further highlighted by using a strengths-based approach (Poulin, 2010).

This chapter will explore the concept of diversity and how it relates to generalist social work practice. From this orientation, all clients (individuals, families, groups, organizations, and communities) are viewed through a culturally aware and responsive lens, and client strengths are recognized and supported at each step of the helping process. We will also discuss the three most common approaches to social work practice: micropractice, mezzopractice, and macropractice. Social workers must be well versed in all three, although their efforts to assist clients may be concentrated in only one or two of these.

6.1 DIVERSITY AND SOCIAL WORK PRACTICE

A hallmark of the social work profession is its insistence on viewing practice within a specific context, commonly referred to as *contextual practice*. As a client-centered approach, contextual practice suggests that all practice methods consider a variety of unique attributes or characteristics, which in turn influence what we do with and on behalf of clients. One type of intervention may work for one person or group, but not necessarily for another. This is further complicated by an ever-changing environment impacting the client and often termed the *client system*, where the client is not viewed as static and cannot be separated from their situation and the people and the places that influence client actions and behaviors. This makes the client's past successes lose their effectiveness when something that worked in the past may no longer work in the current situation. Therefore, problem-solving behaviors cannot remain static.

It should come as no surprise that two significant groups in the social work profession, the Council on Social Work Education (CSWE) (2022) in its EPAS standards and the National Association of Social Workers (NASW), have been active in defining and infusing cultural awareness and competence into curriculum and content. As early as the 1960s, the CSWE noted the importance of diversity and encouraged the social work profession to infuse this information into the curriculum as well as to encourage diversity in hiring faculty and recruiting students (NASW, 2012; see Figure 6.1). This was further reinforced by the NASW Code of Ethics (NASW, 2008), which stated that social workers must honor the ethical responsibility to serve clients in culturally competent ways. In the same tradition, the revisions to the NASW Code of Ethics (NASW, 2018) and the NASW Anti-racism Statement (2022) further expanded this definition, stressing the importance of recognizing differences while acknowledging and avoiding discrimination. Recognizing racism and how it can affect marginalized populations rests firmly in the heart of social work. This heightened level of awareness was noted clearly during the COVID-19 pandemic, for example, when six of eight victims of a mass shooting at an Atlanta spa were Asian women ("8 Dead in Atlanta Spa Shootings," 2021). Lee (2022) reminds us that to facilitate global practice, a tailored-grounded approach is needed that assists immigrants seeking to acculturate in the society. Community-based social movements, such as Black Lives Matter, name racism and other forms of discrimination as insidious social barriers that continue to lead to disproportionate death, illness, and marginalization of Black people across the globe.

Did You Know . . .
To learn more about Black Lives Matter and the Black Lives Matter Global Network Foundation, visit their website.

Throughout its history, the profession of social work has placed great emphasis on understanding culture as inclusive of an integrated system linked to human behavior. Therefore, promoting cultural competence and humility should be reflected in education, research, and practice (NASW, 2018). When a simplified definition of race is coupled with the historical definition that is related to an individual's genetics and color, the recognition of diversity is limited. When diversity is defined from a social work perspective, it is much broader and more nuanced. From a social work perspective, the concept of culture is not viewed as static, and it embodies the beliefs, customs, norms, and other constructs identified within a particular society. Therefore, cultural awareness, responsiveness, and sensitivity are not achieved by recognizing distinctions of gender, age, race, or creed alone, but by allowing inclusive explanations that are never static. In social work, recognizing diversity involves recognizing groups not traditionally seen as diverse and being sensitive to differences within groups, thereby creating subgroupings or recognizing individual responses that may or may not be shared by the group. Critical theory can be one lens that helps to understand how racism affects marginalized populations (Lee, 2022). Critical theories seek to reveal power structures within societies. They can help social workers with their goal of seeking social justice for all.

FIGURE 6.1
Knowledge of cultural awareness and diversity is at the heart of social work practice.

For social workers, the application of knowledge about cultural awareness and diversity requires being vigilant in recognizing cultural differences and using acquired information to adapt helping services to meet the culturally unique needs of the client (NASW, 2018). In social work, the basic premise "Start where the client is" allows for increased understanding and awareness that improve the effectiveness and the fit of the helping strategy. Added to this simple response is the recognition that clients are not located in a silo composed of static simple entities. This makes it essential to recognize and consider the *client within the client system*. As you continue to read this chapter, keep the premise of the client and the client system in mind, because it is the foundation for what is to come.

The characteristics that an individual, family, group, organization, or community bring to the helping relationship are powerful influences in shaping and molding the client and client-system centered intervention. Why? The key to understanding is found in recognizing differences in backgrounds, experiences, ideas, philosophies, and traditions that make all individuals and their situation and support systems unique. A straightforward way to start to understand basic differences in thinking and responding is to read John Gray's classic book *Men Are from Mars, Women Are from Venus* (1992), which details gender differences. Think back to your introductory sociology course in which you learned that norms, mores, and folkways create our individual skeletal system from which our character and behaviors take shape. Now apply this to what we see in gender definitions today.

Historically, it has not been easy to define gender-specific roles and what constitutes gendered behavior, and recently the endeavor has increased in complexity with the addition of the term *nonbinary* (Stonewall, 2021). Spade and Valentine (2014) defined gender simply as "the meanings, practices and relations of masculinities and femininities that people create as we go about our lives in different settings" (p. xiii). The authors warned, however, that this simplistic definition can limit the potential for understanding what is and what could be, suggesting that defining gender is more like looking through a kaleidoscope, where all views are possible and numerous interpretations can flourish.

> ### Did You Know . . .
> For more than thirty years, the organization called GLAAD has provided recommendations and highlighted the needs of lesbian, gay, bisexual, transgender, or queer (**LGBTQ+**) individuals, seeking to influence awareness and acceptance within the community through information, media, advertising, and marketing.

The number of Americans who identify as LGBTQ+ is growing. A 2021 Gallup poll of twelve thousand U.S. adults predicted the proportion of adults who identify as LGBTQ+ will exceed 10 percent of the American population soon, with current rates of 7.1 percent (Jones, 2021). According to the statistics, 21 percent of generation Z Americans (those born between 1997 and 2003) identify as LGBTQ+ as compared to 2.6 percent of those born between 1946 and 1964. In addition to these numbers, it appears that the majority of all LGBTQ+ Americans (57 percent) indicate that they are bisexual. What is most evident in the data is that this population, sometimes referred to as the invisible minority, has been growing more steadily over the past few years than in previous years. The exact reasons for this are unclear, but most would agree that the freedom to come out and be open with one's sexuality has increased over time, along with greater acceptance by the American people and legal protections supporting the rights and lives of LGBTQ+ Americans (Jones, 2021).

Regardless of gender, race, age, or the more inclusive culture of the individual, the first step toward understanding differences is recognizing the life experiences of each client and how these experiences affect the resulting behavior. For example, a person with a disability may not experience an event in the same way as someone who does not have a disability. The person with a disability may have to contend with socially marginalizing beliefs. Mackelprang and Salsgiver (2009) use the term *ableism* (often interchangeably with the term *disablism*) to describe the belief that because of their differences, people with disabilities are inferior to people without disabilities (p. 9). Furthermore, people with disabilities may be vulnerable, requiring the help and assistance of others within the client system simply to meet their daily needs (Fitzsimons, 2009). The author will never forget discussing planning a trip with a client who was paralyzed. The client said that most people have no idea what it is like to fly on an airplane and wonder if your "chariot of fire" (another name for his wheelchair) would arrive and be ready when it was time to leave the airport.

What makes understanding diversity complicated is that there are differences within differences. Hafford-Letchfield and colleagues (Hafford-Letchfield, Simpson, & Reynolds, 2021) remind us that a cross-cultural perspective can be further complicated by a person's age, especially when related to sexuality and expression. Another example is related directly to race and ethnicity and labeling diverse peoples as all acting alike. Labeling diverse peoples as Hispanic or Latino/Latina/Latinx ignores the fact that there are cultural differences among those who are Mexican, Cuban, Puerto Rican, or Spanish, just as there are differences among Asian Americans who are Chinese, Filipino, Japanese, Korean, Vietnamese, or Samoan. And, to further complicate matters, is it fair to say that all Mexicans will act one way and all Puerto Ricans another way? Saying that all Native Americans fall into one group or act the same is equally inaccurate. Defining who and what constitutes these Indigenous peoples is difficult. The term Native American (Indigenous Peoples of North America) is preferable to American Indian, which refers to the Indigenous Peoples of North and South America (not including the Aleut, who inhabit southwest Alaska, and Inuit). Although diverse communities themselves can be diverse, remaining culturally humble and having a learner's mindset can help connect with clients.

According to the 2010 U.S. Census (U.S. Census Bureau, 2011a), the U.S. population included approximately 2.871 million Native Americans and approximately 124,000 Alaska Natives. When Native Americans and Alaska Natives relate to more than one tribal association or if they are considered multiracial, they constitute approximately 5,366,625 people. Native Americans comprise 562 independent tribes that exist as sovereign nations and speak more than two hundred unique languages (Thompson, Johnson-Jennings, & Nitzarim, 2013). In 2020, the U.S. Census listed the American Indian and Alaska Native total population at 2.9 percent, with the majority living in Alaska, with a population of 21.9 percent for the state (U.S. Census Bureau, 2022). This makes communicating between the tribes as well as understanding government-to-government treaties outside the tribal setting a unique cultural challenge not experienced with other cultural groups in the United States. The term *balancing* or *walking between two worlds* remains applicable to Native American students and youth (Thompson et al., 2013).

Did You Know . . .

The Tribal Boundary and Annexation Survey provides information used by the U.S. Census Bureau. The Census Bureau in turn allows tribal, state, and local governments an opportunity to review these data to ensure that boundary names and status information are correct. See the U.S. Census data listed at the American Indian and Alaska Native Programs section of the U.S. Census website to review the reports and other related information.

Identifying diverse cultural groups will always be insufficient if it does not include the awareness of variation in ethnic communities and the impact of these communities on the lives of those involved (Hiller & Barrow, 2011). Avoiding tokenism holds importance, meaning it is imperative not to assume, for example, that one Muslim student in a group represents all Muslims or that one older person in a group represents all older persons (Olcoń, Gilbert, & Pulliam, 2018; Nadir & Dziegielewski, 2001; Rehman & Dziegielewski, 2003). Nothing could be further from the truth, and this type of attitude can be frustrating, and harmful, for all involved. Yet at times this unfortunate mistake continues to be made, and some assume all individuals in certain groupings are alike. It is critical to remember in all attempts at grouping that individual differences and ethnic variations will always exist.

> ### Did You Know . . .
> The term *homophyly* acknowledges that people derive comfort and support from people who are like themselves. Culturally sensitive social work practice recognizes this phenomenon. It is one reason social workers are always encouraged to use a client's own naturally occurring support network whenever possible. Clients are more likely to achieve needed changes when they can work within a system that is familiar to them. But homophyly can also pose challenges with cross-race/ethnicity/gender/cultural work.

The second step in understanding and recognizing diversity involves factoring in individual differences and life experiences as part of the intervention strategy. Since life experiences can vary, people of similar cultures are not raised in the same manner. When we acknowledge differences, even within similar cultural groups, diversity becomes our superpower. In this way, we recognize the uniqueness of the individual and understand the influence and power of these unique dimensions on the human experience. When helping efforts become inclusive of similarities and differences within a cultural context, successful changes become comprehensive. Therefore, before we talk about the types of practice utilized in social work, it is crucial to understand that when being culturally responsive, similarities and differences among "like" groups can exist. Individualized perspectives can influence behavior and can conflict with expected cultural responses, and once identified, these perceptions can be integrated into the most effective generalist practice strategy.

Understanding, recognizing, and integrating diversity into practice strategy is so important in the field that often social work programs, undergraduate and graduate alike, require students to complete one or more courses on this topic, along with incorporating relevant content across their curricula. Information about diversities is included in every course in your undergraduate or graduate program, so do not be surprised if this topic continually resurfaces in this book in one form or another. Sue and Sue (2013) discuss a concept called cultural universality and how it relates to cultural relativism. The term *etic* relates to what is culturally universal, whereas the term *emic* relates to what is culturally specific. From an etic perspective, the social worker emphasizes an outsider view and what is considered important. From an emic perspective, the social worker looks carefully at the customs and beliefs of the local community.

Since it is unrealistic to say that social workers should be experts in all cultural beliefs, listening to the *client's story* becomes essential. Individualized cultural awareness of diversity starts with the client and the client system and the way the story is defined by the client that is influenced by the client system. This makes listening to the client's story the first step in recognizing the role diversity can play in the helping process.

After these values and beliefs essential to the client and the client system are recognized, this information is applied to any future helping activities. The new social worker should always operate from the emic position, where everything is examined regarding the relevant culture and later challenged and explored as it is applied within the larger system. From this perspective, it is important to outline how cultural values, lifestyles, and worldviews can affect how a client thinks and responds, as well as how they are expected to respond within the client system and how this relates to the community and society at large. This is the person-in-environment focus of social work. Space limits our discussion and focus. Although not all racial/cultural/identity groups can be included in our discussion, the authors expect that by the end of this chapter you will understand three key points: (1) how your own cultural perceptions and potential biases can affect problem identification and helping strategy; (2) that cultural, racial, or ethnic dimensions are critical elements of successful professional helping; and (3) not all people who constitute certain similar groups are the same, so all helping efforts must start and end with listening to the client's story and never underestimating the influence of the client system or the surrounding community.

6.2 MEASUREMENT OF DIVERSE PEOPLE—THE U.S. CENSUS

Since 1790, the U.S. Census has been taken every ten years. This count gives the government direction in a variety of matters, such as the number of U.S. representatives assigned to a state or the amount of funding a state receives from the federal government for certain programs. Census data are used by public and private agencies to chart population trends and shifting mobility patterns. These planners then interpret data and project need and response to changing demographic patterns. For example, at the turn of the twentieth century, census data revealed significant migration streams of people from rural communities to the nation's urban areas, and within a few short years most of the nation's population lived in urban areas. In 2006, the census reported an increase in no-employee businesses or small businesses that do not hire employees. This included family-run businesses or spouse/partner teams and illustrated the changing demographic (see the activity below).

Part 2: The Practice of Social Work

> ### Activity
> Try this. Look up the U.S. and world population clock and see how fast the numbers change.

According to the U.S. and world population clock, on October 17, 2022 (at 9:31 a.m.), the U.S. population was 333,213,359, as compared to the 2005 population estimate of 295.5 million. The U.S. and world population clock is updated regularly, and by the time you read the current number, it will already be out of date! After trying the activity above, you might find that the published numbers vary because the actual survey was conducted several years ago and may no longer be accurate.

The population continues to grow, and therefore the growth-related changes that occurred after the numbers were published are not reflected. In addition, regardless of when the information is collected, it remains difficult to count and subsequently categorize the myriad identities of every person in the United States. Questions to consider are: How would you count the homeless or unhoused population, those who do not live in shelters but stay on the street or experience a high degree of transience? How do you count the migrant worker population (see Figure 6.2)? Or the influx of immigrants who are crossing the borders without documentation? And how do we locate every house, home, or shelter in the United States? Although numerous controls are in place to help with this, the basic problem in recording the total picture can affect many aspects of the numbers being reported.

FIGURE 6.2
Scene from a migrant farm worker camp in Michigan during a visit from President Biden. Workers come to Michigan in June to pick strawberries and leave in late fall, after the apple harvest. The workers travel in vans and trucks as they move from one region of the country to another, following the harvest cycles.

For example, in 2021 it was estimated that 11.6 percent of the U.S. population (37.9 million people) lived in poverty, 11 million of whom are children (16 percent of all children nationwide) (The Anne E. Casey Foundation, 2021). The change in the children's poverty rate from the previous year, according to the Supplemental Poverty Measure, was 5.4, which represents a decrease of 4.5 percentage points from 2020. The exact reason for this is not clear, but during the pandemic, stimulus payments and refundable tax credits lifted 4.6 million children out of poverty. In contrast, the number of adults sixty-five years old and older living in poverty increased by 1.2 percent (U.S. Census Bureau, 2021/2022). Although you may find these numbers helpful, caution should always be used. Dated census information and undercounting of poor and underserved individuals in the population are just two reasons why the numbers generated by the census data are not an absolute measure, but should be viewed as one set of data from a fixed point in time.

6.3 DIVERSITY BY RACE AND ETHNICITY IN THE UNITED STATES

The United States is a patchwork quilt of people—including different genders, old and young people, people of multiple or single races, an array of ethnic groups, and rural and urban dwellers. These are just a few ways to identify diversity. The most common denominator of diversity recognized in the United States seems to be race and/or ethnicity. This understanding is further complicated by couples and families with multiple heritages or multiple races (Kelley & Kelley, 2012). People's identities rarely fit neatly and completely into a "box," and although this desire to box people into simple categories may feel helpful for a quick understanding, it may also limit our ability as social workers to view people in a holistic, or well-rounded and complete, manner.

Have you heard of the *Diagnostic and Statistical Manual of Mental Disorders-5-TR*? The "5" refers to the fifth edition of the book and the "TR" indicates that it includes "text revision." Mental health clinicians and others use the book to help identify mental health disorders. For *DSM-5-TR*, the Ethnoracial Equity and Inclusion Task Force, which was tasked with attention to risk factors such as racism and discrimination, recommended updates to diagnostic descriptions and other supportive information in the text. For example, to emphasize cultural awareness, sensitivity, and inclusivity, the revision stressed the addition of the term *racialized* to replace the terms *race* and *racial*. This new term better describes the socially constructed nature of race and the variation and difficulty in using such definitive words to describe a group of people (American Psychiatric Association, 2022). Other terms the American Psychiatric Association (2022) recommended to avoid were *minority* and *non-White* because of the potential that these terms might create a social hierarchy. The term *Caucasian* was also recommended for removal, and to increase gender inclusiveness the American Psychiatric Association recommended the use of the word *Latinx* instead of *Latina* and *Latino*.

In 1997, the federal government's Office of Management and Budget identified five race categories that remained the key organizing groups to identify diversity for the ten-year census categories, starting with the 2000 census: American Indian and Alaska Native; Asian; Black or African American; Native Hawaiian and other Pacific Islander; and White. The term *Hispanic* was denoted as ethnicity. This category on the 2000 survey was different from that on previous surveys because individuals were given the choice of using one or more racial categories to identify their racial identity. This major change in categorization affected our ability to compare the 2000 and later surveys with those that came from the 1990s and before. In addition, for those who could not fit into any of the above categories, an additional category, "Some other race," was added; in this category, a respondent can simply check the box and write in a more specific racial group. This type of reporting continued into the 2020 survey as well. The growth between the 2010 survey and the 2020 survey for persons of Hispanic or Latino origin in the United States was 23 percent, although the Census Bureau urges caution in interpretation as refinements in language use continue (Jones, Marks, Ramirez, & Ríos-Vargas, 2021).

Within each of these racial groupings are subgroups. For example, Asian includes Asian Indian, Chinese, Filipino, Japanese, Korean, Vietnamese, Cambodian, Hmong, Laotian, Thai, and other Asian. Each of these subgroups has additional identifiers: Hmong, for example, includes people who categorize themselves as Hmong, Laohmong, or Mong. For Hispanic or Latino/Latinx individuals, a self-identification question was used. These individuals were asked if they were persons of Spanish/Hispanic/Latino origin. Further classification of this group included Mexican, Puerto Rican, and Cuban, as well as others who indicated that they were from Spain or the Spanish-speaking countries of Central or South America, or that they were other Hispanic or from other Spanish or Latino origins (U.S. Census Bureau, 2011b). As you can see, the U.S. Census information is always changing, and the best way to stay abreast of what is there is to go to the website (census.gov) and look up the information you want to see.

Did You Know . . .

The U.S. Census Bureau has a large, publicly accessible database filled with data and maps, surveys and programs, and a complete resource library. Go to census.gov/en.html and view the resources available.

When issues of diversity are applied in generalist practice, it is crucial to remember that diversity is not limited to racial identity; it also includes a variety of other attributes. Differences may be obvious, such as those in the spoken language, or more subtle, as in cultural expectations and mores. Unless the social worker is aware of potential differences, misunderstandings can easily impair communication. Knowledge and recognition of differences and variation can help the social worker better understand the client and improve practice strategy.

6.4 THE GENERALIST SOCIAL WORKER AND DIVERSITY

Generalist social workers are employed in a variety of agencies, both public and private, and must develop helping relationships with all kinds of clients. Generalist work, therefore, as articulated in the CSWE Curriculum Policy Statement, requires a broad range of knowledge and skills, allowing problems and their solutions to be assessed comprehensively (CSWE, 2022). Furthermore, the definition that we as a profession use to represent diversity goes beyond that outlined in the U.S. Census. In social work, we are genuinely concerned about enunciating a commitment to improving practices and policies, whether intentional or unintentional, related to racism, immigrants, and refugees, people who identify as LGBTQ+, and people who experience discrimination and marginalization. Moreover, generalist social workers extend beyond what would be considered clinical services, bridging the person-in-situation/person-in-environment stance assisting clients and client systems and allowing for the coordination and expansion on the work of other professionals. In such cases, the generalist is an invaluable member of the helping team, not only bridging the person and the environment, but also facilitating communication and fostering continuity of care (Dziegielewski & Holliman, 2020).

> ### Did You Know . . .
> In 2022, the Board Governance Committee of the NASW adopted the NASW Anti-racism Statement (2022), which reaffirmed its commitment to anti-oppressive practice. The full statement can be read on the NASW website.

Taking an Empowering Approach to Practice

In today's social work practice environment, the idea of empowerment and using client-oriented resources and support systems should not be underestimated (Turner, 2011). It is the uniqueness of the individual, group, or community that we must emphasize in each step of the helping process, whatever the method of practice selected. Further, intervention efforts need to be tied to self-empowerment whereby the changes made are fostered for continuance within the system. To put it simply, when the formal intervention ends, the effects and changes always need to be self-sustaining, evidence-supported, and ideally transformative to the systems and/or policies that produced or contributed to the challenge to begin with. Helping efforts and the interventions that follow require both stressing the importance of scientific method with evidence to support what is done and developing productive relationships with clients (Thyer, 2022a, 2022b; Walsh, 2021). Therefore, the changes must be fostered in such a way that they continue long after the social worker is gone. This is what is meant by the phrase "Social workers aim to put themselves out of business eventually," implying that we want to end the circumstances that invite or require social work intervention in the first place. Enhancing the quality of the social worker–client relationship and decisions about how to best proceed will vary based on "personalities of the parties, the presenting problem, and the impact of the external forces on the relationship, including agency policies" (Walsh, 2021, p. 6). Most clients respond favorably when they are acknowledged for their strengths and challenged to achieve their full potential. Also, when they feel there is a plan that will allow the changes to continue, they can feel secure in what can and will continue to be accomplished.

Empowerment, as a central theme of social work practice, reflects the profession's emphasis on strengths and suggests that the client can make decisions and pursue change. Too often, in looking at a problem, we focus on the pathology rather than on the strengths that the client brings to the situation. For example, when addressing the needs of a client with a disability (or, as could be said, "differing abilities"), we may focus on accommodations needed to participate fully at the workplace. This narrow view, however, can ignore valuable information. The client experiencing trouble functioning may have been unsuccessful in some ways, but what about the ways in which they been successful? Individuals with disabilities often overcome barriers that those without disabilities may not notice. Social workers must always assess the strengths a client has and how the client has overcome obstacles in their life. The emphasis is placed on the client's strengths, resiliency, and coping style, with a clear focus on the client's ability to succeed. What makes more sense if you want to motivate and support someone—focusing on strengths and successes or on problems and failures?

Empowerment also requires providing access to the resources and information necessary for success (Fitzsimons, 2009). We cannot expect clients to succeed if they do not have the resources or know how to get them. When resources are provided without the knowledge of how to make changes self-sustaining, the results will be limited. Trust, respect, and treating the client with civility are all part of empowerment. A sensitivity to diversity means that not all clients will respond to services, or service providers, in the same way. Without these core ingredients, we cannot foster the client's sense of self-worth and ability to look realistically at resolving a problem. People often say that "social workers empower their clients"—and wouldn't it be nice if we had a bag of magic dust that we sprinkle on clients? However, empowerment comes from within. Therefore, social workers help clients find and sharpen the skills and tools they already possess and add support, encouragement, and in some cases direct intervention to help them get the additional resources they need to be successful with the change goals they identify for attainment. Social workers facilitate the empowerment process, but it is the individual client who makes it happen. In addition, the cornerstone of all intervention efforts rests on the social worker's ability to understand his or her own values without imposing those values and beliefs on others (Sue & Sue, 2013). Therefore, cultural confidence rests on self-awareness. From this perspective, the social worker recognizes the importance of *not* encouraging the client to change his or her views to reflect those of the social worker and thus achieves client-centered empowerment.

> ### Did You Know . . .
> Historical foundations are important. The Hollis–Taylor report, a study conducted in 1951, showed that the social work profession was becoming increasingly specialized and fragmented in the delivery of services. Many social workers were treating client problems on a case-by-case basis. The report emphasized a more generic orientation to social work practice, with greater concern for social issues and social action. Many objectives set in this report were accepted by the profession and form the basis of what is taught in many schools of social work today (Barker, 2003).

Recognizing Clients and Client Systems through a Systems Perspective

Social work's mission is to engage in a helping activity that enhances opportunities for all people in an increasingly complex environment. From a systems perspective, the essential realization is that human systems are different from other types of systems (Forder, 2008). Social work professionals deal with a variety of human systems—individuals, couples, families, groups, organizations, and communities. In its simplest form, a *system* consists of parts that interact so that a change in one part affects all others and the relations among them.

In future social work classes and texts, you will come across the term *client system*. The addition of the word *system* indicates that an individual, their family, group, and community are all interrelated; all are part of the individual's galaxy of relations, each influencing the others. In considering the client system, we focus on the individual within their relations with and to other parts of their system and seek to understand the extent to which these influence the client (see the activity below).

> ### Activity
> Visit the U.S. Census Bureau web page and download a copy of the short and long forms for the census. Which do you think provides information that gives a better picture of the diversity of the United States? Why?

Although a client may initially seek individual help, the social worker may determine that expanding and including a spouse or a significant other may increase the chances of positive change (see the case of Don in Box 6.1).

> **BOX 6.1**
>
> ### THE CASE OF DON: CONSIDERING THE CLIENT AND THE CLIENT SYSTEM
>
> Don, a fifty-four-year-old Hispanic male, was not following his diabetic diet and was referred to a social worker for discharge planning. Don's medical condition was worsening, and his physician had become very frustrated with Don's noncompliance with his assigned treatment. According to the physician, Don understood he was causing himself harm and might lose his eyesight if he did not change his behavior. In the interview with the social worker, Don appeared resistant and stated he was trying, but found it hard to stick to his diet. He was too busy and tired when he got home from work to worry about the food he ate. He said his wife worked hard to cook what he liked, and he did not want to disappoint her.
>
> During the interview, the social worker explored Don's situation by asking questions about his lifestyle, his job, and whether he lived alone. Don stated that he had been married for thirty years and had no children. Don's wife was a homemaker who prepared most of the meals, which included packing his lunch that he took to work each day. To find out more about Don's support system, the social worker asked Don if his wife had participated in the dietetic counseling he was provided. Don seemed surprised by the question and said, no, his wife did not participate. When asked why his wife had not participated in any of the educational sessions, Don replied that his partner was never invited. Also, since his partner was such an excellent cook, he was not sure this type of class would interest her.
>
> With Don's permission, the social worker called Don's wife to talk about meeting with them both. The social worker set up a meeting with both Don and his wife to discuss Don's diabetic condition with the dietitian and his physician. At Don's request, the social worker joined them in these meetings, helping Don and his wife to explore what they needed to do to safeguard his health. In discussions, it became apparent to the social worker that Don's wife felt that she might have caused his condition, because her mother-in-law told her that her cooking was what caused his health to worsen. Information about the probable causes of the condition was explained and the social worker provided Don's wife with written materials in Spanish about the condition to take to her mother-in-law. A meeting with the dietician was also arranged and copies of meal plans were provided for sharing with relatives, if needed, to assure them that they were working together on his health issues. The counseling the social worker provided helped the couple feel more secure with immediate needs, as well as how to address the concerns of other family members. After this intervention and at a six-week follow-up, Don continued to follow his diet regime. He even joked that his wife was enjoying the cooking classes that she had attended and now he never knew what he was going to eat for lunch or supper. He said he missed the foods he was

CHAPTER 6: RECOGNIZING DIVERSITY AND APPLYING IT TO GENERALIST PRACTICE

> raised on, but knew he had to limit them, so they would have a traditional dinner every other week. He also stated that he wished he could get his mother to attend the cooking classes his wife was attending, but did not think she would consider it. The social worker suggested that Don invite her for a meal, and if she liked it, he could offer to provide her with the recipe written in Spanish that she could try on her own.

Consider the case described in Box 6.1 in which the social worker was given a referral to see one client, Don, but after meeting and talking with him realized the importance of including Don's wife and his dietitian. A basic assessment, intervention plan, and referral process initiated by the social worker with Don's permission and participation helped to harness the strengths of the client system, thereby helping Don to promote his own physical health, while respecting his cultural beliefs.

In addition to addressing Don's particular needs, the social worker believed that advocacy might be needed to help other clients like Don. The social worker talked with other professionals in the hospital to inquire about similar prior occurrences. It soon became apparent that Don's situation was not unusual, but in fact represented a larger pattern in the broader population (macro level). The discussions initiated by the social worker led to the issue being brought before the hospital's quality care management team and the development of a new protocol that required interviewing and assessing all diabetic clients regarding their living situations. It also required that they assess the language they communicated in to ensure that any written materials were consistent with the language spoken by the client and within the client system. This advocacy did not benefit Don directly, but it benefited others who could be prevented from landing in an analogous situation.

For the generalist social worker using a systems perspective, the helping activity assumes four roles: education, advocacy, facilitation, and intervention. Through this perspective, the social worker serves as enabler, broker, mediator, advocate, resource person, gatekeeper, educator, and trainer (Chan & Law, 2008). While performing these functions that often overlap the helping activities, social workers often go beyond working with the originally identified client.

In client advocacy, the first step in the helping process involves education related to factors in the client's situation. Problem-focused education is intended to increase awareness of the services needed and to empower clients to address problems that previously seemed insurmountable. The social worker's practice activities often involve helping clients to secure the information they need and fostering connections that link clients to services and resource systems that contribute to resolving their problems.

Social workers can educate clients in many different areas. In Don's case, the social worker provided education in the meeting with Don and his wife while focusing on the wife's concerns about the family blaming her for making him ill. The couple needed to be educated in an atmosphere where they were comfortable asking questions about the causes of diabetes. The social worker could work with the couple to facilitate communication by exploring questions or having them write down the questions to ask the physician at the next visit. The social worker also saw the wife's frustration with the family and suggested that the wife take home written information to show them that the husband was being taking care of as expected and was "following orders." Facilitating the meeting with the dietitian was important to discuss the medical need for Don to continue the proposed diet and the consequences if it was not followed. Getting written copies of the meal plans in Spanish and English helped to formalize what the wife was trying to do in terms of cooking differently. The worker facilitated the dialogue between the dietitian and the family and helped to support, both in asking questions and clarifying discussion. After the meeting, Don's wife understood what was needed and Don's diet compliance improved dramatically, working toward the overall goal of improving his health. This case demonstrates how a social worker can assist by educating the entire client system—the client, his family, and other members of the delivery team.

Education is important in all practice settings. Child abuse, domestic violence and incest dynamics, parent–child relations, caregiving, homemaker services, and health care, just to name a few, are areas in which education commonly takes place. Social workers understand the importance of going beyond the traditional bounds of simply providing supportive counseling. They can assist in educating clients to better maintain not only their own safety, security, and wellness, but also that of their families. Indeed, social workers are uniquely placed to participate in education, particularly in the areas of prevention and continued health and wellness.

Activity

Look at yourself as a part of a system. Identify the components of your galaxy—family, friends, associations, workplace, and other aspects of your life. Imagine arranging these items with "me" in the middle and drawing a circle around each one to indicate the portion of your environment that it makes up. Do any of the circles overlap? For example, do you work with any members of your family? Is one circle more influential than the others? Why? Do any of the circles influence the others?

Advocacy also helps clients to identify their own strengths and use individual and community resources to support their efforts to change. Advocacy does not always mean doing something for the client; it often means helping or teaching the client how to do things for themself. Issues of individual worth and dignity must always be considered. Therefore, every social worker must know how to maintain cultural integrity while fostering change, allowing diversity to flourish. In social work, the easiest way to remember advocacy is to think of the old saying, "Give them a fish and you feed them for a day; teach them how to fish and you feed them for a lifetime." In social work, advocacy is not just giving the client and client systems a fish; it is teaching them how to fish. The client and client system are encouraged to develop their own goals and resources, and from this perspective, self-reliance and resilience are highlighted. In these cases, when the helping activities end, the change efforts made do not.

Facilitation consists of making connections among different resource systems that enhance responsiveness and usefulness. The social worker may contact agencies to support and mobilize the client and others in the client system. It is here that direct intervention is found, whereby the social worker makes the connections needed to help the client (e.g., arranging transportation services to a medical appointment or registration with programs such as Meals on Wheels). Direct intervention occurs when the client is unable to intervene on their own behalf or simply needs assistance to do so successfully.

6.5 PERSON-IN-SITUATION: GUIDING THE PRACTICE FRAMEWORK

Generalist practice is more than simply combining methods of practice such as casework, group work, and community organizing. It requires a theoretical practice framework involving structured ideas and beliefs that provide a foundation for helping. Within this framework, the applied knowledge and theory are consistent with social work values and ethics from a person-in-situation context. Reamer (2020) reminds us that regardless of how services are delivered, including digital technology, all services are influenced by traditional ethical concepts and values. The long-standing assumption of commitment to multiculturalism, feminism, and anti-racism has not waivered and the ties of these beliefs to a philosophical foundation remain clear (Reamer, 2022). This person-in-situation or person-in-environment context differentiates social work from other helping professions. Additionally, most professional social workers feel strongly that practice should be guided by theory. Therefore, engaging in a theory absent from practice is deficient, helping efforts are decreased, and the client system is deprived of needed professional helping activities.

> ### Did You Know . . .
> Lee Frankel (1867–1931) was an early social work educator and developer of family casework theories and practice. He established the Training School for Jewish Social Work in New York and became a national leader in early health and welfare organizations (Barker, 2003).

Assessing the client and the client system is essential to any application of a conceptual framework used to understand and assess human relations in context in social work. It reflects the person-in-situation or person-in-environment stance that has always reinforced social work practice, focusing attention on an individual, a collective, a policy, a program, a practice, or any concrete or abstract unit in dynamic interaction with an environment.

In social work, the practice framework selected always addresses issues of human diversity. As we have stated throughout this book, social workers always recognize and respect human diversity when forming and maintaining professional relations. Furthermore, social workers are committed to promoting social justice and professional ethical conduct. Social work has historically been concerned with oppressed and disadvantaged populations. The profession's focus on human diversity and social justice reinforces its ethically driven commitment to serving people who do not receive an equitable share of social resources. The commitment and adherence to a professional code of conduct is essential for any type of professional practice, be it generalist or specialist.

For beginning social work professionals, deciding where and how best to engage the client can be difficult because this choice must be linked to the theoretical principles that underlie certain types of helping activities. To accomplish this goal, the social worker reviews the client's situation and, based on the client's needs, decides what theoretical perspective to use. In other words, it is the client's, not the worker's, comfort with or allegiance to a particular practice theory that drives the choice of perspective. The theoretical practice approach and helping strategy are firmly based in the reality of the client's environment.

At times, making this link may seem too difficult or time-consuming, but acknowledging the relation between environment and the selected practice method is critical. For example, one of the authors worked with an elderly male client with a history of alcohol abuse who received treatment, only to be discharged back into an environment that encouraged him to relapse. The return to his previous environment negated much of the influence of the intervention and started a pattern of repeated rehabilitation attempts with numerous admissions to treatment centers. He always seemed to respond well while in the program, but on discharge he quickly relapsed into alcohol abuse. After numerous failed interventions, he was referred to a social worker. The social worker assessed his situation thoroughly and examined the home environment to which he was returning. The social worker discovered that because of his instability and troubles with alcohol, the client was unable to maintain a bank account. Therefore, when it was time to cash his social security check, he used the local bar as his bank. His check arrived each month, he picked it up, and he went to the one place he knew was willing to cash it—that local bar. To complicate matters, the bar would cash checks only upon purchase. It is clear what the consequences were. Assessing the client's discharge environment was critical to applying a helping strategy. To assist the client, the social worker initiated a supervised living arrangement and helped the client to acquire his own bank account, in which his social security check was directly deposited. In addition, it was important to address the client system in which all his social contacts revolved around drinking at the local bar. Helping to create a new social support system became critical to his continued sobriety.

The helping strategy must be congruent with the needs and desires of the client system being served, as well as reflective of the values and ethics of the social work profession. Beginning social workers often feel trapped within a system driven by social, political, cultural, and economic factors that are so powerful that they influence the practice techniques and skills that are utilized. In addressing the needs of poor and disadvantaged individuals and those who are different from the majority culture, recognizing the diversity of problems and how they relate to the people who experience them makes social work practice an art. How can social workers constantly evaluate what is happening to the client and whether societal factors—race, sexual orientation, and so forth—affect the way a problem is viewed? How can the beginning professional consider all system variables that affect the helping relationship? How does a social worker maintain the dignity and worth of each client served and ensure that his or her own feelings and prejudices never enter the helping relationship?

The social work profession celebrates all forms of diversity and recognizes that differences among people provide valuable opportunities and tools in the helping relationship. At the same time, there is another side to diversity that we must address—fear of others and their differences. Sociology refers to this as *xenophobia*, a fear or hatred of foreigners or strangers. Hate crimes are a direct by-product of xenophobia and are directed at people who are *different*—differences are based on characteristics such as race, sex, gender or gender identity, sexual orientation, religious affiliation, or political views. Simply stated, there is no logic to a hate crime other than fear. Social workers recognize that clients are often victims, or at risk of being victims, of hate crimes. If a client has values or beliefs that could lead to hate crimes and actions, the social worker must be able to identify them and help the client address them before a potential hate crime erupts.

> ### Did You Know . . .
> See the website for the Southern Poverty Law Center, which features numerous resources and examples of hate and extremism and policy recommendations for change.

Extreme difficulty accepting and adjusting to differences can lead to hate crimes, and this unfounded fear and hostility are directed at the victim as a member of a group, based on color, creed, gender, or sexual orientation. This makes self-awareness and self-knowledge central to the helping process (Morgaine & Capous-Desyllas, 2015). Understanding our own values and beliefs is the starting point for recognizing the importance of honoring differences in others. There are no easy answers as to how best to address the client in their environment. Addressing each of the questions posed in this section of the chapter and giving it the attention it deserves would require examining different books. Yet it is critical that each client and client system is assessed carefully and treated individually, no matter how similar a case may be to one the social worker has already encountered.

6.6 CULTURAL AWARENESS AND SELECTING A PRACTICE METHOD

A multitude of factors must be considered in selecting the most appropriate practice method. What are the needs of the client? Who makes up the client system? What is the target of change? What resources are available to the client system? What is the probability of success given the many elements that can affect the situation? This already sounds complicated, and in fact it is only a small part of what needs to be addressed when choosing a practice method. Now add to this being aware of cultural diversity and how it can affect the helping efforts. You will learn more about these factors and others in future social work practice classes.

Although it is beyond the scope of this book to explain the many theoretical and practice frameworks available to social workers and how to use them, we will explain the most customary practice methods: *micropractice*, *mezzopractice*, and *macropractice*.

Micropractice, more commonly called direct or clinical practice, with target populations including individuals, families, and groups, primarily uses face-to-face in-person or virtual platforms with clients. Because people deliver services, not programs, emphasis is placed on the highly trained case manager or clinical social worker. It is at the micro level where the emphasis remains on ensuring ongoing supervision, training, and continuing education designed to improve individual skills and strategy (Walsh & Holton, 2008). From this perspective, it is often assumed that the greatest interest lies in the for-profit sector and private practice. The introduction of virtual networks and teletherapy has provided a whole new practice arena for many social workers assisting from a distance and ensuring greater accessibility. Yet, for social workers, special attention should always be given to those who may not have access to this technology, as well as ensuring any virtual therapeutic encounter is protected for client safety and privacy of confidential information.

Mezzopractice involves environmental system variables and agency administration with minimal client contact; it examines agency effectiveness and policy implementation. It can also evaluate the quality of programming, systematic organizational barriers, and organizational management functions, including trends with respect to market stabilization of human capital stressing employee maintenance and well-being (Cabrera & Raju, 2001; Everhart & Wandersman, 2000). When agencies offer adequate material supports such as compensation packages, agreeable working conditions, and adequate agency material supports, workers are more likely to stay and support the programs offered (Walsh & Holton, 2008).

Macropractice defines the client more extensively, to include the community or organizations; it often deals with broader social problems that affect the community. Here, the greatest emphasis is often on working in social change agencies or community-based coalitions and the application of skills designed to change social programs and policies for the betterment of all involved (Segal-Engelchin & Kaufman, 2008).

In the broadest of terms, micropractice is undertaken with individuals, families, and small groups; mezzopractice is directed at organizational administration; and macropractice involves activities and change within larger systems, such as communities and organizations. You might be thinking that we are playing semantic games—that micro, mezzo, and macro are just new names for casework, group work, and community practice. This is not completely true because all three perspectives—micro, mezzo, and macro—apply a client-systems perspective to analyzing the presenting problem. For example, there are not multiple foci in micropractice; the individual's system is the

CHAPTER 6: RECOGNIZING DIVERSITY AND APPLYING IT TO GENERALIST PRACTICE

focus—note the use of singular versus plural. Micropractice involves an individual client with a presenting problem, and our work includes assessment of the system's role in creating, sustaining, or solving the problem—in fact, the system may play all three roles.

As we have discussed in a number of places in this book, social work has two significant professional goals. The first is to help people to achieve their potential and to adjust more effectively to the demands of their situation within their environment. The second is to make social resources more responsive to people's needs, particularly for poor and disadvantaged people who often are avoided or neglected. Incorporating these goals into the helping process reinforces social work's dual focus on personal and social problems and emphasizes the importance of linking micro, mezzo, and macro change efforts.

Micropractice

In micropractice, the focus is on the individual and their system. When individuals are helped directly on the micro level, strengths are highlighted. From the strengths-based approach, the individual is the hero and change agent (Jones-Smith, 2014; see Box 6.2 for the example of Maria).

BOX 6.2

THE CASE OF MARIA: MICROPRACTICE

Maria, at age twenty-two, was a victim of rape at her workplace. At the outset of the criminal investigation, she met a victim's advocate, who was a BSW social worker employed by the police department. The advocate brought Maria to the hospital and became a major support person for her in the following days. During one of their conversations, the advocate learned that Maria had been a victim of sexual abuse during her childhood. The rape, compounded with her childhood experiences, now had put Maria in a very vulnerable emotional and psychological state: she was unable to go to work or meet family or friends, saying that she would rather just stay at home. Maria blamed herself for the rape, stating, "I deserved it. Look at my whole life. I deserve it all." The social worker quickly recognized that Maria needed more in-depth help. She referred Maria to a family service agency, where Maria first took part in individual sessions with an MSW social worker.

After a month, the social worker asked Maria how she felt about joining a group of women who had been raped. At first Maria refused, but with gentle, persistent encouragement from the social worker, she reluctantly joined the weekly group. Maria's group included seven other women aged eighteen to fifty-two. All the participants reached out to Maria and welcomed her. The social worker, who facilitated the group, told Maria that she did not need to talk unless she wanted to. Discussion at Maria's first group meeting focused on the court hearing. Women shared their fears about the hearings, and some who had been through the courts shared their experiences. Subsequent sessions looked at anger control, relationship building, and becoming a survivor. Maria became an active member of the group and after one year joined the police department as a volunteer victim's advocate.

Maria is a client who survived being raped. After the event, Maria was so traumatized that she feared leaving her apartment. A social worker serving as a victim's advocate proved instrumental in helping Maria to overcome many of her initial fears. The social worker provided a supportive role with a constant reassuring presence for Maria during the challenging times following the rape. The advocate explored issues from Maria's childhood and identified unresolved feelings that resurfaced following the rape. Rather than trying to provide in-depth clinical help to Maria, the advocate referred her to a more advanced MSW social worker who had expertise in violence against women. The skilled worker was able to help Maria by using a variety of strategies including both education and supportive therapeutic techniques. When Maria started to stabilize her individual feelings, a referral for group sessions with other survivors helped to validate Maria's experiences and allowed her to share with other group members.

In micropractice, as in all social work methods, social worker and client work together to establish goals and objectives and to develop the steps that must be taken to reach these goals. A typical micro approach has social workers dealing with the client system, which goes beyond the individual client and includes family members and significant others and, at times, other groups of people. In this micro approach, the first step is always deciding what the client wants and taking the action needed to help make it happen (Lanci & Spreng, 2008). Thyer (2022a) warns, however, that all information gathered in addressing the needs of the client should be based on empirical data that clearly outline what has been done and the treatment gains that have been made. Maria, for example, was first seen as an individual and later referred to the group setting to continue the intervention process. Had Maria's family lived in the same geographic area, they too might have become directly involved in the healing process.

Mezzopractice

Mezzopractice involves minimal face-to-face client contact, focusing on administrative intervention within the agency's organizational structure. Some schools of social work recognize this level of practice, whereas others may link this as part of micropractice or macropractice. When mezzopractice is recognized, it typically involves administrative titles including supervisor, unit director, director, executive director, chief executive officer, and president. What is essential in mezzo opportunities is that when the social service agency has a more positive work and service environment, staff turnover will be less, and the delivery of higher-quality services can result (Glisson, 2008).

Many micropractice-level workers do engage in mezzo activities, however. In fact, any competent social worker will be knowledgeable and possess basic abilities in mezzo-level tasks. Organizing the workload, preparing monthly reports, conducting policy analysis, supervising staff, and making public presentations to service groups are all mezzo tasks that micro workers will find themselves undertaking.

Individuals in mezzopractice roles are usually agency focused and develop expertise in several areas, but particularly the following:

- Agency policy formulation and implementation
- Program development, funding, budgeting, and resource allocation
- Management duties such as staff and professional supervision
- Agency representation and linkage with internal and external groups
- Agency representation such as community presentations
- Agency or organizational evaluations of agency effectiveness in process and outcome evaluations.

You will find MSW workers assigned to mezzo positions in agencies, whereas BSW workers are often limited to direct service lines. This may not be the case in rural and small communities, however, where fewer MSW professionals are available and the BSW worker is more likely to find an administrative assignment. Although their knowledge and skills may not be as broad and as deep of those of master-level practitioners, baccalaureate practitioners do possess beginning knowledge and skills in mezzo work.

Macropractice

Macropractice directs the worker's attention to change in the larger community, organizational, and policy arenas (Burghardt, 2014; Hepworth et al., 2023). Like community organization, macro work involves helping individuals, groups, and communities with common interests to deal with "social problems and to enhance well-being through planned collective action" (Barker, 2003, p. 84). In macropractice, the problems identified do not focus on an individual, but rather on a community. The changes often are done on a much larger scale or higher level and can take longer to achieve because they must occur for community good, not specifically for an individual. All needs, concerns, or problems identified are negotiated within the system, and the only benefit to the individual is what is gained through system change. Just as micro practitioners and mezzo practitioners have specialized knowledge and skills, so too does the macro worker.

Did You Know . . .

Mother Jones was Mary Harris Jones (1830–1930), a community organizer and labor union advocate who led many strikes against inhumane treatment of children and adults. She advocated better child labor laws and less dangerous working conditions in the mining and steel industries (Barker, 2003).

The macro worker has expertise in the following areas:

- Communities, their composition, and type—for example, geographic or identity based
- Power structures within communities and their influence within communities

- Policy-making procedures
- Advocating for human service organizations and their purposes, functions, and constituencies
- Dynamics and nuances of social problems
- Macro-specific tasks such as collaboration and capacity building, negotiation, task group dynamics, marketing, research and analysis, and teaching

Macropractice builds on recognizing private issues that have their roots in public matters. Substance abuse, for example, involves individuals. Yet the abuse quickly becomes a public matter when it leads to increased crime related to the selling of drugs, lack of workforce participation or missed work as a result of drug abuse, poor school grades and eventual dropout, and family dysfunction. In the example described in Box 6.3, the macro approach involved a not-so-subtle nonviolent confrontation with a local storeowner.

As outlined in Box 6.3, the owner was not sure which would be worse: the wrath of the drug dealers or the lack of neighbors who would purchase items from his store. He decided the latter, and with help from the local police department, drug sales

---

BOX 6.3

THE CASE OF A DRUG-FREE COMMUNITY: MACROPRACTICE

A drug-related shooting took place in the middle of the day in a poor area of town. A few people gathered that evening in a local church and decided that they had had enough, but they did not know what to do. One of the participants was a social worker from the local neighborhood center. She suggested that the group in fact knew what it wanted—a drug-free community—but now needed to figure out where to begin to make this happen. The group expanded and created a neighborhood drug-free task force to act as a conduit for the community. Neighbors were invited to share their frustrations at meetings held in churches, school halls, and the neighborhood center. Local social service agencies and elected and appointed officials were asked to come and listen to the neighbor's concerns.

Out of these meetings came a plan for a march through the neighborhood, with the police leading the parade and marching with citizens. The social worker took a leadership role in facilitating discussions, but the community group made the decisions on what to do next and how to move forward. The group decided to include a social action activity by marching to the primary spot where drugs were sold, a mom-and-pop convenience store one block from the public elementary school. Once at the store, the marchers, about two hundred people, formed a long, single-file line, and each walked in without saying a word and left one dollar on the counter. The police stood in front of the store and within minutes the drug pushers had disappeared! Over the following weeks, the storeowner worked with the local task force and police; the drug pushers stopped selling in the neighborhood and moved out of the community. The storeowner also joined the task force when it took on other substance abuse issues in the community.

disappeared from the area. As an interesting note, when the group's organizer was told that the dealers were only going to another neighborhood, he responded, "Then that's their problem and they will have to organize them out of the community like we did."

> ## Did You Know . . .
> Hull House is the most famous of all settlement houses, founded in Chicago in 1889 by Jane Addams. Settlement houses were community centers where poor and disadvantaged residents of the area could go for help. These centers were major innovators in social reform.

In this application of macropractice, the social worker helped the group to develop a plan of action and supported the group as it organized itself. The worker facilitated the process, helped to mobilize significant agencies and local leaders, and provided background research—equipping the neighborhood group with the tools it needed to become successful. What began as an individual problem ended up as a community macro issue whose resolution brought about significant changes in the daily lives of individuals, families, and organizations in the neighborhood (see the activity below).

> ## Activity
> Go to the library and find the journal *Social Work*, volume 43, number 6. Think about what the articles in this special issue tell you about the following questions:
>
> 1. What types of contributions did social workers make in micropractice, mezzopractice, and macropractice? How has this changed in practice today?
>
> 2. How do social workers feel about the NASW Code of Ethics, and what does it mean to each area of social work practice discussed in this chapter?
>
> 3. What issues in the history of social work do you believe helped to make the profession what it is today?
>
> 4. What issues in the field of social work identified still need the attention of today's workers?

6.7 RECOGNIZING DIVERSITY AND SHORT-TERM, EVIDENCE-BASED INTERVENTION APPROACHES

This chapter would be remiss if it did not relate recognizing the importance of diversity to conducting micro, mezzo, and macro levels of practice, When looking specifically at the micro- and mezzo-level interventions, whether we like it or not, current social work practice is dominated by short-term, evidence-based practice models where interventions that can clearly document effectiveness remain the focus (Thyer, 2022a, 2022b).

Presentation, suggestions, application, and a more complete discussion of these approaches are for another course in your studies, although knowledge of the focus will assist you in starting your search while remaining mindful of the importance of addressing diversity.

There are many approaches that could fall into this category, but regardless of the methods used, two requirements seem to overlap. The first is that the helping process needs to occur quickly (short duration) and the second is to provide evidence that it works. This means clearly identifying what the client wants to accomplish and working out a system to measure the accomplishments of the goals and objectives outlined (Dziegielewski, 2015). Practice reality dictates that the duration of most practice sessions, regardless of the methodology used or the orientation of the mental health practitioner, remain brief. For social workers, brief treatment must always be sensitive to the client's needs and starts with being culturally aware and recognizing the client's story.

For many practitioners, seeing a client only once (whether in person or virtually) is becoming commonplace, with the realization that most practice encounters are going to be brief and self-contained because they may not occur again. There are many reasons for this trend, but the major influence is money: getting the "biggest bang for the buck." Our current environment is limited in terms of financial and human resources, and there is little chance that this will ever change (Ligon, 2009). Insurance companies, as third-party payers (those who pay a provider for services to another person, thus third party), and health care organizations continue to limit the time during which a client system may receive a service. Simply stated, third-party payers will not underwrite long-term intervention when it is believed that a short-term solution is what is needed, even if the end is less desirable than what a longer-term approach may yield. Many social workers therefore employ time-limited approaches as a major practice model and realize that, to do this, the goals and objectives mutually negotiated with the client and the client system need to be clearly defined and achievable. The goals also need to consider the cultural environment and the influences the client system can have on the outcome.

In other cases, clients simply do not have the time, desire, or money for long-term micro-level social work services. People today are working more hours, sometimes two jobs, and have less time to devote to the self, family, friends, or outside interests. With less time available, they are unwilling to commit extra time and energy to go beyond simply addressing the cause of the problem. The promise of a simple solution is a temptation to begin, but if it is done in haste, reoccurrence remains a concern. Also, some cultures are very protective of personal and family information and what is shared, and this can complicate a simple, logical path to resolution.

Practitioners can become frustrated when the presenting problem and the underlying issues clearly require considering the culture and community perceptions that require a long-term strategy built into the system, not the individual client. Yet so often, and for any number of reasons, the emphasis is placed on the surface issue. In addition, beginning-level social workers may not see the importance of considering the culture

CHAPTER 6: RECOGNIZING DIVERSITY AND APPLYING IT TO GENERALIST PRACTICE

and societal beliefs related to social welfare policy. It is not uncommon for students taking policy courses to complain, "Why do I need this course? It has nothing to do with social work!" Just listen to the news related to the ongoing national debate about health insurance and how diverse individuals are treated within the system, affecting the resulting service. This information outlines clearly why we need to understand policy and how recognizing diversity and cultural influences provides stimulus for its scope and design. Our practice and our ability to help clients succeed grows out of advocating for the needed policy changes. Stated simply, when we change policy, we can change practice. Recognize, modify, and change the ways that third-party payers reimburse clients and professionals for service, and you can change your practice. Consider the individualized needs of the client as part of a culturally diverse client system and success will be enhanced. Over the years, as policies have evolved, social workers, especially those in discharge planning and case management, understand that insurance rarely covers long-term encounters or placements, and yet the pressure for quick fixes remains the expected norm (Dziegielewski & Holliman, 2020).

In generalist practice, we must realize that social work practice encounters are going to be brief, and it may be easy to overlook diverse cultural factors and how they influence problem-solving success. Planning for this short duration in implementing a helping strategy is critical; lack of planning can result in numerous unexpected endings for the client and feelings of failure and decreased job satisfaction or even exit from the job market for the social work professional (Cabrera & Raju, 2001). Limited time and service provision where cultural factors are ignored can result in increased job complexity and fewer defined procedures for achievable successful outcomes.

Name: Dr. Jacqueline Richardson-Melecio, LMSW, PhD
Place of residence: Capital District, New York
College/university degrees: University at Albany, Albany, New York, PhD, MSW, BA
Present position: President and owner, Equity Dynamics, LLC—a diversity, equity, and inclusion consulting firm. We are committed to providing training and consulting programs that support organizations by enhancing knowledge, awareness, and skill in understanding how diversity impacts every component of organizational structure (www.equity-dynamics.org).

Previous work experience/volunteer experience:
- Associate vice president, chief of diversity, SUNY University of Potsdam; executive director, Center for Excellence in Aging University of New York, Quality Technical Assistance Center; assistant executive director, National Association of Social

continues

continued

Workers, NYS; managing director, Mental Health Association in New York State; program director, Hispanic Outreach Services Catholic Charities; member of New York State Office of Mental Health, Multicultural Advisory Committee; training consultant: diversity training, leadership development, and strategic planning.

Teaching/training: Adjunct instructor, University at Albany, St. Rose College, Schenectady Community College, Hudson Valley Community College
- Master-level courses: multicultural counseling, mental health policy, human resource management
- Bachelor-level courses: sociology; Spanish for human service providers; workshops and seminars on diversity, equity, and inclusion

Bio statement:

Dr. Richardson-Melecio, LMSW, PhD, is an author, speaker, consultant, trainer, a diversity, equity, inclusion and belonging (DEIB) expert, doctoral-level researcher, licensed master's social worker (LMSW), and experienced executive. To her work she brings over twenty-five years of executive-level management, program development, delivery of human services, and large-scale workforce development initiatives experience. She has committed her career to supporting organizations in building awareness, knowledge, and skill in developing and sustaining diversity, equity, inclusion, and belonging initiatives.

Her experience extends to founding and presiding over Equity Dynamics LLC, a DEI consulting company. As an experienced consultant, trainer, and educator she has addressed the challenges of social, political, and economic determinants of human conditions and translated this knowledge into solutions for complex systems of care and corporate structures. She has provided consultation and training services to corporate, government, educational institutions, health, and community-based organizations to develop and strengthen the efficacy and overall capacity for diversity, equity, and inclusion across all organizational components. In her book *Belonging: Intentional Inclusivity*, she translates knowledge into strategies, and strategies into solutions for leaders determined to create workspaces that value diversity, employ equity, and practice inclusivity.

What is your favorite social work story? My favorite social work story occurred prior to my career as a social worker. When I reflect upon my community and the people who surrounded me my whole life, I do not have any doubt about what inspired me to be a social worker. Although predominately Hispanic, my neighborhood was wonderfully rich in cultures, customs, and languages, with community members representing diverse racial and ethnic backgrounds. The early evenings of hot summer days were made up of unscheduled gatherings of young and old on the front steps. The crowd would usually extend out into the sidewalk; parked cars would sometimes be used as benches, and folding chairs and steps would also serve as seats. The grown-ups chattered while they rested from a long day at work. The scene is still fresh in my mind, of children playing games like hopscotch, catch, or hide and seek while a few sat and talked and shared a joke or two.

CHAPTER 6: RECOGNIZING DIVERSITY AND APPLYING IT TO GENERALIST PRACTICE

> If I lean into my memories of those days, I can still hear the sounds like the very air around us: the laughter, screaming cheers, music, and pitter-patter of little feet, and the many voices as folks joined in multiple conversations and talked about their day, their hopes, and their dreams. All of this served as the backdrop to what I deem to be social work in its most natural state—resource sharing, capacity building. At these organic gatherings, you see resource sharing in many forms: referrals, housing assistance, job coaching and employment services, and counseling. It all happened so naturally every day and just because you were a part of the community, a neighbor in need, another human being. So, my favorite social work story is also my inspiration for being a social worker: being part of a profession committed to making a difference in the lives of others because it is the right thing to do. The best of our humanity shows up in the ways we are present for others.
>
> *What would be the one thing you would change in the community if you had the power to do so?* It is challenging to think of just one thing to change. Access to health care, homelessness, and hunger, the elimination of bias, racism and discrimination are all things at the top of my list. Absent the magic wand we all wish we had to erase the ills of the world, it is my life's quest never to lose hope and faith in the best of our humanity. And in the spaces, seats, and tables I have the privilege to join during my journey, I want to continue to work towards change, to be the change I want to see in the world, to make a difference.

6.8 WE WILL NEVER HAVE ALL THE ANSWERS!

Several years ago, a T-shirt frequently seen at social work gatherings had a Superman logo on the front and yellow and red lettering that spelled out "Super Social Worker." The apparent exaggeration was ironic, because at times the efforts of social workers really did seem Herculean. No one can dispute, however, that social workers are human beings and therefore, unlike Superman, they are vulnerable. Given the complexity that is required to be culturally responsive, they may not always have the ideal, quick, and easy solution to a problem. Systems are limited and most helping strategies can only go so far. Social workers are only human, and humans are culturally diverse in belief and response!

Therefore, all social workers must be aware of the services available, remain culturally responsive, and try their best to mitigate any potential harm that may come to the clients served. Moreover, when a social worker does not have an answer to a problematic situation, it should be viewed as a *learning moment*. A natural reaction may be to act defensively and to try to blame the standardized protocol, the system, or the lack of services; however, professionals take responsibility for what they do, remaining culturally aware and responsive, and for knowing the services that are available. One important skill of the generalist social worker is learning to recognize what services are available in the system and how the client and the client system can benefit in times of need. When in supervision with a trained professional, the beginning social worker can explore previous helping strategies, as if watching them on videotape. Successful interventions at the micro, mezzo, and macro levels all require evaluating what happened and what might have happened had some other strategy been implemented. To assist with cultural awareness, responsiveness, and sensitivity while implementing time-limited strategy, social workers use professional supervision as a forum for these detailed discussions so that the same or similar mistakes can be avoided in the future. The most powerful resource that a social worker has is the ability to seek supervisory help or peer consultation to better explore cultural awareness and responsiveness in defining a problem.

6.9 CULTURAL AWARENESS, SENSITIVITY, AND INCLUSION IN PRACTICE

In all areas and levels of generalist practice, social workers must help clients to maintain cultural integrity and must respect diversity. The term *ethnic identity* is defined as common heritage, customs, and values unique to a group of people (Fong, 2009). Social science researchers often gather information on race and ethnicity, yet the difference between these two concepts is pronounced and accounts for the changes we already discussed that were implemented by the U.S. Census Bureau. Historically, race has been understood as partly based on physical characteristics of genetic origin (Helms, 1990). Ethnicity embraces a much broader range of commonalities, such as religion, customs, geography, and history. These commonalities between individuals and within a community define and bond members, thereby giving an ethnic backdrop to everyday life. Ethnicity can thus influence thinking and feeling and can pattern behavior in both obvious and subtle ways (Sakamoto & Pitner, 2005). It is easy to overlook the deeper influence of ethnicity because it often is natural and consists simply of daily behavior—for example, what individuals eat or how they react.

The development of ethnic identity occurs on a continuum determined by acceptance of one's ethnicity (Sakamoto & Pitner, 2005). Clients may either embrace or reject their own ethnicity and can be influenced by a particular reference group that is influential in dictating behavior and decision-making practices. Personal identity is how an individual sees themselves, whereas ascribed identity is how society values or perceives her or him. Crucial to understanding the concept of ethnicity is realizing that, although it is a potent factor in the professional helping relationship, it is not easy to identify, and the degree to which it influences life decisions and behavior is not the same for every client.

To provide culturally aware and inclusive practice, social workers must avoid applying a narrow cultural lens that can interpret client-system traditions and problem-solving processes as abnormal or dysfunctional. In mental health, for example, social workers must thoroughly interpret, seek to understand, appreciate, and assess cultural differences to enable providers to develop culturally compatible services. For example, the social worker who works with an Asian client needs to be aware of how they understand and live Asian customs and expectations. In Asian cultures, there may be resistance to outside intervention because family matters are viewed as private. In the mental health area, there is shame and stigma attached to needing these types of services (Ofahengaue-Vakalahi & Fong, 2009). Social workers must be aware of and respect this cultural tradition and know how it can affect the helping relationship. Cultural awareness and humility must extend beyond the general task of making services more accessible and include specifically relevant therapeutic interpretations to guide the framework used.

One last issue in providing culturally sensitive practice from a systems perspective is that the beliefs and values of social workers and other helping professionals reflect those of the greater society (Dziegielewski, 2015). Since all professionals are products of their environment and everyone's story can be different, knowing what the social worker believes is central to not letting these beliefs influence the client's beliefs. Social workers, like other professional helpers, can view a client's actions or behaviors within the client system differently if viewed through their own cultural lens. This self-influenced interpretation, consequently, can lead the social worker to overlook the client's needs or encourage exploring solutions that may not work within the client system. All helping strategy needs to help the client and the client system maintain cultural and ethnic heritage as well as feelings of integrity throughout the intervention process. It is therefore the role of the social worker to acknowledge and facilitate family adjustment and acculturation, whether working with Asians, Latinos, African Americans, or any other diverse groups (Earner & Garcia, 2009; Logan, 2009; Ofahengaue-Vakalahi & Fong, 2009).

If there was a cardinal rule in interpreting, assessing, and providing culturally sensitive services to diverse clients, it is recognizing that all professional helpers need to remain vigilant in avoiding the tendency to assess clients based on the helper's own values, beliefs, biases, and stereotypes. Lack of awareness of ethnicity and culture may distort perceptions of clients and of their family dynamics. The potential danger here is that the client's right to self-determination may be violated (Reamer, 2009, 2022). Providing ethnically sensitive practice requires social workers to assess clients and client systems clearly regarding the effects that culture, environment, and family can have on behaviors and responses. Being aware of ethnicity and culture and accepting diversity are essential in cultural awareness, respect, and sensitivity in practice (Morgaine & Capous-Desyllas, 2015). It can be challenging to understand how one's own values, beliefs, and biases can impact the helping process, because a social worker might not be willing to admit or recognize that this is happening. Getting open and honest feedback from one's supervisor, seeking continuing education on topics related to diversity and bias, and continuing to engage in self-reflective practice can assist in achieving these important aims.

In closing, interpreting, assessing, and exercising culturally sensitive practice requires that the social worker:

- Be aware of the family's identity, values, and norms and note problems related to acculturation or immigration.
- Identify and discuss the impact of psychological problems than can result from adaptation to a new situation or environment.
- Encourage the development of positive and supportive peer relations and culturally consistent ways of seeking help within the client system.
- Encourage relations outside the client system that can help to reduce feelings of isolation and facilitate transition.
- Help the client to develop new coping skills with which to negotiate the unfamiliar environment.
- Explore ways in which culturally sensitive measurements can be conducted and ways that these standardized measures can consider multicultural differences.
- Never forget the importance of recognizing their own values and expectations and how this could affect the counseling strategy provided.

Today, in our global society, so much of what is considered learned is measured through standardized testing for competence. Testing is used now from the earliest grades to later in life. For a complete list of articles and discussion related to measurement instruments and providing relevant and accurate psychoeducational assessments, see *Multicultural Psychoeducational Assessment* (Grigorenko, 2009) or *Culturally and Socially Responsive Assessment: Theory, Research and Practice* (Taylor, 2022). Because it is beyond the scope of this book to address the specifics of how these types of measurements are used, we urge the reader to refer to the chapters in Grigorenko's book. These books can help to break down this complex area and link multicultural assessment across multiple languages as well as multiple domains of functioning.

SUMMARY

To understand the practice of social work within a culturally sensitive and responsive framework, you must appreciate the broad range of activities and areas that practice involves. Choosing from among the varied roles and tasks that social workers perform, as well as identifying what constitutes the client system, is not easy within the dynamic social work practice environment. Therefore, it is not uncommon in generalist practice for new social workers to want to be considered an expert in everything, with skills in the micro, mezzo, and macro areas of practice, only to find that as a beginning professional they struggle with basic practice principles and how best to help the client they serve. Our advice is simple: Do the best you can and do not be afraid to ask for help! Even the most experienced MSW practitioner can feel frustrated. Deciding what helping approach to use and when to apply it requires a delicate balancing act among the needs of the client, awareness of the influences of the client system, the demands of the environment, cultural awareness and responsiveness, the application of professional ethical principles, the skills and helping knowledge available to the social worker, and the sanction of the social welfare agency.

Social workers assist a variety of people, groups, and communities whose issues, concerns, and needs often are unique to their status. The information gleaned from diversity and differences strengthens the social worker's ability to be an effective practitioner and helps develop a specialized intervention reflecting the client system's specific needs.

So where does the social worker begin with matters of diversity? The social worker should begin with the basic premise "Start where the client is," never forgetting that each client can have individual concerns that may or may not be relevant to his or her primary reference group. In addition, the client is always affected by the client system, which can clearly influence client behavior and problem-solving strategies. From a social work perspective, diversity must first be recognized; second it must be understood; and third, this knowledge needs to be applied to provide culturally aware, responsive, and sensitive practice. Once we take hold of diversity from these three avenues, always starting where the client and client system are, we integrate this information into a practice strategy. Recognizing the importance of diversity with the populations we serve, incorporating this knowledge and awareness into our practice skills, and supporting the provision of a diversity of services and programs stands at the forefront of all generalist-level professional helping. Also, with the increasing number of multiple-heritage couples, balancing how to best help these individuals in the micro and mezzo environments becomes essential. Balancing individual needs with societal and political initiatives provides fertile ground for macro interventions.

In closing, realize that recognition, understanding, and acceptance of another person, in this case a client or a client system, will never require the social worker to abandon his or her personal values and beliefs. In the professional helping relationship, our personal beliefs are merely set aside as we embrace those of the client system. Both new and experienced professional social workers struggle with difference and diversity. Such reactions as "Why do they do that?" or "That lifestyle is not for me" or "Their views are very different from mine" are human and natural. As a professional, however, the client is always our primary concern, and this should never require that the client match the worker's individual value and belief system. At the same time, our personal values and beliefs may be in such conflict with those of a particular client that we are not able to help that client. In that case, the most important thing to do is to recognize the conflict and transfer the case to a supervisor or another worker who can effectively work with the client—this is in the client's best interests and reflects the professional's ability to determine his or her own level of effectiveness.

When confronted with a new culture or experience, it is essential that social workers consider diversity and learn about the culture. Pieces of the human experience cannot be disregarded simply because the social worker is not familiar with them. Discovery comes through many avenues—including talking with your supervisor and other colleagues who may be better versed in the culture. Always allow clients to help you learn and develop sensitivity to matters with which you are unfamiliar. Remember, helping is a two-way street and reciprocity is commonplace in a just society.

The numbers from the Census Bureau provide essential information regarding the breadth of diversity and the changes that are occurring in our environment. These numbers, however, do not illustrate the latent issues such as racism, prejudice, and discrimination. Disproportionate levels of poverty, individual and family incomes, and high school and college graduation rates are just some of the indicators that demonstrate that diverse people may be treated differently.

Recognizing and understanding diversity can help the social worker understand how clients can develop anger, hostility, passivity, low self-esteem, poor self-worth, and a sense of hopelessness. The social work relationship should consider and take underlying factors into account, especially those that might not be considered obvious to the untrained eye.

Acknowledging the strength in client-system diversity can assist in the helping process. For example, the strong family and the extended family are hallmarks of the African American community. Acknowledging peer group influences and utilizing this strength will allow a social worker working with an African American client to consider the possible role of the family or extended family in the helping process. Recognizing and understanding diversity is the essence of *contextual practice*—seeing each client as an individual who is set within a specific culture and whose decisions and actions result from his or her life experiences.

Today's society suffers from a multitude of complicated problems that need to be addressed, and social workers, like other helping professionals, are being pressured to assess and address them as quickly and as effectively as possible. Varied social work roles and fluctuating environmental influences reinforce the ongoing need for educational preparation and training in practice. Even after receiving a degree, every social worker needs to enhance their knowledge and skill bases while developing new areas for more effective practice. We must all continue learning and growing to anticipate the needs of our clients.

Social workers believe that competent ethical practice is more than simply helping clients by using what is known. It also involves knowing the client, respecting cultural diversity and the uniqueness of the individual, assessing the environmental situations and resources available, and recognizing the strengths and limitations of the intervention strategy employed. The social worker must decide what method of change to use and at what level the client will be best served—micro, mezzo, or macro.

Micro approaches to social work practice help clients, whether individuals, families, or groups, to feel better about themselves and to address previous relationship experiences affecting new or current relationships. Mezzopractice strengthens an agency's ability to respond more congruently with worker practice needs and client issues. And macropractice confronts larger issues affecting individuals, families, groups, or communities. For social workers and teachers alike, bringing macropractice examples into the classroom is critical to increase awareness, from including relevant census data in the classroom experience (Alston & Grundy, 2022) to representing and discussing relevant social and political issues that can affect practice.

In this chapter and in Chapter 5, we have tried to explain as briefly as possible the basics of social work practice. We have presented a few case scenarios that exemplify how different social workers have tried to help their clients. These cases offer a glimpse of the exciting, challenging, and often frustrating world of the practicing social work professional.

Social workers are needed in the practice arena to address the wide array of social problems. And yes, although social workers face numerous external pressures from funding groups, we cannot allow these to limit our practice strategies. COVID-19 is one recent global event that has helped many to refocus priorities and stress the importance of the role of healthy habits and psychosocial efforts toward wellness (Rico-Bordera, Falcó, Vidal-Arenas, & Piqueras, 2022). Clients need and continue to want supportive services; as the number of people suffering from anxiety and depressive disorders, self-destructive behavior, and life-threatening illnesses continues to grow, so too does the need for social workers who engage in professional practice. In social work, we have a chance to help others to realize that problems are not solved in silos, and as a diverse society, rich with different customs, mores, and beliefs, recognizing and including diversity in all helping efforts can be our superpower.

REFERENCES

Alston, S., & Grundy, A. (2022). *New resources from statistics in schools bring census data into the classroom*. United States Census Bureau. Retrieved from https://www.census.gov/library/stories/2022/08/2022-back-to-school-teachers-guide.html?utm_campaign=20220817msacos1ccstors&utm_medium=email&utm_source=govdelivery

American Psychiatric Association. (2022). *Diagnostic and statistical manual of mental disorders* (5th ed., text rev.). https://doi.org/10.1176/appi.books.9780890425787

The Anne E. Casey Foundation. (2021). *New child poverty data illustrate the powerful impact of America's safety net programs*. Retrieved December 28, 2022, from https://www.aecf.org/blog/new-child-poverty-data-illustrates-the-powerful-impact-of-americas-safety-net-programs

Barker, R. L. (2003). *The social work dictionary* (5th ed.). Washington, DC: NASW Press.

Burghardt, S. (2014). *Macro practice in social work for the 21st century: Bridging the macro micro divide* (2nd ed.). Thousand Oaks, CA: Sage.

Cabrera, E., & Raju, N. (2001). Utility analysis: Current trends and future directions. *International Journal of Selection and Assessment, 9*, 92–102.

Chan, C. L. W., & Law, C. K. (2008). Advocacy. In K. M. Sowers & C. N. Dulmus (Series Eds.) & W. Rowe & L. A. Rapp-Paglicci (Vol. Eds.), *Comprehensive handbook of social work and social welfare: Social work practice* (Vol. 3, pp. 161–178). Hoboken, NJ: Wiley.

Council on Social Work Education. (2022). *EPAS: Educational policy and accreditation standards for baccalaureate and master's social work programs*. Washington, DC: Author. Retrieved December 20, 2023, from https://www.cswe.org/getmedia/bb5d8afe-7680-42dc-a332-a6e6103f4998/2022-EPAS.pdf

Diller, J. V. (2011). *Cultural diversity: A primer for human services* (4th ed.). Belmont, CA: Brooks/Cole.

Dziegielewski, S. F. (2008). Problem identification, contracting, and case planning. In K. M. Sowers & C. N. Dulmus (Series Eds.) & W. Rowe & L. A. Rapp-Paglicci (Vol. Eds.), *Comprehensive handbook of social work and social welfare: Social work practice* (Vol. 3, pp. 78–97). Hoboken, NJ: Wiley.

Dziegielewski, S. F. (2015). *DSM-5 in action*. Hoboken, NJ: Wiley.

Dziegielewski, S. F., & Holliman, D. (2020). *The changing face of health care social work: Opportunities and challenges for professional practice* (4th ed.). New York, NY: Springer.

Earner, I. A., & Garcia, G. (2009). Social work practice with Latinos. In A. Roberts (Ed.), *Social workers' desk reference* (2nd ed., pp. 959–962). New York, NY: Oxford University Press.

8 Dead in Atlanta spa shootings, with fears of anti-Asian bias. (2021, March 17, Updated March 26, 2021). The *New York Times*. Retrieved from https://www.nytimes.com/live/2021/03/17/us/shooting-atlanta-acworth

Everhart, K., & Wandersman, A. (2000). Applying comprehensive quality programming and empowerment evaluation to reduce implementation barriers. *Journal of Educational and Psychological Consultation, 11*, 177–191.

Fitzsimons, N. M. (2009). *Combating violence & abuse of people with disabilities: A call to action*. Baltimore, MD: Brooks.

Fong, R. (2009). Overview of working with vulnerable populations and persons at risk. In A. R. Roberts (Ed.), *Social workers' desk reference* (2nd ed., pp. 925–927). New York, NY: Oxford University Press.

Forder, A. (2008). Social work and system theory. *British Journal of Social Work, 6*, 23–42.

Glisson, C. (2008). Interventions with organizations. In K. M. Sowers & C. N. Dulmus (Series Eds.) & W. Rowe & L. A. Rapp-Paglicci (Vol. Eds.), *Comprehensive handbook of social work and social welfare: Social work practice* (Vol. 3, pp. 556–581). Hoboken, NJ: Wiley.

Gray, J. (1992). *Men are from Mars, women are from Venus*. New York, NY: HarperCollins.

Grigorenko, E. L. (Ed.). (2009). *Multicultural psychoeducational assessment*. New York, NY: Springer.

Hafford-Letchfield, T., Simpson, P., & Reynolds, P. (2021). *Sex and diversity in later life: Critical perspectives*. Bristol, United Kingdom: Policy Press of Bristol University Press.

Helms, J. E. (Ed.). (1990). *Black and white racial identity: Theory, research, and practice*. Westport, CT: Praeger.

Hepworth, D. H., Vang, P. D., Blakey, J. M., Schwalbe, C., Evans, C. B., Rooney, R. H., ... Strom, K. (2023). *Direct social work practice: Theory and skills* (11th ed.). Belmont, CA: Brooks/Cole Cengage Learning.

Hiller, S. M., & Barrow, G. M. (2011). *Aging, the individual and society*. Belmont, CA: Wadsworth.

Jones, J. M. (2021, February 17). LGBT identification in the U.S. ticks up to 7.1 percent. *Politics*. Retrieved from https://news.gallup.com/poll/389792/lgbt-identification-ticks-up.aspx

Jones, N., Marks, R., Ramirez, R., & Ríos-Vargas, M. (2021). *2020 Census illustrates racial and ethnic composition of the country*. Retrieved from https://www.census.gov/library/

stories/2021/08/improved-race-ethnicity-measures-reveal-united-states-population-much-more-multiracial.html#:~:text=The%20Hispanic%20or%20Latino%20population%20grew%20from%2050.5%20million%20(16.3,Latino%20population%20grew%20by%2023%25

Jones-Smith, E. (2014). *Strengths-based therapy: Connecting theory, practice, and skills.* Thousand Oaks, CA: Sage.

Kelley, K. R., & Kelley, M. E. (2012). Contemporary US multiple heritage couples, individuals, and families: Issues, concerns, and counseling implications. *Counseling Psychology Quarterly, 25,* 99–112.

Lanci, M., & Spreng, A. (2008). *The therapist's starter guide: Setting up and building your practice, working with clients, and managing personal growth.* Hoboken, NJ: Wiley.

Lee, S. (2022). Asian critical theory in understanding the women victims of ant-Asian hate crimes. *International Social Work.* https://doi.org/10.1177/00208728221112727

Ligon, J. (2009). Fundamentals of brief treatment. In A. Roberts (Ed.), *Social workers' desk reference* (2nd ed., pp. 215–220). New York, NY: Oxford University Press.

Logan, M. L. (2009). Social work with African Americans. In A. Roberts (Ed.), *Social workers' desk reference* (2nd ed., pp. 962–969). New York, NY: Oxford University Press.

Mackelprang, R. W., & Salsgiver, R. O. (2009). *Disability: A diversity model approach in human service practice* (2nd ed.). Chicago, IL: Lyceum Books.

Morgaine, K., & Capous-Desyllas, M. (2015). *Anti-oppressive social work practice: Putting theory into action.* Los Angeles, CA: Sage.

Nadir, A., & Dziegielewski, S. F. (2001). Called to Islam: Issues and challenges in providing ethnically sensitive social work practice with Muslim people. In M. Hook, B. Hugen, & M. Aguilar (Eds.), *Spirituality within religious traditions in social work practice* (pp. 144–166). Pacific Grove, CA: Brooks/Cole.

NASW Anti-racism Statement. (2022, February 23). *News releases.* NASW. Retrieved from https://www.socialworkers.org/About/Diversity-Equity-and-Inclusion/NASW-Anti-Racism-Statement

National Association of Social Workers. (2008). *Code of ethics.* Washington, DC: Author.

National Association of Social Workers. (2012). *Social work speaks* (9th ed.). Washington, DC: Author.

National Association of Social Workers. (2018). *Code of ethics* (Revised by NASW Delegate Assembly, 2018). Washington, DC: Author.

Ofahengaue-Vakalahi, H. F., & Fong, R. (2009). Social work practice with Asian and Pacific Island Americans. In A. Roberts (Ed.), *Social workers' desk reference* (2nd ed., pp. 954–958). New York, NY: Oxford University Press.

O'Hare, T. (2009). *Essential skills of social work practice: Assessment, intervention, and education.* Chicago, IL: Lyceum Books.

Olcoń, K., Gilbert, D., & Pulliam, R. (2018). Teaching about racial and ethnic diversity in social work education: A systematic review. *Journal of Social Work Education, 56*(20), 215–237.

Poulin, J. (2010). *Strengths-based generalist practice: A collaborative approach* (3rd ed.). Belmont, CA: Wadsworth, Cengage Learning.

Reamer, F. G. (2009). Ethical issues in social work. In A. Roberts (Ed.), *Social workers' desk reference* (2nd ed., pp. 115–120). New York, NY: Oxford University Press.

Reamer, F. G. (2020). *Ethics and risk management in online and distance behavioral health.* San Diego, CA: Cognella Academic Publishing.

Reamer, F. G. (2022). *The philosophical foundations of social work* (2nd ed.). New York, NY: Columbia University Press.

Rehman, T. F., & Dziegielewski, S. F. (2003). Women who choose Islam: Issues, changes, and challenges in providing ethnically diverse practice. *International Journal of Mental Health, 32*(3), 31–50.

Rico-Bordera, Falcó, R., Vidal-Arenas, V., & Piqueras, J. A. (2022). Do healthy habits regulate the relationship between psychosocial dysfunction by COVID-19 and bidimensional mental health? *Journal of Health Psychology 28*(5), 462–476.

Sakamoto, I., & Pitner, R. (2005). Use of critical consciousness in anti-oppressive social work practice: Disentangling power dynamics at personal and structural levels. *British Journal of Social Work, 35*, 435–452.

Segal-Engelchin, D., & Kaufman, R. (2008). Micro and macro-orientation: Israeli students' career choices in an antisocial era. *Journal of Social Work Education, 44*(3), 139–157.

Spade, J. Z., & Valentine, C. G. (2014). Introduction. In J. Z. Spade & C. G. Valentine (Eds.), *The kaleidoscope of gender: Prisms, patterns, and possibilities* (4th ed., pp. xiii–xxiv). Thousand, Oaks, CA: Sage.

Stonewall. (2021). *10 Ways to step up as an ally to non-binary people.* Retrieved December 4, 2022, from https://www.stonewall.org.uk/about-us/news/10-ways-step-ally-non-binary-people#:~:text=Non%2Dbinary%20is%20an%20umbrella,while%20others%20reject%20them%20entirely

Sue, D. W., & Sue, D. (2013). *Counseling the culturally diverse: Theory and practice* (6th ed.). Hoboken, NJ: Wiley.

Taylor, C. S. (2022). *Culturally and socially responsive assessment: Theory, research, and practice.* New York, NY: Multicultural Education Series.

Thompson, M. N., Johnson-Jennings, M., & Nitzarim, R. S. (2013). Native Americans undergraduate students' persistence intentions: A psychosociocultural perspective. *Cultural Diversity and Ethnic Minority Psychology*

, 19, 218–228.

Thyer, B. A. (2022a). What is evidence-based practice? In K. Corcoran & L. Rapp-McCoy (Eds.), *Social workers' desk reference* (4th ed., pp. 693–700). New York, NY: Oxford University Press.

Thyer, B. A. (2022b). Evaluating our effectiveness in carrying out evidence-based practice. In K. Corcoran & L. Rapp-McCoy (Eds.), *Social workers' desk reference* (4th ed., pp. 734–742). New York, NY: Oxford University Press.

Turner, F. J. (Ed.). (2011). *Social work treatment: Interlocking theoretical approaches* (5th ed.). New York, NY: Oxford University Press.

U.S. Census Bureau. (2011a). *The American Indian and Alaska Native Population: 2010.* Retrieved December 28, 2022, from https://www.census.gov/history/pdf/c2010br-10.pdf

U.S. Census Bureau. (2011b). *Overview of race and Hispanic origin: 2010* (2010 Census Briefs). Retrieved December 28, 2022, from https://www.census.gov/content/dam/Census/library/publications/2011/dec/c2010br-02.pdf

U.S. Census Bureau. (2021/2022). Figure 5. Change in percentage of people in poverty using supplemental poverty measure: 2020–2021. *Current Population Survey, 2021 and 2022 Annual Social and Economic Supplements (CPS ASEC)*. Retrieved December 29, 2022, from https://www.census.gov/content/dam/Census/library/visualizations/2022/demo/p60-277/figure5.pdf

U.S. Census Bureau. (2022). *Native American Heritage Day: November 25, 2022* (press release CB22-2SFS.160). Retrieved from www.census.gov/newsroom/stories/native-american-heritage-day.html

Walsh, J. (2021). *The dynamics of the social worker–client relationship*. New York, NY: Oxford University Press.

Walsh, J., & Holton, V. (2008). Case management. In K. M. Sowers & C. N. Dulmus (Series Eds.) & W. Rowe & L. A. Rapp-Paglicci (Vol. Eds.), *Comprehensive handbook of social work and social welfare: Social work practice* (Vol. 3, pp. 139–160). Hoboken, NJ: Wiley.

PART THREE
Settings for Social Work Practice

7

Poverty and Income Maintenance

CHAPTER 7: EPAS COMPETENCIES

Social work programs at the bachelor's and the master's level are accredited by the Council of Social Work Education (CSWE). CSWE's Educational Policy and Accreditation Standards (EPAS) describe the processes and criteria that social work courses should cover. In 2022, CSWE updated its EPAS standards. The following competencies are addressed in this chapter.

Competency 2: Advance Human Rights and Social, Racial, Economic, and Environmental Justice

Social workers understand that every person regardless of position in society has fundamental human rights.

Competency 5: Engage in Policy Practice

Social workers identify social policy at the local, state, federal, and global level that affects wellbeing, human rights and justice, service delivery, and access to social services.

Throughout its history, the core function of the social work profession has been service on behalf of those who are economically, socially, or politically disadvantaged. The International Federation of Social Workers defines human rights as "those fundamental entitlements that are considered to be necessary for developing each personality to the fullest" and states the necessity that the "satisfaction of basic human needs and the equitable distribution of resources" contribute to social work's goal of social justice. This chapter addresses how the United States attempts to meet basic human needs. From the earliest efforts for **charity assistance** were the charity organization societies and settlement houses of the nineteenth century, social workers have tried to help people to achieve their potential and participate in the development of their communities.

As we entered the new millennium, the United States experienced unparalleled economic growth. There were more millionaires and billionaires than at any time in U.S. history. The stock market boomed to new and unexpected heights. Unemployment and inflation reached their lowest levels in decades, and new job opportunities abounded. The United Nations, in September 2000, passed the Millennium Declaration, which included among its eight goals the eradication of extreme poverty and hunger worldwide by 2015 (see United Nations, 2000). Optimism was evident in research think tanks and institutes, such as the Carter Center, which reported the possibility of reducing poverty for all (Carter, 2000). All these developments showed signs of a growing, prospering global economy. But then the worldwide economic walls came tumbling down in 2008 and 2009. Banks collapsed, people lost their homes because of foreclosures, and business and companies closed.

Everyone knew someone who was affected by this economic crisis. The Troubled Asset Relief Program signed into law by President George W. Bush in 2008 achieved success in stabilizing the U.S. economy. A long, slow period of economic growth ensued. Then, in 2020, COVID-19 hit, and the recovery and expansion period following the "Great Recession" ended. The pain of the economic downturns was shared and felt by many, but one group of people sustained the hardest hit: people in poverty.

What do we mean by poverty? On the surface, perhaps the meaning might seem simple. But poverty can be considered in several different ways. Most use *income* as the most common variable. Why income? Because money gives a person the ability and opportunity to purchase goods and services. Money allows you to purchase or access quality health care, decent and safe housing, and an adequately nutritious diet. Income affects who you are and what you can do. As Darby wrote, "Being poor hurts. By itself, poverty diminishes the quality of life" (1996, p. 3). Certainly, there are many heroic examples of people and families who have risen above the limitations of poverty by taking full advantage of public welfare programs and services. But for most people in poverty, this is not possible. Living in poverty is far more often associated with negative life experiences that can leave deep scars. Crime, low educational attainment, inadequate health care, substandard housing, and minimum-wage employment with little opportunity for promotion are among the many debilitating experiences faced by poor populations. For economically disadvantaged individuals—that is, people who cannot financially support themselves and their families—life is not easy.

Imagine what it would be like not to have enough money to feed, clothe, or house yourself and your family. Now imagine what it would be like if, in addition to these troubles, you were viewed negatively and treated differently simply because your income is low. When people are portrayed as not living up to a sometimes-voiced ideal narrative that emphasizes "pulling yourself up by your bootstraps," society marks them with stigma (see Figure 7.1). People living in poverty are often regarded as contributing less than their share to society. Indeed, society emphasizes rugged individualism (i.e., you take care of yourself and your family, and you succeed on your own without outside help). Well-educated people who we believe should know better sometimes make statements such as, "Poor people are disadvantaged because they don't work or try hard enough to better themselves." Reflecting this myth, former and now retired speaker of the U.S. House of Representatives John Boehner (R-OH) said in a talk to the American Enterprise Institute in September 2014,

FIGURE 7.1
Children, and the women who are the most frequent care providers, cannot simply "pull themselves up by their bootstraps."

> We have a record number of Americans not working. We have a record number of Americans . . . stuck if you will. And it is our obligation to help provide the tools for them to use to bring them into the mainstream of American society. I think this idea that has been born out the last—maybe out of the economy last couple of years that, "You know, I really do not have to work. I do not really want to do this; I think I'd just rather sit around." This is a very unfortunate position for our country to take. (Malloy, 2014)

Further reflecting the notion that those who are poor or near poverty have arrived in that situation through their own choices, the current U.S. Senate minority leader Mitch McConnell (R-KY) said in July 2014 that the federal government should not support student loan forgiveness programs: "I think the best short-term solution is for parents to be very cost-conscious in shopping around for higher education alternatives. Not everybody needs to go to Yale. I do not know about you guys, but I went to a regular ol' Kentucky college. And some people would say I've done okay" (Terkel, 2014).

According to the National Conference of State Legislatures (December 12, 2019), the majority of states, at least thirty-seven, issue Temporary Assistance to Needy Families (TANF) through electronic benefit transfer (EBT) cards. In addition to the federal government's restrictions prohibiting EBT card use for liquor purchases, gambling, and gaming businesses, as well as adult entertainment establishments, at least twenty-five states have further restrictions on the use of EBT cards (National Conference of State Legislatures, 2019). For example, in spring 2015, the Kansas senate proposed significant revisions to its existing TANF law, including the following:

No TANF cash aid could be spent out of state or anywhere for expenditures in a liquor store, casino, jewelry store, tattoo or body piercing parlor, spa, massage parlor, nail salon, lingerie shop, tobacco paraphernalia store, psychic or fortune-telling business, bail bond company, video arcade, movie theater, swimming pool, cruise ship, theme park, dog or horse racing facility, or sexually oriented retail business (Rooney, 2015). The bill also limited ATM withdrawals under TANF to $25 per day. Can you find an ATM machine that dispenses $25? And consider that the ATM fee, which ranges from $3 to $5 at most places, could mean nearly a 20 percent tax on the withdrawal.

Let us think for a moment about people who are living in poverty and the common views others have about them. Can you remember any discussions you have had with friends or family about people who are poor? How were these people characterized? How often have discussions of this type become emotionally charged? Now think about pronouncements you have heard politicians make in the heat of political campaigns. How did these politicians present the issue of poverty, and what kinds of plans were proposed to address it? Why do you think people who want to hold office seem to constantly attack poverty-related social programs? We believe that most of the time politicians wish to please their constituents, so they pander to widespread beliefs and attack these programs as costly and wasteful.

Regardless of your opinion about people who live in poverty, poor and disadvantaged populations evoke strong emotions. Views and expectations about people who are living in poverty are founded in myths and stereotypes that many unfortunately assume to be fact. We know quite a lot about poverty, particularly that the state of poverty is persistent. Poverty affects all races and ages. Poverty affects both men and women. Poverty is found in urban, suburban, and rural communities. Those who live in poverty are often disadvantaged or disenfranchised by the greater society. They are seen and treated differently from others. Finally, poverty cannot be isolated within a particular segment of society. Through its effects on educational performance and crime, poverty affects everyone in society each and every day—young and old people, White people, African American people, Latinx/Hispanic people, Asian people, people who live in the city, and people who live in rural America (see Table 7.1).

Did You Know . . .

The means test is the process by which an individual's or family's eligibility for governmental assistance is determined; the test assesses whether the individual or family possesses the means to do without that help.

Table 7.1 Profile of Persons in Poverty, 2020

	Number in poverty (thousands)	Percentage of population
Total	37,247	11.4
White	25,007	10.1
Black	8,472	19.5
Asian and Pacific Islander	1,629	8.1
Hispanic	10,409	17.0
Under 18 years	11,607	16.1
18 to 64 years	20,640	10.4
65 years and older	5,000	9.0
In families	24,282	9.5
Northeast	5,555	10.1
Midwest	6,812	10.1
South	16,619	13.3
West	8,261	10.6
Live in metropolitan area	31,297	11.0
Live outside metropolitan area	5,950	14.1

Source: U.S. Census Bureau (2021a). https://www.census.gov/library/publications/2021/demo/p60-273.html

In this chapter, we will cut through many of the myths that surround poor people and impart critical information to make you a more informed helper. We will then look at several important social programs and assess their effectiveness within a framework of facts rather than myth. Do not become overwhelmed by the numbers and do recognize that the numbers are constantly changing. A good exercise is to search the internet to find updated data regarding poverty rates. One place to start is the U.S. Census Bureau.

Did You Know . . .

In 2020, in the United States, 37.2 million people, 11.4 percent of the population, were living in poverty.

7.1 POVERTY DEFINED

According to the *Social Work Dictionary*, poverty is "the state of being poor or deficient in money or means of subsistence" (Barker, 2014, p. 330). Other definitions similarly stress the link between resources and livelihood: poverty is a "condition of being without basic resources" (Segal & Brzuzy, 1998, p. 78).

Two ideas further refine the concept of poverty: **absolute poverty** and relative poverty. *Absolute poverty* is determined by comparison with a fixed numerical standard that is applied in all situations and usually reflects bare subsistence. *Relative poverty* is determined by comparison with some normative standard that may reflect a living standard far higher than subsistence. On the one hand, absolute measures are usually income based. For example, if a person's annual income is below a certain figure, then the individual is regarded as poor. On the other hand, a relative measure—though still income based—would compare the individual with someone else. A single person with a $45,000 annual income is not absolutely poor, but is poor relative to Bill Gates, one of the richest people in the world. Absolute measures make it easy to count people and minimize the array of subjective variables.

A relative measure is based on the ability, or inability, to meet a standard that is set and approved by the community. For example, if immunizations are expected but a family cannot afford them for their children, then that family is considered poor by this measure. The key is identifying a threshold below which people are counted as poor. Relative measures are much more difficult to formulate or to reach consensus about. They are also difficult to use. For example, a common criticism of poor people in the United States is that they have it easy compared to poor populations elsewhere, in India or the Sudan, for example. But this is like trying to compare apples with oranges. Different countries have different beliefs, values, and economic and social systems, all of which affect the standards by which people are judged to be poor. The bottom line is that poverty affects more than thirty-seven million people in the United States.

Measuring Poverty

The U.S. government measures poverty using a standard called the *poverty threshold*. The measure is based on a formula established in 1963, more than fifty years ago, by Mollie Orshansky, director of the Social Security Administration. She conceptualized the poverty threshold as an absolute measure so that statistical processes could be used to simply count the number of poor people. Orshansky's formula is based on the amount of money that a family must spend on food and on the portion of overall income that this expense constitutes. Orshansky assumed that a family spends one-third of its total income on food. After calculating the cost of a minimum, or economy, food plan as determined by the Department of Agriculture, she multiplied that amount by three to establish the poverty threshold. This value, which is essential in determining benefits, is updated annually and adjusted to reflect inflation, family size, age, and the increased cost of living in Hawaii and Alaska. Its application is simple: a person or family whose gross income falls below the poverty threshold is counted as being in poverty. Learn more about Mollie Orshansky by searching "Remembering Mollie Orshansky—The Developer of the Poverty Thresholds" on the U.S. Government Social Security website.

> ### Did You Know . . .
> Children remain among the poorest people in the United States. Around one in six U.S. children lived in poverty in 2018.

Now that we have explained the poverty threshold calculation, let us complicate matters a bit. The poverty threshold was the government's original attempt to establish a poverty measure under the oversight of the Social Security Administration. Its purpose was to establish a basis for counting retrospectively the number of people who live in poverty. Each year, however, another branch of the federal government, the Department of Health and Human Services (HHS), is responsible for issuing *poverty guidelines* (see Table 7.2). These prospective guidelines, which closely approximate the poverty threshold, are used in determining financial eligibility for certain federal programs.

A crucial point to remember is that the HHS poverty guidelines are used for determining eligibility for many federal programs, but not for all of them. Examples of federal programs that use the HHS guidelines are Head Start, the Supplemental Nutritional Assistance Program (SNAP), the National School Lunch and School Breakfast Programs, Legal Services for the Poor, the Job Training Partnership Act, the Special Supplemental Nutrition Program for Women, Infants, and Children (WIC), and Job Corps. Some of these programs base eligibility on a multiple of the guideline

Table 7.2 2021 Department of Health and Human Services Poverty Guidelines

No. of persons in household	Poverty guideline
1	$12,880
2	$17,420
3	$21,960
4	$26,500
5	$31,040
6	$35,580
7	$40,120
8	$44,660

Source: U.S. Department of Health and Human Services (2021).

percentage, such as 125, 150, or 180 percent. For example, a program may use 125 percent of the HHS guidelines to determine eligibility. In 2022, this eligibility standard for a four-person family was $27,750 × 125$ percent, or approximately $34,687. In other words, a family of four was eligible for the program if its income was below $34,687. The percentages of the HHS guidelines used by different programs are established by congressional committees and, predictably, can create a great deal of confusion between programs. Moreover, several well-known programs—Supplemental Security Income (SSI), Social Services Block Grant, Section 8 housing, the Earned Income Credit, and TANF—are not tied to the HHS guidelines (see the activity below).

One last point about counting people in poverty is that not all people are counted. The Census Bureau does not include or attempt to estimate the poverty status of individuals who fall into the following groups:

- Unrelated individuals under age fifteen, such as foster children (income questions are asked of people of age fifteen and older).
- Individuals under age fifteen who are not living with a family member (maybe a runaway, throwaway, or push-out teen).
- Those who live in institutional group quarters (such as prisons or nursing homes, college dormitories, military barracks, and living situations without conventional housing) and those who are not in shelters—the homeless population.

So here is a key point to remember. When you are looking at the poverty numbers and related rates, recognize that they are underestimates of the real numbers. The extent of the undercount is not known; it may be small—less than one hundred thousand persons—or it may be large—more than a million persons. What we do know is that the official federal numbers are at best low and do not accurately reflect the true number of persons in poverty.

Activity

Using the 2021 poverty guideline (see Table 7.2) for a family of four, $26,500, imagine what life is like. You would have $2,208.33 (before taxes) each month for expenses. Based on Orshansky's formula's assumption, one-third of your income, $736, would go for food, leaving you $1,471 for other expenses, including housing, transportation, health care, clothing, recreation, and so on. Put together a monthly food menu with the $736. Find a place to live and set up other expenses with the remaining $1,471. The two children are five and thirteen years old, and the two adults are the biological parents. And do not forget other costs such as clothing, transportation (car insurance and gasoline), and over-the-counter drug purchases. Now, how realistic are the poverty guidelines? What does this exercise tell you about the level at which poverty guidelines are set? If this were your family of four and these were the resources you had available, could you make ends meet?

Did You Know . . .

A single parent with two children making the minimum wage and working forty hours a week in 2022 would not make enough money to raise their family above the poverty threshold, which was $23,030. This parent would need to make approximately $11 per hour to be above the poverty threshold; the federal mandated minimum wage in 2022 was $7.25 per hour (unchanged since 2009).

Other Considerations in Measuring Poverty

Setting poverty thresholds and thus establishing exactly who will be counted as poor is very controversial. Orshansky's definition, when examined closely, has all sorts of limitations. First, it does not consider geographical differences in cost of living, other than for Alaska and Hawaii—and this is an important consideration in the United States. What do you think: Is it cheaper to live in Los Angeles, California, or in Tallahassee, Florida? Second, the threshold is based on food costs but does not adjust for the different nutritional needs among children, women, women of childbearing age, and men. Third, assuming that one-third of a family's income is spent on food purchases is itself problematic. Over the years, this has not proved to be a well-founded assumption (see the activity below).

Did You Know . . .

In statistics, the mean, median, and mode are indicators of how a set of numbers tends to focus on central values. Applied to income, the mean income is the average income of a population—50 percent of the population has an income above the median income and 50 percent have an income below the median—and the mode income is the most frequently occurring income. Median incomes are the most often reported; in 2020, according to U.S. Census data, the median income was $67,521.

Beyond problems with the formula used to determine poverty is the question of what should or should not be counted as income. For example, should federal cash subsidies such as Social Security retirement payments or monthly checks from SSI be counted as income? Should income be established as the pretax or the posttax (e.g., what you take home after taxes) amount? Should the cash value of in-kind benefits from federal subsidy programs such as SNAP (a.k.a. food stamps) and Section 8 housing be counted as part of a family's income?

> ### Activity
> Determine what the minimum wage in 2022 would need to be for a family to be above the 2022 HHS guidelines (see Table 7.2). A full-time job is generally calculated to a total of 2,087 hours per year. What should the minimum annual salary be for this person?

How income is defined affects actual poverty estimates. Critics of the federal government's income maintenance programs argue that poor people are receiving numerous supports and that these should be counted as income, which in effect raises a number of individuals above the poverty threshold and lowers the number of people in poverty. What do you think would happen to the number of people in poverty based on a combined count that includes earned income credit, means-tested cash transfers, SNAP benefits, Medicaid subsidies, and rent subsidies? Would the number of people in poverty increase or decrease? If you think it would decrease, you are correct—but will this net number portray a realistic picture of the nation's poverty level? Will we have an accurate picture of U.S. poverty if we count the various poverty-related subsidies? Does it really matter if the subsidies are counted? If they are counted and the poverty rate declined from the 2021 rate shown in Table 7.2, would it be a safe bet that the lower rates would be used to justify reductions in welfare programs? And, if welfare programs were reduced, wouldn't the poverty rate rise again?

Nevertheless, agency administrators and welfare advocates often argue that data produced by a standardized process applied consistently from year to year are essential, even if that process is rife with potential measurement flaws. Such numerical measures allow a community to follow trends in poverty and to assess the effects of different attempts to reduce poverty among its citizens. In other words, even though the poverty rate itself may have little intrinsic meaning, it is nonetheless important because its fluctuations over time serve as a barometer of economic well-being.

Number in Poverty versus Poverty Rate

Note that our discussion of measuring poverty started with counting the number of people in poverty but is now framed in terms of the poverty rate. The poverty rate is a more illuminating way to quantify poverty because it provides context by expressing the number of people in poverty as a percentage of the total population. This context is important for two reasons. First, the scale of poverty is difficult to judge if we know only the number of people living in poverty: one thousand people in poverty is a far more severe problem if the total population is two thousand than if it is one hundred thousand, at least as a percentage. The poverty rates expressed in those numbers, 50 percent and 1 percent, show how different the two situations are. Second, trends in poverty cannot be judged by changes in the number of people living in poverty alone. Suppose that over a decade the number of people in poverty rises from one thousand to two thousand. If the total population remains stable at one hundred thousand, the poverty rate has doubled from 1 to 2 percent; if, however, the population grows from one hundred thousand to two hundred thousand, the poverty rate is unchanged at 1 percent—the rate distinguishes between worsening poverty and population growth. As a result, it is more accurate to use the rate (i.e., percentage) than the actual number. As the population increases in number over time, so too will all related indices, including the number of people in poverty. Those who ignore the rate or percentage and solely use the actual number are biasing their arguments.

Table 7.3 shows the different eras in the recent history of poverty. Remember that the U.S. population has grown every year since the nation's founding. You can now "read" different eras in the recent history of poverty. In the 1960s, the number of people in poverty actually declined, a dramatic development, as evidenced by the sharp drop in the poverty rate from 22 to 12.1 percent. This decrease was achieved primarily through the federal government's activist War on Poverty. Over the following years, the poverty rate fluctuated but has remained in the low to mid-teens since 1990. Indeed, although poverty rates are well below the 1960s level prior to the War on Poverty, the numbers in poverty were not far different, and most troubling, poverty continues.

Table 7.3 Poverty Status 2000–2020

Year	Number (in thousands)	Rate (%)
2020	37,247	11.4
2019	33,984	10.5
2018	38,146	11.8
2017	39,564	12.3
2016	40,616	12.7
2015	43,123	13.5
2014	46,657	14.8
2013	46,269	14.8
2012	46,496	15.0
2011	46,247	15.0
2010	46,343	15.1
2009	43,569	14.3
2008	39,829	13.2
2007	37,276	12.5
2006	36,460	12.3
2005	36,950	12.6
2004	37,040	12.7
2003	35,861	12.5
2002	34,570	12.1
2001	32,907	11.7
2000	31,581	11.3

Source: U.S. Census Bureau (2021b). https://www.census.gov/data/tables/time-series/demo/income-poverty/historical-poverty-people.html

7.2 WHO ARE THE POOR?

Intersectionality (Crenshaw, 1991), as a perspective, recognizes that all aspects of individuals' circumstances contribute to their chance of marginalization: race, ethnicity, gender, age, class, sexuality, etc. The confluence of circumstances holds powerful sway over the resources and challenges that help or hinder the health of individuals comprising our society. Poverty cuts across all races, ethnic groups, and ages and darkens the lives of all genders. In this country there has always been a myth that poor people are almost all non-White, yet this is far from true (see Table 7.4). Numerically, there are more White people in poverty than people of any other single race. However, poverty rates for Black people and those of Hispanic origin are much higher than those for White people. Over time, we can see that poverty has declined between 2010 and 2020 (see Table 7.4); however, people who remain in poverty likely take less consolation from that trend than others might. Further, people in poverty are not "others" as myth would have it; in fact, Rank, Eppard, and Bullock (2021) describe research which reported that by the time Americans reach the age of seventy-five years old, almost 60 percent will live below the poverty line for at least one year in their lives.

> ### Did You Know . . .
> In 2020, the number of people living below the poverty threshold totaled 37.3 million Americans. To think about how large this number is, consider that this approximately equals the combined populations of Texas and Tennessee. Another way to consider this number is that the number of people living below the poverty threshold is 2.5 times greater than the total population of New England—Maine, New Hampshire, Vermont, Connecticut, and Rhode Island!

Table 7.4 Poverty Status by Race and Hispanic Origin (Population in Thousands)

Year	All people Number	%	White (not Hispanic) Number	%	Black or multiracial Number	%	Asian Number	%	Hispanic (can be any race, so data overlap race) Number	%
2010	46,343	15.1	19,251	9.9	11,597	27.4	1,899	12.2	13,522	26.5
2011	46,247	15.0	19,171	9.8	11,730	27.5	1,973	12.3	13,244	25.3
2012	46,496	15.0	18,940	9.7	11,809	27.1	1,927	11.7	13,616	25.6
2013	46,269	14.8	19,552	10.0	11,162	25.3	2,255	13.1	13,356	24.7
2014	46,657	14.8	19,652	10.1	11,581	26.0	2,137	12.0	13,104	23.6
2015	43,123	13.5	17,786	9.1	10,797	23.9	2,078	11.4	12,133	21.4
2016	40,616	12.7	17,263	8.8	9,965	21.8	1,908	10.1	11,137	19.4
2017	39,564	12.3	16,619	8.5	10,050	21.7	1,891	9.7	10,816	18.3
2018	38,146	11.8	15,725	8.1	9,695	20.7	1,996	10.1	10,526	17.6
2019	33,984	10.5	14,152	7.3	8,836	18.7	1,464	7.3	9,545	15.7
2020	37,247	11.4	15,942	8.2	9,219	19.3	1,629	8.1	10,409	17.0

Source: Data were drawn/adapted from U.S. Census Bureau, 2021b.

CHAPTER 7: POVERTY AND INCOME MAINTENANCE   215

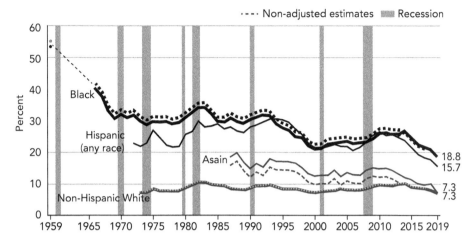

FIGURE 7.2
Poverty rate by race and ethnicity: comparisons over time.
Source: https://www.census.gov/library/stories/2020/09/poverty-rates-for-blacks-and-hispanics-reached-historic-lows-in-2019.html.

Poverty rates in 2020 were disproportionately higher for minority groups compared to the Anglo/White population. Unfortunately, this is not unusual. See Figure 7.2 for a graphical depiction of this circumstance over time.

The data to be presented in Table 7.6 will also challenge the idea that most people living in poverty should be supporting themselves. Using simple mathematics, we can see that children under age eighteen account for almost 32 percent of all poor people, and seniors, people age sixty-five and over, account for more than 9 percent. These are groups not customarily thought of as people who could support themselves. We also see that people in families account for 69.6 percent of all poor people; this statistic alone challenges the common myth that poor individuals are mainly single, middle-aged persons.

Poverty and Location

In 2020, the U.S. Census Bureau reported that the number of people in poverty living in metropolitan areas totaled 31.3 million (11 percent), compared to 6 million (9.1 percent) of those living outside metropolitan areas (Shrider, Kollar, Chen, & Semega, 2021.). Few Americans think of poor people as living in rural areas or small communities, which are generally considered tranquil places for vacation or weekend escapes. Creating successful programs for rural poor populations is a significant challenge; certainly, what works in New York City may not work in rural northwest Wyoming. Payday lenders (see Figure 7.3) commonly charge extraordinarily high interest rates and are often located in poor neighborhoods, more likely in places with higher percentages of populations often considered vulnerable (Gallmeyer & Roberts, 2009).

FIGURE 7.3
Payday lenders can take advantage of cash-strapped people with limited access to other forms of credit, especially in states with few legal safeguards in place, where annual percentage interest rates can top 500 percent.

Poverty and Race

As Table 7.4 shows, poverty rates for Black people and Hispanic people have been nearly twice that for White people for years. Averages by decade show that over time the differences have lessened, but they remain extreme. In 2020, 11.4 percent of Anglos/Whites were in poverty compared to 19.3 for African American or Black/multiracial individuals and 17 percent for Hispanic people (of any race).

Did You Know . . .

The term Hispanic is unique to the United States. No other nation uses this word in the same manner as the U.S. government. "Pertaining to the culture of Spanish- and Portuguese-speaking people . . . this term is often applied to people of Latin American ethnic background. Some people prefer the term Latino" (Barker, 2003, p. 216). Most recently, the term Latinx has come into usage, reflecting a cultural move away from gender specification. According to the U.S. Bureau of the Census, which first used the word Hispanic in 1980, a person of Hispanic origin can be of any race. This means that people who describe themselves as Hispanic can have diverse backgrounds and quite different mores and cultural expectations.

Poverty and Gender

Gender continues to play a crucial role in income distribution. Simply stated, women are more susceptible to poverty than men. Even social workers, members of a profession that proudly advocates for social and economic justice, work in organizations and agencies that discriminate against women. A survey published in 2010 by the National Association of Social Workers and based on data collected in 2009 provided evidence of this continued and pernicious phenomenon. The survey results documented that women social workers (with median salaries of $53,000) earned less than men social workers (with median salaries of $64,000). A systematic literature review (Lane & Flowers, 2015) provided additional evidence of continued gender-associated salary disparities among social workers. Lane and Flowers also identified what sadly looked like a loss of interest in the topic in the early 2000s. The ongoing gender-based salary differentials for social work are the same for society in general. A 2022 Census Bureau publication (Powell, 2022) reported that women earned 30 percent less than men, and the gap widens with age.

During the twentieth century, American family structure underwent significant changes. Two-parent families declined while single-parent families increased, birth rates declined for the general population but rose dramatically among teenagers, and women entered the workforce in substantial numbers. The United States now has many single-parent families that depend on the wages of a female head of household for their income. The COVID-19 pandemic caused the first statistically significant decline in median incomes of U.S. citizens since 2011, from $69,560 in 2019 to $67,521 in 2020, with median incomes of households maintained by women with no spouse present the lowest, at $49,214.

Census Bureau data for 2019 show that families headed by females are over two times more likely to be in poverty than all families—23.4 percent compared to 10.5 percent (Shrider et al., 2021). Even more disturbing are the data for households headed by African American and Hispanic females. Census Bureau data for 2020 reported that for Black female–headed families, 29.9 percent lived below the poverty level. For Hispanic (any race) families the rate was 30.1 percent in 2020 in comparison to the still shocking but significantly lower level of White female–headed families, 19.7 percent below the poverty level.

This hierarchy of poverty faithfully reflects income inequalities. According to the Census Bureau, the nation's median income for all households in 2020 was $67,521. For married-couple families it was $101,517, compared to $49,214 for families with a female head of household. And as you can probably guess, race and ethnicity make a difference; this is not a new finding but reflects a long-term pattern. The median income in 2020 for Anglo/White families was $74,912 compared to $45,870 for African American families and $55,321 for Hispanic (any race) families. As Landrine and Klonoff wrote in 1997 and for which the spirit of the remarks holds true today, ethnic and gender discrimination together generate extremely low salaries for minority women and "impair women's ability to support themselves and their children": "If a job paid Anglo/White men $20,000, then Anglo/White women received $15,000, African American women $12,200, and Latinas $11,000 for the same work. If a job paid Anglo/White men $35,000, then Anglo/White women received $26,250, African American women $21,350, and Latinas $19,250 for the same work. If a job paid Anglo/White men $50,000, then Anglo/White women received $37,500, African American women $30,500, and Latinas $27,500 for the same work" (p. 8).

Poverty and Age

The group with perhaps the greatest risk of poverty consists of children. The Children's Defense Fund (2021) reported that about one in seven children in the United States live in poverty, and about one in sixteen children were living in extreme poverty (defined as an income of $12,963 for a family of four with two children). Child poverty means less food, less stable and safe housing, and less health care. Long-term implications for children experiencing these lacks include lessened cognitive achievement and potentially troubled emotional health.

The younger the person, the more likely he or she is to live in poverty. In 2020, 16.1 percent of children were in poverty. The age cohort with the next largest poverty rate was adults aged eighteen to sixty-four (see Table 7.5). Finally, for people in retirement and relying on fixed incomes, poverty rates fluctuated slightly but hovered around 10 percent 10 percent between 2010 and 2020 (see Table 7.6).

The percentage of older Americans living in poverty was lower than the rate for the entire population—9 percent compared to 16.1 percent in 2020. This was not always the case. In 1959, 35.2 percent of seniors lived in poverty compared with 22.4 percent of all people; between 1967 and 1970, the senior poverty rate ranged from 21.6 to 29.5 percent, compared with a range of 12.6 to 14.2 percent for the whole population. For the most recent decade, 2010 to 2020, the rate ranged from a low of 8.7 percent in 2011 to a high of 10.2 percent in 2013 (U.S. Census Bureau,

Table 7.5 Poverty Rates by Age, Group, and Ethnicity, 2020

Percentage below poverty level			
Group	18 and younger	18–64	65 and over
All	16.1	10.4	9.0
White, not Hispanic	9.9	8.2	6.8
Black/multiracial	26.4	16.4	17.0
Asian	8.4	7.3	11.5
Hispanic (any race)	23.1	14.1	16.6

Table 7.6 Poverty Status of People by Age

Number (in thousands) and percentage below poverty

Year	Children under 18 Number	%	People 18–64 years Number	%	People 65 and older Number	%
2010	16,286	22.0	26,499	13.8	3,558	8.9
2011	16,134	21.9	26,492	13.7	3,620	8.7
2012	16,073	21.8	26,497	13.7	3,926	9.1
2013	15,801	21.5	25,899	13.3	4,569	10.2
2014	15,540	21.1	26,527	13.5	4,590	10.0
2015	14,509	19.7	24,414	12.4	4,201	8.8
2016	13,253	18.0	22,795	11.6	4,568	9.3
2017	12,759	17.4	21,913	11.1	4,893	9.6
2018	11,869	16.2	21,130	10.7	5,146	9.7
2019	10,466	14.4	18,660	9.4	4,858	8.9
2020	11,607	16.1	20,640	10.4	5,000	9.0

Source: Adapted from U.S. Census Bureau, 2021b.

2021b). The average poverty rate among elders between 2010 and 2020 was 9.3 percent (see Table 7.6).

The sharp decline in the poverty rate for older Americans over time was a clear result of specific federal legislation (Jansson, 1993, p. 306). The Older Americans Act of 1965, the Supplemental Security Act, and the indexing of Social Security retirement checks in the early 1970s all helped to raise seniors' fixed incomes above the poverty threshold. Social insurance programs, as DiNitto and Johnson (2012) wrote, "are a primary strategy for preventing poverty among workers and retirees and their dependents or survivors" (p. 120). It is important to recognize that the reductions in senior poverty are primarily the result of federal support that pushes income levels slightly above the poverty threshold.

Of all the statistics we have discussed so far, those that probably disturb people the most are the ones that involve our nation's children. For the better part of twenty years, poverty rates for children hovered around 20 percent—that is, one in five children was poor. In 1990, the poverty rate among children was 20.6 percent, and ten years later, in 2000, it had dropped to 16.2 percent, its lowest point between 1990 and 2017 (see Table 7.6).

Poverty for children increased between 2000 and 2010 and then decreased until 2020—the onset of the COVID-19 pandemic, when poverty increased across the board, including for children. The Children's Defense Fund is an advocacy organization serving as a "voice" for those in the United States who cannot speak for themselves through lobbying and voting. The Children's Defense Fund (2021), in their "State of America's Children 2021," calls child poverty in the United States our "greatest moral disgrace." The Children's Defense Fund also points out research evidence indicating what works to lift children from poverty, research evidence that consistently shows the benefit of government assistance programs.

We know that poverty has negative consequences for those who live in it, but what specific effects does it have on children? What exactly does it mean to be a child raised in an impoverished home? According to the Children's Defense Fund (2015, p. 1), it impairs cognitive, emotional, social, and physical development from the earliest years. It increases the risk for developmental delays, poor school performance, and behavioral issues. Poor children are less likely to graduate from high school and more likely to be unemployed, earn less as adults, and become involved in the criminal justice system. Poverty also compromises children's physical health, increasing the risk for asthma, obesity, diabetes, and a host of other health complications. It increases hunger and homelessness. The nation's high rate of poverty costs at least $500 billion a year in lost productivity and extra health and crime costs. We have seen that race and ethnicity affect poverty rates for women and for the general population, so we should not be surprised to learn that race and ethnicity also affect age-specific poverty rates. In 2020, the poverty rates were 26.4 percent for Black youths, 8.4 percent for Asian youths, and 23.1 percent for Hispanic (any race) youths, compared with 9.9 percent for Anglo/White youths; poverty rates were 17 percent for Black seniors, 11.5 percent for Asian seniors, and 16.6 percent for Hispanic seniors, compared to 6.8 percent for Anglo/White seniors (U.S. Census Bureau, 2021b). These disproportional rates represent long-standing inequalities.

Name: Julie Jackson

Place of residence: Riverview, Florida

College/university degrees:

- MSW advanced generalist from Arizona State University, 2022
- MFA photography from Rhode Island School of Design, 2014
- BA studio art from University of California at Santa Cruz, 2011

Present position: School social worker

What does a typical day at work look like for you? What tasks do you generally complete as a social worker in your area of expertise? On a typical day, I engage in counseling with IEP (Individualized Education Program) students, conduct observations and assessments, meet with parents, attend evaluation meetings for academic or behavior interventions, assist staff, and facilitate referrals. I also offer support for students in crisis.

What do you do in your spare time? In my spare time, I enjoy spending time with my family. My family includes my husband, three bonus daughters, two dogs, and two cats. I love crafting and art making. I build dollhouses and interactive installations. In addition to my social work practice, I am an accomplished installation artist and sculptor. Prior to pursuing my MSW degree, I was an educator and working artist for six years. My work has been exhibited in the United States, Europe, and South Korea. To see my artwork, you can visit my website: www.juliegautierdownes.com.

Why did you choose social work as a career? I chose social work as a profession because I believe that though we may have different backgrounds or experiences that shape our views, our needs and wants are very similar. While I was serving as an AmeriCorps volunteer in eastern Washington State between 2015 and 2017, I worked with low-income individuals and families who were trying to obtain safe, affordable housing. The populations I served were low-income and many had refugee status. The majority lived in rural or suburban areas. Though all the individuals and families that I worked with shared a similar goal of securing housing, their cultural backgrounds and life experiences were vastly different. Over the two years that I served, I was reminded of the importance of community engagement, compassion, and self-determination. This experience taught me that deep down we are more alike than we are different. My experiences as an AmeriCorps volunteer inspired me to pursue a career in social work.

What is your favorite social work story? I inherited a caseload of counseling students from the previous social worker. Despite my efforts to make contact with parents, some were unreachable. I had been working with a student doing counseling as part of their IEP for a couple months. The student happily attended his sessions, but his lack of focus was a barrier. One day, I ran into his parent when he came to pick the student up early. I introduced myself and asked if we could talk while he waited. We ended up having an impromptu meeting while waiting for the student to be brought to the office. He was really struggling to manage working and caring for a child as a single parent. I offered some suggestions to try at home. All of a sudden, the parent did a double take and said, "Wait, are you Miss Julie?" I said yes. He replied, "He talks about you all the time, he really enjoys his sessions." In that moment, I realized that even though I felt challenged, my time spent with the student had meaning.

What would be the one thing you would change in our community if you had the power to do so? If I had the power to change one thing in my community, I would make housing safe, affordable, and accessible available for everyone.

7.3 WHY IS THERE POVERTY IN A WEALTHY NATION?

Entire university courses are devoted to studying how poverty can exist amid great wealth. Countless books and articles also attempt to answer this question. The breadth of this topic allows us only to review some theories put forth to explain why poverty continues to exist. Theories vary as to what causes poverty. In fact, if we knew and agreed to the cause or causes for poverty, we would have long ago ended this very debilitating life experience. But there has not been agreement as to the causes or a long-term commitment to find its foundations and create the necessary opportunities and protections for all people.

Bruening (2014) and Rank (2021) wrote that there are essentially two conflicting theories as to the cause of poverty. One perspective is that poverty is individually and/or culturally caused; that is, the individual and/or their culture is the cause of his/her poverty. Proponents of this school of thought use a variety of data to substantiate their thesis. For example, low educational attainment, unemployment, and low rates of marriage are common characteristics among poor individuals.

The alternative theory that both Bruening and Rank cite is structurally based. The underlying cause of poverty rests with larger, macro issues such as low-paying jobs, schools that are inadequate in teaching, lack of access to health care, and an abundance of crime-filled neighborhoods. Again, specific statistics are used to support this perspective.

Another perspective on poverty (and yes, it is dated) was proposed by Darby (1996, p. 20), who listed four factors that result in poverty:

1. *Decline in low-wage jobs*: Fewer jobs are available for the labor pool.
2. *Immigration*: New immigrants take low-paying jobs away from unemployed residents.
3. *Decline in labor force participation and work effort*: Work effort among men is down over the long term.
4. *Breakdown of traditional family structures*: The number of single-parent families has increased.

Darby believes that these four conditions are intertwined and that one is no more or less important than the others. As a result, programs that address poverty but are narrow in scope, function, and funding will result in minimal changes, if any at all. Rather, Darby argues that antipoverty efforts must be coordinated to target these areas. Bradshaw (2007) argued that five different and competing theories shape social welfare antipoverty programs: (1) individual deficiencies, (2) cultural beliefs (i.e., traditions), (3) political and economic distortions, (4) geographic differences (e.g., rural–urban, and north–south), and (5) cumulative and circumstantial situations.

Another perspective on the causes of poverty was set forth by Johnson and Schwartz (1988), who divided the causes of poverty into three broad areas: economic, social, and political:

- Economic causes relate to unequal distribution of income across society and inadequate income supports in public assistance programs and unemployment programs.
- Social causes of poverty refer to the public's negative views of poor people; the strong belief in self-reliance; and discrimination against people based on race, ethnicity, and gender.
- Political causes include lack of participation in the political process by poor individuals and unjust social policies. Poverty and welfare programs are not popular in political circles and seem to be more vulnerable to public scrutiny and cutbacks than other public programs.

Representing a strong conservative view of poverty is the so-called Tea Party Nation. Their website (teaparty.org) noted that poverty is a condition that stems from a multiplicity of sources, including a culture that celebrates drugs and crime and disdains work as some sort of selling out. Further, the mantra notes that education—which is free and available—is frowned on in America's poorest neighborhoods and communities. This perspective also notes that a sense of entitlement reigns in these places, a sense that "The Man" cheated them out of what was theirs by right of birth. This constitutes poverty, where the reason is not a lack of resource availability.

So, what is the cause of poverty in the wealthiest nation in the world? There is no agreement or consensus as to one specific cause. Statistics are used to support each theory. As a result, the theory you currently subscribe to or may endorse in the future is one that matches your political ideology. There is no way to escape the relationship between the theories of poverty and ideology. Just remember that as a social worker, whichever theory you subscribe to, you must be sure that it supports the tenets of social justice.

7.4 PROGRAMS TO AID THE POOR

It is time to examine current programmatic responses to poverty in the United States and to consider how these programs are viewed and how their recipients are treated. This section will present a brief overview of major public assistance programs. We approach this section with great hesitancy and caution. Programs come and go, eligibility rules change each year, and dollar supports frequently change. As a result, we strongly encourage you to perform an internet search of the various programs for the most current, up-to-date information.

In Chapter 3, we learned that the modern welfare system has its roots firmly planted in the Great Depression of the 1930s and the passage of the Economic Security Act of 1935. A second major federal welfare initiative occurred in the 1960s with the advent of President Johnson's War on Poverty. Finally, a third, dramatic shift in federal social welfare programs for poor individuals took shape with the passage and implementation of the Personal Responsibility and Work Opportunity Reconciliation Act of 1996. This act was a sweeping reform of the role of the federal government in welfare provision. It dramatically restructured programs to aid poor people and ended the nation's six-decade-old guarantee (i.e., entitlement) of cash assistance to poor families.

Temporary Assistance for Needy Families

In 1996, the primary public assistance program was totally changed under the guise of *welfare reform*. Officially known as the Personal Responsibility and Work Opportunity Reconciliation Act, the new federal program, TANF, replaced Aid to Families with Dependent Children (AFDC), the AFDC Emergency Assistance program, and the Job Opportunities and Basic Skills Training programs. More commonly referred to as welfare, TANF is the monthly cash assistance program for poor families with children under age eighteen. The program itself is state based; that is, each state receives funding as a **block grant** from the federal government and is given broad discretion in determining how TANF funds are spent. The differences among the states are represented in the various TANF program names across the country (see Table 7.7).

Table 7.7 Names of State Temporary Assistance for Needy Families (TANF) Programs

State	Name
Alabama	Family Assistance Program
Alaska	Alaska Temporary Assistance Program
Arizona	My Family Benefits Cash Assistance
Arkansas	TANF
California	California Work Opportunity and Responsibility to Kids
Colorado	Colorado Works
Connecticut	Temporary Family Assistance
Delaware	Temporary Family Assistance
Florida	Temporary Cash Assistance
Georgia	TANF
Guam	TANF
Hawaii	TANF
Idaho	Temporary Assistance for Families in Idaho
Illinois	TANF
Indiana	TANF

State	Name
Iowa	Family Investment Program
Kansas	Successful Families Program–TANF
Kentucky	Kentucky Transitional Assistance Program
Louisiana	Family Independence Temporary Assistance Program, Kinship Care Subsidy Program, Strategies to Empower People Program
Maine	TANF
Maryland	Temporary Cash Assistance
Massachusetts	Transitional Aid to Families with Dependent Children, cash assistance; Employment Services Program, TANF work program
Michigan	Michigan Cash Assistance
Minnesota	Minnesota Family Investment Program
Mississippi	TANF
Missouri	Temporary Assistance
Montana	TANF
Nebraska	TANF
Nevada	TANF
New Hampshire	Financial Assistance to Needy Families
New Jersey	Work First New Jersey
New Mexico	TANF
New York	Temporary Assistance
North Carolina	Work First
North Dakota	TANF
Ohio	Ohio Works First
Oklahoma	TANF
Oregon	TANF
Pennsylvania	TANF
Puerto Rico	TANF
Rhode Island	Rhode Island Works
South Carolina	TANF/Family Independence
South Dakota	TANF
Tennessee	Families First

continues

continued

State	Name
Texas	TANF
Utah	Utah Financial Assistance
Vermont	TANF/Reach Up in Vermont
Virgin Islands	TANF
Virginia	TANF
Washington	TANF and WorkFirst Program
Washington, DC	TANF
West Virginia	West Virginia Works
Wisconsin	Wisconsin Works
Wyoming	TANF/Personal Opportunities with Employment Responsibility

Source: Administration for Children and Families, Office of Family Assistance. n.d.a

A federally mandated program that is developed and implemented differently in each state can and does become very confusing. Access to TANF varies by state (there are no federal minimum eligibility standards) and states can and do erect barriers and make cash assistance inadequate and difficult to obtain.

The Congressional Budget Office 2022 projected budget for TANF request was $16.69 billion; in 2004, the actual appropriation was slightly more than $17 billion (U.S. Department of Health and Human Services, n.d., p. 300). The TANF benefits differ by state and the grant awards are not substantial. For example, in 2020 in Alabama, the maximum cash benefit for a family of three with no income was $170; it was $204 in Mississippi, $215 in Alabama, $508 in Colorado, and $923 in Alaska. The HHS Office of Family Assistance reported that the national average monthly TANF benefit for 2020 was $447 (Office of Family Assistance, 2020). For additional information on all the states, visit the TANF website.

Did You Know . . .

To qualify for TANF, the federal assistance program for the poor, a teenage parent under the age of eighteen in most states must live at home with parent(s) or in another state-approved setting.

At the time this book was written (2022), the most current TANF data from the HHS Office of Family Assistance, which has oversight for TANF, was for fiscal year 2020 (i.e., 2019–2020). Some key points included the following:

- The average number of TANF families was 804,117 per month.
- The average size of a TANF family was three persons.

- Around half the TANF families had no adult recipients.
- 80.4 percent of TANF families received SNAP benefits.
- TANF included 26.7 percent Anglo/White families, 29 percent African American families, and 35.7 percent Hispanic families.
- 44.1 percent of TANF recipients were under age twenty-nine.
- 37.5 percent of children receiving TANF were under age five.

TANF does have some minimal requirements that all states must include in their programs, although a state can add to these requirements (U.S. Department of Health and Human Services, n.d.):

- Although, as with all programs, there are exceptions, the participant must work as soon as he or she is *job ready* or no later than two years after coming on assistance.
- Single parents are required to participate in work activities for at least thirty hours per week.
- Two-parent families must participate in work activities for thirty-five or fifty-five hours a week, depending on circumstance.
- Failure to participate in work requirements can result in a reduction or termination of benefits to the family.
- There is a maximum lifetime of five years (sixty months) during which a person may receive benefits.

TANF provides all states the flexibility to structure its programs within broad and flexible guidelines set by the U.S. Congress. As a result, states have different names for the programs, as well as different time limits, program requirements, and cash benefits. Essentially, a person living in Florida is treated differently from a person living in Wisconsin. Even with this flexibility, the lifetime limit (except for child-only cases) of sixty months is a national limit. If a person receives TANF aid for fifty months in one state and then moves to a state with a lower time limit, such as Florida, the second state's limit has already been exceeded and the person receives no further TANF aid there. Even if the person moves to a state that has not lowered its time limit, only ten more months of TANF assistance will be available.

TANF AND FEDERALLY RECOGNIZED INDIAN TRIBES

A separate set of protocols govern public programs for Indian tribes (U.S. Department of Health and Human Services, 2022). The federal office of the Division of Tribal Management, which is part of the HHS Administration of Children and Families, is a crucial point for assisting in implementation and coordination of ongoing consultation with tribal governments relating to TANF. Essentially, these regulations recognize the unique cultural attributes and needs of tribal communities and allow for tribes to develop and administer TANF programs. In 2022, there were seventy-four approved Tribal TANF programs that served 287 federally recognized tribes and Alaska Native Villages (Administration for Children and Families, n.d.).

Food Programs (SNAP, School, WIC)

The primary federal food support program is called the Supplemental Nutritional Assistance Program, or SNAP (U.S. Department of Agriculture, 2022a), and is operated through the U.S. Department of Agriculture. More commonly but incorrectly referred to as food stamps, the federal SNAP is designed to offset hunger and malnutrition. The program's name was changed from the Food Stamp Program in 2008 to reflect a new focus on nutrition. Note, however, that states have the option of not using the federal name and can call the program by another name. Another notable change is that the program no longer uses paper coupons, which were previously known as stamps. In 2009, SNAP benefits were available only on an EBT card; this notable change was made to reduce costs and fraud.

Prior to the Great Depression, no national coordinated effort addressed these fundamental issues. The problem was largely left to the states and local communities. For the most part, antihunger programs distributed actual food items. This practice moved to the national level when, in 1933, the Federal Surplus Relief Corporation was created to distribute surplus food.

> **Did You Know . . .**
>
> In 2022, the average SNAP allotment for a three-person family was $455 per month, or about $5.05 per meal. On average, how much do you spend per meal? Go to your local supermarket and see what you can put together for a week-long meal plan for three people totaling $106.05 ($5.05 multiplied by twenty-one meals in a week).

The first Food Stamp Program project, which ran from 1939 to 1943, used two types of stamps: blue and orange. Blue stamps could be used only for surplus commodities, whereas orange stamps allowed the purchase of any type of food. In 1961, a demonstration Food Stamp Program was started. It led in 1964 to the passage of the Food Stamp Act. Under the auspices of the Department of Agriculture, clients received stamps that allowed them to purchase certain American-grown or American-produced food at certain supermarkets. The current program structure was implemented in 1977 with the goal of alleviating hunger and malnutrition by permitting low-income households to obtain a more nutritious diet through normal channels of trade.

Participation in SNAP in 2021 totaled 41.5 million persons, with an average monthly benefit of $238 per person. Ettinger de Cuba et al. (2019) reported that SNAP decreased food insecurity; lowered the odds of risk of health, developmental, and growth deficits for infants and toddlers; and reduced health care costs for families as a result. The authors concluded that bolstering SNAP benefits could serve as an effective public health intervention. Eligibility for SNAP is based on financial and nonfinancial factors. The application process includes completing and filing an application form, being interviewed, and verifying facts to determine eligibility. With certain exceptions, a household that meets the eligibility requirements is qualified to receive benefits. The basic SNAP income eligibility requirements for 2022 include the following, but these are subject to change (for current information, see the USDA Food and Nutrition Service website).

Households may have $2,500 in countable resources, such as a bank account, or $3,750 in countable resources if at least one person is age sixty or older or is disabled (these amounts can change annually). However, certain resources are not counted, such as a home and lot, the resources of people who receive SSI, the resources of people who receive TANF (formerly AFDC), and most retirement (pension) plans (however, withdrawals from those kinds of plans may count). The values of licensed vehicles (e.g., cars, trucks, or motorcycles) are generally not counted. Almost all types of income are counted to determine if a household is eligible. Most households must have income at or below certain dollar limits before and after deductions are allowed. However, households in which all members are getting public assistance or SSI (or, in some locations, general assistance) do not have to meet the income eligibility tests because of other determinations for other means-tested programs.

For 2022, the monthly income limit for a three-person family was $2,379 (gross income) or $1,830 (net income); income ceilings for all family sizes may be found at the USDA Food and Nutrition Service website. An hourly wage below $14.86 meets the gross income limit for a three-person family. Contrary to the myth, people cannot use SNAP benefits to purchase any items they want. In fact, SNAP has stringent limits on what may be purchased. Eligible items include breads and cereals, fruits and vegetables, meats, fish and poultry, and dairy products. Additionally, seeds and plants that produce food for the household to eat may be purchased with the SNAP benefit. Conversely, one cannot purchase beer, wine, liquor, cigarettes, or tobacco; pet foods; soaps, paper products, and household supplies such as toothpaste and grooming items; vitamins and medicines; food that can be eaten in the store; and hot foods.

SCHOOL LUNCH AND BREAKFAST FOOD PROGRAMS

Other federal food programs we need to consider include the National School Lunch and Breakfast Program, WIC, and Meals on Wheels. Targeted toward poor populations, these programs were developed as supplements for specific vulnerable population groups, particularly children. According to the Children's Defense Fund, in 2019 before the COVID-19 pandemic, more than one in seven children lived in households where children were food insecure, meaning that they lacked consistent access to adequate food (Children's Defense Fund, 2021). A 2019 report by Feeding America, a network of food banks, food pantries, and meal programs, described implications for children of food insecurity that included stunted development, anemia and asthma, oral health problems, lower reading and mathematics test scores, and increased risk for behavioral problems.

The National School Lunch Program (U.S. Department of Agriculture, 2022b), which provides school children in the United States a lunch every school day, was created by Congress following World War II. At that time, the military draft showed a strong correlation between physical deficiencies and childhood malnutrition. In 2022, there were nearly one hundred thousand public and private schools participating in the program providing meals to more than 29.6 million children U.S. Department of Agriculture. 2022b).

Children from families with incomes at or below 130 percent of the poverty level are eligible for free meals. Those with incomes between 130 percent and 185 percent of the poverty level are eligible for reduced-price meals, for which they can be charged no more than forty cents. For 2022, 130 percent of the poverty level was $36,075 for a family of four; 185 percent of the poverty level was $51,338.

The National School Breakfast Program (U.S. Department of Agriculture, 2022c), which operates similarly to the National School Lunch Program, was established by Congress as a pilot program in 1966 in areas where children had long bus rides to school and in areas where many mothers were in the workforce. The program was standardized as a permanent entitlement in 1976 to assist schools in providing nutritious morning meals to the nation's children. Research clearly shows that beginning each day with a nutritious breakfast results in better and stronger learning outcomes. Studies conclude that students who eat school breakfast increase their math and reading scores and improve their speed and memory in cognitive tests. Research also shows that children who eat breakfast at school, especially closer to class and test-taking time, perform better on standardized tests than those who skip breakfast or eat breakfast at home.

Any child at a participating school may purchase a meal through the School Breakfast Program operating at about ninety thousand public and nonprofit private schools (grades PK–12). As with the School Lunch Program, children from families with incomes at or below 130 percent of the federal poverty level are eligible for free meals. The number of children participating in the breakfast program has grown slowly but steadily over the years: 0.5 million in 1970, 3.6 million in 1980, 4.1 million in 1990, 6.3 million in 1995, 8.2 million in 2002, 8.9 million in 2004, 12.1 million in 2011, and more than 12.4 million in 2020.

SUPPLEMENTAL NUTRITION PROGRAM FOR WOMEN, INFANTS AND CHILDREN

The Special Supplemental Nutrition Program for Women, Infants, and Children, often referred to as the WIC program, was enacted in 1972 to provide nutritional counseling and basic food supplements to prenatal and postpartum low-income women and their children. Target populations for WIC are low-income, nutritionally at-risk specific populations (U.S. Department of Agriculture, 2022d), including:

- Pregnant women (through pregnancy and up to six weeks after birth or after pregnancy ends).
- Breastfeeding women (up to the infant's first birthday).
- Nonbreastfeeding postpartum women (up to six months after the birth of an infant or after pregnancy ends).

- Infants (up to the first birthday). Note that WIC serves 53 percent of all infants born in the United States.
- Children up to their fifth birthday.

Coordinated by the U.S. Department of Agriculture's Food and Nutrition Service, WIC is not an entitlement program. It is administered by eighty-nine WIC state agencies, thirty-three Indian Tribal Organizations, the District of Columbia, and five territories (Northern Mariana, American Samoa, Guam, Puerto Rico, and the Virgin Islands). As with TANF and other state-based programs, eligibility requirements and benefits differ by state. According to the Food and Nutrition Service, in 2022, WIC operated through 1,900 local agencies in 10,000 clinic sites with 47,000 authorized retailers. During fiscal year 2018, the number of women, infants, and children receiving WIC benefits each month averaged over 6.87 million per month (U.S. Department of Agriculture, 2022b).

Eligibility for WIC requires participants to receive an income at or below a level or standard set by the state agency or to be determined automatically income eligible based on participation in certain programs. In 2022, the maximum annual income level for a three-person family was $42,606 (U.S. Department of Agriculture, 2022e) and, as with other means-tested programs, the maximum allowable income varies with family size. A state's income standard must be between 100 and 185 percent of the federal poverty guidelines. Some individuals are eligible for WIC because of their eligibility for certain federal programs, including:

- Eligibility to receive SNAP benefits, Medicaid, or TANF.
- Eligibility of certain family members to receive Medicaid or TANF.

According to the Department of Agriculture, WIC supplements participants' diets with specific nutrients. Different foods are provided to each category of participant. These foods include infant cereal, iron-fortified adult cereal, fruit or vegetable juice rich in vitamin C, eggs, milk, cheese, peanut butter, dried and canned beans/peas, and canned fish. Soy-based beverages, tofu, fruits and vegetables, baby foods, whole wheat bread, and other whole-grain options were recently added to better meet the nutritional needs of WIC participants. In recent years, WIC has strongly supported breastfeeding unless there is a medical reason not to breastfeed. Pregnant women and new WIC mothers are provided educational materials and support for breastfeeding through counseling and guidance. Further, WIC mothers who breastfeed receive a higher level of priority for program certification, a greater quantity and variety of foods than mothers who do not breastfeed, a longer certification period than nonbreastfeeding mothers, one-to-one support through peer counselors and breastfeeding experts, and breast pumps and other aids to help support the initiation and continuation of breastfeeding (U.S. Department of Agriculture, 2022f).

Targeted to supplement and improve the nutritional needs of seniors in poverty, the current Meals on Wheels program began in 1972 as part of the federal Older Americans

Act. The first U.S.-based Meals on Wheels program, however, began in Philadelphia, Pennsylvania, in 1954. Coordinated through the Meals on Wheels America, in 2022 there were more than five thousand community-based programs in the United States providing 221 million meals delivered to 2.4 million older Americans each year.

In some instances, meals are provided in the senior's home, whereas in other cases, meals are provided at a central location, such as a senior center. An important and unintended benefit of the program is that seniors, many of whom are isolated, are provided daily contact with others. Volunteers who deliver meals to seniors can check on elderly individuals and ensure that all is fine with them.

Supplemental Security Income

SSI was enacted in 1972 by combining three categorical programs that had been part of the Economic Security Act: Old Age Assistance, Aid to the Blind, and Aid to the Totally and Permanently Disabled. Prior to 1972, these three programs had been run by the states. With the creation of SSI, operations were transferred to the federal government. Recipients of SSI are also eligible for other social services including SNAP, Medicaid, assistance paying Medicare, and other social services.

SSI is a means-tested public assistance program; age is not an eligibility requirement. Potential clients include individuals over age sixty-five who have little or no income, people who are legally blind, people with a disability resulting from physical or mental impairment (including an emotional or learning problem), some people with visual impairment who do not meet the requirements for blindness, addicts and alcoholics in treatment, and children under age eighteen who have an impairment comparable to those that determine eligibility for adults. The 2022 resource limits (e.g., monthly income) were $2,000 for an individual/child and $3,000 for a couple (see SSI eligibility requirements on the U.S. government's Social Security website).

In January 2020, there were 8.0 million SSI recipients who received an average benefit of $576 (Social Security Administration, 2020). Note that each benefit is different depending on the individual's circumstances. In 2022, the maximum federal SSI benefit rate was $841 for an individual and $1,261 for a couple (source: Social Security Administration, n.d.).

Note that SSI benefits do increase on an annual basis because of a cost-of-living adjustment. For example, in 2022, the SSI cost-of-living adjustment was 5.9 percent, although in 2021 it was 1.3 percent (source: Social Security Administration, n.d.). Some states supplement the federal SSI benefit with additional payments.

Immigrants

One of the most significant changes introduced by the 1996 Welfare Reform Act was the sweeping elimination of legal immigrants from all public programs. Legal immigrants become eligible for public assistance only when they become citizens or have worked for forty calendar quarters (ten years). A public outcry led to an amendment to allow legal immigrants receiving SSI on or before August 26, 1996, to continue to receive payments. Yet this was not the case for all programs. The National Immigration Law Center reported that in late 2019 and early 2020 immigrant families were avoiding nutrition programs because of fear and confusion caused by the Trump administration's announcement of planned changes to the public charge of the U.S. Department of Homeland Security. Barofsky, Vargas, Rodriguez, Matos, and Barrows's (2021) analysis of the adoption in February 2020 of the changes to the public charge of the Department of Homeland Security reported that program use was affected for the nutritional programs WIC and SNAP, even for people who were exempt from the rule.

> ### Did You Know . . .
> Words matter. Social workers worldwide are bound together by a simple ethical principle: All people are treated with respect and dignity. This basic ideal is written in the various codes of ethics of social work organizations, such as the U.S.-based National Association of Social Workers and the global International Federation of Social Workers. The words we use to describe people and situations are a clear indicator of how one perceives others. Some words are clearly and tenaciously hateful, while others are less obvious.
>
> For a moment, think about what constitutes an "illegal alien." What image does the word "illegal" conjure up for you? Criminals, drug dealers, hustlers? The list goes on. With the word "alien," many see a terrestrial from another planet who is invading our planet to destroy our way of living and take over our communities. In other words, an "alien" is "different from me" and certainly cannot be trusted in any form or manner. A simple question for you, the reader—How would feel being called an "illegal" or "alien" or "illegal alien"?
>
> As you read this and the following chapters, you'll see the purposeful use of words that demonstrate respect for others. This is not a "woke" mentality, but reflects what we, as social workers, firmly believe in: respecting others no matter who they are, their politics, their gender identity, or any attribute that I or others feel are wrong or uncomfortable. Yes, words matter!

Ginsberg (1998, p. 192) suggested that the rationale behind this decisive move against immigrants is to force legal immigrants to seek and obtain citizenship. Until they are citizens, new immigrants are expected to support themselves or find assistance from private sources, including family or sponsors. As the current immigration reform debates continue, authorized immigrants' ability to access federal "safety net" programs remains fragile at best and impossible at worst.

Undocumented immigrants face an even steeper incline when it comes to getting help. Their very status as undocumented, also called unauthorized (instead of illegal), places them at risk for living in poverty (Becerra, 2020; "Amid plenty, want", 2018). Recently, some policy analysts have suggested that granting citizenship or permanent legal status for undocumented/unauthorized immigrants could actually boost U.S.

economic growth and prevent poverty among that population (see "The Economic Benefits of Extending Permanent Legal Status to Unauthorized Immigrants" on the White House's official website). Therefore, there is a belief that welcoming documented and **undocumented immigrants** could be good for all of us living in the United States!

What it comes down to is that immigration status matters when it comes to accessing employment itself to prevent poverty and social service safety net programs to ameliorate it. Social workers care about vulnerable populations, and immigration status significantly affects people's vulnerability.

Earned Income Tax Credit

The earned income tax credit (EITC) is a tax credit for working families with low to moderate incomes. One of the Clinton administration's major welfare initiatives, it was developed to stimulate work among poor populations. The EITC is a federal income tax credit for workers who are eligible for and claim the credit. The credit reduces the amount of tax an individual owes, and the tax may be returned in the form of a refund. The EITC is viewed as one of the most important antipoverty policies implemented over the past forty years. In most cases, the EITC benefit does not affect other program benefits, such as housing supplements, TANF, SNAP, Medicaid, and SSI.

Eligible working families, either with or without children, pay less federal income tax or receive a larger tax refund. To claim the EITC, families must meet certain rules. Income and family size determine the amount of the EITC. Prior to the June 2015 Supreme Court decision legalizing same-sex marriage, same-sex couples in states that recognized such marriages were treated as married for federal tax purposes and were eligible for the EITC. Qualifying for the credit requires both the earned income and the adjusted gross income for 2021 to be less than the following amounts (Internal Revenue Service, 2023):

- $51,464 ($57,414 married filing jointly) with three or more qualifying children
- $47,915 ($53,865 married filing jointly) with two qualifying children
- $42,158 ($48,108 married filing jointly) with one qualifying child
- $21,430 ($27,380 married filing jointly) with no qualifying children

The maximum allowable tax credit for 2021 was set at the following levels:

- $6,728 with three or more qualifying children
- $5,980 with two qualifying children
- $3,618 with one qualifying child
- $1,502 with no qualifying children

SUMMARY

This chapter has looked at poverty and provided information on just a few of the antipoverty and public assistance programs. Entire courses and books are devoted to this subject. Our purpose is to help you understand the nature of poverty in the United

States in 2022 as well as to review some of the programs that are in place. Over time, poverty has declined as our society paid attention, but those declines were not consistently sustained (Rank, 2021). The biggest success story related to poverty reduction over the sixty-year period from 1959 to 2019 is that related to older Americans; however, the story is not the same for children, whose rates of poverty have remained consistent since the 1970s. Please be careful about pitting one group against another, though.

We can agree that poverty cuts across all races and ethnic groups, all genders, and all age groups. Indeed, more Whites are poor than members of any other group. Nevertheless, poverty rates reveal that some groups are especially vulnerable (Carter, 2000). Women, people of color, and children suffer disproportionately from poverty. Nearly one in seven of all children live in poverty, with rates of one in five children of color and one in twelve for White, non-Hispanic children.

No consensus exists about causes of poverty, and theories to explain it are diverse and controversial (Rank, 2021). Proposed causes of poverty range from an individual's genetic makeup to deep, complicated structures of society. And as we stated, while each is supported by its proponents' statistics, theories of poverty are clearly rooted in political and ideological beliefs.

We also recognize that 1996 was a pivotal year in redirecting the nation's 1960s War on Poverty, as well as the role of the federal government in promoting antipoverty programs. Today, public programs are time limited, with greater state discretion in imposing additional program limits and adding more stringent criteria. In general, a family is left to its own devices once it has exhausted its TANF sixty-month lifetime limit. TANF represented a new direction in welfare programming that stresses employment and penalizes clients who do not work or are unable to meet program requirements on a consistent basis. Some believe that new direction hurt families rather than helped them when it comes to getting out of poverty (Center on Budget and Policy Priorities, 2022).

As social work professionals, what does this mean for us? The social worker's role in public assistance programs is not as clear as it once was. A visit to your local SNAP or TANF office reveals that few, if any, of the workers are professional social workers. The public may believe that social workers run these programs, but the reality is that we do not. The staff are generally called *eligibility workers*, not social workers; their educational degrees may require a bachelor's degree at the most, but often a two-year associate degree meets the requirement.

One of the ongoing historical parts of the social work profession's mission has been its work with and on behalf of poor populations. Although they may not work directly in specific antipoverty programs, social workers do work in agencies and programs that engage poor people and those at risk of becoming poor. To that end, McPhee and Bronstein (2003) outline four critical implications for social workers:

1. Social workers are encouraged to find ways to include the opinions and wishes of program recipients in future changes and continued implementation of the program.

2. The common myths about poor people and women on governmental and state subsidy need to be identified and addressed based on evidence, not opinion.
3. Adequate resources need to be provided to front-line workers to assist them to do their jobs.
4. If TANF proponents are going to claim that it supports families, then the disproportionate concentration on work needs to be addressed, because in many ways this can be counterproductive to basic family reunification.

Poverty and its ravages cannot be washed away by finding people jobs and wishing them well. Nor will it be eliminated by providing minimum-wage jobs for women and children living in poverty because unfortunately, no matter how much effort is made to raise a family out of poverty, these types of efforts will never work (O'Gorman, 2002). Clients need to be linked with appropriate resources—they need professionals who understand the emotional and psychological toll that poverty takes and who can suggest how best to respond to this personal turmoil. Someone with a personal problem expects the best possible professional service from the social worker at the local mental health center. A patient in the hospital expects high-quality care from the hospital's social worker (Dziegielewski & Holliman, 2020). Why should a poor person expect and receive anything less than quality services provided by experts who are compassionate and advocates?

An important question concerns the sixty-month limit set by TANF. What happens at the end of five years? Do we really believe that people without proper education who are forced into low-paying jobs will be self-sufficient within sixty months? And remember, several states have shorter time limits, some as short as twenty-four months. Where will these people go? Will they simply disappear? Of course not. They will remain in our communities—some more visible than others. Some people will say that they were given a chance and we should not do anything else. What is your opinion?

The United Nations put ending poverty as its top "Sustainable Development Goal." Social workers can and should take the lead in promoting just social policies that create opportunities for all people to achieve their full potential and gain economic independence. Our contribution to the attainment of human rights and social justice for all depends on our efforts.

FURTHER READINGS ON THEORIES ABOUT POVERTY

CULTURE OF POVERTY
Banfield, E. C., & Lewis, O. (1966). *The unheavenly city.* Boston, MA: Little, Brown.
Moynihan, D. P. (1965). *The Negro family: The case for national action.* Washington, DC: Office of Policy Planning and Research.

EUGENICS
Jensen, A. R. (1969). How much can we boost IQ and scholastic achievement? *Harvard Educational Review, 39,* 1–23.

Shockley, W. (1976). Sterilization: A thinking exercise. In C. Bahema (Ed.), *Eugenics: Then and now*. Stroudsburg, PA: Doidon, Hutchinson and Ross.

RADICAL SCHOOL

Gil, D. (1981). *Unraveling social policy*. Boston, MA: Schenkman.

Piven, F., & Cloward, R. (1971). *Regulating the poor*. New York, NY: Vintage.

UNDERCLASS

Auletta, K. (1982). *The underclass*. New York, NY: Vintage.

Ricketts, E., & Sawhill, I. (1988). Defining and measuring the underclass. *Journal of Policy Analysis and Management, 7*, 316–325.

Wilson, W. J. (1987). *The truly disadvantaged*. Chicago, IL: University of Chicago Press.

REFERENCES

Amid plenty, want; Poverty in California. (2018, October 27). The Economist, 429(9115), 12(US).

Administration for Children and Families, Office of Family Assistance. (n.d.). *Tribal TANF*. Retrieved from http://www.acf.hhs.gov/programs/ofa/programs/tribal/tribal-tanf

Administration for Children and Families, Office of Family Assistance. (n.d.a). *TANF Program Contact Information*. Retrieved from https://www.acf.hhs.gov/ofa/map/about/help-families#map_states_wrapper

Barker, R. L. (2003). *The social work dictionary* (5th ed.). Washington, DC: NASW Press.

Barker, R. L. (2014). *The Social Work Dictionary*. Washington, DC: NASW Press.

Barofsky, J., Vargas, A., Rodriguez, D., Matos, E., & Barrows, A. (2021). Putting out the "unwelcome mat:" The announced Public Charge Rule reduced safety net enrollment among exempt noncitizens. *Journal of Behavioral Public Administration, 4*(2), 1–15. https://doi.org/10.30535/jbpa.42.200

Becerra, D. (2020). "They say we are criminals": The stress, fears, and hopes of migrant dairy workers as a result of U.S. immigration policies. *Journal of Poverty, 24*(5–6), 389–407.

Bradshaw, T. (2007). Theories of poverty and anti-poverty programs in community development. *Community Development, 38*, 7–25.

Bruening, M. (2014, July 28). Two theories of poverty. *Policy Shop* [Web log post]. Received from http://www.demos.org/blog/7/28/14/two-theories-poverty

Carter, J. (2000). Reducing poverty: It can be done. *New Perspectives Quarterly, 17*, 41–44.

Center on Budget and Policy Priorities. (2022). *Policy basics: Temporary Assistance for Needy Families*. Retrieved from https://www.cbpp.org/research/family-income-support/temporary-assistance-for-needy-families

Children's Defense Fund. (2015). *Ending child poverty now*. Retrieved from https://www.childrensdefense.org/wp-content/uploads/2023/08/The-State-of-Americas-Children-2021.pdf

Children's Defense Fund. (2021). *The state of America's children 2021*. Washington, DC: Author. Retrieved from https://www.childrensdefense.org/state-of-americas-children/

Crenshaw, K. (1991). Mapping the margins: Intersectionality, identity politics, and violence against women of color. *Stanford Law Review*, 43(6), 1241–1299.

Darby, M. R. (1996). Facing and reducing poverty. In M. R. Darby (Ed.), *Reducing poverty in America: Views and approaches* (pp. 3–12). Thousand Oaks, CA: Sage.

DiNitto, D. M., & Johnson, D. H. (2012). *Essentials of social welfare, politics, and public policy*. Upper Saddle River, NJ: Pearson Education.

Dziegielewski, S. F., & Holliman, D. (2020). *The changing face of health care social work: Opportunities and challenges for professional practice* (4th ed.). New York, NY: Springer.

Ettinger de Cuba, S., Bovell-Ammon, A., Cook, J., Coleman, S., Black, M., Childton, M., . . . Frank, D. (2019). SNAP, young children's health and family food security and healthcare access. *American Journal of Preventive Medicine*, 57(4), 525–532. https://doi.org/10.1016/j.amepre.2019.04.027

Feeding America. (2019). *Child food insecurity*. Retrieved from https://www.feedingamerica.org/sites/default/files/2019-05/2017-map-the-meal-gap-child-food-insecurity_0.pdf

Gallmeyer, A., & Roberts, W. (2009). Payday lenders and economically distressed communities: A spatial analysis of financial predation. *The Social Science Journal*, 46(3), 521–538.

Ginsberg, L. (1998). *Conservatives' social welfare policy: A description and analysis*. Chicago, IL: Nelson–Hall.

Internal Revenue Service (2023, November 13). *Earned Income and Earned Income Tax Credit (EITC) Tables.* Retrieved from https://www.irs.gov/credits-deductions/individuals/earned-income-tax-credit/earned-income-and-earned-income-tax-credit-eitc-tables

Jansson, B. S. (1993). *The reluctant welfare state: A history of American social welfare policies* (2nd ed.). Pacific Grove, CA: Brooks/Cole.

Johnson, L. C., & Schwartz, C. L. (1988). *Social welfare: A response to human need*. Boston: Allyn and Bacon.

Landrine, H., & Klonoff, E. A. (1997). *Discrimination against women: Prevalence, consequences, remedies*. Thousand Oaks, CA: Sage.

Lane, S., & Flowers, T. (2015). Salary inequity in social work: A review of knowledge and call to action. *Affilia*, 30(3), 363–379.

Malloy, S. (2014, September 19). Boehner messes up Paul Ryan's image rehab: Attacks unemployed as lazy and unmotivated. *Salon*. Retrieved from https://www.salon.com/2014/09/19/boehner_messes_up_paul_ryans_image_rehab_attacks_unemployed_as_lazy_and_unmotivated

McPhee, D. M., & Bronstein, L. R. (2003). The journey from welfare to work: Learning from women living in poverty. *Affilia*, 18, 34–38.

National Association of Social Workers. (2010). *Summary of key compensation findings*. Washington, DC: Author.

National Conference of State Legislatures. (2019, December 12). *Restrictions on use of public assistance electronic benefit (EBT) cards.* Retrieved from https://www.ncsl.org/research/human-services/ebt-electronic-benefit-transfer-card-restrictions-for-public-assistance.aspx.

Office of Family Assistance. (2020). *Characteristics and financial circumstances of TANF recipients, fiscal year 2019.* Retrieved from https://www.acf.hhs.gov/ofa/data/ofa-releases-fy-2019-characteristics-and-financial-circumstances-tanf-recipients-data#:~:text=On%20average%2C%20TANF%20recipient%20families,in%20cash%20assistance%20per%20month

O'Gorman, A. (2002). Playing by the rules and losing ground. *America, 187*(13), 12–16.

Powell, E. (2022). *Women consistently earn less than men.* Washington, DC: U.S. Census Bureau. Retrieved from https://www.census.gov/library/stories/2022/01/gender-pay-gap-widens-as-women-age.html

Rank, M. (2021). *Confronting poverty: Economic hardship in the United States.* Los Angeles, CA: Sage.

Rank, M., Eppard, L., & Bullock, H. (2021). *Poorly understood: What America gets wrong about poverty.* New York, NY: Oxford University Press.

Rooney, B. (2015, April 7). *Kansas wants to ban welfare recipients from buying . . .* Retrieved from https://money.cnn.com/2015/04/07/news/kansas-welfare-limits/

Segal, W., & Brzuzy, S. (1998). *Social welfare policy, programs, and practice.* Itasca, IL: Peacock.

Shrider, E. A., Kollar, M., Chen, F., & Semega, J. (2021). *U.S. Census Bureau, current population reports, P60-273, income and poverty in the United States: 2020.* Washington, DC: U.S. Government Printing Office.

Social Security Administration. (n.d.). *SSI Federal Payment Amounts.* Retrieved from https://www.ssa.gov/OACT/COLA/SSIamts.html

Social Security Administration. (2020). *2020 annual report of the SSI program.* Retrieved from http://www.ssa.gov/OACT/ssir/SSI14/C_exec_sum.html

Terkel, A. (2014, July 14). Mitch McConnell's solution to soaring student debt: Less Yale, more for-profit schools. Huff Post *Politics.* Retrieved from http://www.huffingtonpost.com/2014/07/14/mitch-mcconnell-student-debt_n_5585521.html?1405371686

United Nations. (2000). *Millennium summit.* Retrieved from https://www.un.org/en/development/devagenda/millennium.shtml.

U.S. Census Bureau. (2021a). *Table A-1: Income summary measures by selected characteristics.* Retrieved from https://www.census.gov/data/tables/2021/demo/income-poverty/p60-273.html

U.S. Census Bureau. (2021b). *Table 3: Poverty status of people, by age, race, and Hispanic origin.* Retrieved from https://www.census.gov/data/tables/time-series/demo/income-poverty/historical-poverty-people.html

U.S. Department of Agriculture. (2022a). *Supplemental Nutrition Assistance Program (SNAP).* Retrieved from http://www.fns.usda.gov/snap/facts-about-snap

U.S. Department of Agriculture. (2022b). *National School Lunch Program (NSLP).* Retrieved from https://www.fns.usda.gov/nslp.

U.S. Department of Agriculture. (2022c). *School Breakfast Program (SBP)*. Retrieved from http://www.fns.usda.gov/sbp/school-breakfast-program-sbp

U.S. Department of Agriculture. (2022d). *WIC—The Special Supplemental Nutrition Program for Women, Infants and Children*. Retrieved from https://www.fns.usda.gov/wic https://www.fns.usda.gov/wic

U.S. Department of Agriculture. (2022e). *WIC income eligibility guidelines*. Retrieved from https://www.fns.usda.gov/wic/ieg-2022-2023

U.S. Department of Agriculture. (2022f). *Breastfeeding is a priority in the WIC program*. Retrieved from https://www.fns.usda.gov/wic/breastfeeding-priority-wic-program

U.S. Department of Health and Human Services, Administration for Children and Families. (n.d.). *Temporary Assistance for Needy Families*. Retrieved December 24, 2023, from https://www.acf.hhs.gov/ofa/programs/temporary-assistance-needy-families-tanf

U.S. Department of Health and Human Services. (2022). *How to become a tribal TANF*. Office of Family Assistance. Retrieved December 28, 2922, from https://www.acf.hhs.gov/ofa/programs/tribal/policy/how-become-tribal-tanf-program

Child Welfare Services

CHAPTER 8: EPAS COMPETENCIES

Social work programs at the bachelor's and the master's level are accredited by the Council of Social Work Education (CSWE). CSWE's Educational Policy and Accreditation Standards (EPAS) describe the processes and criteria that social work courses should cover. In 2022, CSWE updated its EPAS standards. The following competencies are addressed in this chapter.

Competency 2: Advance Human Rights and Social, Racial, Economic, and Environmental Justice

Social workers understand that every person regardless of position in society has fundamental human rights.

Competency 3: Engage in Anti-racism, Diversity, Equity, and Inclusion in Practice

Social workers understand how racism and oppression shape human experiences and how these two constructs influence practice at the individual, family, group, organizational, and community levels and in policy and research.

Competency 8: Intervene with Individuals, Families, Groups, Organizations, and Communities

Social workers understand that intervention is an ongoing component of the dynamic and interactive process of social work practice.

With a 36 percent increase since 1950, children constitute a growing portion of the U.S. population. In 1990, around 64.2 million children under age eighteen made up 26 percent of the U.S. population; in 2000, this number rose to 72.4 million. In 2020, the number continued to rise, to 73.4 million (ChildStats Forum on Child and Family Statistics. (n.d.)). In terms of population numbers, according to the U.S. and World Population Clock, these numbers are already outdated. Go to the U.S. Census population clock and see what the numbers are the day you read this chapter.

Births in the United States are declining. Kearney, Levine and Pardue (2022) reported that between 1980 and 2007 birth rates fluctuated between sixty-five and seventy births per one thousand women. In 2020, the rate had declined to about fifty-six births per one thousand women. These authors expressed their expert opinion that the reasons for the birth rate decline are not simple and likely the explanation is society-wide. The fertility rate for teenagers aged fifteen to eighteen dropped by 8 percent from 2010 to 2011 (Martin et al., 2013). The number of births outside marriage also declined in 2011, falling 3 percent from 2010 (Martin et al., 2013). In addition, the birth rate for teenage mothers reached a historic low in 2011, and this decrease remained consistent for all cultural and ethnic groups (Hamilton & Ventura, 2012). This is very different from 2006, where for the first time in fourteen years the number of teen births increased (Reinberg, 2007).

What is very clear from these evolving birth patterns is that family structure is changing rapidly. When the population shift is superimposed on the changing family structure in U.S. households, it's apparent that the so-called traditional family structure of two biological parents is dwindling. Also, the role of the father as both a single parent and a primary caretaker is gaining increased attention (Coady, Hoy, & Cameron, 2013). In addition, there is an increased diversity in children's living arrangements that can be related to family structure (e.g., single parents, stepparents, adoptive parents, grandparents, or other caretakers such as relatives, friends, or significant others; Kreider & Ellis, 2011). As a result, supporting and caring for these millions of children, considering the limited resources and incomes that many caretakers have, is the single most important investment we can make in the future of our society.

As the baby boomers continue to age, it should come as no surprise that aging people will rely heavily on the children of today to keep the United States prosperous. We cannot overestimate the importance of today's children to tomorrow's society. We can all agree that we need the best and brightest people leading our country. Don't you want competent and self-assured people in the labor force who can take over and move us beyond what has been accomplished? In 2020, the number of childhood deaths resulting from abuse and neglect totaled 1,750, which is about 80 fewer deaths than in 2019 (Administration for Children & Families, 2021). Experts note that these kinds of numbers are often seen as underreported because not all states submit their data.

But the bottom line remains—children are needlessly dying because of abuse and neglect. Certainly, an appropriate and just goal is to end this type of injustice and by helping to protect children from abuse through education and advocacy.

The importance of nurturing children is not a new idea. Indeed, a complex child welfare system exists to give children the opportunity to grow and reach their full potential. Karger and Stoesz (2010) have asserted, however, that child welfare programs and services are controversial because many people see them as an intrusion: "They sanction the intervention of human service professionals in family affairs that are ordinarily assumed to be private matters related to parental rights" (p. 338). In protecting children, when compared to other democratic countries with market-based economies, although the United States ranked 39th of 180 countries worldwide, it was ranked near the bottom for high-income countries on indices of child well-being, behind Montenegro, Belarus, and Bosnia and Herzegovina, both described as upper-middle-income countries (Clark et al., 2022).

Most of us can remember being told that being a child should be fun. Many adults long to return to a simpler time in their lives, when cares and responsibilities were few and far between. For some, Norman Rockwell's images of small-town America capture the ideal childhood. Television, too, has actively promoted the idea of families as caring groups always having fun, even during hard times. Older television shows such as *Father Knows Best, Good Times, The Brady Bunch,* and *The Cosby Show* illustrated life in suburbia and the city within a happy and caring family. When outside help was required, it often came from extended family members, friends, neighbors, religious organizations, and even membership associations.

In this society, we believe, and the media often encourages us to expect, that no child will face the horrors of poverty, homelessness, abuse and neglect, and inadequate health care or live in an environment where crime, alcohol, tobacco, and drug abuse are the norm. This is a worthy goal, but we must be careful because such an ambitious goal can sometimes be satisfied by simply denying that such problems exist. Few sponsors, if any, would want to be the ones to tell America that all is not well with its children. Although it is critical to know how many children's needs are not adequately met, discussing what is needed is easily ignored or denied. But the simple fact is that all is not well with America's children. Even in the United States, considered one of the most advanced of the developed countries, for millions of children life is filled with turmoil. These children are repeatedly forced to face crises that may eventually lead to chaos and tragedy. In this chapter, we will look in depth at America's children. We will examine what life is like for many of them and explore the laws, programs, and services geared toward helping them. In addition, we will discuss how the public and voluntary child welfare systems work together. The role of the social worker in protecting and advocating for the child will be highlighted and concepts such as mandatory reporting will be explained.

Name: Xan Boone

Place of residence: Cincinnati, Ohio

College/university: University of Cincinnati, BS, political science, 1998; MSW, 1995

Present position: Professor educator at the School of Social Work, University of Cincinnati, and assistant director of Ohio's University Consortium for Child and Adult Services; Ohio's state coordinator for the Ohio Child Welfare Training Program and the Ohio Human Services Training System, conducting caseworker and foster parent training that is required by the state.

Previous work experience: 1989–2007: Child welfare professional. Two years as a dependency investigator for Lucas County Juvenile Court; two years as an ongoing caseworker for Hamilton County Children's Services; one year as a family preservation caseworker; four years as a family conference facilitator; and nine years as a new caseworker trainer for Hamilton County Children's Services.

Volunteer experience: Mission trip to rebuild homes for Hurricane Katrina victims; traveled to Ukraine to assist the government in development of an updated child welfare system; study-abroad faculty leader since 2011 for the University of Cincinnati, working in developing countries to build sustainable relationships with communities with a focus on families and social determinants of health (travel programs to El Salvador, Nicaragua, Costa Rica, Mexico, Tanzania, India).

Why did you choose social work as a career? Like many career child welfare professionals before me, I did not choose child welfare as my career initially. I planned to be a juvenile probation officer. However, although I did not get the job that I had hoped to get, the Lucas County Court offered me another position. This would be to work in conjunction with the local child welfare agency to place children in safe family homes. I conducted the assessments of those families for the court and testified regarding their appropriateness to raise a child. I never looked back. That was 1989, and all of these years later my career is still focused on child welfare. I feel that social work is a calling and that social work comes as much from the heart as it does from the head. I was inspired to get my master's degree and am very proud to call myself a career social worker.

What is your favorite social work story? I remember running into a family in downtown Cincinnati on a sunny Saturday. There was something familiar about them. As they approached, I realized that this was a family with whom I had worked when I was doing family preservation several years back. They stopped and looked at me. I knew the mother recognized me immediately. She ran over to give me a hug. The daughter just kept staring at me. Finally, she recognized me. She said, "I remember you; you helped me bake my mom a birthday cake when we didn't have any money." It had been several years, but, yes, I had

> helped her and her brother make their mom a birthday cake. This family was being torn apart by violence, poverty, drug addiction, and mental health issues. When I saw them again, the mother was working, actively sober, the kids were in school, and they appeared to be doing well. There are few times when we have the opportunity to see the results of the work we do with families. Transformation can take years. But when we do see the successes, it helps us avoid burnout and inspires us to keep up the hard work. This was a rare but wonderful glimpse of both the formal and the informal work we do to help others. When successes happen, we might not even know it! I still smile when I think of baking that cake.
>
> *What would be the one thing you would change in our community if you had the power to do so?* I wish people in the world could spend a day walking in the shoes of another. It might be a first step to truly eradicating racism, discrimination, and hate, as well as addressing issues related to poverty and other environmental factors that are causal factors of abuse and neglect.

8.1 THE CHILD WELFARE SYSTEM DEFINED

Let's begin by looking at how the child welfare system is defined.

According to the Children's Bureau (2020), in the United States child welfare is designed as a group of services constituting a system to promote the well-being of children by ensuring safety, achieving permanency, and strengthening families. This system of policies and programs is connected to protect, care, and encourage the healthy development of children. The goal for these services is to ameliorate conditions that put children and family systems at risk, thereby protecting children from future abuse and neglect. Therefore, the goal of child welfare can be simply defined as "to promote the well-being, permanency, and safety of children and families by helping families care for their children successfully or, when that is not possible, helping children find permanency with kin or adoptive families. Among children who enter foster care, most will return safely to the care of their own families or go to live with relatives or an adoptive family" (Child Welfare Information Gateway, 2020b, p. 7).

Put simply, this network of services is offered at the public, private and community-based levels and constitute a complex system of all levels sharing the goal of ensuring child safety and well-being (Bearman, Garland, & Schoenwald, 2014). It encompasses a wide array of programs and policies that address the needs of children, youth, and families. Cross and Risser (2022) go so far as to say that involving the family and community in child welfare services as a best practice related to child welfare services is not just innovative—it should be our standard for practice. Furthermore, the current child welfare system struggles to involve fathers even though research indicates that their active involvement can improve child outcomes (Harty & Banman, 2022).

This inclusive definition of social welfare is not new to social work and was reflected in the earlier writings of Linderman (1995), who also emphasized that the formal organizational aspects of child welfare need to remain inclusive of the interrelated aspects of family and community action. His definition of child welfare characterizes it as both a public and a voluntary effort to coordinate seven interrelated objectives:

1. To protect and promote the well-being of children;
2. To support families and seek to prevent problems that may result in neglect, abuse, and exploitation;
3. To promote family stability by assessing and building on family strengths while addressing needs;
4. To support the full array of out-of-home care services for children who require them;
5. To take responsibility for addressing social conditions that negatively affect children and families, such as inadequate housing, poverty, chemical dependence, and lack of access to health care;
6. To support the strengths of families whenever possible; and
7. To intervene when necessary to ensure the safety and well-being of children.

When looking historically at child welfare organizations, Dobelstein (2002) omitted the voluntary sector and concluded that child welfare involved a broad range of public activities undertaken on behalf of children. Today, however, this definition is much broader and continues to involve private and community organizations. Within child welfare, these services can be viewed as supplementing and supporting family life and in some cases substituting for it (Crosson-Tower, 2012). Services provided involve a multitude of policy sectors, including areas such as health, nutrition, education, and income maintenance. This is further supported by the need for programs to measure effectiveness and track the outcomes that support continued well-being from childhood through adolescence and into adulthood (Hook & Courtney, 2010).

The work of Kadushin and Martin (1988), who wrote a seminal textbook on child welfare, is important because they were among the first to clearly examine these services from a social work perspective. For them, "child welfare is concerned with the general well-being of all children. It encompasses all measures designed to protect and promote the bio-psycho-social development of children" (p. 1). Gil (1985) gave another historic and straightforward definition of child welfare: "In the simplest terms, as well as in a most profound sense, child welfare means conditions of living in which children can 'fare well,' conditions in which their bodies, minds, and souls are free to develop spontaneously through all stages of maturation" (p. 12).

As can be seen in this chapter, over the years, the definitions of child welfare and the resulting child welfare system have changed slightly; some include public and private responsibilities and others do not, but all these definitions of child welfare have several points in common. First, the child welfare system is firmly established within the public sector; when private sector involvement occurs, it will likely have a less prominent role. Second, child welfare policy is closely tied to and directly influenced by family policy. The importance of the family and community connectedness is always a central part of the integration. Third and probably most important is that all policies, services, and programs included in child welfare cover a broad range of interventions and services, but all efforts aim to improve child well-being.

In this way, the child's resilience and ability to cope are maximized and the child is provided with the safest nurturing environment possible, one that fosters growth and full development. Considering all these commonalities, we define the child welfare system as the system of services and programs that protects, promotes, and encourages the growth and development of all children so that they can achieve their full potential and function at their optimal level in their communities. This definition goes beyond the traditional understanding of the term "**child welfare**," which often stops with child protection efforts to include a wider array of services.

As child welfare services continue to develop, the expectation of clear outcomes and the use of performance measures continue to increase. This can be particularly problematic given the variety of programs and services available—all having the common goals of safety, permanency, and well-being, but with each program having numerous variations in how this is accomplished. Samples, Carnochan, and Austin (2013) recognized these differences and called for the implementation of flexibility in federal performance requirements that remain sensitive to local values and priorities, as well as keeping in tune with all stakeholders involved in the delivery of child welfare services. It should come as no surprise that, like other areas of social service, this area of study struggles to bridge the practice/policy gap (Brewsaugh & Prendergast, 2022). This is particularly difficult in this field because of the variety of agencies, standards, and procedures.

8.2 AMERICA'S DIVERSE CHILDREN AND THEIR FAMILIES

The abuse and neglect of children cross all cultural and ethnic groups (Child Welfare Information Gateway, n.d.a). In the United States, minority children are now the majority, surpassing White children (Annie E. Casey Foundation, 2022). Although there are more White children than children of any other racial or ethnic group, population increases for Blacks and Hispanics have been far greater than for Whites. The Hispanic population in the United States has grown quite dramatically, but it is important to note that these rates may be inflated. The term Hispanic is difficult to define. In the U.S. Census, Latinos can classify themselves as Hispanic, Black, or White; in other cases, they may be listed as both Hispanic and Black. Part of the growth in the Hispanic population may reflect resolution of this confusion as individuals switch affiliations.

In addition, according to Tyser, Scott, Readdy, and McCrea (2014), promoting resiliency in American Indian youth has never been more important. Because of the collective nature of their culture, developing and maintaining self-esteem are deeply embedded in their cultural system (Smokowski, Evans, Cotter, & Webber, 2014). For Native Americans, this places the probability of therapeutic success squarely in line with utilizing culturally based interventions (Garrett et al., 2014). With this assumption, it should come as no surprise that the Indian Child Welfare Act (ICWA) passed into federal law in 1978 remains central to the protection of Indian (Native American and Alaska Native) children and, in suspected cases of maltreatment, prohibits the removal of children or adoption of these children by public or private agencies without direct consultation and direction of the child's tribe and family (National Indian Child Welfare Association [NICWA], 2014).

Did You Know . . .

More information related to the ICWA is provided by the National Indian Child Welfare Association (NICWA). The NICWA is an excellent resource for clear, easy-to-read information related to Native American and Alaska Native children. Its section on frequently asked questions about ICWA will be an interesting and informative read for those wanting to know more about protecting the rights of Native American and Alaska Native children (see the NICWA website).

Just as American children have become more diverse, so too have their families. The family is a critical institution in shaping and transmitting from generation to generation the values and rich traditions of culturally and ethnically diverse Americans. The kaleidoscope of families includes those whose roots are Anglo-European, Native Indian, African, Latino, Asian, and Middle Eastern, to mention a few. American families, whatever their ethnic heritage, are expected to respond to the expectations and norms of this society, even though many have very different cultural traditions, values, beliefs, norms, folkways, and mores. Some families hold their distinctive beliefs so strongly that they refuse to change; instead, they pass the same set of rigid expectations from one generation to the next. The key challenge for families is to balance the rich traditions and customs of their cultural heritage with the values and beliefs of the dominant society. To reduce racial inequities and oppression, perceptions of inferiority must be addressed to avoid systematic biases applied to certain groups (Child Welfare Information Gateway, n.d.b). For example, recognition of systemic biases is especially important for immigrant children who may have increased difficulty obtaining food or health care based on negative perceptions related to the immigrant status of their parents (Johnson-Motoyama, 2014).

Family structures are also becoming more diverse. No longer do families mirror the traditional stereotype of a two-parent household in which the father works outside the home and the mother maintains the home. Nontraditional families are growing in number, and it is no longer uncommon for children to be raised in a single-parent household or by lesbian, gay, or transgendered parenting couples. And, as stated earlier, although the number of births is decreasing, increased divorce rates have fueled an increase in the number of single-parent households. Regardless of the type of family or whether the parents are heterosexual, research does appear to suggest that two-parent families appear to be more successful in childrearing (Mallon, 2008). For many couples raising children, however, one parent staying at home with the child has clearly become a luxury, because both parents often work outside the home. For many of these parents, working outside the home, and in some cases having a second job, is not a choice—it is a necessity.

Although divorce rates have declined in recent decades, the United States still possesses one of the highest divorce rates around the globe (Raley & Sweeney, 2020). In the thirty-two years between 1960 and 1992, the number of divorces tripled from 400,000 to 1,200,000 annually, with nearly 50 percent of all marriages ending in divorce (Lindsey, 1994, p. 73). In 2022, the United States was listed as number twenty-two of the top twenty-five countries with the highest divorce rates (Ortiz-Ospina & Roser, 2020). What is of most concern about these high rates of divorce is the effect they can have on children under the age of eighteen (see the activity below). Although some children do just fine and adapt to the divorce, some of the problems that become more likely include abuse and neglect, health problems, behavioral health and emotional problems, crime and drug abuse, suicide, poor school performance, less success in school-related goals and activities, and growing up in poverty (Kayser & Johnson, 2008). Family structure stability acts as a key predictor of child well-being (Raley & Sweeney, 2020).

Activity

Discussion of factors. Following is a list of the circumstances Kayser & Johnson (2008) cited as affecting children after their parents' divorce. Do you agree with them and are there any others that you believe should be added? Be sure to say why you agree or why you don't and what supporting information you have on which to base your opinions.

According to research, children of divorced parents:

- Are more often involved in abuse or neglect;
- Have more health, behavioral, and emotional problems;
- Are more involved in crime and drug abuse;
- Experience depression;
- Perform poorly in reading, spelling, and math;
- Are more likely to repeat a grade, drop out, and be unsuccessful at completing college degrees;
- Will likely earn less as adults than children of intact families;
- Experience low self-esteem, feel abandoned, and experience increased poverty.

Have you ever wondered why so many people worry about the growing number of single-parent households? Why does it matter whether a family has a single parent or two parents? The primary reason is that two-parent families usually have a greater income and therefore greater resources with which to carry out their parenting obligations and responsibilities. Simply stated, by pooling their income, two parents have more money for the family to spend on goods and services. Underlying this concept is the fact that most single parents are women, who have income levels much lower than average. Although fathers are taking a more active role in families, the parent who is primarily responsible for the care of the child generally remains the mother. Involving fathers and helping them to understand the importance of their influence on their children can be central to increasing interactions and relationships (Storhaug, 2013), thereby reducing the pressure on the mother as a single parent. Further, when a child lives in a two-partner family or, in the case of a divorced or missing father, when the other partner is more involved, this supportive relationship allows for more flexibility in child care and supervision. With two adults available, one parent can take a break when the relationship gets too stressful, and whether taking turns or caring for children jointly, more nurturing parent–child time is available. The single parent often has no one to help ease the child care burden. Facing daily problems alone and having to live on one income can be frustrating.

A third significant development in the changing family structure is the rise in blended families. A blended family is one in which the primary caretakers did not give birth to one or more of the children who live in the household. Such families are most often the result of divorce and remarriage. These families can also include parents who simply avoid tying the knot or living in multigenerational households where grandparents or other family members and friends reside (Byron, 2019). With the high rate of unemployment, American divorces, relationship separations, and other lifestyle adjustment, blended families are quite common. These families often face a difficult task because supportive relationships may need to be developed before they can be nurtured. Becoming a blended family requires adjustment because members may enter and leave the family at various times throughout their lives. These adjustments intensify the need to establish and maintain family unison and support. Although all family systems need constant negotiation to maintain equilibrium, blended families face the added struggle of keeping their balance as family-system members come and go.

The kind of family situation regarded as ideal is often shaped by a **political lens**. Think about political candidates and their campaign rhetoric and advertisements. How often have you seen the family play a starring role in a local, state, or national election? Why have children and families become such hot political items? Two reasons come to mind immediately:

1. Every human being was once a child: Having been a child and had experiences that influenced the way you think and feel about things as you grew up helps raise your consciousness in this area. Most of us identify with children's issues simply because of our own experiences. All of us had positive and negative childhood

experiences. Most of us cherish the good times and wish we could have avoided the bad ones. Few, if any, adults believe it is in a child's best interest to suffer physical or emotional pain. Therefore, social workers and other professionals will continue to support and encourage programs and services that prevent and alleviate unfair treatment of all vulnerable groups (Eamon, 2008). Because children are considered a vulnerable population, most adults agree that all children should be protected and have a safe environment in which to grow. Adults are responsible for ensuring that children are shielded from various risks.

2. Everyone has a family: Just as all of us were children once, we were all raised in a diverse family. Our families probably differed vastly. Some people had two parents; others came from single-parent homes. Some people were raised with siblings and others without. Some were raised in foster homes or were adopted; others had aunts, uncles, or other relatives as their primary caretakers; and for some, institutions played the family role. No matter what our family background, our experiences mean we have strong feelings about what "ideal" families should be like.

8.3 THE RIGHTS OF CHILDREN

Children are dependent on their parent(s), and as minors their rights are connected to those of their parent(s). From this perspective, there are two counterbalancing forces at play. On the one hand, we recognize that children generally are not able to make mature decisions. This is not a negative statement about young people, but rather refers to their inexperience. For this reason, children's rights are limited and critical decisions about and responsibility for their lives rest not with them, but with their caregivers. On the other hand, we also recognize that children need protection—sometimes from their own caretakers. As a result, we have established a complex system of child protective services (see Box 8.1).

The interesting history of children's rights for the most part reflects ambivalence. From a legal standpoint, children are treated differently from adults. Children can face *status offenses*, that is, crimes based on status—in this case, age. For example, a child

---

BOX 8.1

CHILD FACT SHEET

Child Welfare in the United States

Number of children who are victims of abuse and neglect: 618,000 (U.S. Department of Health & Human Services, Administration for Children and Families, Administration on Children, Youth and Families, Children's Bureau. (2022). *Child Maltreatment 2020.* https://www.acf.hhs.gov/cb/data-research/child-maltreatment)

Number of children in foster care: 407,000 (www.childwelfare.gov/fostercaremonth/awareness/facts/)

continues

continued

Number of children adopted from foster care: 63,000 (https://www.acf.hhs.gov/sites/default/files/documents/cb/afcarsreport26.pdf)

Number of grandparents raising grandchildren: 2,335,355 (https://www.census.gov/history/www/homepage_archive/2021/june_2021.html)

Youth at Risk in the United States

Averaged freshman high school graduation rate: 86 percent (https://nces.ed.gov/programs/coe/indicator/coi/high-school-graduation-rates)

Number of juvenile arrests: 424,300 (https://www.ojjdp.gov/ojstatbb/crime/qa05101.asp?qaDate=2020)

Number of children and teens in juvenile residential facilities: 36,479 (https://www.ojjdp.gov/ojstatbb/corrections/qa08201.asp?qaDate=2019)

Ratio of cost per prisoner to cost per public school pupil: 7.8 to 1 (https://www.nokidsinprison.org/explore/costs-per-state)

Number of children and teens killed by firearms: 4,357 (https://www.kff.org/private-insurance/press-release/firearms-are-the-leading-cause-of-death-for-children-in-the-united-states-but-rank-no-higher-than-fifth-in-other-industrialized-nations/)

Did You Know . . .

Status offenses hold serious consequences, including commitment to youth corrections facilities. The Annie E. Casey Foundation has been fighting for reform because of the negative outcomes for children who enter locked detention, including re-arrest, longer-term incarceration, mental health problems, worsening of physical health problems, and traumatization. Visit the Juvenile Detention page of the Annie E. Casey website for more information.

---

can be arrested or detained for drinking alcohol, smoking cigarettes, being truant, or being a runaway. An adult cannot be arrested merely for smoking or drinking (unless doing so causes a public disturbance) or for running away from home or being truant.

The overriding principle of parens patriae (which is Latin for "father of the people") under which children can become wards of the state has guided interpretations of children's rights. This principle supported creation of a broad range of juvenile services, including parent–child relationships (Crosson-Tower, 1998, p. 270). Taking this basic position, child advocates were able to argue that children should be viewed in a different light from adults and offered rehabilitation rather than punishment.

In 1899, the first juvenile court was established in Chicago based on the principle of parens patriae and the belief that children could be rehabilitated, which required a legal system far different from the punishment-based adult system. By 1925, all but two states—Maine and Wyoming—had juvenile courts; by 1945, all states had such courts. Prosecution took a back seat to treatment as the primary focus of the juvenile justice system. Hearings were closed to the public to protect the child's right to confidentiality, and all juvenile legal records were sealed once the child reached the legal age of maturity, generally age eighteen. The juvenile court operated very informally. Attorneys were rarely provided for child offenders, and trial by jury and the right to appeal a decision were not available options. In these courtrooms, hearsay evidence was admitted. Remember, the court's purpose was twofold: (1) to identify the problem and (2) to develop and implement an appropriate treatment plan.

The juvenile court changed dramatically because of U.S. Supreme Court decisions in the 1960s. Juveniles were given many of the legal protections enjoyed by adults. Courts were required to allow attorneys to be present, witnesses could be cross-examined, defendants had the right to refuse to incriminate themselves, and guilty decisions (or, in some states, *not innocent* decisions) had to meet the legal standard of reasonable doubt.

Toward the end of the twentieth century, as violent juvenile crime seemed to have worsened (arrests of youth for violent crime have declined since the late 1990s), people had begun to ask whether children should face some of the same penalties as adults. Horrific crimes committed by children left many people in shock. Two young boys, eight and nine years old, in Chicago, Illinois, murdered a young girl to ride her bicycle; two teenagers in Arkansas shot and killed schoolmates; another teenager walked into a school hallway and indiscriminately murdered his junior high school peers. The Chicago youth were released to their parents because state law forbade the incarceration of a child under age ten. Since EducationWeek started tracking school-related violence on K–12 property related to firearms, since 2018 there have been 143 school shootings that resulted in injury or death. The largest number occurred in 2022, with 50 school-related shootings that resulted in injury or death (EducationWeek, 2022).

Cases of youth violence, especially school-related violence, has sparked a national debate over whether teens should be tried in adult courts and, if found guilty, should serve their sentences in adult prisons or even be subjected to the death penalty. Is there an answer? At what age do we stop trying to rehabilitate young people? As you have probably guessed, there are no clear-cut answers to these questions.

In a nutshell, children historically have had few rights, and there has been little agreement on what further rights, if any, they should be granted. In the past, the courts primarily defined children's rights about criminal proceedings against them. In addition, children have the right to financial support and education (Gustavsson & Segal, 1994, pp. 4, 6). Today, the United Nations continues to bring the rights of children to the forefront. The United Nations Convention on the Rights of the Child adopted in 1989 a declaration of children's rights and identified important issues for children. This convention ensured that the rights of children are protected in the areas of health care, education, legal and civil services, and provision of social services. By 2022, 195 countries had formally ratified this act, and the only country yet to do so is the United States. This important declaration is very specific in identifying the issues facing children (United Nations, 1989):

- Preamble: ... Childhood is entitled to special care and assistance.... The child ... should grow up in a family environment, in an atmosphere of happiness, love, and understanding.... The child, by reason of his physical and mental immaturity, needs special safeguards and care, including appropriate legal protection.
- Article 3(1): In all actions concerning children ... the best interests of the child shall be a primary consideration.
- Article 18(1): ... Both parents have common responsibilities for the upbringing and development of the child. Parents or, as the case may be, legal guardians, have the primary responsibility for the upbringing and development of the child.
- Article 19(1): State parties (government) shall take appropriate legislative, administrative, social, and educational measures to protect the child from all forms of physical or mental violence, injury or abuse, neglect or negligent treatment, maltreatment, or exploitation, including sexual abuse, while in the care of parent(s), legal guardian(s) or any other person who has the care of the child.

8.4 THE DESIGN OF THE AMERICAN CHILD WELFARE SYSTEM

Formal child welfare programs and services are found in both public and private settings. Government programs—local, state, and federal—are augmented by both for-profit and nonprofit agencies. In addition, privatization or contracting with nongovernmental agencies for the provision of services continues to grow as these programs are either state or federally funded (Hubel, Schreier, Hansen, & Wilcox, 2013; Huggins-Hoyt, Mowbray, Briggs, & Allen, 2019). Together, these programs form a complex system that starts with prenatal care and ranges to opportunities for teenagers. As we start this section, look carefully at Table 8.1, which provides a snapshot of children most at risk of needing services from our welfare system. Programs are varied, but they can generally be categorized as child protective services, family preservation, out-of-home services, and other services (Figure 8.1).

Child Protective Services

Child Protective Services (CPS) is probably the best known as well as the most controversial children's program. CPS serves children affected by neglect, medical neglect, physical abuse, sexual abuse, and psychological maltreatment. The intent of CPS is to protect children from abusive situations so that they can grow and develop (see Box 8.2). We've all heard stories about abusive CPS workers responding to unfounded charges, taking children from their parents, breaking up families, and ruining the lives of people. In fact, the CPS worker investigates each allegation of abuse or

CHAPTER 8: CHILD WELFARE SERVICES

Table 8.1 America's Most Vulnerable Children: A Snapshot

Numbers (2022)	
Estimated referrals of possible child abuse and neglect	3,643,232
Children substantiated/indicated as abused or neglected	618,399
Children who died as a result of abuse or neglect	1,713
Children living in out-of-home care	631,832
Children adopted from the public foster care system	57,881
Children waiting to be adopted	117,470
Children living with parents who lacked employment	18,833,000
Children living with food insecurity	38,300,000

Source: Child Welfare League of America (2022), *National Fact Sheet 2022*, https://www.cwla.org/our-work/advocacy/national-and-state-fact-sheets/.

FIGURE 8.1
Child welfare cases are heard in civil courts (sometimes termed family court or juvenile court), not criminal courts.

neglect and determines whether the charges are founded or unfounded. A case is opened if the investigation demonstrates that abuse or neglect is indeed occurring. A child is removed from the home only if his or her life is in immediate danger. However, when neglect occurs during critical periods in a child's life, it can have long-term effects on normative development that may extend across the life span (Turner, Vanderminden, & Hamby, 2019).

> **BOX 8.2**
>
> ## THE BEGINNINGS OF CHILD PROTECTIVE SERVICES: THE CASE OF MARY ELLEN
>
> In 1873, Mrs. Etta Angell Wheeler, a church visitor in New York City, learned from people in a neighborhood about a nine-year-old girl, Mary Ellen Wilson, who had been whipped and left alone for hours on end. Neighbors in her apartment building heard the child's cries time and again. The New York City Department of Charities had placed Mary Ellen in this home when she was eighteen months old. There had been no follow-up by the agency to assess the placement. Mrs. Wheeler sought help from several charitable organizations and the police to protect Mary Ellen, but no agency was willing to intervene, and no CPS organization existed. She turned for help to Mr. Henry Bergh, president of the New York Society for the Prevention of Cruelty to Animals. The society intervened with court action and Mary Ellen was removed from the home.
>
> The court found the home to be abusive. The foster mother, Mrs. Mary Connolly, was arrested and found guilty of assault. The court decided that Mary Ellen was to move to a group home, but Mrs. Wheeler asked that the child be placed in her care. Mary Ellen moved in with Mrs. Wheeler's mother and stayed with her until her death. Within a few months of the reported abuse, the New York Society for the Prevention of Cruelty to Children was founded, the first such organization in the world (Watkins, 1990).

Neglect, although chronic in nature, can also end in death and, like physical abuse, should be included in prevention efforts (Damashek, Nelson, & Bonner, 2013). An open case may receive direct services from the agency or from other contract agencies, such as a family service agency. The case is reviewed by CPS staff and is closed once all goals are achieved. All states provide some form of CPS. In 1962, a study of battered children in hospitals recommended that suspected cases be reported so that protective measures could be taken. By 1966, all states had passed legislation concerning abuse (Lindsey, 1994, p. 92).

As of 2020, approximately 3.9 million referrals of child abuse and neglect were received, involving approximately 7 million children (U.S. Department of Health and Human Services, 2022). From the fifty-two states and territories considered in the report that included both screened-in and screened-out referrals, 54.2 percent of the received reports of child abuse and neglect were screened in and the remaining 45.8 percent were screened out because they did not meet the state's standards for investigation. Well over half of these reports (66.7 percent) were submitted by professionals who are termed *mandatory reporters*, such as teachers, police officers, legal staff, and social service staff workers. Nonprofessional reporting, which made up approximately 17 percent of the reports, came from sources including parents, family and other relatives, friends, neighbors, and other interested individuals. There was also a percentage (16.3 percent) of the reports listed as other or nonclassified because the sources of the reports were unknown or anonymous. Children in the first year of life had the highest rate of victimization, at 25.1 per 1,000 children of the same age. Boys accounted for 48.1 percent of the victims and girls for 51.6 percent (U.S. Department of Health and Human Services, 2022).

According to the Children's Defense Fund (n.d.), neglect can often be associated with poverty and is the most common reason for child welfare system involvement. The Children's Defense Fund described an overrepresentation of children of color in child welfare system; for every 1,000 White children, 5.2 are in foster care compared to 9.9 of every 1,000 Black children and 16.9 of every 1,000 American Indian/Alaska Native children.

> ### Did You Know . . .
> Abusing a child or teen is a crime, but these crimes happen in many contexts. Child sex trafficking focuses on the "recruitment, harboring, transportation, provision, obtaining, patronizing, or soliciting of a minor for the purpose of a commercial sex act," according to the U.S. Department of Justice, in other words, selling children and teens for sex. Technological advances in the twenty-first century exacerbated this horrendous problem.

Family Preservation Services

Family preservation services are short-term, family-focused social services that are designed to stabilize troubled families. Family preservation services can vary, but what all programs share is the focus on keeping children safe in their own homes and providing family-based intensive social services. The goal of family preservation is to prevent child removal from the parental home with the expectation that direct services may avoid the need for out-of-home placement, allowing the family to stay together and strengthen family bonds (Tambling & Johnson, 2021; Tracy, 2008).

Gaining in popularity in the 1970s and 1980s, these services received a boost in 1980 with the passage of the Adoption Assistance and Child Welfare Act (Public Law 96–272). The 1980 act called for reasonable efforts to be made to keep children within their families and to minimize family disorder. In Family Preservation Services/Intensive Family Preservation Services, the support services work is intensive, and although programs can vary in content and delivery, it is not unusual for the child serviced to receive anywhere from six to ten hours of direct worker–family contact each week. The typical case requires four to six weeks of contact, and with Intensive Family Preservation Services, a worker's caseload can range from two to six families, providing twenty-four-hour-a-day accessibility.

> ### Did You Know . . .
> The Department of Health and Human Services has a 2018 factsheet available for free download titled "Preventing Child Abuse and Neglect." Numerous other resources can be retrieved from the Child Welfare Information Gateway.

Out-of-Home Services

Out-of-home services are programs for children who are no longer living with their biological or legal guardians, whose parental rights have been or may be terminated. Typical out-of-home programs are foster care, residential or congregate care, and adoption.

FOSTER CARE

Children enter the foster care system because they are unable to get the care they need in their parent's or guardian's home. Removal can be based on numerous factors stemming from abuse and neglectful living conditions or state of care (Font & Gershoff, 2020).

The Social Work Dictionary defined foster care as physical care for children "who are unable to live with their natural parents or legal guardians" (Barker, 2014). This simplified definition remains accurate as the goals of foster care continue to include (1) maximum protection for the child, (2) permanency, and (3) family preservation. Foster care is generally organized through state or county social services, and services may be provided within foster family homes, residential group homes, or institutions (Everett, 2008).

In 1997, the Adoption and Safe Families Act (Public Law 105-89, 1997) was passed with the intention of addressing some of the preexisting problems in the foster care system related to the adoption of special needs children, and later its interpretation emphasized the importance of keeping families together. Thereafter, states were expected to implement the law with emphasis on safety, permanency, and well-being of children who are found to be abused and neglected. In doing this, the act outlined the need for evaluation of the safety of children in foster care and the need for the measurement of child well-being. From this perspective, well-being is a multidimensional construct involving the child's overall functioning levels in terms of health, mental health, and education (Jacobs, Bruhn, & Graf, 2008). Therefore, if protection is needed to ensure the child's safety, a child may need to be placed in a foster home temporarily.

Immediate placement decisions may be needed if at the start of a CPS investigation the worker assesses that the child's life is in imminent danger. This decision is never made lightly because every effort is made to keep families together whenever possible. If the child is to be removed, however, the family is entitled to a court hearing, in most states within twenty-four to seventy-two hours of the time of removal if the child was removed without a court order. In other cases, placement may occur after a court hearing if a CPS investigation finds that this action is in the best interests of the child. Any placement must be in the least restrictive setting (see Box 8.3). For example, a foster home is less restrictive than a residential treatment center; placement with a relative is less restrictive than removal to a nonbiological foster home.

Children in foster care are provided with certain protections, including the following:

- A detailed written plan that describes the appropriateness of the placement, the services to be provided to the child, and a plan for achieving permanence.
- Periodic case review at least once every six months, although a jurisdiction may review a case more often.

- A state inventory of children who have been in care for more than six months to track these children and the goals related to their placement.
- Procedural safeguards that involve parental input in the development of case plans.
- Reunification or permanency planning services, programs that include day care, homemaker services, counseling, parent education, adoption services, and follow-up (Everett, 2008).

BOX 8.3

MYTHS AND FACTS ABOUT OUT-OF-HOME PLACEMENTS

Myth: Foster care is in the best interests of children who have known the hurt of abuse and neglect.

Fact: In some cases, when the child is at great risk, removal from the home is necessary, but it is not necessarily the solution. The devastating norm for foster children is multiple moves, extended stays, and the lack of stable permanent family ties.

Myth: Foster care is principally a problem of poor and minority families.

Fact: Problems leading to abuse and neglect know no race or class boundaries.

Myth: Most children in foster care are placed there because of physical or sexual abuse.

Fact: More than half of child removals are for neglect.

Myth: Child abuse is on the rise.

Fact: Although the number of reports has increased, the evidence does not clearly substantiate that the actual incidence is on the rise. The growing number of reports may be a result of the public's growing awareness of child abuse and of resources to contact.

Myth: Parents whose children are removed from the home do not want their children, do not deserve their children, and cannot or will not change their behavior.

Fact: Experts working with troubled families find that their problems are more extreme versions of similar issues confronting any family. Troubled families often lack resources, knowledge, and skills that most take for granted. Most parents want their children and really want to be good parents. Proper help can benefit many families, but it must be timely.

Myth: Child protective service workers are well-trained professionals but have little authority to protect children.

Fact: The child protective service worker position is an entry-level job requiring minimal education. Most states do not require education in social work and allow a person to work in this position with a degree in music, math, or other non-human service disciplines. Caseloads are usually high, pay and morale are low, and employee turnover is high. Child protective service workers have a wide range of authority, including the power to remove a child from a home, in some instances without supervisor or court approval (Edna McConnell Clark Foundation, n.d.).

For additional information, visit the Edna McConnell Clark Foundation at https://www.emcf.org/news-perspectives/.

For the most part, all states are similar, in that most children in foster care are placed in foster family homes (Everett, 2008). As of November 2021, the Children's Bureau of the U.S. Department of Health and Human Services reported the third straight year of declining numbers of children in foster care and those awaiting adoption. However, they also noted that patterns of racial disproportionality persisted, with disproportionately more children of color in care than White children. According to the National Child Abuse and Neglect Data System, approximately 618,000 children were found to be victims of child abuse and neglect in 2020, and this resulted in about 1.3 million children receiving preventive services. Of those, an estimated 124,360 children received foster care services (U.S. Department of Health and Human Services, 2022).

How are foster parents selected? What is their motivation—money? What about reports that children in foster homes are often subjected to more abuse? Despite the few cases and problems that make the press, for many foster parents there is a calling and a true desire to help the children they serve. Most people choose to be foster parents because of their love for children. Taking in children for the money does not sound like a lucrative proposition, partly because this twenty-four-hour commitment can take extreme time and energy, but also because foster care payments do not actually cover the costs of raising a child in most states (Font & Gershoff, 2020).

We need to keep in mind that children in foster care are coming from what has been judged to be unsafe home situations. Because permanency planning interventions are preferred, only those children in the most unbearable unsafe situations are removed. Most foster children are burdened by a unique set of complex problems that requires understanding and compassion, often including complicated histories of emotional trauma. Being a foster parent is not easy, and it does require a special person. At times, foster parents choose to adopt the children placed in their homes. Evidence suggests that adoption of children in foster care provides socioeconomic advantages for the child as well as less cost to the public for children who do not have the possibility of being reunited with their biological families (Zill & Bramlett, 2014).

RESIDENTIAL OR CONGREGATE CARE

Residential congregate or group care may also be termed institutional care and generally takes place in a facility setting away from the natural parents or legal guardians. Residential settings can include residential treatment centers, state hospitals, detention centers, runaway shelters, and halfway houses. All these facilities provide highly supervised or specialized twenty-four-hour residential care.

Did You Know . . .

The first residential program for children was established in 1729 in New Orleans. The program was developed by Ursuline nuns to care for children orphaned as a result of the battle with Native Americans at Natchez.

What do we know about congregate foster care?

- Younger children, generally speaking, should not be placed in congregate care and should be placed in family-type settings to promote development of healthy attachments.
- Congregate care placements include group homes, residential treatment facilities, psychiatric institutions, and emergency shelters.
- In 2020, a report (National Conference of State Legislatures) indicated that about fifty-five thousand foster children lived in congregate care.

Residential programs are also available for children who no longer live with their legal caretakers, although not necessarily because they've been removed by the state because of abuse or neglect. Typically, such programs are shelters that provide temporary housing and counseling. The purpose of runaway shelters is to get youths off the streets, provide protection, and attempt to reunite children with their families. Social service providers recognize the importance of getting runaways off the streets and into services as quickly as possible to avoid problems related to theft, drugs, prostitution, or pornography (see the activity below).

> ## Activity
> Contact your local runaway youth shelter and ask about the rules of admission and length of stay. Could you find a shelter near you? If you could, ask what happens to youths who leave the shelter but do not return home.

A state-established limit on the length of time that young people may reside in shelters generally restricts these settings to homeless youths. Some programs require parental consent for children to remain in shelters. What happens to youths whose parents do not grant permission for them to remain in the program? Some programs do not allow disruptive youths or youths with mental health problems to enter shelters. What types of community programs, if any, are available for these youths?

ADOPTION

The Child Welfare Information Gateway defines adoption as "the social, emotional, and legal process in which children who will not be raised by their birth parents become full and permanent legal members of another family while maintaining genetic and psychological connections to their birth family" (Child Welfare Information Gateway, n.d.c, p. 1). Adoption creates a "legal family for children when the birth family is unable or unwilling to parent" (Barth, 1995, p. 48). For example, in 2020 there were approximately 117,000 children waiting to be adopted (U.S. Department of Health and Human Services, 2022).

Massachusetts is credited with being the first state to enact an adoption law, in 1851 (Cole, 1985, p. 639), although some cite Mississippi, in 1846, and Texas, in 1850, as having earlier adoption statutes (Crosson-Tower, 1998, p. 356). Whichever state was first, there is consensus that the Massachusetts legislation served as the model for other states (Adoption Law Center, 2017). By 1929, all states had enacted some form of adoption law.

During the nineteenth and much of the twentieth century, most children in need of homes lived in orphanages. Young people were placed in orphanages for any number of reasons, including having poor parents who couldn't afford to raise them, having been born to unwed mothers, or having no parents because of death or abandonment (Crosson-Tower, 1998, p. 357).

Charles Loring Brace, a minister and founder of the Children's Aid Society in New York City, led one of the more compelling child welfare efforts of the nineteenth century (Staller, 2020). Brace developed what became known as the Orphan's Train, through which some fifty thousand to one hundred thousand urban orphans were placed on Midwestern and Western farms (Quam, 1995, p. 2575). The children, who were picked up on the streets of New York City, were put on a wagon train heading west. In town after town, city after city, the train would stop and put the youths up for adoption. Brace (1872) believed that moving waifs off city streets, away from the temptations of urban life to more rural, tranquil lives of work and family, would allow them to be prosperous and productive.

The Orphan's Train was a manifestation of the nation's prevailing belief, no less strong today, that children should live in wholesome environments where caretakers can provide for their needs. Remember the basic child welfare principle: in the best interests of the child. Brace's program and other child-saving programs, including orphanages, were built on this ideal.

Today, adoption takes place in many ways. These include placing children through child placement agencies and through direct agreements between two parties sanctioned by the courts.

Agency-based adoption occurs in government, nonprofit, and for-profit family welfare settings. It entails a rigorous and time-consuming process, which generally includes the following steps:

- Identification of suitable children ensures that all children in need of adoptive homes are included.
- Freeing for placement is the legal process by which custody of the child is removed from one set of parents so he or she can be assigned to the adoptive parents.
- Preparation for adoption involves working with the child before adoption to prepare him or her for the new family. Potential adoptive parents are closely scrutinized by the agency to ensure they have the resources needed to raise a child in a loving, caring environment, usually including the home study process.
- Selection of adoptive parents is conducted by the agency after close review of applications and supporting materials. The agency's goal is to match a child with the adoptive parents who can best meet his or her unique needs.

- Placement with an adoptive family is characterized by many social workers as one of the most exciting days for worker, family, and child. It is a time of joy as the new family begins its life together. Everyone involved often sheds tears!

Postplacement services include a variety of agency-based supports to the family as it makes the transition to a new system of relations. By placing a child with a specific family, the agency is affirming that the placement is in the best interests of the child. To increase the likelihood of success, the agency offers the family continuing supports, ranging from individual and family counseling and support groups to social worker home visits. Although the exact types of intervention may differ, postadoption and permanency support services are widespread. These services support adoptive parents by providing education, training, and information that help the adjustment process. Although the agency wants as few disruptions as possible with the adoption, sometimes the child is removed from the adoptive family's home. When this happens, the social worker does not blame anyone or refer to the original placement as a failure, but instead looks again at what supports are needed for the child and what type of child is best suited for that family.

Legal finalization of the adoption takes place after a period following initial placement. There is a popular myth that adoption is final when the child is placed with the family. This is not so for agency-based adoptions. The final legal assignment of custody is made after an extended period. The period varies among agencies; the norm seems to be six months to one year following placement. The court is the final authority in legally assigning custody of the child to the adoptive parent. The court's decision is reached after review of the agency's reports and recommendations.

Postadoption services provide children with any needed supports, such as counseling, and provides parents with educational or ongoing counseling sessions. Agencies recognize that it may be in the best interests of the child for support services to be provided for extended periods beyond the legal adoption phase (Cole, 1985). Additionally, certain eligible adoptive families may receive financial support, also called a subsidy, provided by the Federal Adoption Assistance and Child Welfare Act of 1980 to facilitate the adoption of children from foster care (Child Welfare Information Gateway, 2020a). If a child is eligible for a federal adoption subsidy, medical assistance via Medicaid is included.

You might have seen advertisements in your college or local newspaper that read something like this: "Loving couple with a great deal to give looking to adopt a newborn. Will pay all fees, including prenatal, delivery, hospitalization, legal, and follow-up costs. Please call..."

Some families resort to private sources, also called independent adoption, rather than using agency-based adoption services. Agreements are reached between the two families involved, and the courts, assisted by attorneys, finalize the legal arrangements. These adoptions can take place much faster and with less red tape than the agency-based process. The prospective adoptive parents usually provide financial support for the pregnant mother and her family, cover all related health costs, and often add a financial stipend—that is, a salary.

Independent adoption is costly, running to tens of thousands of dollars including legal fees, medical expenses, and so on. For-profit adoptions are against the law—that would be "selling" humans! Recognize that with independent adoptions there is less scrutiny and follow-up than with agency-based services. Cole (1985) suggested that problems with independent adoptions can be reduced if the following steps are taken:

- Courts require a detailed statement of all monies that change hands relating to the adoption.
- Violators are vigorously prosecuted and subjected to severe sanctions.
- Communities provide enough financial support to adoption agencies that they can offer the same level of health and maintenance care as independent adoption.

There are three potential pools for adoption: healthy infants, children with special needs, and children from foreign countries (Kadushin & Martin, 1988). Fewer healthy infants are available for adoption because of the increased availability of birth control and abortion (Crosson-Tower, 1998). Unfortunately, it is not uncommon for a couple to be told the waiting period for a healthy infant may be up to ten years!

A special needs child has unique characteristics that can include "race and ethnicity, medical problems, older age (over age 3), attachment to a sibling group, developmental disabilities, and emotional difficulties" (Crosson-Tower, 1998, p. 374). Such children are much harder to place because of their special needs and are more available than healthy infants for adoption.

Sometimes people look to the international community for children to adopt. This has become less common over time. In 2010, 11,058 children were adopted internationally, while in 2021 the number was 1,785 (U.S. Department of State, n.d.). Children born in areas of civil strife or extreme poverty are the main subjects of such adoptions. Over time, Latin America, Vietnam, Korea, the Philippines, India, and other Asian countries have been the principal nations and regions sending children to the United States (Crosson-Tower, 1998).

Did You Know . . .
You can visit the Heart Gallery of America, Inc., to see photo lists of children awaiting adoption.

8.5 CHILDREN WITH SPECIAL NEEDS

As of June 28, 2022, there were 391,098 children in foster care. Many of these children had suffered abuse, abandonment, and/or neglect (U.S. Department of Health and Human Services, 2021). Because of a history of trauma, many or most of these children would be considered *special needs* and required special parenting once placed into either temporary or permanent homes. The term special needs is often associated with children within the U.S. welfare system. Each state's specific criteria may vary slightly, but in general, these children meet special criteria and are either emotionally or physically handicapped. Because of their trauma histories, special needs children require special attention and can be difficult to parent.

Adoption is the permanent legal transfer of full parental rights from one parent or set of parents to another parent or set of parents (Henry & Pollack, 2009, p. 1). The social stigma attached to adoption has a long history in our society and can be fueled by disparaging community attitudes toward adoptive kinship. Many couples would prefer to have their own biological children rather than adopt. When a couple adopts a special needs child, they do not start with a clean slate. Many of these children have had difficult lives, and after suffering either physical or emotional abuse they may have difficulty overcoming past experiences and memories. The negative experiences imbedded in these children and influencing their emotional development can make trusting difficult. This fear of social connections can create a distance between the new parent and the new extended family system. Given the extensive needs of these children, adjustment for the adoptive parents can also be difficult, and attachment is a two-way street. These new parents may go through their own grieving process, experiencing feelings of shock, denial, anger, depression, and physical symptoms of distress and guilt as the dreams of the child they wished for or expected are replaced by the realities of the actual child.

After a brief honeymoon period, the adoptive parents of a special needs child may experience a shocking realization that the new child is unhealthy, either physically or emotionally. Despite the information provided prior to the adoptive placement, many adoptive parents cannot comprehend the full realm of the behaviors and difficulties of the child prior to placement. Consequently, the parents, especially the primary caregiver, may experience shock and bewilderment and may start making excuses for the child's behavior. After living with a child who is unresponsive to them, parents may experience anger or rage. Adoptive caregivers may discover feelings of guilt for not truly loving their adoptive child and for feeling ambivalent or angry toward their child (Forbes & Dziegielewski, 2003).

Many times, the biases of society are as strong, if not stronger, within the nucleus of the immediate family and extended family. Adoption of a special needs child involves integrating adopted children into the entire family social system. Therefore, Henry and Pollack (2009) outline the importance of preplacement training that involves education about adoption issues and feelings that may surface and includes the extended family as part of the preadoptive process. Lack of support from the extended family can undermine the legitimacy of the adoptive placement for the adoptive mother. Therefore, professionals should encourage participation in postplacement services as a necessary part of practice (Henry & Pollack, 2009).

A final but controversial point about adoption is the notion of placement in the best interests of the child and what constitutes "best interests." A particularly contentious child welfare practice around placement of children with adoptive families of the same or different race or ethnicity can arouse strong feelings. Among the many types of adoption, transracial adoptions, also referred to as interracial, biracial, multicultural, or multiracial adoption, have gained and maintained an increased attention over time (Henry & Pollack, 2009; Roberts, 2022; Valenzuela, 2022). The issue is the idea that the cultural needs of a child far outweigh other placement considerations. For example, the National Association of Black Social Workers does not support the placement of African American children in non-Black homes. Similarly, the 1978 ICWA places responsibility for adoption of Native American children within tribes rather than with traditional public child welfare agencies. The 1978 law requires Native American children to be placed with extended family members as a first option and then with other tribal families, regardless of the wishes of the parents.

Should adoption be constrained by race and ethnicity and other cultural factors? Does the compelling need for permanency override the cultural needs of a child? Can a child develop cultural competence and identity in a home of different racial or ethnic origin? What about religion? In Judaism, for example, the religion's law is that a child born to a Jewish mother is always Jewish. Should a Jewish child always be placed in a Jewish home? Should Catholic children always be placed with Catholic families? Is it best to keep a child in a temporary foster home if no culturally similar family can be found? There are no easy answers to these questions, and they may require individual evaluation that clearly considers the best interests of the child. What are your thoughts? How do you feel about this issue?

Other Services

Other child welfare services meet additional needs of children. It is impossible to discuss all of them, but we will touch briefly on one important program area to which social workers often refer children and teens.

YOUTH PROGRAMS

Most of us at one time or another have participated in youth programs sponsored by such groups as the YMCA, YWCA, Boys Clubs, Girls Clubs, Blue Birds, Girls Scouts, Boys Scouts, Brownies, or Little League baseball. Many agencies in our communities work with young people through an array of programs ranging from gym-and-swim to therapeutic prevention.

The YMCA, for example, offers an array of programs including youth development (including sports programs), healthy living (including water safety), and social responsibility (including disaster response). The YWCA offers advocacy and support for anti-oppressive practices benefitting women (e.g., child care, interpersonal violence, and economic empowerment).

Youth programs have four important functions in our communities:

- Youths have positive peer experiences in a formal, supervised atmosphere.
- Youths learn to interact with others in groups.

- Youths can develop their own extended networks outside the family.
- Youths find a safe haven, particularly with after-school, weekend, or evening activities that take place when caretakers may be at work and unable to supervise their children.

8.6 CHILD SEXUAL ABUSE AND TRAUMA

Unfortunately, emotional trauma sustained during childhood and adolescence is not rare. Experiences that can result in negative outcomes associated with emotional traumatization can include bullying, community violence, disasters, exposure to intimate partner violence of caregivers, medical trauma, physical abuse, refugee trauma, sexual abuse, sex trafficking, terrorism, and traumatic grief. The National Child Traumatic Stress Network, funded by the U.S. government, offers up-to-date information and training for professionals, students, parents, and all others who might be involved with children and adolescents.

Sexual victimization stands as one of the most difficult for social workers for many reasons. According to the National Child Traumatic Stress Network, sexual abuse is a type of maltreatment involving a child in sexual activity that provides sexual gratification or financial benefit to the perpetrator. This includes "any interaction between a child and an adult (or another child) in which the child is used for the sexual stimulation of the perpetrator or an observer. Sexual abuse can include both touching and non-touching behaviors. Non-touching behaviors can include voyeurism (trying to look at a child's naked body), exhibitionism, or exposing the child to pornography" (National Child Traumatic Stress Network, n.d.).

Because of the secrecy that surrounds this activity, the abuse of power—often by someone close to and trusted by the child—and the emotional reactions it causes, this continues to be a difficult subject for most people to talk about. As society's awareness of children's issues has grown, so has awareness about child sexual abuse. It is estimated that by the time children reach age seventeen, one of every four females and one of every twenty males has been confronted with sexual abuse (Finkelhor, Shattuck, Turner, & Hamby, 2014). This means that by the time many children reach adulthood, their lives have been affected by some type of sexual abuse.

Social work programs often offer courses where the presence and subsequent signs of child sexual abuse are identified. As mentioned above, this area of practice can be particularly disturbing for social workers. Children represent such a vulnerable population, and the desire to protect them will affect even the most seasoned social worker. This means that all intervention must start with a self-awareness that will result in a greater understanding of others (Morgaine & Capous-Desyllas, 2015) and attention to the potential for secondary traumatization and self-care (van Dernoot Lipsky & Burk, 2009). To start the process, protective service social workers will interview the child, being careful to build rapport and use forensically defensible interview techniques that might include such activities as play that help make the child feel as comfortable as possible when discussing such a disturbing and confusing topic. Medical staff will examine for physical indicators such as bruises or bleeding in the external genital or anal areas, and medical tests will be run for possible venereal diseases and, if relevant, pregnancy. Possible indicators of sexual abuse include an increase in sleep problems, withdrawn behavior, angry outbursts, anxiety, depression, not wanting to be left alone with individuals, and inappropriate-for-age sexual knowledge. Professionals look for patterns of behavior; generally, there is no single behavior that might signal sexual victimization. With the secretiveness and shame that often surrounds sexual abuse, social workers must be skilled at assessing children who are survivors to help them to move past the abuse using evidence-support interventions.

Mandatory Reporting: Who Is Expected to Report?

Social workers, like other professionals, are considered mandatory reporters. Numerous professionals are responsible for mandatory reporting, including all licensed or registered professionals of the healing arts and any health-related occupation who examine, attend, treat, or provide other professional or specialized services including, but not limited to, physicians (including physicians in training), psychologists, social workers, dentists, nurses, osteopathic physicians and surgeons, optometrists, chiropractors, podiatrists, pharmacists, and other health-related professionals. This also generally includes

- Employees and officers in both public and private schools;
- Employees or officers of any public or private agency or institution or other individuals providing social, medical, hospital, or mental health services, including financial assistance;
- Law enforcement agency officials including courts, police departments, correctional institutions, and parole or probation offices;
- Individual providers of child care or employees or officers of any licensed or registered child care facility, foster home, or similar institution;
- Medical examiners or coroners; and
- In some states, employees of any public or private agency providing recreational or sports activities.

As you can see, there is a diverse group of professionals expected to care for and ensure the safety of our children (Child Welfare Information Gateway, 2019).

All social workers, regardless of where they work, must be aware of what is considered reportable and how to make a report. When a report is indicated, it must be made to the child welfare services office or law enforcement. If a social worker, like other professionals, fails to make a report of an incident involving child abuse or neglect, or knowingly fails to provide additional information, or prevents another person from reporting such an incident, they can be found guilty of violations of reporting laws, which are present.

The following types of examples include the indicators that are among those that need to be reported (State of New Jersey, Department of Children and Families, 2024a):

- Inadequate supervision
- Failure to provide food, clothing, or shelter
- Unexplained or suspicious injuries
- Intimate partner violence
- Substance abuse and misuse that affects the child
- Fear or changed behavior in child
- Atypical interest in sex, knowledge of sexual behavior, or acting out sexually
- Rejecting or terrorizing the child

Before you call the child welfare services office in your state (or law enforcement) to make a report of abuse or neglect, you will need to gather certain information. If you are concerned that the report is not needed or if you are not sure if you should make the report, call anyway, and confer with the intake worker. It is not your responsibility to prove that abuse or neglect has occurred, but to report it if you suspect it. If you make a report and the report was made in good faith, you will be immune from liability. In the best-case scenario, the caregivers will not find out who made the report, but this can never be guaranteed. If you do not want your name released, be sure to tell the intake worker that this is your preference. Also, many experienced social workers question whether they should tell the child or the child's caregivers that they are making a report. For the most part, it is best to tell them, but never tell them if you feel it could put you in danger. Your safety is an important priority that should not be underestimated. Whether or not you tell the child's caregivers about the report, you still need to make the report. As you prepare to make the report, be sure that you gather information about the details related to the situation and refer the case as soon as possible. Time is always of the essence, and the sooner you report the case, the less likely it is that the child will be subjected to any further abuse or neglect or to numerous interviews in which the information will have to be repeated multiple times if the case is accepted.

Each state in the United States may vary slightly in procedure, but for the most part the social worker will want to obtain as much of the following information as possible before referring the matter for investigation (State of New Jersey, 2024b):

- Name and date of birth or age for all adults and children involved
- A description of the abuse, including whether the child has current injuries
- Alleged perpetrator's name, location, and access to the child
- Whether the child has Native American or Alaska Native heritage
- Telephone numbers, including area code
- Any cultural or language considerations, race, and ethnicity
- Addresses, directions, or other means to locate the individuals of concern
- Additional information related to family functioning, resources, and supports
- Detailed observations and statements made by the child or others

Once the report is filed, the social worker may be called on to provide any information relating to the incident of abuse or neglect that needs clarification or was not contained in the original report. Sometimes a written report must be submitted following a verbal report. If the social worker is with the child or in the home when the report is made, when the intake worker arrives, the social worker should facilitate the assessment as much as possible by providing a private place for him or her to meet with the child. The intake worker will almost always want to meet with the child alone, without the parents present. He or she will decide whether police intervention is needed. If it is not an emergency and the child is in a protected environment, the police may not need to be called. This decision will depend on the time and the circumstances of the situation, but the social worker should be prepared for what could happen. The social worker may also be asked to testify in court; again, this will depend on the individual situation.

The families and the child involved will be assessed and offered services to assist in addressing and remedying the problem. The goal is to protect the safety and integrity of the child. There are varied services that can be provided; those that are offered will be directly related to the needs determined on the intake and follow-up interviews. Services that can be offered can include diversion services; counseling services; child care/day care; chore services; emergency help such as food, clothing, or rent; and referrals for other services not offered by the department, as well as foster care and foster-care-related cost (e.g., clothing for the child).

If it is determined that the potential for harm does exist, a case plan will be developed and implemented. The case plan will outline the safety issues, goals, and objectives to be accomplished to ensure the protection of the child, as well as the desired outcomes. Indicators and consequences related to success or nonsuccess of the plan will be clearly identified. It is important to find out the reporting procedures for your state before an issue occurs. That way, you will be aware of what is expected and what needs to be done to facilitate the situation and protect the child.

Name: Harun Aslan

Place of residence: Kastamonu, Turkey

College/university degrees: Anadolu University, BBA, BA in sociology (double major); Hacettepe University, PhD in social work

Present position and title: Assistant professor at Kastamonu University, Faculty of Health Sciences, Department of Social Work

What's your story? My interest in social work started with my participation in various volunteering activities during my undergraduate years, and I started to work professionally in the social work profession at the end of 2013. At that time, the number of departments providing social work

education in Turkish universities was rather limited. The Council of Higher Education, which is responsible for the functioning of higher education institutions in Turkey, took an important step to make the social work discipline active in universities in other cities. In order to increase the number of social workers in Turkey, a long-term program was developed through which students would be trained to become academics in social work by receiving postgraduate education and would then go on to train new social workers in the coming years.

Within the framework of this program, the primary goal was to identify and raise successful young social work and sociology graduates. My professional acquaintance with the social work profession and discipline was also realized through this program. Thanks to the economic support I received from the program, in 2014, I was accepted to the postgraduate program in the Social Work Department of Hacettepe University established on July 8, 1967. The department is Turkey's most established and most prestigious social work department. After completing my first year in the master's program, I was transferred from the master's program to the integrated doctorate program. In 2021, I graduated from the integrated doctorate program. During this period, I also served as a research assistant at Hacettepe University, Department of Social Work. Then, I was transferred to Kastamonu University in September 2021. Since then, I have been working as a doctoral faculty member there.

During the years I worked as a research assistant at Hacettepe University Department of Social Work, social work areas I primarily focused on were child welfare, social policy, and migration. I participated in social work practices related to fields of poverty, migration, and children in Ankara Provincial Directorate of Family and Social Services affiliated to the Ministry of Family and Social Services for four semesters and completed my compulsory internship. I have also taken part in many international projects during my professional and academic life. I participated in projects carried out by the United Nations High Commissioner and the International Labor Organization and worked as a researcher in such projects. The projects were on problems related to various areas related to children and migration, such as prevention of sexual abuse of children and protection of children working on the streets in Turkey. In this sense, I prepared various risk maps and made needs analysis and social work practices at various levels, especially for disadvantaged Turkish and immigrant children. Finally, I participated in voluntary activities in various nongovernmental organizations in the field of child welfare.

Why did you choose social work as a career? I think that my interest in the field of social work developed due to the social problems that are constantly present in society, and which we always feel in our bones. The times my friends and I discussed these problems in our university years had a great effect on my developing my interest in social work. However, my own experiences regarding some of these social problems may have been the most important factor. After the age of seven, alongside my education, I worked in various sectors (furniture, textile, retail sales), which I think fed into my decision to choose the

continues

continued

field of child welfare. During those years, during the summer holidays, instead of playing in playgrounds, I spent hours sanding furniture, carrying heavy tools to and from the shop, and was engaging with adults in a masculine environment at a level that was not suitable for children. This left traces on me, which I believe made me choose the social work profession and in particular the field of child welfare. I believe that I can help other children via the knowledge and experience I have in this profession.

What is your favorite social work story? Years ago, a professor of mine and I made an appointment with a family to talk about their children. The family made their living by collecting, sorting, and selling materials thrown away in dumpsters. We visited them in their home. This family could not send their children to school and had to make their children work on the street to contribute economically to the household. My professor and I knew that the family had many young children, like families with a similar sociodemographic structure; thus, we took biscuits, candies, and other snacks with us to gladden them. Before the interview, we offered to give them to the children, after getting permission from the family. Naturally, all of the children saw the snacks and eagerly circled around us. Most families and children consume these kinds of snacks without thinking about it, but these were important gifts for these children. The youngest child (three or four years old) could not get to us as easily as the other older children, so we made a point of offering him any snack he wanted. This boy took some snacks and, as he walked away from us, we saw that he had taken so many that he had stuffed in his pocket. He was holding his sweatpants with his right hand so that they would not fall, and with his left hand trying to prevent things from falling out of his pockets. He looked at us the whole time for fear that his sweatpants would fall off. The greatest knowledge I gained on that day was seeing firsthand the utter poverty I had read in books, articles, and reports throughout my social work professional life. It hit me deeply. I can also say that seeing the happiness of a child closely and being deeply saddened by the absolute poverty he was in at the same time is my unforgettable memory in this profession.

What is one thing you would change in the community if you had the power to do so? My greatest desire is to create a society where women, children, disabled people, the elderly, and other vulnerable groups are free from violence and are not abused. I would like to tell people that violence is an abnormal behavior in daily life, that harming a person should not be such an easy thing, and that many problems can be solved through communication and reconciliation instead of violence, even in ordinary actions in routine life.

SUMMARY

Children are an essential part of our country's future development. What we do with and for them benefits all of us. Homer Folks, in 1940, wrote, "The safety of our democracy depends in large measure upon the welfare of our children" (White House Conference, 1942). Of course, that sentiment holds true today. Our nation's history shows an ongoing sense of caring and responsibility for children, and although we want to protect them—even from themselves—we also want to ensure they are provided as many opportunities as possible. For certain vulnerable groups, especially Native Americans, cultural integrity remains at the heart of successful intervention and building resilience when serving these youth (Corenblum, 2014). How we care for our children tells us a great deal about our society's beliefs, hopes, and aspirations. Involving the family and community support systems as well as understanding spiritual ways and customs provides the foundation for successful integration back into the family and support systems (Garrett et al., 2014).

We do a great deal to care for our nation's children, but we need to do more. We need to find ways to guarantee every child a healthy, caring home. A stimulating environment that encourages growth and development should be the norm for all children. We can accept nothing less. We also need to become aware of our own feelings and how this can affect the helping relationship (Morgaine & Capous-Desyllas, 2015; Singer, Cummings, Moody, & Benuto, 2020). The desire to protect children is strong and this must be balanced with a professional intervention that is always best for the child.

Child welfare is an exciting field. Exploring possibilities for maximizing a highly organized system of care and commitment will remain the challenge (Bargeman, Smith, &Wekerle, 2021; Hubel et al., 2013). Programs still have a long way to go, but more interest in evidence-based outcomes and measures is expected. To further these goals, agencies will need to support professional staff by providing in-services and continuing education on the topic to ensure buy-in from existing employees. When education is combined with connected and well-informed social networks, the fabric to support evidence-based practices will come to the forefront (Horwitz et al., 2014). When this is paired with a well-trained professional workforce, we will have the best recipe for success.

Child welfare is an exciting and rewarding field with one of the noblest purposes—to preserve the well-being of our nation's children. Agency and professional efforts in this area will always be in constant flux, although always under the watchful eyes of the public and of policy makers. Social workers have been, are, and must continue to be significant players in child welfare.

REFERENCES

Administration for Children & Families. (2021). *Child fatalities due to abuse and neglect decreased in FY 2020, report finds*. Retrieved from https://www.acf.hhs.gov/media/press/2022/child-fatalities-due-abuse-and-neglect-decreased-fy-2020-report-finds

Adoption and Safe Families Act of 1997. Pub. L. No. 105–89, 111 Stat. 2115 (1997).

Adoption Assistance and Child Welfare Act of 1980. Pub. L. No. 96–272, 94 Stat. 500 (1980).

Adoption Law Center. (2017). *Significant milestones in the history of adoption in the U.S.* Retrieved from https://adoptmidtn.com/milestones-in-history-of-adoption/

Annie E. Casey Foundation. (2022, October). *Child population by race and ethnicity in the United States*. Retrieved from https://datacenter.kidscount.org/data/tables/103-child-population-by-race-and-ethnicity?loc=1&loct=1#detailed/1/any/false/2048,574,1729,37,871,870,573,869,36,868/68,69,67,12,70,66,71,72/423,424

Bargeman, M., Smith, S., & Wekerle, C. (2021). Trauma-informed care as a rights-based "standard of care": A critical review. *Child Abuse and Neglect, 119*. https://doi.org/10.1016/j.chiabu.2020.104762

Barker, R. L. (2014). *The social work dictionary* (6th ed.). Washington, DC: NASW Press.

Barth, R. P. (1995). Adoption. In R. Edwards & J. G. Hopps (Eds.), *Encyclopedia of social work* (19th ed., Vol. 1, pp. 48–59). Washington, DC: NASW Press.

Bearman, S. K., Garland, A. F., & Schoenwald, S. K. (2014). From practice to evidence in child welfare: Model specification and fidelity measurement of team decision making. *Children and Youth Services Review, 39*, 153–159.

Brace, C. L. (1872). *The dangerous classes of New York and twenty years' work among them*. New York, NY: Wynkoop and Hallenbeck.

Brewsaugh, Katrina, and Sarah Prendergast. 2022. *Ten Key Design Elements for Rigorous Impact Evaluations in Child Welfare: A Desk Reference for Evaluators*. OPRE Report #2022-171. Washington, DC: Office of Planning, Research, and Evaluation, Administration for Children and Families, US Department of Health and Human Services.

Byron, E. (2019, Dec. 15). How the definition of the American family has changed. *The Wall Street Journal*. Retrieved from https://www.wsj.com/articles/how-the-definition-of-an-american-family-has-changed-11576418401

ChildStats Forum on Child and Family Statistics. (n.d.). List of Tables Table POP1. Retrieved from https://www.childstats.gov/americaschildren/tables/pop1.asp?popup=true.

Child Welfare Information Gateway. (n.d.a). *Racial equity resources for child welfare professionals*. Retrieved November 25, 2022, from https://www.childwelfare.gov/topics/systemwide/diverse-populations/racialequity/

Child Welfare Information Gateway. (n.d. b) *Strategies for reducing inequity*. Retrieved November 25, 2022, from https://www.childwelfare.gov/topics/systemwide/cultural/disproportionality/reducing/

Child Welfare Information Gateway. (n.d.c). *Introduction to adoption*. Retrieved December 17, 2022, from https://www.childwelfare.gov/topics/adoption/intro/

Child Welfare Information Gateway. (2019). *Mandatory reporters of child abuse and neglect*. Retrieved from https://www.childwelfare.gov/topics/systemwide/laws-policies/statutes/manda/

Child Welfare Information Gateway. (2020a). *Adoption assistance for children adopted from foster care*. Retrieved from https://www.childwelfare.gov/pubs/f-subsid/

Child Welfare Information Gateway. (2020b). *How the child welfare system works*. U.S. Department of Health and Human Services, Administration for Children and Families, Children's Bureau. Retrieved from https://www.childwelfare.gov/pubs/factsheets/cpswork/

Children's Bureau. (2020). *Factsheet: How the child welfare system works*. Retrieved from https://cwig-prod-prod-drupal-s3fs-us-east-1.s3.amazonaws.com/public/documents/cpswork.pdf?VersionId=1OJwA2lAGsRB.0WoXB_CW9a6Hw1MbGpy

Children's Defense Fund. (n.d.). *Child welfare: The problem*. Retrieved from https://www.childwelfare.gov/topics/safety-and-risk/poverty-and-neglect/

Clark, H., Coll-Seck, A., Banergee, A., Peterson, S., Dalglish, S., Ameratunga, S., ... Costello, A. (2022). *A future for the world's children?* WHO–UNICEF–Lancet Commission. https://doi.org/10.1016/S0140-6736(19)32540-1

Coady, N., Hoy, S. L., & Cameron, G. (2013). Fathers' experiences with child welfare services. *Child and Family Social Work, 18*, 275–284. https://doi.org/10.1111/j.1365-2206.2012.00842.x

Cole, E. S. (1985). Adoption: History, policy, and program. In J. Laird & A. Hartman (Eds.), *A handbook of child welfare: Context, knowledge, and practice* (pp. 638–666). New York, NY: Free Press.

Corenblum, B. (2014). Relationships between racial–ethnic identity, self-esteem, and in-group attitudes among First Nation children. *Journal of Youth Adolescence, 42*, 387–404.

Cross, T., & Risser, H. (2022). Child welfare system: Structure, functions, and best practices. In R. Geffner, J. White, K. Hamberger, A. Rosenbaum, V. Vaughan-Eden, & V. Vieth (Eds.), *Handbook of interpersonal violence and abuse across the lifespan* (pp. 1736–1767). New York: Springer.

Crosson-Tower, C. (1998). *Exploring child welfare: A practice perspective*. Boston, MA: Allyn & Bacon.

Crosson-Tower, C. (2012). *Exploring child welfare: A practice perspective* (6th ed.). Upper Saddle River, NJ: Pearson Prentice Hall.

Damashek, A., Nelson, M. M., & Bonner, B. L. (2013). Fatal child maltreatment: Characteristics of deaths from physical abuse versus neglect. *Child Abuse & Neglect, 37*, 735–744.

Dobelstein, A. W. (2002). *Social welfare: Policy and analysis* (3rd ed.). Pacific Grove, CA: Cengage Learning.

Eamon, M. K. (2008). *Empowering vulnerable populations*. Chicago, IL: Lyceum Books.

Edna McConnell Clark Foundation. (n.d.). *Keeping families together: Facts on family preservation services*. New York, NY: Author.

EducationWeek. (2022). School shootings this year: How many and where. *EducationWeek*. Retrieved December 19, 2022, from https://www.edweek.org/leadership/school-shootings-this-year-how-many-and-where/2022/01

Everett, J. E. (2008). Child foster care. In T. Mizrahi & L. E. Davis (Eds.), *Encyclopedia of social work* (20th ed., Vol. 2, pp. 375–389). Washington, DC: NASW Press.

Finkelhor, D., Shattuck, A., Turner, H., & Hamby, S. (2014). The lifetime prevalence of child sexual abuse and sexual assault assessed in late adolescence. *Journal of Adolescent Health, 55*, 329–333. https://doi.org/10.1016/j.jadohealth.2013.12.026

Font, S. A., & Gershoff, E. T. (2020). An introduction to foster care. In S. Fong and E. Gershoff (Eds.), *Foster Care and Best Interests of the Child* (pp. 1–19). Springer Briefs in Psychology. Cham, Switzerland: Springer. https://doi.org/10.1007/978-3-030-41146-6_1

Forbes, H. T., & Dziegielewski, S. F. (2003). Issues facing adoptive mothers of children with special needs. *Journal of Social Work, 3*, 301–320.

Garrett, M. T., Parrish, M., Williams, C., Grayshield, L., Portman, T. A., Rivera, E. T., & Maynard, E. (2014). Invited commentary: Fostering resilience among Native American youth through therapeutic intervention. *Journal of Youth Adolescence, 43*, 470–490.

Gil, D. (1985). The ideological context of child welfare. In J. Laird & A. Hartman (Eds.), *A handbook of child welfare: Context, knowledge, and practice* (pp. 11–33). New York, NY: Free Press.

Gustavsson, N. S., & Segal, E. A. (1994). *Critical issues in child welfare*. Thousand Oaks, CA: Sage.

Hamilton, B. E., & Ventura, S. J. (2012). *Birth rates for U.S. teenagers reach historic lows for all age and ethnic groups* (NCHS Data Brief (no. 89), pp. 1–8). Hyattsville, MD: National Center for Health Statistics. Retrieved from http://www.cdc.gov/nchs/data/databriefs/db89.pdf

Harty, J., & Banman, A. (2022). Engaging fathers in child welfare and foster care settings: Promoting paternal contributions to the safety, permanency and well-being of children and families. In J. L. Bellamy, B. P. Lemmons, Q. R. Cryer-Coupet, & J. A. Shadik (Eds.), *Social work practice with fathers* (pp. 185–205). Cham, Switzerland: Springer. https://doi.org/10.1007/978-3-031-13686-3_11

Henry, M. J., & Pollack, D. (2009). *Adoption in the United States: A reference for families, professionals, and students.* Chicago, IL: Lyceum Books.

Hook, J. L., & Courtney, M. E. (2010). *Employment of former foster youth as young adults: Evidence from the Midwest study.* Chicago, IL: Chapin Hall at the University of Chicago.

Horwitz, S. M., Hurlburt, M. S., Goldhaber-Fiebert, J. D., Palinkas, L. A., Rolls-Reutz, J., Zhang, J., . . . Landsver, J. (2014). Exploration and adoption of evidence-based practice by US child welfare agencies. *Children and Youth Services Review, 39,* 147–152.

Hubel, G. S., Schreier, A., Hansen, D. J., & Wilcox, B. L. (2013). A case study of the effects of privatization of child welfare on services for children and families: The Nebraska experience. *Children and Youth Services Review, 35,* 2049–2958.

Huggins-Hoyt, K., Mowbray, O., Briggs, H., & Allen, J. (2019). Private vs public child welfare systems: A comparative analysis of national safety outcome performance. *Child Abuse & Neglect, 94.* https://doi.org/10.1016/j.chiabu.2019.104024

Jacobs, M. A., Bruhn, C., & Graf, I. (2008). Methodological and validity issues involved in collection of sensitive information from children in foster care. *Journal of Social Service Research, 34*(4), 71–83.

Johnson-Motoyama, M. (2014). Does a paradox exist in child well-being risks among foreign born Latinos, US-born Latinos and Whites? Findings from 50 California cities. *Child Abuse & Neglect, 38,* 1061–1072.

Kadushin, A., & Martin, J. A. (1988). *Child welfare services* (4th ed.). New York, NY: Macmillan.

Karger, H. J., & Stoesz, D. (2010). *American social welfare policy: A pluralist approach* (6th ed.). Boston, MA: Pearson Education/Allyn & Bacon.

Kayser, K., & Johnson, J. (2008). Divorce. In T. Mizarhi and L. Davis (Eds.), Encyclopedia of Social Work (20th ed.). New York: Oxford University Press.

Kearney, M., Levine, P., & Pardue, L. 2022. The puzzle of falling US birth rates since the Great Recession. *Journal of Economic Perspectives, 36*(1), 151–176.

Kreider, R. M., & Ellis, R., (2011). *Living arrangements of children: 2009* (Current Population Reports P70-126). Washington, DC: U.S. Census Bureau. Retrieved from https://www.census.gov/library/publications/2011/demo/p70-126.html

Linderman, D. S. (1995). Child welfare overview. In R. Edwards & J. G. Hopps (Eds.), *Encyclopedia of social work* (19th ed., Vol. 1, pp. 424–433). Washington, DC: NASW Press.

Lindsey, D. (1994). *The welfare of children.* New York, NY: Oxford University Press.

Mallon, G. P. (2008). Social work practice with LGBT parents. In G. P. Mallon (Ed.), *Social work practice with lesbian, gay, bisexual, and transgender people* (2nd ed., pp. 269–312). New York, NY: Taylor & Francis Group/Routledge.

Martin, J. A., Hamilton, B. E., Ventura, S. J., Osterman, M. J. K., Kirmeyer, S., Mathews, T. J., & Division of Vital Statistics. (2013). Births: Final data from 2011. *National Vital Statistics Reports, 62*(1). Retrieved from http://www.cdc.gov/nchs/data/nvsr/nvsr62/nvsr62_01.pdf

Morgaine, K., & Capous-Desyllas, M. (2015). *Anti-oppressive social work practice: Putting theory into action*. Los Angeles, CA: Sage.

National Child Traumatic Stress Network. (n.d.). *Sexual abuse*. Retrieved December 1, 2022, from https://www.nctsn.org/what-is-child-trauma/trauma-types/sexual-abuse.

National Indian Child Welfare Association. (2014). *Frequently asked questions about ICWA*. Retrieved from http://www.nicwa.org/indian_child_welfare_act/faq

Ortiz-Ospina, E., & Roser M. (2020). *Marriages and divorces*. Our World in Data. Retrieved from https://ourworldindata.org/marriages-and-divorces

Quam, J. (1995). Charles Loring Brace (1826–1890). In R. Edwards & J. G. Hopps (Eds.), *Encyclopedia of social work* (19th ed., Vol. 2, p. 2575). Washington, DC: NASW Press.

Raley, R., & Sweeney, M. (2020). Divorce, repartnering, and stepfamilies: A decade in review. *Journal of Marriage and Family, 82*(1), 81–99. https://doi.org/10.1111/jomf.12651

Reinberg, S. (2007, December 5). Teen birth rates up for the first time in 14 years, U.S. reports. *Healthday News*. Retrieved from https://www.healthday.com/mental-health-information-25/behavior-health-news-56/teen-birth-rates-up-for-first-time-in-14-years-u-s-reports-610651.html

Roberts, D. (2022, November 22). *The Clinton-era adoption law that still devastates Black families today*. Retrieved from https://slate.com/news-and-politics/2022/11/racial-justice-bad-clinton-adoption-law.html

Samples, M., Carnochan, S., & Austin, M. (2013). Using performance measures to manage child welfare outcomes: Local strategies for decision making. *Journal of Evidence-Based Social Work, 10*, 254–264. https://doi.org/10.1080/15433714.2013.788954

Singer, J., Cummings, C., Moody, S., & Benuto, L. (2020). Reducing burnout, vicarious trauma, and secondary traumatic stress through investigating purpose in life in social workers. *Journal of Social Work, 20*(5), 260–638.

Smokowski, P. R., Evans, C. B., Cotter, K. L., & Webber, K. C. (2014). Ethnic identity and mental health in American Indian youth: Examining mediation pathways through self-esteem, and future optimism. *Journal of Youth Adolescence, 43*, 343–355.

Staller, K. (2020). *New York's newsboys: Charles Loring Brace and the founding of the Children's Aid Society*. New York, NY: Oxford University Press.

State of New Jersey Department of Children and Families. (2024a). Indicators of Child Abuse/Neglect. Retrieved from https://www.nj.gov/dcf/reporting/indicators/

State of New Jersey Department of Children and Families. (2024b). How and when to report child abuse/neglect. Retrieved from: https://www.nj.gov/dcf/reporting/how/

Storhaug, A. (2013). Fathers' involvement with the child welfare service. *Children and Youth Services Review, 35*, 1751–1759.

Tambling, R., & Johnson, S. (2021). Personal, familial, and service-related predictors of outcome in Intensive Family Preservation Services Treatment. *Journal of Social Service Research, 47*(5), pp. 616—624. https://doi.org/10.1080/01488376.2020.1861167

Tracy, E. M. (2008). Family preservation and home-based services. In T. Mizrahi & L. E. Davis (Eds.), *Encyclopedia of social work* (20th ed., Vol. 1, pp. 973–983). New York, NY: Oxford University Press/NASW Press.

Turner, H., Vanderminden, J., & Hamby, S. (2019). Child neglect and the broader context of victimization. *Child Maltreatment, 24*(3), 265–274. https://doi.org/10.1177/1077559518825312

Tyser, J., Scott, W. D., Readdy, T., & McCrea, S. M. (2014). The role of goal representations, cultural identity, and dispositional optimism in the depressive experiences of American Indian Youth from a Northern Plains tribe. *Journal of Youth Adolescence, 43*, 329–342.

U.S. Department of Health and Human Services. (2021). *AFCARS report #20: Preliminary FY2021 estimates as of June 28, 2022*. Retrieved from https://www.acf.hhs.gov/cb/report/afcars-report-29

U.S. Department of Health & Human Services, Administration for Children and Families, Administration on Children, Youth and Families, Children's Bureau. (2022). *Child maltreatment 2020*. Retrieved from https://www.acf.hhs.gov/sites/default/files/documents/cb/cm2020.pdf

U.S. Department of State, (n.d.). *Intercountry Adoption*. Retrieved from: https://travel.state.gov/content/travel/en/Intercountry-Adoption/adopt_ref/adoption-statistics-esri.html?wcmmode=disabled

United Nations. (1989). Convention the Rights of the Child. Retrieved from https://www.ohchr.org/en/instruments-mechanisms/instruments/convention-rights-child

Valenzuela, V. (2022, November). *Indigenous transracial adoptee shares her personal struggle amid US Supreme Court Case*. Retrieved from https://www.9news.com/article/news/local/native-american-heritage/indigenous-transracial-adoptee-supreme-court-case/73-fea08568-e5b8-4cc5-ae1a-4ccbf6d7f6c7

Van Dernoot Lipsky, L., & Burk, C. (2009). *Trauma stewardship: An everyday guide to caring for self while caring for others*. San Francisco, CA: Berrett–Koehler.

Watkins, S. A. (1990). The Mary Ellen myth: Correcting child welfare history. *Social Work, 35*, 500–503.

White House Conference on Children in a Democracy (1939-1940: Washington, D. (1942). . . . Final report. [Washington]: [U.S. Govt. print. off].

Zill, N., & Bramlett, M. D. (2014). Health and well-being of children adopted from foster care. *Children and Youth Services Review, 40*, 29–40. https://doi.org/10.1016/j.childyouth.2014.02.008

9

Health Care

CHAPTER 9: EPAS COMPETENCIES

Social work programs at the bachelor's and the master's level are accredited by the Council of Social Work Education (CSWE). CSWE's Educational Policy and Accreditation Standards (EPAS) describe the processes and criteria that social work courses should cover. In 2022, CSWE updated its EPAS standards. The following competencies are addressed in this chapter.

Competency 1: Demonstrate Ethical and Professional Behavior

Social workers understand the value base of the profession and its ethical standards, as well as relevant policies, laws, and regulations that may affect practice with individuals, families, groups, organizations, and communities.

Competency 2: Advance Human Rights and Social, Racial, Economic, and Environmental Justice

Social workers understand that every person regardless of position in society has fundamental human rights.

Competency 4: Engage in Practice-Informed Research and Research-Informed Practice

Social workers use ethical, culturally informed, anti-racist, and anti-oppressive approaches in conducting research and building knowledge.

Competency 8: Intervene with Individuals, Families, Groups, Organizations, and Communities

Social workers understand that intervention is an ongoing component of the dynamic and interactive process of social work practice.

For many of us, starting one career in the helping professions and changing to another is not that unusual. This was Liz's experience. She began her professional career as a nurse, but after several years decided to switch to social work. Liz felt that her knowledge of the medical aspects of a client's condition blended beautifully with mental health considerations. Collaboration in the delivery of health care between nursing and social work is just one route that can lead to improved services promoting health and well-being (Lam, Chan, & Yeung, 2013). Liz's belief is not unique; most health care social workers quickly agree that successful intervention requires awareness of important health and wellness information, as well as interprofessional collaborations that stress the link between the mind and body (Dziegielewski & Holliman, 2020). From this perspective, interprofessional collaborations can benefit both policy and practice.

• • •

In the provision of health and human services, it is clear that over the past decade, the use of social media as a mechanism for providing guidance for health-related decision-making has grown substantially, with a special emphasis on natural disasters and large-scale emergencies (Hiltz et al., 2020; Santoni & Rufat, 2021; Yuan, Li, Liu, Zhai, & Qi, 2021). The provision of health care and social services has been strongly influenced by social media, placing the power of the press and digital information sharing at the forefront of innovation. Whether reinventing care through digital health technologies such as providing direct services electronically or patient monitoring applications, rapid growth in the health care field continues (Dowell, 2020). Along with these innovative systems of delivery and easily accessible and shared information, the need for social work services has never been greater. This combination of health and social services supports the contention that mind and body cannot be separated. From this perspective, each client and client system must be treated wholistically, with a focus on continued wellness and prevention. The health care social worker, who often works as part of a collaborative team, brings knowledge and understanding of the importance of focusing on more than just the medical condition a client is suffering from. Each client is part of a system, and the social worker uses his or her knowledge and skills to link the client to the environment. This emphasis is central to treatment as well as discharge planning and case management.

According to the U.S. Census Bureau American Community Survey (2019), health care workers are the largest and fastest-growing sector for employment in the United States and account for 14 percent of all workers (United States Census Bureau, 2019). These twenty-two million professionals, health care practitioners, and health care support workers have faced numerous challenges, with one of the greatest in the past few years being the support needed in the fight against COVID-19 (Laughlin, Anderson, Martinez, & Gayfield, 2021).

> **Did You Know . . .**
> Which industry had the highest employment and annual payroll in 2018?
> According to the U.S. Census Bureau's County Business Patterns, the 907,426 businesses in the Health Care and Social Assistance sector topped all others, with 20 million employees and over $1.0 trillion in annual payroll in 2018 (U.S. Census Bureau, 2020).

The U.S. Bureau of Labor and Statistics reported in 2021–2022 that there were 173,860 social workers employed in the health area in the United States. Most of these social workers were employed in general or surgical hospitals ($n = 43,120$), followed by 22,040 in individual and family services, home health care ($n = 21,350$), nursing care facilities (skilled nursing facilities, $n = 13,510$), and outpatient care centers ($n = 13,480$). With the remaining social workers listed as being employed in psychiatric and substance abuse hospitals ($n = 2,420$) and community food and housing and emergency relief services ($n = 2,250$), the top-paying positions were related to scientific research and development ($n = 130$), dentist offices ($n = 8$), and insurance carriers ($n = 5,260$) (U.S. Bureau of Labor Statistics, 2023).

Given the sheer numbers of social workers working in health care as a profession, they provide many supportive services. When mixed with all the innovations in this century, providing supportive services to clients and client systems can pose challenges for health care social workers. Traditional medical services are delivered in hospitals, clinics, doctor's offices, extended care homes, and residential services. The previous expectations of the shortest stays and most cost-effective approaches continue. What has escalated, however, is the expansion of supporting telemedicine and virtual therapy sessions. Today, in traditional health care settings, acute care hospitals and ambulatory health care facilities employ more social workers than other settings, such as individual and family services, schools, and state and local government agencies (Bureau of Labor Statistics, 2018). Therefore, the number of practicing health care professionals continues to rise, and the health care industry remains the largest employer in the United States (Thompson, 2018).

When relating this information directly to social workers, expectations related to behavioral-based coordinated care, downsizing and reorganization of hospital social work staffs, limited availability of services to insured and uninsured populations, and increased demand for brief interventions make health care a formidable setting for creative social work practice (Dziegielewski & Holliman, 2020).

Clear demonstration and documentation of desired outcomes has taken on increased weight in today's health and social care arenas. In nonprofit organizations, social workers in mezzopractice have been called on to assist with showing that expected outcomes are being achieved and that readmissions are for similar problems (recurrences) that were incompletely treated or inaccurately assessed are down. In attempting to demonstrate "return on investment" through measurement of program success, agencies face a struggle for survival. That means that social workers serving as program administrators must identify outcome measures that provide evidence of sound fiscal management strategy (Burke, 2008).

Americans have simply come to accept rising prices and limited and often stagnating services in health care, but Rugy (2014) and other key social policy advocates continue to ask, Does it really have to be that way? There are other hard-to-answer questions:

- Is there a way to cut costs in the system we currently have while maintaining essential services?
- Is there a belief that all Americans truly need and deserve the same level of health care availability and affordability? And, based on this belief, how is service provision influenced?
- Do we provide health care to groups such as uninsured homeless people—and, if so, to what extent? How will these costs be managed?
- What about people in prison? Do we provide health care to those serving life sentences with no possibility of parole? In addition, is there a belief that prison inmates deserve the same health care as law-abiding citizens? If not, how does this affect health care provision to this population?
- How do we ensure that people in rural and sparsely populated areas have access to high-quality health care? Do they have the transportation or technology to access it?
- Should we continue to move efforts toward a refined national health insurance model rather than the one in existence today?
- Should we finance elective, alternative, nontraditional health interventions?

These questions are very thought provoking and there will be no easy answers. For the generalist social worker, the activities required could span the micro-, mezzo-, and macropractice areas. At the center of this and any future discussion is acceptance of the premise that health care is costly, and access will always have limitations. How can the best compromises be made so that all get the greatest benefit?

Name: Faith Sills, CBHCMS, LCSW
Place of residence: Orlando, Florida
College/university degrees: BS in interpersonal communication; BS in psychology, MSW
Present position: Supervisor of social services, Office of the Public Defender, 9th Circuit, Florida

What does a typical day at work look like for you? What tasks do you generally complete as a social worker in your area of expertise? On a typical day, I first check my phone and email for any emergencies. Since my work involves jails and mental health hospitals that are open twenty-four hours a day, 365 days a year, problems don't adhere to any schedule.

Additionally, since we support about one hundred attorneys who have court each weekday morning, when a fire does start, it needs to be put out immediately. Next, I see what cases are in queue to be assigned to social workers. The referrals are usually in regard to indigent criminal defendants who need help with various issues including substance abuse, homelessness, medical issues, and/or mental health disorders. The clients that I assign to myself are for death penalty mitigation for individuals accused of first-degree murder. Mitigation includes getting to know a client very well and interviewing their friends, family, neighbors, teachers, and other collateral sources to get a full picture of their life before the alleged offense. We also gather tons of records, photos, and other documents to support our findings and create genograms and timelines to demonstrate the full picture of a client's life story. We then develop comprehensive reports to provide to a team of homicide attorneys. The attorneys will then utilize our work to try to save the client from death row. Additionally, over the years I have taken on other responsibilities that are on the more macro or administrative side of the spectrum, which is less clinical (and therefore less interesting to me personally) but equally as important. For example, I have roles that include audits related to funding and roles that are closer to human resources than clinical social work (though at times HR feels surprisingly like social work). Forensic social work is a fairly new field at the intersection of criminal justice and mental health and encompasses a lot of nuanced and varied roles and responsibilities. Never a dull moment!

What do you do in your spare time? I'm the mom of the coolest kid in the world, I like to nerd out on nonfiction, and I enjoy writing songs and poetry.

Why did you choose social work as a career? I knew that I wanted a job where I could look at myself in the mirror at the end of the day (and at the end of my life) and know that I had done my part to help people and to make the world a better place. I think I succeeded and that I'm part of the solution. After eighteen years, I'm proud of my contributions and I feel that my time has been well spent.

What is your favorite social work story? My favorite fiction story is "The Starfish Story" because I think it represents so many of our success stories. For example, I had a client named Larry who was on hospice but was in criminal trouble for not paying some old fines. The work we did with him led to a macro-level change in the system that helps indigent individuals to this day. Larry was very proud of his last hurrah. He'd felt marginalized by an inequitable system his entire life and just months before he passed he finally got to "speak truth to power" for the first time and be a part of a change that he wanted to see in this world. His pride and his smile were priceless. There is a plethora of similar stories where perhaps there wasn't a fantastic happily-ever-after ending but at least one chapter of a client's life was improved, or they got a second chance and made good use of it. Small wins add up and the ripple effects of positive change are incalculable.

What would be the one thing you would change in our community if you had the power to do so? If I could only change one thing, I would still have to change two! I would require that mindfulness be taught in schools and secure more funding for housing.

9.1 EFFORTS TOWARD INCLUSIVE HEALTH CARE ACCESS

During the early 1990s, politicians were responsive to the American public's demand for health care reform (see Figure 9.1). During his first term, President Bill Clinton made a campaign promise to address this issue and formed a major task force chaired by his wife, Hillary Clinton, which began to develop a national health care policy (Mizrahi, 1995). The task force considered proposals for health care reform from single-payer systems to limited forms of universal coverage. The eventual proposal was not a single-payer approach, but a type of *managed competition* in which purchasing alliances were formed that would have the power to certify health plans and negotiate premiums for certain benefit packages (The White House Domestic Policy Staff, 1993). Payment for these plans was financed by employer–employee premiums.

The actual consumer out-of-pocket cost would vary based on the benefit package chosen. The Clinton proposal eventually failed after concerted attacks by the health care industry and conservative members of Congress. As you begin to read the information on the Affordable Care Act below, this new plan will sound like this original failed proposal. Some political commentators felt this was the last chance to change the health care system, yet during the 2000 presidential campaign, health care resurfaced as a hot topic, with arguments over insurance coverage and a patient's bill of rights. This led to renewed interest in finding something, possibly not as ambitious, that would take us closer to universal health care. The struggle continues into the twenty-first century.

Given increasing health care costs, the Affordable Care Act (ACA), often commonly referred to as *Obamacare*, provides a major example of the effort to ensure that

FIGURE 9.1
Delegates for family health care at the 1992 Democratic Convention; the demand for inclusive, affordable health care access is nothing new.

Americans have access to health care (Centers for Medicare & Medicaid Services, n.d.). To address affordability, ACA was the topic of vigorous debates in March of 2010, and Congress ultimately chose to enact the ACA (Centers for Medicare & Medicaid Services, n.d.). The purpose of the ACA was to give the American people back some degree of control related to their health care by providing coverage options that provide stability, flexibility, and informed choice (U.S. Department of Health & Human Services, 2014). Box 9.1 highlights the basic bill of rights coverage and care information. To read more about the law and learn more about the ten titles that outline the premises for inclusion within the ACA outlined in 2009, see the activity below.

BOX 9.1

AFFORDABLE CARE ACT (PATIENT'S BILL OF RIGHTS)

Coverage Highlights

- *Ends preexisting condition exclusions for children*: Health plans can no longer limit or deny benefits to children under the age of nineteen because of a preexisting condition.
- *Keeps young adults covered*: Those under age twenty-six are covered under the parent's health plan.
- *Ends arbitrary withdrawals of insurance coverage*: Limits canceling coverage for mistakes.
- *Guarantees the right to appeal*: Can further the right to appeal denial of payment decisions.

Cost Highlights

- *Ends lifetime limits on coverage*: Lifetime limits on most benefits are banned for all new health insurance plans.
- *Reviews premium increases*: Insurance companies must now publicly justify any unreasonable rate hikes.
- *Maximizes health care expenditure premiums*: Premiums relate more directly to health care benefits than to administrative costs.

Care Highlights

- *Covers preventive care at no cost to the covered person*: May also have preventative health services with no copayment.
- *Protects consumer choice of doctors*: Choose primary care doctor from plan's network.
- *Removes insurance company barriers to emergency services*: Can seek emergency care at a hospital outside the health plan's network.

Source: U.S. Department of Health and Human Services (2014).

> **Activity**
>
> The ACA has ten titles that outline the purpose of the law and what it is designed to accomplish. The ten titles of the ACA are listed with the amendments to the law called for by the reconciliation process.
>
> Go to the U.S. Department of Health and Human Services website and read the "About the Affordable Care Act" page to review the different information available; you will also find the full-text PDF of the Affordable Care Act and Reconciliation Act. Take the time to read each section. Do you believe that this law will continue to be able to meet what it was intended to do in terms of the factors (cost, care, and coverage) outlined in Box 9.1? Why or why not?
>
> The ACA, section by section:
>
> Title I. Quality, Affordable Health Care for All Americans
>
> Title II. The Role of Public Programs
>
> Title III. Improving the Quality and Efficiency of Health Care
>
> Title IV. Prevention of Chronic Disease and Improving Public Health
>
> Title V. Health Care Workforce
>
> Title VI. Transparency and Program Integrity
>
> Title VII. Improving Access to Innovative Medical Therapies
>
> Title VIII. Community Living Assistance Services and Supports Act (CLASS Act)
>
> Title IX. Revenue Provisions
>
> Title X. Reauthorization of the Indian Health Care Improvement Act

As a result of political compromise through the ACA, "[Americans'] health insurance options are provided through a disconnected, patchwork of programs including employment-based insurance, Medicare, Medicaid, S-CHIP, the Veterans Health Administration, the Indian Health Service, the Public Health Service and community mental health centers" (Moniz & Gorin, 2014, p. 10). This law reached its full implementation as planned in 2014 and seeks to hold insurance companies accountable by setting standards for reform that allow for lower health care costs as well as the guarantee of more choices that enhance quality of care. At present, this plan continues to remain in effect, and websites and other supporting structures are in place to facilitate enrollment and coverage options. In addition, as of 2022, most efforts to repeal this act have been abandoned and employers are urged re-examine their existing ACA Employer Mandates responsibilities (Sheen, 2022b).

Most professionals agree that ACA supports health care changes as well as improvements in health care access, quality, and service. The expectation was that this program would support the coverage of 32 million Americans who currently did not have health care coverage while opening doors for accessible health care (Ofosu, 2011). As of 2022, the numbers were at 14.5 million Americans who elected to receive this health care coverage during the open enrollment period (Sheen, 2022a), with a total of 31 million benefiting from ACA-related benefits (U.S. Department of Health and Human Services, 2022). Innovative programs such as this continue to evolve and require that all health care professionals be open to change while balancing quality of care and utilizing evidence-based practices that are effective and cost-efficient (Dziegielewski & Holliman, 2020). One of the greatest challenges for social work in health care was the shortage of data that support social work services effectiveness (National Association of Social Workers [NASW], 2016).

> ### Did You Know . . .
> HealthCare.gov is the government website that is designed to assist with establishing eligibility, enrollment, application, and cost information. There is also a section on frequently asked questions that may be extremely helpful to consumers preparing for application.

From your own experiences buying medication or paying for medical treatment, you know that, even with the advent of the ACA, appropriate covered services remain costly. This program also requires that even healthy young adults carry health insurance, regardless of the wages they make, whether they use the health care system, whether they see the need, or whether their employer provides a health care plan. However, young people may not realize the risks of lacking health insurance. The U.S. Centers for Medicare & Medicaid Services (2022) reported that one in six young adults suffers from a chronic illness and nearly half of young adults encountered challenges covering their own medical bills. If taxpayers do not possess or purchase health care coverage from the marketplace, they will pay a penalty when filing taxes. Therefore, social workers have a key role in helping clients navigate, identify, and obtain the services they need. One reason so many Americans have no form of health insurance and are willing to risk paying a fine for not adopting provider coverage under the ACA is the expense! Even with programs such as the ACA, large deductibles and copayments can be a problem. This, in combination with states that have not accepted the Medicaid waivers, can place our poorest individuals and those with lower-middle-level incomes at the greatest risk. Even with the increased access afforded by the ACA, there is no reason to expect that health care delivery costs will ever go down. It is common to hear social workers in the health care field discuss the complexity of the system and the frustration they experience when they try to connect clients to the services they need.

Although it is beyond the scope of this chapter to describe the ACA in detail, establishing and agreeing on a unified definition of health care social work remains critical for survival in today's service delivery environment. What seems to have remained consistent over the years is that service reimbursement is clearly linked to performance indicators. This means that there must be a clear linkage to consumer outcomes, service events, resource acquisition, and efficiency (Poertner & Rapp, 2007). We do not want to paint a bleak picture, but we do want to give a realistic one. The continual changes and swirling controversies contribute to a turbulent health care environment. Declining hospital admissions, reduced lengths of stay, and other restrictions and methods of cost containment are common threats that unite all health care social workers.

Miller (2008) rated our health care system as "complex, under-funded, disparate, inconsistent, state of the art, miraculous, successful, unjust, illogical and more" (p. 219). Today, the ACA has provided one step toward ensuring adequate health care services in the United States. Unfortunately, system changes and differing plan requirements in each state, as well as challenges with the implementation of ACA, remain. The complexity encountered in trying to meet individual needs, especially with regard to access and affordability problems, remains a central issue.

> ### Did You Know . . .
> In current health care practice, the term *patient* has returned to the vocabulary of social workers, especially those in the health care area. In this setting, varying titles such as patient, consumer, and client can be used, but it depends on the setting. To best talk the talk and walk the walk, social workers are keenly aware that using context-accepted terminology helps to bring them to the table as part of an interdisciplinary collaborative team that uses similar terminology when referring to the individuals being served.

9.2 DEFINING HEALTH CARE SOCIAL WORK

Health care social work, historically called *medical social work* and today overlapping with *clinical social work* (the term can also be used to describe the work of some mental health focused practitioners, also commonly referred to as clinical social workers), is one of the oldest, best-established fields of professional social work practice.

Tom Carlton, a major social work thinker and advocate in health care social work during the 1970s and 1980s, defined health care social work in its broadest sense as "all social work in the health field" (1984, p. 5). Carlton felt that social workers interested in this area must be prepared to do more than engage solely in direct clinical practice. His vision of health care practice included program planning and administration; preparation, supervision, and continued training for social workers and other health care professionals; and social research. It is not surprising that the term health care social work has historically been used interchangeably with the term medical social work. Using these two terms interchangeably, however, can obscure a subtle difference in meaning.

In 2003, *The Social Work Dictionary* defined medical social work as a form of practice that occurs in hospitals and other health care settings. This type of practice facilitates good health and prevention of illness, and it aids physically ill clients and their families in resolving the social and psychological problems related to disease and illness (Barker, 2003). Today, health care social work is more encompassing, and although hospitals may be one of the largest employers, service provision can take place in other supportive settings.

According to the U.S. Bureau of Labor Statistics (2021), social work is defined as providing individuals, families, and groups with psychosocial support, helping consumers get the support needed to cope with chronic, acute, or terminal illnesses. "Services include advising family caregivers. Provide patients with information and counseling and make referrals for other services. May also provide case and care management or interventions designed to promote health, prevent disease, and address barriers to access to healthcare" (U.S. Bureau of Labor Statistics, 2021).

With so many different health care settings, all of which have varying service expectations, it is not surprising that so many social workers serve as members of professional collaborative teams. For example, as part of a **multidisciplinary team**, the social worker can help link the services provided by each of the helping disciplines. In the interdisciplinary team, the shared roles and responsibilities allow the social worker to share his or her expertise as part of the team. Regardless of the type of team effort utilized to help the client, the role of the social worker is essential in sensitizing the other team members to the social-psychological aspects of illness. For other examples of collaborative teams, see Table 9.1.

Activity

Do you know anyone who has worked as a health care social worker? Using the definitions in Table 9.1, ask the social worker what their perceptions are of collaborative teamwork. What does the social worker see as the strengths and weaknesses of the approach?

Health care social workers are expected to address the psychosocial aspects of client problems. They are also expected to alert other team members to these psychosocial needs and to ensure adequate service provision within the discharge environment. In performing these functions, social work professionals not only represent the interests of clients, but also often become the moral conscience of the health care delivery team. According to Leipzig et al. (2002), although provider satisfaction with interdisciplinary teamwork was often high, client satisfaction was low. Information such as this further reinforces the role of the social worker as one of the primary providers responsible for increasing communication and understanding for all involved. For health care social workers, whether they work independently or as part of a collaborative team, service provision rests on addressing the needs of the current problem as well as plans and strategies for continued health and wellness (Fink-Samnick, 2021).

	Table 9.1 Types of Collaborative Teams
Multidisciplinary teams	A group of professionals working together for a common purpose, working independently while sharing information through formal lines of communication to better assist the patient/client/consumer
Interdisciplinary teams	A group of health care professionals who work together for a common purpose, working interdependently with some degree of sharing roles, tasks, and duties that overlap with both formal and informal lines of communication to better assist the patient/client/consumer
Intradisciplinary teams	This type of collaborative team is made up of individuals from one discipline. These professionals in the same discipline work collaboratively to assist the client. Although this type of team can include all groups of professions, it is seen in hospitals, physician's offices, and wellness clinics.
Transdisciplinary teams	A group of health care professionals and the patient/client/consumer and identified members of his or her support system freely share ideas and work together as a synergistic whole, where ideas and sharing of responsibilities are commonplace in routine care.
Pandisciplinary teams	A group of health care professionals who work together in a specialized area where each member of the team is seen as equal in the delivery of care with similar skills for assisting the client. Professionals are considered experts in an area, not necessarily in a professional discipline. For example, when working in geriatrics, all individuals are skilled professionals listed by subject area, rather than by profession.

Source: Content modified from Dziegielewski and Holliman (2020).

Did You Know . . .

In the early days, hospital nurses performed medical social work services. These nurses were convenient choices for this employment because they were easily accessible, already knew agency procedure, and were aware of community resources. Later, however, when it was established that more specialized training in understanding social conditions was needed, the employment of social work professionals began. Some social workers worry the pendulum might be swinging back to the past. Health care social workers do not believe this would be in the best interest of health care consumers.

The struggle to define exactly what health care social workers are expected to do reflects the changing nature of the health care system. Striving to obtain a clear definition of what the health care social worker does can help lay the groundwork for acceptance as part of the team by the other professionals (Dziegielewski & Holliman, 2020). Part of the struggle involves trying to establish concrete cost-containing goals and objectives that clearly represent the diverse and often unique service(s) provided. This inability to document a concrete service strategy has long been a thorn in the side of health care administrators, who need this information to justify and compete for continued funding. Yet short stays and poorly planned discharges that do not involve the client system can result in even quicker readmissions. It becomes a delicate dance when even the simplest descriptions of service provision can vary depending on the client population served, the client support system, and the actual services needed, while trying to avoid the prospect of readmission for the same concern.

Health care social workers practice in a setting where doctors are expected to fix what is broken and do so with unrealistic speed and incredible competence. This has resulted in the push for quick and sometimes incomplete solutions, such as a pill to address a situation rather than more comprehensive behavioral types of treatment interventions (Dziegielewski & Holliman, 2020). This is further complicated by delivering services through telehealth and other digital mechanisms. For example, older adults' fear of accessing such technology can turn this technological blessing into a curse (Alignment Health Care, 2022). Social workers assist clients as quickly as possible, yet given the complexity of the human situation, this task is not at all straightforward. Also, to avoid readmissions for the same or a similar problem, it is necessary to consider the client system. In adapting services to address the needs of clients while anticipating changes in the health service environment, social work professionals must employ flexible and constantly updated skills.

9.3 THE PRACTICE OF HEALTH CARE SOCIAL WORK

Simply stated, health care social work practice deals with all aspects of general health and strives to promote and restore social functioning for clients, families, and small groups. This type of integrated care requires considering all aspects of people's physical health as well as their mental well-being (Dziegielewski & Holliman, 2020). According to NASW (2016), the profession plays a leadership role in the U.S. health care system, especially in psychosocial service provision.

Did You Know . . .

In 1918, the National Conference of Social Work in Kansas City included a series of discussions that result in the formation of the American Association of Hospital Social Workers (Virginia Commonwealth University Libraries Social Welfare History Project, n.d.). This was the first professional social work organization in the United States.

In health care practice, as in other areas of social work, the tasks performed are collaborative, yet diverse and unique. Social workers serving in health care settings need expert training to guide service provision because they are competing in a service provision environment that is overcrowded with health care professionals. Moreover, today's health care social workers are exposed to all the turbulence and change of seeking coordinated health care (Dziegielewski & Holliman, 2020). In this environment, insurance reimbursements often dictate the level of service; no longer are recommendations from physicians or other professionals treated as sacrosanct. Pressures to cut costs mean that health care service must be provided in the briefest, most effective manner possible (Dziegielewski, 2015; Dziegielewski & Holliman, 2020).

> ### Did You Know . . .
> In 1928, the American College of Surgeons developed and included a minimum standard of service provision for social service—that is, social work—departments.

There is also a movement to provide what is referred to as *wraparound services*. More traditionally conceptualized for use in children's services, although they are being extended to other patient groups (Maestre & Fernandez, 2019), these services involve a team-based, collaborative process for the implementation of individualized care plans capable of addressing the needs of an entire client system (patient and/or families or other caregivers) (Walker, Bruns, & Penn, 2008). From this perspective, the needs of the consumer to ensure continuance of care are linked, retained, and supported. In its most basic form, consumers may be taken to appointments when transportation is an issue or assisted with getting/taking their medications. Wraparound services can include housing support, transportation, child care assistance, and therapy to address psychological and emotional stressors (Jackson, 2022). Familiar to social workers, the wraparound system of care highlights the importance of the client-in-situation or the client-in-environment. From this perspective, addressing clients' problems includes identifying the client and the client system and recognizes supports that are available upon their return home, such as family and friends and other resources in the community (Summers, 2012). As a result of interdisciplinary approaches, all health care providers, including social workers, must work in a versatile, flexible manner to complete tasks with limited resources. The varied tasks coupled with the dynamic environment and limited fiscal resources complicate our simple definition of health care practice as well as the practice itself and the roles and responsibilities of the worker.

9.4 A BRIEF HISTORY OF HEALTH CARE SOCIAL WORK

Medical social work can be traced back to the nineteenth-century public health movement. As a result of industrialization, with urban growth came overcrowding and the spread of disease. In Trattner's (1989) graphic words,

> American cities were disorderly, filthy, foul-smelling, disease-ridden places. Narrow, unpaved streets became transformed into quagmires when it rained.

Rickety tenements, swarming with unwashed humanity, leaned upon one another for support. Inadequate drainage systems failed to carry away sewage. Pigs roamed streets that were cluttered with manure, years of accumulating garbage, and other litter. Slaughterhouses and fertilizing plants contaminated the air with an indescribable stench. Ancient plagues like smallpox, cholera, and typhus threw the population into a state of terror from time to time while less sensational but equally deadly killers like tuberculosis, diphtheria, and scarlet fever were ceaselessly at work. (p. 57)

Overall, this was not a suitable place or time to live. It soon was evident that public sanitation programs were needed. The resulting laws and health care efforts helped doctors and related medical professionals gain stature (Segal & Brzuzy, 1998, p. 108). Hospitals, too, changed dramatically during this era. Once a haven for the poor, the hospital became a "scientific center for the treatment of illness" where physicians provided oversight and subsequent control of the helping activities and services provided (Popple & Leighninger, 1990, p. 436). Medical social work was first practiced in 1900 in Cleveland City Hospital, when the workers helped to discharge patients with chronic conditions and homeless Civil War veterans from overcrowded wards (Poole, 1995; see Figure 9.2).

Social work subsequently developed as a specialization through the efforts of Richard Cabot and, shortly thereafter, Ida Cannon, a new graduate from Simmons College. In 1905, Cabot set up the first social service (work) department in a hospital. Though trained as a physician, Cabot recognized the unique and important contributions of

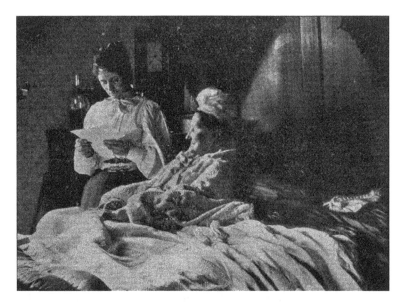

FIGURE 9.2
In the 1990s, social workers were first recognized for their contributions to improving health in the hospital setting.

social workers when he served as director of the Boston Children's Aid Society. The social worker's skill in linking social environment to disease, thought Cabot, would be extremely helpful in medical diagnosis. The social work department established at Boston's Massachusetts General Hospital is regarded as the debut of medical social work.

> ## Did You Know . . .
> Johns Hopkins Hospital established its first social work program in 1907. The first social worker to be employed there was Helen B. Pendleton (Nacman, 1977).

Health care social work today, as in Cabot's time, takes place in a *host* setting—that is, an organization whose primary purpose is something other than providing social work services. You will find social workers in hospitals (a hospital accreditation requirement), intermediate and skilled care facilities, neighborhood health centers, physicians' offices, health clinics, city public health departments, veterans' hospitals and clinics, military hospitals and clinics, and nonprofit and for-profit health-related organizations.

> ## Did You Know . . .
> The U.S. Veterans' Bureau, now the Department of Veterans' Affairs, began hiring social workers to work in its hospitals in 1926.

One increasingly important aspect of today's health care social work is that it is team based and interdisciplinary in nature. Health care social workers need to be invested in both the process and the structure of the services that are to be performed (see the activity below). Each discipline needs to be competent in the practice and approach utilized. Competency involves being able to link the knowledge, values, and skills and integrate them into practice (Damron-Rodriquez, 2008).

> ## Did You Know . . .
> In the 1920s and 1930s, the U.S. military started to add social workers to its ranks. Military social workers usually work in mental health, health, and protective service settings.

In interdisciplinary collaborations, social workers can help the team of professionals communicate with one another and the client to be served. The social worker can also help members of the team become aware of their own values, behaviors, habits, and emotions that can affect the helping process. Creating an atmosphere of self-knowledge yields a deeper awareness that results in a more culturally sensitive approach for the client (Morgaine & Capous-Desyllas, 2015). From this perspective, diversity is viewed as a superpower. In addition, the social worker can help to connect those clients entering the system with the supports needed. This intervention from start to finish builds continuity of care and links the client to helping networks that can continue long after the service has ended. The concept of ensuring continuity of care, however, is complicated because what constitutes quality care fluctuates. With new discoveries, improved technology, and improvements in access, ensuring efficient and effective quality care can vary. Furthermore, measuring what constitutes the provision of quality care that is not static can elude even the best measurement practices of service provision (Johnson & Sollecito, 2020). Changes in service provision and measurements for success seem to favor purpose-oriented health care networks to address increasing demands for health care and controlling expenditures (Peeters, Westra, van Raak, & Ruwaard, 2022).

Did You Know . . .

In 1965, the United States launched its first community health centers to improve health care access, regardless of individuals' ability to pay. In 1965, President Lyndon B. Johnson made them part of his Great Society policy initiatives designed to help eliminate poverty and racial injustice. These centers are the largest health care providers in the country, providing services to twenty-nine million Americans each year (one in eleven people across the country). These centers are the bedrock of our public health system and were a vital part of the nation's response to the COVID-19 pandemic (U.S. Census Bureau, 2022).

Social workers are part of a professional team that may include physicians, nurses, vocational rehabilitation workers, psychologists, and psychiatrists. Today's social worker must therefore understand and value the contributions that other professionals offer. For our clients and ourselves, we can no longer see what matters solely through our individual professional lens. As part of a collaborative team, the social worker becomes an active player who stays mindful that all services we provide must yield "outcomes" and performance standards derived, identified, and measured as part of the service provision (Steketee, Ross, & Wachman, 2017).

Activity

Have you ever been admitted to a hospital? While you were there, did you see a social worker? If you did not, would you have liked to? If you did, what services did he or she provide? Make a brief list of the services that you believe social workers can provide in the hospital setting.

Name: Jamshid Khoshnoodi, PhD, LCSW
Place of residence: Nashville, Tennessee
College/university degrees:
- University of Tennessee, College of Social Work, MSSW (2015–2017)
- Vanderbilt University, leadership education in neurodevelopmental disabilities (2015–2016)
- Swedish University of Agricultural Sciences, PhD in molecular cell biology (1992–1997)
- Uppsala University, Sweden, bachelor of science in biology (1987–1991)

Present position: I am currently working as a psychotherapist in my own private practice in middle, Tennessee. I am also honored to serve as a special guest reviewer for the *Journal of Social Services Research*, where I am a blind reviewer for research-based articles in social services.

Previous positions and work experience:
Since I graduated from the University of Tennessee's School of Social Work in 2017, I have worked as a primary therapist and clinical director in several inpatient recovery centers in Tennessee. As a primary therapist, I provide clinical assessments and treatment of trauma and mental health disorders using a variety of therapy modalities including EMDR therapy, Gestalt therapy, CBT, DBT, schema therapy, internal family systems, and group psychodrama. I also facilitate psychoeducational workshops on family systems theory, attachment disorders, neuroscience of addiction, childhood trauma and brain development, and relapse prevention strategies.

In my role as a clinical director, I have provided clinical supervision and education for the clinical staff and performance evaluation of their professional development. I have also served in clinical administration, helping with identifying levels of clinical care, monitoring guidelines, utilization audits, and streamlining policies and procedures of the clinical program.

Before entering the profession of social work, I was an academic research scientist and scholar. For many years as a biochemist and a molecular cell biologist, my research interests have shifted from plant molecular biology to genetic kidney diseases and cardiovascular disorders. Throughout my academic career, I have served as research assistant professor of medicine and biochemistry at Vanderbilt Medical Center (2002–2009) and postdoctoral researcher at Karolinska Institutet in Stockholm, Sweden (1998–2002).

What does a typical day at work look like for you? What tasks do you generally complete as a social worker in your area of expertise? A typical day in residential setting usually starts with a group therapy. After a guided meditation, the group can either continue processing feelings, thoughts, concerns, or I can share educational information on topics like the neuroscience of addiction, childhood trauma, and brain development, or attachment disorders and emotion dysregulation. In my experience working with families, there is a general misunderstanding and social stigma around addiction and mental health disorders. Having a scientific background in biology has definitely helped me to explain in simple terms the balanced forces between nature and nurture, and how early adverse childhood experiences can lead to maladaptive thinking styles (mental health issues) and self-soothing behaviors such as misusing substances (addiction).

Individual therapy is a big part of my private practice during which I often use a combination of EMDR therapy, Gestalt therapy, or internal family systems to help clients overcome traumatic memories and internal conflicts.

What do you do in your spare time? I read, hike, or work on oil paintings or drawings.

Why did you choose social work as a career? After leaving academia in 2009, I faced a personal crisis and fell into a deep depression. After seventeen years of academic life, it was inconceivable for me to see myself in roles other than a researcher. It took me several years of painful soul-searching and inner struggle to finally accept the fact that "I am not my career." I realized that in order to rethink my new path, I needed to reflect on my personal life. Born and raised in Iran, I was forced to leave my home country to avoid social and political persecution that affected millions of people following the 1979 revolution. Sweden became my second homeland for nearly seventeen years before relocating to the United States in 2002. As a trilinguist who has lived in the Middle East, Europe, and North America, I knew that I cherished my multicultural life experience of living in different parts of the world. Being able to learn and educate others has been a central theme throughout my life, so choosing a career path in social work felt not only a good fit but also a personal quest I take very seriously.

What is your favorite social work story? During my social work studies, I enrolled in a program called Leadership Education in Neurodevelopmental Disabilities at Vanderbilt University. The program is an advanced and interdisciplinary effort meant to facilitate collaboration across medicine, psychology, social work, occupational therapy, nutrition, and more.

What would be the one thing you would change in our community if you had the power to do so? Help to create a publicly funded health care system that meets the needs of everyone independent of age, gender, or income.

9.5 UNDERSTANDING THE CURRENT HEALTH CARE ENVIRONMENT

The human coronavirus disease of 2019 (COVID-19) and its many mutations have had an unprecedented effect both globally and nationally. The COVID-19 pandemic disrupted normal life activities (e.g., employment, education, and recreational) as well as the health facilities and workers delivering these services (Schleicher, 2020). To limit the spread of the virus, most countries, including the United States, instituted containment strategies (Bitler, Hoynes, & Schanzenbach, 2020; Xu, Pompili, & Sampogna, 2021); the burden this placed on health care facilities, services, and the workers who support them was truly unprecedented. The efforts to control the spread of the virus, from lockdowns to social distancing mandates (Carter & May, 2020), caused tremendous unintended human suffering. Terminally ill individuals died alone, and family members were kept apart because of travel restrictions or social distancing mandates. Not being able to say goodbye to loved ones is a trauma that will leave lasting scars. When the COVID-19 pandemic is coupled with spiraling costs, distrust and fear of governmental control, and uninsured/underinsured people, the challenges for the American health care system remain formidable. And with new variations of the virus and the aftereffects of past responses, the crisis has been slow to abate.

According to Dziegielewski and Holliman (2020), the importance of health care social workers rests firmly in the events that surround us.

1. The number of older adults is growing larger, and these older adults often need more supportive care resources as well as costly health care services.
2. Americans are resistant to paying additional fees for medical services, maintenance, or wellness care. Large yearly insurance deductibles can detract from seeking service provision.
3. The insurance industry is highly fragmented, with managers trained under different environmental conditions. Also, the profit motive is clear and marketing strategies may not support the best interests of clients being served.
4. There is excessive pressure to fill any oversupply of hospital inpatient beds when they exist.
5. There is still a focus on treating acute illness rather than a more holistic, wellness, or preventive perspective that can lead to more costly treatment.
6. Insufficient medical outcome data exist, especially on the importance of addressing psychosocial concerns, which impairs decision-making.
7. Too many heroic attempts are made to implement expensive procedures without regard to quality of continued life.
8. Professionals try to be cautious and can order unnecessary tests and procedures to avoid malpractice suits. Medical information is often posted electronically, and complete patient-friendly explanations are often neglected.

Additional changes have been brought about by COVID, such as distrust of the government, vaccine mandates, the psychological stressors experienced with the current health situations, and the fear of future health-related crisis. Even though these events have triggered underlying health and wellness factors that are difficult to change, all require a supportive response of one type or another.

It is beyond the scope of this chapter to identify all the practice issues related to health care delivery and reform. The most salient issue in need of reform for the overall health care system is the refined use of enhanced state-of-the-art information technology to be shared not only across health care settings, but also in an easy, understandable way with those being served. The health care sector has languished behind all other industries in adopting a shared system of information technology and in sharing this within one patient portal, with access and explanations that are user-friendly. For example, service providers can use limited electronic technology, and these records may not be easily accessed by other providers in different settings, or sometimes even the same setting; this can result in errors and costly duplication of effort. Other agencies provide electronic access to patients but do not teach patients how to use the system or access the data. Electronic service delivery options are improved by providing online education to consumers and providers alike, as well as online group participation and networking (Nicholas et al., 2007). With all the electronic technology available, providers often expect that all individuals are well versed in computer usage. Nothing could be further from the truth, especially when it relates to getting information related to the delivery of services. The technology that is supposed to make our lives easier often does the reverse.

A second issue, and the most daunting of health care challenges, is providing care to uninsured and underinsured Americans. Ways of increasing inclusion for the uninsured population involve extending health coverage to all residents through the provision of tax credits designed to offset the costs of eligible participants' insurance premiums and monitoring and coordinating the patchwork availability of current plans and high deductibles and copays. Another way to confront this issue may be to consider expanding **Medicaid** in states that currently have not adopted the Medicaid waiver under the ACA and the State Children's Health Insurance Program to cover a broader range of participants. If states adopted unifying criteria rather than different requirements for each state, it might be easier to implement across-the-board planning, rather than deal with the complications of state-specific rules. Among the anticipated benefits is coverage of families under a single plan and access to a personal clinician, both of which increase the likelihood that patients will receive appropriate, timely care in the right setting.

Measuring the number of underinsured people and improving access to care is a much more complicated concept. The term *underinsured* refers to people who have medical insurance but whose employers try to save dollars by cutting back policy coverage or benefits. To reduce costs, employers can eliminate benefits, reduce benefits for family members, or increase employees' contributions to insurance benefits. This is also complicated by the fact that health insurance coverage is relative to the number of hours a person works; many part-time or temporary workers may still not be able to afford health insurance and remain uninsured, regardless of the potential fines imposed.

A third area is malpractice reform. It has become commonplace to see debates over malpractice insurance and refusal by physicians to provide care because of what they perceive to be unreasonable rates for this insurance. This debate and subsequent refusal to provide services has resulted in limited access to care for patients in rural and other underserved communities. This professional fear of liability has also impeded efforts to identify sources of error so that they can be prevented. Moreover, the tort system frequently does not result in compensation of injured patients, and those who are compensated often experience lengthy delays. One way to address this issue might be to have states create injury compensation systems outside the courtroom that are client centered and focused on safety. These systems would set reasonable payments for avoidable injuries and provide fair, timely compensation to a greater number of clients while stabilizing the malpractice insurance market by limiting health care providers' financial exposure.

Another area of growing concern that needs attention relates to the recognition of the quality and appropriateness of patient care, given the rising prevalence of chronic conditions such as diabetes and heart disease. In the early twenty-first century, 120 million Americans have one or more chronic conditions, many of which could have been prevented or delayed through education or other interventions that promote healthy behaviors. Improving lifestyle behaviors can help to reduce the risks of diabetes and other chronic conditions. Interventions that recognize the importance of lifestyle on behavior include behaviorally based changes as a crucial component designed to assist individuals suffering from chronic disease (Gross et al., 2007). The physical and psychological implications are that living with a chronic condition can disrupt every area of a client's life. From the moment a client is diagnosed with the condition, the social and psychological factors will become key areas for the health care social worker to recognize and help the health care delivery team to access (Zabora, 2009).

As stated earlier, all too often, health care practices focus on physical symptoms. When these symptoms are acute and reflective of episodic problems, this type of focus cannot effectively provide the ongoing treatment and coordination among multiple care providers and settings needed by those with chronic ailments. Moreover, health care still focuses on treatment of the physical symptoms rather than the psychological ones. A focus on treatment that lacks an emphasis on prevention can be equally problematic. For example, many people with diabetes still do not receive foot examinations to check for nerve damage, and smokers fail to receive counseling about quitting smoking and the health benefits that quitting can bring.

Last, the need remains to enhance primary care facilities, because this is where most clients enter the health care system and where most of their health care needs are met. The reliance on the primary care facility and receiving care in this way is critical to achieving goals related to treatment of acute and chronic conditions, prevention, and health promotion. For example, to improve delivery, community health centers need to undertake initiatives to reinvent and enhance primary care through new models of care delivery, support for patient self-management, and other strategies. As access and transition points, these centers need to build on their existing innovations in electronic record keeping and management of chronic diseases. New incentives can enable centers and their staffs to share in the rewards of the cost savings they generate by eliminating waste.

When confronted with challenges, it is easy to unequivocally state that "we are at a crossroads" or "we are facing a crisis." Yet social work is full of challenges, no matter what the setting—health care or another area of practice. And even the most experienced health care social workers have felt that no matter how hard they try, health care organizations represent large bureaucracies that seem impossible to change. As a result, we can become stuck at the crossroads, never moving, and believing that others control our destiny—or we can begin to understand and identify the problems and explore potential solutions for change.

9.6 ROLES AND TASKS OF THE HEALTH CARE SOCIAL WORKER

According to *The Social Work Dictionary*, health care workers can be defined in a generic sense as all "professional, paraprofessional, technical and general employees of a system or facility that provides for the diagnosis, treatment and overall wellbeing of patients" (Barker, 2003, p. 192). Nevertheless, a clear distinction must be made between health care workers and allied health care professionals. Health care workers are nonprofessional service support personnel such as home health aides, medical record personnel, nurse's aides, orderlies, and attendants (Barker, 2003). Allied health care providers, by contrast, are professionals such as social workers, psychologists, audiologists, dietitians, occupational therapists, optometrists, pharmacists, physical therapists, and speech pathologists.

It is as allied health care professionals that you will find social workers practicing in health care settings. Health care social workers serve this area well because of their broad-based training in evaluating, based on behavior, the biological, psychological, and social factors that can affect a client's environmental situation—that is, the behavioral **biopsychosocial approach**. The beginning generalist (BSW) and advanced specialist (MSW) levels of education help to make the social work professional an invaluable member of the health care delivery team. In social work, either a BSW or an MSW degree from an accredited program certified by the Council of Social Work Education and state-level licensure are required (NASW, 2016). The services that health care social workers provide can be divided into two major areas: direct practice and support or ancillary services.

Where do physicians and nurses, the most recognizable health care providers, fit in? Physicians and nurses are not considered allied service providers. Because their services are necessary to any type of medical care, they are called *essential health care providers*—they are the major players in the host environment (Dziegielewski & Holliman, 2020).

9.7 DIRECT PRACTICE

Today, social workers can be found in every area of our health care delivery system. The ACA and the Patient Protection and Affordable Care Act (2010), with its emphasis on prevention, coordinated care, and client centeredness, have created opportunities for social workers to take an accelerated role in integrated primary care and behavioral health settings (Putney et al., 2017).

Providing culturally aware and responsive practice while affirming the worth and dignity of all clients served is at the core of what social workers do (NASW, 2016). Therefore, do not be surprised if you find yourself in a situation in which providing culturally responsive practice can become a balancing act between client self-determination and respect for cultural expectations. For most social workers, listening to the client's story, considering the client system, and realizing the need to start from where the client is provides a firm basis for any intervention to follow (see the activity below).

Activity: Being Culturally Aware and Responsive in the Medical Setting

Read and process the following case. Consider getting the opinions of other classmates in terms of their perception of this case and how to best address the needs of the client. Based on the input and ideas you receive, as well as class discussion, prepare a plan for how to best assist in the client situation described.

When the social worker arrives in a client's hospital room to gather some routine admission information, she walks in on a couple having a very heated discussion. Jon is a forty-year-old Hispanic male who is in the hospital for routine, same-day exploratory surgery. Jon's wife is visibly upset and crying. The social worker feels a bit awkward for intruding and asks if the couple would like her to leave. Jon motions that he would like her to stay and begins to tell her that he is furious that his wife has decided to go on a trip alone to see her mother. When questioned as to whether he is disappointed because he wants to go with her, he quickly says no. He is angry because she made plans without getting his permission first. His wife states that she is sorry for not asking him first, but she felt that the decision had to be made quickly. The couple asks the social worker for her opinion.

In view of her need to respect cultural diversity and maintain professional integrity, what types of responses and/or assistance could the social worker provide? What types of responses should be avoided?

Dziegielewski and Holliman (2020) identified several areas in which practitioners typically provide a wide variety of services to clients and their families:

- *Case finding and outreach*: Assist the client in identifying and securing the services they need.
- *Preservice or preadmission planning*: Identify barriers to accessing health care services.
- *Assessment*: Identify service needs and screen to identify health and wellness concerns.
- *Direct provision*: Secure concrete services such as admission, discharge, and aftercare planning. Assess whether the client is a candidate for teletherapy/telemedicine services if needed.

- *Psychosocial evaluation*: Gather information on the client's biopsychosocial, cultural, financial, and situational factors for completion of the psychosocial assessment or social history.
- *Goal identification*: Establish mutually negotiated goals and objectives that address the client's health and wellness issues.
- *Counseling*: Help the client and family to deal with their situation and problems related to health interventions needed or received.
- *Short- and long-term planning*: Help the client and family to anticipate and plan for the services needed based on the client's current or expected health status.
- *Community Connections and Service access assistance*: Identify preventive, remedial, and rehabilitative service needs and assist the client and family with overcoming potential barriers to service access.
- *Education*: Instruct the client and family on areas of concern regarding their health and wellness. Be sure to assess for any language barriers, especially when providing written information.
- *Wellness training*: Help the client to establish a plan to secure continued or improved health based on a holistic prevention model.
- *Referral services*: Provide information about services available and make direct connection when warranted.
- *Continuity of care*: Ensure making proper connections among all services needed, with careful examination of how the problems are viewed by multiple health care providers.
- *Advocacy*: Teach and assist clients to obtain needed resources or, on a larger scale, advocate for changes in policy or procedure that directly or indirectly benefit the client.
- *Case management and discharge planning*: Ensure that clients are connected to the services they need after leaving the general health care facility. Also, how will these services be received in the client support system?

The clinical services that health care social workers provide have clearly expanded far beyond the traditional core of discharge planning. Health care is a changing environment in which even the classic definition of discharge planning has been altered. Social workers not only coordinate discharges, but also oversee the collaborative teams of which they are members to be sure that clients are getting the services they need. Because discharges can involve numerous individual, family, and community factors, counseling services for the client to facilitate placement are often needed (Summers, 2012). Social workers often provide more than just concrete services, and supportive services such as counseling are delivered to prepare the person for discharge. Furthermore, once the team agrees that a client is ready for discharge, it is often the social worker who is responsible for ensuring that the transfer is complete and goes smoothly. Often, this involves the connection of services to ensure continuity of care and any client and family education needed.

Focus on the Interprofessional Approach

With all the complex needs of a client within the client system, it is not a surprise that in the health care professions the emphasis on education that supports collaborative practice continues to grow. Many schools of social work are now looking into enhancing education for the health care social worker in direct practice by encouraging interprofessional (IP) team-based models of care. From an IP perspective, it is assumed that each different discipline brings unique skills that complement and enhance those of the other team members (Zerden, Jones, Day, & Lombardi, 2021). This area of practice is continuing to grow while it directly attacks the assumption that disciplines act in silos. Unfortunately, Lutfiyya, Brandt, Delaney, Pechacek, and Cerra (2016) warn us that the practice is not growing as quickly as it could because of resistance (perhaps related to "turf"?) and that its roots must be planted deeply in the formal education of these disciplines, helping them to realize the contributions the other disciplines can make. To help stimulate growth in behavioral training programs, the Health Resource Service Administration (2014–2015) awarded funding, and in the first year of Leadership in Public Health Education, nearly 29 percent of the supported public health students graduated, 100 percent of whom reported the intention to pursue employment or further training in medically underserved communities. The Health Resource Services Administration (2022) continues to fund training and enhancement opportunities in mental and behavioral health.

As part of the IP team, social workers can fill distinct roles. As part of a collaborative team, contributions are significant because of their long-standing commitment to recognition of the person-in-situation and the person-in-environment. This focus starts where the client is, considers the client system, and reflects on how to best provide inclusive and comprehensive helping services. Depending on the health care setting, these roles may vary, but three primary areas identified are behavioral health specialist, care manager, and community engagement specialist (Fraser et al., 2018). In behavioral health, the experienced social worker will use their behavioral health training to assess people for mental health and substance use diagnoses. As care managers, they will work directly with the team and the client system to coordinate care planning, with special attention given to clients with complex health problems and psychological stressors. Working closely with care managers, community engagement specialists connect the individual, family, or family system to community resources (Zerden et al., 2021).

IP is gaining in popularity and schools of social work encourage these collaborations. As part of a collaborative team, social workers will continue to serve a key role on these teams, assisting in improving care planning outcomes. This is especially important for clients who suffer from chronic conditions that require constant reassessment and adjustment to existing care plans. One promising area for further study is directly measuring the role of the social worker and the effectiveness of the services provided within these collaborative teams (Zerden et al., 2021).

9.8 SUPPORT SERVICES

Social workers can also provide health-related services that are not considered direct practice. Social workers practicing in the health care setting are expected to take responsibility for continuous professional development in the state or jurisdiction in which they practice (NASW, 2016). Leadership roles in these support or ancillary services include staff supervision, administration, and community-based services:

- *Direct supervision*: Provide direct professional social work supervision through direction, guidance, and education on case services and counseling.
- *Consultation*: Provide consultation services to other social workers and multidisciplinary and interdisciplinary teams.
- *Agency consultation*: Provide consultation to agency administrators on how to enhance service delivery to clients and organizations.
- *Community consultation*: Provide consultation services to communities to assist with the development of community-based services.
- *Policy and program planning*: Assist in formulation and implementation of health care policies and programs that will help to meet client needs.
- *Program development*: Assist the agency to refine and develop new and improved programs.
- *Quality improvement*: Assist the agency to ensure that continuous quality services are provided that meet standards of professionalism and efficiency.
- *Service advocacy*: Assist the agency to recognize the needs of clients.
- *Service outreach*: Identify unmet needs and services that are not available to clients; advocate for improved programs and services; provide home visits.
- *At-risk service outreach*: Identify clients at risk of decreased health or illness and advocate securing services for them.
- *Health education*: Participate and instruct communities on developing and implementing health education programs.
- *Agency liaison*: Serve as a liaison to the agency on behalf of the client, ensuring that connections are made among client, supervisor, and community.
- *Community liaison*: Serve as a contact or connection among the client, family, and community.

Support services often go beyond what we consider the core of health care social work, and social workers often extend beyond the agency setting and, when needed, go directly into the home of the client and visit with caregivers and families. They may also need to help clients access telemedicine or teletherapy sessions with their primary care and other medical providers. We must recognize the importance of all practitioners who do this type of work day in and day out. These tasks and functions cannot be overemphasized, particularly in this era of coordinated care.

Direct Supervision

Staff supervision is a major support activity with a long and rich history in health care social work. The NASW (2013) maintains that supervision and continuing education are essential for competent practice and the skillful development of professional practice. Supervision requires specialized knowledge that builds on years of practice. It also requires updated information because the environment and the practice setting are constantly in flux. To support the requirements for advanced knowledge and oversight experience, most social workers performing supervision, whether it is clinical or administrative oversight, have an MSW degree. On occasion, you may find a BSW worker in a supervisory role, but this is the exception.

Supervision is a complicated activity, but it is necessary for the professional growth of all social workers. Reamer (2022) reminds us that a commitment to ethical practice should always integrate with our practice efforts. Supervisors are mentors, or teachers if you will, who can act as sounding boards, share practice frustrations, and look at diverse ways of collaborating with a particular client or group. When the social worker is working as part of a collaborative team, individual and/or team-related supervision efforts should always emphasize client skill building and strength enhancement. A team approach helps to build satisfaction among members and provides leadership that enhances satisfaction among all team members (Baran, Shanock, Rogelberg, & Scott, 2012).

The supervisor has varied roles in health care, but he or she oversees the services provided and can help to coordinate, develop, and evaluate the individuals he or she supervises, as well as perform administrative, educational, and supportive functions (NASW, 2013). In health care, repeated policy changes and consequent organizational instability, which lead to rapid changes, reorganization, and cutbacks, can make supervision a challenging role to assume. For the social worker, whether a new or an experienced practitioner, such uncertainty can be difficult to manage. Let's be honest—no one likes to be in an uncertain work environment where the rules may change from one day to the next. In health care, social workers must continually modify details of their practice.

In social work, supervision is a tool to help the new social worker develop and refine skills with the help of a more senior professional knowledgeable and skilled in the area (Gelman, 2009). In mediating between supervisees and clients, coworkers, or the larger community, the supervisor should always try not to adopt the opinion of any side. Supervisors must be sensitive to their staff's ongoing struggles to create initiative-taking, client-directed services within the constraints set by payers. Supervisors must also balance the demands of their jobs with those of third-party payers. To say the least, the supervisor's role is difficult. Flexibility and the time to provide proper oversight, as well as good practice skills, are central to competent supervision. The need to be flexible, however, and the environment that creates this need are major sources of stress. Stress and its management are therefore prominent issues for both supervisors and staff.

Supportive supervision addresses such issues as stress, staff morale, and work-related anxiety and worry, which, if left unaddressed, can lower job satisfaction and commitment to the agency. Supportive supervision builds worker self-esteem and emotional well-being. Overall, it can reduce stress levels and thus the dissatisfaction that results in employee burnout (Sheafor & Horejsi, 2014).

As if system uncertainty were not enough of a problem for the health care supervisor, let's add another challenge to the job: lack of clarity in staff roles and responsibilities. What are the differences in the work conducted by BSWs and by MSWs in the practice setting? You may find that what BSWs do in one setting is accomplished only by MSWs in another setting, or, in today's competitive environment, services are conducted by another professional altogether with vastly different training and background. This lack of clarity about functions means that supervisors must be careful in assigning cases and tasks. In social work, supervisors must ensure that tasks assigned to BSWs are within their scope of practice. The fact that another organization assigns a particular task to BSWs is no guarantee that the activity is appropriate for an entry-level practitioner. Rather, that organization may not be able to assign or even hire an MSW, but the task must be done, so it must be given to a BSW. Although professionally unsound, this task assignment can be made less daunting by discussing it with the supervisor.

In active supervision, advice and direction are given on the best way to handle client care for the supervisee, the multidisciplinary or interdisciplinary team, the agency, and the community. Mediation requires the supervisor to recognize that conflicts are not intentional and to help supervisees to address them in the most ethical, moral, and professional way possible. In advocacy, the supervisor empowers the supervisee to assist with the development of needed services for clients, their families, and significant others; this requires keeping current on the services available and keeping in mind changes that occur rapidly and without warning.

As brokers, social workers must establish a link for clients with community services and other agencies. Remember, when most people come into a medical setting, such as a hospital, their stay is limited. The social worker must elicit a great deal of information on the client's environment quickly and concisely. Information on social, emotional, and physical factors and their relation to the illness is a critical factor in understanding the person in his or her situation. From the early days of medical social work, Richard Cabot saw this as the most significant role of social work practice in health care. The social worker may discover that a client needs a variety of follow-up support services to sustain his or her family through the recovery period or ongoing illness. The social worker seeks out these community-based services through brokering and develops a case plan that is tailored to the client.

Health Education and Health Counseling

Social workers were part of the nineteenth-century public health education movement, also called the *sanitation movement*. Therefore, providing education and instruction is not new to social work—although recognition and emphasis of the importance of health care counseling were limited. Attention was not directed toward counseling until training became institutionalized in colleges and moved to an educational model. Joubert and colleagues (2022) remind us that social workers are adaptable, and as large-scale changes occur, such as natural disasters or in regard to immigration and human suffering as a result of conflict and mass movement of populations, educational strategies must be broadened to prepare social workers to take on this necessary expanded role.

Psychoeducation involves a wide array of services, but in health care, as in other areas of practice, this type of supportive intervention involves helping clients identify the challenges they are facing and develop social support and coping skills to address them (Walsh, 2009). Health care counseling is especially important with the increased participation of social work professionals as educators in new health care areas, such as weight reduction and smoking cessation, that we might call *nontraditional social work*. The worker continues to teach new patterns of behavior, but then employs counseling theory and skills to help the client negotiate the period of change. The worker calls on a variety of skills and strategies ranging from support to confrontation. According to Strom-Gottfried (2009, p. 721), effective educational practice relies on six essential components:

1. The development of clear and appropriate objectives
2. An understanding of the learner's needs and abilities
3. An atmosphere that is conducive to learning
4. Knowledge of the material to be conveyed
5. The skill to select and use teaching methods appropriately
6. The ability to evaluate one's performance and the learner's acquisition of the educational outcomes

Administration

Administration and related tasks have not been considered core practice areas of health care social work. In fact, most prospective social workers shy away from studying administration, focusing instead on client-related courses. If you do not believe us, ask your classmates how many of them plan to major in or develop a specialization in administration. You will find that everyone agrees that someone should study administration—"but not me." Yet administration, particularly in health care, directly affects the types of services offered in a setting. The role that administration plays in strengthening direct practice cannot be overstated. For the social worker serving as an administrator, training in time management, organizational management and operations, and sound fiscal awareness is only the start of the skills needed.

Social work administrators, like other health care administrators, must respond to often-competing management philosophies. These conflicting styles can affect the provision of client care. For example, the social work administrator may receive a directive from the hospital central administration to increase the participation of professional staff members in the organization's decision-making processes. The idea behind this directive is that greater involvement will strengthen commitment to the hospital. The social work administrator decides that quality circles and total quality management will best achieve the outcomes that central administration is seeking. While the social work administrator is attempting to put total quality management in place with quality circles among staff members, central administration announces that reimbursement from third-party payers and census data (e.g., patient bed days) are down. These announcements are an unmistakable sign of financial pressure (always remember that a hospital is a business and, like all businesses, must attend to the "bottom line"). Therefore, the social work administrator must now be concerned with generating significant patient numbers to justify and sustain the department. The new goal is to maximize reimbursement potential. If numbers decrease, then the department administrators will cut back on staff while raising workloads for those who stay. A *do more with less resources and support* mentality takes hold while the edict to develop staff loyalty remains in place.

Does this sound frustrating? Does stressing a financial motive seem unfair, or does it simply not make sense? This example may help you to understand why so many health care social work administrators become frustrated and feel trapped. Double-edged and conflicting messages sent by central administration, fueled by the pressure for reimbursement, can make social work administration one of the most difficult, frustrating, and challenging jobs in our field. However, the situation is not as dismal as it seems. Health care social work administrators do have some individual power, in that they can assume a leadership role in balancing these pressures while influencing the agency's policy decisions. Miller (2008) reminds us that policy drives practice, so being part of policymaking can help to bring about needed changes. Serving on agency committees or boards allows the administrator to help construct new policy directions and provides an opportunity to meet funding bodies to explain practice realities and discuss ways to enhance service delivery. This strategy is called *practice policy*. It reflects the understanding that social work activities are born of policy decisions. As social workers, we must be informed about and involved in the development of organizational policy—our clients are stakeholders in the policymaking and implementation process. Our practice knowledge, advocacy skills, and ability to mediate between conflicting parties are all contributions that we as social workers can make to the health care policymaking process.

Acute and Long-Term Care Settings

Social work has long been at the forefront of providing health care services to clients in acute care and long-term care settings (Beder, 2006; Chapman & Toseland, 2007). In a national survey of licensed social workers, Whitaker, Weismiller, Clark, and Wilson (2006) reported that general and acute care medical facilities are the most common employment settings for health care social workers. U.S. Census Bureau (2020) data cited hospitals as the largest employer. Therefore, as the number of practicing health care professionals continues to rise (Jansson, 2011), the role and influences of the health care social worker in the acute practice setting will remain pronounced (Dziegielewski & Holliman, 2020).

Important roles and responsibilities for health care social workers are as follows:

- To aid with treatment plans and compliance issues
- To assist clients and families with discharge planning and referral
- To provide counseling and support for clients and significant others in the areas of health, wellness, mental health, bereavement, and so forth
- To ethically assist clients and their families to make tough decisions that can affect physical health and mental health
- To educate clients, their families, and significant others about psychosocial issues and adjusting to illness and to assist in resolving behavioral problems
- To assist in identifying and obtaining entitlement benefits
- To secure nonmedical benefits and assist with risk management and quality assurance activities
- To advocate for enhanced and continued services to ensure client well-being

Long-term and transitional care restorative settings may not be very familiar to you. Let us try some other names that you are more likely to recognize, such as rehabilitative hospitals and clinics, nursing homes, intermediate care facilities, supervised boarding homes, home health care agencies, hospices, and hospital home care units. These settings require careful attention to ensuring continuity of care from one transitional facility to another, creating an assessment that will need to change as the patient's condition and situation change (Diwan, Balaswamy, & Lee, 2012). These settings are usually multidisciplinary, and social workers provide services within the areas of assessment, treatment, rehabilitation, supportive care, and prevention of increased disability of people with chronic physical, emotional, or developmental impairments. The use of transitional care options continues to gain popularity because transitional facilities such as long-term and community-based **home care** can help to save money for hospitals by reducing acute care services such as those provided in the emergency department (Dziegielewski & Holliman, 2020).

Because of the variability of tasks to be performed in these settings, the importance of staff participation. The role of the social worker is essential in helping to create a welcoming environment, act as a resource for the family, and facilitate communication about the resident with all care providers, including those in the facility (Dziegielewski & Holliman, 2020). Creating a climate of *re-enablement* allows the patient to be viewed as a person with abilities who is once again empowered to regain what was lost as a result of illness or injury (NursingTimes.net, 2012).

Empowering clients to reach their maximum level of independence reflects the core values and ethics set out in the code of ethics. The social work code of ethics reminds us how important it is to maintain sensitivity and respect for people served, to be aware of individuals' rights and abilities to make decisions for themselves (in most situations), and to maximize clients' strengths and resources. In building self-awareness for the social worker, the helping activity becomes more client sensitive and maximizes self-determination (Morgaine & Capous-Desyllas, 2015).

The phrase *long term* indicates that the client has a chronic condition that may affect his or her abilities. Unfortunately, many chronic conditions are unlikely to improve. Furthermore, people living in poverty and communities of color experience higher rates of acute and chronic illness (NASW, 2016). The sheer utility of placement in a long-term care facility is the provision of twenty-four-hour care and support. Therefore, most of the individuals served in these facilities will be older adults, and providers will often be specialists in geriatric care and focus their care provision services in this area (Temkin, 2009). This may be a particular problem for younger adults in need of these services; therefore, it is essential to be aware of the services a facility provides, as well as the age group it serves. Other populations served in these settings can include persons with disabilities and children with serious medical illnesses that require twenty-four-hour care. Care needs may be intensive and long term, but that does not mean that the social worker and other team members give up hope or stop trying to ensure that the client receives the highest quality of professional treatment. We must be realistic, but optimistic. We should not hide information from clients or discount their feelings. Remember, we are all people who think, feel, and care.

Health care social workers employed in long-term care must develop specialized knowledge of various chronic conditions and learn to identify and assess signs and symptoms of the expected progression of various diseases (Dziegielewski & Holliman, 2020). Such information is critical to being an effective practitioner with the client, family, and friends. Family, friends, and significant others often need assistance to participate in the care of their loved ones. Many people do not know what to say or how to say it and, as a result, feel overwhelmed and even useless. We should never underestimate the importance of others in the healing or sustaining process. Emerging evidence indicates that the involvement and support of family and friends and teaching about the importance of incorporating the whole person contribute to the overall wellness and satisfaction of all involved (Zechner & Kirchner, 2013). One last thought: When addressing the needs of a client who suffers from a chronic condition, the beginning professional should strive not to be afraid. Rely on what you have learned in school, and always be a compassionate person who uses skills and theory grounded in values and ethics that allow for the celebration of the entire human experience.

Hospital Emergency Room Social Work

Social work services are offered in hospital emergency rooms across the country, but in this challenging environment the actual services provided can differ greatly. For the social worker assigned to the emergency room, the employment setting is fast paced. Crises, deaths, and severe client problems must be assessed and addressed as quickly and efficiently as possible. Once the emergency medical crisis is stabilized, the social worker needs to assist with the psychosocial protocol (Boes & McDermott, 2005). The social worker can provide psychosocial services such as education and support to the client being admitted to the hospital, as well as to the client's family and friends (Beder, 2006).

In cases of disaster, terrorism, and other trauma-based occurrences, clients often present in the emergency room. Having a strong skill set relating to immediately addressing the needs of the client is essential; this needs to be combined with clear clinical standards on how to provide the best psychosocial care (Brake & Duckers, 2013). This was evident during the COVID pandemic when hospital social workers were required to take on new tasks and adapt new practices to mitigate the risk of infection (Gan, Lim, & Coh, 2020). The pressure for immediate action in this setting is intense, and the social worker must remain in a constant state of readiness, prepared for whatever might come through the door next. According to Van Wormer and Boes (1997), working in emergency room settings is different from working in other settings in the hospital because of the speed and intensity with which services must be assessed and provided. With increased pressure on the health care system and scarcity of resources, social workers may be forced to question the services that can be provided and struggle morally if they are inconsistent with ethical standards, professional values, and beliefs (Greenberg, Docherty, Gnanapragasam, & Wessely, 2020). Numerous types of cases can be seen in the emergency room; among the most common are (1) trauma-related events, which are often complex problems ranging from individual events to more global ones; (2) acute or chronic mental health and chronic medically related conditions; (3) substance-related conditions; (4) family-related events such as domestic violence or rape; and (5) family-related events such as child abuse and neglect. This can be further complicated by working with vulnerable populations such as homeless individuals or those who do not have the resources to help themselves. Continuity services are needed so that once the acute crisis is addressed, the client will be provided ongoing support and referral that maintains the level of care and avoids readmission and more extended hospital stays.

For many social workers in the emergency room setting, it is common to work as part of a collaborative interprofessional team (Dziegielewski & Holliman, 2020; Dziegielewski & Jacinto, 2016). Teamwork in this setting often involves a variety of professionals, including physicians, nurses, respiratory technicians, health unit coordinators, X-ray technicians, nurse case managers, social workers, and other health care professionals. One especially helpful team approach is the nurse–social worker collaboration (Lam et al., 2013). Some emergency departments divide this team further into what is often termed a case management subteam or dyad that utilizes the combined services of a nurse and a social worker (Bristow & Herrick, 2002). In this setting, the case management subteam members work together to provide social services and discharge planning and to ensure that continuum of care needs are met for each client served.

Historically, the presence of a social worker in the emergency room setting has been important from a supportive/clinical perspective, as well as to provide direct case management and discharge planning services (Beder, 2006). Supportive services for helping clients include discharge planning or counseling services for the family support system of the client. In the emergency room, the problems for which clients seek treatment are multifaceted and complex. The types of problems addressed are diverse, ranging from auto accidents to other types of accidental and nonaccidental injuries. Many individuals may have acute or chronic episodes of an illness, first or repeated episodes of a physical or mental illness, or suicide attempts related to health and/or emotional issues. Treatment of these individuals by health care professionals, especially for vulnerable populations who are subject to stigma, has never been more important (Schroeder, 2013).

According to Bristow and Herrick (2002), the services that social workers provide in this setting include psychosocial assessments, bereavement counseling and support, substance abuse assessment and referral, discharge planning, referrals for community resources, emotional support, and educating and advocating for patients. In addition, the emergency room social worker can assist with case management by gathering contact information for family and friends, as well as finding additional means for meeting the client's health needs. Unfortunately, some believe that the emergency room has become a dumping ground for those who lack insurance or are homeless. This group of individuals has a unique set of circumstances requiring short-term intensive support designed to facilitate the discharge process and decrease the chance of recidivism (Dziegielewski & Holliman, 2020). Because many individuals who seek care in the emergency room lack or have inadequate health care coverage, the hope is that the ACA will help to assist with the catastrophic costs that result from noncoverage.

Social work in the emergency department plays a key role in providing for the psychosocial needs of patients in a time of crisis. Although this role is important, emergency room social workers warn that medical staff may overlook social work services because of their focus on the medical needs and not the psychosocial needs of the client being served. Thus, to better utilize the services of social workers in the emergency department, emergency room staff as well as hospital administrators must be educated about the role of the social worker in their department.

Home Care Services

Home care agencies have been providing high-quality in-home services to Americans and have remained an integral part of the provision of health services since 1905. Health care social workers help patients and their families cope with chronic, acute, or terminal illnesses and handle problems that may stand in the way of recovery or rehabilitation.

Home care refers to health care and the social services that are provided to individuals and families in their home or in community and other home-like settings (Dziegielewski & Holliman, 2020). Home care includes a wide array of services such as nursing, rehabilitation, social work, home health aides, and other services. This rapidly expanding area of health care social work can be traced back as far as the early nineteenth century (Cowles, 2003). In 1955, the U.S. Public Health Services endorsed a physician-oriented and organized home health care team designed to provide medical and social services to patients within their homes. The team consisted of a physician, nurse, and social worker (Goode, 2000). Since that time, social workers have continued to provide social services in the home care setting, and this area of health care social work remains a diverse and dynamic service industry. The demand for home care services is increasing as hospital stays are decreasing.

Most home care services are provided by a third party and reimbursable by Medicare, Medicaid, private insurance policies, health maintenance organizations, and group health plans. Payments are determined by factors including client diagnosis and the types of services required. **Medicare** recipients are the largest group of clients needing home health care services. Furthermore, Medicare beneficiaries, referred to as the *duals* because they are also eligible for Medicaid, often reflect a vulnerable population and one of the largest high-risk groups (Frank, 2013). More frequently than not, the services they need involve social as well as medical supports, making the role of social work crucial in the field of home care. Unplanned discharges where an individual's psychosocial needs go unmet put the client at risk for readmission.

Cowles (2003) identified six categories of home care client problems: (1) barriers to service admissions; (2) service adjustments; (3) diagnosis, prognosis, or treatment/care plan adjustments; (4) lack of information to make informed decisions; (5) lack of needed resources; and (6) service barriers related to discharge. Rossi (1999) described home care social workers' duties as the following:

> (1) helping the health care team to understand the social and emotional factors related to the patient's health and care; (2) assessing the social and emotional factors to estimate the caregiver's capacity and potential, including but not limited to coping with the problems of daily living, acceptance of the illness or injury or its impact, role reversal, sexual problems, stress, anger or frustration, and making the necessary referrals to ensure that the patient receives the appropriate treatments; (3) helping the caregiver to secure or utilize other community agencies as needs are identified; and (4) helping the patient or caregiver to submit paperwork for alternative funding. (p. 335)

McLeod and Bywaters (2000) validate the need for social workers in health care and report that there is substantial scope for social work involvement by working toward greater equality of access to existing health and social services. Equally important is participation in shaping how social workers are viewed, establishing their role as a knowledgeable, positive, and supportive resource to support staff, coworkers, and administration (Neuman, 2000).

One additional concern relates directly to older adults. Maust, Oslin, and Marcus (2014) found that oftentimes older adults were prescribed mental health medications without an existing mental health condition to support the prescription. This makes the role of the social worker essential in protecting the rights of older adults in this setting, avoiding stigma and the overprescribing of dangerous medications that may not be relevant to the care needed.

Hospice Social Work

Hospice care is a distinct way of caring for people who are terminally ill and their families. The goal of hospice is to care for the client and the family with open acknowledgment that no cure is expected for the client's illness. Hospice care includes physical, emotional, social, and spiritual care; usually a public agency or private company that may or not be Medicare approved provides this service. All age groups are serviced, including children, adults, and the elderly, during their final stages of life, and most of this care occurs at the client's home. In 2018, according to a National Hospice and Palliative Care Organization report, 53.8 percent of Medicare beneficiaries received hospice care for thirty days or less in 2018. It was determined that this brief period of services may not have been long enough to fully benefit from the person-centered care available from hospice (National Hospice and Palliative Care Organization, 2020). That number remained roughly stable in 2022 (National Center for Health Statistics, 2022). In the hospice setting, both in-patient and in-home services can be provided. In this setting, the individual is prepared for a dignified death that is satisfactory to him or her and to those who participate in his or her care (McSkimming, Myrick, & Wasinger, 2000).

In hospice, the role of the social worker is crucial to the family planning process, and efforts are made to help family members deal with the client's illness and impending death in the most effective way possible. The social worker tries to facilitate open communication between the patient and his or her family and assess levels of stress—especially those that affect coping and prognosis. In addition, special attention is given to assessing the spiritual needs of the client and his or her family and helping them to adjust and accept. In the hospice setting there is a strong interdisciplinary focus, with a team approach that will continually assess environmental safety concerns. One of the first tasks of the social worker is to address grieving, with an initial bereavement risk assessment for the caregiver, thereby assisting the patient and family in identifying strengths that help cope with loss (Dziegielewski & Holliman, 2020). Families are supported over time as the patient and family progress through the stages of grieving. Other duties of the hospice social worker involve updating bereavement care plans and assessing the type of bereavement program to be initiated upon the death of the patient. Referrals are also provided for bereavement support services.

9.9 WHY DO IT?

By now you may be wondering why anyone would want to work in the changing, often unsettling, health care system. This is a fair question, so let us try to find an answer.

Social workers are among the many allied health professional groups that make up the health care army. Given the interdisciplinary nature of today's work, it is incumbent on the social work profession to promote a clear understanding of its purpose and role to maintain a place in health care delivery. What we bring to the health care arena is vital. History shows this. Nevertheless, we must always define our role and be players in this process. Social workers cannot afford to let others decide what they can do with and on behalf of clients and their families. The roots of health care social work, as part of the social work profession, lie in serving poor and disenfranchised populations. As the medical arena has changed over the years, so too has the role of the health care social worker.

And now, as the social environment changes, expectations for health care are becoming clouded. Is health care a right or a privilege? Should the government guarantee a minimum standard of health care for all people? Who would establish such a standard? What role should the insurance industry have in such deliberations? Should a patient's bill of rights be developed as a new initiative? (In New York City taxicabs you will find a rider's bill of rights. It is interesting that taxicab riders are provided certain guarantees, but not people in the health care system!) While the public debates these issues, the day-to-day work of the social worker in health care is daunting. Flexibility is a prerequisite for helping our clients and for adjusting to the constantly renegotiated health care environment.

All health care social workers—whether in the role of clinical practitioner, supervisor, or administrator—face the challenge of understanding and anticipating health care trends. Social workers need to know how society operates and have an appreciation for the causes of diseases and an understanding of psychological processes (Rosenberg, 2008). Each worker's skills must therefore be current, flexible, and proactive with clients. And yes, all health care social workers must also understand macroeconomics and its influence on health care delivery. The current economic environment is characterized by a shifting tension between quality of care and cost containment. Although the goal of the social work profession is to provide high-quality care, these services are overshadowed and influenced by cost containment strategies. Health care social workers are expected to include cost containment among their practice principles whether they serve as direct practitioners, professional supervisors, administrators, or community organizers (Dziegielewski & Holliman, 2020).

The viability of health care social work rests on two points. First, medical settings must place greater emphasis on the macro perspective in health care. Policy and practice are clearly linked (Miller, 2008). Whether it is as part of a collaborative team or independently, people in the social work profession must work actively to help the larger community understand the responsibility to create a cradle-to-grave health care system like those in other countries. Believing that the health care system will eventually solve its own problems is ludicrous. Health care social workers, whatever roles they choose for practice delivery, must take the lead in developing a more humane health care system that meets the needs of all people, regardless of their financial capabilities.

The second point central to all areas of health care social work practice is that advocacy leads to client empowerment (NASW, 2016). Health care social workers must change the mindset that coordinated care and the policies dictated by it are all bad. Social workers must recognize that there are benefits in a coordinated care system for both clients and providers. The greatest strength of the ACA and coordinated care is coverage in a catastrophic situation. Advocating for systems of care that help provide a comprehensive approach stands at the forefront of providing comprehensive efforts, and advocacy in this area remains central.

We must recognize, however, that coordinated care also has pitfalls, starting with large monthly premiums, extensive copays, and large deductibles. In these areas, health care social workers must advocate for clients. Workers must always stress development of new and needed services within the managed care framework. They must also teach clients how to obtain needed resources and help them to do so. On a larger scale, social workers are bound—by their code of ethics—to advocate changes in policies or procedures that will directly or indirectly benefit clients.

Working as a health care social worker is far from easy. If you decide, nonetheless, that it is the area for you, the question is, How do you best respond to the challenge? You will be tempted to switch areas and collect a paycheck in a less volatile setting. Health care social work is suited to people who will relish the changing environment, want to maximize resources for clients, look to serve on boards and committees to influence policy and practice, and enjoy the idea that every day will be different. If that is you, the health care setting is worth considering.

Name: Dodie M. Stein

Place of residence: Indianapolis, Indiana

College/university degrees: PhD, University of Iowa; MSW, Indiana University; MA, University of Southern California; BS, Syracuse University; Licensed Clinical Social Worker (LCSW), State of Indiana.

Present position and title: Psychotherapist, private practice (current); retired 2021 from medical social work, most recently with DaVita Kidney Care

Previous work/volunteer experience:

- Medical social worker: home dialysis as well as in-center dialysis; hospice social worker (also as a volunteer prior to social work career)
- Fellow, Fairbanks Center for Medical Ethics, Indiana University Health (formerly Clarian Health)
- Adjunct faculty, technical communications, School of Engineering Technology, Indiana University–Purdue University Indianapolis (1993–2002)
- Various executive positions in business, technology, nonprofit community organizations
- Clinical and educational audiologist in private practice and universities, special education, community speech and hearing center, and medical practices
- Member, National Committees for Quality Assurance (serious illness)
- Various volunteer roles for the National Kidney Foundation–Indiana, including chair of the chapter's unit. Grant reviewer, U.S. Department of Education
- Editor and reviewer, Sertoma, various professional journals and publishers in communication disorders
- Committee and board activities in audiological organizations, Kentucky technology assistance projects, National Governors Association

continues

continued

- National Kidney Foundation–Indiana Chapter: chair, Council of Nephrology Social Workers (2015–2021); various event committees (current)
- National Association of Social Workers–Indiana Chapter: Program Committee, Ethics Committee (current)

Why did you choose social work as a career? I was in an allied health field working with babies, young children, and older adults ("womb to tomb," as they say) for many years. After leaving the field and working in other governmental and not-for-profit organizations, I found I missed health care. This was about the time I spent a last year with a friend who was dying from breast cancer, and I volunteered for hospice at a local hospital. That's what inspired me to go into social work—working with hospice patients and those with life-threatening chronic diseases, having the honor of helping them manage their illnesses whether they were in a transition in their lives (starting dialysis) or at the end of their lives (hospice). Currently, since retirement as a medical social worker in dialysis, I am in private practice in a therapy group providing psychotherapy to adults with a variety of mental health issues. All of my prior work experiences provided me the experience and skills to transition to private practice.

What is your favorite social work story? The series of events that I used to see every day for seventeen years as a renal social worker were inspiring: Patients waiting for years, then finally getting a transplant; patients feeling better and feeling like they have more control over their lives with home dialysis; patients who are depressed and not coping well getting better with appropriate meds and counseling and feeling more sense of control and contentment. These are patients who constantly dealt with dialysis as their lifeline, their many comorbidities, and the many meds they took to manage the renal disease . . . not to mention the financial aspects of insurances, high monthly copayments, or having to pay full price for very expensive meds, juggling work and dialysis if they were well enough; multiple physicians' appointments, family demands; transportation difficulties; other activities. I have enormous respect for them and all they cope with and juggle. I always wonder if I could do it if I were faced with all of it. At least I know I helped them learn to manage, "stay steady," and get back to enjoying what they used to enjoy before renal disease changed their lives. The social work counseling services I provided to dialysis patients helped prepare me for private practice, the environment I've recently chosen in the final years of my social work career.

What is one thing you would change in the community if you had the power to do so? Universal health care (as in health care for all living in this country), preferably single-payer health care, to provide "health," not "sick" care, including preventative care at all ages, is critical for health care equality. This also assumes physicians and other health care providers are making decisions with their patients, not insurance or government bureaucrats "practicing medicine without a license!"

SUMMARY

Health care social work is a dynamic, exciting, constantly changing field of practice. The past twenty years have brought changes and events both nationally and globally. The most experienced social workers can feel frustrated when forced to address specific issues in an environment where the rules are evolving. Health care social work's history is an extensive one, deeply rooted in the activities of pioneers such as Ida Cannon and Richard Cabot. These early practitioners linked social work practice to the medical model considered the core of health care practice.

Today, health care social workers strive to restore the highest level of functioning for each client, family, small group, and community served. The struggle with integrating practice and theory continues, and translating academic practice into successful helping activities is the key (Brake & Duckers, 2013). Opportunities to include interprofessional collaborative practice remain rich in helping to enhance integrated care (Zerden et al., 2021). Health care social work remains central to building the profession. Starting long ago and continuing to this day, health care social work is an important and vital force, both in the profession and in communities across the country and around the world. People with medical illnesses often have other related problems and may need help re-establishing their routines once they arrive home from the hospital, or they may have trouble paying their bills. Families who lose a loved one may need counseling to process their grief, and those with hereditary conditions may need help sorting through their fears and concerns about the future. The health care social worker is viewed as the bridge between the client, the client system, and the success of the services provided. When this is complicated with increased workloads and restrictive communications such as requiring masks or other face coverings, advocating for patients can require increased attention (Joubert et al., 2022).

Health care social workers use a wide range of skills in all these settings, employing both a family- and a systems-oriented approach to psychosocial care. The incorporation of health and wellness strategy goes beyond just addressing emergent health care needs and takes us one step closer to achieving what some could term a balanced life (Zechner & Kirchner, 2013). Social workers, like other helping professionals, provide counseling, help families develop strengths and resources, and run programs for patients who have diseases such as AIDS and heart disease (Centers for Disease Control and Prevention, 2014). The settings these workers occupy vary from acute short-term settings to extended-care long-term settings (U.S. Census, 2020). Regardless of the type of clientele served or the area of practice, health care social work is a challenging and essential area of practice. For social workers, like other health care professionals in the United States and globally, especially when facing a pandemic, avoiding burnout and finding the right work–life balance is not an easy task (Tuğsal, 2020).

Today's health care system is imbued with knowledge, expertise, equipment, and technologies never dreamed of or thought possible. Within our lifetime, we have seen transplants go from headline news to no news, diseases eradicated, and life expectancy dramatically increased. Yet we all know that the health care system is challenged. Costs have risen, and continue to rise, to levels that require health insurance to help make care affordable. Tough decisions will need to be made by scores of individuals and families when they are forced to weigh the importance of simple decisions such as "Do I put food on the table tonight or buy the prescription for my child?"

Let us for a moment consider what the health care system *should* be like—reflecting on Ida Maude Cannon's ideals and imagining how they would translate to a health care system at the outset of the twenty-first century. One way to consider *what might be* is to identify core principles that you feel are central to your organization's purpose. Integrate these policies without bias or consideration of who is or is not favored and begin to think about what is in the best interest of the whole, nationally and internationally. Areas for future thought include the following:

1. Given the most recent strides with the ACA, health care modification efforts must be affordable to individuals and families, businesses, and taxpayers, and consistency among the states in providing these benefits is the key.
2. Health care must be as cost-efficient as possible, with the maximum amount of dollars spent on direct patient care.
3. Health care must provide comprehensive benefits that are culturally sensitive and responsive, including benefits for mental health and long-term care services, along with technological connectedness.
4. Health care must promote prevention and early intervention.
5. Health care provisions and services must eliminate disparities in access to quality health care (NASW, 2016).
6. Health care must address the needs of people with special health care requirements, particularly those within underserved populations in both rural and urban areas.
7. Health care must promote quality and better health outcomes, while examining national and global trends and connections for clients and client systems.
8. Health care services must be inclusive by having adequate numbers of qualified health care caregivers, practitioners, and providers to guarantee timely access to quality care.
9. Health care must ensure adequate and timely payments to guarantee access to providers.
10. Health care services must be comprehensive, fostering a strong network of health care facilities, including safety net providers.
11. Health care services must maximize consumer choice in terms of health care providers and practitioners.
12. Health care services must ensure continuity of coverage and care.
13. Clients receiving health care services must have access to telemedicine and/or teletherapy to foster or supplement treatment.

REFERENCES

Alignment Health Care. (2022). *2022 Social threats to aging in America*. Orange, CA: Author. Retrieved from https://www.alignmenthealthcare.com/files/2022-ALHC-Social-Threats-to-Aging-Well

Baran, B. E., Shanock, L. R., Rogelberg, S. G., & Scott, C. W. (2012). Leading group meetings: Supervisors' actions, employee behaviors, and upward perceptions. *Small Group Research, 43*, 330–335.

Barker, R. L. (2003). *The social work dictionary* (5th ed.). Washington, DC: NASW Press.

Beder, J. (2006). *Hospital social work: The interface of medicine and caring*. New York, NY: Routledge/Taylor & Francis.

Bitler, M. P., Hoynes, H. W., & Schanzenbach, D. W. (2020). *The social safety net in the wake of COVID-19*. Brookers Papers on Economic Activity, Special Editon, September 2020(2), 119–158. Retrieved from https://www.nber.org/papers/w27796

Boes, M., & McDermott, V. (2005). Crisis intervention in the hospital emergency room. In A. R. Roberts (Ed.), *Crisis intervention handbook* (3rd ed., pp. 543–565). New York, NY: Oxford University Press.

Brake, H. T., & Duckers, M. (2013). Early psychosocial interventions after disasters, terrorism, and other shocking events: Is there a gap between norms and practice in Europe? *European Journal of Psychotraumatology, 4*, 1–10.

Bristow, D., & Herrick, C. (2002). Emergency department: The roles of the nurse case manager and the social worker. *Continuing Care, 21*(2), 28–29.

Bureau of Labor Statistics. (2018). *Occupational outlook handbook*. Retrieved from https://www.bls.gov/ooh/community-and-social-service/social-workers.htm#tab-3

Burke, T. N. (2008). Nonprofit service organizations: Fidelity with strategic plans for financial survival. *Journal of Human Behavior in the Social Environment, 18*, 204–221.

Carlton, T. O. (1984). *Clinical social work in health care settings: A guide to professional practice with exemplars*. New York, NY: Springer.

Carter, D. P., & May, P. J. (2020). Making sense of the U.S. COVID-19 pandemic response: A policy regime perspective. *Administrative Theory and Praxis, 42*(2), 265–277. https://doi.org/10.1080/10841806.2020.1758991

Centers for Disease Control and Prevention. (2014). *Recommendations for HIV prevention with adults and adolescents with HIV in the United States*. Retrieved from http://stacks.cdc.gov/view/cdc/26065

Centers for Medicare & Medicaid Services. (n.d.). *Patient's bill of rights*. Retrieved December 28, 2022, from https://www.cms.gov/CCIIO/Programs-and-Initiatives/Health-Insurance-Market-Reforms/Patients-Bill-of-Rights

Chapman, D. G., & Toseland, R. W. (2007). Effectiveness of advanced illness care teams for nursing home residents with dementia. *Social Work, 52*, 321–329.

Cowles, L. A. (2003). *Social work in the health field: a care perspective* (2nd ed.). Florence, KY: Routledge.

Damron-Rodriquez, J. (2008). Developing a competence for nurses and social workers. *Journal of Social Work Education, 44*(3), 27–37.

Diwan, S., Balaswamy, S., & Lee, S. E. (2012) Social work with older adults in health-care settings. In S. Gehlert & T. Browne (Eds.), *Handbook of health social work* (2nd ed., pp. 392–425). Hoboken, NJ: Wiley.

Dowell, E. K. (2020). *Census bureau's 2018 county business patterns provides data on 1,200 industries*. United States Census Bureau. Retrieved from https://www.census.gov/library/stories/2020/10/health-care-still-largest-united-states-employer.html

Dziegielewski, S. F. (2015). *DSM-5 in action*. Hoboken, NJ: Wiley & Sons.

Dziegielewski, S. F., & Holliman, D. (2020). *The changing face of health care social work: Opportunities and challenges for professional practice*. (4th ed.). New York, NY: Springer.

Dziegielewski, S. F., & Jacinto, G. A. (2016). *Psychopharmacology and social work practice: A person-in-environment approach* (3rd ed.). New York, NY: Springer.

Fink-Samnick, E. (2021). The social determinants of mental health: Definitions, distinctions, and dimensions for professional case management: Part 1. *Professional Case Management, 26*(3), 121–137. https://doi.org/10.1097/NCM.0000000000000497

Frank, R. G. (2013). Mental illness and a dual dilemma. *Journal of the American Society of Aging, 37*(2), 47–53.

Fraser, M. W., Lombardi, B. M., Wu., S., Zerden, L. D., Richman, E. L., & Fraher, E. P. (2018). Integrated primary care and social work: A systematic review. *Journal for the Society of Social Work Research, 9*(2), 175–215. https://doi.org/10.1086/697567

Gan, W. H., Lim, J. W., & Koh, D. (2020). *Preventing intra-hospital infection and transmission of COVID-19 in healthcare workers*. Safety and Health at Work, *11*(2), 241–243.

Gelman, S. R. (2009). On being an accountable profession: The code of ethics, oversight by boards of directors, and whistle-blowers as a last resort. In A. R. Roberts (Ed.), *Social workers' desk reference* (2nd ed., pp. 156–162). New York, NY: Oxford University Press.

Goode, R. A. (2000). *Social work practice in home health care*. Binghamton, NY: Haworth Press.

Greenberg, N., Docherty, M., Gnanapragasam, S., & Wessely, S. (2020). Managing mental health challenges faced by healthcare workers during COVID-19 pandemic. *British Medical Journal BMJ (Clinical research ed.), 368*, m1211. https://doi.org/10.1136/bmj.m1211

Gross, R., Tabenkin, H., Heymann, A., Greenstein, M., Matzliach, R., Portah, A., & Porter, B. (2007). Physician's ability to influence the life-style behaviors of diabetic patients: Implications for social work. In S. Dumont & M. St. Onge (Eds.), *Social work health and international development: Compassion in social policy and practice* (pp. 191–204). Binghamton, NY: Haworth Press.

Health Resource Service Administration. (2014–2015). *Behavioral health training programs: Academic year 2014–2015*. Retrieved from https://bhw.hrsa.gov/sites/default/files/bureau-health-workforce/data-research/behavioral-health-training-2015.pdf

Health Resource Service Administration. (2022). *Behavioral health workforce education and training (BHWET) program for professionals*. Retrieved December 28, 2022, from https://www.hrsa.gov/grants/find-funding/HRSA-21-089

Hiltz, S. R., Hughes, A. L., Imran, M., Plotnick, L., Power, R., & Turoff, M. (2020). Exploring the usefulness and feasibility of software requirements for social media use in emergency management. *International Journal of Disaster Risk Reduction, 42*, Article 101367. https://doi.org/10.1016/j.ijdrr.2019.101367

Jackson, T. (2022, July 29). We won't end the HIV epidemic until we help the most vulnerable. *New York, NY: Global Health, Health Equity, Rabin Martin Newsletter.* Retrieved from https://rabinmartin.com/insights/we-wont-end-the-hiv-epidemic-until-we-help-the-most-vulnerable/

Jansson, B. S. (2011). *Improving healthcare through advocacy: A guide for health and helping professionals.* Hoboken, NJ: Wiley.

Johnson, J. K., & Sollecito, W. A. (Eds.). (2020). *McLaughlin and Kalunzny's continuous quality improvement in health care* (5th ed.). Burlington, MA: Jones & Bartlett Learning.

Joubert, L., Hampson, R., Acuto, R., Powell, L., Latiff, M. L., Tran, L., . . . Simpson, G. (2022). Resilience and adaptability of social workers in health care settings during COVID-19 in Australia. *Social Work in Health Care, 61*(4), 199–217. https://doi.org/10.1080/00981389.2022.2096170

Lam, W., Chan, E. A., & Yeung, K. S. (2013). Implications for school nursing through inter-professional education and practice. *Journal of Clinical Nursing, 22*(13/14), 1988–2001.

Laughlin, L., Anderson, A., Martinez, A. & Gayfield, A. (2021). *22 million employed in health care fight against COVID-19.* United States Census Bureau, Washington, DC. Retrieved from https://www.census.gov/library/stories/2021/04/who-are-our-health-care-workers.html?utm_campaign=20220808msprts1v1pupnl&utm_medium=email&utm_source=govdelivery

Leipzig, R. M., Hyer, K., Ek, K., Wallenstein, S., Vezina, M. L., Fairchild, S., . . . Howe, J. L. (2002). Attitudes toward working on interdisciplinary healthcare teams: A comparison by discipline. *Journal of the American Geriatric Society, 50,* 1141–1148.

Lutfiyya, M. N., Brandt, B., Delaney, C., Pechacek, J., & Cerra, F. (2016). Setting a research agenda for interprofessional education and collaborative practice in the context of United States health system reform. *Journal of Interprofessional Care, 30*(1), 7–14. https://doi.org/10.3109/13561820.2015.1040875

Maestre, G., & Fernandez, F. (2019). Wrap-around services to older adults with dementia: Collaboration, education, and prevention as a model for integration of primary care and neurobehavioral health. *Alzheimer's & Dementia, 15*(7, Suppl.), 205. https://doi.org/10.1016/j.jalz.2019.06.4543

Maust, D., Oslin, D. W., & Marcus, S. (2014). Effect of age on the profile of psychotropic users: Results from the 2010 National Ambulatory Medical Care Survey. *Journal of the American Geriatrics Society, 62,* 358–364.

McSkimming, S., Myrick, M., & Wasinger, M. (2000). Supportive care of the dying: A coalition for compassionate care—conducting an organizational assessment. *American Journal of Hospice & Palliative Care, 17,* 245–252.

McLeod, E., & Bywaters, P. (2000). *Social work, health, and equality.* New York, NY: Routledge.

Miller, P. J. (2008). Health-care policy: Should change be small or large? In K. M. Sowers & C. N. Dulmus (Series Eds.) & I. C. Colby (Vol. Ed.), *Comprehensive handbook of social work and social welfare: Social policy and policy practice* (Vol. 4, pp. 219–236). Hoboken, NJ: Wiley.

Mizrahi, T. (1995). Health care: Reform initiatives. In R. Edwards. (Ed.), *Encyclopedia of social work* (19th ed., Vol. 2, pp. 1185–1198). Silver Spring, MD: NASW Press.

Moniz, C., & Gorin, S. (2014). *Health care policy and practice: A biopsychosocial perspective* (4th ed.). New York, NY: Routledge.

Morgaine, K., & Capous-Desyllas, M. (2015). *Anti-oppressive social work practice: Putting theory into action.* Los Angeles, CA: Sage.

Nacman, M. (1977). Social work in health setting: A historical review. *Social Work in Health Care, 2,* 407–418.

National Association of Social Workers. (2013). *Best practice standards in social work supervision.* Washington, DC: Author.

National Association of Social Workers. (2016). *NASW standards for social work practice in health care settings.* Retrieved December 29, 2022, from https://www.socialworkers.org/LinkClick.aspx?fileticket=fFnsRHX-4HE%3d&portalid=0

National Center for Health Statistics. (2022). Post-acute and long-term care providers and services users in the United States, 2017–2018: Analytical and epidemiological studies. *Vital and Health Statistics, 3*(47), 1–84. Hyattsville, MD: U.S Department of Health and Social Services.

National Hospice and Palliative Care Organization. (2020). *NHPCO releases new facts and figures report on hospice care in America.* Alexandria, VA: National Hospice and Palliative Care Organization. Retrieved December 29, 2022, from: https://www.nhpco.org/hospice-facts-figures/

Neuman, K. (2000). Understanding organizational reengineering in health care: Strategies for social work's survival. *Social Work in Health Care, 31,* 19–32.

Nicholas, D. B., Darch, J., McNeill, T., Brister, L., O'Leary, K., Berlin, D., & Koller, D. (2007). Perceptions of online support for hospitalized children and adolescents. In S. Dumont & M. St.-Onge (Eds.), *Social work health and international development: Compassion in social policy and practice* (pp. 205–224). Binghamton, NY: Haworth Press.

NursingTimes.net. (Practice Comment). (2012). *Expand HCA role to focus on older people's rehabilitation.* Retrieved from http://www.nursingtimes.net/nursing-practice/clinical-zones/older-people/expand-hca-role-to-focus-on-older-peoples-rehabilitation/5048850.article?blocktitle=Practice-comment&contentID=6854

Ofosu, A. (2011). Implications for health care reform. *Health & Social Work, 36,* 229–231.

Patient Protection and Affordable Care Act. (2010). 42 U.S.C. § 18001 et seq.

Peeters, R., Westra, D., van Raak, A. J. A., & Ruwaard, D. (2022). So happy together: A review of the literature on the determinants of effectiveness of purpose-oriented networks in health care. *Medical Care Research and Review, 80*(3), 266–282. https://doi.org/10.1177/10775587221118156

Poertner, J., & Rapp, C. A. (2007). *The textbook of social administration: The consumer centered approach.* Binghamton, NY: Haworth Press.

Poole, D. (1995). Health care: Direct practice. In R. Edwards & J. G. Hopps (Eds.), *Encyclopedia of social work* (19th ed., Vol. 2, pp. 1156–1167). Washington, DC: NASW Press.

Popple, P., & Leighninger, L. (1990). *Social work, social welfare, and American society.* Needham, MA: Allyn & Bacon.

The White House Domestic Policy Staff. (1993). *The president's health security plan: The Clinton blueprint.* New York, NY: Times Books/Random House.

Putney, J. M., Sankar, S., Harriman, K. K., O'Brien, K. H., Stanton, D., Hecker, R., & Hecker, S. (2017). An innovative behavioral health workforce initiative: Keeping pace with an emerging model of care. *Journal of Social Work Education, 53*(Suppl. 1), S5–S16. https://doi.org/10.1080/10437797.2017.1326329

Reamer, F. G. (2022). *The philosophical foundations of social work* (2nd ed.). New York, NY: Columbia University Press.

Rosenberg, G. (2008). Social determinants of health: Twenty-first-century social work priorities. In K. M. Sowers & C. N. Dulmus (Series Eds.) & I. C. Colby (Vol. Ed.), *Comprehensive handbook of social work and social welfare: Vol. 4. Social policy and policy practice* (pp. 237–247). Hoboken, NJ: Wiley.

Rossi, P. (1999). *Case management in healthcare*. Philadelphia, PA: Saunders.

Rugy, V. D. (2014). Where is the innovation in health care? Fairfax, VA: Mercatus Center, George Mason University. Retrieved from http://mercatus.org/expert_commentary/where-innovation-health-care

Santoni, V., & Rufat, S. (2021). How fast is fast enough? Twitter usability during emergencies. *Geoforum, 124,* 20–35. https://doi.org/10.1016/j.geoforum.2021.05.007

Schleicher, A. (2020). *The impact of COVID-19 on education: Insights from education at a glance 2020*. Paris, France: Organization for Economic Cooperation and Development (OECD) Education and Skills Today. Paris, France: OECD Publishing, OECD.org.

Schroeder, R. (2013). The seriously mentally ill older adult: Perceptions of the patient–provider relationship. *Perspectives in Psychiatric Care, 49,* 30–40.

Segal, W., & Brzuzy, S. (1998). *Social welfare policy, programs, and practice*. Itasca, IL: Peacock.

Sheafor, B. W., & Horejsi, C. R. (2014). *Techniques and guidelines for social work practice* (10th ed.). Boston, MA: Allyn & Bacon/Pearson.

Sheen, R. (2022a, February 2). ACA open enrollment reaches record-breaking 14.5 million. The ACA Times. Retrieved from https://acatimes.com/aca-open-enrollment-reaches-record-breaking-14-5-million/

Sheen, R. (2022b, October 13). Employers take note: ACA no longer being repealed. *The ACA Times*. Retrieved from https://acatimes.com/employers-take-note-aca-no-longer-being-repealed/

Steketee, G., Ross, A. M., & Wachman, M. K. (2017). Health outcomes and costs of social work services: A systematic review. *American Journal of Public Health, 107,* S256–S266. https://doi.org/10.2105/AJPH.2017.304004

Strom-Gottfried, K. (2009). Enacting the educator role: Principles for practice. In A. R. Roberts (Ed.), *Social workers' desk reference* (2nd ed., pp. 720–725). New York, NY: Oxford University Press.

Summers, N. (2012). *Fundamentals of case management practice: Skills for the human services* (4th ed.). Belmont, CA: Brooks/Cole.

Temkin, M. (2009). *Aging and developmental disabilities strategic issues for service agencies*. Victoria, British Columbia: Garth Homer Society. Retrieved from http://www.garthhomersociety.org/sites/default/files/imce/FinalAgingReport_GarthHomer_2009.pdf

Thompson, D. (2018). *Health care just became the U.S.'s largest employer: In the American labor market, services are the new steel.* The Atlantic: https://www.theatlantic.com/press-releases/. Retrieved from https://www.theatlantic.com/business/archive/2018/01/health-care-america-jobs/550079/.

Trattner, W. (1989). *From poor law to welfare state: A history of social welfare in America* (4th ed.). New York, NY: Free Press.

Tuğsal, T. (2020). The mediator role of social support amid work–life balance and burnout of employees in the context of coronavirus pandemic precautions and social isolation. *Beykent Üniversitesi Sosyal Bilimler Dergisi, 13*(1), 6–18. https://doi.org/10.18221/bujss.718383

United States Census Bureau. (2019). *U.S. Census Bureau Releases 2014-2018 ACS 5-Year Estimates.* Retrieved from: https://www.census.gov/programs-surveys/acs/news/updates/2019.html

U.S. Bureau of Labor Statistics. (2023). *Occupational employment and wages, May 2021, 21-1022 Health care social workers.* Retrieved October 20, 2022, from https://www.bls.gov/oes/current/oes211022.htm

U.S. Census Bureau. (2020). *Health care still largest U.S. employer.* Retrieved December 28, 2022, from https://www.census.gov/library/stories/2020/10/health-care-still-largest-united-states-employer.html

U.S. Census Bureau. (2022). *National Health Center Week: August 7–13, 2022.* Retrieved from https://www.census.gov/newsroom/stories/health-center-week.html?utm_campaign=20220808msprts1v1pupnl&utm_medium=email&utm_source=govdelivery

U.S. Centers for Medicare & Medicaid Services. (2022). *Young adults and the Affordable Care Act: Protecting young adults and eliminating burdens on families and businesses.* Retrieved from https://www.cms.gov/CCIIO/Resources/Files/adult_child_fact_sheet.

U.S. Department of Health and Human Services (HHS). (2014). New HHS data shows major strides made in patient safety, leading to improved care and savings. South Washington, DC: Health and Human Services. Retrieved from https://www.cms.gov/priorities/innovation/files/reports/patient-safety-results.pdf

U.S. Department of Health and Human Services. (2022). *New reports show record 35 million people enrolled in coverage related to the Affordable Care Act.* Retrieved from https://www.hhs.gov/about/news/2022/04/29/new-reports-show-record-35-million-people-enrolled-in-coverage-related-to-the-affordable-care-act.html

Van Wormer, K., & Boes, M. (1997). Humor in the emergency room: A social work perspective. *Health and Social Work, 22*(2), 87–92.

Virginia Commonwealth University Libraries Social Welfare History Project. (n.d.). *National Association of Social Workers: History (1917–1955).* Retrieved December 29, 2022, from https://socialwelfare.library.vcu.edu/social-work/national-association-social-workers-history/

Walker, J. S., Bruns, E. J., & Penn, M. (2008). Individualized services in systems of care: The wrap-around process. In B. A. Stroul & G. M. Blau (Eds.), *The system of care handbook: Transforming mental health services for children, youth, and families* (pp. 127–155). Baltimore, MD: Brookes.

Walsh, J. (2009). Psychoeducation. In A. R. Roberts (Ed.), *Social workers' desk reference* (2nd ed., pp. 474–478). New York, NY: Oxford University Press.

Whitaker, T., Weismiller, T., Clark, E., & Wilson, M. (2006). *Assuring the sufficiency of a front-line workforce: A national study of licensed social workers* (Special report: Social Work Services in Health Care Settings). Washington, DC: NASW Press.

Xu, T., Pompili, M., & Sampogna, G. (2021). Psychological distress of international students during the COVID-19 pandemic in China: Multidimensional effects of external environment, individuals' behavior, and their values. *International Journal of Environmental Research and Public Health, 18*(97580), 1–18. https://doi.org/10.3390/ijerph18189758

Yuan, F. X., Li, M., Liu, R., Zhai, W., & Qi, B. (2021). Social media for enhanced understanding of disaster resilience during Hurricane Florence. *International Journal of Information Management, 57*, Article 102289. https://doi.org/10.1016/j.ijinfomgt.2020.102289

Zabora, J. R. (2009). Development of a proactive model of health care versus a reactive system of referrals. In A. R. Roberts (Ed.), *Social workers' desk reference* (2nd ed., pp. 826–832). New York, NY: Oxford University Press.

Zechner, M., & Kirchner, M. P. (2013). Balanced life: A pilot wellness program for older adults in psychiatric hospitals. *Psychiatric Rehabilitation Journal, 36*, 42–44.

Zerden, L. D., Jones, A., Day, S., & Lombardi, B. M. (2021). Interprofessional collaboration: An evaluation of social work students' skills and experiences in integrated health care. *Journal of Social Work Education, 57*(4), 758–770. https://doi.org/10.1080/10437797.2020.1743219

10

Mental Health

CHAPTER 10: EPAS COMPETENCIES

Social work programs at the bachelor's and the master's level are accredited by the Council of Social Work Education (CSWE). CSWE's Educational Policy and Accreditation Standards (EPAS) describe the processes and criteria that social work courses should cover. In 2022, CSWE updated its EPAS standards. The following competencies are addressed in this chapter.

Competency 1: Demonstrate Ethical and Professional Behavior

Social workers understand the value base of the profession and its ethical standards, as well as relevant policies, laws, and regulations that may affect practice with individuals, families, groups, organizations, and communities

Competency 2: Advance Human Rights and Social, Racial, Economic, and Environmental Justice

Social workers understand that every person regardless of position in society has fundamental human rights.

Competency 4: Engage in Practice-Informed Research and Research-Informed Practice

Social workers use ethical, culturally informed, anti-racist, and anti-oppressive approaches in conducting research and building knowledge.

Competency 8: Intervene with Individuals, Families, Groups, Organizations, and Communities

Social workers understand that intervention is an ongoing component of the dynamic and interactive process of social work practice.

There were 173,860 documented jobs held by social workers in the United States in 2021 in health and mental health, with 2,420 of these listed as being employed in psychiatric and substance abuse hospitals (Bureau of Labor Statistics, 2021). Social workers are the nation's largest providers of mental health services. Yet there are so many areas of practice where social workers may be underutilized. For example, in a recent study, Jung, Jamie, and Lee (2022) noted that when interviewing employees in subsidized housing units, the mental health needs of the residents were not always met. These needs could have been better addressed by an integrated health care approach that involved social workers assisting with the multilevel barriers to receiving health and mental health care.

In the United States in 2021, it was estimated that there were 181,600 jobs for psychologists (Bureau of Labor Statistics, 2022a), 65,300 for marriage and family therapists (Bureau of Labor Statistics, 2022b), and a fast-growing body of substance abuse, behavioral disorder, and mental health counselors, estimated at 351,000 jobs (Bureau of Labor Statistics, 2022c). Furthermore, according to the *Occupational Outlook Handbook* (Bureau of Labor Statistics, 2022d), there were 74,700 openings for social workers each year, with the job outlook for social workers projected to grow 9 percent from 2021 to 2031, which is faster than the average of all the previously mentioned occupations. When compared to other mental health disciplines, social workers constitute the largest group of mental health providers who can help people to overcome a variety of mental health problems such as depression, anxiety, and other disorders (National Association of Social Workers [NASW], 2022).

Social workers are employed in a variety of settings, including health care and mental health and substance abuse settings. The field is expected to grow in the areas of supportive care in health and mental health. Social workers have a long history of leadership in this area, advocating at multiple levels with targeted interventions for individuals, families, groups, and communities and at the macro level with larger provider systems (NASW, 2012). For social workers, ensuring that clients have access to mental health services remains an important aspect of client advocacy. The profession clearly supports mental health parity.

In 2020, the NASW Delegate Assembly updated the policy statement by the Delegate Assembly from August 2011. In this statement, the NASW continues its commitment to enhancing the well-being of people with mental illness and pushes for increased access to the services and interventions needed. From this perspective, physical health is deeply affected by mental health and the two should not be separated in treatment. The social work profession affirmed its commitment to improving direct mental health services such as availability, quality of care, and reimbursements, as well as adopting a more macro perspective advocating for public policies designed to improve research and education in mental health (NASW Delegate Assembly, 2020). This statement continued to support the policy of mental health parity, which requires both public and private insurance plans to provide comparable coverage for physical and mental health conditions. Supporting efforts toward mental health parity would give individuals suffering from a mental illness equal access to health-related treatments and services. In addition, achieving mental health parity could help to dispel the widespread fears and stigma associated with suffering from a mental illness. It could also give consumers equal access to health care in a system that often limits mental health and substance-related treatments. Although some states have adopted laws to ensure mental health parity, we still have a long way to go.

> ### Did You Know . . .
> The complete revised policy statement updated by the Delegate Assembly in 2020 mentioned above is available for download and review. To download a copy of this document, see https://www.socialworkers.org/LinkClick.aspx?fileticket=4efHh0QO3ZE%3d&portalid=0.

In mental health practice, social workers are essential service providers, helping individuals meet their daily needs. Services provided include treating individuals with mental illness and other mental health and substance abuse–related problems. Social workers in substance abuse treat many individuals suffering from abuse of alcohol, tobacco, and other legal and illegal substances. Social workers practicing in this area engage in numerous services and functions, including mental health counseling in community mental health centers, private practice, psychiatric hospitals and psychiatric units, long-term care facilities, mental health courts, and prisons; case management; discharge planning, intake, or admission evaluation; high social risk case identification and patient education, support, and advocacy; crisis intervention; and interdisciplinary collaboration (Dziegielewski & Holliman, 2020).

Assessment and diagnostic services are considered an essential part of social work education and practice (Williams, 2009). Services are provided to all clients and their families, and all major psychiatric disorders are addressed, including schizophrenia, and affective and mood disorders such as depression, neuropsychiatric disorders, eating disorders, personality disorders, phobias, substance abuse, childhood disorders, and organic psychoses (Dziegielewski, 2015). With events such as COVID-19, creative ways of reaching isolated adults became a challenge, and when in-person assistance was not possible, telephone-based reassurance programs became an option for continued assistance (Fields et al., 2022).

Social workers serving in the field of mental health usually have either a baccalaureate or a master's degree from an accredited social work education program. Social work in general is not a highly paid profession, but of all the practice areas, those who work in the hospital setting seem to fare the best. For example, the U.S. Bureau of Statistics listed the median salary for mental health social workers at $50,390 in May of 2021 (Bureau of Labor Statistics, 2022d). Unfortunately, the labor statistics do not break down income by degree.

> ### Did You Know . . .
> Massachusetts General Hospital in Boston pioneered hospital and psychiatric social work, starting a social service department in 1905 and hiring social workers to collaborate with patients who suffered from mental illness in 1907 (NASW, 1998).

When a social worker employed in a local mental health clinic outside Orlando, Florida, was asked how she felt about her job, she said she could describe it best as "challenging, rewarding, and most of the time quite frustrating." She believed that the role of the mental health social worker is complicated because allegiances must be divided, and always placing the needs of the client first forced her to maintain a delicate balance between the needs of the family, the agency, and the society. Because clients with mental impairment often cannot manage their own affairs, the social worker must ensure that the rights of these clients in terms of respect for individual dignity, worth, and self-determination are not violated, thereby finding a balance between encouraging autonomy and minimizing risk (Scheyett et al., 2009). Working to get clients access to mental health treatment and to keep families together in the home are emphasized (Barth, Kolivoski, Lindsey, Lee, & Collins, 2014).

The mental health social worker must also be aware of *duty to warn*. If a client is perceived as a *danger to self or others*, action is taken to protect any person or persons who may be at risk (Fox, 2009). Duty to warn may force a social worker to violate the confidence of the client to protect others in the immediate environment or, if the client is threatening suicide, to protect the client. Therefore, mental health social work practitioners must always strive for balance between the rights of the client and the needs of the client and family. Social workers must be advocates for clients with mental impairment; these clients will often be provided services through facilitation and referral, especially when they are not capable of representing themselves.

Oftentimes, beginning social work professionals are attracted to the area of mental health because they aspire to do therapy with the clients they serve. The NASW (2011, p. 1) described six essential components of psychosocial psychiatric services as:

1. Determining client eligibility for services
2. Conducting timely **biopsychosocial** assessments and social histories
3. Assessing clients for substance use, support systems, physical and emotional functioning, financial stability, safety, suicidal and homicidal ideation, etc.
4. Developing and implementing treatment and discharge plans that adhere to client self-determination
5. Providing direct therapeutic services to clients such as individuals, families, and groups, related to specific mental health issues
6. Performing crisis management and other types of administrative, supportive, and management functions all designed to aid in providing ethical client care

This early stance by the NASW is still in use today and highlights how important it is for the social worker to understand diagnosis and assessment, particularly because most social workers serve as advocates, facilitating and ensuring as part of the interdisciplinary team that the client gets the services needed.

In this chapter we will introduce the role of social worker in mental health. We will also introduce a multidimensional psychosocial assessment that allows the social worker to gather information needed to understand the client and his or her environment. In closing, we will examine potential areas of practice for the social worker interested in working in mental health.

10.1 MULTIDIMENSIONAL PSYCHOSOCIAL ASSESSMENT

In the area of mental health, the profession of social work did not develop in isolation. To survive and compete in the mental health practice environment, social workers have adapted to the dominant culture. This means that the practice approaches and methodologies employed by social workers at all levels may be influenced by expectations delineated by a team approach or agency designation. Furthermore, expectations that outline the connection between service provision and reimbursement become significant contenders in the delivery of care. For example, outcome measures, which dictate service reimbursement, have become mandatory (Dziegielewski & Holliman, 2020), and the more client focused these measures can become, the better (Pike, 2009). Moreover, it is common for all health care professionals to feel forced to reduce services to clients, focusing their efforts instead on clients who are covered by insurance or able to pay privately. Clients who cannot pay privately or afford the copayments required by selected insurance plans may self-terminate services if they are viewed as too costly (Dziegielewski & Holliman, 2020).

This problem can be further complicated for older adults, whom Frank (2013) terms the *duals*. The term duals is used to represent individuals who qualify for both Medicare and Medicaid services. These individuals tend to be a highly heterogeneous, vulnerable, high-cost group requiring a multitude of services. Accurate psychosocial assessment is therefore a critical tool for all mental health and health care social workers because it documents a client's needs and can support not only the efficiency but also the continued necessity of a chosen intervention. Such assessments not only open the door for services, but also can help to justify the need for the service, determining who will receive initial and continued services as well as what will be provided.

Social workers who work with clients who suffer from mental illness range from the baccalaureate-level practitioner, who is active in case management, initial assessment, and discharge planning, to the master-level social worker, who is an active participant in completing assessments and diagnoses (see Box 10.1 for a case application). Regardless of the social worker's degree and subsequent level of practice, he or she must be aware of the assessment tools and expectations characteristic of the field (Jordan

> **BOX 10.1**
>
> ### MENTAL ILLNESS CAN STRIKE ANYONE AND THE CONSEQUENCES CAN BE DEVASTATING: A TRUE CASE STORY
>
> Fort Worth—Jane fell so far so fast. A woman of education with a soft spot for the underdog, Jane combined a master's degree in social work with a compassion for the homeless that propelled her into Austin's power circles. She drove an expensive car, lived a full life, and was devoted to a loving family. And she lost it all as a victim of mental illness. The petite, blue-eyed, blonde-haired person who once turned heads was beaten to death Saturday, left alone on a dirty sidewalk among those she once helped. At age forty-three, she died penniless and homeless, all her possessions in two plastic grocery bags.
>
> For those who knew Jane, the tragic end was no surprise. Jane suffered from bipolar and personality disorders that left her without a family, unable to work, and on the street. "It is sad to say, but we feared something like this would happen," said her friend of twelve years. "She was so out of control, and no matter how hard we tried to help, she wouldn't take it."
>
> Early Saturday, Jane was found slumped over in front of the Mental Health Services day resource building. An autopsy showed she died from blunt force injuries to her head. Her killer remains a mystery, and there were leads in the case. Witnesses told police they saw Jane talking to an unidentified man about an hour before she was found dead, said the homicide detective. A composite of the man has been posted on fliers and tacked up around the shelters and known hangouts for local indigents. "He could be a witness or a suspect, and right now we just want him for questioning."
>
> Jane's daughter said the fact that her mother would not accept help from loved ones adds to her sadness. "A lot of people ask me, 'Why didn't you help? Why didn't you do anything?' Well, what they do not know is that it is harder than that," her daughter said.
>
> Jane's former social work professor, who taught and served as a mentor, said Jane is proof that mental illness can tear apart lives. "I do not think the public knows just how vicious mental illness is. It can destroy you ... It destroyed her to the end."
>
> Her daughter stated that family members had not seen Jane for two years. Jane had avoided seeing loved ones, but managed to stay connected through phone calls and letters. Jane's daughter described her mother as someone who had inner and outer beauty, a person with a profound sense of humor who was articulate and who made sure the family went to church. "During the summer she used to make me volunteer. She was just that way. She really cared about others. But the mental illness tore our relationship apart," she said.
>
> "I had a real good conversation with her, a week ago," Jane's daughter continued. "It was the best we had in a long time. I was beaming for days afterward. Since it was the last time we talked, it was a gift from God." News about Jane's slaying unnerved the night shelter residents, who expressed fear that the killer might be among them.
>
> "Women who are street-wise know how to protect themselves," said the executive director of the shelter. "Unfortunately, Jane did not. Jane did not fit the stereotypes

continues

continued

of a homeless person. She was educated and not addicted to drugs or alcohol. But the mental illness left her destitute. Jane did not say anything to anybody. She kept to herself and roamed all over the city. I was really crushed when I heard what happened to her. She did not deserve this." "About 60 percent of the homeless in this country suffer from some form of mental illness, and about 40 percent have a substance abuse problem," said the chief of mental health and addiction services. Jane was first diagnosed with depression when she was about eighteen, relatives and friends said. She was in and out of treatment facilities repeatedly, beating the illness long enough to fall in love, get married, and raise a family. When Jane, who was adopted, sought out her birth mother, the reunion proved devastating when her mother rejected her. The illness resurfaced and her marriage failed. She divorced her husband and lost custody of her daughter.

She remarried and enrolled in college while in her thirties. Her friend remembered the days when they went to the state capitol to lobby for welfare reform and how easily Jane fit into the social work community and the jobs that followed. But Jane left the work she loved in 1993, when she learned she was pregnant with her second child. After the birth, manic depression took its toll, relatives and friends said. The marriage failed and her second husband took custody of her son, who is now four. Those close to her said those events may have triggered her depression and mood swings. And by the spring of 1996, Jane found comfort living on the streets, traveling between Fort Worth, Las Vegas, and San Diego.

Her friend tracked her down at a psychiatric facility in Fort Worth and found Jane staring blankly at daytime television through a fog of medication. She said, "Hi, what are you doing here?" And I said, "I came to see you. What are you doing here?" And she said, "Well, this is where I belong." This memory left her friend feeling helpless and frustrated. "Jane used to work hard to help people who had fallen through the cracks and were unemployed or near homeless," her friend said. "She was a good person who took everything to heart. To me, this is proof that if it can happen to Jane, it can happen to the rest of us." (This is a modified case story. Names were either deleted or changed and the text was abridged.)

& Franklin, 2021). The importance of the initial psychosocial assessment should not be underestimated because it provides the foundation and the framework for any current and future intervention.

Assessment is defined as determining a comprehensive understanding of a client's situation and identifying what causes it, what maintains it, and what needs to be changed to address it. Social workers assume that assessment is a key component to the start of any intervention and always begin with the first client–worker interaction (Austrian, 2009). The information that the social worker obtains determines the requirements and direction of the helping process.

> **Did You Know . . .**
>
> *Words matter.* Social workers worldwide are bound together by a simple ethical principle: All people served are treated with respect and dignity. This basic ideal is written in the various codes of ethics of social work organizations, from the U.S.-based National Association of Social Workers to the global International Federation of Social Workers. In all areas of social work, especially mental health, a complete assessment starts with considering how the words we use to describe a client or client system can be a clear indicator of how one perceives others. Some words are clearly and tenaciously hateful, while others are less obvious.
>
> For a moment think about suffering from a mental illness. Would you like it if someone you love who suffers from schizophrenia was referred to as "a schizophrenic" or someone with a problem with chemical dependency as "an alcoholic?" What does the word "schizophrenic" conjure up for you? Do you think of a violent and insane person who cannot be controlled? Do you see that person as "different from me," someone who certainly cannot be trustable in any form or manner? A simple question for you, the reader—How would you feel if others simply referred to you as an "alcoholic" or a "schizophrenic"?
>
> As you read this and the following chapters, you'll see the purposeful use of words that demonstrate respect for others. An individual with schizophrenia should be referred to with respect. Being careful to use proper terminology is not a "woke" mentality, but reflects that we, as social workers, firmly believe in respecting others no matter who they are, their politics, their gender identity, or any attribute that I or others feel are wrong or uncomfortable. As social workers, when starting the assessment process, remember . . . yes, words matter.

The mental health social worker gathers information about the present situation, elicits history about the past, and anticipates service expectations for the future. This assessment should always include creative interpretations of alternatives to best assist the client to obtain the services needed (Dziegielewski, 2015; Dziegielewski & Holliman, 2020).

In mental health assessment, as in all social work assessments, the client is regarded as the primary source of data. Although the client remains the primary data source, social workers cannot afford to ignore inclusion of the effects the client system may have on the situation. This means asking the client important questions that will help to assess individual health as well as client system components that may affect the treatment process to follow.

In most cases, the client is questioned directly, either verbally or in writing. Information about the client is also derived from direct observation of verbal and physical behavior and interaction patterns between the client and other health and mental health collaborative team members, family members, significant others, or friends in

FIGURE 10.1
This woman was previously hospitalized for schizophrenia. With family support, she was able to live outside an institution, enjoy her grandniece, and live a fuller life.

the support system. Viewing and recording these patterns of communication can be extremely helpful in later identifying and developing strength and resource considerations (see Figure 10.1). In addition, background sheets, psychological tests, and tests to measure health status or level of daily functioning may be used. Furthermore, in keeping with social work's traditional emphasis on including information about other areas, the worker talks with family members and significant others to estimate planning support and assistance. It may also be important to access secondary sources such as the client's medical record and other health care providers.

To facilitate assessment, the social worker must be able to understand the client's medical situation or at least know where to go for information and help. Knowledge of certain mental health conditions, as well as common accompanying medical conditions, can help the social worker to understand the breadth of what is affecting the client's behavior. Referrals for a complete medical checkup should always be considered (Dziegielewski, 2015). Social workers should not hesitate to ask for clarification of medical problems and the complications they can present regarding a client's care, especially when they are unsure about how the information may enhance their understanding of the client's situation.

Five expectations guide the start of the assessment process in the health and mental health settings (Dziegielewski & Holliman, 2020):

1. *Clients must be active and motivated in the treatment process.* As in all forms of intervention, the client is expected to be an active participant. The client must often expend serious energy in attempting to make behavioral changes. Clients therefore must not only agree to participate in the assessment process, but also be willing to

embark on the intervention plan that will produce behavioral change. Social workers usually practice verbal therapy; however, clients who are unmotivated or unwilling to talk or discuss change strategies may require more concrete goals and objectives to bring about specific behavior change.

2. *The problem must guide the approach or method of intervention used.* Social workers must be aware of different methods and approaches to practice. It is crucial to ensure that the approach favored by the social worker is not what guides the intervention that follows. The approach that best addresses the client's circumstance should be what guides the choice of the intervention. The social worker must always be careful to avoid becoming overinvolved and wasting valuable time in trying to match a particular problem to a particular theoretical model or approach. Regardless of the degree, MSW or BSW, health and mental health social workers must never lose sight of the ultimate purpose of the assessment process, that is, to complete an assessment that helps to establish a concrete service plan that addresses the client's needs (see the activity below and the definition of assessment).

Activity

Review the definition of assessment and look at the reasons given for social workers to participate in this function. Discuss these issues with your classmates and decide whether you believe it is essential for social workers in health care and mental health to participate in assessment. Explain both what you see as reason for participation and what you see as problems that might be caused by taking this active stance as a member of a collaborative health team. Do you think there is a difference in the assessment process for a social worker with a bachelor's degree and one with a master's degree? What differences would you expect based on degree training?

3. *The influence of values and beliefs must be made apparent in the process.* Each of us, professional or not, is influenced by our own values and beliefs. These beliefs are the foundation of who we are. In the professional practice of social work, however, it is essential that these personal beliefs and values do not override the outcome of the assessment and subsequent intervention process. This requires considering the social worker's personal values and beliefs and being aware of how these beliefs could influence practice strategy. The professional helping strategy should always be guided toward what is best for the client and not founded on preset personal assumptions or beliefs that the client does not hold.

For example, what if an unmarried client in a psychiatric hospital has tested positive for pregnancy and is not sure if she wants to have an abortion? The social worker will realize that, because of the client's mental health condition, life circumstances, and other factors, she may have limitations in her capability to parent the child. The social worker personally believes that abortion is wrong. This personal value is so strong that the social worker feels that she cannot objectively or in good conscience discuss abortion as an option. The client is unsure about what to do, although she realizes she cannot stop taking her medications to address the hallucinations and delusions. The social worker also knows that if the client continues to take these medications in the formative stages of the pregnancy (the first three months in particular), the fetus could be negatively affected. The client realizes her current limitations and states that she would not be a good parent and cannot take care of herself without help. She asks the social worker for help in deciding what to do and what her options are.

From a personal perspective this can be a difficult case, but from a professional perspective the answer becomes clearer. From the professional perspective, the ultimate assessment and intervention strategy must be based on the client's needs and desires, not those of the social worker. Therefore, guided by the profession's code of ethics, the social worker will not tell the client of her personal feelings and will explore all options. If the personal perspective is so pronounced that the social worker feels she cannot fully empower the client to make the best decision and explore all potential options available, he or she must refer the client, in such a way as to avoid harm to the client, to another social work professional who can be more objective. Our value of self-determinations means that clients have the right to make their own decisions. Clients exercise this right especially when they are aware of their situation and want to participate in their own individualized health care plans. Whatever their own feelings, social workers must do everything possible to protect this right and to keep their private opinions from preventing a proper assessment.

The beliefs and values of the members of the collaborative team must also be considered. Social workers must recognize value conflicts that arise among the other team members and make team members aware of how their personal feelings and opinions may keep them from exploring all viable options for a client. This is not to suggest that social workers are more qualified to address this issue or that they always have an answer. It means that social workers should strive to assist these professionals and should always keep the goal—how to best serve the client in a nonjudgmental way—at the forefront. Furthermore, social work has a very comprehensive code of ethics, and at times this may be different or have a different emphasis from that used by other professionals on the team. Good, sound ethical decision-making is expected, and educating other professionals about ethical conduct in social work may be warranted (Strom-Gottfried, 2008).

4. *Issues of culture and race should be addressed openly in the assessment and treatment.* The understanding of racial identity and the effect it can have on psychological well-being should not be underestimated (Woods & Kurtz-Costes, 2007). In addition, social workers must be aware of their own cultural heritage as well as that of their clients to create the most open and receptive environment possible. To facilitate the assessment, the following basic guidelines are suggested:

- Note cultural factors and remain open to cultural differences (Locke & Bailey, 2014).
- Recognize the integrity and the uniqueness of the client, respect self-determination, and provide services within a nonjudgmental framework (Dziegielewski, 2015).
- Empower the client using his or her own learning style, including use of his or her own resources considering the client system of support (Dziegielewski & Holliman, 2020).

> **Did You Know . . .**
> The fifth edition of the *Diagnostic and Statistical Manual of Mental Disorders*, which was released in May 2013 and is considered the major reference for the diagnosis of mental disorders and related mental health conditions, stresses that cultural factors must be considered before establishing a diagnosis. To assist with this, cultural concepts of distress that can mimic a mental disorder but are related to an individual's culture are outlined and an interview format, called the Cultural Formulation Interview, is provided to identify and measure cultural factors. All social workers must know how cultural and ethnic factors can affect assessment. In addition, the *Diagnostic and Statistical Manual of Mental Disorders Text Revision*, released in 2022, further clarifies wording to address racism, along with updating and including culturally sensitive terminology (e.g., racialized instead of racial).

5. *Assessment must focus on client strengths and highlight the client's own resources.* Identifying how to use the client's own strengths and resources is central to creating sustained change (Corcoran & Walsh, 2022). Clients can have enormous difficulty identifying and planning to use their own strengths. Clients are no different from the general population in this regard; people in general tend to focus on the negative and rarely praise themselves for the good they do. Also, admitting to a mental health problem may carry stigma the client may not want to accept. This stigma may be carried over to family and friends as *courtesy stigma*, and that may disturb the supportive helping networks the client needs (Rosenzweig & Brennan, 2008). The client's perceptions are important to the helping relationship, especially whether he or she believes that the provider is listening and understands what is being said (Schroeder, 2013).

Empowering the client's by using a strengths-based assessment is considered critical (Corcoran & Walsh, 2022; Morales, Sheafor, & Scott, 2012). For many clients, especially those with mental health problems, their opinions of the world around them can become distorted. Also, it is always important for the social worker to avoid confusing the boundaries between normal human behavior and pathology because this can cause false diagnoses and a medicalization of what might be considered adaptive behavior

(Frances & Jones, 2013). The way clients see and think of themselves and the tasks that need to be accomplished can become clouded. An all-or-nothing approach may cause them to feel lost, alone, and ineffective in what they have done or tried to do. Therefore, it is the role of the social worker to assist the client in identifying positive behaviors and accomplishments. Social workers also feel strongly about the importance of teaching life skills and expanding on this area to increase psychosocial functioning (Reddon, Hoglin, & Woodman, 2008).

In today's high-pressure health and mental health environments, social workers cannot spend time exploring issues and the related behaviors that do not contribute to the client's well-being. They must quickly utilize a strengths-based assessment by helping the client to identify his or her own strengths and thereby maximize skill-building potential. Because most treatment is currently time limited, individual resources are essential for continued growth and maintenance of wellness after the formal treatment period has ended. Although there are several time-limited approaches to practice, most social workers agree that their first task is to clearly identify the client's strengths to use them as part of the treatment planning process. Focusing on a client's strengths can help the client to become empowered and make changes that otherwise may have seemed impossible (Corcoran & Walsh, 2022).

10.2 PLACING A DIAGNOSIS AND USE OF THE *DSM*

The *Diagnostic and Statistical Manual of Mental Disorders* (*DSM-5*; American Psychiatric Association, 2013) and its latest version, the *Diagnostic and Statistical Manual of Mental Disorders Text Revision* (*DSM-5-TR*), released in June 2022 (American Psychiatric Association, 2022), are valuable tools for social workers in the mental health arena. It is beyond the scope of this chapter to describe how to use this book in practice, but awareness of it and its use is essential for the beginning social worker. The *DSM* is considered an advanced tool to assess mental health disorders and supporting conditions. Its use is covered in graduate courses, and in some schools, entire courses are devoted to its study and application and its relationship to social work practice. In the beginning of both the *DSM-5* and the *DSM-5-TR*, the list of professionals who are expected to use the book includes social workers. Based on the number of different professionals that use the book and given that the *DSM-5* and the *DSM-5-TR* are written and revised by the American Psychiatric Association, one major concern is related to the lack of input from other professional disciplines, especially social workers.

The companion to this diagnostic resource is the *International Classification of Diseases, 10th Edition, Clinical Modification* (*ICD-10-CM*), with the updated text to include the *International Classification of Disorders, 11th edition* (*ICD-11*). The *DSM* is designed primarily for use in the United States and Canada, whereas the *ICD* is considered international in scope. These two books (the *DSM* and the *ICD*) are intimately connected because U.S. insurance companies, including Medicare and Medicaid, use the coding from the *ICD* for insurance reimbursement purposes. In *ICD-11*, the development of the chapter on mental, behavioral, or neurodevelopmental disorders provides a widespread global testament regarding mental health disorder classification. The aim of this latest revision of the *ICD* is to provide updated global applicability, scientific validity, and clinical utility (Gaebel, Stricker, & Kerst, 2020).

When using the *DSM-5-TR* or its predecessors, one major reason social workers can be conflicted is the fear that diagnosing a mental disorder can result in a label for a client that will be carried indefinitely. For example, once placed, several of the diagnoses, such as schizophrenia, will stay with the individual indefinitely, and if the symptoms of the disorder are no longer present, the client is referred to as being "in remission." When placing a diagnosis is coupled with negative media attention or societal myths, a real concern develops over how such diagnoses can affect a person's employment and other responsibilities. For a more detailed explanation of the *DSM-5* and the implications of certain recurrent diagnoses in treatment planning and practice, see Dziegielewski (2015).

In addition, when using the *DSM-5* and the *DSM-5-TR*, supportive information critical to the client and the client system should always be included. The supporting information needs to codify the environmental factors considered when looking at an individual's situation. In summary, regardless of what type of mental health problem is presented, mental health professionals must recognize and later systematically address mental health problems and behavioral difficulties. In your continued course work, you will see how a clear relationship between completing a diagnostic assessment and how it relates to the treatment that will follow is essential to client progress and subsequent change behaviors.

10.3 THE BEHAVIORAL BIOPSYCHOSOCIAL APPROACH

Social work practice in assessment and intervention today (Dziegielewski & Holliman, 2020), as in the past (Carlton, 1984), should recognize three factors: the biomedical, the psychological, and the social. A social worker who understands the **biopsychosocial approach** to health and mental health practice strives to ascertain for each client the appropriate balance among biomedical, psychological, and social considerations (Austrian, 2009). Balance, however, does not mean that these factors are treated as equal for every client. The unique situation experienced by the client determines where emphasis must be placed and what area must be addressed first. In today's practice environment, with its insistence on an observable, measurable outcome, the mental health social worker addresses the biopsychosocial factors in the client's life through the behavioral aspects of the client's condition. For social workers, the person-in-environment outlined within the psychosocial approach is one of the most popular ways of viewing clients in a comprehensive assessment (Jordan & Franklin, 2021).

One of the first and most important aspects is to begin with a careful risk assessment. Because the most significant risk factors for suicide include suffering from a severe mental disorder or a mood disorder combined with substance abuse, this type of assessment should always come first (Yeager, Roberts, & Saveanu, 2009). This involves creating a culture of safety for assessing the client as well as the physical environment. Yeager et al. (2009) stress that to assess for suicidality the social worker must identify psychiatric signs and symptoms, as well as past and current suicidal ideation, past attempts, and current plans (see the activity below for a sample treatment plan with a client who is suicidal).

Activity

Recognizing the potential for suicide is a critical factor in the mental health assessment. Here is a sample treatment plan for a client who is suicidal. In reviewing this plan, what surprises you about it? What seems like common sense to you?

Sample Treatment Plan for Suicidal Ideation/Behavior

Definition: Suicide is a human act of self-inflicted, self-intentional cessation. Simply stated, it is the wish to be dead with the act that conducts the wish.

Suicide ideation: Thinking about suicide.

Suicide verbalization: Talking about suicide.

Parasuicide: Attempting suicide.

Suicidal intent: A clear plan to act on ideas and the means of completion, which requires immediate action.

Signs and symptoms to note in the record (document any of these signs in the record):

Changes in eating and sleeping.	Changes in friends and social programs.
Changes in grades or job status.	Changes in love relationships.
Changes in usual daily activities.	Constant restlessness or unshakable depression.
Neglected appearance or hygiene.	Increase in drug or alcohol use.
Giving away of material possessions.	Recurrent thoughts or preoccupation with death.
Recent suicide attempt.	Current suicidal ideation?
Previous attempts or present plans.	History of suicide attempts in the family.
Sudden mood changes.	Past suicide attempts and what was done.
History of drug abuse.	

Goals:

1. Stabilize suicidal crisis.
2. Place client at appropriate level of care to address suicidal crisis.

3. Re-establish a sense of hope to deal with the current life situations.
4. Alleviate suicidal impulses and intent and return to higher (safer) level of functioning.

Objective	Intervention
Client will no longer feel the need to harm self	Assess for suicidal ideation and concrete plan of execution. Then make appropriate disposition/referral. Complete no-risk assessment and document in record.
Client will discuss suicidal feelings and thoughts	Address suicidal thoughts or impulses. Determine level of depression or suicide precaution.
Identify positives in current life situation	Assess and monitor suicide intervention.
	Assist client to develop awareness of negative self-talk patterns and encourage positive images and self-talk.
Help client to identify consistent eating and sleeping patterns.	Educate client in deep-breathing and relaxation techniques. Assist client in developing coping strategies.
Take medications as prescribed and report any inconsistencies or side effects	Monitor for medication use and misuse and confer with treatment team on a regular basis.
Complete assessment of functioning.	Arrange or complete Activities of Daily Living assessment. Determine services needed for community placement.

Note: The period for completion of the intervention is to be individualized to the client, and if suicidal ideation becomes intent, immediate action to avoid danger to self or others is required.

10.4 WHEN MEDICAL AND MENTAL HEALTH CONDITIONS COEXIST

A client suffering from both a physical and a mental health condition can present unique challenges. For example, if a client is newly assessed as having schizophrenia while also being HIV positive, many issues must be addressed. At first, the emphasis may be placed on the biomedical or biological area. The client must be told immediately that the medical test for HIV is positive and given information about what a positive test means. The task can be complicated by the client's mental condition. The schizophrenia may produce periodic breaks from reality, such as hallucinations and delusions that keep him or her from accurately interpreting medical information. The client may have difficulty understanding how far the disease has progressed and what can be expected medically, for example. Nevertheless, every attempt must be made to help the client to understand the medical aspects of his or her condition and what being infected with the virus and receiving treatment means. It is critical to ensure that the client understands terms such as T-cell count, future self-protection from illness, and opportunistic infectious diseases. It is also important to examine the client system and whether sexual activity with a partner(s) could benefit from the importance of stressing safe sex practices as well as from pre-exposure prophylaxis. These medications can help keep sexual partners from contracting HIV. While this sort of information about the medical condition is shared, a constant vigil is needed to maintain client safety, with assessment and reassessment as needed (Yeager et al., 2009).

Once the biomedical situation and support for what the client is experiencing emotionally are addressed, emphasis may shift to the social and psychological aspects of the client's condition. Because HIV is clearly communicable, the client must realize quickly that his or her behavior can have significant effects on people in his or her support system. Early education about how the virus is transmitted can be critical. Because HIV is most often sexually transmitted, the client's past and present sexual partners must be considered. Alone or with help, the client must face telling loved ones about the diagnosis and what it will mean for future social relations.

The client may also be frightened by the changes in his or her mental status and unsure of how to control the symptoms related to schizophrenia. First, the client must understand what is happening. Second, the client must be helped to realize what schizophrenia means and how it can influence self-behaviors and actions toward others. Valuable information must be shared with family and friends. The social perspective of the biopsychosocial approach focuses on the individual client together with the family, significant others, and friends—not only on how best to protect them, but also to involve them in problem-solving. The psychological perspective focuses directly on the fears and concerns of the individual—on how to help him understand his mental health and the emotions he exhibits.

As you can see, if a client has a **dual diagnosis**, helping can become extremely complicated. In our example, the dual diagnosis of HIV (physical medical condition) and schizophrenia (mental health condition) means that the client may be losing touch with reality at a time when his knowledge and awareness are especially important. Once the immediate needs of the client and client system have been addressed and a risk assessment has been completed, the focus of intervention should shift to the functional/situational factors affecting the individual client. A functional assessment allows the social worker to determine the level at which the client can respond to a concrete, intervention-based plan.

It is essential that assessment and intervention be related to the needs and abilities of the client. The social worker begins with exploration to examine and organize the unique aspects of the client (Austrian, 2009). A complete assessment is designed to help the client better understand himself or herself, and the factors identified during

Table 10.1 Biomedical or Biological Factors to Be Considered in Mental Health Assessment

Area	Explanation
General medical condition	Describe the physical illness or disability from which the client is suffering. Client is to evaluate his or her self-reported health status and level of functional ability.
Overall health status	Describe what the client can do to meet his or her daily needs.
Overall level of functioning	Concrete tasks are assessed and documented for focus on future change effort.
Maintenance of continued health and wellness	Measure the client's functional ability and interest in preventive medical intervention.

the procedure are shared with the client to assist in self-help or continued skill building (Eamon, 2008). Tables 10.1 and 10.2 list factors to be considered in the mental health assessment. The assessment process is used to examine the situation and initiate the helping process; later it contributes to an intervention plan.

When There Is More Than One Mental Health Diagnosis: The Dual Diagnosis

When a physical medical condition exists with a mental health one, as outlined in the previous section of this chapter, providing adequate and comprehensive care for both

Table 10.2. Social Factors to Be Considered in the Mental Health Assessment

Area	Explanation
Social/societal help-seeking behavior	Is the client open to outside help? Is the client willing to accept help from those outside his or her immediate family or the community?
Occupational participation	How does the client's illness or disability impair or prohibit functioning in the work environment? Is the client in a supportive work environment?
Social support system	Does the client have support from neighbors, friends, or community organizations (church membership, membership in professional clubs, etc.)?
Family support	What support or help can be expected from relatives of the client?
Support from significant other	Does the significant other understand and show willingness to help and support the needs of the client?
Ethnic or cultural affiliation	If the client is a member of a certain cultural or religious group, will affiliation affect medical treatment and compliance issues?

FIGURE 10.2
Completing a comprehensive assessment requires taking into account the uniqueness of the individual and starting where the client is.

conditions can be complicated. Furthermore, with any population or in any field of practice, social workers are increasingly confronted with dually diagnosed clients who suffer from the symptoms of more than one mental health diagnosis. These clients have more than one mental health problem that affects their behaviors, and therefore each disorder and/or problematic behavior must be equally addressed in the intervention process. For mental health social workers to work successfully with dually diagnosed clients, they must stay cognizant of client problems, diagnostic assessments, clinical interventions, and current case studies. For example, clients with psychiatric and co-morbid substance use disorders may be best served by utilizing a more holistic strengths-based perspective that avoids placing labels and seeks policy change and advocacy (Reedy & Kobayashi, 2012). This is especially important when noncompliance with treatment occurs upon return to the outpatient setting. Returning to a similar environment without system-level intervention can leave these individuals vulnerable to a variety of negative clinical ramifications, including problems with relapse and rehospitalization. In the assessment process, this also requires carefully identifying problematic behaviors and familiarity with multiple measures, such as rapid assessment instruments that can comprehensively identify problematic behaviors that support evidenced-based practice (Jordan & Franklin, 2021).

Although addressing the needs of a client with more than one mental health problem will be covered in more depth in your clinical courses, such clients can often be misdiagnosed and/or given inadequate treatment because of the limited period allowed for mental health–related inpatient care. For example, when medications are used as a principal element of treatment, it can take weeks to see a clear effect on problematic behaviors (Dziegielewski & Jacinto, 2016). In cases such as this, rushed discharges resulting from limited inpatient stays make intense outpatient follow-up critical, and this degree of follow-up may simply not be available. Resources and at times intervention strategy are shaped and influenced by cost containment, with an emphasis placed on time-limited, outcome-oriented interventions (Dziegielewski, 2015). As health care delivery changes, funding for mental health is limited and the need for programs specializing in integrated treatment is clear.

Daley and Zuckoff (1998) highlighted the following adverse effects that can transpire for noncompliant, dually diagnosed clients:

- Poorly compliant clients are more likely to experience clinical deterioration of their psychiatric condition, relapse to alcohol or other drug use, and return to the hospital because of severe depression, thoughts of suicide or homicide, mania, or psychotic decompensation.
- Missing outpatient appointments often leads to failure to renew medication prescriptions, which in turn contributes to exacerbations of psychiatric and substance use symptoms.
- Poor treatment compliance causes the loss of supportive relationships and contributes to frustration among professionals and family members, who can end up watching helplessly as their loved one's condition deteriorates.

Because of the increased risk of hospitalization, poor outpatient compliance leads to increased costs of care because more days are spent in expensive inpatient treatment facilities. Assessing the impact of trauma and other life events is necessary, especially those factors that could affect the performance of the individual with mental illness. Trauma exposure can have physical and behavioral outcomes that affect mental health (Liu, Li, Liang, & Hou, 2021; O'Donnell et al., 2017). Although emotional trauma is well recognized and practice recommendations exist for providing early psychosocial care, embedding these recommendations into assessment guidelines with clear standards could be of widespread benefit (Brake & Duckers, 2013). A comprehensive assessment must identify conditions that can make the current situation worse, such as sexual victimization, medical emergencies, car accidents, overdoses from prescribed medications or illegal drugs, and other events and sudden losses that can complicate the mental health condition (O'Hare & Sherrer, 2009). In the treatment of psychotic disorders alone, multiple medications have been introduced that can affect an individual's behavior, with little emphasis on classifying the pharmacological properties (Zhou, Nutt, & Davies, 2022) and how other systems of the body can be affected. Furthermore, when dealing with older adults, Maust, Oslin, and Marcus (2014) found that the medications prescribed, which could have dangerous side effects, were often not clearly related to any mental health condition being treated. This makes knowledge of medications essential (Dziegielewski & Jacinto, 2016). In addition, mental health social workers must be educated and trained in the treatment of clients who suffer from more than one mental health problem and/or condition. For the dually diagnosed client, treating one condition without recognition of the comorbid or contributing factors is not considered acceptable (see Box 10.2 for an overview of questions to guide the assessment and intervention process and Box 10.3 for important professional contact information).

BOX 10.2
MENTAL HEALTH SOCIAL WORK PRACTICE IN THE NEW MILLENNIUM

Questions to Guide Assessment and Intervention Success

1. Are you able to complete a diagnostic assessment of the individual and show the relationship between the mental illness and the behaviors that resulted?
2. Can you show that the identified condition is treatable with a realistic chance of success?
3. Have you developed specific goals and objectives for the treatment of the client?
4. Do you provide a clear rationale for the level of care, modality, types of intervention, and duration of treatment?
5. Is there a process for updating and periodic review of goals and objective attainment?
6. Is the client involved in the treatment development process?
7. If treatment is to be longer than originally expected, is a rationale for extension provided?
8. What specific things will happen to indicate that treatment goals and objectives have been met?
9. Is the intervention plan utilized consistent with social work values and ethics?

BOX 10.3
PROFESSIONAL CONTACT INFORMATION AND EMAIL ADDRESSES

Professional Organization

National Association of Social Workers, 750 First St. N.E., Suite 700, Washington, DC, 20002-4241

Accredited Social Work Programs

To determine whether individual social work programs have either specialized courses or a concentration in mental health, contact the Council on Social Work Education, 1725 Duke St., Suite 500, Alexandria, VA 22314-3457, or use their website.

Information on licensing requirements and testing procedures for each state may be obtained from state licensing authorities, or from the Association of Social Work Boards, 400 South Ridge Pkwy., Suite B, Culpeper, VA 22701.

10.5 MENTAL HEALTH AND WORKING WITH THE FAMILY IN ACUTE CARE SETTINGS

As early as 1903 at Massachusetts General Hospital, Richard C. Cabot realized the importance of addressing psychosocial factors in medical illness. From this early perspective, the assigned duties of the medical social worker included focusing on the economic, emotional, social, and situational needs of patients and their families (Cabot, 1913). To accomplish the assigned tasks in the late 1800s and early 1900s, health care social workers were required to have adequate medical knowledge, an understanding of disease and factors that affected mental health, and a firm comprehension of public health. With the medical advances of the late 1950s, the social worker was expected to bridge "the gap between the hospital bed, the patient's home and the world of medical science" (Risley, 1961, p. 83).

In health and mental health today, the role of the social worker continues along the same path, with extensive focus also on meeting the needs of the client and his or her family members. In social work education, a competency-based approach is stressed and this perspective rests firmly in developing a shared view of the nature of competence (Council on Social Work Education [CSWE], 2022a). Therefore, although the family members are not the actual client being served, it is common for services to be provided to them that include education, supportive interventions, and referrals, as well as reporting of problematic social conditions, assisting and ensuring treatment compliance with the established medical regime, and providing linkages between the acute care setting and the appropriate community agencies. Table 10.3 lists psychosocial factors to be considered in the mental health assessment. Often it is the family who first recognizes the problem and seeks help for the client (Brennan, Evans, & Spencer, 2008).

Other areas of service provision in these acute health care settings include case consultation, case finding, case planning, psychosocial assessment and intervention, collaboration, treatment team planning, group therapy, supportive counseling, organ donation coordination, health education, advocacy, case management, discharge planning, information and referral, quality assurance, bereavement, and research (Dziegielewski & Holliman, 2020; Holliman, Dziegielewski, & Datta, 2001).

In this challenging environment, all professionals are forced to deal with numerous issues that include declining hospital admissions, reduced lengths of hospital stay for medical as well as mental health conditions, and numerous other restrictions and methods of cost containment (Dziegielewski & Holliman, 2020). Struggling to resolve these issues has become necessary because health care spending has far exceeded any hopes of budget negotiations. As Yeager and Latimer (2009) pointed out, the concern for reducing expenditures in an environment that also requires maximizing scarce and dwindling resources continues to prevail. This is further complicated by continued expectations for state-of-the-art care in the United States (Anderson & Frogner, 2008). Technological advances have clearly increased and changed the way clients and

Table 10.3 Psychological Factors to Be Considered in Mental Health Assessment

Area	Explanation
Life stage	Describe the development stage in life at which the individual is functioning.
Mental functioning	Describe the client's mental functioning. Complete a mental status measurement. Can the client participate knowledgeably in the intervention experience?
Cognitive functioning	What does the client think and reason about what is happening to him or her? Is the client able to participate and make decisions regarding his or her own best interest? Does the client understand what is happening to him or her?
Level of self-awareness and self-help	Is the client capable of assisting his or her level of self-care? Is the client capable of understanding the importance of health and wellness information? Is the client open to help and services provided by the health care team?

professionals view expected treatment and care (Palmo, 2011). Yet, regardless of these expectations and resources, receiving quick, cost-cutting services can also be linked to increased rates of high-risk patient relapse, especially around mental health concerns. Therefore, it should come as no surprise that family members of someone who has mental health problems are constantly frustrated as their loved ones are admitted and readmitted with the same mental health issues in one of the most technologically advanced countries in the world.

When a client is discharged from a facility, an important part of discharge planning is ensuring an appropriate follow-up service plan for return to a lesser level of care. In the past, the role of the social worker was often expected to end once the client was discharged from the facility (Simon, Showers, Blumfield, Holden, & Wu, 1995). Today, however, social workers are finding that these traditional roles have expanded to cover a broader function. In the area of mental health, extended care placement options are limited and returning clients to the family system for care can cause strain because support resources, especially those that are not classified as disabled, range from limited to nonexistent. It is necessary to develop specific plans that link a client with mental health concerns to other systems of care, as well as specific care plans that focus on continuity of care.

A significant issue to consider when dealing with a client's mental health issues is not only the label of having a mental illness that is placed on the client but also the psychological and social burden that is often placed on the client's family. This burden can either lead to or exacerbate higher rates of mental health problems. For example, recent incidents and increased threats of violence and victimization in our schools are rising, and the behaviors of the assailants have been strongly associated with antisocial behavior, deviant peers, antisocial attitudes, victimization, and peer rejection (Turanovic, Pratt, Kulig, & Cullen, 2022).

This makes addressing mental health issues of paramount importance, and exploring ways to manage and control school violence remains an essential task for helping professionals (Giordano, 2022). Mental health concerns cannot be ignored, and addressing school violence starts with understanding how this unbridled anger and frustration occurs (Turanovic et al., 2022). From an environmental or situational (micro/mezzo/macro) perspective, not only are the victims and the victim's client system affected, but also the violent assailant and their extended family system. Those within all affected client systems may be traumatized and at increased risk for psychological disturbances and should always be included in the treatment process (Pieterse et al., 2022). This, in turn, may require larger-scale policy changes that advocate beyond controlling and punishing behavior, addressing preventive recognition and treatment before the behavior occurs. Mental illness and its chronic nature can strain family relationships at a time when neither clients nor the family system may see signs of the illness or the potential for violence that exists. As educators, combating hatred and adopting transformational educational strategies are crucial (Furin, 2022).

When dealing with the family of a client with mental illness, the social worker must assume a flexible and diverse role. Special challenges when working with families include finding treatment goals and objectives that are not only effective for the client, but also of interest and importance to the members of the family. This opens the door for evidence-based practice: "a scientific paradigm that encompasses clinician expertise, client characteristics, and client values and preferences" (Jordan & Franklin, 2021, p. 6). Helping to make all goals and objectives mutually negotiable for all is central because, at times, different expectations may lead to blurring and overlapping of the services provided. Simply telling a family system that a client is ill and they need to understand is not productive and will not work.

It is crucial for the social worker to examine each family member's sense of personal well-being, ability to self-care, and level of family and environmental support because many times these factors become essential to the discharge of the client. If these personal/social and environmental issues are not addressed, a client with mental instability may be put at risk for harm. Furthermore, whether the client is discharged to a home or to a correctional facility, mixed feelings can be experienced on all levels. For example, when clients are discharged home to a family that does not want them, they are more at risk of abuse and neglect. Family members can feel responsible for the actions of a loved one, and this leads to feelings that a situation is hopeless or inescapable, or the parents themselves can have a history of trauma that places them at greater risk for depression, anxiety, or posttraumatic stress disorder (Pieterse et al., 2022).

The social worker must always recognize the importance of culture and environmental factors as paramount to efficient and effective practice. When cultural differences exist, they can clearly influence the therapeutic process (Duckworth, 2009). For example, depression that results in suicide can be viewed differently in some societies and by certain ethnic and racial groups. The importance of culture as a variable in suicide is modest at best, but understanding culture can help the clinician to gain a more robust assessment of suicidal reasoning and purpose (Leach, 2006). Another example of a situation in which cultural and environmental factors play a part in patient care is that in which family members of a sick infant object to a blood transfusion for religious reasons or the family refuses life support because it is viewed as disturbing the natural life progression. The de-emphasis or denial of this consideration can result in the delivery of substandard care.

In today's environment of behavioral managed care and evidence-based practice, capitation, fee for service, and decreased number of hospital inpatient beds, health care social work continues to hold a place in the acute care hospital setting. According to Dziegielewski and Holliman (2020), the challenge for acute medical hospitals is to combine the humanitarian objective of practice with the hospital's agenda for cost control and rationing of resources. In addition, recognition that the client is part of a family system places importance on the overall health and wellness of the individual. Often, family members need assistance, and the acknowledgment and addressing of family problems can help to improve and maintain quality of life for the mentally ill client and his or her support system (Marshall & Solomon, 2009).

The functions of the mental health social worker in this setting include psychosocial evaluations (assessment for the treatment plan), casework (counseling and supportive intervention), group work (education and self-help), information and referral, facilitation of community referrals, team planning and coordination, and clients and family education, as well as advocacy for clients within the setting or beyond, with local state and federal agencies (NASW, 2008). Social workers provide the backbone for front-line services that create a safety net for all clients served (Hoffler & Clark, 2012). In addition, with the numerous service cutbacks and cost-effectiveness strategies, many social workers are now being required to expand their duties (Yeager & Latimer, 2009). Many are being asked to serve as financial counselors to ensure that the client and the service agency will receive adequate reimbursement for services needed. These services can involve assisting clients with applying for outside insurance carriers to cover additional services not directly covered under their current policy.

Dziegielewski and Holliman (2020) believe that social workers in acute care mental health settings need essential skills and practice techniques. The social worker remains integral in aiding with:

- Providing comprehensive diagnostic assessments utilizing a strengths-based biopsychosocial approach that assists in resolving behavioral problems.
- Providing supportive treatment to individuals, families, and groups, such as counseling for clients and significant others in the areas of health, wellness, mental health, bereavement, and so on.

- Aiding and providing guidance to clients and their families in making ethical and morally tough decisions that can affect health and mental health.
- Educating clients, their families, and significant others about psychosocial issues and adjusting to illness.
- In a case management role, assisting clients and families with discharge planning and referral, as well as identifying and obtaining entitlement benefits and securing nonmedical benefits.
- Assisting with risk management and quality assurance activities.
- Advocating for enhanced and continued services to ensure continued client well-being.

Last, to comprehensively address mental health concerns in this fast-paced setting, social workers must go beyond focusing on the traditional view of problem identification and realize that successful helping activities are seen as developmental and dynamic, which evolve over time (CSWE, 2022a). When developmental and dynamic responses are required, the vigilance needed to monitor or change the helping strategy can be stressful. Although it is beyond the scope of this chapter to carefully discuss the means of addressing stress through self-care, the importance of recognizing the signs of impaired performance related to stress is central to effective helping. Since social work can be an incredibly stressful occupation, recognizing the signs and symptoms to avoid compassion fatigue and burnout is important, because they can affect job performance (Hlavatska, 2020). Compassion fatigue occurs when people listen with empathy to the troubles of others (Cuatero & Campos-Vidal, 2019).

Activity

Review the "Social Worker Burnout: 8 Self-Care Tips" article on the Florida State University College of Social Work website for more information on how to recognize burnout. Of the eight self-care tips listed, which do you think would most likely affect you?

Name: Sharon Williamson
Place of residence: Umatilla, Florida
College/university degrees: MSW, University of Cincinnati; BA in sociology, University of Florida
Present position and title: Mental health therapist at a rural community behavioral health clinic; licensed mental health therapist
Present work/volunteer experience: Provide mental health assessments and therapy in an outpatient setting to adults with mental illness.

continues

> *continued*
>
> *Why did you choose social work as a career?* I have been blessed to have several wonderful women social workers in my life as role models, including my wife (thirty years together and legally married for six of them)! I have always been involved in the "helping profession" so it made sense to finally go to graduate school at an old age (fifty years young!) and get my MSW, so I could do more in the "helping" field than just case management.
>
> *What is your favorite social work story?* Not sure if it is my favorite story, but it is one which helped me to grow. I was doing an intake for a gentleman in his mid-forties and asked him the questions about exposure to violence in intimate relationships. He started crying during the yes/no questions and finally admitted that he was currently involved in an abusive relationship with a woman he had been dating and living with for the past two years. He said she has been diagnosed as being bipolar, and during her manic phases she could become very aggressive toward him. He said he does not want to leave her because when she is stable on her medications, she is a nice person. It is not that I was unaware domestic violence can be directed toward men, but to know that he *wanted* to stay so they could remain a couple made it clear how important the relationship was to him. He stated that he wanted to try and help her stay on her medications. It was obviously a codependent relationship, but it gave me more insight into how this man still wanted to be the one to take control of his needs.
>
> *What would be the one thing you would change in our community if you had the power to do so?* Medical/behavioral health care for all! It is ridiculous that whether people receive health care is based on politics. I worked in Cincinnati, Ohio, for many years, and that state offered Medicaid expansion, which helped a great deal in providing care for the underserved populations. Here in Florida, they do not offer it. Therefore, there are so many folks out there who need medical care (including behavioral health care; after all, the head is attached to the body!) and cannot receive it due to a lack of any type of insurance. The walking wounded do not go far when they mentally and physically cannot walk!

10.6 TELEMENTAL HEALTH AND THE ELECTRONIC AGE

Telehealth (TH) and telemental health (TMH) gained in popularity with the 2020 onset of COVID-19. In TH and TMH, electronic communication equipment uses technology to go from one site to another to transmit medical information for the purpose of benefitting the client or client system (Totten et al., 2016). These days, those communications can range from old-fashioned phone calls to videoconferencing, digital transmission of specialized images, and texting. The National Institute of Mental Health further defined TMH as using telecommunications such as videoconferencing to support and provide mental health services (National Institute of Mental Health, 2021).

Along with this convenience and increased accessibility, however, comes concerns about maintain client information privacy. When delivering services through TH or TMH, it is paramount to ensure compliance with the protection of health information. This includes following the Health Insurance Portability and Accountability Act (HIPAA) of 1996 and the Patient Protection and Affordable Care Act (ACA), which expanded HIPPA requirements, as well as the Administrative Simplification Compliance Act (ASCA), which required that all claims submitted to Medicare be done electronically, with certain exceptions. To ensure privacy protection when delivering TM or TMH services, it is required to only use covered websites that secure confidentiality of client–helper communications and information. As a beginning social worker, it is important to protect the privacy of client information, and familiarity with these legal expectations prior to releasing protected client information holds importance.

For more information related to these public laws, see the "helpful hint" that follows. Considering these public laws, whether receiving traditional in-person assistance or technology-enhanced professional services, requires release of *protected health information* (PHI; medical or mental health covered under HIPAA) as the practice standard to ensure consumer confidentiality and privacy. In addition, these policies are not static and can change, so awareness and knowledge of the updates is important. For example, during COVID-19, with the many isolation efforts in place to ensure greater access in the delivery of mental health services, especially to those in rural areas, adjustments were made to HIPAA compliance requirements and the audiovisual platforms under Medicare and Medicaid (Lepkowsky, 2020).

Along with HIPAA, PHI, ACA, and ASCA requirements, the days of recording in a paper record are all but gone. Since ACSA requires that all reimbursement billing for Medicare (with limited exceptions) be done electronically, electronic communications and protecting the rights of consumers in releasing records and maintaining efforts toward confidentiality are now the state of practice. In addition, there is great concern related to the rapid expansion of mobile health (mmHealth) and mental health (mHealth) apps and how to securely maintain the copious amounts of sensitive data available (Benjumea, Ropero, Rivera-Romero, Dorronzoro-Zubiete, & Carrasco, 2020). It should come as no surprise that electronic protections for confidentiality and privacy are clearly outlined for social workers in the NASW Code of Ethics (2018). This increased accessibility also introduces the possibility of the need for consumer support in not only accessing these technologically supported health-related options but also accessing their own health-related information and interpreting results. When this information is posted and made accessible, it can be very confusing to patients to try to determine what details about a certain X-ray result or lab result are important to note. Assisting clients in this area is an important aspect of providing support to clients that requires that the social worker be versed in technology access to help empower clients to interpret their own information and data.

10.7 THE MENTALLY ILL IN THE CRIMINAL JUSTICE SYSTEM

The practice of deinstitutionalization, which resulted in the closing of many federal and state mental health facilities, has had devastating effects on the provision of mental health services, including those in the criminal justice system (Byron, 2014). Some were shocked when in 2004 the sheriff of Los Angeles County told the press he ran the largest mental hospital in the county (Lopez, 2005). Today, this remains applicable because illicit drug use and inmates with mental illness are common in prison; when these inmates are released, they are also more likely to reoffend and be reimprisoned (Stewart et al., 2022). When this information is coupled with how individuals with mental illness are handled in the criminal justice system, it is clear that the criminal justice is overburdened and ill-prepared to best address the special needs of this population. For example, the death in July 2015 of Sandra, who exhibited signs of mental illness after being taken into custody and entering the criminal justice system, documents the ongoing nature of the problem. Her case was included with research that linked 10,667 civilian deaths in the criminal justice system between January 1, 2005, and October 30, 2020, finding that inmates with mental illness were at the highest risk of death while in custody (Pollock, Sibilla, Frantzen, Luo, & Carmen, 2022). According to the data supplied by Pollock et al., however, at later stages in the criminal justice system and placement in jail or prison, the indicators of a mental illness leading to death in custody are reduced.

The need for social workers to assist with civilians with mental illness entering the criminal justice system has never been greater. As the number of inmates suffering from mental illness in our prison's increases, more social workers interested in mental health have begun to accept positions in this area.

The implementation of deinstitutionalization provides a perfect example of how a political and economic proposal that is not thoroughly explored prior to implementation can have devastating effects on those caught in the system. Many professionals in mental health passionately believe that deinstitutionalization has put tremendous pressure on families to care for their loved ones, as well as to bear the stigma of having done something wrong or, worse yet, causing the problem (Olson, 2006). For some, the inability of the family and community to address the needs of these individuals has resulted in utilizing the prison system as a holding tank for those with serious mental disorders. From this, prisons can be viewed as a replacement for the mental hospitals that have been closed (Butterfield, 1998).

Furthermore, the mental health services that are provided within the prison system are limited because of the lack of public concern for rehabilitation of offenders. When an individual with mental illness is incarcerated, the stigma is twofold, first as a prisoner and then as a person suffering from a mental illness (Slate, Buffington-Vollum, & Johnson, 2013). Regardless of the exact reason, the number of offenders with mental illness continues to grow in our prisons, jails, and the probation and parole system (Stewart et al., 2022).

Moreover, closing state mental health facilities and trying to treat chronic offenders in the community has left many individuals with mental illness homeless and without care (Slate et al., 2013). Individuals with mental illness may also be unfairly arrested and jailed because their behaviors present a danger or risk to those around them. To help avoid unfair arrests, programmatic responses have included collaborations among criminal legal professionals and those providing mental health services. One such collaboration is related to information sharing related to mental health, with the hope that having this information available will help to explain behavior, avoid unnecessary actions, and lead to safer interactions. In a recent study, when a group of consumers were asked their impressions of this practice, there was staunch support for information sharing while expressing concerns about the perceived stigma around mental illness and the potential consequences this stigma could have (Pope et al., 2022).

Regardless of the benefit or detriment of information sharing, finding the most appropriate placements, such as mental health centers in the community, may be complicated because these centers may be either unwilling or unable to help as a result of the indigent status of people with chronic mental illness and their subsequent inability to pay for services. When this problematic disconnect is identified, regardless of the reason, the importance of linking to direct services must be initiated along with macropractice activities that advocate for public awareness of the direct linkage between release and transition back into the community.

To help address this issue, social workers have advocated for the development of case management services as a humane, effective, and efficient way of interpersonal connection and information gathering (Frankel & Gelman, 2012). Furthermore, recent evidence based on a systematic review of the literature found that when referral mechanisms were increased that linked discharged inmates to community mental health services, the outcomes were promising. In addition, when these programs were tailored to the complex and unique problems of those individuals related to previous illicit drug use and mental health problems, outcomes that reduced recidivism improved (Stewart et al., 2022). For social workers, immediate connection to supportive services upon discharge can be used to help offenders return successfully to the community; assertive case management and collaboration between mental health providers and the criminal justice system encourage joint problem-solving. The CSWE also supports providing training on trauma-based care, particularly at the graduate level. To support this emphasis that stress and trauma are so influential on clinical practice and mental health, at the yearly conference for social work educators (2021–2023), sponsored by the CSWE, the clinical practice sequence of the annual program meeting included trauma as a central issue to be addressed (CSWE, 2022b). In recognizing the importance of trauma in the legal system, social workers are taking a more active role in police departments, as well as correctional facilities.

In police departments, social workers can help with multiple types of crimes, assisting trauma victims, survivors, and family members (Knox & Roberts, 2009). Whether it is offered in police departments or in other types of correctional facilities, this type of professional activity and coordination of specialized services upon release is important for improved living and social relationships for the mentally ill offender (Stewart et al., 2022). Social workers are encouraged to seek the most appropriate placements for those with mental illness through assertive case management, with the presumption that this type of service can bring about beneficial results when compared with the cost of re-incarceration.

Like problems occurring in the health care system, recidivism, or the readmission of individuals to the penal justice system, has presented a sincere concern (Stewart et al., 2022), and some offenders may be more at risk than others for rearrest (especially those with comorbidity involving depression and substance abuse). For mental health social workers in this area, a partnership between criminal justice professionals and social workers and other counseling professionals is blossoming (Kirschman, Kamena, & Fay, 2014). The role of the social worker is paramount, especially when this partnership is coupled with anti-oppressive strategies that shift punishment-centered practices to decarceration, health and wellness, and community empowerment (Willison & O'Brien, 2022).

This collaboration could result in early identification and treatment of those who might otherwise end up in the criminal justice system because of the lack of support in diagnosing and assessing mental health symptoms that can lead to criminal behaviors. This can also help to address any racial disparities in terms of sentencing (Gabba et al., 2022).

Without such a partnership, offenders with mental illness will continue to be rotated from mental health centers to jails in a cycle that causes further disease deterioration and increased criminality (Harrington, 1999). Jails are not staffed as mental hospitals, and a brief period of incarceration can compound the problems of an offender with mental illness because the jail is not geared toward providing treatment or achieving stabilization. Therefore, planned efforts to achieve better community treatment would result in fewer costly hospital stays and less jail time for these offenders. Furthermore, encouraging voluntary treatment of the individual is the best way to avoid a crisis that might lead to legal concerns (National Alliance on Mental Illness, 2008). Mental health courts are an emerging strategy designed as an alternative to incarceration, providing a means to avoid placing individuals with mental illness directly into the criminal justice system (Gabba et al., 2022). These courts are designed to assist clients who suffer from severe mental illness.

Another important concept leading to this advocacy for unification of the disciplines revolves around societal cost, financial and otherwise. The spending for mental health services is often below that for other types of health care. With deinstitutionalization, many individuals with mental illness were diverted into substance abuse programs funded by the federal government because the community programs were unprepared to manage the influx of patients (Slate et al., 2013). Those individuals with serious mental illness who were not placed in residential treatment facilities were criminalized because the mental health providers were actively involved with treating societal coping skills (Harrington, 1999). Assessing for functional situational factors in the mental health assessment is paramount to helping clients within the mental health system (see Table 10.4).

Table 10.4 Functional/Situational Factors to Be Considered in a Mental Health Assessment

Area	Explanation
Financial status	How does the health condition affect the financial status of the client? What income maintenance efforts are being made? Do any need to be initiated? Does the client have savings or resources to draw from?
Entitlements	Does the client have health, accident, disability, or life insurance benefits to cover his or her cost of health service? Has insurance been recorded and filed for the client to assist with paying of expenses? Does the client qualify for additional services to assist with illness and recovery?
Transportation	What transportation is available to the client? Does the client need assistance or arrangements to facilitate transportation?
Placement	Where will the client go after discharge? Is there a plan for continued maintenance when services are terminated? Is alternative placement needed?
Continuity of service	If the client is to be transferred to another health service, have the connections been made to link services and service providers appropriately? Based on the services provided, has the client received the services he or she needs during and after the treatment period?

This union of the disciplines will never succeed unless both disciplines acknowledge its importance and strongly advocate for collaboration and information sharing between the various professionals as well as the organizations involved in the process (Kirschman et al., 2014). Because there is no single system or organization that can meet all the conditions needed for optimal treatment of those with mental illness (Schnapp & Cannedy, 1998), sharing information is critical. Awareness of or familiarity with the police culture and collaboration fosters more supportive and integrated planning, as well as policy development and facilitation of the highest degree of complete and accurate information for decision-making (Kirschman et al., 2014).

SUMMARY

Regardless of the setting, most professionals would agree that the role of the mental health social worker involves complex decisions often linked to collaborative teamwork (Campbell, Brophy, & Davidson, 2022). CSWE emphasizes a competency-based approach that requires that competence be multidimensional, with interrelated competencies that link practice efforts (CSWE, 2022a). For social workers going beyond the traditional view of problem identification, starting and ending with the client falls short of considering the effects helping activities can have on the client system. Also, recognizing that problems are not static opens the door to assessing the developmental and dynamic changes needed. Therefore, it comes as no surprise that social work can be a stressful occupation. Recognizing the signs and symptoms to avoid burnout is important (Hlavatska, 2020; Salvagioni et al., 2017).

More information is needed on the link between mental health problems and structural issues, such as poverty, racism, and gendered inequalities. Despite views of mental illness or how it is defined, formulating the diagnosis, assessment, or diagnostic assessment and the psychosocial assessments performed by mental health and health care social workers are essential (Dziegielewski, 2015). Assessment is the critical first step in formulating a plan for intervention. It thus sets the tone and framework for the entire mental health social work process. With this acknowledgment, however, there needs to be a transition to ensure the mental health services provided are more inclusive, equitable, and rights based (Ungar & Theron, 2020). From this perspective, a more culturally aware and responsive approach starts by listening to the client's story and the needs and perceptions within the client system.

To compete in today's mental health environment, social work professionals must play a twofold role: (1) ensure that high-quality service is provided to the client and the client system and (2) ensure that the client and the client system have access so that the mental health needs for all are addressed. Neither of these tasks is easy, nor will they make a social worker popular in today's environment. Mental and other health services must now be delivered with limited resources, and the pressure to reduce services is intense. There are also the dangers of false diagnosis and overmedicalizing or placing a label on what might otherwise be considered adaptive behavior (Frances & Jones, 2013). Social workers must know the assessment and treatment planning tools that are used in the field and be able to use them, always being careful not to falsely support a diagnosis or place a label that may affect the client for the rest of his or her life. Assessment and treatment planning are together the first step in providing services, a step that social work professionals cannot afford to neglect.

Numerous ways to codify mental health conditions exist to assist social workers in the mental health assessment process, and use of the **DSM-5-TR** is the most popular classification system. Utilizing a systematic assessment that considers the client and the client system can provide social workers with a framework for practice. In addition, when using standardized measurement instruments to assess problems, social workers should exercise caution, and information related to reliability and validity should always be gathered (Jordan & Franklin, 2021). As you will learn in practice courses yet to come, when placing a formal mental health diagnosis, even the most experienced social workers fear that these methods can place labels on clients that are exceedingly difficult to remove. These fears are well founded, but they should not cause social workers to shun assessment. Indeed, the fact that social workers are aware of such dangers makes their participation in assessment essential. In addition, the social worker brings a wealth of information to the collaborative team about a client's environment and family situation. Social workers who focus on building the skills and strengths of the client are well equipped to help design a treatment plan that is realistic and effective. Although assessments completed today may initially appear to have a narrower focus, it is essential that utility, relevance, and salience be maintained (Dziegielewski & Holliman, 2020).

Because social workers practice in a variety of health and mental health settings and perform many different duties, it is not surprising that the processes of assessment and treatment planning shows great diversity. Assessment and subsequent treatment plan development depend on a multiplicity of factors, including client need, agency function, practice setting, service limitations, and coverage for provision of service. The scope of assessment and intervention must be narrowed in response to reductions in economic support. Therefore, overall practice in the mental health setting must continually be examined to ensure high quality. If the process of helping is rushed, superficial factors may be highlighted while significant ones are overlooked. All social workers, regardless of their mental health care setting, must establish services that are quality driven, no matter what the administrative and economic pressures may be. Last, Kourgiantakis et al. (2022) remind us that good practice techniques for improving mental health require strengthening professional training on recovery, especially with individuals who have a history of substance addiction. Along with advocating for the reduction of coercive treatment policies, equitable practices that reduce stigma and discrimination must be increased.

QUESTIONS TO CONSIDER

1. Based on the information provided in this chapter, what do you see as the most important tasks for the social worker in starting the assessment process?
2. To avoid the stigma related to suffering from a mental health disorder, what strategies should social workers employ?
3. When a client suffers from mental health problems, do you believe that a complete assessment and treatment planning framework requires considering the client and the client system? In what ways do you believe taking the client system into account will help to make interventions for the client more successful?

REFERENCES

American Psychiatric Association. (2013). *Diagnostic and statistical manual of mental disorders, DSM-5* (5th ed.). Washington, DC: Author.

American Psychiatric Association. (2022). *Diagnostic and statistical manual of mental disorders, DSM-5* (5th ed., text rev.). Washington, DC: Author.

Anderson, G. F., & Frogner, B. K. (2008). Health spending in OECD countries: Obtaining value per dollar. *Health Affairs, 24*, 903–914.

Austrian, S. G. (2009). Guidelines for conducting a biopsychosocial assessment. In A. R. Roberts (Ed.), *Social workers' desk reference* (2nd ed., pp. 376–380). New York, NY: Oxford University Press.

Barth, R. P., Kolivoski, K., Lindsey, M. A., Lee, B. R., & Collins, K. S. (2014). Translating the common elements approach: Social work experiences in education, practice, and research. *Journal of Clinical Child and Adolescent Psychology, 42*, 301–311.

Benjumea, J., Ropero, J., Rivera-Romero, O., Dorronzoro-Zubiete, E., & Carrasco, A. (2020). Privacy assessment in mobile health apps: Scoping review. *JMIR mHealth and uHealth, 8*(7), e18868. https://mhealth.jmir.org/2020/7/e18868

Brake, H. T., & Duckers, M. (2013). Early psychosocial interventions after disasters, terrorism, and other shocking events: Is there a gap between norms and practice in Europe? *European Journal of Psychotraumatology, 4*, 1–10.

Brennan, E. M., Evans, M. E., & Spencer, S. A. (2008). Mental health services and support for families. In J. M. Rosenzweig & E. M. Brennan (Eds.), *Work, life, and mental health system of care* (pp. 3–26). Baltimore, MD: Brooks.

Bureau of Labor Statistics, U.S. Department of Labor. (2021). *Occupational employment and wages, May 2021, 21-1022 Health care social workers*. Retrieved December 29, 2022, from https://www.bls.gov/oes/current/oes211022.htm

Bureau of Labor Statistics, U.S. Department of Labor. (2022a). *Occupational outlook handbook, psychologists*. Retrieved December 29, 2022, from https://www.bls.gov/ooh/life-physical-and-social-science/psychologists.htm

Bureau of Labor Statistics, U.S. Department of Labor. (2022b). *Occupational outlook handbook, marriage and family therapists*. Retrieved December 29, 2022, from https://www.bls.gov/ooh/community-and-social-service/marriage-and-family-therapists.htm

Bureau of Labor Statistics, U.S. Department of Labor. (2022c). *Occupational outlook handbook*. Retrieved December 29, 2022, from https://www.bls.gov/ooh/community-and-social-service/substance-abuse-behavioral-disorder-and-mental-health-counselors.htm

Bureau of Labor Statistics, U.S. Department of Labor. (2022d). *Occupational outlook handbook, social workers*. Retrieved December 29, 2022, from https://www.bls.gov/ooh/community-and-social-service/social-workers.htm

Butterfield, F. (1998, March 5). Prisons replace hospitals for the nation's mentally ill. *New York Times*, p. A1, A26.

Byron, R. (2014). Criminals need mental health care: Psychiatric treatment is far better than imprisonment for reducing recidivism. *Mind & Brain, 25, 2*, 1–7.

Cabot, R. C. (1913). Letter. *Journal of the American Medical Association, 60*, 145.

Campbell, J., Brophy, L., & Davidson, G. (2022). Editorial: International perspectives on mental health and mental health social work. *International Journal of Environmental Research and Public Health, 19*(12), 7387. https://doi.org/10.3390/ijerph19127387

Carlton, T. O. (1984). *Clinical social work in health care settings: A guide to professional practice with exemplars*. New York, NY: Springer.

Corcoran, J., & Walsh, J. (2022). *Clinical assessment and diagnosis in social work practice* (4th ed.). New York, NY: Oxford University Press.

Council on Social Work Education. (2022a). *Accreditation standards*. Retrieved December 29, 2022, from https://www.cswe.org/accreditation/standards/2022-epas/

Council on Social Work Education. (2022b). *Clinical practice, APM assignments*. Retrieved December 29, 2022, from https://www.cswe.org/events-meetings/2023-apm-643c4518123761ba32a8f0af52504210/education/proposals/2023-apm-tracks/clinical-practice/

Cuatero, E., & Campos-Vidal, J. (2019). Self-care behaviours and their relationship with satisfaction and compassion fatigue levels among social workers. *Social Work in Healthcare, 58*(3), 274–290. https://doi.org/10.1080/00981389.2018.1558164

Daley, D. C., & Zuckoff, A. (1998). Improving compliance with the initial outpatient session among discharged inpatient dual diagnosis clients. *Social Work, 43*, 470–474.

Duckworth, M. P. (2009). Cultural awareness and culturally competent practice. In W. T. O'Donohue & J. E. Fisher (Eds.), *General principles and empirically supported techniques of cognitive behavior therapy* (pp. 63–76). Hoboken, NJ: Wiley.

Dziegielewski, S. F. (2015). *DSM-5™ in action*. New York, NY: Wiley.

Dziegielewski, S. F., & Holliman, D. (2020). *The changing face of health care social work: Opportunities and challenges for professional practice* (4th ed.). New York, NY: Springer.

Dziegielewski, S. F., & Jacinto, G. A. (2016). *Psychopharmacology and social work practice*. New York, NY: Springer.

Eamon, M. K. (2008). *Empowering vulnerable populations*. Chicago, IL: Lyceum Books.

Fields, N. L., Lee, K., Cassidy, J., Kunz-Lomelin, A., Stringfellow, M. K., & Feinhals, G. (2022). It gave me somebody else to think about besides myself: Caring callers volunteer experiences with a telephone-based reassurance program for socially isolated older adults. *Journal of Applied Gerontology, 42*(1), 49–58. https://journals.sagepub.com/doi/abs/10.1177/07334648221123302

Fox, R. D. (2009). The essential elements of private practice social work. In A. R. Roberts (Ed.), *Social workers' desk reference* (2nd ed., pp. 53–60). New York, NY: Oxford University Press.

Frances, A., & Jones, K. D. (2013). Should social workers use the *Diagnostic and Statistical Manual of Mental Disorders-5*? *Research on Social Work Practice, 24*, 11–12.

Frank, R. G. (2013). Mental illness and a dual dilemma. *Journal of the American Society of Aging, 37*(2), 47–53.

Frankel, A. J., & Gelman, S. R. (2012). *Case management. An introduction to concepts and skills* (3rd ed.). Chicago, IL: Lyceum Books.

Furin, T. L. (2022). *Combating hatred for the soul of America: Watershed moments for transformational educators*. Lanham, MD: Rowman & Littlefield.

Gabba, A., Schaffer, P. M., Andre, M., Pinals, D. A., Drawbridge, D., & Smelson, D. (2022). Racial and ethnic differences in behavioral health, criminal legal system involvement, and service delivery needs among mental health court participants: Implications for service delivery. *Psychological Services, 19* (4), 637–647.

Gaebel, W., Stricker, J., & Kerst, A. (2020). Changes from *ICD-10* to *ICD-11* and future directions in psychiatric classification. *Dialogues Clinical Neuroscience, 22*(1),7–15. https://doi.org/10.31887/DCNS.2020.22.1/wgaebel

Giordano, G. (2022). *Parents and school violence: Answers that reveal essential steps for improving schools*. Lanham, MD: Rowan & Littlefield.

Harrington, S. (1999, May/June). New bedlam: Jails not psychological hospitals now care for the indigent mentally ill. *Humanist, 59*, 9–13.

Hlavatska, O. (2020). Self care for social workers in avoiding burnout. *Social Work and Education, 7*(1), 35–45.

Hoffler, E. F., & Clark, E. J. (2012). *Social work matters: The power of linking policy and practice*. Washington, DC: NASW Press.

Holliman, D., Dziegielewski, S. F., & Datta, P. (2001). Discharge planning and social work practice. *Social Work in Health Care, 32*(3), 1–19.

Jordan, C., & Franklin, C. (2021). *Clinical assessment for social workers: Quantitative and qualitative methods* (5th ed.). New York, NY: Oxford University Press.

Jung, H., Jaime, J., & Lee, S. (2022). Mental health in subsidized housing: Readiness to assist residents with mental health issues in subsidized housing from the perspectives of housing employees. *Qualitative Social Work, 21*(5), 850–868. https://doi.org/10.1177/14733250211027630

Kirschman, E., Kamena, M., & Fay, J. (2014). *Counseling cops: What clinicians need to know.* New York, NY: Guilford Press.

Knox, K. S., & Roberts A. R. (2009). The social worker in a police department. In A. R. Roberts (Ed.), *Social workers' desk reference* (2nd ed., pp. 85–94). New York, NY: Oxford University Press.

Kourgiantakis, T., McNeil, S. R., Hussain, A., Logan, J., Ashcroft, R., Lee, E., & Williams, C. (2022). Social work's approach to recovery in mental health and addiction policies: A scoping review. *Social Work in Mental Health, 20*(4), 377–399.

Leach, M. M. (2006). *Cultural diversity and suicide: Ethnic, religious, gender and sexual orientation perspectives.* Binghamton, NY: Haworth Press.

Lepkowsky, C. M. (2020). Telehealth reimbursement allows access to mental health care during COVID-19. *The American Journal of Geriatric Psychiatry, 28*(8), 898–899.

Liu, H., Li, T. W., Liang, L., & Hou, W. K. (2021). Trauma exposure and mental health of prisoners and ex-prisoners: A systematic review and meta-analysis. *Clinical Psychology Review, 89*, 102069.

Locke, D. C., & Bailey, D. F. (2014). *Increasing multicultural understanding* (3rd ed.). Thousand Oaks, CA: Sage.

Lopez, S. (2005, December 11). Mentally ill in the jail? It's a crime. *Los Angeles Times.*

Marshall, T. B., & Solomon, P. (2009). Working with families of persons with severe mental illness. In A. R. Roberts (Ed.), *Social workers' desk reference* (2nd ed., pp. 491–494). New York, NY: Oxford University Press.

Maust, D., Oslin, D. W., & Marcus, S. (2014). Effect of age on the profile of psychotropic users: Results from the 2010 National Ambulatory Medical Care Survey. *Journal of the American Geriatrics Society, 62*, 358–364.

Morales, A. T., Sheafor, B. W., & Scott, M. (2012). *Social work: A profession of many faces* (12th ed.). New York, NY: Pearson.

National Alliance on Mental Illness. (2008). *Beyond punishment: Helping individuals with mental illness in Maryland's criminal justice system.* Charleston, SC: BookSurge.

National Association of Social Workers. (1998). *Centennial information: Celebrating 100 years of social work practice* [pamphlet]. Washington, DC: Author.

National Association of Social Workers. (2011). *Social workers in mental health clinics & outpatient facilities: Occupational profile.* Washington, DC: Author.

National Association of Social Workers. (2012). *Social work speaks* (9th ed.). Washington, DC: Author.

National Association of Social Workers. (2018). *Code of ethics.* Washington, DC: NASW Press.

National Association of Social Workers. (2022). *Social work promotes healthy minds and bodies.* Retrieved December 29, 2022, from https://www.socialworkers.org/Events/Campaigns/Social-Workers-Promote-Healthy-Minds-and-Bodies

National Association of Social Workers Delegate Assembly. (2020). *Policy statement, mental health.* Retrieved December 29, 2022, from https://www.socialworkers.org/LinkClick.aspx?fileticket=4efHh0QO3ZE%3d&portalid=0

National Institute of Mental Health. (2021). *What is telemental health?* Retrieved December 29, 2022, from https://www.nimh.nih.gov/health/publications/what-is-telemental-health

O'Donnell, M. L., Schaefer, I., Varker, T., Kartal, D., Forbes, D., Bryant, R. A., . . . & Steel, Z. (2017). A systematic review of person-centered approaches to investigating patterns of trauma exposure. *Clinical Psychology Review, 57,* 208–225.

O'Hare, T., & Sherrer, M. V. (2009). Impact of the most frequently reported traumatic events on community mental health clients. *Journal of Human Behavior in the Social Environment, 19,* 186–195.

Olson, M. E. (2006). Family and network therapy training for a system of care. In A. Lightburn & P. Sessions (Eds.), *Handbook of community-based practice* (pp. 135–152). New York, NY: Oxford University Press.

Palmo, A. J. (2011). *Foundations of mental health counseling.* Springfield, IL: Charles C. Thomas.

Pieterse, D., Kim, B. K., Klomhaus, A., Comulada, W. S., Lopez, S. A., Bath, E., . . . Milburn, N. G. (2022). PTSD among families of juvenile justice-involved youth: Relation to mental, emotional, and behavioral health problems. *Journal of Child and Family Studies, 31*(7), 1947–1956.

Pike, C. K. (2009). Developing client focused measures. In A. R. Roberts (Ed.), *Social workers' desk reference* (2nd ed., pp. 351–357). New York, NY: Oxford University Press.

Pollock, W., Sibila, D., Frantzen, D., Luo, F., & Carmen, A.D. (2022). *A systematic examination of the influence of indicators of mental illness on deaths in the Texas criminal justice system.* Los Angeles, CA: SAGE.

Pope, L. G., Warnock, A., Perry, T. H., Langlois, S., Anderson, S., Boswell, T., . . . Compton, M. T. (2022). Information sharing across mental health service providers and criminal legal stakeholders: Perspectives of people with serious mental illness and their family members. *Social Science & Medicine, 307,* 115178. https://doi.org/10.1016/j.socscimed.2022.115178

Reddon, J. R., Hoglin, B., & Woodman, M. (2008). Immediate effects of a 16-week life skills education program on the mental health of adult psychiatric patients. *Social Work in Mental Health, 6*(3), 21–40.

Reedy, A. R., & Kobayashi, R. (2012). Substance use and mental disorders: Why do some people suffer from both? *Social Work in Mental Health, 10,* 496–517.

Risley, M. (1961). *The house of healing.* London, England: Hale.

Rosenzweig, J. M., & Brennan, E. M. (2008). The intersection of children's mental health and work-family studies. In J. M. Rosenzweig & E. M. Brennan (Eds.), *Work, life, and mental health system of care* (p. 3–26). Baltimore, MD: Brooks.

Salvagioni, D. A. J., Melanda, F. N., Mesas, A. E., González, A. D., Gabani, F. L., & Andrade, S. M. (2017). Physical, psychological and occupational consequences of job burnout: A systematic review of prospective studies. *PloS One, 12*(10), e0185781. https://doi.org/10.1371/journal.pone.0185781

Scheyett, A., Kim, M., Swanson, J., Swartz, M., Elbogen, E., Dorn, R. V., & Ferron, J. (2009). Autonomy and the use of directive intervention in the treatment of individuals with serious mental illnesses: A survey of social work practitioners. *Social Work in Mental Health, 7*, 283–306.

Schnapp, W. B., & Cannedy, R. (1998). Offenders with mental illness: Mental health and criminal justice best practices. *Administration and Policy in Mental Health, 25*, 463–466.

Schroeder, R. (2013). The seriously mentally ill older adult: Perceptions of the patient–provider relationship. *Perspectives in Psychiatric Care, 49*, 30–40.

Simon, E. P., Showers, N., Blumfield, S., Holden, G., & Wu, X. (1995). Delivery of home care services after discharge: What really happens. *Health and Social Work, 20*, 5–14.

Slate, R. N., Buffington-Vollum, J. K., & Johnson, W. W. (2013). *Mental illness: Crisis and opportunity for the justice system*. Durham, NC: Carolina Academic Press.

Stewart, A. C., Cossar, R. D., Quinn, B., Dietze, P., Romero, L., Wilkinson, A. L., & Stoove, M. (2022). Criminal justice involvement after release from prison following exposure to community mental health services among people who use illicit drugs and have mental illness: A systematic review. *Journal of Urban Health, 989*(4), 635–654.

Strom-Gottfried, K. (2008). *The ethics of practice with minors: High stakes, hard choices*. Chicago, IL: Lyceum Books.

Totten, A. M., Womack, D. M., Eden, K. B., McDonagh, M. S., Griffin, J. C., Grusing, S., & Hersh, W. R. (2016). Telehealth: Mapping the evidence for patient outcomes from systematic reviews. *Agency for Healthcare Research and Quality, 16*, 26.

Turanovic, J. J., Pratt, T. C., Kulig, T. C., & Cullen, F. T. (2022). *Confronting school violence: A synthesis of six decades of research*. Cambridge, UK: Cambridge University Press.

Ungar, M., &Theron, L. (2020). Resilience and mental health: How multisystemic processes contribute to positive outcomes. *Lancet Psychiatry, 7*, 441–448. https://dx.doi.org/10.1016/S2215-0366(19)30434-1

Williams, J. B. (2009). Using the *Diagnostic and Statistical Manual of Mental Disorders* (4th ed., text rev.). In A. R. Roberts (Ed.), *Social workers' desk reference* (2nd ed., pp. 325–334). New York, NY: Oxford University Press.

Willison, J. S., & O'Brien, P. (2022). *Anti-oppressive social work practice & the carceral state*. New York, NY: Oxford University Press.

Woods, T. A., & Kurtz-Costes, B. (2007). Race identity and race socialization in African American families: Implications for social workers. *Journal of Human Behavior and the Social Environment, 2*(3), 99–116.

Yeager, K. R., & Latimer, T. R. (2009). Quality standards and quality assurance in health settings. In A. R. Roberts (Ed.), *Social workers' desk reference* (2nd ed., pp. 194–203). New York, NY: Oxford University Press.

Yeager, K. R., Roberts, A. R., & Saveanu, R. (2009). Optimizing the use of patient safety standards, procedures, and measures. In A. R. Roberts (Ed.), *Social workers' desk reference* (2nd ed., pp. 174–186). New York, NY: Oxford University Press.

Zhou, C., Nutt, D. J., & Davies, J. C. (2022). Visualizing classification of drugs used in psychotic disorders: A subway map representing mechanisms, established classes and informal categories. *Journal of Psychopharmacology, 36*(9), 1007–1015. https://doi.org/10.1177/02698811221115758

Older Adults

CHAPTER 11: EPAS COMPETENCIES

Social work programs at the bachelor's and the master's level are accredited by the Council of Social Work Education (CSWE). CSWE's Educational Policy and Accreditation Standards (EPAS) describe the processes and criteria that social work courses should cover. In 2022, CSWE updated its EPAS standards. The following competencies are address in this chapter:

Competency 1: Demonstrate Ethical and Professional Behavior

Social workers understand the value base of the profession and its ethical standards, as well as relevant policies, laws, and regulations that may affect practice with individuals, families, groups, organizations, and communities.

Competency 3: Engage in Anti-racism, Diversity, Equity, and Inclusion in Practice

Social workers understand how racism and oppression shape human experiences and how these two constructs influence practice at the individual, family, group, organizational, and community levels and in policy and research.

Competency 4: Engage in Practice-Informed Research and Research-Informed Practice

Social workers use ethical, culturally informed, anti-racist, and anti-oppressive approaches in conducting research and building knowledge.

Competency 7: Assess Individuals, Families, Groups, Organizations, and Communities

Social workers understand that assessment is an ongoing component of the dynamic and interactive process of social work practice.

Let's begin by exploring your thoughts about aging. To start, answer these questions about getting older and let us explore your impressions of aging and what it means.

1. For me, getting older means . . . Close your eyes and imagine yourself at various ages.
   What do you see?
   a. At age sixty, I am . . .
   b. At age seventy, I am . . .
   c. At age eighty, I am . . .
   d. At age ninety, I am . . .
   e. At age one hundred, I am . . .
2. Name a person who is sixty-five or older whom you admire or have admired. What is so special about this person? How can this person be a role model for you?

No one escapes the aging process. In fact, from the moment we are born, aging begins. During the aging process, as in all phases of human growth and development, people must adjust to changes in their life circumstances. Unfortunately, these changes are viewed negatively in our society (Algilani et al., 2014). Declines in physical functioning, changes in physical appearance, loss of income, retirement, and loss of partner and social supports are all associated with aging (Heckhausen et al., 2021). But not everyone experiences these shifts in quite the same way. Although aging is often thought of as an individual process, it can also include a more comprehensive reference, including its potential effects as the numbers of older individuals increase in a society (Moody & Sasser, 2012). Most professionals agree that to understand aging, we must look at more than just a person's chronological age—that is, how old they are. The study of older adults therefore embraces varied life circumstances and issues and must consider physical and psychosocial factors (Dziegielewski & Holliman, 2020).

Did You Know . . .

One myth about aging is that all older people age in the same way and display predictable patterns of age-related behavior that can easily be studied. Nothing could be further from the truth. As we age, the shifts can differ dramatically based on individual factors, including mental health and social factors, as well as other factors, such as diet and overall health.

Over the years, however, use of a chronological age cutoff has been the most common way to decide who is an older adult. Although this is an easy way to define old age, the number is highly dependent on who you ask. If you ask people who are forty-five or younger, the answer will be sixty-one and older, but if you ask people who are quite a bit older than sixty-one, they may see the age as young (*Huffington Post*, 2012; Taylor, Morin, Parker, Cohn, & Wang, 2009).

> ### Did You Know . . .
> At one time, people used to talk about retiring at age sixty-five. Well, retirement age has increased for most people. Can you retire at any age? Sure, but if you retire in the United States before full retirement age and plan to collect a monthly Social Security check, the amount you receive will be reduced. An eligible person may begin receiving retirement checks at age sixty-two or delay receiving checks while working past retirement age. Note that the longer you wait to collect your benefits, if you keep a stable income, the larger your monthly Social Security checks will be.

You may also know people who began to receive retirement information from various groups shortly after their fiftieth birthdays. You can join the American Association of Retired Persons at age fifty with a traditional membership, or today you can also join if you are between the ages of eighteen and under the age of fifty. For younger adults, you can now receive full membership benefits unless restricted by law or contract (American Association for Retired Persons, 2022). Several major airlines offer *senior discounts* to people who are fifty-five or older. The senior golf tour has a minimum age of fifty, and other senior games and athletic contests in various states have ages that differ (fifty to fifty-five and older). Most political scientists agree that the definition of senior status began with the Economic Security Act of 1935 and was based on the German precedent, which established sixty-five years (depending on your date of birth) as the appropriate age for benefits to begin (Brieland, Costin, & Atherton, 1980). And indeed, this simple definition is administratively useful because it establishes clear eligibility standards for programs such as Social Security, which historically began at age sixty-five (see Figure 11.1).

> ### Did You Know . . .
> According to the World Bank, in 2020, the general life expectancy was 77 years, slightly down from the previous year. According to Social Security 2019 (2022 Trustee Report), the average age from birth is 76.22 for males and 81.28 for females (Social Security, 2022).

Nothing lasts forever, and people born after 1959 will have to wait until age sixty-seven to collect full benefits. For people born earlier, the benefit rate can vary depending on age. For example, if you were born in 1955, you will have to wait until you

Part 3: Settings for Social Work Practice

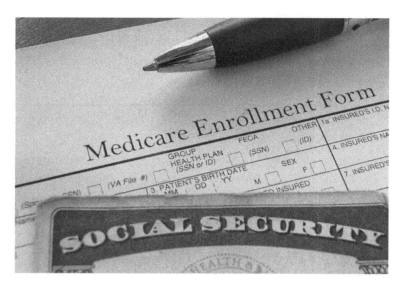

FIGURE 11.1
Medicare and Social Security are two essential programs for older adults in the United States.

are sixty-six years and two months to collect full benefits from Social Security (see the activity below and visit the official Social Security website to calculate retirement benefits based on age).

Activity

When can I collect Social Security Benefits? Go to the Social Security website and enter your year of birth to determine how old you will need to be to collect 100 percent of your social security benefits. Also, enter your parents' birth years and see how old they will need to be to retire with full, 100 percent Social Security benefits. Review your partner/spouse's (if you have one) benefit eligibility as well.

The population shift, referred to as *population aging*, occurs as the population of older adults' increases. This shift is so striking it is attracting widespread attention. According to the U.S. Census Bureau (2018), starting in the year 2030, the current baby boomers will all reach the age of sixty-five. By 2034, it is expected that the number of children under eighteen will be less than the number of older adults. This trend will continue to increase, and in 2060 it is estimated that children under age eighteen will comprise 19.85 percent of the population, whereas older adults sixty-five and older will comprise 23.4 percent. When this happens, those adults sixty-five and older will be the largest percentage of the U.S. population (U.S. Census Bureau, 2018). Despite life expectancy declines observed since 2014 (Woolf & Schoomaker, 2019), population-level aging has been increasing in the United States, as in other countries. When the number of older adults is outpacing the number of all younger cohorts, it can have major implications for the overall population. In addition, the earlier predictions of life expectancy—approximately 81.1 years for women and 76.2 years for men—remain realistic (U.S. Census Bureau, 2018).

> ### Did You Know . . .
> As the population numbers change, so do the social support programs. When the Economic Security Act was passed in 1935, age sixty-five marked the 95th percentile of the U.S. age distribution. By 1986, age sixty-five marked the 76th percentile. As the share of the U.S. population that is age sixty-five has continued to increase dramatically, the age at which benefits are offered has changed as well.

The aging of our population has had far-reaching effects, and it is no surprise that the sheer number of older adults has attracted significant interest (Cass, 2022). The simplest way for administrators and policy planners to define what constitutes older adults is using chronological age and population numbers. However, this definition is deficient when used alone because it cannot reflect changes in the composition of the older adult population. As a result of such changes, older adults have become a much less homogeneous group. About seventy years ago, males and females aged within resulting in equal numbers of people age sixty-five or older. As Americans enjoy longer life spans and lower death rates, the numbers of women who live longer than men continue to increase. Although women have a longer life expectancy than men, the number of older men is expected to grow as of 2010 (Ortman, Velkoff, & Hogan, 2014). The exact reason for the increased number of older males is not clear, but may be related to the fact that most males are married and do not live alone. This changing demographic may lead to more options for home care and for spouses to take care of each other in the community setting. After retirement, women often assume the role of primary caregiver within a family unit, taking primary responsibility for helping the partner or other aged family members in need of care. This burden for females can put additional stress on an aging couple.

When looking at living in skilled facilities, because women often outlive men, it is no surprise that in 2021 females outnumbered males in nursing homes. The average age of a nursing home resident is approximately eighty-one, making up 46 percent of the residents (approximately 1.5 million Americans). In 2020, over 40 percent of the COVID-19 deaths in the United States occurred in nursing homes (El, 2022).

With regard to health domains specifically, older adults in Canada were most concerned about independent functioning, followed by fears of suffering from diseases and increased pain (Lazarevic & Quesnel-Vallee, 2022). In both Canada and the United States, the importance of social support and connection to family supports, including an intimate partner, appears to be a major factor in recovery from illness.

Name: Ms. Lecia Gray, MSL, MSW, CBT

Place of residence: Native Floridian, born and raised in Palm Beach County, currently residing in Orlando, Orange County

College/university degrees:

- Palm Beach Atlantic College, BS in psychology, double minor in sociology/gerontology
- Barry University, MSW (concentration, mental health and substance abuse)
- Belhaven College, MSL
- Currently DSW candidate, Barry University

Present position and title: Chief community resource specialist (CCRS), Light of Life Consultants, Inc. (nonprofit); Lighthouse Publishing and Promotions, LLC, Webcast Host of *Setting It Straight w/Ms. Gray*

Previous work/volunteer experience: For thirty years, I have worked in the field of mental health for adults and the elderly in Palm Beach, and in Orange, Osceola, and Seminole Counties. I was recruited by Children's Services Council for my mental health and social welfare skill set and learned how to write grants. I felt that I took the field of social work to a whole different level and didn't foresee how that new skill would impact my life. I retired from that agency and realized that I needed a break from the mental health arena, so I joined AmeriCorps, and once again, my life changed forever.

Once I remarried in 2001, I moved to Orlando and began working with disabled adults through Agency for Persons with Disabilities. The door also opened for me to begin providing therapy for kids with learning disabilities and I began working at Children's Medical Services. I was an adjunct professor back home and was able to teach here in Orlando at a Christian university. For balance, I became a cameo and voice-over actor, performing at our History Center and in commercials. I soon was led by God to return to the nonprofit world by starting my own, and then later forming another company where I would have products to sell, e.g., my books, candles, and blessed oils, to name a few. I have been on the radio and now have returned to media with my show, *Setting It Straight w/Ms. Gray*, which is a place where we discuss societal ills, and we provide solutions to those who are hurting and feeling hopeless.

I volunteer with and/or am a member of NASW, NAACP, OCCPTA/PTSA, CEC, and the Amputee Coalition.

Why did you choose social work as a career? I did not choose social work; it chose me. A high school classmate introduced me to the field and even though I was four years behind her, I followed in her footsteps and entered this beautiful world of service.

What is your favorite social work story? Wow, there are so many stories of impact and change affecting children, families, and professionals. For me, it's the fact that my love for this field has made an impact by influencing over fifty individuals to pursue the field, including licensure as well.

> *What is the thing you would change in the community if you had the power to do so?* I want to bring awareness to our aging Black Americans. There are not enough services, resources, or evidenced-based research for and on the ethnic group. I intend to change that by getting my DSW in trauma-informed care, including direct service and resources through ministry, my businesses, and my social media.

11.1 DEFINING THE OLDER ADULT AND AVOIDING AGEISM

There are several factors that complicate a simple definition of the term *older adult* and how these individuals are viewed by society. Using terms such as "baby boomer" to describe older adults encompasses a wide range of ages. According to the U.S. Census Bureau, 30 percent of males and 22 percent of females age sixty-five to seventy-four remain active in the labor force (Roberts, Ogunwhole, Blakeslee, & Rabe, 2018). The number of Americans who are eighty-five years old or older is growing. As this oldest age group continues to age, they are more likely to have significant health problems than adults aged fifty-five through sixty-five and even those in their seventies. This makes it exceedingly difficult to treat all these older adults equally and lump them into one category. Furthermore, Hafford-Letchfield, Simpson, and Reynolds (2021) and the authors in their edited work remind us that for older adults, beyond the physical differences there are societal expectations that do not receive the same attention as do those for younger adults. For example, sexual discourse for older adults who remain sexually active is addressed differently than it would be for a younger adult. Discussing sexual needs with a partner can be exceedingly difficult because it is complicated by societal expectations as well as physical changes that may not be fully understood. Although they are so important in any type of sexual relationship, these types of discussions are often subtle to avoid negative societal attitudes and expectations.

To further identify age-related groups, older adults have been divided for purposes of simplicity into the terms *older adults* and *aged* to refer to all people of age sixty-five or older and baby boomers to include those born between 1946 and 1964 as defined by the U.S. Census.

During the late 1990s, the John A. Hartford Foundation, a national foundation that supports gerontological efforts, financially supported the development of both master-level and baccalaureate-level educational initiatives in aging. In schools and departments of social work, gerontology field placements, elective courses, and concentrations (at the graduate level) were developed as a direct result of support by the Hartford Foundation. In 1998, the Hartford Foundation partnered with the Council on Social Work Education (CSWE, 2001) and developed curriculum standards and a clearinghouse for geriatric resources and teaching tools. This Gero-Ed center continues today, and the website offers multiple resources and grant opportunities for supporting education and training in this area (John A. Hartford Foundation, 2022).

> ### Activity
> Visit the John A. Hartford website and dissemination center and look up some of the grant opportunities/resources for social workers in the area of aging.

In this chapter, we will introduce you to the topic of aging, a normal and universal stage of human development. As the number of older citizens continues to increase, so does the need for culturally aware and responsive social work services. Fortunately, services provided to older adults, within specific limits, are considered human rights, and the benefits have limited dependence on the means testing so common elsewhere in the social service arena. We will highlight issues and trends essential to an understanding of America's aging population.

11.2 AGING: WHAT CAN BE EXPECTED

Dziegielewski and Holliman (2020) along with Van Hook (2014) and others are clear in pointing out the implications of the increasing numbers of older adults for practice in the twenty-first century. One factor contributing to this increase is the substantial portion of the population that will fall into the category of older adults; this segment of the population is often referred to as baby boomers (see the activity below).

> ### Activity
> Explore the concept of aging by visiting the Census Bureau website. You can use this website to compare the national levels of older adults in your home state or county.

Prior to World War II, large numbers of young immigrants came to America. The immigrants who came legally were counted in the national statistics, whereas those who came illegally were not. All of these immigrants (legal and illegal) are now reaching retirement age. This group of people born after World War II (between 1945 and 1955), as well as those officially classified as baby boomers (born between 1946 and 1964), will now reach retirement age (Barr, 2014).

Another factor underlying the growth in the number of aged individuals is the number of births relative to the number of deaths. The trend in recent years has been fewer births and longer and healthier lives, resulting in lower death rates (U.S. Census Bureau, 2014). It is predicted that death rates will continue to decline, leaving more aged individuals in society, especially the *old-old*, or those older than seventy-five.

As the numbers of older adults continues to rise, so will health care utilization (Tompkins & Rosen, 2014). As older adults retire from the workforce, there will be fewer young adults to step up and supplement the financing of our health care system. With the recent influx of immigrants reaching 44.9 million in 2019, it is not clear whether this pattern will change (Esterline & Batalova, 2022).

Regardless, the effects of aging for the boomers will be pronounced, especially as people develop more chronic conditions that require ongoing treatment. Social workers have become keenly aware of the need for providers to look carefully at the needs of older clients to ensure that quality of life is maximized for both older adults and their caregivers (Gellis, 2009). As Kim, Hayward, and Kang (2013) remind us, the spiritual, physical, and social well-being of older adults and their caregivers are intimately connected. Taking this connection into account makes it essential that any intervention efforts with a client also include caregivers using a multifaceted team approach (Prasher, Davidson, & Santos, 2021).

The aging process and working with older adults as a field of study, known as gerontology, did not become popular until the end of the 1930s (Shock, 1987). This increased attention to older adults was related to three major events: (1) the implementation of the Economic Security Act, (2) the development of a scientific basis for the study of the aged, and (3) the dramatic population trends involving older people.

To track this development, it is important to recognize that in the 1930s the United States was experiencing the aftermath of major social changes. As World War I ended, many people were thrust into poverty. The Great Depression made destitute many people who had never been poor before. Faced with these newly and unusually impoverished fellow citizens, American society showed increased willingness to help certain disadvantaged groups, particularly older people and young children (Frank, 1946). At the same time, the country still held a strong work ethic; regardless of age or circumstances, every person was expected to be a productive part of society. It was during this period that the public, among whom social workers were active, began to insist that government take the necessary steps to ensure that the older adults and children did not, through their inability to work, become burdens on society (Stern & Axinn, 2011).

The Economic Security Act of 1935 was a societal response to the problem of widespread unemployment caused by the Great Depression. This act mobilized an unprecedented redistribution of income within society. As a result of this legislation, older citizens were provided with a government-assisted income because they were officially designated as unemployable (Stern & Axinn, 2011). This new guaranteed income helped to make this *worthy* group prosperous enough to command additional professional and societal attention. Also in the 1930s, an improved scientific basis for the study of the aged developed. The year 1942 saw the publication of *Problems of Aging* by E. Cowdry, a collection of papers by eminent scientists from many disciplines that represented the first compilation of scientific data on aging (Shock, 1987, p. 34). It is interesting to note that, following Cowdry's publication, the first issue of the *Journal of Gerontology* appeared in January 1946. This journal claimed to be the first in the field of gerontology and was designed "to provide a medium of communication and of interpretation in our efforts to gain a much surer knowledge of human growth and development" (Frank, 1946, p. 3). The journal represented the Gerontological Society, whose primary interest was to assist older citizens "against the present almost brutal neglect of the aged, by which many have been misused" (Frank, 1946, p. 3). These two publications highlighted the point that science and technology could assist in providing preventative health care for this vulnerable population.

Now, over a half century later, a large body of literature reflects the popularity of aging as a subject of study. Numerous books, textbooks, and classes are offered in this area. Furthermore, chemists, physicians, economists, dentists, psychologists, and social workers are among the professionals who have all contributed to existing knowledge about the aging population. With the increase in technology, it should come as no surprise that according to the 2018 Census approximately 80 percent of older adults live in a household with a computer and 75 percent live in a household with access to the internet (Roberts et al., 2018). The highest rates of internet access were among those aged sixty-five to seventy-four.

Did You Know . . .

The social work profession has a long-standing interest in aging. This interest was expressed as early as 1947 at the National Conference of Social Work. Issues in aging were also included in the 1949 Social Work Yearbook (as cited in Lowry, 1979).

One last reason for the increased attention focused on the needs of older adults was the growth trend predicted for this population. Data collection had reached such a level of sophistication that it was able to track population trends within the 1930s showing that this population group was sure to grow. The growing numbers of older individuals in the late 1930s were clearly documented (Stern & Axinn, 2011), causing much concern, because this group was not always considered capable of contributing to the national economy in terms of work (Frank, 1946). Today, this fear has taken a new direction as many professionals worry that these early attempts at meeting the needs of older individuals and the resulting programs to support them may not be enough. The programs born of good intention under the Economic Security Act to assist this population may no longer suffice. This fear is inspired primarily by expected increases in the numbers of older adults and the extended life spans that older people will enjoy, along with the population growth trends already noted. Given the open advocacy and concern expressed for older adults today as well as the severe financial constraints in our economy, a sense of cautious optimism has developed. However, resistance to providing these services for older adults continues because their problems are often complex and involve an integrated approach to care that highlights health and mental health as well as the social and cultural dimensions (Dziegielewski & Holliman, 2020).

11.3 THEORETICAL FRAMEWORKS FOR PRACTICE WITH OLDER ADULTS

A cornerstone of all social work programs is the acknowledgment of the influence of human growth and development theory. This theoretical framework became popular in the 1970s because its broad approach considers the benefits and challenges that individuals encounter as they mature. The personality of an individual is assumed to be consistent with the way life tasks are developed and managed throughout his or her lifetime (Rhodes, 1988). For older adults, there is a great need to be accepted and participate fully within families and communities (Podnieks, 2006). For social workers borrowing from this psychological theory, the most comprehensive and widely used work reflective in social work courses is that of Erik Erikson (1959). Erikson looked at the psychosocial aspects of human development and outlined eight stages that individuals experience. His model extended beyond childhood and adulthood and recognized the stages that older individuals are most likely to experience (see Box 11.1).

Erikson believed that once an individual had successfully completed all eight stages, he or she would accept the self and take responsibility for his or her own life. In the last developmental stage, integrity versus despair, an individual's life goals reach finalization, and reflection and contemplation become important tasks. Ryff (1982), among others, expanded on Erikson's last developmental stage for older adults by including such tasks as adjusting to their inability to supplement their sense of identity through work. Therefore, individuals become accepting of the physical limitations imposed by the aging process and learn to cope with death while embracing spirituality. Encouraging the connectedness that is often found through spirituality may be one way of staying engaged (Stinson, 2014).

Human growth and development theories are often covered in social work classes and have displaced older theories about how older individuals adjust to their changing societal role. Two of these older theories that deserve mention concern the patterns of behavior related to healthy aging: disengagement theory and activity theory.

BOX 11.1

ERIKSON'S STAGES OF HUMAN DEVELOPMENT

Basic trust versus mistrust
Autonomy versus shame and doubt
Initiative versus guilt
Industry versus inferiority
Identity versus identity diffusion
Intimacy versus self-absorption
General activity versus stagnation
Integrity versus despair

Historically, in their quest to understand the aging process and the milestones that older people attain, social workers considered the concepts of disengagement and activity. These theories postulate that both activity and disengagement from traditional life experiences are normal and natural parts of the aging process.

Disengagement theory, introduced by Cumming and Henry (1961), focused on the normal process of withdrawal from the social environment. It was believed that the aging person would initiate withdrawal from usual life events and acknowledge his or her impending death, reduced physical energy, or poor health. The process of acknowledging the life situation and resulting disengagement was considered beneficial to both the individual and society (see Box 11.2).

Disengagement theory can clarify the need for changes in roles and life transitions. However, most social workers, although they are aware of this theoretical perspective, do not embrace it wholeheartedly. This is especially true because the research on disengagement theory has been limited, controversial, and contradictory. The extent to which older adults will practice disengagement after leaving mainstream society remains unclear. Furthermore, some individuals do not separate, but stay engaged by changing the focus of their activities. More research is needed to determine whether disengagement is a natural part of the aging process while recognizing that the concepts can be helpful in identifying the transitions that could occur.

The roots of activity theory are based in the idea that the older adult has the same social and psychological needs as the middle-aged adult. Early proponents of activity theory believed that professional intervention involved helping the client to continue an active existence. For example, a social worker might encourage an older adult to do volunteer work to replace previously paid employment (see Box 11.3).

Today, most social workers collaborating with older people should be aware of these older theories and of the influence they have had on current perceptions of the aging process. To date, there are newer theoretical perspectives that can help to better explain the process of aging that help to create a direct link between measuring the level of activity and life satisfaction. The unique aspects relative to successful aging are linked to specific goal recognition, identification, and acquisition. One such model is *goal systems*

BOX 11.2

DISENGAGEMENT THEORY

According to proponents of disengagement theory, the role of the social worker is to help the client to disengage from mainstream society. This allows a natural transition by physically separating the individual from mainstream life and fostering an adjustment period. Disengagement is viewed as an inevitable process that every aging individual must undergo. If a person resists this natural process of letting go, then problems in adjustment to the elderly years will develop (Cumming & Henry, 1961).

> **BOX 11.3**
>
> **ACTIVITY THEORY**
>
> The concepts of activity theory were introduced before disengagement theory, but activity theory was not formalized until 1972 with the work of Lemon, Bengston, and Peterson. These authors were among the first to evaluate activity theory in relation to reported life satisfaction. They hypothesized that, as activity increased, life satisfaction would also increase; conversely, as role loss increased, life satisfaction would decrease. Basically, getting older is characterized by the desire to remain middle aged. Therefore, for aging to be successful, older individuals need to continue to participate in activities like those that were important in middle age (Lemon, Bengston, & Peterson, 1972).

theory, which helps to conceptualize human motivation. From this perspective, goals are organized in a hierarchical structure and the means to attaining them are outlined (Heckhausen et al., 2021). A goal system is developed, either *multifinal* (achieving several goals at the same time) or *equifinal* (different paths can all lead to achievement). When developing a goal system, progress is defined as maximizing attainment as the measure of success.

Two other approaches that are related to goal awareness and attainment are the *motivational theory of life-span development* and the *selection, optimization, and compensation model*. The first approach, goal systems theory, tends to be more focused on motivation, and the other two models are more focused on healthy aging and adopting life-span developmental processes of goal change. For an excellent resource on the application of these models, see Heckhausen et al. (2021).

Taking these historical and current goal acquisition perspectives into account, the social worker has a significant role in highlighting the need for older adults to maximize the positive experiences in their lives while minimizing the negative ones. All conceptual frameworks, especially those related to goal setting, provide avenues for intervention that can support activities related to measuring change. To assist people with transition in the older years, social workers help to create an environment where successful aging can occur. Assistance with this transition is so important as people are working longer and the age of retirement continues to increase. From a healthy aging perspective, under the pressure of working longer, older adults may try to continue previous levels of activity while possibly experiencing mobility-limiting chronic health conditions (Vanajan, Bultmann, & Henkens, 2022).

In summary, the above theories have all been described to help you focus on ways to better understand normal aging and how to best assist older adults in identifying the transitions that will need to be addressed. Whatever theoretical practice framework is used, more empirical research is needed to support the utility of developmental theories in working with all populations, including older adults. For setting up treatment plans, the goal-based theories may respond best to research-related endeavors.

Ryff (1982) argued that to better understand which model works best, the factors that result in accomplishment of Erikson's developmental stages should be isolated and those that allow older adults to achieve optimal levels of performance should be examined. This argument is still valid. However, it is important to add another caution about these theories, especially the older ones such as disengagement and activity theory, namely that, because of when they were written, they could incorporate underlying classist and racist or sexist biases. Research has not proven that one single theory is comprehensive enough to explain all life changes experienced by older adults. Furthermore, although many interventions that were originally developed for younger persons may work well with older adults, modifications may be needed, especially in adjusting goals and how the older adult may respond to challenges (Heckhausen et al., 2021).

Social workers believe that theory must be consistent with social work values and expectations and provides the cornerstone of the interventions that emerge. When selecting an intervention, social workers must recognize how societal perspectives on aging can influence all intervention outcomes. Whether or not these theories are valid, the fact that professionals and laypeople believe them may strongly affect their expectations and behavior. Keeping an open mind and avoiding uncritical adherence are central to keeping practitioners thinking about alternative explanations for clients' behavior and trying innovative problem-solving techniques. Furthermore, each older adult is indeed an individual, and circumstances can vary. What they share, however, is that all will have to face objective losses in the body and the mind, and anything that helps to address these expected changes may lay a foundation for future acceptance (Heckhausen et al., 2021).

As individuals age, it is common for them to become frustrated with what their bodies can and cannot do and with their lack of ability to complete tasks that used to be so much easier. As the older adult continues to age, his or her ability to act and manage independent living activities is sure to be affected; therefore, including the family and recognizing the role of supportive networks are critical to situation betterment and treatment success (Dziegielewski & Holliman, 2020).

11.4 HEALTH, MENTAL HEALTH, AND THE OLDER ADULT

How often have you heard someone describe an aged loved one as "dying of old age?" How often have you heard professionals encourage this notion? How often have you seen or heard of an older person who consulted a physician about a certain ache or pain only to be told that the pain was simply related to old age? Dying of old age is a myth that should not be propagated (see Box 11.4).

Social workers must always give older clients the respect they deserve, allowing them to state their concerns in a nonjudgmental atmosphere. Remember that no one ever died of old age! The aging process is further complicated by the stigma that can be

> **BOX 11.4**
>
> **THE PAIN IN MY ELBOW**
>
> A ninety-year-old man visits a physician for pain in the elbow joint of his right arm. After the client explains his symptoms to the physician, the physician says, "You are ninety years old. It is possible that the pain is merely related to your age, and there may be no plausible medical explanation for your pain." After hearing this theory, the patient thought for a moment and asked, "If your idea is tenable, why doesn't my other elbow hurt? It is the same age."

placed on getting older. This focus on the negatives can affect not only older individuals themselves, but also how they are perceived by the community as well as other health professionals and contribute to the perpetuation of ageism, both internalized and toward others. Avoiding stereotyping and actively listening to older individuals, including those with severe mental illness, can improve patient–provider relations (Schroeder, 2013). There are many causes of social isolation in older persons, including such serious conditions as chronic illness and visual, hearing, or cognitive impairment or decreased physical functioning and medical frailty that may be caused by heart disease, cancer, and stroke (Aldwin & Gilmer, 2013). When death occurs as the result of a medical condition, it should never be dismissed as dying of old age. This attitude can lead to actual diseases going undetected if clients and medical providers assume that symptoms characteristic of disease are simply related to the aging process.

> ## Helpful Point . . .
>
> Social workers should encourage clients who are approaching retirement to contact the Social Security Administration and obtain a copy of their lifetime earnings report. They should do this each year to verify the amount earned and credited toward their retirement. Any problems can be corrected with documentation of salary, but it is best to catch errors early rather than waiting until retirement.

> ## Did You Know . . .
>
> The knowledge that no one dies of old age is not new. For example, Mosher-Ashley (1994), in an archival study of records on 298 clients treated by a mental health center, found that issues surrounding death often revolved around life situation problems such as: (1) family conflicts, (2) poor physical health, and (3) feeling that they were not in control of their lives.

The recognition of how functional decline is attributable to medical or mental disorders rather than normal aging has made it easier to diagnose certain disorders and to establish subsequent treatment modalities. Older adults deserve the same professional treatment as any other age group, and social work professionals have a role in educating and helping all clients to secure the specific health services they need.

The increased numbers of older adults have led to increased concern related to health care services utilization. The 2022 Social Threats to Aging Well in America survey is an excellent resource that makes a compelling case that client system factors referred to as environmental factors clearly have an effect on the health and mental health of older adults. These social determinants of health can be important in identifying the factors that contribute to providing respectful and deserved health care opportunities. In this 2022 study, the top three social barriers identified related to access of care were economic instability, loneliness, and food insecurity (Cass, 2022).

In addition, Dr. Dinesh Kumar, Alignment Healthcare chief medical and chief operating officer (cited in Cass, 2022), said there were seven things all professionals should know when working with older populations. First, many older adults may see other priorities that affect daily living as more important than their own health and medical care. The priorities varied, with other expenses such as housing, family, and other concerns coming first. A second concern was paying for medication or related medical supplies. The third and fourth concerns related to paying existing medical bills or having unpaid medical debt. The fifth concern related to feeling lonelier and isolated from others than they did in the previous year. It is important to note, however, that this survey was done when many older adults may have been ill with COVID-19 and under isolation precautions. A sixth concern related to the increased cost of groceries and being able to select from healthier, high-cost food alternatives. The final concern was that it was often too difficult to get consistent access to transportation to and from medical care visits. This concern was coupled with limitations on their access to technology (phones, internet, telecare services) (Alignment Health Care, 2022). Since older individuals are more likely to experience medical concerns and chronic conditions that require continued care, these concerns related to accessing and affording medical care can be well founded.

Based on sheer numbers, older adults are important consumers of health care. Tan (2009) warned, however, that regardless of all the research on the subject, a clear consensus is lacking among studies regarding the measurement of service use. This concern continues today because service use is often defined by the type of service utilized. For example, hospital use by older individuals received a strong boost in 1965 with the initiation of Title XVIII (Medicare), one of the amendments to the Economic Security Act of 1935, which provided health insurance for older adults, a high-risk group in terms of vulnerability to illness and poverty (Stern & Axinn, 2011), and Medicare was viewed as one of the largest health insurance programs in the world (National Bureau of Economic Research, n.d). Medicare's introduction in 1965 was, and remains to date, the single largest change in health insurance coverage for older adults in U.S. history.

Medicare is the closest program we have in the United States to universal health insurance, providing services to adults age sixty-five and older as well as to many with disabilities, resulting in recent calls for Medicare for all.

As people age, they are more likely to need health care services. Since 1965 and the implementation of Title XVIII, however, regardless of the difficulty in defining what is meant by services, the increase in health care consumption at age sixty-five has been dramatic. Medicare brought health care benefits to older people who could not afford them otherwise; physicians and hospitals also benefitted from the greater assurance of payment for providing needed health care services. The benefits to health care recipients and providers, however, came at a particularly high price for the federal government. As the cost of services continued to escalate, the government became determined to control Medicare expenditures (Starr, 1982).

In 1983, Congress mandated a radical change in the payment structure for hospital care to rescue the Hospital Insurance Trust Fund from imminent bankruptcy (Lee, Forthofor, & Taube, 1985). The original system required Medicare to pay whatever hospitals charged for a particular service. Faced with these various and fluctuating costs, the government wanted to achieve uniformity and predictability. To control costs and develop an equitable payment system, diagnostic related groups (DRGs) were developed (Begly, 1985).

The formal DRG system instituted in the past served as the basis for grouping individuals who had similar diagnoses, regardless of age or general health status. Each diagnostic category was assigned a particular standard of care, including the length of stay for which the government was willing to pay—for example, gallbladder removal was allowed seven days of hospital treatment. This system thus had a fixed payment schedule, and hospitals knew how much money they would receive for everyone. Unfortunately, for older people, who are more fragile and often have chronic or complicating conditions, this system and its newer derivatives remain problematic.

Today, similar problems exist because little incentive exists for hospitals to accept patients who may require extended stays. When hospitals do accept older patients, many social workers have noted that they are discharged as quickly as possible. Quick discharges are problematic because discharge options may be limited, especially for weakened older adults who also have limited incomes and few community-related supports. Extended care facilities may be reluctant to take these recently discharged individuals because their current condition is medically less stable. In addition, facility staff become stressed when these new patients require much more care and observation. Inadequate placement options can lead to readmission, which is costly for the individual and for the hospital.

The Affordable Care Act

To help address health care financing concerns and out-of-control spending, legislation such as the Affordable Care Act (ACA) was passed (Centers for Medicare and Medicaid Services, 2012). The ACA, enacted in 2010, seeks to hold insurance companies accountable by setting standards for reform that allow for lower health care costs while guaranteeing more choices that enhance quality of care. The ACA supports health care changes as well as improvements in health care access, quality, and service. At present, this plan remains in effect and websites and other supporting structures are in place to facilitate enrollment and coverage options. As of 2022, most efforts to repeal this act have been abandoned and employers are urged to re-examine their existing ACA Employer Mandates responsibilities (Sheen, 2022a). As of 2022, 14.5 million Americans elected to receive this health care coverage during the open enrollment period, with a total of 31 million now benefiting from ACA-related coverage, such as Medicaid and Medicare purchased from the marketplace (Sheen, 2022b). Programs such as this continue to evolve and require that all health care professionals be open to change while balancing quality of care and utilizing evidence-based practices that are effective and cost-efficient.

Effectiveness in working specifically with older adults involves patient/client/consumer advocacy at the most basic level. In this system of care, health care professionals will decide, with the input of consumers, who will qualify for and receive services (Dziegielewski & Holliman, 2020). Therefore, education about and awareness of the services offered have never been more important. Social workers are trained to address the psychosocial needs of the patients served and to support an important continuum of care that is essential for linking the person to the environment (Ofosu, 2011). The time has come for social workers to embrace illness prevention that can help to minimize the effects of chronic illness on individuals, families, and their support systems (Zabora, 2011). These efforts have been hailed as critical to tertiary prevention; when applied properly, they can lead to the detection of psychological distress. When the stresses related to chronic illness are not identified and addressed, they can magnify medical symptoms experienced, such as pain and other somatic complaints (Zabora, 2011).

Medicare, Medicaid, and the ACA—and insurance reimbursement in general—are of particular interest to social workers working with older adults because they are the ones who generally handle the discharge and placement of older clients in both nursing home and hospital settings. Social workers must be aware of community supports for discharge back into the community and the availability of special treatment or services. Discharging older people who cannot complete their own activities of daily living may place great stress on the family and home services extended care staff. Few experienced professionals would argue that, with discharges back to the community, long term care admissions could be more likely when family stressors with providing care to loved ones increases. Measures should be taken to allow families to communicate needs, problem solve, and participate in support groups. Social workers provide an excellent entry point for supportive and educational services for both older adult clients and caregivers. Placing an older client who needs a great deal of individual care into a long-term care facility can also create great stress for the staff. Support groups and regular in-service training on how to treat these clients is mandatory. If additional staff is needed to facilitate placement, social workers should recommend such support.

Ryan and Super (2003) refers to Medicare beneficiaries who are also eligible for Medicaid as duals. This high-risk group is of sufficiently low income to qualify for Medicaid and tends to have more health-related problems than nondual older adults. The chronic conditions from which older adults often suffer are either physical (biological or physiological) or mental (psychological) in nature. We make this distinction only for simplicity's sake; it is important to remain aware that physical and mental health conditions are often related and interdependent. For example, a physical event such as a stroke may develop into the mental health condition dementia. Also, several stress-related conditions can complicate the medical condition an individual is suffering from.

The worst fear for so many frail older adults is that of developing a chronic health condition because it can impair activity and hamper independence. Fear of drug dependence and living in pain can be difficult for the older adult to overcome. Because of this fear of medications and the recent acceptance by many states of the use of medical marijuana, older adults are increasingly turning to cannabis to treat many medical and chronic conditions (Manning & Bouchard, 2021).

> **Did You Know . . .**
> A chronic condition is defined as a condition or disease that lasts a long time. An acute condition, in contrast, often starts quickly and affects the individual greatly, but generally lasts for only a short duration once treatment has been received. Weakened older adults are affected more by chronic than by acute conditions.

Physical Health Conditions and the Older Adult

The older adult faces many challenges in aging, including declines in cognitive and physical abilities (Heckhausen et al., 2021). As the numbers of older adults are growing globally, so are the numbers of physical and mental health-related illnesses (Tiwari et al., 2013). Many older people fear the loss of individual unaided activity or perceived independence. When assessing an older adult, the social worker must first look carefully at the signs and symptoms that occur and whether these symptoms can be explained by medically related factors (Aldwin & Gilmer, 2013). For example, has the individual been placed on a new medication? Medications should be monitored carefully for all individuals, but in older people, for whom slower metabolisms are the norm, metabolizing drugs and the way the older person responds to a medication may not be as easy to predict as they are for younger people (Dziegielewski & Jacinto, 2016). Furthermore, Maust, Oslin, and Marcus (2014) found that although many older adults were less likely to have a psychiatric disorder, they were often prescribed mental health medications. The authors therefore advocate more control of the medications that are being prescribed to this population. To address this issue completely, it is important to ensure that a general medical practitioner has been consulted with completion of a general medical exam.

Of all physical health conditions, heart disease remains the leading cause of death among those aged sixty-five or older in the United States and worldwide (Nichols, 2019). This is followed by cancer, according to the American Cancer Society, with the most common cause in males and females being lung and bronchus cancer (American Cancer Society, 2019). Although these conditions (excluding cancer) are considered acute, patients often gradually fall prey to chronic conditions such as paralysis and mental impairment that result in some type of major neurocognitive condition. Other major chronic conditions that result in the restriction of activity include arthritis, hearing, and vision impairments.

Among vision conditions, cataracts and glaucoma are the most common. Social workers should always encourage older clients suffering from vision impairments to receive regular checkups to aid in detecting such conditions before permanent damage results. It is also important for social workers to consider how decreased vision can affect the counseling relationship (Dziegielewski, 2015). For example, an older client may not want to admit that he cannot easily read written material or navigate in a particular setting. Even for the oldest-old adults with vision impairment, exercises and activities adapted to their capabilities are always encouraged (Hackney, Hall, Echt, & Wolf, 2013).

Special attention should also be paid to hearing loss in clients. Someone who seems withdrawn and unresponsive to conversation may simply be suffering from hearing loss; they may be hearing only part of what is said and guessing the rest (Dziegielewski, 2015). If the client's response is not appropriate, it can seem like confusion. Family members may believe that their aged relative is becoming confused or simply ignoring them. Communication problems tend to increase the stress felt by family members (Dziegielewski & Holliman, 2020).

Social work professionals should always be aware that older adults are often shocked and embarrassed by changes in their health and that these feelings may lead to denial. We can all understand reluctance to admit individual inadequacy. Counseling and interviewing should include an initial assessment to determine whether health concerns are affecting the interview process.

Mental Health and the Older Adult

Older individuals suffer many life circumstances that can affect their mental health. According to the Centers for Disease Control, good mental health is essential to overall health and well-being and should be addressed for all adults, including older adults, with the same level and urgency as physical health. Although all older adults can experience mental health concerns that are treatable, some racial and ethnic minorities may experience increased obstacles in maintaining positive mental health (Centers for Disease Control, 2022a). Since the onset of COVID-19, for example, rates of mental health concerns for some racial and ethnic minorities have increased when compared to that of non-Hispanic White people (Thomeer, Moody, & Yahirun, 2022).

As people age, it is virtually impossible not to experience traumatic life-changing events. Common stressful life events include loss of a spouse, social and occupational losses, and physical health problems. They may also be affected by criminal victimization and any health concerns that may result from such attacks and injuries. Because of the sheer number of life tragedies that older people have faced, it would seem logical that they would seek more mental health services than other population groups; however, this is often not the case. Many older individuals do not openly seek mental health services. One reason for this is the method of delivery. When living in the community, older psychiatric clients go to community mental health centers for checkups and medication; many older adults refuse these services because they do not want to leave their homes (Dziegielewski & Holliman, 2020).

DEPRESSION

For many social work practitioners, clients who report symptoms of depression are commonplace, with older adults being at increased risk of experiencing depressive symptoms (Centers for Disease Control, 2022b). Nearly thirty million people in the U.S. adult population may be affected with major depression, and many of them are classified as severely depressed. Because depressive feelings are reported so frequently during routine medical visits and throughout the course of psychological treatment, depressive symptoms can seem like the common cold of mental health. Therefore, it comes as no surprise that depression is a significant mental health problem for older adults, one frequently associated with physical symptoms and illness.

Although depression may be a common symptom, it is not a normal part of the aging process (Casey, 2017). The symptoms of depression are considered important indicators for general health and wellness. Depressive disorders in the older population are prevalent and can be highly associated with medical conditions, particularly those of a chronic nature (Woodward, Taylor, Abelson, & Matusko, 2013).

Although it is obvious that depression occurs in older adults, measuring what it means to everyone is not easy. Unfortunately, many older adults may deny what they are feeling and avoid seeking treatment for depression or any other mental health condition. Yet depression in older adults remains a treatable medical condition (Casey, 2017). Depression is also believed to be related to suicide rates. Older adults aged seventy-five and older account for less than 10 percent of suicides, but they have the highest suicide rate (19.1 per 100,000), with men aged seventy-five and older having the highest suicide rate overall (40.5 per 100,000) when compared to other age groups (Centers for Disease Control and Prevention, 2022).

Common signs and symptoms of depression include feelings of sadness, loneliness, guilt, boredom, marked decrease or increase in appetite, increase or decrease in sleep behavior, and a sense of worthlessness (Dziegielewski, 2015). For older adults, as the circadian rhythms change with advanced age, getting good, restful sleep becomes more difficult (Rybarczyk, Lund, Garroway, & Mack, 2013). Insomnia, characteristic of disturbed sleep, can easily affect mood as well as cognitive and behavioral responses.

When depression occurs in response to life circumstances, it is called *situational*. Situational depression is a particular risk for older adults because they endure many tragedies, including loss of loved ones, jobs, status, and independence, as well as other personal disappointments. Feelings of depression can be triggered by such experiences as bereavement for a deceased loved one or frustration with a medical condition (Dziegielewski & Holliman, 2020). Of particular concern when working with older adults are the additional problems that can accompany increased mortality and chronic medical conditions. Older individuals who have increased limitations in mobility and the ability to carry out activities of daily living, self-perceived poor health, life dissatisfaction, and cardiac problems are at the highest risk for poor outcomes and recovery (Woo & Keatinge, 2008).

Social work intervention and counseling can help older clients to deal with situational depression and achieve greater life satisfaction. For example, social workers can teach older adults how to control the frequency of their depressive thoughts and to use relaxation techniques, such as imagery and deep muscle relaxation, to calm themselves during anxious times. Concrete problem-solving and behavioral contracting can be used to help the older client change problem behaviors. Whenever possible, family members should be included in treatment contracting because they can provide support and assist in recording and observing behaviors that the older client is seeking to change.

Caution should always be used, however, because not all cases of depression in older individuals are situational. Some cases of depression may arise directly from internal causes; these are called *endogenous* depression. Furthermore, the etiology of depression in older adults is not always distinct; depression may be the result of a combination of situational and endogenous factors. For example, many chronic medical conditions, such as hypothyroidism, Addison's disease, Parkinson's disease, Alzheimer's disease, and congestive heart failure, are often accompanied by depression. It is also possible that symptoms of depression are by-products or side effects of medication taken for another condition (Dziegielewski, 2015; Dziegielewski & Jacinto, 2016) or symptoms of something else. The American Psychiatric Association (2022) has warned that the diagnosis of depression in older adults can be particularly problematic because the symptoms of dementia in its initial stages and those of depression are remarkably similar. Symptoms such as loss of interest and pleasure in usual activities, disorientation, and memory loss are common to the two conditions. There is one significant difference, however. Although many signs and symptoms are the same, a person in the initial stages of dementia will rarely improve with treatment.

For the beginning social work professional, working with clients who are depressed can be frightening. You may feel uncertain about what questions to ask or what to do if they tell you they would like to harm themselves. This makes it a practice necessity to gather a detailed social, medical, and medication history as soon as possible. In addition, older clients with depression should always be referred for medical examination to rule out any physical reasons for depressive symptoms. Depression is most dangerous when it is unrecognized. When implemented, treatment for depression in the older adult is as effective as it is with other age groups (Dziegielewski & Holliman, 2020).

Continued Care Options and the Need for Extended Care

The current trend is for many older people with mental impairment who cannot be handled at home or in the community to be discharged to rehabilitation and/or long-term care facilities. This practice has increased because of the deinstitutionalization that over the past thirty-three years has reduced state mental health hospitals to one-third their former capacity and thus eliminated an important placement option (Dziegielewski & Holliman, 2020). In response to the consequent need for more constricted placement, many privately run long-term care facilities, including adult congregate living facilities (boarding homes) and nursing homes providing intermediate and skilled care, have been opened. In the past thirty years, the number of nursing homes has increased dramatically in the United States, with 2016 numbers reporting 15,600 facilities; the proportion of nursing homes that are for profit is 69.3 percent (National Center for Health Statistics, 2019). These homes provide a discharge option for older clients with mental impairment that other population groups do not have. Most patients admitted to long-term care facilities are older than sixty-five.

Dziegielewski and Holliman (2020) warn that long-term care facilities, although convenient, are inappropriate placement options for older adults with mental impairment because these facilities do not provide mental health services. Furthermore, too many long-term care facilities provide minimal psychosocial interventions, with medication being the primary method of treatment. Beginning social work professionals must exercise caution when placing a client in a long-term care facility, especially if the client needs mental health services. Each facility is different. Social workers must be aware not only of what long-term facilities exist in an area but also which services the different facilities offer to older clients with mental impairment. Because many older adults fear functional activity loss, social workers must be aware of this fear, regardless of whether such loss has occurred. Such worries have a real foundation. Because many older individuals suffer from chronic conditions, the probability that these conditions will improve is low. It is important to support the individual client as well as his or her caregiver by giving him or her as much freedom of choice as possible when selecting a facility and the treatment to be received (Zegwaard, Aartsen, Grypdonck, & Cuijpers, 2013).

Older adults who do not need inpatient or round-the-clock care still may require caregiving assistance to allow them to leave the home and continue working. Caregiving can be as serious an issue for older couples as for younger couples. Working with both the client and the caregiver highlights the connection that fosters well-being for both (Kim et al., 2013). For all extended families, the need for eldercare services will become a reality (Dziegielewski & Holliman, 2020). Upon the client's return to home or community living, the provision of older adult day care services, similar to child day care services, can help these families. Social workers should advocate for companies to consider adding elder care as a standard option in employee benefit packages.

Our society tends to deny that problems may be terminal. Family members and some professionals may tell aged people that they will get better, rather than helping them to develop ways to cope (Dziegielewski & Holliman, 2020). It is important for social work practitioners to be knowledgeable about common chronic conditions, their signs and symptoms, their expected progression, and when and where to refer clients for additional treatment. There is considerable evidence that the involvement and support of family members is important in creating a general sense of well-being for older adults (Dziegielewski & Holliman, 2020). The social worker is essential in educating aged clients and their family members to cope with and understand changes that will occur. A comprehensive assessment of the individual, including health conditions and environmental factors, is critical.

11.5 COMMUNITY CARE AND CASE MANAGEMENT

Case management is a collaborative process that assesses, plans, implements, coordinates, monitors, and evaluates the options and services required to meet an individual's health needs, using communication and available resources to promote high-quality, cost-effective outcomes (Mullahy, 1998). Case management services for older individuals are considered an important and necessary service for the continuity of care often designed to address loneliness and isolation (Austin & McClelland, 2009). Case management services with older individuals, like those provided to recipients of all ages, seek to ensure that all clients receive the services they need in a system that sometimes appears fragmented and difficult to navigate. The tasks in case management can vary; however, for older adults these services can include the concrete tasks of completing psychosocial assessments, initiating, and implementing advanced directives, connecting to resources, obtaining insurance verification for hospital stays, accessing community resources, and obtaining referrals for services and durable medical equipment. They can also include more supportive services, such as counseling. All these services are designed to help the individual maintain his or her status in the community. Social support and connectedness remain important ingredients in continued well-being and can provide the support needed (Waite, Iveniuk, & Laumann, 2014).

> ### Did You Know . . .
> Two general terms are often used in the medical community to describe the process of getting older. The first, aging, is defined as the condition of growing older regardless of chronological age; the second, senescence, is used to characterize the process of deterioration that occurs in the later years of an individual's life.

For the older adult, community-based care and case management services often begin with assessing the person-in-situation. This clearly involves addressing the client and the client system together. For example, what type of support system does the older adult have to stay in the community safely? When support systems are severely limited or do not exist, a client can refuse to consider more restrictive care. Therefore, it is a delicate issue when a client who is unable to handle activities of daily living or personal affairs refuses to go to a nursing home.

In the broadest sense, the social work case manager is the person who links the client and the client system to the health care system, thereby influencing both the quality of the outcome and the cost. Roles are diverse, but the case manager can facilitate an earlier, more supported, and stable discharge when a client has been hospitalized; negotiate a better fee from a medical equipment supplier; or encourage the family to assume responsibility for assisting with the day-to-day care for an older relative. In addition, the social worker can serve as a catalyst for change by seeking solutions that promote identification, improvement, or stabilization of the client's concerns. Often the social worker may have to arrange home health care for the patient, nursing home placement, provision of medical equipment, hospice care, transplants, or simply transportation (Nelson & Powers, 2001). To ensure that individual worth, dignity, and safety are maintained, the social worker must consider the wishes of the client and the client's system, including the client's family, the needs of the client, and the potential for future growth in this environment.

11.6 EMPLOYMENT AND OLDER ADULTS

Today, problems associated with unemployment in the United States are inspiring social work professionals to look seriously at the social and economic consequences of being without a job. The number of older Americans, people aged seventy-five and older, is expected to grow by 96.5 percent in the next decade (Yee, 2022). At the same time, a growing number of low-paying and minimum wage jobs are not being filled. Having to address these problems has made the public aware of the specific experiences of certain groups, such as older adults. Currently, the trend toward early retirement, in conjunction with the diminishing number of youths entering the workforce (because of lower birth rates), has created interest in older adults as a potential source of labor to help fill this gap. When people live longer and maintain good health employment remains possible and can assist with an underutilized labor pool (see Figure 11.2). In addition to societal need, many older individuals who enjoy good health see continued employment as desirable. Loss of the work role and the steady income it provides can be a big step for anyone to take. Furthermore, it is common for an older adult to be called on to help younger extended family members.

Living Longer, Working Longer

Over the past forty years, older individuals have become better educated and wealthier than previous generations. With ten thousand adults turning sixty-five each day, it is essential to understand the needs of older adults and what could impede their health

FIGURE 11.2
People who are living longer and healthier remain viable employees and constitute an underutilized labor pool.

and wellness (Cass, 2022). Attracting those who have retired back into the workforce, especially those individuals who may seek continued employment to supplement income can serve to assist financially while also creating an opportunity for continued meaningful engagement. Unfortunately, if an older adult decides to return to work, there is no guarantee that he or she will get a job or be able to use the skills learned from their years of previous employment. Regardless of protective legislation, age discrimination can and still does exist in the job market. There are many ways to subtly avoid hiring older adults, especially in nontrained positions that require physical agility. In addition, many jobs now require an application and search process that involves the use of a computer and access to the internet. The expectation of online application has increased and now most positions require an internet application process. For older individuals, particularly those with low income, this can be problematic and serve as a block to seeking employment.

Until recently, Social Security rules created an unnecessary barrier for seniors who wished to work. Seniors who worked full- or part-time and earned income over a certain level were penalized for working by having their Social Security checks reduced (see Box 11.5). The U.S. Congress continues to address this issue while proposing strategies that would decrease and/or eliminate this penalty and allow seniors to earn as much as they can while retaining their retirement checks.

Social work professionals assist older clients returning to the workforce in several ways. First, social workers must encourage older clients to update or learn new skills so that they can remain competitive throughout their careers. This is especially important because of the rapid technological advances occurring today, as well as the use of computer and automation technologies in most occupational settings. For an older client,

> **BOX 11.5**
> **SOCIAL SECURITY RETIREMENT BENEFITS**
>
> At one time, people talked about retiring at age sixty-five. Retirement age has increased for most people, as indicated in the following table. Can you retire at any age? Sure, but if you retire earlier than full retirement age, your monthly Social Security check will be reduced. An eligible person may begin receiving retirement checks at age sixty-two or delay receiving checks while working past retirement age. Note that the longer you wait to collect your benefits, the larger your monthly checks will be.
>
> | Year of birth | Full retirement | Age (years) | Reduction of benefits for retiring early* |
> |---|---|---|---|
> | 1937 or earlier | | 65.0 | 20% |
> | 1940 | | 65.6 | 22.5% |
> | 1943–1954 | | 66.0 | 25% |
> | 1960 and later | | 67.0 | 30% |
>
> *Source*: U.S. Social Security Administration (n.d.). *Retirement Planner: Benefits by Year of Birth*. Retrieved from http://www.socialsecurity.gov/retire2/agereduction.htm
>
> *Early retirement is at age sixty-two. An advantage of early retirement is that you collect your benefit for a longer period (if you live). The disadvantage is that your monthly check is permanently reduced by some percentage for the remainder of your life.

learning and maintaining these types of skills can be frightening. This apprehension creates the need for the next point of social work intervention.

Second, social workers must work with employers to make job sites more worker friendly while linking older clients to larger support systems. Programs are often needed to accommodate older workers. These may include work schedule modifications such as job sharing between two or more workers, flextime schedules, and reduced workweeks. Furthermore, programs that are designed to build worker skills, motivation, and self-confidence need to be made available, either by the employer through in-house programs or through community-based programs. Programs that create specialized job assistance provide an excellent practice environment in which social workers can help older workers to become re-employed.

Retirement Life Changes

Retirement from the workforce has been viewed in diverse ways over the years. Attitudes toward retirement have changed with changes in social, emotional, political, and cultural climates. To illustrate how the view of retirement has changed, we will present a brief history of the role of older adults in the labor force.

> **Activity**
> Go to the Social Security Administration web page and use the online retirement planner to estimate your monthly Social Security benefit check. What do you find? Is this what you thought you would get? Can you live on this amount of money?

The early twentieth century saw a shift from an agrarian to an urban industrial economy in the United States (Stern & Axinn, 2011). In an agrarian society, all family members were viewed as contributing members of a cohesive unit. The family was responsible for meeting all the needs of its individual members, including older family members. Industrialization changed this perspective, establishing different expectations and roles, and many left the farm community to seek other types of income.

During the age of industrialization (1890–1912), one member's income was not enough to support the entire family, and often work outside the home by all family members, including women, children, and the aged, became mandatory (Stern & Axinn, 2011). The participation of all these groups in the labor force did not last long, however. Family members left the workforce for two primary reasons: (1) industrialization required fewer workers in the production of output and (2) an influx of new immigrants made far more workers available (Morrison, 1982). Women, children, and older adults were no longer needed to supplement the workforce. It was in this era that the public became increasingly aware of the growth in the number of older adults. Morrison (1982) attributed this increased interest to worries that this large population might compete with younger workers for limited jobs.

The Economic Security Act of 1935 was the first time the government acknowledged responsibility for providing the elderly with an income that did not depend on continuing participation in the labor market. "The Social Security Act . . . set up a national system of old age insurance . . . which legitimized retirement at age 65" (Morrison, 1982, p. 9). This act supported limited, although permanent, economic guarantees to elderly adults. According to Morrison, Social Security helped to ensure that retirement benefits would moderate the reduction in income that workers faced when they left the labor market, and it helped to establish sixty-five years as the encouraged or expected retirement age.

The lives of older adults have not changed radically over the past fifty years; what has changed, however, is society's view of these individuals and how it acts on this view. In working with older clients, social workers must be aware of the following aspects of retirement and how they can affect the lives of the aged. Over the short span of forty years, retirement has become an important concern of the American people; every day, articles and commentaries appear in publications throughout the country on the economic, social, and psychological consequences of retirement (see the activity below).

In the past, it was clear that this interest in retirement was heightened by the rising costs of public and private retirement benefits, and now fluctuating investment opportunities make confidence in sustained viability almost impossible. Today, this concern about the viability of the Social Security System continues, and added to it is the fear of many individuals that they will not be able to afford to retire because of the rising cost of living and health care expenses.

As baby boomers approach retirement age, fiscal concerns increase related to whether the Social Security system can handle the inevitable growth in the number of beneficiaries in view of the recent downturns in our economy. Social work intervention can be critical in helping an aged client make a successful transition from the role of worker to the new role of retiree. It is important, however, that the social worker clearly communicate with older clients about their role in the delivery of services. For example, preretirement planning is one of the services a social worker can provide to assist in the transition process. Through counseling and more specific assistance, the social worker can help aged clients to plan for the role adjustment they will face. Since many people gain status or identity through employment providing internal and external rewards, giving up gainful employment may not be easy. Some older people can afford to retire, but given the current reality, both politically and socially, people may simply be afraid to do so. Regardless of the reason for retirement, it is important to plan leisure time as carefully as previous work time. Social workers must be sensitive to the desire for leisure time but understand that it may need to be planned to make it fulfilling.

Activity

Retirement involves both endings and beginnings. Look at your own retirement and think about your beginnings and endings. To assess your endings, consider what your life will be like when you retire. Think about your paycheck, alarm clock, commute, and other aspects of your life that will change.

What Will End	Will You Miss It?	
	Yes	No
1. _____	_____	_____
2. _____	_____	_____
3. _____	_____	_____
4. _____	_____	_____

When you think about your beginnings, consider what you will miss from your work environment and what can you replace it with. For example, you might miss managing projects, and you might replace this task with volunteering in a program that requires management skills.

continues

continued

Miss	Replace
1. _____	_____
2. _____	_____
3. _____	_____
4. _____	_____
5. _____	_____

Source: Arnone, Kavouras, and Nissenbaum (2001).

To plan leisure time, the degree and type of activity that a client can perform (and afford) must be considered. The social worker and client can together create a list of options and discuss each option in a problem-solving, decision-making manner. Once they have chosen an appropriate leisure activity, they can develop an individual contract. The contracting of leisure time activity can give the client permission to engage in restful activities that can provide structure to an otherwise ambiguous period in life.

Financial concerns, including the fear of not having enough income or of being inundated with medical bills and having difficulty securing health insurance, may also deter an older individual from entering retirement. Concerns such as this can mount and may cause an individual approaching retirement to delay it, if possible. There has not been a clear link between suicide and retirement, but the changes in the economic, social, and emotional contexts of a client's life can be severe, causing difficulties in any transitions that are yet to come (Dziegielewski & Holliman, 2020). A social worker must be aware of the resources available to the older client and must help the client to obtain adequate financial counseling. Employers often will provide such counseling on request. Insurance brokers can be consulted about health and life insurance. These brokers can discuss numerous policy options because they represent several different companies.

When conducting retirement counseling, social workers should always remember that people often resist change and avoid what they cannot predict. Many people approaching retirement have grown comfortable in their careers and established job patterns that are integral parts of their lives. Older adults need to be made aware of the options available to them in retirement, especially regarding leisure activities.

Planning retirement is a crucial step in transition, yet many people avoid it. Most social work interventions in this area come after the fact and are supportive in nature. Some older adults could benefit from preretirement counseling to decrease their anxiety about what retirement will bring. Social workers can take a more active role in preretirement counseling by telling clients about its importance, as well as how to plan and what to expect in the way of benefits and activities. The way an individual approaches retirement and the attitude developed can be especially important in determining life satisfaction during retirement.

Name: Brianna Wren **Place of residence:** Hoover, Alabama
College/university degrees: Alabama State University, BSW; Alabama A&M University, MSW
Current position: Middle Alabama Area Agency on Aging as a Medicaid Waiver Program case manager

What inspired you to be a social worker? What inspired me to become a social worker is growing up with cousins who previously were in foster care. Hearing their story sparked an interest in me to look into the field of social work. I began exploring opportunities to serve my community and obtain a degree in social work. In 2017, I volunteered with Alabama Partnership for Children where I worked closely with the program called Help Me Grow. This program assisted parents in identifying development delays in their child(ren) across the state of Alabama. Becoming familiar with the complexity of child development, my work with parents led to my interest in volunteering with Jefferson County Committee for Economic Opportunity Head Start Program. I assisted with program enrollment and providing resources for families as well as engaging with children in the classroom. These experiences led to me ultimately obtaining a master's in social work with a concentration in family and child welfare.

What does a typical day at work look like for you? What tasks do you generally complete as a social worker in your area of expertise? Upon graduating with my MSW, I started working for the Department of Human Resources (DHR) as a family preservation caseworker. I managed a caseload of thirty-five to forty clients where I provided in-home services that addressed parenting and rearing issues to reduce opportunities for child abuse and neglect. The goal of services is to provide parents and caregivers with tools that promote healthy and sustainable home environments for children to grow and develop. Working at DHR provided a solid foundation for understanding social services and prompted my transition to work with elderly and disabled individuals at Middle Alabama Area Agency on Aging. As a Medicaid waiver case manager, I manage a caseload of thirty-five to forty-two clients to maintain independence within the home and provide personal and home health care through direct service providers (DSP) or personal preferences where the client is the employer. My work days consist of scheduling visits, communication with DSPs on possible workers in the area to serve clients, printing out paperwork for upcoming redetermination to get clients reapproved for services, completing paperwork for approved redetermination clients, and submitting any referrals for clients.

What is your favorite social work story? One story that easily comes to mind is a time where I was in a one-on-one session with my client and she expressed to me that she was being bullied at school. She mentioned that she did not have clothes like the other kids, and it impacted how she made friends and felt about herself. Listening to her story brought back memories of my time as a little girl who went through a similar experience with bullying and going without. I had the opportunity to lean in and help her purchase clothes to

continues

> *continued*
>
> wear. Being able to see the client for who she was and providing her the space to be heard and appreciated reminded me of why I chose to be a social worker.
>
> *What do you do in your spare time?* In my spare time, I like to watch movies, read books, spend time with family/friends, and explore new adventures.
>
> *What would be the one thing you would change in our community if you had the power to do so?* I would like to change the lack of resources within my state for clients who are elderly and individuals who have disabilities. Some of the main issues my clients face are food insecurities and mobility. With strict laws and legislation surrounding welfare services such as food stamps, home health resources, and transportation, it is difficult for individuals who rely on social services to become self-sufficient and sometimes the resources available are not always beneficial to my client population. I am interested in equity and access for all so that the resources improve their quality of life.

11.7 ABUSE, NEGLECT, RISK OF EXPLOITATION, AND AGING

Vulnerable older adults can easily become targets for financial, physical, and psychological abuse (U.S. Department of Justice, 2011). Elder abuse and neglect remain a significant concern of practitioners as well as policy makers and program planners. The definition of exactly what constitutes abuse in older adults can vary widely, whether it is financial abuse and someone taking their funds or domestic violence, homicide, or homicide–suicide. The term *elder justice* is used to signify the connection between Adult Protective Services (APS) and the criminal justice system and the assurance that, when victimization rises to a criminal standard, it will be addressed and, if needed, fully prosecuted (Dubble, 2006). While many are familiar with child abuse reporting, fewer are aware of the similar process in place for vulnerable adults. The process of taking reports of elder abuse, assessing and substantiating the reports, and providing intervention rests with the APS agencies.

Individuals with cognitive impairment disorders such as dementia are at increased risk of abuse because these disorders can disturb intellectual functioning and can be the most difficult for APS workers to assess because of an elder's right to choose, which social workers call self-determination. This is vastly different from working with children, where intervention is expected regardless of choice. Older adults who are mentally competent can make their own choices and decisions, and for social workers it can be difficult to decide what to do if the older adult does not want intervention. There is only one reason cited by APS workers for disregarding a client's right to choose, and that is when the client is deemed to be mentally incompetent (Bergeron, 2006). As mandatory reporters, social workers must be sure that every effort has been made to protect the client and to determine whether the client who is refusing services is capable of rational thought. Both violent behaviors between caregivers and care recipients and self-neglect often require cases to be reported to APS.

In assessing potential abuse of older adults, the following questions should be considered.

1. Client safety: Is the client safe in the current situation?
2. Assistance: Does the client and the client system seem open to helping efforts?
3. Mental capacity: Does the client seem capable of making informed choices regarding his or her own safety or wellness?

Drifthnery (2000) examined abuse, neglect, and exploitation of the elder population and found that factors such as self-imposed neglect, endangering behaviors, financial mismanagement, and environmental dangers as well as physical illness and/or disability, along with mental health conditions such as alcohol or other substance abuse, can increase cases of abuse of older adults. Social workers are in a unique position to recognize and assess on behalf of this vulnerable population throughout the distinct levels of care.

One way to ensure client safety is to involve the client system in any intervention efforts. Assisting caregivers to better navigate the system and the resources available can be invaluable for helping the client in his or her current environment or situation. In the community care setting, social workers can provide education to older adults, their families, and the public to prevent elder maltreatment. Also, greater advocacy to increase funding for prevention, detection, support, and intervention in older adult abuse and neglect is needed. This trend is in its infancy because law enforcement agencies have just begun to see the need to develop programs to investigate and identify crimes against older people. According to the U.S. Department of Justice (2011), in 2009, 11 percent of older adults living in the community who responded to a phone survey reported that they had experienced at least one form of mistreatment that involved physical abuse, emotional abuse or neglect, or sexual abuse. Financial exploitation by a family member was reported by 5.2 percent of older people in one year. In 1999, 3.8 of every 1,000 persons sixty-five and older were victims of crime. Unfortunately, many older adult victims, especially those who live alone, worry that reporting crime can bring embarrassment, along with additional harassment. Even worse, victims think that concerned family members may use the incident as leverage to put them in a nursing home. Social workers must review warning signs, such as withdrawal of large sums of money from the bank accounts of older adults; family members and financial institutions should also watch for these transactions. Because agencies and victim support services are ill prepared to deal with an increase in victims, advocacy to avoid crimes against the vulnerable older adult is necessary and urgent.

11.8 ASSESSING SUICIDE RISK AND PLANNING FOR DEATH

In general, people with serious mental illness have a life expectancy that is eight to thirty-two years shorter than that of the general population (Druss, Zhao, Von Esenwein, Morrato, & Marcus, 2011). When this is coupled with rising suicide rates among the aged, suicide risk should always be assessed in individuals with a history of mental illness.

Why are the rates so high in this group, and will they continue to grow? There is no conclusive reason for these trends, but there is a definite connection between stress levels among older adults and illness (Onose et al., 2013). It makes sense that when stress is high, usual methods of coping and problem-solving become ineffective. Another factor is that religious organizations and family and friends may be uncomfortable even mentioning suicide with a loved one because they fear it may make the situation worse. Furthermore, dissatisfaction with functional abilities caused by ill health can negatively affect emotions and feelings of resilience. Finally, the tremendous number of life stressors that older adults may experience in a short amount of time—for example, death of spouse, relatives, or friends and changes in social status and employment status—cannot be overemphasized (Dziegielewski & Holliman, 2020).

Suicide rates are usually considered indicative of the mental health, satisfaction, and well-being of a population. But society does not always view suicide among older adults in the same way as suicide involving young people. For example, the increase in suicide rates among adolescents has raised much alarm and led many to a call for solutions. However, suicide with older people may not be treated as seriously. The older individuals at the greatest risk are those who report feeling lost, trapped, and alone. Fear of declining physical health coupled with increased health care costs can make older adults feel that options are limited. The methods for completion of suicide are similar in the young and old, including inappropriate use of prescription medications or alcohol, delaying medical treatment for a life-threatening condition, or risk-taking behavior such as driving recklessly (Zarit & Zarit, 2007). In older adults, however, the self-destructive behaviors tend to be more subtle and range from taking too much prescription medication to not taking any at all. We must ask ourselves as a society—Why do we seem to care less about suicide risk with this population group? Is it ageism?

The death of a partner presents a particular coping problem because it may require the older adult survivor to assume new, unfamiliar duties: managing finances, driving, shopping for groceries, and so forth. These new tasks and the adjustments they imply, in conjunction with the loss of a life partner, can place unbelievable stress on older people. They may feel isolated from married friends and fear dependence on family or friends. These feelings of isolation can be considered a significant risk factor to continued well-being (Cacioppo & Cacioppo, 2014). Widowhood particularly affects older women because they more often outlive their male partners (Federal Interagency Forum on Aging-Related Statistics, 2012). Widowhood may not be linked to suicide; however, when the male partner outlives a female spouse, the suicide rates are higher for older males than for older females. Nevertheless, Zarit and Zarit (2007) warned that widowhood is likely to have negative effects, including impairment of physical, psychological, and social well-being. Suicide among older adults is always a result of major life stresses and accumulated losses; therefore, widows and widowers have a high probability of committing suicide (see Box 11.6).

> **BOX 11.6**
>
> ## GETTING COMMITMENT AND FORMULATING A SAFETY PLAN
>
> Social work professionals often help clients to complete professional agreements even when clients have no actual plans to harm themselves. This is not a legal contract; it is completed to document clearly what has been said and to help the client articulate a plan that can be monitored. If used, this should always be part of a larger and more comprehensive safety plan included in the client's record and should not stand alone. It can assist as part of the standard of practice and documentation of a plan.
>
> I _____ agree that I will not kill myself or someone else and that I do not have any plans to do so. If I start to feel as though I might want to try to kill myself or someone else, I have voiced my intent to immediately seek help at [insert the name and address of a twenty-four-hour emergency room that manages indigent clients where the client can receive assistance].
>
> *Helpful hint*: Be sure to get permission from the client to call a family member or notify the support system, so they too are aware of the pending situation. Document this clearly in the record (Dziegielewski & Holliman, 2020).

Research indicates that the first year after the death of a spouse is the hardest time of adjustment (Erlangsen, Jeune, Billie-Brahe, & Vaupel, 2004). During this especially stressful period, social workers should keep aware of a client's abilities or problems in coping with grief.

The social worker plays an essential role with potentially suicidal older clients. First, if a client, young or old, expresses a wish to commit suicide and has a concrete plan, steps to ensure active intervention must be taken immediately. The person needs to be in a safe place. Unfortunately, criteria for hospital admission are not always clear, and the social worker may not know how likely the client is to turn suicidal verbalizations into actions. In any case, some type of intervention, perhaps counseling, must take place. For dealing with aged clients, Perkins and Tice (1994) emphasized a counseling strategy that focuses on client strengths. In this method, client and social worker identify the client's preexisting coping and survival skills to help him or her to accept the role of survivor. This approach, in conjunction with crisis services and bereavement counseling, can help the older client to regain control of his or her life.

Much of the confusion in our society regarding death can be linked to the atmosphere of denial, secrecy, and fear that we have created around this inevitable part of life. Many people attempt to ignore or avoid it, at least until it affects them indirectly. For example, have you prepared for your own death? Do you have a will? Is your family aware of your wishes? For most of us the answer is no. Our reasons vary from "I'm too young to worry about that now" to "I have plenty of time." Now, if you, the helping professional, said no, what do you think your clients will answer? If you did say no, you are not alone, but do not take comfort in this—it is evidence that you need to address these issues in your own life.

No one rationally desires to be dying or to have a terminal illness. Indeed, most people resist even the idea of being ill. For some people, however, regardless of age, there comes a time when they truly do want to die. Many older people fear the chronic conditions that can make them dependent on family and/or friends. Family members also fear this new independent health-related decision-making and can be daunted by the prospect of making decisions without the input of their loved one, especially regarding continuing or terminating life. The older person and family members often turn to science and medicine for the answers. Physicians, as representatives of the scientific and healing community, are sought out and expected to supply answers and make decisions. Some physicians may feel unprepared to deal with the psychosocial aspects of dying, and when trained to help people avoid death, these professionals may see their role as to prolong life, thereby avoiding death (Dziegielewski & Holliman, 2020). It is the social worker, often as part of an interdisciplinary team, who will be asked to help the client or family to cope with death.

Before a social worker can successfully help a client and his or her family deal with death, several issues should be addressed. First, the social worker must explore his or her own feelings about death and address any uncomfortable feelings he or she may have. By examining alternative conceptions of death and the legitimization of the role of death, social workers can disperse some of the mysticism that surrounds death in the United States. Once the social worker feels comfortable talking about death, these concepts must be discussed with the client as well as family members.

Second, the social worker must know what community resources and services might assist older clients in preparing for death. One example is a hospice program (National Hospice and Palliative Care Organization, 2022). Hospice, which is funded by Medicare, offers services to people suffering from terminal illnesses who are expected to live six months or less (Dziegielewski & Holliman, 2020). This and similar programs do not focus on prolonging life beyond its natural end. In providing services through such programs, the social worker serves on an interdisciplinary team designed to help the client and family members to prepare for natural death.

Finally, the social worker should learn about living wills and decide whether such a measure is appropriate for the client. Most people are aware of the need for a will and some complete a will that declares who is to receive their money, property, and other possessions. However, the concept of a living will is less familiar (Dziegielewski & Holliman, 2020). Simply stated, a living will allows a person to document, in advance, his or her preferences relating to the use or avoidance of life-sustaining procedures in the event of a terminal illness. This type of documentation is especially helpful to family members burdened with making such decisions when an older relative is mentally incapacitated. Without it, they may avoid making any decision because they feel that doing so gives them too much control and responsibility. Owens (2020), in her book titled *Be Your Own Hero: Senior Living Decisions Simplified*, makes a compelling case for helping older adults to be proactive in making life decisions as opposed to waiting till reactionary health care decisions are required. Books such as this can empower clients to be proactive in making important health care decisions that are well planned and not crisis driven.

SUMMARY

We all face the prospect of growing older, yet older people often suffer as the result of societal attitudes that devalue old age. Our society fears aging, and confronting ageism is essential. We must promote attempts to overcome negative stereotypes that affect our perceptions of aging on the human body and the mind. The focus on the losses of functioning that come with aging often dominate expectations, and little attention is given to promoting optimal functionality geared toward the individual's capabilities (Algilani et al., 2014). Such prejudices spring from both rational and irrational fears. Rational fears about worsening health, the loss of loved ones, and declining social status can be intensified by negative stereotypes of older people. And irrational fears about changes in physical appearance, loss of masculinity or femininity, and perceived mental incompetence are not unusual. For older people, misinformation and myth, as well as biological, psychological, social, and economic challenges, can impede self-help and the pursuit of individual contentedness. The fear of isolation can weigh heavy on the mind of the individual, having a toxic effect on his or her well-being (Cacioppo & Cacioppo, 2014). Setting clear goals and remaining flexible and open to change may hold the key to measuring treatment success (Heckhausen et al., 2021). Advocating for all older clients, particularly those with serious mental illness, to receive adequate medical care should always be a top priority (Bartels et al., 2013).

Aging today creates complexities, both in policy and in the human experience. Advances in medicine allow people to live longer. You will find families that have three generations of seniors: the granddaughter in her late fifties, her father in his early eighties, and her grandmother in her one hundreds, for example. Talk about perplexing family dynamics! As we age and live longer, we will spend more years in retirement. Retirement now can last forty and even fifty years. Income, health care, socialization, loneliness and happiness, and support are among the areas that policy makers and senior advocates struggle with today.

The good news is that older people are turning more often to mental health professionals to address the problems they are facing (Dziegielewski & Holliman, 2020). In addition, the COVID-19 pandemic and the many restrictions placed on social contact forced older adults to use teletherapy/telemedicine services. For example, during the first twelve months of the pandemic, Medicare beneficiaries increased their usage of telehealth services (U.S. Department of Health and Human Services, 2022). There were also restrictions that were lifted for those using Medicare and Medicaid services, policies easing restrictions that require HIPAA compliance on audio/visual platforms used in telehealth as well as policies that limited access to only certain rural facilities (Lepkowsky, 2020). Although these expectations assisted in acquiring services for older adults, those that did not have information technology fluency were often left out. With the use of this technology being expected of older adults, assuming equivalency of use to younger cohorts, aspects of ageism were unintentionally introduced, especially for those over the age of eighty who did not previously use the technology (Lepkowsky, 2022). In the future, retaining telephonic access to health care, especially for older adults, is critical for providing the most inclusive care possible (Lepkowsky, 2020).

When working with older adults, at a minimum, social workers must examine their own attitudes about aging and how these attitudes can affect their practice with older clients and their families, especially in the expected use of technology. According to Lepkowsky and Arndt (2019), it was expected that 93 percent of the people over the age of seventy and 98 percent of the individuals over the age of eighty do not use the internet to communicate with health care providers. For the most part, these older adults use face-to-face meetings and the telephone for communication. Social workers must remember that just because information technology service is available, it may not be accessible, especially when working with older adults.

As mandatory reporters, we should be familiar with our roles and what we must do to protect those who cannot protect themselves. We should be keenly aware of the types of discrimination that can occur, often unintentionally, and we must never contribute, directly or indirectly, to any discriminatory practices based on age. All helping professionals must recognize that each aged person is a valuable resource in our society. Our role is to provide services and advocacy that will help older people in need of services to maximize their life satisfaction and well-being.

REFERENCES

Aldwin, C. M., & Gilmer, D. F. (2013). *Health, illness, and optimal aging: Biological and psychosocial perspectives* (2nd ed.). New York, NY: Springer.

Algilani, S., Ostlund-Lagerström, L., Kihlgren, A., Blomberg, K., Brummer, R. J., & Schoultz, I. (2014). Exploring the concept of optimal functionality in old age. *Journal of Multidisciplinary Healthcare, 7*, 69–79.

Alignment Health Care. (2022). *2022 Social threats to aging in America*. Orange, CA: Author. Retrieved from https://www.alignmenthealthcare.com/files/2022-ALHC-Social-Threats-to-Aging-Well

American Association of Retired People. (N.D.) *AARP membership FAQs*. Retrieved December 21, 2023, from https://www.aarp.org/membership/faqs/#:~:text=How%20old%20do%20I%20have%20to%20be%20to%20join%3F&text=All%20people%20age%2050%20and,The%20Magazine%2C%20and%20much%20more

American Cancer Society. (2019). *Facts & figures 2019: US cancer death rate has dropped 27% in 25 years*. Retrieved from https://www.cancer.org/latest-news/facts-and-figures-2019.html

American Psychiatric Association. (2022). *Diagnostic and statistical manual of mental disorders, DSM-5-TR* (5th ed., text rev.). Washington, DC: Author.

Arnone, W. J., Kavouras, F., & Nissenbaum, M. (2001). *Ernst and Young's retirement planning guide: New tips and strategies for building wealth* (2nd ed.). New York, NY: Wiley.

Austin, C. D., & McClelland, R. W. (2009). Case management with older adults. In A. R. Roberts, (Ed.) *Social workers' desk reference* (2nd ed., pp. 797–801). New York, NY: Oxford University Press.

Barr, P. (2014, January 14). The boomer challenge. *H&HN (Hospital and Health Networks), 88*(1), 22–26.

Bartels, S., Aschbrenner, K. A., Rolin, S. A., Cimpean, H. D., Naslund, J. A., & Faber, M. (2013). Activating older adults with serious mental illness for collaborative primary care visits. *Psychiatric Rehabilitation Journal, 36*, 278–288.

Begly, C. (1985). Are DRGs fair? *Journal of Health and Human Resources Administration, 8*, 80–89.

Bergeron, L. R. (2006). Self-determination and elder abuse: Do we know enough? *Journal of Gerontological Social Work, 46*(3/4), 81–102.

Brieland, D., Costin, L. B., & Atherton, C. R. (1980). *Contemporary social work* (2nd ed.). New York, NY: McGraw–Hill.

Cacioppo, J. T., & Cacioppo, S. (2014). Social relationships and health: The toxic effects of perceived social isolation. *Social & Personality Psychology Compass, 8*(2), 58–72.

Casey, D. A. (2017). Depression in older adults: A treatable medical condition. *Primary Care, 44*(3), 499–510.

Cass, A. (2022). *Social threats to older adults' healthcare: 7 things to know.* Becker's Hospital CFO Report. Retrieved from https://www.beckershospitalreview.com/finance/social-threats-to-older-adults-healthcare-7-things-to-know.html

Center for Disease Control. (2022a). *Prioritizing minority mental health.* Retrieved December 28, 2022, from https://www.cdc.gov/healthequity/features/minority-mental-health/

Centers for Disease Control. (2022b). *Depression is not a normal part of growing older.* Retrieved December 28, 2022, from https://www.cdc.gov/aging/depression/

Centers for Disease Control and Prevention, National Center for Injury Prevention and Control. (2022). Web-based Injury Statistics Query and Reporting System (WISQARS) [February 17, 2022]. Retrieved from https://www.cdc.gov/injury/wisqars

Centers for Medicare and Medicaid Services. (2012). *Affordable Care Act implementation FAQs—set 8.* Retrieved December 28, 2022, from http://www.cms.gov/CCIIO/Resources/Fact-Sheets-and-FAQs/aca_implementation_faqs8.html

Council on Social Work Education. (2001). *Strengthening the impact of social work to improve the quality of life for older adults and their families: A blueprint for the new millennium.* Alexandria, VA: Council on Social Work Education.

Cowdry, E. V. (Ed.). (1942). *Problems of aging: Biological and medical aspects.* Baltimore, MD: Williams & Wilkins.

Cumming, E., & Henry, W. (1961). *Growing old: The process of disengagement.* New York, NY: Basic Books.

Drifthnery, F. (2000). Work history and U.S. elders. Transitions into poverty. *Gerontologist, 40*, 469–479.

Druss, B. G., Zhao, L., Von Esenwein, S., Morrato, E. H., & Marcus, S. C. (2011). Understanding excess mortality in persons with mental illness: 17-year follow-up of a nationally representative U.S. survey. *Medical Care, 49*, 599–604.

Dubble, C. (2006). A policy perspective on elder justice through APS and law enforcement collaboration. *Journal of Gerontological Social Work, 46*(3/4), 35–55.

Dziegielewski, S. F. (2015). *DSM-5™ in action*. Hoboken, NJ: Wiley.

Dziegielewski, S. F., & Holliman, D. (2020). *The changing face of health care social work: Opportunities and challenges for professional practice* (4th ed.). New York, NY: Springer.

Dziegielewski, S. F., & Jacinto, G. A. (2016). *Social work practice and psychopharmacology: A person and environment approach* (3rd ed.). New York, NY: Springer.

El, S. (2022). *What percent of elderly people live in nursing homes? Plus, over 101 nursing home statistics*. Retrieved December 28, 2022, from https://www.simplyinsurance.com/nursing-home-statistics/

Erikson, E. (1959). Identity and the life cycle: Selected papers. *Psychological Issues, 1*, 1–171.

Erlangsen, A., Jeune, B., Bille-Brahe, U., & Vaupel, J. W. (2004). Loss of partner and suicide risks among oldest old: A population-based register study. *Age and Ageing, 33*, 378–383.

Esterline, C., & Batalova, J. (2022) *Frequently requested statistics on immigrants and immigration in the United States*. Migration Policy Institute. Retrieved December 28, 2022, from https://www.migrationpolicy.org/article/frequently-requested-statistics-immigrants-and-immigration-united-states?gclid=Cj0KCQjwnvOaBhDTARIsAJf8eVOoLSvJjh3rdKRDQvpj7XLqM-CUMvrgoMUlW2mV4vDdF02DCerRaC4aAszHEALw_wcB

Federal Interagency Forum on Aging-Related Statistics. (2012). *Older Americans 2012: Key indicators of well-being*. Washington, DC: U.S. Government Printing Office. Retrieved from https://agingstats.gov/docs/PastReports/2012/OA2012.pdf.

Frank, L. (1946). Gerontology. *Journal of Gerontology, 1*, 1.

Gellis, Z. D. (2009). Evidence-based practice in older adults with mental health disorders. In A. R. Roberts (Ed.), *Social workers' desk reference* (2nd ed., pp. 376–380). New York, NY: Oxford University Press.

Hackney, M., Hall, C., Echt, K., & Wolf, S. (2013). Dancing for balance: Feasibility and efficacy in oldest-old adults with visual impairment. *Nursing Research, 62*(2), 138–143.

Hafford-Letchfield, T., Simpson, P., & Reynolds, P. (2021). *Sex and diversity in later life: Critical perspectives*. Bristol, United Kingdom: Policy Press of Bristol University Press.

Heckhausen, J., Brandstätter, V., Fishbach, A., Freund, A., Lachman, M. E., & Robert, P. (2021). Goal changes and healthy aging. *The Journals of Gerontology: Series B, 76*(2), 105–114. https://doi.org/10.1093/geronb/gbab038

Huffington Post. (2012, May 2). The elderly vs. the middle age: Who is a senior citizen, who is middle aged and why? Retrieved from http://www.huffingtonpost.com/2012/05/02/elderly-senior-citizens-middle-age-aged_n_1471176.html

John A. Hartford Foundation. (2022). *National Center of Gerontological Social Work Education transition grant*. Retrieved December 28, 2022, from https://www.johnahartford.org/grants-strategy/national-center-for-gerontological-social-work-education-transition-grant

Kim, S., Hayward, R., & Kang, Y. (2013). Psychological, physical, social, and spiritual well-being similarities between Korean older adults and family caregivers. *Geriatric Nursing, 34*, 35–40.

Lazarevic, P., & Quesnel-Vallee, A. (2022). Rating health and rating change: How Canadians rate their health and its changes. *Journal of Aging and Health, 35*(7–8), 535–542.

Lee, E., Forthofor, R., & Taube, C. (1985). Does DRG mean disastrous results for psychiatric hospitals? *Journal of Health and Human Services Administration, 8*, 53–78.

Lemon, B. L., Bengston, V. L., & Peterson, J. A. (1972). An exploration of activity of aging: Activity types and life-satisfaction among in-movers to a retirement community. *Journal of Gerontology, 27*, 511–583.

Lepkowsky, C. M. (2020). Telehealth reimbursement allows access to mental health care during COVID-19. *The American Journal of Geriatric Psychiatry, 28*(8), 898–899.

Lepkowsky, C. M. (2022). Ageism, mentalism, and ableism shape telehealth policy. *American Journal of Geriatric Psychiatry, 31*(3), 235–236.

Lepkowsky, C. M., & Arndt, S. (2019). The internet barrier to healthcare for older adults? *Practice Innovation, 4*(2), 124–132.

Lowry, L. (1979). *Social work with the aging: The challenge and promise of later years*. New York, NY: Harper & Row.

Manning, L., & Bouchard, L. (2021). Medical cannabis use: Exploring the perceptions and experiences of older adults with chronic conditions. *Clinical Gerontologist, 44*(1), 32–41.

Maust, D., Oslin, D. W., & Marcus, S. (2014). Effect of age on the profile of psychotropic users: Results from the 2010 National Ambulatory Medical Care Survey. *Journal of the American Geriatrics Society, 62*, 358–364.

Moody, H. R., & Sasser, J. R. (2012). *Aging concepts and controversies* (7th ed.). Thousand Oaks, CA: SAGE.

Morrison, M. (1982). *Economics of aging: The future of retirement*. New York, NY: Van Nostrand Reinhold.

Mosher-Ashley, P. M. (1994). Diagnoses assigned and issues brought up in therapy by older adults receiving outpatient treatment. *Clinical Gerontologist, 15*(2), 37–64.

Mullahy, C. (1998). *The case manager's handbook*. Gaithersburg, MD: Aspen.

National Bureau of Economic Research. (n.d.). *Medicare and its impact*. Retrieved from http://www.nber.org/digest/apr06/w11609.html

National Center for Health Statistics. (2019). Long-term care providers and services users in the United States 2015–2016. *Vital Health Statistics, 3*(43), 1–80. https://www.cdc.gov/nchs/data/series/sr_03/sr03_43-508.pdf

National Hospice and Palliative Care Organization. (2022). *About NHPCO*. Retrieved from https://www.nhpco.org/about-nhpco/

Nelson, J., & Powers, P. (2001). Community case management for frail, elderly clients: The nurse case manager's role. *Journal of Nursing Administration, 31*, 444–450.

Nichols, H. (2019). *What are the leading causes of death in the US?* Retrieved December 28, 2022, from https://www.medicalnewstoday.com/articles/282929

Ofosu, A. (2011). Implications for health care reform. *Health & Social Work, 36*, 229–231.

Onose, G., Haras, M. A., Sinescu, C. J., Daia, C. O., Andone, I., Onose, V. L., ... Blendea, C. D. (2013). Basic wellness features and some related actions propensive for active and healthy ageing. *World Medical Journal, 59*(4), 155–160.

Ortman, J. M., Velkoff, V. A., & Hogan, H. (2014). *An aging nation: The older population in the United States* (Current Population Reports, P25-1140). Washington, DC: U.S. Census Bureau. Retrieved from https://www.census.gov/library/publications/2014/demo/p25-1140.html.

Owens, C. L. (2020). *Be your own hero: Senior life decisions simplified.* London, England: Legend Times, Hero Publishing LLC.

Perkins, K., & Tice, C. (1994). Suicide and older adults. The strengths perspective in practice. *Journal of Applied Gerontology, 13,* 438–454.

Podnieks, E. (2006). Social inclusion: An interplay of health: New insights into elder abuse. *Journal of Gerontological Social Work, 46*(3/4), 57–79.

Prasher, V. P., Davidson, P. W., & Santos, F. H. (Eds.). (2021). *Mental health, intellectual and developmental disabilities, and the ageing process* (2nd ed.). Cham, Switzerland: Springer.

Rhodes, C. (1988). *An introduction to gerontology: Aging in American society.* Springfield, IL: Thomas.

Roberts, A., Ogunwole, S., Blakeslee, L., & Rabe, M. (2018). *Most older adults lived in households with computer and internet access.* U.S. Census Bureau. Retrieved December 28, 2022, from https://www.census.gov/library/stories/2018/10/snapshot-fast-growing-us-older-population.html

Ryan, J. and Super, N. (2003). Dual eligible for Medicare and Medicaid: Two for one or double jeopardy. Washington, DC: National Health Policy Forum, 2003 September 30, No. 794. Retrieved from: https://www.ncbi.nlm.nih.gov/books/NBK559780/

Rybarczyk, B., Lund, H. G., Garroway, A. M., & Mack, L. (2013). Cognitive behavioral therapy for insomnia in older adults: Background, evidence, and overview of treatment protocol. *Clinical Gerontologist, 36,* 70–93.

Ryff, C. D. (1982). Self-perceived personality change in adulthood and aging. *Journal of Personality and Social Psychology, 42,* 108–115.

Schroeder, R. (2013). The seriously mentally ill older adult: Perceptions of the patient–provider relationship. *Perspectives in Psychiatric Care, 49,* 30–40.

Sheen, R. (2022a). Employers take note: ACA no longer being repealed. *The ACA Times.* Retrieved from https://acatimes.com/employers-take-note-aca-no-longer-being-repealed/

Sheen, R. (2022b). ACA open enrollment reaches record-breaking 14.5 million. *The ACA Times.* Retrieved from https://acatimes.com/aca-open-enrollment-reaches-record-breaking-14-5-million/

Shock, N. W. (1987). The International Association of Gerontology: Its origins and development. In G. L. Maddox & E. W. Busse (Eds.), *Aging: The universal experience* (pp. 21–43). New York, NY: Springer.

Social Security. (2022). *Actuarial life table.* Retrieved December 28, 2022, from https://www.ssa.gov/oact/STATS/table4c6.html

Starr, P. (1982). *The social transformation of American medicine.* New York, NY: Basic Books.

Stern, M. J., & Axinn, J. J. (2011). *Social welfare: A history of the American response to need* (8th ed.). New York, NY: Pearson.

Stinson, A. M. (2014). Spiritual life review with older adults: Finding meaning in late life development. *Dissertation Abstracts International: Section A, 74*(11-A) (E) 2014.

Tan, J. (2009). Measurement issues of service use among elders. *Journal of Human Behavior in the Social Environment, 19*, 171–185.

Taylor, P., Morin, R., Parker, K., Cohn, D., & Wang, W. (2009). *Growing old in America: Expectations vs. reality*. Washington, DC: Pew Research Center. Retrieved from https://www.pewresearch.org/social-trends/2009/06/29/growing-old-in-america-expectations-vs-reality/

Thomeer, M. B., Moody, M. D., & Yahirun, J. (2022). Racial and ethnic disparities in mental health and mental health care during the COVID-19 pandemic. *Journal of Racial Ethnic Health Disparities, 22*, 1–16. https://doi.org/10.1007/s40615-022-01284-9

Tiwari, S. C., Srivastava, G., Tripathi, R. K., Pandey, N. M., Agarwal, G. G., Pandey, S., & Tiwari, S. (2013). Prevalence of psychiatric morbidity amongst the community dwelling rural older adults of northern India. *Indian Journal of Medical Research, 138*, 504–514.

Tompkins, C. J., & Rosen, A. L. (2014). *Fostering social work gerontology competence: A collection of papers from the first national gerontological social work conference*. New York, NY: Routledge.

U.S. Census Bureau. (2014). *65+ in the United States: 2010* (Current Population Reports P23-212). Washington, DC: U.S. Government Printing Office. Retrieved from http://www.census.gov/content/dam/Census/library/publications/2014/demo/p23-212.pdf

U.S. Census Bureau. (2018). *An aging nation: Projected numbers of children and older adults*. Washington, DC: U.S. Government Printing Office. Retrieved from https://www.census.gov/library/visualizations/2018/comm/historic-first.html

U.S. Department of Health and Human Services. (2022). *Telehealth was critical for providing services to Medicare beneficiaries during the first year of the COVID-19 pandemic*. Retrieved from https://oig.hhs.gov/oei/reports/OEI-02-20-00520.asp

U.S. Department of Justice. (2011). *OJP fact sheet, elder abuse, and mistreatment*. Washington, DC: Office of Justice Programs. Retrieved from http://ojp.gov/newsroom/factsheets/ojpfs_elderabuse.html

U.S. Social Security Administration. (n.d.). *Retirement planner: Benefits by year of birth*. Retrieved December 28, 2022, from http://www.socialsecurity.gov/retire2/agereduction.htm

Van Hook, M. P. (2014*Social work practice with families: A resiliency-based approach*

).. Chicago, IL: Lyceum Books.

Vanajan, A., Bultmann, U., & Henkens, K. (2022). How do newly diagnosed chronic health conditions affect older workers' vitality and worries about functional ability? *Journal of Applied Gerontology, 41*(12), 2426–2434.

Waite, L. J., Iveniuk, J., & Laumann, E. O. (2014). Social connectedness at older ages and implications for health and well-being. In C. R. Agnew & S. C. South (Eds.), *Interpersonal relationships and health: Social and clinical psychological mechanisms* (pp. 202–231). New York, NY: Oxford University Press. https://doi.org/10.1093/acprof:oso/9780199936632.003.0010

Woo, S. M., & Keatinge, C. (2008). *Diagnosis and treatment of mental disorders across the life span*. Hoboken, NJ: Wiley.

Woodward, A. T., Taylor, R. J., Abelson, J. M., & Matusko, N. (2013). Major depressive disorder among older African Americans, Caribbean Blacks, and non-Hispanic Whites: Secondary analysis of the national survey of American life. *Depression & Anxiety, 30*, 589–597.

Woolf, S. H., & Schoomaker, H. (2019). Life expectancy and mortality rates in the United States, 1959–2017. *Journal of the American Medical Association, 322*(20), 1996–2016. https://doi.org/10.1001/jama.2019.16932

Yee, A. (2022). Older Americans go back to work in next frontier of the labor force. *BloombergUS Edition,*. Retrieved from https://www.bloomberg.com/news/articles/2022-07-21/older-americans-go-back-to-work-in-next-frontier-of-labor-force?leadSource=uverify%20wall

Zabora, J. R. (2011). How can social work affect health care reform? *Health & Social Work, 36*, 231–232.

Zarit, S. H., & Zarit, J. M. (2007). *Mental disorders in older adults: Fundamentals of assessment and treatment* (2nd ed.). New York, NY: Guilford Press.

Zegwaard, M. I., Aartsen, M. J., Grypdonck, M. H., & Cuijpers, P. (2013). Differences in impact of long term caregiving for mentally ill older adults on the daily life of informal caregivers: a qualitative study. *BMC Psychiatry, 13*, 1–9.

12

Intimate Partner Violence

By Amber Sutton, Debra Nelson Gardell and Sophia Dziegielewski

CHAPTER 12 EPAS COMPETENCIES

Social work programs at the bachelor's and the master's level are accredited by the Council of Social Work Education (CSWE). CSWE's Educational Policy and Accreditation Standards (EPAS) describe the processes and criteria that social work courses should cover. In 2022, CSWE updated its EPAS standards. The following competencies are addressed in this chapter.

Competency 1: Demonstrate Ethical and Professional Behavior

Social workers understand the value base of the profession and its ethical standards, as well as relevant policies, laws, and regulations that may affect practice with individuals, families, groups, organizations, and communities.

Competency 2: Advance Human Rights and Social, Racial, Economic, and Environmental Justice

Social workers understand that every person regardless of position in society has fundamental human rights.

Competency 3: Engage in Anti-racism, Diversity, Equity, and Inclusion (ADEI) in Practice

Social workers understand how racism and oppression shape human experiences and how these two constructs influence practice at the individual, family, group, organizational, and community levels and in policy and research.

Competency 5: Engage in Policy Practice

Social workers identify social policy at the local, state, federal, and global level that affects wellbeing, human rights and justice, service delivery, and access to social services.

Competency 6: Engage with Individuals, Families, Groups, Organizations, and Communities

Social workers understand that engagement is an ongoing component of the dynamic and interactive process of social work practice with and on behalf of individuals, families, groups, organizations, and communities.

Competency 7: Assess Individuals, Families, Groups, Organizations, and Communities

Social workers understand that assessment is an ongoing component of the dynamic and interactive process of social work practice.

With the increasing accessibility of technology, behaviors and experiences that were once believed to be private matters are not so private after all. Forms of gender-based violence including intimate partner violence (IPV) and sexual assault have gained considerable attention, particularly in the wake of social media movements such as #WhyIStayed, #MeToo, and #TimesUp. For women specifically, violence occurs at alarming rates (McMahon, Postmus, Warrener, Plummer, & Schwarts, 2013). In 2021, while embarking on a cross-country trip with her fiancé Brian Laundrie, Gabby Petito was reported missing. During the investigation, it was found that a police report about a domestic violence incident had been filed as the couple was driving through Moab, Utah (Maxouris, 2022). Further evidence supplied by body cam footage showed Gabby sobbing and afraid and police suggesting the two separate for the evening. Gabby's family reported her missing in September, after she stopped answering calls and texts. Her body was later discovered, and it was determined she was murdered as the result of manual strangulation. A warrant was issued for Brian's arrest and a weeks-long search ensued. The search ended in October 2021 after his remains were located. He died by suicide from a gunshot wound to the head. This case grabbed national media attention and highlights another tragic example of domestic murder–suicide (Salvatore, 2022).

Similarly, in 2014, an ABC news release story headlined a football player, Ray Rice, who was caught on video in an elevator deliberately punching his girlfriend twice in the face after an argument (Murray, 2014). After knocking her unconscious, he emerged from the elevator dragging her body. Rice initially explained that she had passed out from drinking too much, until a video taken in the elevator revealed a vastly different picture. Cases like these are nothing new, and social workers have a unique and significant role to play in addressing IPV. Social workers have long been advocates in addressing IPV, with the National Association of Social Workers mandating in 1975 that gender-related disparities be prioritized (Sutton & Carlson, 2019).

• • •

Over the past fifteen years, the problems of domestic violence and legal system intervention, as well as the roles of assessment and social work practice, have gained wide recognition within the social work profession. Many social workers have experienced IPV personally or have learned about it by doing the work (Wahab, Mehrotra, Kimball, Ng Ping Cheung, & Meyers, 2021).

In this chapter, we will discuss the issues related to IPV and the role social workers can play in addressing this problem. We first begin by defining IPV and the types of abuse. We then discuss the risk factors for perpetration, assessing lethality risks, and barriers to escaping violence. Throughout the chapter, we discuss the role of social workers in responding to survivors and their children and advocacy models in a legal and social service context. We conclude by offering case scenarios and practical strategies such as comprehensive safety planning tools that social workers can implement in their practice.

12.1 INTIMATE PARTNER VIOLENCE DEFINED

Even though the terms ***domestic violence*** and ***intimate partner violence*** are used interchangeably throughout the literature and within systems, this chapter brings specific attention to IPV (see Figure 12.1). Intimate partner violence focuses on intimate partnerships and does not include cases referring to violence in relationships between siblings, neighbors, or other related individuals (Moorer, 2021). Intimate partner violence can be defined as an ongoing pattern of coercive control that is maintained through fear-inducing tactics such as physical, psychological, sexual, and/or economic abuse (Centers for Disease Control and Prevention, 2022; Sutton, Beech, and Nelson-Gardell, 2020a; Warshaw, Sullivan, Rivera, & U.S. Department of Health and Human Services, 2013, p. 2).

FIGURE 12.1
Awareness ribbons have been around for a long time—the purple color of this one reminds people to stay aware of the epidemic level of domestic violence in society.

Data from the National Intimate Partner and Sexual Violence Survey reveal that about one in four women and one in ten men have experienced some form of violence or stalking by an intimate partner (CDC, 2021). Intimate partner violence is the leading cause of severe injury to women in the United States, costing them on average $103,767 compared to only $23,414 for male victims (CDC, 2022; L. Miller, 2008).

> ### Did You Know . . .
> The lifetime economic costs of IPV including lost time from paid work and education, the cost of injuries, and physical, mental, and legal fees are $110 billion across the United States (Peterson et al., 2018).

Although any person can experience IPV, women occupying certain social identities who experience racism, classism, sexism, and other systems of oppression are disproportionately impacted (Breiding & Armour, 2015; Messing, 2014). For instance, partner homicide is one of the leading causes of death for Black women ages fifteen to thirty-five, and the rate for Indigenous women is six times higher than that of White women (Grant, Dechart, Wimbish, & Blackwood, 2021). Additionally, IPV affects LGBTQI+ communities, and for these couples, it is no easier to leave an abusive relationship, and the love, caring, and remorse remain a part of all relationships (Shernoff, 2008). Although the violence patterns may be similar, LGBTQI+ couples face the additional burden of social stigma; the fear that they will not be believed; or, worse yet, the fear that their concerns will not be given adequate attention by law enforcement or the judicial system (L. Miller, 2008).

A growing body of research has linked coercive control as a means of keeping the victim from escaping the situation. Coercive control occurs when one partner manipulates and intimidates the other to exert power and is a risk factor for severe abuse, including intimate partner homicide (Myhill & Hohl, 2019; Stark, 2007). Threatened actions can include harming children, pets, and relatives and the use of weapons (Faver & Strand, 2003; Fridel & Fox, 2019). Although males do not always perpetrate IPV, 85 percent of victims identify as women (Jones, 2014). An analysis of FBI data for accounted female homicides in 2018 showed that in cases where a relationship between the perpetrator and victim could be identified, 63 percent of women were killed by current husbands, ex-husbands, or current boyfriends (Violence Policy Center, 2020). These data translate into almost three women being killed each day in the United States, which is drastically different compared to men who are killed by other men in 75 percent of cases (Hackman, 2021). Table 12.1 illustrates the various components of abuse and expands our thinking of IPV beyond just physical acts.

See the comprehensive list created by Women against Abuse, the National Domestic Violence Hotline, and the Stalking Resource Center.

Table 12.1 Types of Abuse

Type of abuse	Example behaviors
Psychological	Name calling, extreme jealousy, intimidation, isolation, humiliation
Physical	Hitting, slapping, strangulation, use of weapons, sexual abuse, reproductive coercion
Economic/financial	One partner monitors the other's spending, gives them an allowance, affects their ability to work, takes money earned by them and controls where it is spent
Tech	Hacking into personal accounts, using tracking devices to monitor, demanding passwords to email and social media
Spiritual	Ridicules religious or spiritual beliefs, forcing children to be raised in a faith that the other partner has not agreed to, using religious text/beliefs to rationalize abuse
Stalking	Sending unwelcome gifts; showing up repeatedly at home, work, or school; communicating persistently via phone, text, or social media

12.2 RISK FACTORS FOR PERPETRATING IPV

Intimate partner violence encompasses multiple types of abuse by men and by women toward romantic partners of the same or opposite sex, with differing levels of severity (Capaldi, Knoble, Shortt, & Kim, 2012). Social workers must understand that IPV perpetration occurs through a combination of individual, relational, community, and societal factors, and addressing violence at the micro, mezzo, and macro levels is crucial for identifying prevention and intervention opportunities. There is no single factor that causes IPV; rather, an assembly of many factors can cause abuse depending on the circumstances.

Some characteristics relating to those who become perpetrators of IPV include:

- Low self-esteem,
- Low education or income,
- History of physical or emotional abuse in childhood,
- Belief in strict gender roles,
- Aggressive behavior as a youth,
- Parents with less than a high-school education,
- Witnessing violence between parents as a child,
- Communities with high rates of poverty and limited educational and economic opportunities,
- Communities with easy access to drugs and alcohol,
- Communities with low involvement among residents,
- Income inequality, and
- Cultural norms that support aggression (CDC, 2022).

A high correlation exists between substance abuse and domestic violence (Liutkus, 1994; Siegler, 1989; Stith, Williams, & Rosen, 1990; Tolman & Bennett, 1990). Alcohol and other drug-related problems were identified in two-thirds of the offenders who committed or attempted homicide (Green & Macaluso, 2009). Men who physically abuse their partners expect their partners to be subordinate to them and adhere to traditional, stereotypic gender or sex roles where gender expectations lead to the perception that male power and privilege are normal and natural (Anderson & Umberson, 2014). It is worth noting that IPV results from structural violence in which health, economic, gender, and racial disparities act as impediments to safety and security, further allowing abusive partners to maintain power and control (Lee, 2019). This perspective helps reframe the narrative that IPV is not simply an individual pathology, but rather the result of social inequities. One potent example is inadequate gun laws that allow easy access to firearms, the most common weapon used to kill intimate partners (Fridel & Fox, 2019).

The role of economic stress in IPV cases cannot be ignored, and work, masculinity, and violence can be intertwined in ways that help us understand why IPV is more prevalent among low-income couples, specifically when men are either unemployed or underemployed (Goodmark, 2018). Male unemployment is one of the most important demographic risk factors for intimate partner homicide as violence becomes the vehicle for re-establishing masculinity (Campbell et al., 2003; Goodmark, 2018). Additionally, abusers are often pathologically jealous; prone to addiction; and passive, dependent, and antisocial (Gelles & Cornell, 1990). Histories of sexual aggressiveness and violence toward others, poor impulse control, isolation, and poor relationship skills are also common (Finkelhor, Hotaling, & Yllo, 1988). Educational level, occupational status, and income are customarily low, and in fact, unemployment or underemployment increases the likelihood of abuse (Gelles & Cornell, 1990; Siegler, 1989).

> ### Did You Know . . .
> Although there is no consensus about the causes of domestic violence, the typical characteristics defined by Straus (1980) remain relevant:
>
> | | |
> |---|---|
> | Partner unemployed | Concerns about economic security |
> | Social isolation | Disagreements over children |
> | Partners from violent families | Couples married less than ten years |
> | Partners under thirty years of age | High levels of family and individual stress |
> | Partners verbally aggressive | Frequent alcohol use |

12.3 BARRIERS TO ESCAPING IPV

In the book *Safety Planning with Battered Women: Complex Lives/Difficult Choices*, the authors outline the various risks that are generated by the abusive partner as well as ongoing challenges that the survivor faces in addition to the violence resulting from oppressive systems (J. Davies, Lyon, & Monti-Catania, 1998). The chart listed in Table 12.2 is vital in helping to understand the barriers and the complex nature of abuse as it relates to the survivor, their loved ones, and service providers.

Table 12.2 Risk Identification

Batterer-generated risks	Life/oppression-generated risks	Intervention-generated risks (because of action or inaction)
Physical Physical injury Death HIV, sexually transmitted disease Pregnancy	Economics Impact on job Ability to get/hold a job Welfare issues	911 Failure to assess risk to victim Dispatch priority for domestic violence calls Language accessibility
Psychological Psychological harm Substance abuse Long-term trauma effects Suicide threats (victim, partner)	Education/training Access to education/training Language issues	Police response Failure to determine context of violence, history/risk Arresting the wrong person No primary aggressor determination Inadequate evidence collection
Children Physical injury or psychological harm Loss of children Parenting impact	Discrimination Racism Classism Heterosexism Ageism Differently abled	Booking/release from custody Bail determination not related to risk/danger Victim notification of release not timely
Relationship Loss of relationship implications (cultural, religious) Loss of caretaker/child care	Housing Discrimination Affordability Eviction/homelessness	Arraignment Lack of offender information Criminal history Protective order information
Family, friends, community Cultural implications Threat or injury to them Loss of support, isolation Ostracization	Physical health Substance abuse Lack of health insurance	Victim advocate/witness contact Confusion about confidentiality Timing of referral to advocacy services Lack of culturally relevant services

Batterer-generated risks	Life/oppression-generated risks	Intervention-generated risks (because of action or inaction)
Financial Standard of living Loss of income/job Housing issues Loss/damage to possessions	Mental Health Lack of resources, affordable treatment Provider biases	Prosecution Reliance on victim to prosecute Retaliation by batterer
	Access to servicesLocation/transportation Child care Culturally relevant	Sentencing Ignoring history and risk Victim—blaming judicial demeanor
	Legal status Her arrest Partner's arrest Family court orders Immigration/residency status	Probation/supervision Inappropriate treatment referrals Lack of culturally relevant services for abusive party No victim follow-up
		Child protection Coercing victim to get Order For Protection (OFP) Ignoring violence in custody issues Damaging relationship with children

Source: Adapted from J. Davies, Lyon, and Monti-Catania (1998), Praxis International (https://www.praxisinternational.org), and Battered Women's Justice Project (https://www.bwjp.org).

Survivors face risks whether they stay in the relationship or attempt to escape it. Probably one of the most sobering statistics outlines the very real danger that can occur in leaving or escaping a violent relationship. One in five women is severely injured or killed by a partner without warning. Oftentimes, the fatal or life-threatening incident was the first of its kind, and in 45 percent of the homicides, the partner was trying to leave the relationship (Green & Macaluso, 2009). Therefore, the decision to escape must be thoroughly explored to enhance the survivor's safety.

In many cases, the victim wants to believe that the abusive partner will reform, and promises that it will never happen again can be very seductive. The cycle of abuse created by Lenore Walker in 1979 is used to describe patterns in an abusive relationship that include periods of tension building, violence, and reconciliation (Walker, 1979). Although this is not representative of all abusive relationships and there are various iterations, it is one tool for illustrating that there is not a time in IPV where some element of IPV is not occurring (whether visible or not). Experiencing IPV can be compared to attempting to walk through water without getting wet—it is impossible to not be affected. Women survivors may doubt their ability to obtain and maintain economic stability and may worry about what will happen to them and her children if she leaves. Research has found that women subject to IPV are also at risk for reproductive coercion and as a result may also have a child with the abuser (Messing, Thaller, & Bagwell, 2014). Reproductive coercion is defined as behavior that interferes with a woman's right to make autonomous decisions about her reproductive health and can include actions such as birth control sabotage and pregnancy coercion (E. Miller, Jordan, Levenson, & Silverman, 2020; Sutton et al., 2020a). Therefore, as stresses increase in an abusive relationship, pregnancy may escalate potentially assaultive behavior patterns (Green & Roberts, 2008). Pregnant survivors often experience increased violence during pregnancy, and research has revealed that partner homicide is the leading cause of death of pregnant women (Lawn & Koenen, 2022). Awareness of this potential situation and knowledge of what questions to ask and when to ask them in the assessment can be beneficial in uncovering such situations while avoiding any future negative consequences to the child (Messing et al., 2014).

Additionally, survivors can face issues such as poor employment options and the possibility of homelessness (Mullins, 1994), as well as difficulty finding and affording adequate day care for their children (Dziegielewski, Campbell, & Turnage, 2005; Gelles & Cornell, 1990). It has been speculated that the greatest deterrent for women is the fear of economic hardship and inadequate care for their children. This makes creating a protective environment and strengthening economic support for families crucial (CDC, 2022). On average for all women, not just abused women, marital separation often leads to a significant drop in the standard of living within the first year. To complicate this further, child support payments are often not made regularly, and consistent alimony payments are rare even when they are awarded. Economic disparity alone amply explains why women remain trapped in abusive relationships. Social and economic factors indicate the need for therapeutic intervention that is intersectional and considers the entire context of survivors' lives.

In the discussion of treatment for IPV, it is contended that too little attention is given to working with the perpetrator, especially because violence directed at an intimate partner will often reoccur (Westmarland & Kelly, 2013). There are two primary types of intervention often used with batterers: perpetrator groups and couples counseling. In the groups designed specifically for men who batter, relationship issues and the power and control relationship are clearly defined. For example, Pence and Paymar (1993) use a tool called the power and control wheel, which helps the individual identify methods of coercion such as threats, economic abuse, intimidation, emotional abuse, minimizing, denying, blaming, isolation, male privilege, and threats toward children.

Traditional couples counseling emphasizes focusing on how to react to stressful situations with nonthreatening behaviors while showing respect, honesty, and accountability.

It is hoped that intervention efforts to increase trust and support will ultimately result in responsible parenting and shared responsibilities for the domestic partnership. However, it is important to understand the unique dynamics of IPV and the risks for any survivor attending couples counseling with an abusive partner. Most mental health professionals report not being adequately trained in IPV (Sutton, Beech, Ozturk, & Nelson-Gardell, 2020b) and abusers commonly use gaslighting tactics to deflect responsibility and shift blame, therefore making the entire process ineffective and unintentionally dangerous for the survivor. Intimate partner violence is not a relationship problem; it is a power and control problem. Survivors are highly encouraged to process therapeutic options with a trained advocate so that they are fully informed of all risks and to safety plan accordingly.

12.4 HELPING SURVIVORS OF ABUSE

Social workers often provide direct clinical services for survivors of abuse. Because such experiences can result in upheaval in all aspects of a person's life, providing comprehensive and holistic services should be paramount (Haeseler, 2013). The types of services can vary from direct counseling to outpatient services such as community-based domestic violence fatality review teams as well as coordinated community response teams. These teams are designed to coordinate the provision of community services to prevent IPV (Chanmugam, 2014). The pooling of resources among this diverse group of disciplines allows for greater awareness and coordination of services.

To facilitate healing and decrease isolation, oftentimes group sessions are offered, either in a shelter or through community outreach programs. Providing group as well as individual counseling for the survivor is designed to empower them to make decisions about the future. Support groups can provide additional support to survivors through the sharing of experiences, vital resources, and connections.

The most important principle guiding all interventions with the survivor is client safety and, if children are involved, the children's safety. Devising a safety and escape plan is often the first order of business in the initial interview (Walker, 2017). A safety plan is an integral part of the intervention process. It is also crucial to respect the survivor's choices and not judge or blame her (Green & Macaluso, 2009). The social worker must honor self-determination by helping the client explore all options while ensuring safety for all involved. One example of a safety planning tool that includes valuable input from the survivors is the VIGOR (the Victim Inventory of Goals, Options, and Risks) created by Sherry Hamby. This plan assesses risks as well as coping strategies and is personalized to each survivor's situation (Hamby, 2015).

Using this model, the social worker helps the survivor to explore the following areas:

- Hopes they have for themselves and their families.
- Identifying actual and possible risks.
- Identifying their strengths and resources.
- Identifying their options and reflecting on their choices.

Children: The Forgotten Victims

More than fifteen million children in the United States experience childhood domestic violence (Child Domestic Violence, 2022). Research has shown a direct link between a mother's mental health and her children's health and the impacts of experiencing negative interactions in the home (Chamberlain & Levenson, 2011). Because children growing up in abusive homes are not just passive witnesses, one of the greatest concerns is how the repeated violence and domestic abuse occurring in a family affect the child. Whether children being raised in such a home are abused or just witnessing the abuse, can this have a lasting effect? The sad fact is that studies seem to support that it does indeed affect the child. Using four waves of longitudinal data in a three- to five-year study, Yoo and Huang (2013) found that, particularly for preschool children, the internalizing and externalizing behavior problems were indicative of intervention and prevention efforts. Children raised in violent homes seem to be more vulnerable and can exhibit a range of problems related to adjustment difficulties and anxiety (Green & Roberts, 2008). However, these same children may be less likely to talk about their experiences, even though sharing those experiences could have great therapeutic value (Cater, 2014). Because children get many of their reaction cues from their parents, being in this type of chaotic environment can leave a deep and lasting impression.

Mothers affected by IPV have been observed to be more responsive toward their children as a protective factor against violence, but for some women experiencing IPV, it can impact their ability to parent, which can increase the likelihood of distress in the children (Graham-Bermann, Lynch, Banyard, DeVoe, & Halabu, 2007; Levendosky & Graham-Bermann, 2000). There is a myth that children under the age of three are generally not affected by this type of behavior. Children as young as one year old can display distress in response to observing violent and coercive behavior toward their mother (Lieberman, Van Horn, & Ghosh Ippen, 2005; Øverlien, 2010), and exposure to IPV has been associated with trauma symptoms and other issues, including depression, increased risk of alcoholism, and drug use later in life (Cannon, Bonomi, Anderson, & Rivara, 2009). Yet at this age children develop the capacity to experience, regulate, and express emotions as well as to learn from the environment and develop trusting and secure relationships (Kamradt, Gilbertson, & Jefferson, 2008).

Regardless of the age of the child, the social worker should always explore the possible effects of the experience and ensure that the child too receives intervention and assistance. J. Davies and Lyon (2014) provide an extensive list of applying standards of safety when working with children. As much as possible, the nonabusive parents should be involved in this process because adult pathology may continue to be reflected in the parent–child relationship (Novick & Novick, 2005). In child welfare, considering witnessing violence and the impact it can have on the child and his or her current or future behaviors is essential to consider when completing a risk assessment (Forgey, Allen, & Hansen, 2014). Collaboration between child welfare workers and IPV advocates is essential for determining strengths, risks, options, and next steps.

The Legal System

There is a gap between written law and contemporary practice. Traditionally, the justice system has been unwilling to intercede or intrude in family matters, and society has preferred it that way. Survivors of abuse can feel helpless trying to persuade police officers and the courts to act to control their partners if violence has not occurred; police officers, for their part, are often frustrated by the situation and by not knowing how to intervene, and this is often complicated by a victim who refuses to admit that abuse occurred or does not want to see his or her partner arrested. Additionally, research has revealed that African American women survivors often do not elect for police intervention because of a long, tenuous history between their community and law enforcement (K. Davies, Block, & Campbell, 2007; Leone, Johnson, & Cohan, 2007; C. Miller & Vittrup, 2020; Waller, Joyce, Quinn, Hassan Shaari, & Boyd, 2022; West, 2021).

> **Did You Know...**
>
> A woman could not legally refuse her spouse's conjugal rights until the 1970s, when some states legally recognized the concept of marital rape.

In recognition of this weakness in the law, the federal **Violence against Women Act** of 1994 (VAWA) was designed to improve the response to violent crimes against women by strengthening collaboration amongst the criminal justice system, researchers, advocates, and social service providers (National Resource Center on Domestic Violence and Battered Women's Justice Project, 1994; Sacco, 2015; see Figure 12.2). The purpose of the VAWA is to create policies to prevent domestic violence and increase victim services. VAWA was first a part of the Violent Crime Control and Law Enforcement Act, which required a coordinated community response (CCR) to address violent crimes such as domestic violence, sexual assault, and stalking (Sacco, 2015). Since its inception in 1994, it has been reauthorized four times, with the most recent in 2022. Provisions of VAWA have been expanded to include strengthened protections for immigrants and LGBTQ survivors, as well as provisions for protective orders and criminal and civil jurisdiction for American Indian tribes (Sacco, 2015).

It treats domestic violence as a major law enforcement priority and funds improved services to victims of domestic violence. Title II of the bill, the Safe Homes Act, increases federal funding for battered women's shelters and related programs. It also provides a federal

FIGURE 12.2
The Violence against Women Act stands as a crucial part of the U.S. response to interpersonal violence. Its renewal has not always been a smooth process.

criminal statute for spouse abuse committed during interstate travel (Mullins, 1994). By creating emergency and long-term solutions for shelter and survival needs, the VAWA is a key step in the government's commitment to responding to IPV. However, as with any policy, there can be unintended consequences. Today, police officers have mandatory arrest policies and must make an arrest if it is believed that either party has committed an assault (L. Miller, 2008). Therefore, if a domestic assault has occurred, an arrest will be made regardless of whether the victim wants the arrest, further limiting survivor-informed intervention options (Dichter, Cerulli, Kothari, Barg, & Rhodes, 2011).

If the primary aggressor cannot be identified, both the victim and the abuser can be arrested. This has led to a new trend. Mandatory arrest laws have inadvertently caused more women victims to be arrested, leading to lower arrest rates of perpetrators and retraumatization, specifically for women of color (Hirschel & Buzawa, 2009). Discretionary arrest laws, which outline situations in which officers "may" make an arrest but allow decisions on a case-by-case basis, could prove to be a more beneficial response, particularly within communities of color (Hirschel, 2008).

Another issue is that the laws that currently exist are complex, contradictory, and at times unenforceable. The law regards property division, divorce, child custody, financial obligations, and criminal culpability as separate matters. Just as marriages can be deemed successful, so can divorces. Unfortunately, in many of these cases, divorces go badly, and children are forced to face parental conflict, aggression, and anger (Johnston, Roseby, & Kuehnle, 2009). In domestic violence cases, however, many of these issues continue to overlap. In terms of domestic violence courts, three primary objectives come to the forefront: (1) victim safety, (2) offender accountability, and (3) a mixture of other related goals (e.g., deterrence, rehabilitation, and administration of justice) (Center for Court Innovation, 2009). Domestic violence courts and greater organization, along with new domestic violence statutes, will continue to help reduce confusion and hopefully integrate the jurisdictions.

The assistance provided by police at the domestic violence scene is critical. As first responders, officers must be aware of mediation, listening to the events as presented by both sides, restating key points, and suggesting viable solutions (L. Miller, 2008). Police intervention can be strengthened by incorporating advocate-initiated responses, in which an advocate contacts the survivor to provide information and support. If an assault has occurred, charges must be processed. Policies that favor the arrest of abusers may address the immediate situation by stopping further violence at that moment, but do little to stop future incidents of abuse from occurring (Roberts, 1996b). Frisch and Caruso (1996) warn, however, against the opposite extreme: even the most complete legal plan to address an abused survivor's needs is useless if those responsible for carrying it out have no enforcement power.

The Role of the Social Worker

Oftentimes, it is the social worker who first sees the survivor of IPV, because social workers are employed in various service sectors where they interact with survivors and their families. Survivors of domestic violence may not openly state their concerns, and clear assessment questions may be needed to facilitate this process (Messing et al., 2014). One of these service systems can include a court setting. Mullarkey (1988) identified five areas in which social workers can join the criminal justice system and prosecutors to assist domestic violence survivors. First, the social worker can help the system to understand the client by completing a detailed and accurate assessment, thus providing more information about the type of abuse, the history of abuse, and the circumstances and repercussions of the abuse. Recognizing potential indicators of abuse, the social worker can assess and identify the high-lethality cases while screening, evaluating, and subsequently contributing to potential treatment outcomes. By using a risk assessment, the social worker may be able to voice concerns to a prosecutor, judge, or probation officer (Messing & Thaller, 2014). The social worker can also help the client to understand the system. Abuse victims have varied needs for legal services, social services, and psychological services. A well-documented community service awareness approach that utilizes domestic violence response teams, coordinated by the social worker, can help to integrate the efforts of health, mental health, social service, judicial, and law enforcement agencies for the benefit of survivors of IPV (Chanmugam, 2014).

The second type of assistance the social worker can provide is education, support, and psychosocial adaption strategies to help get through the crisis (Green & Roberts, 2008). These clients can suffer from self-esteem problems as well as concerns related to their safety and the survival of themselves and their children, and this can affect any action or reaction they can have (Dziegielewski et al., 2005). Working closely and supporting and educating the client each step of the way is essential to helping them request and access the services that they need. Social workers must educate their clients and in turn to be educated by system participants such as police telephone operators and dispatchers, police officers and staff, prosecutors, judges, and those directly involved, such as the survivors, the abusers, and family and support system members. They need to be aware of pro-arrest and mandatory arrest policies and what they involve, as well as the potential of electronic monitoring as part of a coordinated community effort (Roberts, 1996a).

It also helps to apply an intersectional understanding to IPV so that social workers are aware of how systems of oppression may impact survivors' help-seeking behaviors; for example, calling the police may not be an immediate strategy (Waller et al., 2022). In addition to helping the client, social workers also must educate and train police telephone operators, dispatchers, and police officers. Operators and dispatchers are the first to receive the call for help and the officer is usually the first on the scene. This education and training should include telephone training for screening and assessment, basic techniques of police safety, how to identify a primary aggressor in IPV cases, dispute management and crisis intervention techniques, and the ability to provide referral links with the social service worker (Fusco, 1989). Training sessions in these skills can influence police officers to take seriously their role in protecting the abused (Roberts, 1996a).

When conducting training, the social worker is responsible for creating an atmosphere for a team intervention that reflects respect, support, cooperation, and feedback. Moreover, the social worker plays a crucial role in advocating for the rights of the client, particularly in ensuring equality of access, discouraging sex-role stereotyping, explaining the social and emotional effects of discrimination, and identifying the dynamics of victimization and other relevant psychosocial factors (Martin, 1988). Working in this area can be incredibly stressful for the social worker, and particular care should always be given to recognizing feelings of apathy, frustration, and cynicism, often referred to as compassion fatigue or professional burnout (Knoll, 2009). The social worker must also be aware of their feelings related to the domestic violence situation. This self-awareness will allow the social worker to help others involved in the situation become aware of their value systems and behaviors and how they might affect any subsequent helping efforts (Morgaine & Capous-Desyllas, 2015).

In addition to front-line workers, court clerks, case managers, legal advocates, and judges should receive education and training (Roberts, 1996b). Professionals in the legal system often focus on conviction as the primary means for accomplishing justice. The pain that the abuser has caused the survivor, their children, and their family can be minimized or overlooked. The social worker, therefore, has a twofold task: first, to educate people in the legal system about the dynamics and issues within the abusive situation and, second, to remind everyone to address the psychosocial effects that have occurred regardless of the legal outcome (Green & Roberts, 2008).

From assessment to treatment, the third role that the social worker can assume is as a safe individual whom the survivor can trust and feel comfortable with. It is crucial for the professional helper to communicate clearly to the client the purpose of the therapy and to see the sessions as a safe place that is violence and judgment free (Walker, 2017). One dynamic in abusive relationships is for survivors to become isolated from their family and friends. They have often been taught to fear and avoid contact with others outside the abusive relationship. This isolation is problematic even when a survivor has started to receive relief from the legal system. This survivor must face their abuser and others who may threaten retaliation if the abuser faces conviction and possible incarceration. Anticipating this outcome of the legal process may leave the survivor feeling a mixture of relief and guilt, and these contradictory emotions can hamper her testimony and make her look like an unreliable witness. The prosecutor is usually rushed, however, and cannot build the rapport needed to get the survivor to trust him or her; therefore, the social worker can be a critical bridge between the prosecutor and the survivor.

> ## Activity
>
> It is important to understand the difference between types of abuse that are perpetrated and how best to handle the situations. Break into groups and examine the following two case examples. Decide what types of abuse are present. As a social worker presented with

continues

continued

this situation, how would you best intervene to help? What referrals would you make in each situation and for whom would the referral be made?

Scenario 1: A verbal dispute between two partners resulted in one partner threatening to get a knife and stab the other if the intimate partner tried to leave the house with the children. For fear that the partner might act on the threat, the partner who originally threatened to leave stayed behind.

Scenario 2: During an altercation, two intimate partners yelled and pushed each other repeatedly. Upon being pushed down, one partner's head was cut on an end table, and the other partner, who was smaller in size, later developed bruises on the shoulder and arms where their partner had grabbed them in anger.

The fourth role the social worker embraces is that of an advocate. This role has always been critical for social work professionals, and advocating for the survivor within the legal system through all stages of the criminal process is essential. Social workers have the right to serve as advocates for the survivor even before an arrest is made or while a case is awaiting trial or on appeal (Mullarkey, 1988). The role of the survivor's advocate (or victim's advocate) is to assist the client in acting as her representative whenever possible (Martin, 1988). When it is not possible—perhaps because the survivor is too distraught or incapacitated by the fear of retribution—the advocate can speak with the client's permission. Many states now permit the survivor or the survivor's advocate to address the judge at sentencing (Mullarkey, 1988). When situations are highly lethal, the professional helper has a responsibility to share and be honest about concerns for the client's safety, especially when the client is planning to return to the abusive situation (Walker, 2017). (See the activity below to identify the needed services and rank their priority.)

Activity

In the classroom, break into small groups of three or more students. As a group, review these potential goals for domestic violence programs and rank in order what you consider the top three most important goals. Compare your group's choices with those of the other groups. Was it difficult for your group to agree? Why? Why not?

Goals for Domestic Violence Programs

- To ensure safe surroundings for survivors and their children
- To increase access to material resources—income, housing, and food
- To establish and enhance legal support and other multiagency collaborations
- To build social contacts and support networks for survivors and their children
- To engage in prevention work that decreases violence and other systemic injustices
- To provide trauma-informed interventions for children and the survivors of domestic violence

CHAPTER 12: INTIMATE PARTNER VIOLENCE   427

The successful advocate for an abuse survivor must not only address a safety plan to help keep the client safe but also recognize and prepare the client for the potential complexities of the legal system. The social worker must be aware of the variety of system components that are involved—in particular, law enforcement, prosecution, and corrections. The social worker must also advocate with family members and additional support systems. Part of advocacy is helping to educate those closest to the survivor on the most effective ways to offer support and to increase understanding of the complexities of abuse, including reasons for leaving or staying.

The fifth role the social worker plays is serving as an expert witness. The social worker can assess the situation and help others to understand the underlying reasoning behind the resulting behaviors. Although social workers welcome any opportunity to assist their clients, they may worry that acting as a witness will compromise their duty to protect their client's legal rights. Counseling sessions and written notes may contain information that the social worker does not want to share because its disclosure might harm the survivor's case. For example, many times the survivor is angry with the abuser and voices this anger to gain emotional distance from the abuser. Nevertheless, the social worker should always take careful case notes despite full awareness that these notes can be subpoenaed by a court of law. As stated by Mullarkey (1988, p. 49), "The constitutional guarantee to confront accusers provided by the SIXTH AMENDMENT can be interpreted by any competent court to override any privacy statute or shield law."

Without a court order, social workers are not required to speak to defendants, attorneys, or investigators outside the courtroom. Mullarkey (1988) recommended that when social workers are summoned to court they recognize the importance of (1) appearing and being professional and nonpartisan; (2) answering all questions directly or fully; (3) immediately asking for clarification of unclear questions; (4) going over possible questions with the prosecutor before testifying; and (5) ensuring that every note, professional conversation, and report they have prepared is discoverable by the defendant and his legal representatives.

Name: Amber Sutton
Place of residence: Prattville, Alabama
College/university degrees:
- Doctorate, University of Alabama
- MSW, Washington University in St. Louis
- BSW, University of Montevallo

Present position: Assistant professor of social work, Auburn University at Montgomery

What does a typical day at work look like for you? What tasks do you generally complete as a social worker in your area of expertise? I would say within social work, there is no such thing as a typical day, but on average I spend my time teaching

continues

continued

various courses to social work students, conducting and publishing my research that focuses on intimate partner violence including overseeing grants and an independent study, applying to conferences by preparing proposals, providing professional advising and advocacy to students, engaging with the community, and delivering therapeutic services via telehealth to adult clients.

What do you do in your spare time? I spend time with those I care about deeply, including my partner, my son, my dog, friends, and colleagues. I enjoy boxing, taking care of my plants, organizing, reading, and teatime.

Why did you choose social work as a career? I've always been a natural advocate and social work as a profession was my way to continue that advocacy. I think of social work as the melding of art and activism, which is a great fit for me.

What is your favorite social work story? I have been honored to meet so many incredible individuals through my work and I never stop learning. I don't have a specific moment, but I will say that the times when I have been able to secure a resource for a survivor or advocate in a way that empowers them is what keeps me going. I also love facilitating support groups! Every survivor has taught me something.

What would be the one thing you would change in our community if you had the power to do so? Legal responses to intimate partner violence. The current system has severe gaps in how the laws are written, interpreted, and implemented. Responses are not always survivor-informed, nor do they encapsulate an intersectional lens and, therefore, resources are lacking to assist survivors and their families when escaping violence. One example would be firearm laws and keeping guns away from abusive partners. There is a ton of research on the intersection of IPV, guns, mass shootings, and intimate-partner homicides, not to mention strategies for addressing these issues, and yet there is a reluctance to take the necessary steps that could save lives. I believe the bigger issue is getting people to see how all these problems are interconnected and to care enough about women in particular. Prioritizing and honoring women is where the change starts.

12.5 PRACTICE APPLICATION: THE ROLE OF THE WOMEN'S SHELTER SOCIAL WORKER

Susan and her partner have been together for ten years. During that time, Susan's partner abused her physically on several occasions and she sustained injuries that needed medical attention. As a result, she has been treated in the local hospital emergency room. On several occasions, Susan called the police to intervene, but when they arrived at the domestic violence scene, she usually refused to press charges. Susan stated that she once began to press charges but soon dropped them when her partner called from jail apologizing and making promises to never abuse her again. The police are dispatched to the scene so often that they refer to Susan and her partner by their first names.

Susan has tried to escape the relationship several times, but the partner always tracks her down and persuades her to return. Her partner constantly calls her on her cell phone and texts her repeatedly throughout the day, asking her where she is and what she is doing. Susan's family is aware of the abuse. Both Susan's mother and her sister have started to refuse her calls asking for help. Susan often calls them when she and her partner are fighting, asking for an "understanding ear or a safe place to stay." Her family is frustrated because no matter what they do, Susan always seems to return to the abusive situation. Whenever they do take Susan in, the partner arrives and tries to intimidate Susan's mother. Susan's mother does not think her health is strong enough to handle the repeated stress.

On a referral from her employer, Susan called a domestic violence shelter during her lunch break at work and spoke with a shelter social worker. She confided in the social worker that she felt lost and abandoned. After hearing her options, Susan decided to go to the shelter. During the intake session, Susan told the social worker that she wanted to kill her partner. When asked how she would do it, Susan immediately broke down and cried that she would probably be better off killing herself. When questioned further, she said that she had not planned to harm herself, but that ending her life would make it easier for all. The event that precipitated Susan's crisis was a fight with her partner on the previous night. The partner insisted that she climb a ladder and help paint the house. Susan refused because she is four months pregnant and is afraid of heights. The partner became frustrated and hit her across her back with the ladder.

Based on the information Susan provided, the social worker can make the following assessment. Susan has experienced multiple forms of abuse, including the possibility that her pregnancy resulted from reproductive coercion. She fears for her life, is threatening to take the life of another, and might also take her own life if she could. Susan is alienated from her family and has no support system available to her. There are several entry points where the social worker can begin engaging with Susan to build rapport, inform Susan of her available options, and work toward empowering Susan to create a safer environment for herself. Because Susan has made vague threats to hurt herself, the social worker must gather more information about her intent to effectively address Susan's previous comments. Addressing this concern can be a part of her comprehensive safety plan. Susan, the social worker, and other shelter staff all collaborate to determine Susan's strengths, her needs, and her desired outcomes (see the VIGOR model noted above). The social worker informs Susan of the free resources that the shelter can provide, including individual and group therapy, assistance with filing for an order of protection, and case management services.

With the help and support of the social worker, Susan decides to file an order of protection and seek legal services because she has questions about filing for a divorce. The social worker connects Susan with a court advocate and an attorney offering pro bono services through the shelter. While participating in individual therapy, Susan decides she wants to reconnect with her estranged family members and is thinking about moving in with an aunt who lives in a different city. After she regains the recognition and assistance of her family, Susan decides to move in with her aunt and is considering her options for what to do with the baby. The social worker assists with arranging transportation for Susan, securing her a cell phone and reviewing technology safety steps to protect her information, filing paperwork for the address confidentiality program, connecting her to community resources in the new city, and discussing safety strategies once she leaves the shelter. The social worker also sets up follow-up calls to check in on Susan post shelter discharge.

Clevenger and Roe-Sepowitz (2009) reported that most women utilize shelter services if they have children to care for at the time of an abusive incident, call for assistance from a place other than their home, do not have a current order of protection in place, and have been injured during the domestic violence incident. In the case described above, the social worker provided support in various ways. First, the social worker found a safe environment where the client received help in dealing with her crisis. The social worker also provided counseling and supportive services. Second, the social worker helped the client to create and carry out a plan of action in her dealings with the legal system and other community services. Women who have been abused by their partners need supportive services, and this includes being well-informed about the available options, what each process looks like, and how interacting with selected resources impacts their overall safety. The role of the social work professional is crucial. Whether working within the shelter system or another agency, the social worker can make a true difference for survivors.

SUMMARY

Because social workers practice across the public and private sectors, they have enormous potential for influencing approaches with IPV. Social workers play a crucial role by providing multiple services to survivors of abuse. First, they complete detailed assessments that give information about the type of abuse, the history of abuse, and the circumstances and repercussions of the abuse. Second, they actively educate and are educated by law enforcement and justice system participants and people directly involved, such as survivors, abusers, and family and support system members. Third, they act as safe individuals whom survivors can trust. Fourth, they advocate for survivors through all stages of criminal prosecution (Green & Roberts, 2008). Last, they can assist prosecutors and aid survivors by acting as victim advocates or expert witnesses.

As with other types of specialized practice, social workers must strive to develop a team approach with other professionals and act as an integral part of the intervention team by offering support services, engaging in prevention work that helps to improve attitudes and beliefs about IPV, and engaging in coordinated community efforts. When children are involved, especially preschool children, working with the mother and the child together may assist in the adjustment process (Yoo & Haung, 2013). Services such as counseling, social service assistance, and protection must be carefully coordinated and available to the abuse survivor. It is encouraged that social workers make personalized referrals when providing resources to clients to build stronger rapport and trust, which includes timely response rates and comprehensive and individualized safety plans. Additionally, the profession must continue to demand and advocate for changes in our laws and legal system that will prevent IPV as well as provide better services for those who perpetrate abuse. Social workers recognize the importance of counseling and supportive services. However, to plan, they must never lose sight of the importance of social policy change in assisting the survivors of IPV.

REFERENCES

Anderson, K. L., & Umberson, D. (2014). Masculinity and power in men's accounts of domestic violence. In J. Z. Spade & C. G. Valentine (Eds.), *The kaleidoscope of gender: Prisms, patterns, and possibilities* (4th ed., pp. 494–504). Thousand Oaks, CA: SAGE.

Breiding, M. J., & Armour, B. S. (2015). The association between disability and intimate partner violence in the United States. *Annals of Epidemiology, 25*(6), 455–457. Retrieved from https://www.sciencedirect.com/science/article/abs/pii/S1047279715001271?via%3Dihub

Campbell, J. C., Webster, D., Koziol-McLain, J., Block, C., Campbell, D., Curry, M. A., . . . Laughon, K. (2003). Risk factors for femicide in abusive relationships: Results from a multisite case control study. *American Journal of Public Health, 93*(7), 1089–1097. https://doi.org/10.2105/ajph.93.7.1089

Cannon, E., Bonomi, A., Anderson, M., & Rivara, F. P. (2009). The intergenerational transmission of intimate partner violence. *Archives of Pediatric and Adolescent Medicine, 163*, 706–708. https://doi.org/10.1001/archpediatrics.2009.91

Capaldi, D. M., Knoble, N. B., Shortt, J. W., & Kim, H. K. (2012). # 4 A systematic review of risk factors for intimate partner violence. *Partner Abuse, 3*(2), 1–27. https://doi.org/10.1891/1946-6560.3.2.e4

Cater, A. K. (2014). Children's descriptions of participation processes in interventions for children exposed to intimate partner violence. *Child Adolescent Social Work, 31*, 455–473.

Center for Court Innovation. (2009). *A national portrait of domestic violence.* Retrieved from http://www.courtinnovation.org/research/good-courts-case-problem-solving-justice-0

Centers for Disease Control and Prevention. (2020, April 30). *Infographic about Intimate Partner Violence.* Retrieved from https://www.cdc.gov/violenceprevention/communicationresources/infographics/ipv.html#:~:text=When%20we%20teach%20skills%20and,intimate%20partner%20in%20their%20lifetime.

Centers for Disease Control and Prevention. (2022, October 11). *Fast facts: Preventing intimate partner violence.* Retrieved December 28, 2022, from https://www.cdc.gov/violenceprevention/intimatepartnerviolence/fastfact.html

Chamberlain, L., & Levenson, R. (2011). *Healthy moms, happy babies: A train the trainers curriculum on domestic violence, reproductive coercion and children exposed.* Healthy Moms, Happy Babies. Retrieved December 29, 2022, from https://www.futureswithoutviolence.org/userfiles/file/HealthCare/HV_Trainer%27s_Guide_Low_Res_FINAL.pdf

Childhood Domestic Violence. (2022, October 14). *You are not alone.* CDV. Retrieved December 29, 2022, from https://cdv.org/what-is-cdv/you-are-not-alone/

Chanmugam, A. (2014). Social work expertise and domestic violence teams. *Social Work, 59*, 73–79.

Clevenger, B. J., & Roe-Sepowitz, D. (2009). Shelter service utilization of domestic violence victims. *Journal of Human Behavior in the Social Environment, 19*, 359–374.

Davies, J., & Lyon, E. (2014). *Domestic violence advocacy: Complex lives/difficult choices* (2nd ed.). Thousand Oaks, CA: SAGE.

Davies, J., Lyon, E., & Monti-Catania, D. (1998). *Safety planning with battered women: Complex lives/difficult choices.* Thousand Oaks, CA: Sage.

Davies, K., Block, C. R., & Campbell, J. (2007). Seeking help from the police: Battered women's decisions and experiences. *Criminal Justice Studies, 20*(1), 15–41. https://doi.org/10.1080/14786010701241317

Dichter, M. E., Cerulli, C., Kothari, C. L., Barg, F. K., & Rhodes, K. V. (2011). Engaging with criminal prosecution: The victim's perspective. *Women & Criminal Justice, 21*, 21–37.

Dziegielewski, S. F., Campbell, K., & Turnage, B. (2005). Domestic violence: Focus groups from the survivor's perspective. *Journal of Human Behavior in the Social Environment, 11*(2), 9–24.

Faver, C. A., & Strand, E. B. (2003). Domestic violence and animal cruelty: Untangling the web of abuse. *Journal of Social Work Education, 39*, 237–253.

Finkelhor, D., Hotaling, G., & Yllo, K. (1988). *Stopping family violence.* Newbury Park, CA: Sage.

Forgey, M. A., Allen, M., & Hansen, J. (2014). An exploration of the knowledge base used by Irish and U.S. child protection social workers in the assessment of intimate partner violence. *Journal of Evidence-Based Social Work, 11*(1/2), 58–72.

Fridel, E. E., & Fox, J. A. (2019). Gender differences in patterns and trends in U.S. homicide, 1976–2017. *Violence and Gender, 6*(1), 27–36. https://doi.org/10.1089/vio.2019.0005

Frisch, L. A., & Caruso, J. M. (1996). Criminalization of Woman Battering: Planned Change Experiences in New York State. In A. R. Roberts (Ed.), *Helping battered women: New perspectives and remedies* (pp. 102–131). New York, NY: Oxford University Press.

Fusco, L. J. (1989). Integrating systems: Police, courts, and assaulted women. In B. Pressman, G. Cameron, & M. Rothery (Eds.), *Intervening with assaulted women: Current theory, research, and practice* (pp. 125–135). Hillsdale, NJ: Erlbaum.

Gelles, R. J., & Cornell, C. P. (1990). *Intimate violence in families.* Thousand Oaks, CA: Sage.

Goodmark, L. (2018). *Decriminalizing domestic violence: A balanced policy approach to intimate partner violence.* Oakland, CA: University of California Press.

Graham-Bermann, S. A., Lynch, S., Banyard, V., DeVoe, E., & Halabu, H. (2007). Community-based intervention for children exposed to intimate partner violence: An efficacy trial. *Journal of Consulting and Clinical Psychology, 75*, 199–209. https://doi.org/10.1037/0022-006X.75.2.199

Grant, E., Dechart, L., Wimbish, L., & Blackwood, A. (2021). (rep.). *Missing and murdered Indigenous People.* Retrieved from https://www.niwrc.org/sites/default/files/images/resource/wy_mmip_report.pdf

Green, D. L., & Macaluso, B. (2009). The social worker in a domestic violence shelter. In A. R. Roberts (Ed.), *Social workers' desk reference* (2nd ed., pp. 95–102). New York, NY: Oxford University Press.

Green, D. L., & Roberts, A. R. (2008). *Helping victims of violent crime: Assessment, treatment, and evidence-based practice.* New York, NY: Springer.

Hackman, R. (2021, September 26). Femicides in the US: The silent epidemic few dare to name. *The Guardian.* Retrieved from https://www.theguardian.com/us-news/2021/sep/26/femicide-us-silent-epidemic

Hamby, S. (2015). *The VIGOR safety plan for victims of domestic violence | Sherry Hamby.* Retrieved from https://www.familyjusticecenter.org/wp-content/uploads/2019/11/The-VIGOR-The-Victim-Inventory-of-Goals-Options-Risks.pdf

Haeseler, L. A. (2013). Organizational development structure: Improvements for service agencies aiding women of abuse. *Journal of Evidence-Based Social Work, 10*(1), 19–24. https://doi.org/10.1080/15433714.2013.751000

Hirschel, D. (2008). *Domestic violence cases: What research shows about arrest and dual arrest rates.* U.S. Department of Justice Programs (NIJ ePub). Retrieved from https://www.ojp.gov/ncjrs/virtual-library/abstracts/domestic-violence-cases-what-research-shows-about-arrest-and-dual

Hirschel, D., & Buzawa, E. (2009, October). *An examination of the factors that impact the likelihood of arrest in intimate partner violence cases.* Paper presented at the annual meeting of the Justice Research Statistical Association, St. Louis, Missouri.

Johnston, J., Roseby, V., & Kuehnle, K. (2009). *In the name of the child: A developmental approach to understanding and helping children of conflicted and violent divorce* (2nd ed.). New York, NY: Springer.

Jones, F. (2014, September 10). Ray Rice: Black women struggle more with domestic abuse. *Time.* Retrieved December from https://time.com/3313343/ray-rice-black-women-domestic-violence/

Kamradt, B., Gilbertson, S. A., & Jefferson, M. (2008). Services for high-risk populations in systems of care. In B. A. Stroul & G. M. Blau (Eds.), *The System of Care Handbook: Transforming mental health services for children, youth, and families* (pp. 469–490). Baltimore, MD: Brookes.

Knoll, J. (2009). Treating the morally objectionable. In J. T. Andrade (Ed.), *Handbook of violence risk assessment and treatment: New approaches for mental health professionals* (pp. 311–346). New York, NY: Springer.

Lawn, R. B., & Koenen, K. C. (2022). Homicide is a leading cause of death for pregnant women in US. *British Medical Journal, 379*(2499). https://doi.org/10.1136/bmj.o2499

Lee, B. X. (2019). Structural Violence. In B. X. Lee (Ed.), *Violence. An interdisciplinary approach to causes, consequences, and cures* (pp. 123–142). Hoboken, NJ: Wiley.

Leone, J. M., Johnson, M. P., & Cohan, C. L. (2007). Victim help-seeking: Differences between intimate terrorism and situational couple violence. *Family Relations, 56*(2), 427–439.

Levendosky A., & Graham-Bermann S. (2020). Trauma and parenting in battered women: An addition to an ecological model of parenting. *Journal of Aggression, Maltreatment, & Trauma, 3,* 25–35. https://doi.org/10.1300/J146v03n01_03

Van Lieberman, A., Horn, P., & Ghosh Ippen, C. (2005). Toward evidence-based treatment: Child–parent psychotherapy with preschoolers exposed to marital violence. *Journal of American Academy of Child and Adolescent Psychiatry, 44*, 1241–1248. https://doi.org/10.1097/01.chi.0000181047.59702.58

Liutkus, J. F. (1994, April). Wife assault: An issue for women's health. *Internal Medicine, 7*, 41–53.

Martin, M. (1988). A social worker's response. In N. Hutchings (Ed.), *The violent family: Victimization of women, children, and elders*. New York, NY: Human Science Press.

Maxouris, C. (2022, January 21). A timeline of 22-year-old Gabby Petito's case. *CNN*. Retrieved November 14, 2022, from https://www.cnn.com/2021/09/16/us/gabby-petito-timeline-missing-case/index.html

McMahon, S., Postmus, J. L., Warrener, C., Plummer, S., & Schwarts, R. (2013). Evaluating the effect of a specialized MSW course on violence against women. *Journal of Social Work Education, 49*, 307–320.

Messing, J. T. (2014). Intimate partner violence and abuse. *Encyclopedia of Social Work*. Oxford, UK: Oxford University Press. https://doi.org/10.1093/acrefore/9780199975839.013.1151

Messing, J. T., & Thaller, J. (2014). Intimate partner violence risk assessment: A primer for social workers. *British Journal of Social Work, 45*(6), 1804–1820. https://doi.org/10.1093/bjsw/bcu012

Messing, J. T., Thaller, J., & Bagwell, M. (2014). Factors related to sexual abuse and forced sex in a sample of women experiencing police-involved intimate partner violence. *Health & Social Work, 39*, 181–191.

Miller, C., & Vittrup, B. (2020). The indirect effects of police racial bias on African American families. *Journal of Family Issues, 41*(10), 1699–1722. https://doi.org/10.1177/0192513X20929068

Miller, E., Jordan, B., Levenson, R., & Silverman, J. G. (2020). Reproductive coercion: Connecting the dots between partner violence and unintended pregnancy. *Contraception, 81*(6), 457–459.

Miller, L. (2008). *Counseling crime victims: Practical strategies for mental health professionals*. New York, NY: Springer.

Moorer, O. (2021, January 5). *Intimate partner violence vs. domestic violence*. YWCA Spokane. Retrieved December 29, 2022, from https://ywcaspokane.org/what-is-intimate-partner-domestic-violence/

Morgaine, K., & Capous-Desyllas, M. (2015). *Anti-oppressive social work practice: Putting theory into action*. Los Angeles, CA: Sage.

Mullarkey, E. (1988). The legal system for victims of violence. In N. Hutchings (Ed.), *The violent family: Victimization of women, children, and elders* (pp. 43–52). New York, NY: Human Science Press.

Mullins, G. P. (1994). The battered woman and homelessness. *Journal of Law and Policy, 3*, 237–255.

Murray, R. (2014). NFL player Ray Rice released after disturbing new video surfaces. *ABC News*. Retrieved from http://abcnews.go.com/Sports/ray-rice-cut-ravens-video-elevator-punch/story?id=25347953

National Resource Center on Domestic Violence and the Battered Women's Justice Project. (1994). *The Violence against Women Act 1994*. Harrisburg, PA: Author.

Novick, K. K., & Novick, J. (2005). *Working with parents makes therapy work*. Lanham, MD: Rowman & Littlefield.

Øverlien, C. (2010). Children exposed to domestic violence: Conclusions from the literature and challenges ahead. *Journal of Social Work, 10,* 80–97. https://doi.org/10.1177/1468017309350663

Pence, E., & Paymar, M. (1993). *Education groups for men who batter*. New York, NY: Springer.

Peterson, C., Kearns, M. C., McIntosh, W. L. K. W., Estefan, L. F., Nicolaidis, C., McCollister, K. E., . . . Florence, C. (2018). Lifetime economic burden of intimate partner violence among U.S. adults. *American Journal of Preventive Medicine, 55*(4), 433–444. https://doi.org/10.1016/j.amepre.2018.04.049

Roberts, A. R. (1996a). Police responses to battered women: Past, present, and future. In A. R. Roberts (Ed.), *Helping battered women: New perspectives and remedies* (pp. 85–95). New York, NY: Oxford University Press.

Roberts, A. R. (1996b). Court responses to battered women. In A. R. Roberts (Ed.), *Helping battered women: New perspectives and remedies* (pp. 96–101). New York, NY: Oxford University Press.

Sacco, L. N. (2015). *The Violence against Women Act: Overview, legislation, and federal funding*. Washington, DC: Congressional Research Service.

Salvatore, T. (2022, October 5). Domestic murder–suicide: A compound tragedy. *FBI.* Retrieved November 14, 2022, from https://leb.fbi.gov/articles/featured-articles/domestic-murder-suicide-a-compound-tragedy

Shernoff, M. (2008). Social work practice with gay individuals. In G. P. Mallon (Ed.), *Social work practice with lesbian, gay, bisexual, and transgender people* (2nd ed., pp. 141–178). New York, NY: Taylor & Francis/Routledge.

Siegler, R. T. (1989). *Domestic violence in context: An assessment of community attitudes*. Lexington, MA: Heath.

Stith, S. M., Williams, M. B., & Rosen, K. (1990). *Violence hits home: Comprehensive treatment approaches to domestic violence*. New York, NY: Springer.

Sutton, A., Beech, H., & Nelson-Gardell, D. (2020a). Intimate partner violence and reproductive coercion. In *Encyclopedia of social work*. Oxford, UK: Oxford University Press. https://doi.org/10.1093/acrefore/9780199975839.013.1368

Sutton, A., Beech, H., Ozturk, B., & Nelson-Gardell, D. (2020b). Preparing mental health professionals to work with survivors of intimate partner violence: A comprehensive systematic review of the literature. *Affilia, 36*(3), 426–440. https://doi.org/10.1177/0886109920960827

Sutton, A., & Carlson, C. (2019). Advocating for self-determination, arriving at safety: How social workers can address ethical dilemmas in intimate partner violence. In S. Marson & R. McKinney (Eds.), *Routledge handbook of social work ethics and values* (pp. 127–134). London: Routledge.

Tolman, R. M., & Bennett, L. W. (1990). A review of quantitative research on men who batter. *Journal of Interpersonal Violence, 5,* 87–118.

Violence Policy Center. (2020). *When men murder women: An analysis of 2018 homicide data*. Retrieved December 28, 2022, from https://vpc.org/studies/wmmw2020.pdf

Wahab, S., Mehrotra, G., Kimball, E., Ng Ping Cheung, S., & Myers, K. (2021). Resistance and submission: A case study of the training of DV advocates. *Journal of Progressive Human Services, 32*(3), 243–262.

Walker, L. E. (1979). *The battered women*. New York, NY: Harper & Row.

Walker, L. E. (2017). *The battered woman syndrome* (4th ed.). New York, NY: Springer.

Waller, B. Y., Joyce, P. A., Quinn, C. R., Hassan Shaari, A. A., & Boyd, D. T. (2022). "I am the one that needs help": The theory of help-seeking behavior for survivors of intimate partner violence. *Journal of Interpersonal Violence, 38*(11–12), 7063–7888. 088626052210843. https://doi.org/10.1177/08862605221084340

Warshaw, C., Sullivan C., Rivera E., & U.S. Department of Health, and Human Services. (2013). *A systematic review of trauma-focused interventions for domestic violence survivors*. Chicago, IL: National Center on Domestic Violence, Trauma & Mental Health.

West, C. M. (2021). Widening the lens: Expanding the research on intimate partner violence in Black communities. *Journal of Aggression, Maltreatment, & Trauma, 30*(6), 749–760. https://doi.org/10.1080/10926771.2021.1919811

Westmarland, N., & Kelly, L. (2013). Why extending measurements of success in domestic violence perpetrator programmes matters for social work. *British Journal of Social Work, 43*, 1092–1110.

Yoo, J. A., & Huang, C. (2013). Long-term relationships among domestic violence maternal mental health and parenting and preschool children's behavior problems. *Families in Society, 94*, 1–9.

13

Social Work Advocacy in the Political Arena

Economic and Environmental Justice

By Sarah R. Young, Debra Nelson-Gardell, and Sophia Dziegielewski

CHAPTER 13: EPAS COMPETENCIES

Social work programs at the bachelor's and the master's level are accredited by the Council of Social Work Education (CSWE). CSWE's Educational Policy and Accreditation Standards (EPAS) describe the processes and criteria that social work courses should cover. In 2022, CSWE updated its EPAS standards. The following competencies are addressed in this chapter.

Competency 2: Advance Human Rights and Social, Racial, Economic, and Environmental Justice

Social workers understand that every person regardless of position in society has fundamental human rights.

Competency 5: Engage in Policy Practice

Social workers identify social policy at the local, state, federal, and global level that affects wellbeing, human rights and justice, service delivery, and access to social services.

Think for a moment about politics and the impression of glamor of being an elected national politician, someone who goes to Washington, DC, and walks the halls and conducts meetings in the Capitol. For a nostalgic reference, if you have not seen it, please check out the classic 1939 movie *Mr. Smith Goes to Washington*; you can find it on Netflix using the search function and keying in "Jimmy Stewart." Ok, the movie is a bit old, and yes, it is in black and white and not high definition, but overall, it still is a fun movie. The venerable actor Jimmy Stewart plays a young, idealistic politician who goes to Washington to represent the people and do what is right. He embraces his new job driven by a simple philosophy—government is the friend of all the people, works for all the people, and represents all the people. He believes that elected leaders are simply an extension of our neighbors who act on our behalf and place the community's need above their personal interests. Their overriding purpose is to help achieve what is best for the country. But Mr. Smith finds something else in Washington, DC. He sees a place filled with corruption as people, lobbyists and elected officials alike, solely seek power and money. Mr. Smith is challenged to hold onto his idealism and core principles of doing good for and on behalf of others.

Is Mr. Smith's uncompromising view of politics and government the popular perspective held by most of us today? We suspect not. The riots at the U.S. Capitol on January 6, 2021, show us at minimum that our country feels politically divided. It is likely that few people today believe that Mr. Smith's principled vision accurately depicts the motivations of politicians as we approach the end of the first quarter of the twenty-first century. Rather, the view of former president Ronald Reagan is more widely held: "Government is not the friend of the people." This sentiment creates "strange bedfellows" where people on both ends of the political spectrum, from conservative to progressive, may lose faith in the role of government for an equitable and reliable distribution of resources. Beyond that, recent election polling shows that Republicans and Democrats (the two major political parties in the United States) view the other party and their supporters in an increasingly negative light, with some scholars describing America as "exceptional" compared to other nations for its level of political or partisan divide (Dimock & Wike, 2021). This political polarization may make it even more difficult to get things accomplished politically, leading to increasing frustration at the gridlock and a feeling of a self-fulfilling prophecy.

• • •

For many social workers, especially given our current political climate, the political arena is not an enticing place. For example, the events on January 6, 2021, clearly highlighted this political polarization and lack of faith in the system. On that date, the U.S. Capitol in Washington, DC, was stormed by an angry group of President Trump's supporters protesting his loss of re-election. This event provides a demonstration of how passions run high and how ignoring politics and political opinions can have disastrous results, whether it is related to racial injustice, COVID prevention measures, or voting rights for all Americans. Many of these events and protests recently have been fueled by political figures (SPLC Southern Poverty Law Center, 2021). When this political climate is added to the Council on Social Work Education (CSWE)'s professional educational standards, we see that it is no easy task to advance **human rights** in relation to social, racial, and economic justice in a climate with a history of oppression and strong political agendas. Therefore, social workers need to have knowledge and understanding of the change efforts needed, as well as how to critically apply this understanding toward any advocacy for change.

Politicians can have a profound influence on current opinion, and just the thought of "playing politics" to achieve social and economic justice conjures up ideas of backroom deal making, abuses of rank and power, payoffs, and other unethical activities. Political scandals and allegations of wrongdoing over the past years have reached every level of political office and branch of the government. It is not surprising that you may hold politics in low esteem. In 2022, the national discourse was filled with rancor and partisanship, with seemingly little work getting done. Even so, we believe that all social workers should and must be actively engaged in their political environments, from the local city/county governments to the federal government (see Figure 13.1). And, as we will discuss in this chapter, the so-called political world is not limited to electoral politics and government, but also extends to community action and mobilization, as well as working in our social service agencies.

As we begin our exploration of social work advocacy for social, economic, and environmental justice in the political arena, we recognize a basic belief widely held among social workers: we must continue to rise our passions and use this energy to directly engage in the political process, no matter if it is at the national, state, or local level of government. We social workers are obligated to work on behalf of our clients and promote social policies and economic justice principles that strengthen our communities, our neighborhoods, and our nation (see, for example, Section 6 of the National Association of Social Workers (NASW) Code of Ethics (2018), which discusses social workers' obligation to broader society).

FIGURE 13.1
Jeannette Rankin was a suffragist, a peace advocate, and the first social worker elected to the U.S. Congress, in 1917.

13.1 WHAT IS MEANT BY POLITICS?

We throw around the word *politics* as if we all agree to its meaning. Plain and simple, politics has to do with power, especially the power to access, use, and allocate (often scarce) resources. Certainly, politics and the political arena include all elected offices and the officials who fill them at the local, county, state, and federal levels. Yet getting to hold one of these positions involves a process referred to as *electoral politics*. Electoral politics involves getting elected, which by its very nature is incredibly difficult. Electoral politics encompasses a range of activities such as fundraising, getting out the vote, face-to-face communications, political advertisements, recruiting and sustaining volunteers, and communicating a clear message that reflects the candidate's vision.

> ### Did You Know . . .
> The first woman to hold a presidential cabinet position was a social worker, Frances Perkins, who held the position from 1933 to 1945. She held that post longer than any other person in the department's history. She played a key role in the creation of the Social Security Act of 1935.

Politics, however, is much more comprehensive and moves beyond just electoral politics. It incorporates informal and formal interactions that are politically and strategically charged and often not tied to one's ideals. Rather, the "winds of the moment," that is, public opinion, often drive politics and its outcomes. To understand these "winds," it may also be helpful to understand ideology, or the values and ideals that animate political actions, communications, and tendencies. A savvy social worker (and citizen) goes beyond electoral politics to understand the values behind the policies, norms, and tendencies. For example, if someone believes in the ideology of "pulling oneself up by their bootstraps" and being "independent," they may oppose policies that offer social welfare benefits or a redistribution of wealth. If someone holds the ideology that a person is embedded in their social environment and that there is power in community and mutual aid, they may oppose policies that benefit individuals but harm the community at large. Politics is also alive and well in social welfare organizations, in agencies, and even on social work practice teams. How often have you heard someone say, "The politics here stink" or "They're just playing politics" or "You have to understand the politics of the situation"? Some of our friends left their jobs primarily because of the agency's politics. This was likely referring to ideology and conflicting values and the way that it informed decisions, behaviors, and actions.

So, what is meant by politics? We see politics as being diverse and embracing many of our day-to-day activities. Haynes and Mickelson (2009) have gone further, contending that our helping activities make all social work political. Ideas and services are needed like providing gender-affirming care to transgender individuals, discussing race and the legacy of racism in public classrooms, and advocating for individuals to have access to abortion care. These practice expectations are commonly endorsed and in line with commonly held conceptions of social work ethics. These practices, however, although they are expected in social work, are not universally endorsed and can become contested in public opinion. These practices, which are rich in social work ethics but controversial in public opinion, can make what we do as social workers seem ever more radical and politicized. In this chapter, we will look at politics and its relation to social work practice. Our discussion will examine political strategies, including electoral ones, that we hope can serve as a primer for social workers on politics and political activities.

> ### Did You Know . . .
> The first women ever elected to the U.S. Congress was a social worker. Jeannette Pickering Rankin was first elected in 1916 (before women had the right to vote) and again in 1940.

13.2 WHY POLITICS AND SOCIAL WORK?

First, let us take a brief look at social and economic justice in the political arena and its relation to social service agencies. What guides or directs the activities of social workers in their agencies? We must understand that social workers are not always able to take liberties in their practice and provide any type of service they see fit. An organization's policies set forth its programs and services, which in turn direct the social worker to the actual day-to-day work with and on behalf of clients. No one agency offers the comprehensive range of social work activities; rather, an agency's programs grow out of its specific function. Let us say, for example, that a practitioner in a child welfare agency wants to offer group therapy to senior citizens in a local housing project. The intervention may be worthy, but the agency likely will decide that a seniors' group falls outside the agency's purpose and function. It is also important to note the concept of "mission creep." This is when an agency's original purpose or focus "creeps" or extends to issues that stray from the original focus or, in some cases, expands beyond the organization's expertise. Many times, this is the result of funding opportunities (for example, when efforts that support the funding for the original focus on an issue "dries up," the organization will need to pursue other funding streams to survive). The focus on an issue can also change when leaders or the staff or board of directors at a for-profit or nonprofit agency change. There is debate among scholars and practitioners about whether mission creep is "bad" or "good," but one concern is that the reputation an organization may build on one issue may be diluted if they switch focus to a different issue. They may lose political capital or the ability to influence the political process if the mission creeps too far, stretching the organization and its staff beyond their limits or expertise ("New Opportunities or Mission Creep?," 2021).

An agency's function is set forth in its mission statement and operationalized by its policies. Policies do not just spring forth; rather, they are the result of a political process, be it an agency board of directors or an elected body such as a state legislature. And who are these people? Are they social workers? Are they expert enough in human services that they should be shaping social work practice? Unfortunately, most people who develop an agency's broad social policies have little, if any, direct social work experience, and even fewer have an educational background in social work or human services. When professional social workers choose to avoid the political aspects of the field, one outcome is inevitable: people who are not social workers will govern that area of social work practice. As a result, social workers need to engage in the political world to help shape social policy. This can be done in three ways: (1) by electing individuals who are sympathetic to the profession's interests, (2) by engaging in lobbying and education efforts with those who form social policy, and (3) by encouraging social workers to run for elected office (see the activity below).

Activity

Find out how many social workers there are in your state legislature, both in the House and in the Senate. You can do this by checking with your state's secretary of state office. Then look at the House and Senate committees that oversee social problems; they may have titles such as Committee on Health and Human Services. Now, look to see how many committee members are social workers. Look at their staff: How many employees are social workers? What do your findings tell you about the development of social policies in your state? What potential is there for interprofessional or interdisciplinary work?

13.3 SOCIAL WORK VALUES AND POLITICAL ACTIVITY

Some social workers allow negative images of politics and political activity to outweigh their responsibility to engage in the political arena. Yet the Code of Ethics of the NASW (2018) clearly states our obligations and political responsibilities in two separate places in Section 6, "The Social Worker's Ethical Responsibilities to Society":

1. Social workers should facilitate informed participation by the public in shaping social policies and institutions (Sec. 6.02).
2. Social workers should . . . advocate for changes in policy and legislation to improve social conditions in order to . . . promote social justice (Sec. 6.04[a]).

The 2022 Educational Policy and Accreditation Standards (EPAS) of the CSWE (2022) also supports the profession's political involvement and refers to this as "policy practice." Specifically, competency 5 reminds us that social workers understand that human rights–based policies are needed to advance social, economic, racial, and environmental justice and how these factors can affect social policy.

Social work practitioners understand that policy affects service delivery, and they actively engage in policy practice. Social workers know the history and current structures of social policies and services, the role of policy in service delivery, and the role of practice in policy development. Social workers analyze, formulate, and advocate for policies that advance social well-being and collaborate with colleagues and clients for effective policy action.

Why does the NASW Code of Ethics, as well as similar ethical codes for other professional social welfare organizations and the CSWE's EPAS, emphasize practitioner involvement in the political arena? First and foremost, remember that the definition of social work includes working to bring about a just community built on the tenets of social and economic equality. Second, many of the problems experienced by clients are created by forces external to them and can be remedied only through amended social policy or additional funding for social services. Third, the best advocates for change are those who deal with problems day in and day out. Through direct practice, social workers see firsthand the debilitating effects of problems on clients.

Now this is where it can get a bit messy for social workers. Some groups contend that the social work profession is nothing more than a left-wing group of ideologues who want socialistic style programs and a big government. Is this belief true? Or do experienced social workers familiar with the system vote the issues they feel are most germane in helping the clients served? Just look at where social work educational programs are located: some are in our nation's most conservative faith-based universities, whereas others are found in the most liberal universities. In other words, social work crosses the political and ideological spectrum. The social work tent includes conservatives and liberals, Democrats, Republicans, Greens, Independents, Tea Party members, and others from the dozens of political parties that are active in politics. In other words, the social work ideology of justice for all people is not owned by one political party. Our political ideologies and philosophies merely frame different pathways to achieve justice for all.

Several scholars have attempted to study the political diversity of social workers, and their articles may be worth exploring (see, for example, Ringstad, 2014; or Rosenwald, Wiener, Smith-Osborne, & Smith, 2012) The political diversity in social work can be difficult to accept, but if we use our critical thinking approaches, we can engage in thoughtful debate that will result in answers that benefit the greater good. And that is ultimately what politics is about: doing what is right for the greater good.

13.4 A HISTORICAL OVERVIEW OF POLITICAL ACTIVITY BY SOCIAL WORKERS

Social work has had separate but significant waves of political involvement: the Progressive Era of the nineteenth century, the 1930s New Deal, and the 1960s War on Poverty, with their emerging social justice and economic and racial equity movements. In each of these periods, social work's involvement in politics mirrored the profession's growth and internal conflict over mission, scope, and function. In all three periods, leaders disagreed about the causes of social problems and how best to solve them. The Progressive movement was attractive to many social workers and provided a political focus for their philosophical beliefs and commitments. Social workers such as Jane Addams and Florence Kelley used the political system to address social problems. Settlement house workers seemed to be more partisan than other social workers. Weismiller and Rome (1995) noted that settlement workers ran political campaigns, organized neighborhoods to support particular candidates, lobbied, and worked on welfare reform. In contrast, Mary Richmond, a leader in the charity organization society movement, believed that social workers should be nonpartisan and confine their efforts to helping clients to resolve their individual issues (Weismiller & Rome, 1995).

The Great Depression of the 1930s created ample opportunity for social workers to venture into the political arena. Schools of social work were more organized than their forerunners during the Progressive Era, and macro content, which focused on political concerns, was included in the curriculum. The federal government's Children's Bureau and Women's Bureau provided social workers with a setting to address significant social issues. In fact, many parts of the Economic Security Act of 1935 were written by social workers (Weismiller & Rome, 1995).

Frances Perkins, a social worker who was President Franklin Delano Roosevelt's secretary of labor in the 1930s and 1940s, was instrumental in bringing about significant social welfare changes such as the forty-hour workweek, minimum wage, worker's compensation, child labor laws, unemployment relief, and social security (Downey, 2010, p. 1). The profession was beginning to accept political activism as a suitable response to crisis; however, social work remained ambivalent regarding political activity as an appropriate long-term social work methodology (Haynes & Mickelson, 2009).

The third wave of political activism by social workers came in the 1960s. With the emergence of the Peace Corps and VISTA, a domestic version of the Peace Corps program, and the burgeoning civil rights movement, social workers actively promoted a political agenda. Community organization, both as a practice and as an educational specialization, took shape in the late 1950s and 1960s. This activity challenged social workers to view systems from the much broader macro prospective. Federal dollars were funneled to initiatives that encouraged neighborhoods and local people to engage in problem-solving and community action.

> ### Did You Know . . .
> A Congressional Social Work Caucus was founded in 2010. It is bipartisan (including both Democrats and Republicans) and bicameral (House and Senate members), presently at over forty members.

Within the profession, the debate continues and the role and scope of political activity within the profession and its professional activities remain. Weismiller and Rome (1995) reported in one study that NASW members agreed to pay increased organizational dues if it would bring about greater political activity by members. Yet this somewhat overzealous characterization did not affect the entire profession, and members continued to debate the merits of efforts at the political level, particularly considering the massive problems facing individuals and families.

In 1976, the NASW organized its first conference on politics in Washington, DC. Aimed primarily at social work political activists, the meeting gathered NASW members from around the country for a political training institute. The NASW then supplemented this national meeting with regional institutes. By the end of the twentieth century, the NASW discontinued these gatherings and left training to the state chapters and other professional associations.

The 1990s seemed to be a watershed decade for social workers involved in electoral politics. Never in the profession's history were social workers and their professional organizations as active in political campaigns as in the last decade of the twentieth century. "Lift Up America" was the NASW's 1992 presidential project theme, augmented by numerous national, regional, and state election activities (Landers, 1992), and NASW's political action committee, Political Action for Candidate Election (PACE), endorsed more than one hundred candidates for national office (Hiratsuka, 1992) and contributed approximately $200,000 to national campaigns while state PACE committees dispensed in excess of $160,000 to state and local candidates (D. Dempsey, personal communication, November 30, 1992; Dempsey, 1993).

In 1991, the NASW reported that 113 social workers held elected office (Weismiller & Rome, 1995); by 1992, 165 social workers in forty-three states had won a variety of races (NASW, 1992); and by 1998, there were more than 200 social workers holding political office in the nation! They held elected office at all levels of government, from city councils to the U.S. Senate. With each succeeding election, individual social workers and their professional associations gained new experiences, built on previous knowledge, and strengthened themselves as active players in the political arena.

In 2003, 175 social workers nationwide held a variety of local, state, and federal offices, and as of February 2009, according to the NASW, 177 social workers held elected office. In 2013 the NASW reported that there were 190 individuals elected to various offices (see the "Did You Know?" that corresponds to this information), whereas in the 117th Congress (2021–2023), social workers held five positions, two in the U.S. Senate and three in the U.S. House of Representatives (Lewis, 2022).

There are several more recent and noteworthy accomplishments of social workers in Congress. First, the so-called dean (e.g., longest-serving person) of women in the U.S. Senate prior to her retirement in 2017 was a social worker, Barbara Mikulski (D-MD), who was first elected in 1986. Senator Mikulski was also the longest-serving woman in the history of the U.S. Senate, having served for thirty years. In 2022, former congresswoman (elected in 2010) and social worker Karen Bass became the first woman and second Black person to be elected to the role of mayor of Los Angeles. In December 2022, Senator Kyrsten Sinema (who was elected to the House of Representatives in 2012) announced she was leaving the Democratic Party and would register as an Independent.

Although still evolving and emerging, several contemporary movements in the United States and beyond have animated social workers, involved them, and encouraged debates about the best and most equitable path forward. Summarizing an evolving history is a challenging task, so we will focus on two noteworthy social movements: the Occupy Wall Street (OWS) movement and the Black Lives Matter movement. The OWS movement is a protest movement that saw advocates occupy Wall Street (a symbol of global finance in New York City) and other financial centers across the United States and world as an attempt to interrupt the vast economic disparities that exist between what leaders of OWS called the "1%" (or wealthiest people) and "the 99%" (referring to the population that is most at risk of economic exclusion and disparity). The term "We are the 99%!" was a rallying cry to build community and political action, raising political consciousness about the impact of Wall Street and "Big Finance" on predatory loans, student loan debt, housing foreclosures, low-paying wage work, and other systemic issues.

Officially founded in 2013 after the murderer of a thirteen-year-old Black youth named Trayvon Martin was acquitted, Black Lives Matter (or #BLM) has been a highly visible organization and wider social movement calling for the elimination of anti-Black racism in society (see Figure 13.2). Utilizing social media, mainstream media, and community-based organizing tactics, #BLM has also had notable electoral victories, such as initiating police reform at the local and state levels, the passage of "Breonna's Law" in Kentucky following the murder of Breonna Taylor during a police raid, and a political action committee (or PAC) that works to elect officials whose goals align with

FIGURE 13.2
Black Lives Matter (#BlackLivesMatter) formed as a social and political movement focused on anti-racism and racial justice in the United States in reaction to persistent systemic violence perpetrated against people of color.

the mission of #BLM (Menjevar, 2020). Although advocates for centuries, led by people of color and White allies, have named and decried systemic racism, the suffocation and murder of George Floyd by police officers in Minneapolis, Minnesota, in May 2020 was a flashpoint and rallying cry to end racism and examine the ways that White supremacy animates our society from a micro to a macro level.

As you continue to learn about the social work profession, you will note the changes in the 2022 CSWE EPAS that highlight anti-racism, diversity, equity, and inclusion. It is the opinion of these authors that the #BLM and racial justice movements of late have pushed a shift in language to name anti-racism as an explicit social justice goal.

Name: Samantha Fletcher
Place of residence: Upstate New York
College/university degrees: University of Tulsa, BA; University at Albany, State University of New York, MSW, PhD
Present position: Executive director, National Association of Social Workers, New York State (NASW–NYS)

What does a typical day at work look like for you? What tasks do you generally complete as a social worker in your area of expertise? For me, the beauty of macro social work means no days look the same. At NASW–NYS, I support our team and volunteers in several areas including political advocacy,

continues

continued

professional development, multiple social justice initiatives, and networking. I am in meetings at least five to six hours each day, strategizing and implementing our initiatives. I am responsible for leading the research needed to support our legislative agenda items. For example, I author reports for the New York State legislature highlighting workforce issues. Advocacy typically begins with research. It is our job to tell the stories and provide data to the decision makers when we want to see policy change.

What do you do in your spare time? I like to spend time with my family. We are deeply connected to the land and enjoy hiking, kayaking, climbing mountains, etc.

Why did you choose social work as a career? The values of the profession, especially social justice, closely matched my lived experiences. I connect with the mission of the profession to change the systems that cause and perpetuate oppression.

What is your favorite social work story? My organizational perspective and leadership approach are grounded in Indigenous culture. As a Cherokee, this is my culture. As such, leadership is tied to service. I view my role as building stages with my team and inviting social workers to step on the stage and lead efforts for needed change. Shortly following the public murder of George Floyd in May 2020, our team embedded several racial justice initiatives at the NASW–NYS chapter. One of our student board members didn't think we went far enough in combatting racism. During a meeting with her, we developed an initiative called Revolutionize the Profession. The plan was to hold a series of town halls to identify how racism presents in schools of social work, NASW–NYS, clinical social work, and macro social work. During town halls, we elevated the voices of social workers who face racism. White allies joined us but were asked to listen and communicate in the chat feature. We thought we would end the town halls and begin a series of work groups to create a white paper to present to stakeholders who have the power to make organizational changes. We didn't anticipate the town halls themselves becoming an intervention. Within a few months of implementation, we had social workers from all fifty states and several countries participating in the town halls. We received feedback from participants that they didn't feel alone anymore, they now recognized racism as racism, and they felt empowered to speak up and call it out. The participants also started a peer support group for only social workers who face racism to process the trauma they have experienced in the workplace. A student started this initiative that has made meaningful change in the lives of social workers around the world. What is more powerful than that?

What would be the one thing you would change in our community if you had the power to do so? I would like to see the social justice value more at the center of all our work. We are called to work with and on behalf of people from oppressed membership groups. This is what differentiates us from other helping professions. I don't believe people are voiceless or unable to communicate the issues in their communities. People with lived experience are the most invested in their community and are the best people to describe the needed changes. We need to create opportunities for them to advocate for change, especially in the political arena.

13.5 ELECTORAL AND LEGISLATIVE POLITICS

Political social work has two sides that are intricately related; both are important to the social work profession's realization of its goals. First, social workers identify and support candidates who are friends of the profession and support issues that are of direct concern to the profession. By making contributions and working in candidates' campaigns, social workers can help pro–human service candidates win elections. This is referred to as electoral politics. Second, social workers collaborate with elected officials during the ongoing legislative sessions on policy proposals. This is commonly referred to as lobbying or education.

> ### Did You Know . . .
>
> The NASW keeps track of the elected officials at various levels who are social workers. This list is updated on a regular basis. For more information, see the "Social Workers in Elected Office" section of their website. It can be reached directly at: https://www.socialworkers.org/Advocacy/Political-Action-for-Candidate-Election-PACE/Social-Workers-in-State-and-Local-Office. Political activity is generally viewed through the lobbying lens. Richman (1991), Haynes and Mickelson (2009), Mahaffey and Hanks (1982), and Wolk (1981), among others, emphasize the lobbying side of politics. Little attention is paid to electing candidates to public office. De-emphasizing electoral politics violates two important legislative lessons, however:
>
> - *Lesson 1*: Lobbying is much easier with supporters and friends of social work than with its detractors and antagonists.
> - *Lesson 2*: Lobbying for prevention proposals is a much better use of energy than lobbying against negative proposals and rectifying previous legislative errors.
>
> You might view the political process as a cycle (see Figure 13.3). In a rational logical model, the political life cycle begins with candidate identification and then progresses through participation in electoral politics, educating the candidate on social work issues and advocating certain positions, lobbying the candidate to support the profession's stance, and back to candidate identification and re-election.
>
> This becomes an ongoing, uninterrupted circle. Not surprisingly, the real-life political cycle is not so rational and not so logical; in fact, you can typically enter the process and begin your efforts at any given point. Suppose, for example, that legislation regarding critical race theory in education is up for debate in the state senate. First, you attempt to educate your legislator on the issue from a social work perspective; the representative decides not to support your view. You soon realize that a new elected official is needed to better serve the interests of your district and the profession, and you begin to seek an alternative candidate for the next election. And the cycle continues.

continues

continued

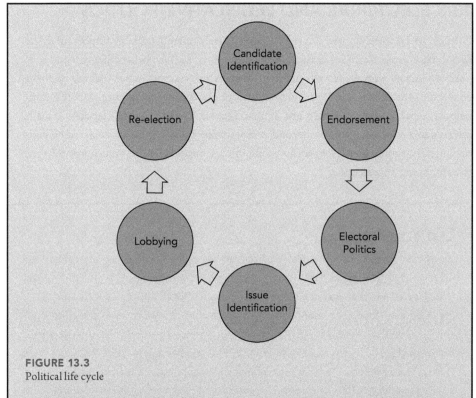

FIGURE 13.3
Political life cycle

Although elected officials are responsible primarily to their constituencies, they are also receiving advice and counsel from their campaign supporters and lobbyists. A long-held political adage, "Money buys access," is true. Even so, active campaign support establishes a relationship between the candidate and possible next officeholder and the social work community. When this is achieved, rather than having to adopt a defensive lobbying posture—protecting what they have from social work antagonists—social workers can influence the development and enhancement of social services through public policy. Conversely, when they do not have supporters and advocates in the legislative body, social workers must put most of their efforts into attempting to block or modify coercive public policies.

13.6 SOCIAL WORK ORGANIZATIONS AND ELECTORAL POLITICS

Nonprofit organizations, such as those in which social workers are most typically employed, are not allowed to directly campaign, lobby, or give money to a political candidate. Further, campaign financing laws severely restrict the amount of money a person or group can give to a candidate, campaign, or political party.

Political action committees evolved as a mechanism organized to spend money for the election or defeat of a candidate. The first PAC was created in 1944 by the Congress of Industrial Organizations so that contributions could be made to pro-union candidates while skirting the federal law that precluded unions giving money to candidates. Political action committees have been and remain very controversial. Federal laws limit the amount of money any one group can donate to an individual. The U.S. Supreme Court in its 2010 decision, *Citizens United v. Federal Election Commission*, overturned key sections of the Campaign Reform Act of 2002 (also known as the McCain–Feingold Act) that had prohibited corporate and union political expenditures in political campaigns. After this decision, private groups could spend dollars from their general treasuries to finance campaigns. And in 2014, the Supreme Court further opened the door to funding candidates by abolishing limitations on election spending, striking down a decades-old cap on the total amount any individual can contribute to federal candidates in a two-year election cycle (Liptak, 2014).

Another Supreme Court decision, this time in 2012, allowed an individual to give $2,600 per candidate in primary and general elections. The Supreme Court also said that imposing overall limits of $48,600 by individuals every two years for contributions to all federal candidates violated the First Amendment, as did separate aggregate limits on contributions to political party committees, currently $74,600 (Liptak, 2014).

The Center for Responsive Politics reports that the top donor PAC for the 2021–2022 fiscal cycle was the National Association of Realtors, which gave $3,594,000. The top donor to Democratic candidates was the American Federation of State, City, and Municipal Employees, with approximately $2.2 million in contributions; the largest donor to Republican candidates for the same period was the Majority Committee PAC, with approximately $2.2 million in donations (Center for Responsive Politics, 2022b).

Social work itself has been actively engaged since the early 1970s in organizing PACs. As with any PAC, the profession's political advocacy group acts as a mechanism to identify candidates who support social work while often providing financial support for their election. And, as shown in Box 13.1, PACs have their own language.

Education Legislative Network

In 1971, the Education Legislative Network was organized by the NASW as a vehicle to bring together divergent and often contentious social work groups, in particular, clinical and macro-level social workers. The premise of the Education Legislative Network was that a united social work community would strive together for the good of the whole, and as it did so, separate groups would become more friendly toward each other, thus creating broader support for each group's issues.

As a beginning effort, the Education Legislative Network was successful in educating NASW members on a number of national policy issues. It used a progressive strategy in which NASW members were (1) informed on issues and (2) encouraged to lobby their elected representatives in Washington. It became obvious, however, that more friendly elected leaders were needed. Concurrent with the association's first organized political efforts, PACs took on greater importance in American politics overall.

> **BOX 13.1**
>
> **TERMS AND DEFINITIONS USED BY POLITICAL ACTION FOR CANDIDATE ELECTION (PACE), 2014**
>
> **Contribution:** When PACE gives money to a candidate running for office.
>
> **Candidate:** A person running for election.
>
> **Endorsement:** A stamp of approval for someone running for office, which means that PACE wants him or her to win the election.
>
> **Challenger:** A person running for election against an incumbent.
>
> **Incumbent:** A person who is already elected to the office for which he or she is seeking re-election.
>
> **Fundraiser:** An event to raise money for a candidate; takes place at various times of the year; counts as a contribution.
>
> **Hard money:** A slang term that refers to campaign and political action committee funds that are subject to limitations and reporting requirement by the Federal Election Commission. The PACE money is hard money that is unaffected by the new campaign finance law. Indirectly, it will put more pressure on PACE for its funds.
>
> **Open seat:** A situation when the incumbent is not running for re-election or the district was newly created during redistricting and reapportionment.
>
> **PACE trustees:** The national PACE board of trustees consists of seven NASW members who make decisions about endorsements of and contributions to federal candidates.
>
> **Partisan:** Relating to a particular political party. (Bipartisan relates to the two major political parties; nonpartisan does not relate to any political parties; multipartisan relates to more than one political party.)
>
> **Political:** Relating to government, making or influencing governmental policy, party politics, or the art or science concerned with winning and holding control over a government.
>
> **Reapportionment and redistricting:** An activity that occurs every ten years after the U.S. Census, during which congressional districts are allocated to states and congressional district lines are redrawn to reflect shifts in population.
>
> *Source:* National Association of Social Workers (n.d.).

Political Action for Candidate Election

In 1976, the NASW organized PACE, which served as the association's national effort to raise money and endorse candidates for national office who supported the profession's agenda. In other words, PACE was the NASW's PAC. Through its bylaws, PACE is a separate organization from NASW, which as a nonprofit organization is not allowed to engage in political activity such as lobbying. However, it is interesting to note that an employee of a nonprofit organization may educate a candidate on an issue. The difference is that to lobby is to get someone to adopt a particular position, whereas to educate is to provide an individual with basic facts without endorsing a particular stance. The difference is subtle, perhaps, but vital in order not to violate any laws or regulations.

Political Action for Candidate Election has a threefold purpose. First, it endorses those candidates who are most supportive of social work issues. Second, it sometimes makes campaign contributions to endorsed candidates. And third, it educates NASW members about candidates and encourages electoral participation (see the activity below).

> ## Activity
> Contact your state PACE unit through the NASW. Find out who serves on the PACE board of trustees or committee. What is the track record of PACE endorsements? Do endorsed candidates get elected? How many Republicans, Democrats, or candidates from other political parties were endorsed in the last election? How much money was contributed to the candidates? What criteria do they use when endorsing candidates?

The national PACE is limited to endorsing and contributing to national candidates, that is, candidates for the presidency, the U.S. House of Representatives, and the U.S. Senate. A board of trustees (seven to thirteen in total), each appointed by the national NASW president, governs PACE. The board, with consultation from NASW members and state chapters, screens candidates for national elections, endorses candidates, and in some but not all instances makes financial contributions. After a candidate is endorsed, NASW members in the candidate's state or district are encouraged to work in his or her campaign and make additional campaign contributions.

Even as the national PACE effort grew in strength, the NASW recognized the truth of former House speaker Tip O'Neill's (D-MA) statement, "All politics is local." The NASW therefore encouraged state chapters to organize their own PACE units to endorse local and statewide candidates and raise funds for their campaigns.

By 1998, every state had a PACE unit working to help candidates who support social work positions. The state PACE units are structured in a manner like the national PACE: each has a board of trustees or committee, appointed by the state chapter president, that screens and endorses candidates. The efforts and activities of the state PACE units are separate from each other and from the national PACE; there is no formal mechanism or means for accountability to the national professional association, although PACE state units may consult with the national PACE if it advances their collective work.

In theory, a state PACE unit could work against the interests of the NASW national office by endorsing candidates who do not support the social work positions outlined at the national level. If this happened, there would be no recourse for the NASW national office or the chapter membership. As trustees, the board members are ultimately responsible for all endorsements and for disbursements of campaign contributions, and they are accountable only to themselves. Nevertheless, the nationwide network of social work PACE units provides an important opportunity to identify, support, and work to elect individuals who can be advocates for social work issues and friends of the profession. Your membership and active involvement in NASW brings your voice into the effort.

> ### Did You Know . . .
> Several graduate and undergraduate academic programs offer courses focusing on politics and social work. There are also several professional social work organizations that focus on macro practice, such as the Association for Community Organization & Social Action, which has a macro social work student network for social work students interested in macropractice.

POLITICAL ACTION FOR CANDIDATE ELECTION ENDORSEMENT PROCESS

Each state unit as well as the national PACE develops its own endorsement process and procedures. Remember that the state PACE units are not tied to each other or to the national PACE; they are separate entities, each with its own set of bylaws. A state's PACE unit is separate even from the state's NASW chapter. You can learn more about your own state PACE organization by visiting your NASW state chapter website; look for links directly to PACE or look for a link to *advocacy*. Sometimes you will need to look under the "About Us" link to find the PACE information.

Colby and Buffum (1998) found what seems to be a typical format for state endorsement (but recognize that not all states follow this procedure). The board or committee puts together a survey that is distributed to all candidates (see Box 13.2). Candidates are given a specified period in which to respond; if a survey is not returned, someone calls the candidate's office asking to have the survey completed. If the candidate is seeking re-election, the board will also review his or her voting record. Finally, members of local NASW units will be asked to provide input to the process. Some state PACE units also hire professional lobbyists to help assess candidates. Professional lobbyists work the legislative halls every day, attempting to convince legislators to vote one way or another on specific legislation. As a result, they often have a more detailed understanding of candidates than PACE trustees.

Based on the information it accumulates from the survey, the board or committee decides which candidates to endorse. Once endorsements are made, the board then determines whether a financial contribution will be made. For example, in 2022, NASW–PACE endorsed 112 candidates for office. Of the 112 candidates endorsed, there were 77 wins, 28 losses, and 6 races that were too close to call (NASW, 2022). The board looks at many issues in deciding whether to contribute: Is the candidate opposed in the election? Does the candidate need the money? Is the candidate themselves a social

BOX 13.2
EXAMPLE OF A CANDIDATE SURVEY

Currently, Texas is ranked last (fiftieth) of the fifty states and the District of Columbia in the delivery of mental health care (National Public Radio, 2022). At the same time, Texas also ranks near or at the top of the list of all states in terms of the severity of many health and social problems, including teen pregnancy, school dropouts, the number of AIDS cases, infant mortality, and the lack of rural health care.

During the spring Texas legislative session, numerous bills were introduced to address these issues. As with most states, however, the ongoing state deficit forced cuts in social services. Public education to housing and health care were all cut. Nevertheless, the legislature spent three special sessions, at a cost of $1.5 million per session, to redraw congressional district maps to eliminate congressional seats held by Democrats and increase the number of Republicans in the U.S. House of Representatives. Clearly, the majority of the members in the Texas legislature were more concerned about political self-interest than providing for the public good.

Do you support or oppose the following 2023 Legislative Priorities?

Support Oppose

1. Advocate for equitable accessibility in social work licensing process within the Texas State Board of Examiners.
2. Support social workers in educational settings by codifying school social work services.
3. Expand eligibility and funding for mental health Loan Repayment Program to address the current workforce shortage.
4. Promote policies and funding opportunities that create pipeline workforce programs for early career social workers, especially compensation for undergraduate and graduate level practicum students.
5. Establish reimbursement parity at 100% of the Medicaid rate for licensed Clinical Social Workers (LCSWs) and other mental health professionals for psychotherapy services, aligning Health and Human Services Commission (HHSC), and Texas Department of insurance (TDI) rules.
6. Expand the Medicaid mental health network to include reimbursement for Licensed Masters Social Workers (LMSWs) under supervision at 70 percent the Medicaid rate for psychotherapy services.
7. Enhance the experience, resources, and outcomes of individuals and families engaging in child welfare, education, healthcare, immigration, and criminal justice systems by increasing the social work workforce.
8. Ensure licensed social workers from other state jurisdictions have the authorization to provide mental health services in Texas, and that Texas providers can legally6 serve clients out of state.

continues

continued

Equity, Health, and Human Rights

1. Promote ongoing racial justice efforts to advance practices that address systematic oppression and increase accountability across institutions.
2. Support increased access to affordable, quality health care, including reproductive care and rights, with an emphasis on low income and at-risk populations, and implement a state-wide expansion of Medicaid for enhanced eligibility and access.
3. Partner with allies to ensure all children and families involved in the immigration process receive supportive services, are treated humanely, and allowed all due process the law allows.
4. Support culturally responsive policies within the child welfare system that ensure client safety, well-being and development through trauma-informed practices.
5. Promote and protect the civil rights of all Texans, ensuring that all services remain available to those who identify as LGBTQIA+.
6. Support policies that reduce barriers to voting and expand access to registration.
7. Partner with allies to support restorative justice efforts within the education system and eliminate the school-to-prison pipeline. Source: NASW Texas Chapter. (2023). 2023 Legislative Priorities. Austin, TX: NASW Texas Chapter. Retrieved from: https://www.naswtx.org/page/LegislativePriorities

On a separate piece of paper, please answer the following questions:

1. If elected, (a) what would be your main legislative priorities, and (b) what committee assignments would you seek?
2. Are you, any member of your family, or a close personal friend a professional social worker?
3. Would you support the seven premises outlined under Equity, Health and Human Rights?

worker? If unopposed, does the candidate need help in retiring a campaign debt? There are no correct answers to these questions; they simply serve as discussion points to help the trustees to make a final decision.

Did You Know . . .

Bundling is a campaign loophole that allows organizations to get around legal financial caps on contributions. For example, a state PACE unit may contribute the maximum amount for a person running for the state house, say $500. When the PACE check is presented, additional checks from individual NASW chapter members are given at the same time (thus, the

> idea of a bundle of checks). So, a candidate may receive $500 from the organization and perhaps thirty checks for $50 each, for a total of $2,000. In effect, the organization, with member support, has increased its level of financial support to the candidate. And the candidate is more likely to remember a $2,000 contribution than individual $50 checks.

Once endorsements are made and the level of contributions is determined, NASW members are informed of the PACE decisions. Checks may be presented directly to the candidate by social workers from the candidate's district; this provides an opportunity for local social workers to make a direct connection with the candidate and to strengthen the relations for future lobbying efforts.

Social Workers and Political Campaigns

Volunteers and paid campaign staff provide critical support to a candidate's electoral bid. Commitment to a candidate and his or her ideas is the only prerequisite. It does not matter where the individual's competence lies: a campaign has room for a volunteer to perform an array of tasks—answering phones, preparing bulk mailings, putting up yard signs, conducting social media campaigns, and canvassing neighborhoods.

Social workers can contribute many skills typical of their profession to a political campaign. These include planning, decision-making, consensus building, group management, research, assessment, relationship building, crisis intervention, and communication. In terms of roles, or functions, that social workers perform, eight are appropriate for political campaigns (see Table 13.1).

The following are a few simple things that social workers can do to strengthen the presence of the social work profession in a political campaign.

VOLUNTEER AT A CAMPAIGN HEADQUARTERS

Traditionally, a campaign begins on Labor Day and concludes with the general election in November, a ten- to eleven-week period. But now this traditional election cycle has been thrown out. The day after President Obama was re-elected in 2012, political pundits were already predicting who would be in the running for the Democratic and Republican nominations in 2014. And, as of 2022 when this text was in revision, predictions for the November 2024 elections were coming fast and furious for both Democratic and Republican candidates.

A campaign relies on volunteers to staff an office, with much of the work taking place during evenings and on weekends. You might organize ten to fifteen social workers and commit to providing a volunteer for one night each week at the campaign office for the duration of the campaign. Say you select Tuesday evening; this can become known as Social Work Night to the candidate and key staff. The potential value to future lobbying efforts of even such a brief commitment is incalculable. The candidate will be much more open and sympathetic to a group that worked throughout the campaign.

Table 13.1 Voting: What Can a Social Worker Do in a Political Campaign?

Role	Tasks
Advocate	Speaks on behalf of the candidate and represents his or her position to various constituent groups
Teacher/educator	Instructs staff and volunteers about campaign strategy and issues; in conjunction with advocacy, educates potential supporters about the candidate
Mobilizer	Energizes staff and volunteers; prioritizes and assigns individuals to needed campaign activities
Consultant	Provides expertise in problem-solving and strategizing; helps candidate and staff to develop strategies for the campaign
Planner	Identifies key community players and activities; assesses strengths of potential relationships and overall prospects for electoral victory
Caregiver	Provides emotional support to candidate, his family, friends, staff, and supporters (relations can become strained)
Data manager	Develops and implements a data structure that allows for quick and easy access; designs a user-friendly system for staff, volunteers, and candidate
Administrator	Develops and implements a well-operating campaign structure that is functional and not overwhelming; keeps the structure simple, efficient, and consistent with the candidate's best interests

MAKE YOUR OWN SOCIAL WORK BUTTONS AND T-SHIRTS

Make a modest investment to purchase buttons or T-shirts printed with a simple slogan. Social workers for (candidate's name)—what an effective message! Be sure to wear the buttons or T-shirts on Social Work Night/Day at the campaign office. Let others know who you are and where you stand.

HOST A FUNDRAISER

All candidates need money to run a campaign. A bare-bones efficient run for the state House costs at least $100,000 (with variation in costs between states), and these costs continue to escalate with each new electoral cycle. Plan a fundraising event with other social workers. Be sure to coordinate the event with the candidate's campaign staff—there is usually one person who is responsible for scheduling the candidate's time. Make the event brief—the candidate has no extra time during the heat of a campaign and often needs to be in four places at once. Try to make the event fun as well. Be creative. For example, one interesting fundraiser was a *nonevent fundraiser*; people donated $25 not to attend! If you host an event with the candidate present, be sure to wear your buttons or T-shirts.

WORK ON ELECTION DAY

Election Day is the longest day in the campaign. With polls opening as early as 6:00 a.m. in some states and closing as late as 8:00 p.m., campaign volunteers work up to eighteen hours! Volunteers are needed to work near the polling places, passing out candidate literature; to put up last-minute candidate yard signs; to provide voters with transportation to the polls (be sure to wear your buttons or T-shirts and to talk about your candidates with those you are driving); and to staff the campaign office, answering phones and dealing with last-minute glitches and crises. When the polls close, go to the candidate's headquarters or wherever the party is being held. You deserve to celebrate after all the energy you have put into the campaign. And be sure to wear your buttons or T-shirts.

HELP WITH SOCIAL MEDIA

The power of social media in the political world is undoubtedly on full display at the time of writing this chapter. The 2008 Obama presidential campaign is credited with being the first presidential campaign to effectively use email and other related technologies on a national scale. Political organizers are becoming more and more savvy about the diverse uses of social media. For example, in September 2014, the Republican National Committee launched a new Voter Challenge Facebook application. The election of Donald Trump, who himself was a media icon and notorious Twitter user for some period, saw ever-evolving use of social media as the new frontier of the "public square." Campaigns from the local to the federal level often scour opponents' social media histories looking for material to be used against the candidates. Social media can also be a new way to engage with candidates by messaging, boosting support for, and debating the candidates. Although the traditional door-to-door campaigning, handing out literature, and putting up yard signs will remain a significant part of the electoral process, social media are fast becoming the quickest and most nimble way to communicate with current and prospective supporters.

Lobbying for Social Work Legislation

Lobbying is an act of persuasion in which you educate someone about an issue with the goal of gaining active support. According to the Center for Responsive Politics (2022a), in 2022 there were 12,098 lobbyists registered to persuade and educate the U.S. Congress and the various federal agencies. That is slightly more than 22 lobbyists for each of the 535 members of the U.S. Congress (100 senators and 435 members of the House of Representatives). You might think that is a lot of people who are paid to influence (e.g., lobby) the U.S. Congress. Yes, it is, but there were far fewer lobbyists (about 20 percent less) in 2022 than in 2007, when there were 14,837 registered lobbyists. But these numbers are only for the federal government! Every state, county, and city/town government also has its own sets of lobbyists. So, what do all these individuals who are paid hundreds of millions of dollars by their clients to lobby have in common? They are the experts with key information and access to support, both financial and people. And you, too, can be a lobbyist with specialized information around a specific social issue.

Lobbying takes many different forms in the attempt to find the best way to communicate a clear and persistent message. Typical activities include emailing, writing postcards and letters, making telephone calls, making personal visits, and giving public testimony. Each is an effective and important part of the lobbying process. With computer technology, letter writing is not difficult—a mass mailing to the legislature does not take too much longer to compose than a single letter. Given the trend away from using phones, telephone calls are particularly effective because of the perceived effort and the personal voice involved. Both emails and comments posted on an elected official's web page or Facebook page are quick and easy. Personal visits are expensive if you do not live in or near the state capital, and they also require a great deal of time for what are generally brief meetings, but face-to-face meetings are effective. Remember that elected officials have local offices, and you can meet with them there if you are not able to travel to the state capitol. No matter which form of lobbying you select, be sure to be brief, dignified, sincere, and, most important, respectful.

LETTER WRITING

Write early, before the legislator has made up his or her mind. Write a letter of one page or less; legislators (nor their staff) do not have time to read dissertations! Get to the point quickly and be concise. Attach handouts to support the key points. Make sure you educate, educate, and educate the legislator on the issue. If you are writing about a specific bill, be sure to include the bill number. Note how the legislation will affect the legislator's district, mention the names of key supporters of your position from the district or from the legislator's campaign, provide reasons to support the bill, and request an answer to your letter indicating how the legislator plans to vote on the issue. Be sure to say thank you at the beginning and end of the letter and be sure to use the appropriate salutation (see Box 13.3). Be sure to get your agency's written permission before using its letterhead for a letter. Using letterhead indicates that you are writing on behalf of the agency or, at a minimum, that your views reflect those of the organization.

A typical but not useful letter-writing strategy is the prewritten postcard approach. This involves using preaddressed postcards with a prewritten message that requires the person only to sign her or his name. This does not work, nor do duplicated copies of the same letter with a signature line. Politicians know that people have not taken time to share their views and that this is a quick and dirty mail method. The basic lesson is that mass duplicated mailings are a 100 percent waste of time and energy. Write a personal handwritten note; this is your most effective strategy and your best bet to be heard.

EMAIL

Now all elected officials have websites that post a variety of information, including a "Contact Us" section. This is useful if you organize a large group to send a series of emails in concert with a letter-writing campaign. But if you plan on writing one email to let off steam, that is about all that will occur—you will let off steam but nothing much will happen. You will get two email responses. The first one will come back almost immediately, thanking you for writing to the senator or representative. You might get a

BOX 13.3
SALUTATIONS FOR LETTER WRITING

Governor

1. Writing:
   The Honorable (full name)
   Governor of (State)
   Address: Dear Governor (last name)
2. Speaking: Governor (last name)

Lieutenant Governor

1. Writing:
   The Honorable (full name)
   Lieutenant Governor of (state)
   Address: Dear Lieutenant Governor (last name)
2. Speaking: Lieutenant Governor (last name)

Speaker of the House

1. Writing:
   The Honorable (full name)
   Speaker of the House
   Address: Dear Mr./Madame Speaker:
2. Speaking: Mr./Madame Speaker

State Senator

1. Writing:
   The Honorable (full name)
   The (State) State Senate
   Address: Dear Senator (last name)
2. Speaking: Senator (last name)

State Representative

1. Writing:
   The Honorable (full name)
   The (State) House of Representatives
   Address: Dear Mr./Ms. (last name)
2. Speaking: Representative (last name) or Mr./Ms. (last name)

second email a month or so later, maybe sooner, thanking you "for sharing your views." You might be fortunate enough to get the personal email address of an elected official. If so, use it sparingly unless the elected person tells you otherwise, and certainly do not give it out to others. As with letter writing, be sure to get your agency approval before sending any messages to an elected official's email address using your agency's email domain.

TELEPHONE CALLS

You will probably talk with a legislative aide, so don't take it personally if you don't speak with the legislator. Also, if there is a phone blitz on the bill you're calling about, the aide may be rather short with you and may cut you off in the middle of your presentation. Again, do not take it personally. Be brief and to the point; try to take less than three minutes. Make notes before you call and practice what you want to say. Introduce yourself and mention your address, especially if you are from the legislator's home district. Follow the same principles as in letter writing: identify the bill number and describe how it will affect the legislator's district. Ask how the legislator plans to vote on the issue; if the person you speak to does not know, ask when you can call back to learn of the decision. End by thanking the legislator or aide for his time and support.

PERSONAL VISITS

Personal visits are the most time-consuming, frustrating, and potentially most effective form of lobbying. Meetings are as a rule very brief, lasting from a few minutes to no more than fifteen. They usually take place in the legislator's office, but do not be surprised if you find yourself walking down the hall to accompany the representative or senator to a meeting while you lobby for a few short minutes. Most often you will meet with an aide, but if you have a good relationship with the legislator—in particular, if you were a good campaign volunteer—you will probably be able to meet with him or her. You will need to be pleasant, brief, concise, and convincing. Discuss only one legislative issue during your meeting. Be sure to follow up with a phone call and a letter of appreciation. These meetings may be short, but many social workers have found that they have been able to change a politician's stance on an issue because of a face-to-face meeting. Your sincerity, knowledge, and compassion about the issue speak volumes to politicians.

GUEST SPEAKERS

Check with your faculty to have them invite elected officials to your school, for a class lecture or a noon presentation. Most elected officials enjoy visiting with college students and try to work in the time, if possible. Such visits provide a wonderful opportunity to develop a relationship with an elected official as well as for him or her to learn more about social work. There is one basic rule of thumb for such visits—do not get into arguments. Listen, be courteous, and most of all remember that you are representing the social work profession.

PUBLIC TESTIMONY

In general, when considering legislation, a committee must allow opportunities for public input. Such testimony usually lasts less than five minutes per speaker. The committee will have rules that govern the testimony's length—check them out beforehand by contacting the committee's staff person in the legislative offices.

Be sure that your testimony is in a word-processed format, distribute copies to the committee members, and have a few extra copies available for others who are interested in your comments. Be sure your name, address, and phone number are easily found on the cover page of your testimony in case someone wishes to contact you after the hearing. This is important because you may not have time to get all your ideas across; the written testimony allows you to do so. In effect, your public testimony is an abstract or abbreviated version of your written statement.

As with writing letters and sending emails, be sure to get your agency's approval if you are in any way offering testimony in a professional capacity. Your agency may ask that you refrain from referencing your employment or they may encourage you to do so. Again, always check with your supervisor or agency executive director prior to giving any testimony at a hearing.

Do not be surprised if the legislators ask you no questions after your presentation. There may be twenty to thirty people offering testimony, each speaking three to five minutes. Asking questions only prolongs the process. If a question is asked, be sure of your answers. Do not make up an answer; if you are not sure what the answer is, tell the committee you'll find out and get back to its staff person within twenty-four hours. And be sure you do! Nothing is more damaging to your credibility in the legislature than to give inaccurate or misleading information or to make a promise and not follow up.

Finally, do not argue with the legislators! You are a guest in their workplace. You are there to convince and make friends, not to argue and make enemies. Your legislative opponent today may be your key supporter tomorrow on another issue. Try not to burn your bridges, but build and strengthen them.

> ### Did You Know . . .
> Although not focused exclusively on electoral politics, the Community Tool Box from the University of Kansas offers a free resource to build community-based organizing skills, including how to get your "Issues on the Public Agenda." More information can be found by searching "the Community Tool Box."

13.7 COMMUNITY ORGANIZATION: LINKING THE POLITICAL TO THE COMMUNITY

To best link social and economic justice in the political arena to the needs of the community, a strategy must first be outlined. By strategy we mean the action options that are open to the social worker to help reach the change goals identified. Rothman, Erlich, and Tropman (1995) remind us to start by researching the history and the evolution of strategies that have been applied in the past. The old adage "History can repeat itself" can complicate any type of intervention plan. Second, the social worker must explore the societal climate or environment. What is important to the individuals who live in the community? What are the values, the norms, and the expectations of the constituents to be served? To discover this, the community itself must be examined. The stakeholders must be identified. Small groups, both formal (such as church members) and informal (such as neighborhood support systems), within this community will affect the change efforts to be implemented. These players must be identified, and all efforts must be made to ensure that their needs are addressed. In community organizations, the needs and wishes of the community always provide the cornerstone for all helping efforts. Therefore, it is important not to have helping efforts thwarted by individual or institutional agendas that do not operate for the best efforts of the community. To completely describe the fundamentals of this type of practice is beyond the scope of this chapter. Although it is a critical part of social work macropractice, a beginning social worker is encouraged to obtain more specialized training and education before engaging in this type of practice.

SUMMARY

Weismiller and Rome (1995, p. 2312) noted that "despite residual skepticism about the appropriateness of political work, there has been a resurgence of political action in recent years" among social workers. This continues to hold true. Courses in schools of social work, ongoing efforts by national and state PACE units, direct participation in political campaigns, and election of social workers to political office are among the many ways social workers are developing much-needed political savvy.

We have learned through many, often painful, experiences that attempts to influence the development of public policy must begin well before the legislative process. Identifying and working for the election of people who are in favor of human services initiates the lobbying effort; having the right people in place makes lobbying that much easier. We know that trusting in the election process with all the repeated controversy about election outcome deniers can make it difficult. However, analysis results from the Center for Justice indicate that in many of the key battleground states, those that tried to control election administration fared the worst (Norden & Parker, 2022). Having faith in the system is important, but challenging process will always be the right of those who run and serve. Participation in the election process helps the social worker see the internal workings and better understand why and how challenges occur.

Moreover, elected officials are influenced by groups that "vote regularly and are active in the electoral process" (Parker & Sherraden, 1992, p. 27). Social workers and their membership organizations are making significant contributions to political campaigns. As campaign workers, social workers can translate their agency-based practice expertise to the political arena.

The years since 2001 have been tumultuous at best, and this trend continues with concerns related to future elections. Wars and economic crisis have continually overshadowed all efforts, no matter the profession or ideological beliefs. Trillions of dollars were spent to re-energize the American economy, pay for the ongoing wars, and fund antiterrorism efforts while, at the same time, in 2022, the nation's debt continues to grow to unprecedented levels. The continued wars in the Middle East and the ongoing terrorism threats drove much of the political discourse after the 2001 terrorist attacks and certainly will do so for years to come. The world since the COVID-19 pandemic emerged in 2020 seems difficult to describe, and the impact of the pandemic on our social and political fabric continues to unfold. At the time of the writing of this edition of this text, the U.S. Attorney's Office reported that our government continued in its investigation of an attack on our U.S. Capitol that disrupted a joint session of Congress during the presidential election certification process. World political circumstances were further complicated by the 2022 onset of the war between Russia and Ukraine, and an unprecedented $21.9 billion was given in military assistance, along with additional monies for security assistance (U.S. Department of State, 2022). In recovering from the COVID-19 pandemic, disagreement among the American people runs high as to whether these funds should be used to assist our allies or be applied to the needs of U.S. citizens.

But what of social welfare? Isn't it important to support our allies? Yet, how do we solve our most perplexing internal problems? How will Americans fund (or not fund) their medical services for aging and/or vulnerable people? Will full funding for public education continue to be kept at bay? What will happen with student loan debt? Will the Congress establish proactive immigration reform that strengthens and extends individual civil liberties to all people? Will new laws expand hate crime statutes? Will Congress create a living wage law rather than continuing to support the minimum wage statutes? Perhaps, with the ever-increasing speed of change in our lives, you might know some of answers to these questions as you read this chapter.

Social work students too will be challenged when they move into the practice world. Current and future social workers must have knowledge and skills in economic and financial literacy, not just around macro policy issues, but also in the day-to-day work with those whose homes are in foreclosure, those who have lost their jobs, or retirees whose fixed incomes and pension plans have been devastated.

Even with the daunting global circumstances swirling around us, social workers must pursue legislative agenda for social work education. Social work education must advocate for new ways to increase and broaden access to higher education through new fellowship and scholarship programs; seek ways to strengthen existing loans, create new loan forgiveness programs, advocate for the full and complete funding of Pell grants, and seek to repair the faulty federal student loan assistance program; and argue for the deepening and expansion of funding streams to our colleges and universities to ensure that the necessary financial support is available for our programs to address their missions in the education of undergraduate and graduate social work students.

Social work practice requires advocacy for social and economic justice, and all efforts are directly affected by politics. We cannot ignore this simple reality. Every two years, close to a half million offices are up for election, involving hundreds of thousands of candidates. These individuals represent the broad spectrum of political ideology and views of humankind. Sadly, most of these individuals are not social workers. Although the number of social workers holding elected office increased significantly over the past quarter of a century, policy decisions are made by non–social workers and those with little knowledge or desire to recognize the importance of achieving social, economic, and environmental justice of the human condition. These uninformed and often misinformed elected individuals with committed agendas continue to influence the work in our social service agencies.

Social workers face a simple choice: to remain on the sidelines, while others make decisions that determine how the social service community operates, or to participate aggressively at all levels of political activity to open the door for progressive lobbying efforts that critically address social, economic, and environmental justice. Simply put, social workers can sit in the audience watching others advocate change or they can be pivotal actors who build on the rich experiences of political campaigns.

REFERENCES

Center for Responsive Politics. (2022a). *Lobbying database.* Retrieved December 22, 2022, from https://www.opensecrets.org/federal-lobbying

Center for Responsive Politics. (2022b). *Top PACs.* Retrieved December 28, 2022, from https://www.opensecrets.org/political-action-committees-pacs/top-pacs/2022

Colby, I., & Buffum, W. (1998). Social work and political action committees. *Journal of Community Practice, 5*(4), 87–103.

Lewis, C. J. (2022). Macro social workers gather at Brown School. Washington, DC: Congressional Research Institute for Social Work and Policy. Retrieved December 21, 2023, from https://crispinc.org/

Council on Social Work Education. (2022). *2022 EPAS—Educational Policy, and Accreditation Standards for baccalaureate and master's social work programs.* Alexandria, VA: Author. Retrieved from https://www.cswe.org/accreditation/standards/2022-epas/

Dempsey, D. (1993, March 10). *Letter to chapter presidents.* Washington, DC: NASW Press.

Dimock, M., & Wike, R. (2021, March 29). *America is exceptional in its political divide: The pandemic has revealed how pervasive the divide in American politics is relative to other nations.* https://www.pewtrusts.org/en/trust: Trust Magazine. Retrieved from https://www.pewtrusts.org/en/trust/archive/winter-2021/america-is-exceptional-in-its-political-divide

Downey, K. (2010). *The woman behind the new deal, the life and legacy of Frances Perkins, social security, unemployment insurance, and the minimum wage.* New York, NY: Anchor Books.

Haynes, K. S., & Mickelson, J. S. (2009). *Affecting change, social workers in the political arena* (7th ed.). New York, NY: Pearson.

Hiratsuka, J. (1992). 114 more races backed. *NASW News, 37*(9), 1, 10.

Landers, S. (1992). NASW steps up efforts to elect Clinton. *NASW News*, 37(9), 1.

Liptak, A. (2014, April 2). Supreme Court strikes down overall political donation cap. *New York Times*. Retrieved from https://www.nytimes.com/2014/04/03/us/politics/supreme-court-ruling-on-campaign-contributions.html?_r=0

Mahaffey, M., & Hanks, J. (Eds.). (1982). *Practical politics and social work and political responsibility*. Silver Spring, MD: NASW Press.

Menjevar, J. (2020). *Black Lives Matter protests: The fight for racial equality continues, but these are some victories the movement has already earned*. New York, NY: DoSomething.org. Retrieved from https://www.dosomething.org/us/articles/black-lives-matter-protests-whats-been-achieved-so-far

National Association of Social Workers. (n.d.). *NASW—PACE tip sheet*. Retrieved December 28, 2022 from https://www.yumpu.com/en/document/read/46260729/nasw-pace-tip-sheet-national-association-of-social-workers

National Association of Social Workers. (2018). *Code of ethics of the National Association of Social Workers*. Washington, DC: Author. Retrieved from https://www.socialworkers.org/About/Ethics/Code-of-Ethics/Code-of-Ethics-English

National Association of Social Workers. (2022). *2022 PACE endorsements*. Retrieved December 22, 2022 from https://www.socialworkers.org/Advocacy/Political-Action-for-Candidate-Election-PACE/Elections/2022-PACE-Endorsements

National Public Radio. (2022, June 4). *Texas ranks last in mental health care among U.S. states*. Retrieved from https://www.npr.org/2022/06/04/1103075887/texas-ranks-last-in-mental-health-care-among-u-s-states

New opportunities, or mission creep? (2021). *Board & Administrator for Administrators Only*, 37(11), 2–2. https://doi.org/10.1002/ban.31260

Norden, L. & Parker, M. (2022, November 11). *Election deniers running for secretary of state were this election's biggest losers*. Center for Justice. Retrieved from https://www.brennancenter.org/our-work/analysis-opinion/election-deniers-running-secretary-state-were-elections-biggest-losers?ms=gad_election%20results_635869236409_8628877148_144570830398&gclid=CjwKCAiAnZCdBhBmEiwA8nDQxWGrrTRJ1q2ZLQEOzypGJNUnffiad_sUZSx8gD8ElR8_29viwmGTORoCIugQAvD_BwE

Parker, M., & Sherraden, M. (1992). Electoral participation of social workers. *New England Journal of Human Services*, 11 (3), 23–28.

Richman, W. (1991). *Lobbying for social change*. New York, NY: Haworth.

Ringstad. R. (2014). Political diversity among social work students. *Journal of Social Work Values and Ethics*, 11(2), 13–22.

Rosenwald, M., Wiener, D. R., Smith-Osborne, A., & Smith, C. M. (2012). The place of political diversity within the social work classroom. *Journal of Social Work Education*, 48(1), 139–158. https://doi.org/10.5175/JSWE.2012.201000062

Rothman, J., Erlich, J. L., & Tropman, J. E. (1995). *Strategies for community intervention*. Itasca, IL: Peacock.

SPLC Southern Poverty Law Center. (2021). *The road to Jan.6: A year of extremist mobilization*. Retrieved December 22, 2022, from https://www.splcenter.org/news/2021/12/30/road-jan-6-year-extremist-mobilization

U.S. Department of State. (2022). *Press statement Anthony J. Blinken, Secretary of State. $1.85 billion in additional U.S. military assistance. Including the first transfer of patriot air defense system.* Retrieved December 22, 2022, from https://www.state.gov/1-85-billion-in-additional-u-s-military-assistance-including-the-first-transfer-of-patriot-air-defense-system/#:~:text=The%20Department%20of%20Defense%20is,the%20beginning%20of%20the%20Administration

Weismiller, T., & Rome, S. H. (1995). Social workers in politics. In R. L. Edwards et al. (Eds.), *Encyclopedia of social work* (19th ed., pp. 2305–2313). Washington, DC: NASW Press.

Wolk, J. (1981). Are social workers politically active? *Social Work, 26,* 283–288.

PART FOUR
Expanding Horizons for Social Work

14

Global Social Welfare

By Kenan Sualp, Sophia Dziegielewski, and Debra Nelson-Gardell

CHAPTER 14: EPAS COMPETENCIES

Social work programs at the bachelor's and the master's level are accredited by the Council of Social Work Education (CSWE). CSWE's Educational Policy and Accreditation Standards (EPAS) describe the processes and criteria that social work courses should cover. In 2022, CSWE updated its EPAS standards. The following competencies are addressed in this chapter.

Competency 1: Demonstrate Ethical and Professional Behavior

Social workers understand the value base of the profession and its ethical standards, as well as relevant policies, laws, and regulations that may affect practice with individuals, families, groups, organizations, and communities.

Competency 2: Advance Human Rights and Social, Racial, Economic, and Environmental Justice

Social workers understand that every person regardless of position in society has fundamental human rights.

Competency 3: Engage in Anti-racism, Diversity, Equity, and Inclusion in Practice

Social workers understand how racism and oppression shape human experiences and how these two constructs influence practice at the individual, family, group, organizational, and community levels and in policy and research.

Competency 5: Engage in Policy Practice

Social workers identify social policy at the local, state, federal, and global level that affects wellbeing, human rights and justice, service delivery, and access to social services.

• • •

Our world is a global community. We need to always remember to think of our world on a large scale. Our interests, concerns, influences, and obligation relate to a community that extends far beyond the confines of our geographic neighborhood. As in the past, we continue to call this phenomenon *globalization*, with the creation of an international system that affects domestic economies, politics, and cultures (Midgley, 1997). For social workers, the protection of human rights and the promotion of social justice are at the core of our profession. Global stresses and inequalities affect all societies, and social workers must position and reposition us to prepare for addressing these challenges (Palattiyil et al., 2019).

The human coronavirus disease (COVID-19), for example, disrupted many normal life activities such as employment, education, recreational activities, and socialization. These transformations were so profound that people's lives were changed in significant ways, challenging the basics of human well-being (Schleicher, 2020). This pandemic required a global response in which most countries, including the United States, instituted policies and procedures designed for containment of the virus (Bitler, Hoynes, & Schanzenbach, 2020; Xu, Pompili, & Sampogna, 2021). In the United States, as well as in other nations throughout the world, measures were taken to contain the spread of the virus at individual and community levels; these measures included lockdowns, restrictions on travel, masking in public places, social distancing mandates, and establishing community testing and vaccination sites (Carter & May, 2020). In the educational arena, the emphasis on increased distance education and electronic connections as the preferred style of communication forced us to more completely rely on modern technologies and software to mitigate these barriers. Now we can only wonder what the world will look like by 2050.

Most of us would agree that we live in a global neighborhood, as clearly shown by the COVID-19 pandemic, which crystalized the requirement of a global response. Friedman's (2005) classic work *The World Is Flat* vividly describes the shrinking world and shows how our nations' borders have virtually disappeared. Technology has opened the doors to new possibilities for peoples throughout the world. Email, texting, and social media platforms allow us to communicate in a manner that was unthought of at the beginning of the 1990s. As electronic communication has progressed, the COVID-19 pandemic created a rapid launch into technology and global linkages heretofore never experienced. For example, during the lockdown period, social work educators across the globe scrambled to ensure their students' learning needs were met via online delivery and virtual platforms such as Zoom, Blackboard, Microsoft Teams, and

Google Meets. Educators realized early on that this response brought its own set of potential inequities because not all social work students had the same technological access (Mclaughlin, Scholar, & Teater, 2020). This expanding technology and restrictions of the pandemic were confounded by a widening gap in the wealth of countries; according to the World Social Report (2020), more than 70 percent of the global population resides in countries where the gap in wealth continues to grow at unprecedented levels. As the global economy faces a major downturn as a result of the COVID-19 pandemic (Oxfam Novib, 2021), social work services, especially those related to serving vulnerable populations puts this group at risk for losing opportunities to gain or maintain employment within the labor market (International Labour Organization, 2020).

Did You Know . . .

As of October 24, 2022, approximately 624 million confirmed COVID-19 cases and over 6 million deaths had been reported to the World Health Organization (WHO) and posted on the WHO Coronavirus (COVID-19) Dashboard. There were also 12.8 billion vaccine doses administered. A total of 6.5 million people throughout the world lost their lives as a result of the COVID-19 pandemic between the years 2019 and 2022 (World Health Organization, UNICEF, and World Bank, 2022). This pandemic caused global connections to soar as so many different people in different areas of the world were forced to process it together.

Like what we saw with COVID-19, twenty-first-century history has shown how regional conflicts and disasters can quickly escalate into global issues. Another familiar example from the twentieth century, the Great Depression of the 1930s, reverberated worldwide, not just in the United States where the early effects were concentrated. Later in the 1930s, after the German and Japanese war machines had conquered many of their neighboring countries and beyond, the United States, which had originally assumed an isolationist position, became one of the leading allied nations. The collapse of the Berlin Wall in November 1989 signaled upheavals in many Communist bloc nations that have had significant social and economic consequences around the world. In 2014, the Russian Federation annexed parts of Ukraine to begin rebuilding the former Russian empire (Shoichet, 2014), and in 2022, Russia once again attacked Ukraine, with this invasion resulting in major economic, social, and political impact, not only in the region but also across the globe. The winter of 2022–2023 brought major hardship across Europe as food and energy costs soared.

Did You Know . . .

In October 2022, the National Association of Social Workers (NASW) launched its first chapter in the central district of Kamenets Podisk in the Ukraine (International Federation of Social Workers [IFSW], 2022).

As a by-product of this invasion, there was a devastating impact on prices globally, with the United States seeing an undeniable increase in the cost of gas and other types of energy, as well as building materials and food supplies. The Ukraine war significantly increased the economic and social burden that started with the COVID-19 pandemic (Birrell, 2022). With the impact of the pandemic exacerbated and later combined with acts of war like the invasion of Ukraine, these acts have generated a collective response to a global economic crisis, triggering high inflation that directly impacts the lives of billions of people throughout the world. Certainly, other examples of global events exist, and the message is clear: what happens across the oceans affects all of us, no matter where we live.

> ### Did You Know . . .
> COVID-19 exacerbated the challenge of providing proper maternity care. A survey by WHO stated that half of the 105 participating countries reported partial disruptions in antenatal care.

COVID-19 pandemic responses may have differed globally, but the ease of information sharing via technology reminded us of the opportunity to learn from other societies and cultures about how to strengthen our own approach to social living. Studying how other countries approach social problems and examining their successful strategies can be fruitful for application in our communities. Some people believe that the United States has nothing to learn from the rest of the world about technology, education, and other social advancements, but this is not true! Technology makes global news and updates that may have been delayed in the past almost immediately available to anyone with internet access. This tremendous digital enhancement, however, has been accompanied by digital inequality and is such a concern that the United Nations called for full digital equality (United Nations, 2019). Across the globe, digital resources, such as home computers, internet connectivity, and access to digital education programs, remain accessible to those with the resources to acquire them. When these resources are not accessible as personal property and people are unable to purchase this technology, those in need of services may be left with social means–tested acquisition, charitable donations, or inadequate governmental support. This has made it critical to support individual initiatives such as one-to-one laptop programs (where all students in respective settings are provided with laptop computers) around the world (B. Zheng, Warschauer, Lin, & Chang, 2016). However, there is an overriding reluctance to use virtual services even when they are made available. This is further complicated by difficulties accessing the internet and by cybersecurity and privacy concerns (Southey & Stoddart, 2021). Although hindrances exist to the use of digital technology, the access and global connections made support international social welfare and move us closer to a connected, cooperative world community.

Name: Beth Okantey

Place of residence: Mataheko-Afienya, Greater Accra Region, Ghana, West Africa

College/university degrees: Pacific Lutheran University, BSW; Walla Walla University, MSW; current social work doctoral student at Florida State University

Present position: Director of International Programs at Palm Institute (Ghana, West Africa) and BSW/MSW adjunct instructor at Florida State University, Portland State University, University of Alabama, and the University of Nevada at Reno

What does a typical day at work look like for you? What tasks do you generally complete as a social worker in your area of expertise? Providing supervision to American social work students completing a field placement in Ghana does not have a typical day. Prior to students arriving in Ghana, I provide pre-departure support preparing them for their experience with a focus on limiting expectations, adaptability, openness, and respect despite the differences. While students are in Ghana, I check in with them consistently and help them to process and problem-solve their personal and professional experiences in Ghana. We meet weekly to debrief and discuss the difficulties of being away from home, the biases and assumptions present based on a Western lens, the role of saviorism and Western-based cultural understanding, the complex cultural challenges that exist at their field placement or in their housing situation, and how to gain the needed awareness to ensure cultural sensitivity and humility in each interaction. I provide monthly field trips for students to gain a greater perspective of social problems present in Ghana and the way social work is done outside of their individual field placement. I also encourage engagement in various cultural experiences to gain a further understanding of Ghanaian culture.

What do you do in your spare time? In my spare time, I enjoy spending time with my family. I also enjoy jogging, socializing with friends, and working to understand Ghanaian culture on a deeper level through conversation by asking, questioning, comparing, and processing.

Why did you choose social work as a career? I chose social work as a career to be able to empower vulnerable individuals to make a difference in their own lives. Much of my career (fifteen plus years) has led me abroad to work in community development, health education, and child protection. I enjoy spending time in other cultures, learning from other cultures to increase my own cultural understanding, and gaining a different perspective on social work. In Ghana, I was interested in providing students with an immersive experience that will significantly impact those they work with in their future social work practice. As an adjunct instructor, I try to incorporate the importance of cultural awareness in each course that I teach.

What is your favorite social work story? My favorite social work stories are about students who are profoundly changed by an international experience in Ghana. I once supervised a

continues

continued

student who had never traveled on an airplane nor had left the United States and was phenomenal at adapting on his own, being open and flexible, navigating and respecting Ghanaian culture, and developing strong connections with those he lived and worked with. Another favorite story was when two students were napping in their hotel room and a baboon opened their door and entered inside in search of food!

What would be the one thing you would change in our community if you had the power to do so? If I had the power to change my community, I would ensure social workers are keen to partner with, listen to, learn from, and recognize the expertise that all individuals have within their own lives. I would also reiterate the importance of connection and ensuring culturally relevant practice that considers engagement, assessment, and intervention from different cultural perspectives.

14.1 SOCIAL WORK IS EXPANDING GLOBALLY

As the profession of social work continues to expand globally, China provides a strong example of a complex path to professionalization different from Western countries such as the United States. Wang and Jin (2009) referred to this as top-down professionalization. With great support from the government, the number of certified social workers in China continues to grow (see Figure 14.1; Niu & Haugen, 2019). The Ministry of Civil Affairs reported that there were 669,000 licensed social workers nationwide in 2020, which is an increase of approximately 135,000 from the 534,000 social workers listed in 2019 (Ministry of Civil Affairs of the People's Republic of China, 2020). The role of these social workers in assisting to ensure the well-being of the people remains central. However, even as the number of professional social workers continues to increase internationally, maintaining a supported workforce of trained professionals

FIGURE 14.1
Significant government support means that the number of certified social workers in China continues to grow.

is not assured. For example, in China, although the number of social workers is growing, there is often a labor shortage with a high turnover rate (Gao & Yan, 2015; Lei, Luo, Chui, & Lu, 2019). The high turnover rate among social workers reflects their lack of professional identity (Jiang, Wang, Chui, and Xu, 2019). In addition, the number of jobs did not grow, nor did salaries, which presented major challenges for Chinese social work graduates (Tang, 2016).

For social workers in China, although social work is a productive developing profession, concerns related to work schedules and decisions as well as professional autonomy influenced by administrative power when delivering social services remain obstacles that must be addressed (Daniel & Wheatley, 2017; G. Zheng, Liu, Wang, & Chen, 2021).

As international awareness and acceptance of social workers continues to grow, some U.S. social workers have been reluctant in their commitment. Despite their awareness of the ever-changing world community and their recognition of its importance in our daily lives, American social workers remain ambivalent in their commitment to the international arena. As technology brings global concerns and solutions to the forefront, the profession must prepare to meet international challenges and opportunities and be more aggressive in benefiting from those opportunities. In other words, as the world experiences globalization, so too must the social work profession in the United States.

Did You Know . . .

The global population was 2.8 billion in 1955, 7.1 billion in 2014, and 7.97 billion in 2022. Estimates indicate that the world population will reach 9.6 billion by the year 2050.

In this chapter, we will touch on the many international facets of social work. Although we cannot delve into details of cultural differences and economic and demographic trends, we hope to raise your awareness of these issues. By the end of the chapter, you will recognize that social work is a global profession facing the persistent challenge of promoting social and economic justice.

14.2 HOW DO WE COMPARE DIFFERENT NATIONS?

A general question that seems simple enough to answer is, How many nations are there in the world? We could look at the United Nations (UN), but not all nations are UN members. We could search the web to see what comes up—why not do that now and see what number you find? For example, when this sentence was being written on September 2, 2022, a web search produced a few answers ranging from 193 to 197. These numbers include 193 members of the UN (with an additional 2 so-called *observer states*). In total, the UN recognizes 195 nations. But these numbers only get more confusing depending on your information source. For example, there is a general recognition that the United Kingdom, which includes Northern Ireland, Scotland, and Wales, among other world states, is one nation. Yet, FIFA (the Fédération Internationale de Football Association) notes that Northern Ireland, Scotland, and Wales are separate nations. And what about the Vatican City and Palestine—although they are not recognized as separate nations by the UN, they are viewed as individual sovereign global states. And then there is Kosovo, which in 2008 declared its independence from Serbia. Yet, Kosovo is not listed as a separate nation by the UN.

A second point to consider is that the world's nation states are not static, but susceptible to change. A nation emerges in any number of ways, from the spoils of war to a nation giving up its governance over land. Enriquez (2005, pp. 22–23) reminds us that, in 1909, a little over one hundred years ago, the British Empire included 11.5 million square miles, which was 20 percent of the world's land mass—this led to the saying that the "sun never sets on the British Empire." Within fifty years, the British Empire has shrunk by more than 11.4 million square miles, to about 94,248 square miles. Let us not forget that in 1991 the Union of Soviet Socialist Republics splintered into Russia and fourteen other republics. And who is to say that the United States will always consist of fifty states? Maybe Puerto Rico and/or Guam will join the country at some point. In 2021, legislation was introduced in the U.S. Congress to make Washington, DC, the fifty-first state. Remember that Hawaii and Alaska joined the United States in 1959.

To make international comparisons, it is helpful to have a framework for grouping nations based on similarities. Otherwise, comparisons may not be meaningful and can lead to inaccurate conclusions. For example, there is little that can be learned by comparing the economic systems of the United States and Nepal. The vast political, economic, social, historical, and cultural differences between these two nations make such a comparison impossible.

Did You Know . . .

According to the *New York Times*, as of August 24, 2022, military losses in the Russia–Ukraine war have been heavy on both sides, with about 9,000 Ukrainians and as many as 25,000 Russians said to be killed. Ukrainian civilians have paid a heavy price, too, with 5,587 civilians killed.

One framework for comparison is based on a nation's technological level, which incorporates three tiers: preindustrial, industrial, and postindustrial (Bell, 1973). This framework can be visualized as a core with circles, or concentric zones, surrounding it. Core nations include those in western Europe and North America; a second group of nations surround the core, which then is encircled by the outermost group of nations (Chatterjee, 1996). The second group of nations includes former Communist countries and various nations in Asia and South America; the outermost ring includes the remaining Asian and South American countries and Africa. Chatterjee called these three groups of nations the First World, the Second World, and the Third World (see Box 14.1).

CHAPTER 14: GLOBAL SOCIAL WELFARE

> **BOX 14.1**
> ### THE WORLD SYSTEM
>
> *First World*: Also known as the core, it includes North America, western Europe, Australia, and Japan. It is wealthy, capitalist, industrial, and based on the traditions of a market economy and individualism.
>
> *Second World*: Somewhat outside the core, it consists of eastern Europe, Central and Northern Asia, and Cuba. It is neither wealthy nor poor and it is socialist, selectively industrial, and based on the traditions of a planned economy and collectivism. A substantial part of the Second World has been attempting to convert to a market economy since 1991.
>
> *Third World*: It includes nations mostly in Africa, southern and Southeast Asia, and South America. It is mostly poor, often nationalist, selectively industrial to preindustrial, and based on a mixed economy and regional loyalty.
> *Source*: Chatterjee (1996, p. 46).

The World Bank, an international organization that promotes economic development and productivity to raise the standard of living in less-developed nations, uses a different framework. The World Bank categorizes nations into six regions: South Asia, Middle East and North Africa, Latin America and the Caribbean, Europe and Central Asia, East Asia and the Pacific, and the Africa Region (see Box 14.2).

> **BOX 14.2**
> ### REGIONS OF THE WORLD AS DEFINED BY THE WORLD BANK
>
> *South Asia*: Afghanistan, Bangladesh, Bhutan, India, Maldives, Nepal, Pakistan, Sri Lanka.
>
> *Middle East and North Africa*: Algeria, Bahrain, Egypt, Iran, Jordan, Kuwait, Lebanon, Morocco, Oman, Qatar, Saudi Arabia, Syrian Arab Republic, Tunisia, Yemen, United Arab Emirates.
>
> *Latin America and the Caribbean*: Antigua and Barbuda, Argentina, Belize, Bolivia, Chile, Colombia, Costa Rica, Dominica, Dominican Republic, Ecuador, El Salvador, Grenada, Guatemala, Guyana, Haiti, Honduras, Jamaica, Mexico, Nicaragua, Panama, Paraguay, Peru, St. Kitts and Nevis, St. Lucia, St. Vincent and the Grenadines, Suriname, Trinidad and Tobago, Uruguay, Venezuela.
>
> *Europe and Central Asia*: Albania, Armenia, Azerbaijan, Belarus, Bosnia and Herzegovina, Bulgaria, Croatia, Czech Republic, Estonia, Georgia, Hungary, Kazakhstan, Kyrgyz Republic, Latvia, Lithuania, the Republic of North Macedonia, Moldova, Poland, Romania, Russian Federation, Slovak Republic, Slovenia, Tajikistan, Turkey, Turkmenistan, Ukraine, Uzbekistan.
>
> *East Asia and the Pacific*: Cambodia, China, Fiji, Indonesia, Kiribati, Korea, Lao People's Democratic Republic, Malaysia, Marshall Islands, Federated States of

continues

continued

Micronesia, Mongolia, Myanmar, Palau, Papua New Guinea, Philippines, Samoa, Solomon Islands, Thailand, Tonga, Vanuatu, Vietnam.

Africa: Angola, Benin, Botswana, Burkina Faso, Burundi, Cameroon, Cape Verde, Central African Republic, Chad, Comoros, Congo, Democratic Republic of Congo, Republic of Côte d'Ivoire, Djibouti, Equatorial Guinea, Eritrea, Ethiopia, Gabon, Gambia, Ghana, Guinea, Guinea-Bissau, Kenya, Lesotho, Liberia, Madagascar, Malawi, Mali, Mauritania, Mauritius, Mozambique, Namibia, Niger, Rwanda, São Tomé and Principe, Senegal, Seychelles, Sierra Leone, Somalia, South Africa, Sudan, Swaziland, Tanzania, Togo, Uganda, Zambia, Zimbabwe.

Question: *What countries are missing from the list and why?* Connect with the World Bank's web page for additional information and read the organization's purpose for the answer.
Source: The World Bank (2022). Retrieved from https://projects.worldbank.org/en/projects-operations/project-country?lang=en&page=

Did You Know . . .

In 2022, China's population was estimated to be 1,425,887,337 persons and the Pitcairn Islands had the smallest population, 50 people.

It is important to be sensitive to our use of words and how they may be interpreted by others. For example, what does it mean to be called *developed* versus *undeveloped*? Even more important, what are we implying when we call a nation undeveloped or even underdeveloped? Are we holding that country to our standards or to their standards? At best this reference is paternalistic and at worst it suggests cultural elitism.

We have described two frameworks here, but there are several alternative approaches to comparing nations. For example, another model speaks of nations in the north and the south, using the equator as a global dividing line. What we want to accomplish is to organize the world's countries to facilitate discussions that are consistent and appropriate. In other words, we want to compare apples with apples, not apples with peaches!

Did You Know . . .

You can see just how much you don't know that you think you know about the rest of the world! The Gapminder Worldview Upgrader web page will entertain and educate you on some common misconceptions about the world.

Let us use Chatterjee's classification to demonstrate how a framework can be applied to make international comparisons. As shown in Table 14.1, Chatterjee identified social issues and then tabulated how the First, Second, and Third Worlds respond to them. Chatterjee (1996, p. 78) also went a step further by asking the following questions about the three worlds and then compiling responses, listed in Table 14.2:

1. Once a person has been socially defined as unemployable, can he/she ask the state for help?
2. Once a person has been socially defined as employable but is unemployed, can he/she ask the state for support?
3. Once a person has been socially defined as employed but is marginally employed, can he/she ask the state for support?
4. If the state is providing support, is it means tested?
5. If the state is providing support, it is related to past or potential earnings?
6. If the state is providing support, it is a flat rate or with a minimum or maximum or is it linked to an index of fluctuating living costs?
7. Is the state committed to seeing that each citizen receives a basic package of health care, or has it engaged other qualified parties to do so?
8. Is the state committed to seeing that each citizen receives a basic education? If so, has it set up a formal structure to provide such education itself, or has it engaged other qualified parties to do so?
9. Is the state committed to seeing that each citizen receives basic housing? If so, has it set up a formal structure to provide such housing, or has it engaged other parties to do so?
10. Is the state committed to providing protection to various vulnerable groups (children, elderly, developmentally disabled, and mentally ill)? If so, has it set up a formal structure to provide such protection, or has it engaged other qualified parties to do so?
11. Have one or more occupational groups emerged within the state that are self-appointed advocates for vulnerable groups and are seeking increased professionalization?

Table 14.1 Welfare Trends on Selected Issues in the Three Worlds

Issue	First World	Second World	Third World
Housing	Public housing for the poor; some rent control or subsidy	Rationed housing for all	No such concept
Education	Supported; often uneven in various localities and regions of a country	State supported	State efforts do not reach all
Income	Almost all countries	Almost all countries	Minimal, with largest number of people living on less than $2 every day
Health care	Almost all countries; rising costs	Almost all countries; supplies and equipment problematic	Crisis-based care to the poor from charitable clinics and hospitals

Table 14.2 Comparison of Eleven Welfare State Variables

Question	First World	Second World	Third World
1	Yes	Mostly yes	Mostly no
2	Yes	Mostly yes	No
3	Mostly yes	Mostly yes	No
4	Mostly yes	Mostly yes	Does not apply
5	Mostly yes	Mostly yes	Does not apply
6	Mostly yes	Mostly yes	Does not apply
7	Yes, except in the United States	Yes	No
8	Mostly yes	Mostly yes	No
9	Mostly yes	Yes	No
10	Yes	Mostly yes	No
11	Yes	Partly yes	Partly yes

Source: Chatterjee (1996, p. 80).

Did You Know . . .

The definition of literacy (reading, writing, and counting skills) is changing and now includes identification, understanding, interpretation, creation, and multiple communication forms, including digital and text mediated. Being literate is often linked to increased successes, such as greater participation in the labor market and improved access to health and life opportunities. The World Bank estimates that 773 million adults worldwide are illiterate (United Nations Educational, Scientific and Cultural Organization, 2017).

14.3 HOW DO WE LOOK AT INTERNATIONAL SOCIAL WELFARE?

For educators and students alike, the literature detailing international social welfare issues is, to say the least, interesting and stimulating. For educators, international awareness increases judgement capacity, proactiveness, and innovativeness (Crowther & Quoquab, 2022). For students, it expands horizons and fosters practice and actions for social change that are culturally responsive and sensitive to the client and client system under the mores and expectations of the surrounding society. In this type of social entrepreneurship, the activities are geared to benefit society by improving local communities. This may at first seem in direct contrast to the profit motive in a capitalist system. Social entrepreneurial activities are not profit driven, but these activities provide a catalyst for social change (Crowther & Quoquab, 2022).

> ### Did You Know...
> Twenty-six percent of the world population still lacked safe drinking water in 2020. This number is equal to over two billion people across the globe (WHO, UNICEF, and World Bank, 2022).

Consistent themes in international social welfare journals include peace and social justice, human rights, and social development. These areas are critical for all social workers to understand. In fact, the accreditation standards of the Council on Social Work Education (CSWE) require that these topics be included in both baccalaureate and graduate social work programs. Our fascination with international issues transcends our educational mandates, however, and is evident in our day-to-day conversations. How often have we heard people compare the United States with other countries? Typically, the conversation will include a statement such as, "The poor in the United States have it easy compared with the poor in India." Although sentiments like these are inappropriate and pejorative at the very least, they do open the door for a critical thinking analysis to form the basis of comparative social welfare discussions.

Midgley's (1995) work remains central when promoting locality-relevant approaches whose emphasis does not rely solely on Western-based assumptions. He identified five basic types of international social welfare studies:

1. Comparative studies of social need
2. Comparative studies of social policies and human services
3. Typologies of welfare states
4. Studies of the genesis and functions of social policy
5. Studies related to the future of the welfare state

Comparative studies of social need are reports that collect and assess a variety of social and economic data from different countries. These reports are usually quantitative in nature and present tabular data on a variety of topics. Typical studies include data on income, education, birth rates, poverty, and migration.

Comparative studies of social policies and human services are most often qualitative or descriptive presentations of issues. The topics explored are like those addressed by comparative studies of social needs, but the discussion includes analysis of political issues, funding patterns, eligibility standards, types of services, and provision or delivery of services.

Typologies of welfare states discuss the ideological and philosophical bases for the welfare systems of different countries. Typology studies, which are qualitative or descriptive, can shed light on a nation's view of people and social issues and, at the same time, provide important insight into the direction of its social welfare program. According to Midgley (1995), the most common typology is the Wilensky and Lebeaux conceptual model of residual versus institutional social welfare.

Studies of the genesis and functions of social policy are closely related to welfare typology studies. They focus on three areas: how welfare organizations emerged, what forces affect the development of social policy, and what are the functions of social policy in society (Midgley, 1995). Such studies may be either quantitative or qualitative. They form the theoretical basis for social welfare endeavors.

Studies of the future of the welfare state have become more common recently. Midgley (1995) believed this increased popularity is in response to international criticism of social welfare and worldwide attempts to rethink national social welfare commitments and responsibilities. Such reports integrate the other four types of welfare studies and forecast the future.

14.4 INTERNATIONAL SOCIAL WELFARE ASSOCIATIONS

Many social work practitioners and students are surprised to learn that numerous long-standing social welfare associations exist around the world. The number of international social welfare associations increased following World War II, primarily to help rebuild war-torn countries and to assist poor countries in gaining greater economic stability (Healy, 1995). Healy classified international associations into three groups: (1) UN structures, (2) U.S. government agencies, and (3) private voluntary bodies.

UN Structures

The UN was originally organized in 1945 by 51 nations to provide a forum to help stabilize and maintain international relations and to give peace among nations a more secure foundation. By 2014, 193 nations were members and there were 2 observer nations, the Holy See (or the Vatican) and Palestine. The newest member of the UN was Montenegro, which joined in 2006, the same year that it separated from Serbia.

The UN is most recognized for its peacekeeping forces, which have been deployed throughout the world to help mediate conflict. In addition to its peacekeeping mission, however, the UN conducts a variety of activities (fifty different areas are listed on its web page), with 80 percent of its work taking place in developing nations. Typical of these services are programs for AIDS, children, women, environmental protection, persons with disabilities, human rights, health and medical research and services, poverty and economic development, agricultural development, family planning, emergency and disaster relief, air and sea travel, use of atomic energy, and labor and workers' rights.

Although the UN participates in an array of activities, seven specific agencies address social welfare issues:

1. *United Nations Children's Fund*: The best-known UN social welfare program, it provides a variety of child-directed services in such areas as health, child abuse, neglect and exploitation, child nutrition, education, and water and sanitation. You may know it by its acronym: UNICEF. In 1965, UNICEF received the Nobel Peace Prize for its efforts on behalf of children (United Nations Children's Fund, 2014).
2. *World Health Organization*: This specialized UN agency, also often referred to as WHO, focuses on worldwide health issues. It works to establish international health standards in a variety of areas, including vaccines, research, and drugs. It monitors and attempts to control communicable diseases, and it has a special focus on primary health care.
3. *UN High Commissioner for Refugees*: This commission oversees protection, assistance, and resettlement aid. In 1981, it was awarded the Nobel Peace Prize for its work with Asian refugees.
4. *Economic and Social Council*: The council coordinates several economic and social activities, with specific commissions for focusing on social development, human rights, population, the status of women, and drugs.
5. *Department of Economic and Social Affairs*: As part of the Social Perspective on Development Branch of the UN, the Department of Economic and Social Affairs focuses on numerous social issues, including aging, civil society, cooperatives, disability, employment, family, Indigenous peoples, inequality, poverty, social inclusion, sport for development and peace, and youth.
6. *UN Developmental Programme*: This agency works with around 170 countries to help them achieve the UN's Sustainable Development Goals. They focus on sustainable development, democratic governance, and climate disaster resilience.
7. *UN Population Fund*: This agency supports reproductive health. It also includes work in the areas of safe childbirth, prevention of gender-based violence, female genital mutilation, prevention of child marriage, and data collection for development planning.

Did You Know . . .

The United Nations and its organizations and staff have been awarded the Nobel Peace Prize on fifteen separate occasions—1950, 1954, 1957, 1961, 1965, 1969, 1974, 1981, 1982, 1988, 2001, 2007, 2008, 2013, and 2020.

The UN provides many other social welfare services. Typical activities include scores of annual conferences and conventions, as well *special years* dedicated to a specific issue. Over the years, recent special issues included:

- 2024 International Year of Camelids
- 2023 International Year of Millets

- 2022 International Year of Artisanal Fisheries and Aquaculture, International Year of Glass, International Year of Basic Sciences for Sustainable Development, International Year of Sustainable Mountain Development

Similarly, conferences focus on specific themes:

- World Summit for Children (1990)
- Conference on the Environment (1992)
- Fourth World Conference on Women (1995)
- Earth Summit (1997)
- World Food Summit (2002)
- Forum on the Eradication of World Poverty (2006)
- World Conference on Indigenous Peoples (2008)
- UN Conference on Sustainable Development (2012)
- UN Framework Convention on Climate Change: 21st Conference of Parties (COP21) (2015)
- UN Climate Action Summit (2019)

The UN also sponsors significant special days each year, such as the International Women's Day, held on March 8 each year, and World Water Day on March 22.

Of particular interest to social work is the UN's sponsorship of Social Work Day at the UN, which is typically held in March each year (note that March is recognized as Social Work Month throughout the world; this annual meeting brings together about one thousand social workers to discuss and advocate on global human issues). In 2022, Social Work Day at the UN held its thirty-eighth annual gathering. Social work students from around the United States participate at the UN event; check with your social work program to see if a student delegation may be attending the next UN Social Work Day.

Did You Know . . .

The headquarters for the International Federation of Social Workers is in Maiengässli 4, 4310 Rheinfelden, Switzerland, and can be reached via email: global@ifsw.org.

U.S. Government Agencies

The United States conducts a variety of international social welfare efforts through federal agencies:

- *Administration for Children and Families*: A subsection of the Office of Public Affairs, this agency is the primary conduit for international affairs and social work. Activities include meetings, research, professional exchanges, and cosponsorship of welfare programs.

- *Office of Refugee Resettlement*: This office coordinates resettlement of refugees in the United States. Since 1975, more than three million people, of whom 77 percent are either Indochinese or citizens of the former Soviet Union, have been assisted in the United States because of persecution in their homelands because of race, religion, nationality, or political or social group membership.
- *Social Security Administration*: This agency examines social insurance programs worldwide.
- *U.S. International Development Finance Corporation*: This corporation has two responsibilities: international private investment and operating the Agency for International Development (AID). The AID provides funding for international projects and is concerned about AIDS, child welfare, population growth, and basic education. It has given money to welfare groups, including the NASW, to sponsor international programs.
- *Peace Corps*: First organized in 1961, the Peace Corps sends American volunteers to different nations to assist in a variety of social, economic, and agricultural projects.

Private Voluntary Bodies

Private or nongovernmental groups provide a variety of services and activities throughout the world. Human service organizations such as the YMCA and YWCA sponsor direct services and programs. In addition, nonprofit organizations consult with international agencies and groups about human service issues.

14.5 INTERNATIONAL PROFESSIONAL SOCIAL WELFARE ORGANIZATIONS

There are a variety of international social welfare organizations around the world. Some are social work membership associations, like the NASW. Others are national and regional educational associations, similar in purpose and function to the CSWE.

Three worldwide organizing bodies cross national boundaries and encourage partnerships: the IFSW, the International Association of Schools of Social Work, and the International Council on Social Welfare.

International Federation of Social Workers

The IFSW was founded in 1956 to promote social work on the world stage. The organization is divided into five geographical regions: Africa, Asia and the Pacific, Europe, Latin America and the Caribbean, and North America. Membership is open to one professional social work association in each country. In 2022, it was composed of 141 professional associations representing over 3 million social workers. A total of 116 countries with more than 750,000 members reported belonging to the federation (see Box 14.3). Individuals and organizations may join the IFSW to take part in the Friends Program. As a friend, a social worker receives the IFSW newsletter, published three times annually, policy papers, and a discount on registration for IFSW international and regional conferences.

BOX 14.3
MEMBERS OF THE INTERNATIONAL FEDERATION OF SOCIAL WORKERS, 2014

Albania	Hong Kong	Norway
Andorra	Hungary	Palestine
Argentina	Iceland	Papua New Guinea
Armenia	India	Peru
Australia	Indonesia	The Philippines
Austria	Ireland	Poland
Azerbaijan	Iran	Portugal
Bahrain	Israel	Puerto Rico
Bangladesh	Italy	The Republic of North Macedonia
Belarus	Japan	Romania
Belgium	Kenya	Russian Federation
Benin	Korea	Rwanda
Bolivia	Kosovo	San Marino
Botswana and Herzegovina	Kuwait	Serbia
Brazil	Kyrgyz Republic	Sierra Leone
Bulgaria	Latvia	Singapore
Canada	Lebanon	Slovakia
Chile	Lesotho	Slovenia
China	Liberia	South Africa
Colombia	Libya	Spain
Costa Rica	Lithuania	Sri Lanka
Croatia	Luxembourg	Sudan
Cuba	Macau	Swaziland
Cyprus	Madagascar	Sweden
Czech Republic	Malaysia	Switzerland/Liechtenstein
Denmark	Malta	Tanzania
Djibouti	Mauritius	Thailand
Dominican Republic	Moldova	Turkey

Estonia	Mongolia	Uganda
	Monaco	Ukraine
Faeroe Islands	Montenegro	United Kingdom
Fiji	Morocco	United States of America
Finland	The Netherlands	Uruguay
France	Netherlands Antilles	Vietnam
Georgia	New Zealand–Aotearoa	Yemen
Germany	Nicaragua	Zambia
Ghana	Niger	Zimbabwe
Greece	Nigeria	

The IFSW represents global social work in a variety of international arenas. For example, the IFSW is granted *special consultative status* by the UN and the United Nations Children's Fund. The IFSW has a long history working with the WHO and the United Nations' Office of the High Commissioner for Refugees and the High Commissioner of Human Rights. In addition to these international associations, partner organizations of the IFSW include Amnesty International, the Conference of Non-governmental Organizations, Commonwealth Organisation for Social Work, Council of Europe, ENSACT, European Union, the International Association of Schools of Social Work, the International Council on Social Welfare, Public Services International, the UN Department of Economic and Social Affairs, and the United Nations Children's Fund.

With the International Association of Schools of Social Work (see below), the International Federation of Social Workers (IFSW) generated a definition of social work that is used around the world. The global definition, which was approved at the IFSW general meeting and International Association of Schools of Social Work general assembly was approved in July 2014, took several years to write and gain approval by the various member associations. For a moment, think how difficult it is in your class to reach agreement; now transpose this to a worldwide discussion that involves a variety of cultural frameworks and different meanings of words set within historical patterns of mistrust between regions and nations. The idea that people from around the world were able to find common ground speaks volumes about the authenticity and commitment of social workers, no matter where they live and work. Reflecting sensitivity to the diversity of languages and its membership, the IFSW posts the definition in several languages on its website (see Box 14.4).

> **BOX 14.4**
>
> **GLOBAL DEFINITION OF SOCIAL WORK AS POSTED IN VARIOUS LANGUAGES BY THE INTERNATIONAL FEDERATION OF SOCIAL WORKERS, 2014**
>
> **Afrikaans:** Maatskaplike werk is 'n praktyk-gebaseerde professie en 'n akademiese dissipline wat maatskaplike verandering en ontwikkeling, maatskaplike kohesie, en die bemagtiging en bevryding van mense bevorder. Beginsels van maatskaplike geregtigheid, menseregte, kollektiewe verantwoordelikheid en respek vir diversiteit is fundamenteel in maatskaplike werk. Versterk deur teorieë vir maatskaplike werk, sosiale wetenskappe, geesteswetenskappe en inheemse kennis1, betrek maatskaplike werk mense en strukture om lewenseise te hanteer en welsyn te bevorder. Die bogenoemde definisie kan verder uitgebou word op nasionale en/of streekvlakke.
>
> **Arabic:**
>
> وافقت اللجنة التنفيذية للاتحاد الدولي للأخصائيين الاجتماعيين ومجلس الاتحاد الدولي للمدارس الخدمة الاجتماعية من وضع تعريف عالمي للخدمة الاجتماعية وستعرض اللجنة التنفيذية التعريف الجديد المقترح لأعضاء كلتا المنظمتين في الاجتماع العام / للجمعية في ملبورن يوليو 2014.
>
> وتود اللجنة التنفيذية للاتحاد الدولي للأخصائيين الاجتماعيين أن تعرب عن شكرها للعديد من المنظمات الأعضاء والأخصائيين الاجتماعيين من مختلف أنحاء العالم الذين شاركوا في عملية المراجعة الشاملة.
>
> كما تعرب عن تقديرها للاتحاد الدولي للاخصائيين الاجتماعيين ومجلس الاتحاد الدولي لمدارس الخدمة الاجتماعية المنظمة الشقيقة لاشتراكهم في تسهيل العملية ولكونها دائما على استعداد للعمل على إيجاد حلول مما كانت المهمة معقدة.
>
> كما نود أيضا أن نعترف بالجهد الكبير من المتطوعين وأعضاء الأمانة الذين قاموا بتيسير العمل يوما بعد يوم في استعراض ووضع التعريف نيابة عن اللجنة التنفيذية.
>
> ونحن سعداء أن أدت عملية التشاور إلى التعريف المقترح الجديد الذي نعتقد أنه يدل على تطور المهنة.
>
> وسوف يكون اجتماع الجمعية العمومية للاتحاد الدولي للاخصائيين الاجتماعية 6 و7 يوليو 2014 في ملبورن.
>
> **English:** Social work is a practice-based profession and an academic discipline that promotes social change and development, social cohesion, and the empowerment and liberation of people. Principles of social justice, human rights, collective responsibility, and respect for diversities are central to social work, social sciences, humanities, and Indigenous knowledge. Social work engages people and structures to address life challenges and embrace wellbeing.

The above definition may be amplified at national and/or regional levels.

Espanol: El trabajo social es una profesión basada en la práctica y una disciplina académica que promueve el cambio y el desarrollo social, la cohesión social, y el fortalecimiento y la liberación de las personas. Los principios de la justicia social, los derechos humanos, la responsabilidad colectiva y el respeto a la diversidad son fundamentales para el trabajo social. Respaldada por las teorías del trabajo social, las ciencias sociales, las humanidades y los conocimientos indígenas, el trabajo social involucra a las personas y las estructuras para hacer frente a desafíos de la vida y aumentar el bienestar.

La siguiente definición se puede ampliar a nivel nacional y/o regional.

Francaise—Les professionnels du travail social ont pour mission de favoriser le changement et le développement social, la cohésion sociale, le pouvoir d'agir et la libération des personnes. Les principes de justice sociale, de droit de la personne, de responsabilité sociale collective et de respect des diversités, sont au coeur du travail social. Etayé par les théories du travail social, des sciences sociales, des sciences humaines et des connaissances autochtones, le travail social encourage les personnes et les structures à relever les défis de la vie et agit pour améliorer le bien-être de tous.

Hebrew:

> **העבודה הסוציאלית** היא מקצוע מעשי ויישומי ותחום דעת (דיסציפלינה) מדעי, המקדם שינוי חברתי, פיתוח חברתי, לכידות חברתית ופועל להעצמתם של בני אדם, תוך שימת דגש על חירותם וכבודם. עקרונותיה המרכזיים של **העבודה הסוציאלית** הם צדק חברתי, זכויות אדם, אחריות כלל חברתית, הדדיות, מתן כבוד לשונות, ושוויון. בהתבסס על תיאוריות בעבודה סוציאלית, במדעי החברה והרוח, ועל ידע נלמד מתוך ההתנסות של הנעזרים בשירותיהם של עובדים סוציאליים, **העבודה הסוציאלית** רותמת ומפעילה מוסדות של החברה ואנשים, על מנת להתמודד עם אתגרי חיים, ולקדם את רווחת הפרט, המשפחה, קבוצות, קהילות וכלל החברה.

isiZulu: Ezenhlalakahle ziwumkhakha ombandakanya ukwenza umsebenzi ophathekayo, uqeqesho lwezemfundo olukhuthaza uguquko lwezenhlalo nokuthuthukiswa komphakathi, ubumbano lomphakathi, ukugqugquzela nokukhulule ka kwabantu. Imigomo yobulungis wa, amalunge lo e s intu, ukubamba iqhaza, nokuhlonipha ukwehlukana kwezinhlanga kuseqhulwini emkhakheni wezenhlalakahle. Ngokusekelwa imibono ehlukahlukene yezenhlalakahle, ubuchwepheshe bezenhlalo, ubuntu, nolwazi loMdabu, ezenhlalakahle zixhumanisa abantu nezakhiwo ezilwisana nezingqinamba zempilo ziphinde zithuthukise nempilo jikelele.

Lencazelo engenhla ingaguquguqulwa ngokwamazinga ezwe futhi/noma awezifunda.

Italian: Il servizio sociale è una professione basata sulla pratica e una disciplina accademica che promuove il cambiamento sociale e lo sviluppo, la coesione e l'emancipazione sociale, nonchè la liberazione delle persone. Principi di giustizia sociale, diritti umani, responsabilità collettiva e rispetto delle diversità sono fondamentali per il servizio sociale. Sostenuto dalle teorie del servizio sociale, delle scienze sociali, umanistiche e dai saperi indigeni, il servizio sociale coinvolge persone e strutture per affrontare le sfide della vita e per migliorarne il benessere.

La definizione di cui sopra pu essere ampliata a livello nazionale e/o regionale.

continues

continued

Portuguese: O Serviço Social é uma profissão de intervenção e uma disciplina académica que promove o desenvolvimento e a mudança social, a coesão social, o empowerment e a promoção da Pessoa. Os princípios de justiça social, dos direitos humanos, da responsabilidade coletiva e do respeito pela diversidade são centrais ao Serviço Social. Sustentado nas teorias do serviço social, nas ciências sociais, nas humanidades e nos conhecimentos indígenas, o serviço social relaciona as pessoas com as estruturas sociais para responder aos desafios da vida e à melhoria do bem-estar social.

Esta definição de Serviço Social pode ser ampliada ao nível nacional e/ou ao nível regional.

Russian:

> Социальная работа является практической профессией и академической дисциплиной, которая способствует общественным изменениям и развитию, содействует социальной сплоченности и укреплению способностей к самостоятельному функционированию людей в обществе, их освобождению. Принципы социальной справедливости, прав человека и уважения многообразия являются центральными в социальной работе. Опираясь на теории социальной работы, общественные и гуманитарные науки, специализированные знания, социальная работа вовлекает людей и структуры в решение жизненно важных проблем и повышение благополучия.
>
> Данное определение можно расширять на национальном и/или региональном уровнях

The IFSW sponsors meetings throughout the world (see Box 14.5). In addition to its biennial international meetings, it sponsors regional meetings that focus on specific area issues; participant costs are much lower for these meetings. Since 1966, there have been more than twenty regional meetings in Europe and in Asia and the Pacific and approximately fifteen meetings in Africa. Both regional and worldwide gatherings provide social workers from around the world with a chance to share research findings as well as program ideas.

The IFSW also provides critical leadership in the pursuit of human rights for individual social workers, social work students, and social service workers. In 1988, the IFSW established a Human Rights Commission with members representing each region. The commission works with several international human rights groups, including Amnesty International.

> **BOX 14.5**
>
> ## MEETINGS SPONSORED BY THE INTERNATIONAL FEDERATION OF SOCIAL WORKERS
>
> 1966 Helsinki
>
> 1970 Manila
>
> 1974 Nairobi
>
> 1976 Puerto Rico
>
> 1978 Tel Aviv
>
> 1980 Hong Kong
>
> 1982 Brighton
>
> 1984 Montreal
>
> 1986 Tokyo
>
> 1988 Stockholm
>
> 1990 Buenos Aires
>
> 1992 Washington, DC
>
> 1994 Colombia
>
> 1996 Hong Kong
>
> 1998 Jerusalem
>
> 2000 Montreal
>
> 2002 Harare
>
> 2004 Australia
>
> 2006 Germany
>
> 2008 Brazil
>
> 2010 Hong Kong–joint meeting with the International Association of Schools of Social Work (IASSW) and International Council on Social Welfare (ICSW)
>
> 2012 Sweden–joint meeting with the IASSW and ICSW
>
> 2014 Australia–joint meeting with the IASSW and ICSW
>
> 2016 Seoul, Korea–joint meeting with the IASSW and ICSW

The IFSW is the primary organization to set forth position papers on behalf of the global social work community on a range of social welfare topics. Examples include three 2014 statements regarding the Israeli/Palestinian conflict (see Caissie & Wheeler, 2014; IFSW, 2014a; Kimura & Henderson, 2014). The IFSW also issued a statement of support for the people of Turkey following the May 2014 mine explosion (IFSW, 2014b).

Another noteworthy activity of IFSW is its research and publication of policy papers that explore social issues that social workers face day in and day out. In addition to the following issues, policy papers are planned to explore Indigenous peoples and international adoptions:

- Advancement of women
- Welfare of elderly people
- Child welfare
- Health
- HIV/AIDS
- Human rights
- Migration
- Peace and disarmament
- Protection of personnel
- Refugees
- Rural communities
- Self-help
- Youth

International Association of Schools of Social Work

As the name suggests, the International Association of Schools of Social Work (IASSW) is the focal point for social work education around the world. The IASSW does not set international accreditation standards for social work education; rather, it promotes social work education and the development of high-quality educational programs around the world. In a 1928 worldwide meeting, attended by more than three thousand people from 42 nations, the participants agreed that social work was a mechanism that could professionalize and achieve better outcomes from charitable activities (Hokenstad & Kendall, 1995). In the following year, the IASSW was organized, and today membership is open to national associations, such as the CSWE and its specific educational programs. By 1995, IASSW membership totaled 450 schools from 100 countries (Hokenstad & Kendall, 1995), and in 2009 membership had grown to more than 600 programs in more than 115 nations. Member schools are divided into five regions—Asia–Pacific, Africa, European, Latin American, and North America–Caribbean—which facilitates development of regional educational initiatives.

> **Did You Know . . .**
> The journal *International Social Work* is sponsored jointly by the International Association of Schools of Social Work, the International Federation of Social Workers, and the International Council on Social Welfare. A full list of school members, individual members, individual life members, and affiliate members can be found on the International Association of Schools of Social Work website.

The IASSW sponsors a biennial meeting, the International Conference of Schools of Social Work, and supports a variety of educationally directed projects. In addition, the association publishes a newsletter and texts. Those who are interested in viewing the global social work documents that outline the definition of global social work and the standards for social work education and training are encouraged to visit the IASSW website.

Like the IFSW, the IASSW is sensitive to the language barriers in a global community. To that end, the IASSW, as part of its organizational structure, includes a language committee that continually assesses and proposes new ways to communicate across the world. The IASSW recognizes that there is and should be no difference in value and importance among any languages and that all languages on this earth should be treated equally. However, English is the dominant language.

Based on the nature of social work and the IASSW's mission to promote social work education, as well as its history and membership distribution, the following policy was adopted as the Global Definition of Social Work: "Social work is a practice-based profession and an academic discipline that promotes social change and development, social cohesion, and the empowerment and liberation of people. Principles of social justice, human rights, collective responsibility, and respect for diversities are central to social work. Underpinned by theories of social work, social sciences, humanities and Indigenous knowledges, social work engages people and structures to address life challenges and enhance wellbeing" (retrieved October 2022 from https://www.iassw-aiets.org/global-definition-of-social-work-review-of-the-global-definition/).

International Council on Social Welfare

As stated on its website, the International Council on Social Welfare (ICSW) is a global nongovernmental agency "focused on advocacy, knowledge-building and technical assistance projects in various areas of social development carried out at the country level and internationally." The primary thrust of the council is to promote social and economic development activities that will reduce poverty, hardship, and vulnerability. The council was founded in Paris in 1928, and today its office is in London, England. Like the IFSW and IASSW, the council holds a biennial conference as well as regional meetings.

The ICSW is subdivided into five regions—Africa, Asia and Pacific, Latin America and Caribbean, North America, and Europe. From 2020 to 2024, the ICSW has been shaped by three considerations.

1. The founding objectives of the ICSW,
2. The Global Agenda for Social Work and Social Development, and
3. The new global economic and political circumstances, including the COVID-19 pandemic, the UN Sustainable Development Goals, and the climate crisis.

Among its crucial functions, the ICSW publishes a journal, *Global Social Policy*, which includes a creative section titled "Observatory on the Global South." This section highlights social welfare trends in the Global South and draws attention to many of the issues that otherwise are left unrecognized.

Name: Kenan Sualp
Place of residence: Orlando, Florida
College/university degrees: University of Central Florida, MSW, PhD
Present position: Lecturer and assessment coordinator, University of Central Florida

How did you choose social work as a career? What is the focus of your research in social work? My roads crossed with the field of social work when I was doing my internship. I was doing my bachelor's in Turkey as a junior psychology student. I was an ambitious student and with the reference of my clinical psychology professor I was able to arrange an interdisciplinary internship at the biggest university hospital in Turkey. Besides working with amazing professionals from various fields I was also excited for the opportunity of learning about various disciplines including psychiatry, psychology, pedagogy, and social work. My experience with different services was great. Therefore, my experience with social work was a bit different—in a good way. I was thrilled to see the empowerment and inclusion of environmental factors and resources that provided people with multidimensional care. Starting that moment, my goal was to learn more about the social work profession. Following my graduation and internship, I worked as a psychologist for two years and provided counseling for disabled people and their caregivers in the form of various therapy modalities, including individual, group, and family therapies. After multiple successful exam scores, the opportunity arose for a fellowship. I decided to take it and come to the USA for my Master of Social Work (MSW). Following that, my path crossed with the University of Central Florida, from which I received my master's degree.

During my master's program I learned about various populations and social issues, and this helped me to shape my research interests and gave me a research focus for my PhD.

I started focusing on the role of the environment and I was looking to the various underserved populations in the United States and trying to understand how environmental resources and burdens are disproportionately impacting these people. I realized the value of understanding environmental risk factors for mental health and access to care. I was confident that further investigations and research into this area would significantly contribute to the profession at the national and global level, and thus understand the importance of studying it further. This resonated with my research focus on this area. While doing that I became more familiar with various techniques (e.g., GIS) and resources that helped me to have a better understanding of the issue through using advanced methodologies.

What does a typical day at work look like for you? What tasks do you generally complete as a social worker in your area of expertise? As an academic, a portion of my daily routine is preparing the class material, grading, and learning about new software and developments about teaching strategies. Besides that, my work routine consists of assessment planning, analysis, and reporting. In addition to these activities, I am actively doing research in my area of interest. Designing programs and writing grant proposals are other activities that take place in my daily routine. I also help community organizations to develop and evaluate programs. This helps organizations to improve their programs and provide better services to their community.

What do you do in your spare time? In my spare time I like to be in nature. For me, volunteering activities to help people, plus the environment, meditation in nature, reading books, and spending time with friends and family are the best ways to relax and decompress from stress. I enjoy doing volunteer activities and working toward leaving a better environment for the future generations, and stopping climate change and disproportionate environmental burden across various populations. It makes me feel better because I feel I am doing something that makes the lives of the next generations easier in my community in the United States and across the globe.

Why did you choose social work as a career? Helping people was always my goal because helping people has changed me and helped me to grow and become the person I always wanted to be. In other words, helping people helped me to find satisfaction and purpose. When I realized this, I decided to chase this ideology and when my roads crossed with social work, I knew that this is what I was going to do as a career, and what would help me to find my purpose.

Now, looking back, I am very happy with the decision I made. I was planning to help people by touching various dimensions of their lives. Now with research that I am conducting and teaching philosophy I apply in the classroom settings to educate future social workers, I feel that directly and indirectly I am touching lives at micro and macro levels. I believe I am being part of that macro change through positive direction. Regardless of the recognition and other important dimensions of job satisfaction, having self-awareness for taking part in touching people's lives to make them better provides a great job satisfaction. I always believed that life and job satisfaction is very possible if you are a social work

continues

Part 4: Expanding Horizons for Social Work

continued

educator or researcher who is aware of the impact of their job on other people's lives. This belief made me choose social work as my career.

What would be the one thing you would change in our community if you had the power to do so? I would like to reduce the disproportionate burden of environmental hazards on certain disadvantaged communities (e.g., air and water quality and exposure to other environmental risk factors).

14.6 INTERNATIONAL INITIATIVES OF THE NASW AND CSWE

National Association of Social Workers

The NASW is active in pursuing and promoting international relations. The association is guided by its International Activities Committee, which was formed in 1986. This committee seeks to adopt a variety of mechanisms to increase the globalization of the NASW.

As part of its international outreach activities, the NASW has sponsored international meetings and travel opportunities. For example, in 1992, the NASW, as part of that year's annual meeting, cohosted the World Assembly, the biannual international conclave of social workers, in Washington, DC. During the 1980s and 1990s, many state NASW chapters forged partnerships with social workers and associations in other

FIGURE 14.2
The National Association of Social Workers' headquarters in Washington, DC

countries. In fact, by 1992, twenty-one state chapters had formal relationships with other associations around the world. In addition, the national association and several state chapters have sponsored study tours in various countries around the world.

Council on Social Work Education

The CSWE is also extremely active in international circles. It includes the Commission on Global Social Work Education, which works with other international organizations, including the IASSW, to promote international programs and projects and to develop the international dimension of the social work curricula. The commission also is responsible for advising the Foreign Equivalency Determination Service and for maintaining relationships with foreign students and schools. In addition to linking the CSWE with international groups, the commission strongly advocates that schools internationalize curricula and provide students with worldwide opportunities. The commission also sponsors the Katherine A. Kendall Institute for International Social Work Education, which serves as a conduit for the generation of educational materials for social work educators. For example, the Kendall Institute sponsored a disaster management meeting in the Caribbean with educators and relief workers from around the world. This led to the development of curriculum programs on social workers and disaster relief. The Kendall Institute sponsored similar meetings that were held in South Africa and China. The institute also actively promoted the CSWE–China Collaborative, which created partnerships between U.S. and China social work programs. The U.S. schools agreed to establish a five-year partnership that included student–faculty exchanges. This supported the Chinese programs in developing educational programs based on their unique cultural attributes while not allowing the U.S. schools to "export" their degree programs to China. This collaboration, which involved seven U.S. social work educational programs (Arizona State University, Case Western Reserve University, Fordham University, University of Alabama, University of Chicago, University of Houston, and University of Southern California) and fifty-two Chinese universities in seven different regions, began in 2012 and ended in 2017. With the impetus of numerous linkages as of 2018, according to the Ministry of Civil Affairs, China has trained over a million individuals in social work and employs 218,000 social workers (Niu & Haugen, 2019).

CSWE has sponsored many international study trips. Most recently, social work educators have been developing linkages with colleagues in Cuba through trips that first began in 2012. And in 2014, CSWE organized a social work educators' group to Costa Rica.

The CSWE's research and publications around global matters has significantly increased as the profession has become more attuned to the growing global interconnectedness (Finn, Perry, & Karandikar, 2013; Hokenstad, Healy, & Segal, 2013; Lager, Mathiesen, Rodgers, & Cox, 2010). Examples of publications include *Guidebook for International Field Placements and Student Exchanges* (2010), *Teaching Human Rights: Curriculum Resources for Social Work Educators* (2013), and *Gender Oppression and*

Globalization (2013). The Kendall Institute offers numerous resources supporting global and international competence for social work students.

Other Programs

Several social work programs offer international student exchanges, field placement opportunities, and study tours. These opportunities are usually open to students and faculty from different colleges and universities; check with your social work faculty to learn more about recent and upcoming international study opportunities either in your program or in other programs. (Remember that you can transfer credit back to your home college or university, but you need to check with your academic advisor to see how such study opportunities will affect your degree plan.) The following list is just a small sample of the activities that social work programs have undertaken in recent years; check directly with your own social work program about any international opportunities it may offer.

- University of Alabama: international field placements, summer travel courses (Mexico, Spain)
- University of North Carolina–Chapel Hill: study tour of Ireland, Wales, and Scotland
- University of Houston: academic exchange program with City University of Hong Kong and travel courses to Wales, Turkey, South Africa, Mexico, and China
- University of Central Florida: summer course in Mexico
- Florida State University: summer course in England and Spain
- East Carolina State University: summer course in Bristol, England
- University of South Carolina: study tour of Greece

SUMMARY

According to the online world population clock that updates regularly, the Earth is home to an ever-growing population of 7,929,158,049 people. Since the astronauts first circled the moon in 1968 and took one of the most exciting pictures of the planet Earth (called *Earthrise*), there has been a growing awareness of the interconnected complexities that exist in our world. In exploring space and upon the Earth as we saw in the COVID-19 pandemic, there have been numerous landmark events such as these that have helped to connect all peoples and nations economically and technologically.

There is great diversity among the earth's people, governments, and experiences. Furthermore, creating a global community has been complicated by great concern relating to sensitivity resulting in conflicting views. Therefore, something as simple as a designation of land borders can provide highly separate and rigid boundaries affecting change, especially when countries directly border each other. The spread of COVID-19 sparked awareness of both the weaknesses of borders (the virus crossed borders easily) and the challenges of borders (the travel restrictions that accompanied the efforts to limit the pandemic (Collins, Duffy, & Kim, 2022). As we study these changes and plan for a global response, awareness and the widely differing economic and social disparities remain an important topic in social work education. And yet within this great diversity, despite the looming threats, there are common social problems that afflict people day in and day out as well as solutions we can learn from each other. Poverty, homelessness, mental illness, inadequate housing, hunger, poor health care, physical violence, and neglect are among the many problems that know no geographic borders.

> ### Did You Know . . .
> According to the World Health Organization, approximately 38.4 million people were living with HIV in 2021.

Events from the past, such as the terrorist attack of September 11, 2001, and the recent COVID-19 pandemic, have caused awareness of the importance of global connections to grow. These events, however, cannot be used as an excuse to turn away from the issues so germane to the globalization of our society. Problems of substance abuse, child abuse and neglect, spouse battering, poverty, inadequate mental health and health care, and the isms of race, age, and gender continue to be found in every region of the world. Social workers, too, are found throughout the world, helping individuals, families, and communities to confront these and other social issues. We experience the effects of globalization every day. We can cross the oceans in a matter of hours; we can talk to a friend in another nation simply by sending an email, video chatting, or placing a telephone call. With electronic communications we can send messages around the world to any number of people in mere milliseconds.

Social work and social welfare are part of this fast-paced, ever-changing world. Terry Hokenstad and Katherine Kendall (1995), both recognized as significant leaders in the development of social work on the global level, noted early on that social work students had limited exposure to international issues. Certainly, social work education, through the EPAS, and NASW with its ongoing international work with the IFSW, have attempted to broaden the educational experience to include global relevance, but should we be doing more? And if so, what, and how?

The social work educational curriculum is already packed with required content. It is easy to say that international content is required in all social curricula, but at what expense? Will existing content need to be dropped or modified? Are social work educators and practitioners willing to decide whether international content, although important in our world today, is necessary for effective social work practice? How to fit the knowledge all social workers need into social work education remains a challenge.

Social work practitioners often claim that they are stretched to the limit by work obligations and wonder how they could continue to manage the rigors of work if they were required to move into the international arena. As one practitioner stated, "Do not get me wrong, I am genuinely concerned about poverty in India and the clear mistreatment of people based on a caste system. BUT I just do not have enough time in a day to do what needs to be done for my child welfare clients. What is important for me is that my kids can get back with their families and no longer feel the pain of abuse and neglect."

Attending his or her first international meeting can be an eye-opening experience for the American social worker. It is common to hear social workers from around the world speak in negative terms about the American social work community. Many believe that American social workers do not value the international experience. Whether this is true or not, they perceive that American social welfare journals discriminate against international authors by declining to publish their manuscripts. They feel that U.S. social work programs do not value international journals and texts, an idea reinforced by the absence of international materials among required readings in social work courses.

There is some truth to allegations that American social workers are undereducated about the perplexing issues faced in the international social welfare arena. They are surprised to learn that there are social work organizations like the NASW and CSWE throughout the world. And yes, they are surprised to discover that social work extends beyond the borders of North America and some parts of Europe.

Rather than berate the profession and each other, we must commit ourselves to professional globalization. In the classroom, we need to look at issues and conduct discussions in an international context. That does not mean that the focus of all efforts should be global, but it does mean that we should consider topics through an international lens when appropriate.

But what are specific things we can do? First, we can support the NASW in its organizational efforts on a national level as well as in the state chapters and local units. Dedicating continued education efforts to an international issue with either a guest speaker or a film will enhance our efforts.

Second, while more ambitious than looking for a guest speaker, a study-travel course organized in conjunction with the NASW or offered by a social work program is a worthwhile activity. Third, we can work to develop a sister program with an international social welfare association or school that can lead to professional exchanges for practitioners and students alike. Such partnerships allow students to meet with students from other countries through social media, and the opportunities for potential collaborations on projects are endless.

Fourth, each year most colleges sponsor an international week on their campuses. The local social work student group can sponsor an activity that highlights international social welfare. Alternatively, a program might consider sponsoring an international event during March, National Social Work Month in the United States.

Fifth, social work programs can sponsor global forums by inviting individuals to speak with students and faculty. The list of speakers is endless and can include members of a foreign consulate, Peace Corp volunteers, and representatives from various international organizations such as UNICEF or CARE. Also, a social work program can easily use any number of social media platforms, such as Zoom or Skype, to host a speaker from another country. And finally, a social work program can encourage its students to organize an international student group to become the central organizing home for student global work. Examining hot topics as they are viewed across the globe can result in a fruitful discussion and help to identify commonalities and differences. For women, equality has been placed on the political agenda and this will require widespread support and awareness (Connell, 2014). International experiences have a way of changing who we are and how we approach our work and daily life circumstances. One of this text's authors wrote the following to his college's alumni describing a trip he took to Israel in January 2009 during the height of the Gaza war:

> For ten days in early January, I traveled around Israel as part of a five-person delegation invited by the Israeli Foreign Ministry. Other delegation members came from Harvard, Georgetown University, Virginia Commonwealth University, and the University of Illinois–Chicago. We met a variety of people including Knesset members, the minister for social welfare, former ambassadors, think tank professionals, educators, lawyers, and leaders of social agencies. The war in Gaza was in its full fury during our visit and framed our conversations. I was particularly impacted by a meeting with a colleague who teaches at Sapir College, located in S'derot, approximately 4.8 kilometers from Gaza. She described classrooms built like bomb shelters, the air raid sirens going off 15 to 20 times in a typical class; students and faculty know a siren means a rocket will hit within 15 seconds—everyone falls to the floor and waits for the rocket blast. Everyone then gets back in their chairs and resumes class until the next siren goes off. The morning of our discussion she described the college reopening after being closed for three weeks; she described the constant buzz of helicopters flying over the campus while watching smoke rising in the near distance. She said that women do not wear heels—they need to be able to run as fast as possible to a bomb shelter; or people do not use bathrooms all day simply because they are not bomb proof. My colleague noted that approximately 3,000 of the 7,000 students suffer from PTSD.
>
> I cannot imagine teaching a class in an environment like that of my colleague in S'derot. How do you pick yourself off the floor and resume teaching as if nothing happened? How different my life would be knowing that at any moment a siren may go off and I will have 15 seconds to find a safe place. As our evening together concluded I said to her that I was having an exceedingly challenging time trying to fully understand what she was describing. She interrupted me and said, "I pray you never have to experience what I am in order to understand what our lives are like."

Most certainly I came away from Israel with a greater understanding of the Mid-East conflict and all its complexities. While that is important, I also no longer take for granted the safe and secure environments that many of us enjoy both at work and at home. I hope that my colleague's wish is realized and that I, we, will never have to experience an air raid siren or dive to the floor for safety.

But even more than that, this one international experience only serves to reinforce my profound respect and admiration for those who teach and work in war-torn and unsafe areas. They are true heroes and remind us all that our mission in social work, the promotion of justice for all, is important and necessary. As the Reverend Dr. Martin Luther King Jr. said, the hopes for a livable world rest with those who strive for peace and justice. (Colby, Ira 2009. Spring comments to alumni. University of Houston Graduate College of Social Work.)

What we do as social workers is limited only by our creativity and our willingness to grow. Social enterprise and social entrepreneurship are gaining in popularity, which has attracted approval from society, governments, and the media as well as from consumers and the public. This is a global phenomenon that shows signs of expanding rather than shrinking (Crowther & Quoquab, 2022). These factors are concepts that can have a real impact on social change that is rich with social responsibility, making the future look promising (Halsall, Oberoi, & Snowden, 2022).

Did You Know . . .

"The USA has yet to ratify the International Covenant on Economic, Social and Cultural Rights, including Article 12, that expands upon health as a human right (Gable 2011; UN-CESCR 2000; United Nations Office of the High Commissioner Human Rights n.d.). Despite this, the social work profession operates from the notion that health is a human right." (Bernhardt, Forgetta, & Sualp, 2021)

But before doing anything, we must first commit to the belief that we live in a global community. We need to embrace the notion that our work influences and is influenced by the global community. Then, and only then, will we be able to confront the social ills that plague the world and have any chance of achieving social justice for all people, no matter where they live or what their social and economic status.

REFERENCES

Bell, D. (1973). *The coming of post-industrial society*. New York, NY: Basic Books.

Bernhardt, C., Forgetta, S., & Sualp, K. (2021). Violations of health as a human right and moral distress: Considerations for social work practice and education. *Journal of Human Rights and Social Work, 6*(1), 91–96.

Birrell, I. (2022). *World's top medical journal finally says COVID-19 COULD have come from lab leak*. Daily Mail. Retrieved September 17, 2022, from https://www.dailymail.co.uk/news/article-11223335/Covid-19-Worlds-medical-journal-finally-says-virus-come-lab-leak.html

Bitler, M. P., Hoynes, H. W., & Schanzenbach, D. W. (2020). *The social safety net in the wake of COVID-19*. National Bureau of Economic Research. Retrieved from https://www.nber.org/papers/w27796

Caissie, M., & Wheeler, D. (2014). *Statement by the North American region of IFSW on the Israeli/Palestinian conflict*. International Federation of Social Workers. Retrieved from https://www.ifsw.org/statement-by-the-north-american-region-of-ifsw-on-the-israeli-palestinian-conflict/

Carter, D. P., & May, P. J. (2020). Making sense of the U.S. COVID-19 pandemic response: A policy regime perspective. *Administrative Theory and Praxis, 42*(2), 265–277. https://doi.org/10.1080/10841806.2020.1758991

Chatterjee, P. (1996). *Approaches to the welfare state*. Washington, DC: NASW Press.

Collins, M. E., Duffy, J., & Kim, S. H. (2022). Borders: An international comparative analysis of social work's response. *The British Journal of Social Work, 52*(4), 2063–2081.

Connell, R. W. (2014). Change among the gatekeepers: Men, masculinities, and gender equality in the global arena. In J. Z. Spade & C. G. Valentine. *The kaleidoscope of gender: Prisms, patterns, and possibilities* (4th ed., pp. 564–579). Thousand Oaks, CA: Sage.

Crowther, D., & Quoquab, F. (2022a), Introduction: Social entrepreneurs and social change. In D. Crowther & F. Quoquab (Eds.), *Social entrepreneurs: Mobilizers of social change* (Developments in Corporate Governance and Responsibility, Vol. 18, pp. 1–10). Bingley, UK: Emerald. https://doi.org/10.1108/S2043-052320220000018001

Enriquez, J. (2005). *The United States of America*. New York, NY: Crown.

Finn, J. L., Perry, T. E., & Karandikar, S. (2013) *Gender oppression and globalization: Challenges for social work*. Alexandria, VA: Council on Social Work Education.

Friedman, T. L. (2005). *The world is flat: A brief history of the twenty-first century*. New York, NY: Farrar, Straus & Giroux.

Gao, J., & Yan, M. (2015). Social work in the making: The state and social work development in China. *International Journal of Social Welfare, 24*(1), 93–101. https://doi.org/10.1111/ijsw.12089

Halsall, J. P., Oberoi, R., & Snowden, M. (2022). Social enterprise, social innovation and sustainable future: A driver for policy change. In D. Crowther & F. Quoquab (Eds.), *Social entrepreneurs* (Developments in Corporate Governance and Responsibility, Vol. 18, pp. 13–27). Bingley, UK: Emerald. https://doi.org/10.1108/S2043-052320220000018002

Healy, L. (1995). International social welfare: Organizations and activities. In R. L. Edwards et al. (Eds.), *Encyclopedia of social work* (19th ed., Vol. 2, pp. 1499–1510). Washington, DC: NASW Press.

Hokenstad, T., Healy, L., & Segal, U. (Eds.) (2013) *Teaching human rights: Curriculum resources for social work educators*. Alexandria, VA: Council on Social Work Education.

Hokenstad, M. C., & Kendall, K. A. (1995). International social work education. In R. L. Edwards (Ed.), *Encyclopedia of social work* (19th ed., Vol. 2, pp. 1511–1520). Washington, DC: NASW Press.

International Federation of Social Workers. (2014a). *Social work for peace and self-determination in Palestine and Israel.* Retrieved from https://www.ifsw.org/social-work-for-peace-and-self-determination-in-palestine-and-israel/

International Federation of Social Workers (2014b). *Statement of IFSW Europe e. V. supporting the people of Turkey following the coal mine tragedy.* Retrieved from http://ifsw.org/news/statement-of-ifsw-europe-e-v-supporting-the-people-of-turkey-following-the-coal-mine-tragedy

International Federation of Social Workers. (2022). *National Association of Social Workers launched in Ukraine.* Retrieved from https://www.ifsw.org/national-association-of-social-workers-launched-in-ukraine/

International Labour Organization. (2020, June). *COVID-19 and the world of work: Ensuring no one is left behind in the response and recovery* [ILO policy brief]. Conditions of Work and Equality Department, Ilo.org: Gender, Equality and Diversity & ILO/AIDS Branch. Retrieved from: https://www.ilo.org/wcmsp5/groups/public/---dgreports/---gender/documents/publication/wcms_750309.pdf

Jiang, H., Wang, Y., Chui, E., & Xu, Y. (2019). Professional identity and turnover intentions of social workers in Beijing, China: The roles of job satisfaction and agency type. *International Social Work,* 62(1), 146–160. https://doi.org/10.1177%2F0020872817712564

Kimura, M., & Henderson, R. (2014). *Public statement by IFSW Asia Pacific regional president and member-at-large concerning the humanitarian disaster currently taking place in Gaza.* International Federation of Social Workers. Retrieved from http://ifsw.org/news/public-statement-by-ifsw-asia-pacific-regional-president-and-member-at-large-concerning-the-humanitarian-disaster-currently-taking-place-in-gaza

Lager, P., Mathiesen, S., Rodgers, M., & Cox, S. (2010). *Guidebook for International field placements and student exchanges: Planning, implementation, and sustainability.* Alexandria, VA: Council on Social Work Education.

Lei, J., Luo, M., Chui, E., & Lu, W. (2019). Whether professional training matters: Attitudinal antecedents to the turnover intentions of social workers in Guangzhou, China. *Journal of Social Service Research,* 45(3), 444–454. https://doi.org/10.1080/01488376.2018.1480569

Mclaughlin, H., Scholar, H., & Teater, B. (2020). Social work education in a global pandemic: Strategies, reflections, and challenges. *Social Work Education: The International Journal,* 39(8), 9756–9982.

Midgley, J. (1995). International and comparative social welfare. In R. L. Edwards (Ed.), *Encyclopedia of social work* (19th ed., Vol. 2, pp. 1490–1499). Washington, DC: NASW Press.

Midgley, J. (1997). Social work in international context: Challenges and opportunities for the 21st century. In M. Reisch & E. Gambrill (Eds.), *Social work in the 21st century* (pp. 59–67). Thousand Oaks, CA: Pine Forge Press.

Ministry of Civil Affairs of the People's Republic of China. (2020). *Statistical bulletin on civil affairs development in 2020.* https://chinadevelopmentbrief.org/: CDB Reports Civil Affairs, Chima Development Brief. Retrieved December 20 2023, from https://chinadevelopmentbrief.org/post-tag/civil-affairs/

Niu, D., & Haugen, H. O. (2019). Social workers in China: Professional identity in the making. *The British Journal of Social Work,* 49(7), 1932–1949.

Oxfam Novib (2021). *The inequality virus. Bringing together a world torn apart by coronavirus through a fair, just, and sustainable economy.* Oxfam GB. https://doi.org/10.21201/2021.6409

Palattiyil, G., Sidhva, D., Pawar, M., Shajahan, P. K., Cox, J., & Anand, J. (2019). Reclaiming international social work in the context of the Global Agenda for Social Work and Social Development: Some critical reflections. *International Social Work, 62*(3), 1043–1054.

Schleicher, A. (2020). *The impact of COVID-19 on education: Insights from education at a glance 2020.* OECD. Retrieved from https://web-archive.oecd.org/2020-09-08/562941-the-impact-of-covid-19-on-education-insights-education-at-a-glance-2020.pdf

Shoichet, C. E. (2014, August 7). What is Putin's endgame in Ukraine? *CNN.* Retrieved from https://www.cnn.com/2014/08/07/world/europe/russia-putin-ukraine-endgame/

Southey, S. J., & Stoddart, K. P. (2021). Clinical intervention with autistic adolescents and adults during the first two months of the COVID-19 pandemic: Experiences of clinicians and their clients. *International Social Work, 64*(5), 777–782. https://doi.org/10.1177/00208728211012462

Tang, N. (2016). *Attitudinal professionalism among social work license holders in China* (Publication No. 10240180) [Doctoral dissertation, University of Alabama]. ProQuest Dissertations and Theses Global.

United Nations. (2019). *The age of digital interdependence.* Retrieved from https://www.un.org/en/pdfs/DigitalCooperation-report-for%20web.pdf

United Nations Children's Fund. (2014). *Levels and trends in child mortality, report 2014.* New York, NY: Author.

United Nations Educational, Scientific and Cultural Organization. (2017). *Literacy rates continue to rise from one generation to the next.* Fact Sheet, No. 45. UNESCO Institute for Statistics. Uis.unesco.org, Retrieved from: https://uis.unesco.org/sites/default/files/documents/fs45-literacy-rates-continue-rise-generation-to-next-en-2017_0.pdf

U.S. Census Bureau. (2022). *U.S. and world population clock.* Retrieved from https://www.census.gov/popclock/

Wang, H., & Jin, P. (2009). Analysis on the characteristics of professionalization of social work in China. *Social Sciences in Xinjiang, 4*,106–109.

Wheatley, D. (2017). Autonomy in paid work and employee subjective well-being. *Work and Occupations, 44*(3), 296–328. https://doi.org/10.1177%2F0730888417697232

World Health Organization (WHO), UNICEF, World Bank. (2022). *State of the worlds drinking water: An urgent call to accelerate progress on ensuring safe drinking water for all.* Geneva, Switzerland: World Health Organization.

World Social Report. (2020). *Inequality in a rapidly changing world.* Department of Economic and Social Affairs, United Nations. https://www.un.org/development/desa/dspd/world-social-report/2020-2.html#:~:text=The%20challenge%20of%20inequality%20in,change%2C%20urbanization%20and%20international%20migration.

Xu, T., Pompili, M., & Sampogna, G. (2021). Psychological distress of international students during the COVID-19 pandemic in China: Multidimensional effects of external environment, individuals' behavior, and their values. *International Journal of Environmental Research and Public Health, 18*(97580), 1–18. https://doi.org/10.3390/ijerph18189758

Zheng, B., Warschauer, M., Lin, C. H., & Chang, C. (2016). Learning in one-to-one laptop environments: A meta-analysis and research synthesis. *Review of Educational Research, 86*(4), 1052–1084.

Zheng, G., Liu, H., Wang, Y., & Chen, B. (2021). The embedded paradox of organizational turnover and professional autonomy. *Research on Social Work Practice, 31*(6), 662–670. https://doi.org/10.1177%2F1049731520984535

15

Conclusion

CHAPTER 15: EPAS COMPETENCIES

Social work programs at the bachelor's and the master's level are accredited by the Council of Social Work Education (CSWE). CSWE's Educational Policy and Accreditation Standards (EPAS) describe the processes and criteria that social work courses should cover. In 2022, CSWE updated its EPAS standards. The following competencies are addressed in this chapter.

Competency 1: Demonstrate Ethical and Professional Behavior

Social workers understand the value base of the profession and its ethical standards, as well as relevant policies, laws, and regulations that may affect practice with individuals, families, groups, organizations, and communities.

Competency 2: Advance Human Rights and Social, Racial, Economic, and Environmental Justice

Social workers understand that every person regardless of position in society has fundamental human rights.

Competency 3: Engage in Anti-racism, Diversity, Equity, and Inclusion in Practice

Social workers understand how racism and oppression shape human experiences and how these two constructs influence practice at the individual, family, group, organizational, and community levels and in policy and research.

Competency 5: Engage in Policy Practice

Social workers identify social policy at the local, state, federal, and global level that affects wellbeing, human rights and justice, service delivery, and access to social services.

Competency 6: Engage with Individuals, Families, Groups, Organizations, and Communities

Social workers understand that engagement is an ongoing component of the dynamic and interactive process of social work practice with and on behalf of individuals, families, groups, organizations, and communities.

The title of a book can tell the reader a great deal about the contents and the views of its authors. Margaret Truman's *Murder at the CIA*, for example, is a murder mystery set within the government. Carl Berstein and Bob Woodward's *All the President's Men* is a work exploring a president, Nixon in this case, and his staff. However, titles may mislead you. *Hunt for Red October* is not a story about fall in New England. J. D. Salinger's classic *Catcher in the Rye* is not a baseball story about the exploits of Yankee legend Yogi Berra.

In social work, you can also tell a lot from book titles. Look at the following titles from the 1960s to the present and think about what they say to you:

- *The Professional Altruist* (Lubove, 1965)
- *Social Work, the Unloved Profession* (W. Richan & Mendelsohn, 1973)
- *Introduction to the Drama of Social Work* (Bloom, 1990)
- *Unfaithful Angels* (Specht & Courtney, 1994)
- *Maneuvering the Maze of Managed Care: Skills for Mental Health Practitioners* (Corcoran & Vandiver, 1996)
- *Economics for Social Workers: Social Outcomes of Economic Globalization with Strategies for Community Action* (Prigoff, 2000)
- *Taking Charge: A School-Based Life Skills Program for Adolescent Mothers* (Harris & Franklin, 2008)
- *Empowering Vulnerable Populations* (Eamon, 2008)
- *Combating Violence and Abuse of People with Disabilities: A Call to Action* (Fitzsimons, 2009)
- *Social Work, a Profession of Many Faces* (Morales, Sheafor, & Scott, 2009)
- *Service Delivery for Vulnerable Populations: New Directions in Behavioral Health* (Estrine, Hettenbach, Arthur, & Messina, 2011)
- *Introduction to Social Work: An Advocacy-Based Profession* (Cox, Tice, & Long, 2018)
- *Days in the Lives of Social Workers: 62 Professionals Tell "Real-Life" Stories from Social Work Practice* (Gobman, 2019)
- *The Changing Face of Health Care Social Work: Opportunities and Challenges for Professional Practice* (Dziegielewski & Holliman, 2020).
- *Introduction to Social Work: The People's Profession* (Dziegielewski, Nelson-Gardell, & Colby, 2024)

Each title should tell you something about the author's or authors' view of the profession and the population they seek to serve. Lubove (1965) recognizes social workers as people who want to help others, but looks beyond the philanthropic model to someone who is professionally trained in this important art and science. *Social Work, the Unloved Profession* depicts the larger community's negative view of social work, one in which the profession's activities are not held in high regard (W. Richan & Mendelsohn, 1973). *Introduction to the Drama of Social Work* by Bloom (1990) unpacks the many struggles that social workers face in providing care. *Unfaithful Angels* is a critical look at the social work profession by two social workers who strongly assert that professionals have abandoned advocacy efforts on behalf of the poor in favor of for-profit and private psychotherapeutic services (Specht & Courtney, 1994). As can be seen by the title, *Maneuvering the Maze of Managed Care* by Corcoran and Vandiver (1996) explored social workers' struggles in a fragmented system of delivery that emphasizes time-limited interventions and clearly defined and measured clinical outcomes, with the ultimate responsibility belonging to the funding source.

Economics for Social Workers by Prigoff (2000) speaks clearly to the need to recognize economic concerns and the movement toward globalization through community action. Eamon (2008), in *Empowering Vulnerable Populations*, highlights the strong focus of many schools of social work on cognitive behavioral therapy and assisting and empowering vulnerable populations. Other books present a call to action for social workers to help vulnerable populations, from combating violence and abuse for people suffering from disabilities (Fitzsimons, 2009) to calling on adolescent mothers to take charge of their lives through empowerment and skill building (Harris & Franklin, 2008). Estrine and Hettenbach (2011) emphasized assisting those in need utilizing a behavioral health concept while avoiding the notion that a "one-size-fits-all" approach is going to work.

In *Introduction to Social Work: An Advocacy-Based Profession*, Cox, Tice, and Long (2018) remind us of the importance of advocacy as well as the importance of empowering clients to incorporate and maintain those helping efforts. *Days in the Lives of Social Workers: 62 Professionals Tell "Real-Life" Stories from Social Work Practice* (Gobman, 2019) helps to highlight what social workers experience in the field. *The Changing Face of Health Care Social Work: Opportunities and Challenges for Professional Practice*, by Dziegielewski and Holliman (2020), investigates health care delivery, outlining how managed behavioral health has been replaced with coordinated care although many of the same health care premises remain. They also outline the expanding roles social workers can assume in health care and the flexibility that is needed to embrace what is often termed coordinated care.

Furthermore, consider the work of Morales, Sheafor, and Scott (2009), who see social work as a profession of many faces, with numerous varied roles and contributions to society. And, last, the authors of the current introductory text deliberately chose the title *Social Work: The People's Profession* in its first edition and kept it across the subsequent editions because social work remains an exciting and fascinating profession that works on behalf of all people in need.

When these books listed above are taken individually or viewed as a timeline, they remain inspirational and thought-provoking, linking the past foundations of the profession to the present. And although the main purpose of each of these texts is to educate, advocate, and inform, a text should also get its readers to think about the subject matter in a more critical, insightful manner.

After reading this book, we hope you can see why we chose the title *Social Work: The People's Profession*. Have you learned something new about the social work profession? Do you have a better understanding of the profession, its varied practice methodologies, and the issues faced by today's professionals?

The practice of social work can be so varied, from direct practice with individuals, families, groups, and communities to advocacy in advancing human rights and social and economic justice. In addition, Hoefer and Watson (2021) remind us that social workers need to use their professional abilities, skill-building activities and knowledge of development and leadership skills in policy planning, program evaluation, budgeting, and fund development. Issues in the news related to sexuality and health-related behaviors and the reproductive rights of women are just a few of the central issues where social workers can contribute and heighten multilevel integrated health care and policy (Rice et al., 2022).

The primary purpose of this book is to help the reader to develop a better understanding of social work as a profession, including the many intriguing areas of practice and advocacy that social work involves. In providing a reality-based approach to practice, we hope to give the beginning social work professional a toolkit for examining the client and client system and how problems and concerns can be addressed from a person-in-environment or person-in-situation perspective resulting in change efforts that make the world a better place for all.

Name: Becky S. Corbett
Place of residence: Rockville, Maryland
College/university degrees: University of Alabama, MSW and BS, human development & family studies
Present position: President & CEO, BSCorbett Consulting, LLC

What does a typical day at work look like for you? What tasks do you generally complete as a social worker in your area of expertise?
I am a systems social worker who connects people and processes for a living and am fiercely dedicated to inspiring others to lead and help communities, organizations, and individuals move ideas to action. A typical workday includes strategy and future thinking for my training and coaching business. Every morning, I wake up and start the day counting my blessings, and every evening before I go to sleep, I reflect on my Victory List from the day and what I can do tomorrow to intentionally improve myself. Some days

the list is shorter than others and some days the list is longer—what matters to me is how meaningful our work outcomes are to the communities and clients we serve.

I am an entrepreneur who serves clients through inspirational speaking engagements, customized trainings, and strengths-based coaching to help them with their intentional growth and development. My ideal week includes the harmony between my professional and personal lives. The typical workday includes a mix of coaching, facilitating, mentoring, advising, and operational consulting in the areas of leadership development, time management, and proDUCKtivity®. My ideal week includes a mixture of curriculum development, direct service, and program evaluation for the Leading ME Principles℠, proDUCKtivity®, The Bridge to Hope & Healing®, and Self-Care Starts with ME℠; our passion Mentoring project, and my own wellbeing and breath work.

What do you do in your spare time? I spend quality, meaningful time with family, and friends who I have chosen to become family along the way. Activities that I enjoy immensely include smiling; collecting inspirational quotes; traveling; listening, singing, and dancing to 70s music; shopping for little gifts for my friends, family, and colleagues; watching a good Alabama football game; playing backgammon, Rummikub, and cards while sipping on bourbon; watching the sunset over the water; watching movies or streaming specific television shows with good popcorn and a Dr. Pepper; going for a low-impact hike in the mountains; overseeing my aging parents' care; and being available to anyone in my network seeking assistance for their salary and benefits negotiation.

Why did you choose social work as a career? After obtaining my undergraduate degree in human development and family studies, from the University of Alabama (UA), I set out on a journey to become a marriage and family therapist. While completing informational interviews with psychology, counseling, and the social work departments—as well as talking to supervisors and mentors at the mental health center where I was working—I choose social work. Good thing I did, because after completing the first year of my MSW program at UA School of Social Work (UASSW), I realized I no longer wanted to focus on micro-level social work and therapy services. I was so very fortunate that UASSW administrators and faculty saw something in me that I did not necessarily see in myself—I was to become a nonprofit exec. Thirty plus years later, I have blended my family business background with my deep devotion to the mission of nonprofit organizations.

What is your favorite social work story? There are so many—it is extremely difficult to choose only one. The one I want to share highlights several social work foundational concepts I learned in school: a strengths-based perspective, person-in-environment, and the client's right to self-determination. While serving as the chief operating officer of the NASW National Office, I worked alongside two amazing associates. Their areas of expertise were similar; however, they had different strengths related to their delivery of services. Both are detailed-oriented and the best project managers and program developers I know. However, one specialized in overseeing the coordination of one hundred tasks on our to-do list and the other implemented four cross-functional projects at one time. When

continues

> *continued*
>
> asked to walk in the shoes of the other, they both said, "No way and no thank you." We would experiment and have them change roles while one or the other was out on vacation or sick leave. They were right: each was not as effective in this new role. Supervising these individuals is one of the highlights of my career. They taught and showed me what it meant to support, coach, mentor, and advise alongside people, always remembering a strengths-based perspective, person-in-environment, and the client's right to self-determination.
>
> *What would be the one thing you would change in our community if you had the power to do so?* Every social worker would see and believe they are a leader; believe in their own intentional growth, self-worth and negotiate their next salary and benefits opportunity; and move to action their organizational, professional, and personal growth.

15.1 THE TIME TO DECIDE IS APPROACHING

From the outset, we have made some assumptions about you as the reader of this text and as a beginning social work professional. First, we believe that you are reading this book because it is assigned for a class. We realize this is not the book of choice for evenings, weekends, or vacations! Second, we think that you are taking a social work course called Introduction to Social Work or something similar because you are interested in learning more about the field. Whatever the title of the course, the class you are taking is one of the first, if not the first, social work class in a series of required courses for a degree in social work. Third, we have assumed that, although you or some of your classmates may have had some experience with social work professionals, for the most part you agree that most people do not really have a detailed understanding of the social work profession, including its mission, purpose, and function.

FIGURE 15.1
The time to decide is approaching, and selecting the best path to take is never easy.

Fourth, some of you are seriously exploring social work as a career and have registered for this course with that purpose in mind. For others of you, however, this may have been the course that was available at the right time in person or online or you may have heard that the instructor was interesting, so you decided to try it. Trying to address the needs implicit in these assumptions was at times a daunting task, but it was an effort we enjoyed. It feels good to have put together a text that meets the social work accreditation standards, helps people to gain a clear understanding of the social work profession, supports the faculty members' direction, and helps the individual student to make a crucial career decision: Is social work for me?

Making a career decision is not easy, nor should it be (see Figure 15.1). For the seven hundred thousand social workers across the United States (National Association of

Social Workers [NASW], 2022a), entry into this profession is not just a job, it is a calling. We will be very forthright with our advice to you: Do not make yourself miserable with worry. What you decide today does not obligate you for the rest of your life or even through next week! You can change your mind at any time about your career goals. It is not unusual for college students to change majors a few times before completing their baccalaureate studies.

To be fair, it is true that family, friends, and college teachers and counselors put unnecessary pressure on today's students. Why is it so important to select a major by the end of your sophomore year? When you say that you are going to college, "What's your major?" is often the first question you hear. The reasons for this question vary. Family and friends are excited that you are pursuing a college education, and naturally they are interested in what courses you plan to take and what career path you will follow. Those of us who teach in higher education see the potential major to sustain the field. Academic programs are under constant pressure—intense pressure—to maintain student enrollments. Declining student enrollments jeopardize continuation of a major. Look at what happened to sociology at several colleges in the 1980s: it was discontinued as a major, untenured faculty were released from their jobs, and tenured faculty members were moved to other departments.

Years ago, the preference was for a student to get a liberal arts education as an undergraduate. To be considered educated, that is, to develop a broad worldly view of people and their settings, a person must have studied a variety of subjects in the arts, sciences, and humanities. The idea was that a liberal thinker, in the literal rather than the political sense, is better suited to participate in society. For some occupations, this broad-based education was sufficient. People could get good jobs without having majored in a specific area. Training for a specific position or workplace happened on the job. People who chose to continue their studies in a specialized field did so in graduate programs.

By contrast, today's undergraduate students are asked to declare their majors early, sometimes even at the time of application. Is it fair to ask someone who is just beginning his or her college education to select a career? We could argue the merits and drawbacks of this practice until we are all blue in the face. The fact is that you must select a major or be cast into the land of the general major (different colleges have different terms for this group; it usually includes all students who have not chosen a career path).

By this point, most readers of this text have made some decisions about social work. We will not take sole credit for influencing the decision-making process. Class lectures and discussions, guest speakers, field trips, and other learning opportunities, in addition to this text, have helped you to make your decision, or at least a partial decision.

The Non–Social Work Major

We want to offer a few words to those of you who have decided that social work is not for you. First, we are glad you have made a decision that is right for you at this time. Do not be disappointed that you have learned that social work is not your profession of choice.

By looking at yourself in the light of information gleaned from this text, you may find yourself challenged on many fronts; the resulting decisions require you to take an especially crucial step in your life. And you can always revisit your decision. When you make career choices, the door never closes for good: you can always reconsider your options.

We hope you have a better understanding and appreciation of social work and the issues that drive our profession. Although you feel that social work is not your career choice, you can nevertheless help to increase other people's understanding. You have learned how to better communicate with people having difficulty and you know the strengths and weaknesses of our social welfare system to help you advocate for positive change. You are better informed about several social issues and several myths that shroud public policy. When you hear others attack social welfare, listen carefully to what is being said and always be sure to take your time and respond with accurate information. At the very least, be slow to judge and be sure to look up or research what others say if it does not sound like what we have discussed thus far. You can be part of the myth-busting squad that dispels misinformation. Let people know the facts about poverty, child welfare, domestic violence, health and mental health, and the many other areas discussed in this text. When using telehealth or teletherapy services, do not assume all people are familiar with the technology and capable of utilizing it. Stay informed about the issues: keep up with the news in whatever way fits your lifestyle and always visit reputable websites for updated information. Information and facts are among the most powerful tools you can have at your disposal. Do not let yourself or others be victims of gaslighting, where one person tries to manipulate another, suggesting the problems that are being experienced are their own fault.

Did You Know . . .

Gaslighting is a term that is often seen in the recent literature. Gaslighting can be used to describe any argument in which there is disagreement. Be careful, however, because it can also be considered a form of emotional abuse where one individual tries to manipulate another, suggesting the fault lies in the person who disagrees with the gaslighter's opinion.

Source: WebMD (2022). Retrieved from https://www.webmd.com/mental-health/ss/slideshow-gaslighting-what-it-is-and-how-to-stop-it#

Did You Know . . .

The website WebMD has a helpful page, "What Is Gaslighting in Relationships?," with more information on gaslighting, its effects, warning signs, and treatment.

You can also be invaluable as a social service volunteer. Most social agencies need people who want to help others. All it takes is one phone call to a specific agency asking if it needs help. Or if you just want to volunteer a few hours a week and the organizational setting does not matter, simply call and volunteer at a local service agency. You will be placed in the areas of greatest need where your awareness of the profession and what could help the most will help you to make a meaningful, client-empowered contribution.

> ### Did You Know . . .
> In 1998, the field of social work in the United States celebrated a century of professional social work education and recognized more than one hundred years of contributions to the well-being of individuals, groups, families, communities, and the natural environment. This was such an important event that volume 43, number 6, of the NASW journal *Social Work* was dedicated to accomplishments in social work practice.

The Social Work Major

You are about to enter a very structured educational experience. Remember what we learned earlier about the demands of accreditation by the Council on Social Work Education (CSWE)? (If you do not remember, you may want to reread Chapter 2, especially before your final examination!) With restrictions and expectations related to accreditation and professional practice, you can plan on your academic schedule being outlined for you for the remainder of the program. Because the coursework is so prescribed, be sure to meet with an advisor to discuss the courses you plan to take. This will prevent any surprises as you get ready to graduate. Be sure you are aware of how the courses in your program are sequenced by semester or quarter. You can look at your program's student handbook or ask the course instructor or your academic advisor to review the academic program.

Some aspects of your program are set in stone, with little room for modification or negotiation, and coursework will follow the CSWE EPAS standards (CSWE, 2022a). Additionally, there are some considerations for you to keep in mind:

1. For most students at the graduate or the undergraduate level, the program will take two years of full-time study. Oftentimes, courses are sequenced in a certain order. You cannot take these classes out of order and there is generally no way to double up and graduate in one year. We have found over the years that some students spend an inordinate amount of time challenging and trying to change a structured educational program. They often become angry with the faculty and program, calling them inflexible, yet so many of these decisions are beyond the control of the instructor and program. Before you sign on the dotted line and make the decision to become a social work major at either the graduate or the

undergraduate level, be sure to check the curriculum model, the sequencing of courses, and the specific requirements. This includes mapping out a course of study and accepting the length of time that will be needed to complete the program. Be sure to explore all aspects that may affect your ability to meet these financial and structural requirements. If you are concerned about the requirements, meet with a social work advisor and determine whether your needs can be accommodated.

Do not select this major without planning out the time you will need to complete the degree and explore all possible scenarios. Plan your schedule carefully and make any necessary arrangements, such as those for needed child care or employment, to complete all the program requirements (see item 3 below on field placement). Look carefully to see if there are online options for some classes and if this will help you to plan your schedule. If you are in an online program, are there synchronous or only asynchronous opportunities for classes? Keep in mind that the beauty of online courses is flexibility; however, you will still have to plan carefully to meet all program requirements. Whether in person, online, or a hybrid of the two, if you feel you cannot commit to the full-time option, check to see if there is a part-time option. It may take you twice as long to complete the program, but living and working between classes may warrant a slower but steady pace for your course of study.

2. Academic credit will not be given for life experiences, according to CSWE accreditation standards. There are no ifs, ands, or buts on this point. Academic credit is awarded for successful completion of specific college courses and activities only. It does not matter if you have lots of experience in the field, worked in the Peace Corps for two years, or worked in a human service agency for five years—no academic credit or course waivers can be awarded for these activities.

3. In social work there is an expectation that each graduate will have supervised work in the field upon graduation. Therefore, you will have a field placement, which is strategically scheduled in your academic program to allow demonstration of specific knowledge and skills learned in the classroom. Your field experience will be sequenced after you have completed certain courses. You will not be able to take the field course any earlier in the program, nor can your field course be waived in recognition of previous work experience. Remember that the CSWE does not accept experience in lieu of classwork and that this applies to all facets of the educational program, including the field placement.

Be sure to meet the field coordinator in your school; an appointment just to say hello is always a promising idea. Meet with the field coordinator as early as possible to discuss your concerns (for example, if you cannot or prefer not to work in any agency or require special considerations in your placement options). Most programs will be as flexible as possible to help meet your needs. You will also need to be flexible in field placement selection. A program will work with you to find the best site to meet your academic needs, but the final field assignment depends on the social work program and what is available in the community. We have heard students say that, for them to get a job, their placement must be in a certain agency. Although programs are concerned about your prospective employment, the primary issue in field assignment is your learning—employment comes later. Be sure to work closely with your field placement director or coordinator and always consider that some programs may have limited resources to meet all or even some of your field placement needs. Remember what we said about planning in advance and making sure that your plan is doable. It is incredibly sad when students cannot receive a BSW or MSW degree simply because they did not complete their field placement hours. Although programs and agency placements try to be flexible, you may not be able to get an evening or weekend placement, and it would be a shame if noncompletion of the field hours stopped you from graduating.

4. Remember that your peers in social work courses are in the same place you are. Although everyone's circumstances are different—some are older or younger, some have agency experience whereas others have none—these differences really have minimal importance in the educational setting; all of you are evolving as you begin the process of becoming a professional social worker. No one is better off than anyone else because of life experiences. Do not be intimidated by what others say or do or how they come across in class. Try to listen objectively to what others say, and process accordingly as you start to question your own assumptions. Allow yourself to expand your previous assumptions as you embrace this professional perspective.

5. The purpose of your baccalaureate educational program is to prepare you for beginning practice. It is not to prepare you for a specialization, which takes place at the graduate level. At this level of your academic career, your course instructor and academic advisor care primarily about your development as a beginning social worker.

6. Do not tell an instructor that you need an A in the course for your own personal satisfaction or to get into graduate school. There is a saying in Texas that fits this type of situation: "That dog won't hunt!" You certainly have the right to talk with a faculty member about a grade and how it was determined, but it does not do any good to be argumentative. The instructor's responsibility is to assess your answers and summarize the quality of your responses with a grade. Grading is not easy—to say the least—and many teachers struggle to ensure that their grades are fair and consistent. Rather than arguing your position, you should use your energy positively, incorporate your social work skills to clarify the situation, and seek a remedy if you feel one is needed. Can you redo the assignment? Is there extra credit work you can do for the course? What changes can you make to do better next time? If you feel that your grade is incorrect, review the student grievance policy in the program. But we emphasize—use this only as a last resort.

Remember that your instructors are faculty members who were once students and, like you, they at one time or another felt that an instructor had graded them unfairly. Grading is not an easy task, and it is commonplace for a student to be upset or angry when receiving a low grade. Why do we get upset about a grade? The simple reasons are that people do not like getting negative feedback, such as a low grade. Before going to the faculty person's office, we suggest you step back for a moment and look at what the course instructor is saying: What didn't you do on the assignment? What could you have done to get your point across more clearly? What have you learned from this experience that you can apply to future assignments or experiences?

Your goal should be the same as your faculty's goal for you: to develop competence and expertise in entry-level generalist social work practice. Your energy should be directed toward developing critical knowledge and skills necessary for effective practice. Learning to be a professional is not easy; it means relooking at your old ways of doing things and applying this new professional strategy. You are a student striving to learn, and if mistakes are made, this is the place where you want to make them.

There are two questions to ask around grades: (1) How will my challenging a grade for a paper, test, or final exam make me a better social work professional? (2) Is there an error in the grading that I can demonstrate to the course instructor that justifies the assignment of another grade?

Name: Karen Winston

Place of residence: Bellaire, Texas

College/university degrees: BA in communications, University of New Mexico; master of social work, LCSW, University of Houston

Present position: Currently I am a clinical social worker in private practice in Houston, Texas. I am also a clinical assistant professor in the Menninger Department of Psychiatry and Behavioral Sciences, Baylor College of Medicine,  Houston, Texas. Formerly I was an instructor for the National Football League (NFL), helping players navigate the transition from college to the NFL. I was also formerly the team psychotherapist for the Houston Texans.

What does a typical day at work look like for you? Currently I am seeing psychotherapy patients both online and in the office. I see individuals for forty-five minutes and couples for sixty minutes. I start at 8:00 a.m. and usually finish by 4:00 p.m. I only take insurance for NFL players or former NFL players and their families or employees of an NFL team. This requires my calling the insurance carrier and getting their free sessions approved. This also requires my giving them a diagnosis. While it's helpful to these patients to have free care, it also can be very limiting because of the number of sessions the insurance company approves. Also, during breaks or at the end of the day I return calls from new referrals and calls from current patients who may have a question or have an appointment change request. Additionally, I may need to make calls to help a patient find some resources for themselves or a family member. As an example, I have a patient whose husband was a former NFL player, and he has been diagnosed with dementia. She is completely overwhelmed caring for him and needs help with options to give her a break. At times I also collaborate with my patients' other psychiatric providers, with their written permission. For example, I may have a patient who is severely depressed, and I may want to consult with their psychiatrist so we can put our heads together to see how to best help them. (Two heads can be better than one.)

What task do you generally complete as a social worker in your area of expertise? What I do in a typical day, as referenced above, also includes some additional tasks. In my daily private practice, I am meeting with patients, whether couples or individuals. The first few sessions involve making a thorough evaluation and gaining an understanding of what they are wanting to think about and to make sure we are a good fit. I need to know that I am the right person with the right skill set for their situation. Then we get to the task of psychotherapy, which means we together, the patient and me, commence in a process and in a relationship to try to understand and make sense of the issues they are concerned about. For example, a couple comes in extremely stressed as the wife has discovered her husband has been having an affair. I evaluate them to see if they want to stay or go and whatever they decide I can help them navigate those choppy waters. Another example is a professional athlete, who is making a minimum salary, and is struggling to meet the financial demands his family is placing on him. The family feels entitled to his salary and setting limits and boundaries is very difficult for him. He feels very guilty and angry at the same time.

What is your favorite social work story. One particular story that stands out to me I call the Porch Light Metaphor. I was working with a couple and the husband was a surgeon and often worked late. In the winter, when the sun goes down early, he would arrive home in the dark and had trouble seeing the keyhole on the front door. He asked his wife if she would turn on the porch light so he could see. She said yes. Week after week they would come to my office, and he would report that the light had never been turned on. She had lots of reasons/excuses each week. Over time we were able to eventually understand that the porch light was a metaphor for him. If she turned it on, then he would know his wife had him in her mind. He grew up with a mother he felt did not have him in her mind, thus it was extremely important that he knew his wife did.

A second favorite story is when I was working with a rookie football player. He was desperately trying to make the team. He was a standout in college, but the NFL is a whole different level of skills and challenges. During a preseason game, which is a serious evaluative time for who does and does not make the team, the player made a major mistake. He was pretty sure he would not make the team as the coach was clearly mad at him. He came to see me as he started having panic attacks. We didn't have a lot of time to think through. I suggested he might consider going to the coach and tell him he will never make that mistake again and he will work really hard on his skills and learning his playbook. He was

continues

continued

apprehensive, terrified, and felt very vulnerable. Ultimately, he was also very brave and talked to the coach. The coach was appreciative and believed in him, and he made the team. He felt his own advocacy was the turning point.

Why did you choose social work as a career? I owned a retail store and spent my time shopping for merchandise and selling it. It was a successful travel store, but I felt empty and that the deeper parts of myself were not being attended to. One Sunday, three different friends called me and asked me if they could come over to talk to me about something personal. By the end of that day, I knew where I needed to be and what I wanted to be doing. I was thirty-eight years old and making another career change, so I knew I had to get this right. Social work was the obvious choice with its diversification and the ability to get licensed for private practice, which was my ultimate goal.

What's the one thing you would change in our community if you had the power to do so? If I could advocate for one change, I would want to encourage more men of color to get their master's in social work. Having worked in professional football and most professional sports for several decades, I see what a gift it would be for some of these male athletes to have a therapist who looks like them and have some relatability around culture and community.

15.2 THE FUTURE AND YOU

We are now in a new century and the second hundred years of social work practice. In an environment where concepts such as "cancel culture" most evident when one political party lead the charge with information shared, they can cancel the opinions of another (Foundation for Economic Education, 2022). When cancel culture is rooted in historically marginalized and disenfranchised groups that seek social justice, the relationship and advocacy efforts in social work become clear. As an up-and-coming social worker, you will lay the foundation for the twenty-first century. You represent our future, and what you do and say will shape the profession for years to come. As we bring the text to a close, we want to spend our remaining time looking at two premises. First, as you begin your professional career, you should remember always to start each professional activity by applying the knowledge you have learned about social work. Be sure to explore how you can update your knowledge base because environments are not static, and all efforts should be relevant to the person-in-situation stance.

A commitment to ethics and the philosophical foundations within the literature are intertwined in our practice efforts (Reamer, 2022). Whether online or in person, the foundations of the social work profession remain strong (Reamer, 2020). Finding the best evidence-based practices is essential (Drisko & Grady, 2019; Hall & Roussel, 2022; Howlett, Rogo, & Shelton, 2021). These evidence-based practice strategies should always consider the best available evidence or data to support the outcome results, the social worker's knowledge and skills, and what the client and/or client system wants or needs.

Always use this knowledge to guide your helping efforts in the years to come. And second, consider how you can best use these skills to work with clients individually and collectively to provide client-centered care from a micro, mezzo, or macro perspective.

Social Work as a Profession: Future Considerations

You have seen how social work evolved from volunteer efforts geared toward poor people to a multifaceted profession working with a variety of client groups. Education was initially limited to on-the-job training, with no oversight of work other than the agency's internal safeguards. Men were the supervisors and women were the caseworkers. Today, social work education is formal (and some say too rigid) because this professional designation must be earned within colleges and universities. There is public regulation in every state for some, but not all, levels of social work practice. Many states are seeking or already have title protection, which means that you cannot use the title of social worker unless you have the professional training and qualifications to do so. Social work remains a female-dominated profession. Therefore, it comes as no surprise that, throughout the first hundred years of the profession, it was women's critical contributions to the theory, practice, and politics that made social work what it is today. In the twenty-first century, we find women holding critical positions, leading the profession in academic institutions, professional associations, and social welfare agencies.

The profession's first century required commitment, passion, and vision to achieve its current stature. Although we have come a long way, as the poet Robert Frost wrote, "we have miles to go before we sleep." What are some areas into which the profession should move more aggressively? Let us consider a few ideas:

1. *Social work is not designed just to help the individual family or small group.* With all the societal upheaval and changes around us, the twenty-first century provides fertile ground for social workers to assume a pivotal position to create positive social change. Seeking a clear definition of social work and a solid unifying identity is difficult because of the expansiveness of the profession (Forenza & Eckert, 2018). Therefore, an inclusive definition starts with empowerment for all individuals. Eamon (2008) identified four goals: (1) accessing and enhancing social resources, (2) acquiring and increasing economic resources, (3) increasing self-determined behavior, and (4) influencing the social policies and organizational and community practices that affect the lives of people from vulnerable groups. To achieve these goals, providing services at the micro and mezzo level only is insufficient; therefore, it is critical to also focus on helping efforts at the macro level. Macro-level interventions require social change and advocacy that can be most easily accomplished by holding elective office at the local, state, and national levels. We need more of our colleagues to take this chance and run for office and to advocate for policy change. When these efforts are combined with recognizing the phenomenon of cancel culture (FAA, 2022), macro interventions can become critical in recognizing how historically marginalized people can be ignored while supporting those who have been systematically disenfranchised.

The advice of W. C. Richan (2006) remains relevant today as we are reminded that social problems follow a logical sequence. To start the process, the social problem must be recognized and analyzed. Once this is completed, the policy is formalized and later implemented. Since it is possible that the way people apprise and relate to stress can be related to their political ideology, this aspect of societal response should not be underestimated (Wright, Faul, Graner, et al., 2022). Therefore, once the policy is in effect, expected results and consequences must be evaluated and monitored. This stepwise process creates an interlocking cycle in which one step leads to the next. To create policy, at either the formulation or the evaluation stage, who is better qualified than social workers with their knowledge of and experience with families, children, and underserved, low-income, sick, and at risk populations? Social workers and lawyers make an effective team. Therefore, social workers should never be afraid of being called *bleeding-heart liberals*. Instead, they should be proud of it. If assuming the role of a bleeding-heart liberal means that we stand for fairness and equity for all people, shelter for the homeless, food for the hungry, and education for all children, then we should stand proudly to acknowledge that role. Wouldn't you love to run against an opponent who claims to oppose care for sick children, to want homeless seniors to live unprotected on the streets, to want people (children in particular) to starve, and to oppose making all children the best educated in the world? In other words, the profession must use its assets. If we are a people's profession, our assets start with our attention to human rights and striving to protect the rights of all people.
2. The profession of social work must recognize the importance of unification and work together, especially on critical issues, presenting a unified front. Social work is a diverse field, and there are those who believe we need special-interest groups and membership associations to focus on specialized practice matters. But we are fast approaching a crossroad, if we have not already reached it, where practice membership associations conflict with each other and with the overall interests of the profession. Tension between members of the different membership groups is not healthy for the profession or, more important, for the public and the clients we serve. Social work membership groups must find common ground if the profession is to become more effective in its public efforts.
3. The entry degree in the field of social work is the BSW, yet there are far too few at this level who are active in professional membership organizations such as the NASW. Those at the BSW level make important contributions to the field, and their voices need to be heard. We must seek out more BSWs to join the NASW. Because there are too few BSW members in the association, their practice interests are not fully represented at all levels of the association. Annual membership dues certainly are expensive—in particular, for BSWs at lower pay levels—and the NASW has tried to address this by revising the dues structure. But efforts to attract BSWs must go far beyond lower dues. It is essential that MSWs make BSWs

feel that they are accepted and recognized as key members within the profession. Elitism and professional ethnocentrism will only weaken our efforts.

Social work programs can play a critical role by involving BSW students in the NASW. First, programs could promote membership. Student dues are relatively inexpensive and are far outweighed by the association's benefits. Second, social work programs, together with state chapters and local units, can look at developing student units that proactively involve students. Third, social work programs can work with local NASW units to cohost continuing education efforts or facilitate connections between student groups and the NASW. The key is for professional groups and social work programs to be aggressive in recruiting students, to value BSW students as future members, and to involve them in association activities.

4. In Chapter 14, we spent time exploring the global social welfare arena. Social work is a worldwide profession that helps people, families, communities, and social systems to deal with issues that cut across national boundaries. Each of these groups comes from a different culture, which requires that a social worker be able to understand and integrate the differences that occur. Focusing on Western culture may deter the development of social work as a profession in other countries. For example, as social work continues to grow in China, the influence of Western culture can conflict with cultural expectations there taking a different path to professionalization (Niu & Haugen, 2019). For social work to globally develop, it is crucial to acknowledge that the social worker helps to interpret how all these individuals view the world, and Western culture is not the only way. As we grow closer together and the boundaries become more easily crossed, practitioners in the twenty-first century are challenged more than at any other time in the world's history to understand the influence of the international community and be influenced by it. The phrase "Think globally, act locally" probably best captures the direction we must go. Yet social workers have little exposure to international social welfare. International course content is sparse in both undergraduate and graduate programs. There are exceptions, of course; some schools sponsor study-abroad programs, offer educationally directed travel programs, or have a greater international emphasis. But most social work programs do little more than include brief mentions of international issues as part of a course or courses.

Professional associations also need to work harder to promote international issues. Again, through study tours and publications, we become more aware of the international community. But is this enough? The authors do not think so. Many in the social work community support the goal of global understanding and activism. Expanding our understanding will help us to be knowledgeable members of the world community. Enhancing global learning and understanding of others will help us to better appreciate the strength and potential of seemingly different people while developing greater awareness of the struggles that will need to be engaged. Global activism builds on knowledge. Once we understand others, we are in a better position to offer effective assistance and support. Social workers in the United States must enhance their valuing of the learning we gain from abroad that can help us help here at home.

There are many mechanisms we can implement to pursue the goal of global understanding and activism. The expansion of BSW and MSW curriculum content would help us work toward this goal. International content in each course and an additional specific international course would help enhance our knowledge base. We can also become more creative in our approach. Social work educational programs can sponsor annual activities that highlight one or two aspects of international social welfare. Utilizing information technology and the internet can make many of these opportunities more accessible. Professional associations, both at the national and the state level, can sponsor international activities each year. Hosting continuing education workshops virtually or in person, dedicating parts of association newsletters to international issues, and developing dedicated international handouts and brochures will help us to become more global.

Social work focuses on change and change affects social work practice. Social justice stands as a historical focal area of interest for the profession, but changes in our society have brought social justice issues to the fore in what seems like every area of our lives. The social work profession is a place where we prepare individuals to extend social justice—we are ready! Some exciting areas of social work practice emerging in this first third of the twenty-first century include sports social work, corporate social work, remote technologically assisted social work, and environmental justice– and climate change–focused social work. Whether you join the profession or become one of its beneficiaries, the future of social work holds tremendous promise.

The American Social Welfare System: The Future

What a fascinating history we have in social welfare! The overview in Chapter 2 was just that, an overview. Even from that brief foray, we can see emerging the long-held myths that underpin the current U.S. social welfare system. First is the myth that people of lower socioeconomic status, historically referred to as poor people and people in need, are different from the rest of us. Some say poor people are morally inferior and lazy; others say they are poorly educated and lack the motivation to change. This negative stereotyping can justify the lack of attention and service provision the system affords. Recognizing efforts to ignore and further disenfranchise individuals requires confronting such efforts (Foundation of Economic Education, 2022). For social workers, this can be done through micro and mezzo interventions that can assist the client and the client system, as well as community-level and other political efforts that expose and create an environment of free expression.

Second, there is a strong belief by the critics of welfare that social services are best left to the local community and private groups. Americans have often been reluctant to support federal involvement in the social welfare system. Social agencies, churches, volunteer associations, and informal networks are seen as more acceptable vehicles for social welfare. Yet, as a society we must be careful not to discriminate against others based on lifestyle or religious preference; this makes suspect service provision provided by those motivated by religious custom and dogma (Blackwell & Dziegielewski, 2005).

These beliefs can lead to hate crimes such as the Pulse Night Club shooting in 2016, where forty-nine people were killed and fifty-three more were wounded in a gay nightclub (Ellis, Frantz, Karimi, & McLaughlin, 2016), and more recently with the attack on the gay nightclub in Colorado Springs, where five people were killed and at least nineteen others were injured (Wolfe & Andone, 2022). Hate crimes such as these speak loudly to the fact that advocacy for fairness and justice for all people cannot be ignored.

Third is the myth that social welfare is not something that everyone deserves, but a temporary support given only to the worthiest individuals. Over time, women, infants, children, the elderly population, and people with disabilities have fallen into the category of the *worthy poor*. Fourth is the myth that work is the primary way to achieve self-sufficiency. Some believe that all anyone needs is a job, not even a good-paying job at first, because the early experience will lead to higher-paying jobs.

These views are not necessarily those of most social workers, but they do express the expectations of much of the American public. In Chapter 2, we discussed the modern welfare system and, in Chapter 7, we examined the 1990s welfare reform package, along with more recent developments. We all should remember that in the presidential election of 2000, a new welfare concept came on the national scene: *compassionate conservatism*. These discussions of the late 1990s and early 2000s showed how the four myths described above have become well ingrained into the American welfare system. When compassionate conservatism is followed by the health care reform of 2010, particularly what is popularly called Obamacare, which allowed many more individuals to obtain health care coverage than ever before. When health care reform is coupled with efforts to avoid anti-racist activities and humane policies at our borders with respect to immigration, addressing these events will require humanitarian-focused, and effective responses.

So, where does the American welfare system go from here? Is the current system working? Here are some underlying assumptions that could support the need for changes to our social welfare programs.

First, the welfare system must be just and treat all people with respect and dignity. How do we explain compassion for those who are less fortunate when we have in each state a federally mandated and binding welfare program known as Temporary Assistance to Needy Families (TANF)? Although there are some differences among states, this program allows only a maximum of five years of assistance in a lifetime. Some people, no matter what we do, will not be able to care for themselves. Why do we penalize an unborn baby by denying it welfare benefits because the mother was already on assistance? What kind of life are we promising that child? A comprehensive welfare system embraces people and their strengths. We should move away from a punitive system to one based on hope.

Second, American welfare recipients continue to carry an enormous stigma. Every day, politicians, radio talk show hosts and callers, and newspaper columnists, among others, rail against poor people. With this constant barrage, it would be a wonder if welfare clients did not hide from the general public. Being poor and receiving public assistance is not the fulfillment of a lifelong ambition. We should work to remove the stigma associated with public aid.

Third, the goal of the welfare system should be to help all people with adequate benefits and supports. If the system works, then people who can do so will move to sustainable work. The purpose of the welfare system's benefits and supports is simple: to help clients meet their daily needs so they can focus their energies on becoming self-sufficient. The welfare system should concentrate on meeting basic needs: food, shelter, and protection.

The ideal social welfare system includes, at a minimum, the following five core pieces: (1) The level of these benefits must be comprehensive. (2) Services must include high-quality health care and child care and ongoing support to adults in their efforts to work. (3) Programs must help people develop the necessary knowledge and skills to become self-sufficient in a technological society. (4) Reliable transportation is needed to ensure that people can get to training programs, work, or school. (5) Jobs must be permanent (e.g., not seasonal) and offer a living wage, not a minimum wage.

Fourth, a comprehensive welfare system is expensive. But if we genuinely want to help poor and less fortunate individuals to achieve social, economic, and environmental justice, the price tag should be a burden that, as a society, we accept. Funding decisions for programs are made in a political context. The decision to fund roads and highways at one level and after-school child care at a much lower level is a clear statement about our beliefs. Funds could be available to support a comprehensive welfare system that encompasses social, economic, and environmental justice for all citizens, but it would be accomplished by changing government spending patterns and/or by raising taxes. Throughout the text, we have referred directly and indirectly to the influence of the political system on social welfare, and in Chapter 13 we outlined the role that social workers can assume in politics. As we consider the role of politics in social welfare and questions related to funding, we must first answer two questions: (1) What is the goal of our welfare system? (2) What commitments are we willing to make to achieve that goal?

Last, social welfare and social work should do no harm to any person, group, or community. The *do no harm* philosophy is a fundamental value embraced by the medical community and its ideas should resonate throughout our helping systems. Do we want to create social policies that harm people? Of course, we would never want to do this. Yet most agree that the first thrust of TANF is to make it clear that women (particularly unwed teen mothers) do not take personal responsibility for having children. To overcome this and place responsibility for the loss of support on the mother, TANF has a lifetime limit in place on the number of months a person can receive federal assistance (Day & Schiele, 2013). Why do we allow millions of our children not to be fully immunized? Under a do no harm philosophy, we would ensure that all children would be fully immunized. Do no harm is a core concept that serves as a pivotal girder in the foundation of a just, compassionate society.

15.3 SOCIAL WORK PRACTICE

Of all the practice professions, social work has one of the most comprehensive codes of ethics (NASW, 2018). The profession makes statements such as "Once a client, always a client" and "Start where the client is" and in every professional encounter holds paramount the individual worth and dignity of each client. Not all social workers are employed as team members or in group practice where they can process ethical dilemmas (Reamer, 2020, 2022). In this situation, a social worker may contact an ethics hotline or former colleagues or classmates to discuss the situation in confidence and gain advice. When working as part of a collaborative team, the social worker may note an ethical problem when no one else does. Having such a comprehensive code of ethics can be both a blessing and a curse, especially when other professionals do not view the problem in the same way. This can make ethical practice decisions difficult for the new social worker, especially in an environment of cost containment and evidence-based behavioral coordinated care strategies. To practice in this competitive environment, social workers must either accept this challenge for change or lose the opportunity to be players. Regardless, whether making the decision alone or as part of a team, social workers must be able to show that what they do is necessary and effective while maintaining their own ethical and moral standards for the helping relationship.

As discussed in several chapters of this book, culturally responsive practice is essential, and listening to a client's story remains the starting point of any intervention. The nuances of culture can range in subtlety from the differences in meaning of certain nonverbal gestures to the differences in perception of the roles and responsibilities of the practitioner (Arden & Linford, 2009). All groups must be treated equally, especially groups that have been disenfranchised through preconceived notions and discriminatory practices. Learning more about diverse groups such as gay, lesbian, bisexual, and transgender individuals is just one way we can provide more culturally sensitive practice (Dziegielewski & Jacinto, 2013).

For social work practice to truly make a difference, all social workers must take a proactive stance, regardless of their practice area. This book is designed to serve as a practical guide for understanding and applying this philosophy in our social work practice environment. Simply stated, all social workers must embrace the following imperatives at all levels of practice (see Figure 15.2; adapted from Dziegielewski & Holliman, 2020):

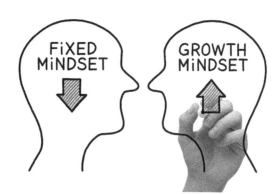

FIGURE 15.2
Becoming a proactive social worker requires you to embrace a new mindset.

- *P*: PRESENT and POSITION themselves as competent professionals with POSITIVE attitudes in all service settings, whatever the type of practice. Social workers are excellent communicators, which makes them excellent choices for leading collaborative team activities.

- *R*: RECEIVE adequate training and continuing education in the current and future practice area of social work; RESEARCH time-limited treatment approaches that can provide alternatives for social workers struggling to provide high-quality services while cutting costs. RELATIONSHIPS that connect the mind to the body and therefore understand how neuroscience can explain the behaviors that result.
- *O*: ORGANIZE individuals, groups, and communities to help them to access efficient, effective, evidence-based, safe, and affordable services; ORGANIZE other social workers to prepare for the changes that are occurring and develop strategies to continue to provide ethical, cost-effective service. Social workers understand that the gift of organization rests with empowering those we serve to act. Therefore, it is not doing for the client, but teaching the client to do for the self.
- *A*: ADDRESS policies and issues relevant to providing ethical, effective, and efficient service. Be aware of the social issues and concerns in terms of how these circumstances can affect individuals, families, and communities.
- *C*: COLLABORATE with other helping professionals to address client concerns and needs utilizing a client-centered and culturally sensitive approach; COMPLEMENT practices by utilizing holistic practices and alternative strategies that can help clients achieve increased well-being.
- *T*: TEACH others about the value and the importance of including social work services and techniques; TAKE TIME to help ourselves holistically by preventing professional burnout, thus remaining productive and receptive and serving as good role models for clients and other professionals.
- *I*: INVESTIGATE and apply INNOVATIVE approaches to client care problems and issues; INVOLVE all social workers in the change process that needs to occur in traditional social work, while empowering clients as active participants in the helping process.
- *V*: VISUALIZE and work toward positive outcomes for all clients and potential clients; VALUE the roles of all other helping professionals and support them as they face similar challenges and changes.
- *E*: EXPLORE supplemental therapies and strategies that clients can self-administer at little or no cost to preserve and enhance well-being; EMPOWER clients and us by stressing the importance of EDUCATION for self-betterment as well as individual and societal change.

We will need to face the many changes that continue to challenge social workers as helping professionals, and we must recognize that social welfare has been and will remain the primary target for budget cuts, and that in this area of budget cutting and cost containment, we can be viable players. Even so, the NASW Code of Ethics (NASW, 2018) encourages us to charge reasonable fees and base our charges on ability to pay. This means that the fees social work professionals charge remain competitive with those of psychiatrists, psychologists, family therapists, psychiatric nurses, and mental health counselors, who provide similar services. This lower-cost model may entice health and other service delivery agencies to contract with social workers instead of other professionals to provide services that have traditionally fallen in the domain of social work practice.

15.4 SPECIAL TOPIC: REGULATION OF SOCIAL WORK PRACTICE

In practice we are expected to be accountable professionals, especially because we work with vulnerable populations (Gelman, 2009). To help ensure accountability, the government regulates all professions throughout the United States. Regulation is important to ensure that the public is protected from harm caused by unqualified persons. Credentialing is a part of the government's regulatory functions and licensing rules are maintained in the administrative code (Marks & Knox, 2009). Licensing is designed to ensure the public is protected (Association of Social Work Boards [ASWB], 2022a).

Why Do We Regulate Occupations and Why Is Credentialing Important?

A regulated occupation's activities are such that the average citizen may be harmed physically, emotionally, or financially if he or she is exposed to the practice of an unqualified person. Credentialing suggests that a specific educational background is needed to make a person qualified to carry out the tasks in a regulated occupation. Through regulation, the public is assured that all regulated persons meet minimum standards of competence as set forth by the state. Additionally, the public is assured that mechanisms are available for the pursuit of grievances against regulated workers. Consider what professions are regulated and how this outlines the scope of practice for the services provided (see the activity below).

> **Activity**
> Visit the web page or contact your state's social work licensing board or regulatory body and ask for information about the regulation of social work practice. Are all levels of social work practice licensed? Does the board represent the social work profession's broad range of work, or is its membership restricted to one or two types of practice? Attend a licensing board meeting (they are open to the public) and determine how the board protects the public interest. Finally, how does the local social work community perceive licensing? (Check this out at a local NASW unit meeting.)

Think for a moment about the types of occupations that are regulated by the government. Because decisions about which professions need to be regulated are left to state governments, you will find that some occupations are licensed in one state but not in

Table 15.1 Partial List of Occupations Regulated by the State of Florida

Architect	Interior designer	Barber
Public accountant	Pool contractor	Solar contractor
Building contractor	Chiropractor	Nail specialist
Cosmetologist	Hair braider	Dental hygienist
Dentist	Electrical contractor	Alarm system contractor
Embalmer	Talent agency	Physician
Optometrist	Podiatrist	Veterinarian
Nurse	Auctioneer	Athletic trainer
Respiratory therapist	Midwife	Nutrition counselor
Surveyor and mapper	Audiologist	School psychologist
Mental health counselor	Asbestos contractor	Physical therapist
Occupational therapist	Liquor salesperson	Building inspector

another. When a profession is regulated by more than one state, the criteria for certification may differ. Types of educational degrees and years of experience required and the use of exams to test competence vary by state and occupation.

The list of occupations that states regulate seems endless. Each state oversees a wide array of occupations that can affect people's lives for good or bad (see Table 15.1, for example, for regulated professions in Florida).

The profession of social work is regulated in all fifty states. By that we mean that some form of social work practice is licensed or certified by each state government. Regulation does not completely mirror the two levels of social work practice, the BSW (generalist practice) and the MSW (specialist practice). For example, several states license both BSW and MSW practitioners together, whereas other states limit licensing to MSW practitioners who specialize in clinical social work. Each state sets its own rules and regulations for licensure, and social workers must meet the qualifications and standards in the state or province in which they will practice (ASWB, 2022b) These rules can change because state requirements can be modified and updated. Most, but not all, states require successful completion of a written examination, and most, but not all, states require ongoing continuing education after licensure; the exact courses needed will vary and depend on the state.

The regulation of social work practice is subject to several complications. First, it is tied to the intricacies of the political process. As with any law passed by a state legislature, it reflects political interests. What seems to be a logical, straightforward piece of legislation may end up being defeated for any number of reasons. Some social workers are against formal licensure for the profession, but if we license and regulate hair braiders and surveyors, doesn't it make sense also to regulate a profession that is concerned with the emotional and psychological well-being of people?

Licensing requires social work professionals to overcome their own biases and to act in the best interests of the profession. This has been further complicated because in social work there is one body, the Association of Social Work Boards (ASWB) that creates, oversees, and administers the exams social workers are required to take (ASWB, 2022a). In 2020, all fifty states in the United States used some level of this exam. After numerous concerns were voiced by social work academics and practitioners that this exam could be biased against certain groups, the ASWB, in its "2022 ASWB Exam Pass Rate Analysis," posted the results (ASWB, 2022c). The data revealed glaring disparities in the pass rates of certain racial groups, particularly among Black, Indigenous, and other people of color when compared to White test-takers as well as older social workers (CSWE, 2022b). The CSWE will continue to monitor this to ensure the full diversity of the profession is represented and will explore models that eliminate the need for a licensing exam that is considered redundant since graduation from an accredited program ensures that the core competencies within the profession were covered (CSWE, 2022b). Since the profession of social work and its professional organizations (NASW and CSWE) clearly advocate to openly confront racism within the profession, review of these data will continue to receive further attention and scrutiny. Examining and determining how to best address this information is essential for protecting the public without unfair and unnecessary gatekeeping and discriminatory practices (NASW, 2022a).

Licensing BSW and MSW practice can become very cumbersome and confusing. Although licensing protects the public from nonprofessional practice, state regulation also carves out specific practice areas or *turf* for professions, making transfer or reciprocity of a social work license difficult from state to state. One major advance toward addressing this concern occurred in 2022 when the NASW supported the creation of an Interstate Compact for Social Work Licensure. This draft legislation will assist social workers to be licensed and able to practice under their respective license in multiple "pacts" agreed on by the states. This would avoid the problems that occur when trying to transfer qualifications from one state to another. It also includes several other important aspects, such as facilitating interstate or interterritory telemental health and improving continuity of care when clients travel or relocate. The passage of this pact would encourage cooperation among compact member states and territories in regulating the practice of social work, while preserving and strengthening state licensure systems. Efforts toward licensure portability, especially after the limitations to access highlighted during the COVID-19 pandemic, would clearly enhance the ability of social workers to service clients in more than one state (Apgar, 2022). In summary, this agreement would support accessibility and continuity of care by allowing supportive counseling through teletherapy services that could be more easily available and delivered (NASW, 2022b).

Name: Montavious Bryant
College/university degrees: MSW, Florida State University, class of 2022
Present position: Registered clinical social work intern and mental health professional

What do you do in your spare time? In my spare time, I enjoy listening to podcasts, painting, cooking, and surfing the internet. Also, I enjoy spending time building and maintaining relationships with friends and family.

Why did you choose social work as a career? It's important to note that I didn't choose social work as a career; it chose me. For most of my life, I have spent time helping friends and family analyze life problems, issues, and goals. For this reason, continuing education in the field of social work was a natural fit. Also, I previously obtained a master's in psychology in education with a focus on clinical psychology. It appears that my choices have always aligned with the way that my mind naturally works.

What is your favorite social work story? There is no one story that is my favorite. Since experiencing many stories that clients have shared, I can say that I have related to them all. If I were to share, I would say that a past client who was raised in the foster care system eventually became a popular YouTuber who shares his experience with others to motivate them to focus on progress, not perfection. His story is particularly personal since I have known friends who have triumphed from a similar past.

What would be the one thing you would change in our community if you had the power to do so? If it were in my power, I would allow individuals in the community to appreciate the benefits of therapy and social work through pro bono work and increased funding at the state/federal level. In addition, I would use some of the funds to promote advertising aimed at reducing the stigma of mental health disorders. Last, I would collaborate with prescribing psychiatrists to increase holistic methods of treatment in an effort to reduce and/or curtail the immediate use of medicines to treat disorders while promoting meditation, spirituality, improved diet, consistent sleep, and exercise as primary treatment modalities for mental health disorders.

SUMMARY AND FINAL THOUGHTS

Now that you have read the chapters in this book, as our future, it is time for you to start writing the next chapters. As future social workers and members of the global community, you will be responsible for how the social welfare system continues to develop in the twenty-first century. The types of programs, levels of assistance, and clients eligible for benefits will all be issues you will address. Helping clients to access services is central to what we do. Be sure to recognize that all attempts at using technology and increasing services through teletherapy and telemedicine may be a tremendous asset to providing care, but may unintentionally introduce access limitations, especially for those who are not versed in its use, such as many older adults (Lepkowsky, 2020, 2023; Lepkowsky & Arndt, 2019).

The social work profession will always be part of our community if complex human social problems persist. As social workers, our challenge is to remain relevant to our nation's goals and our clients' needs. We can do this by vigorously pursuing competence in practice, by discovering and validating innovative interventions, and by ensuring that our educational and training programs continue to excel.

As you tackle social welfare issues, remain passionate in your convictions, ethical in your actions, knowledgeable about your discipline, and, above all, committed to the view that all people have a right to social justice. Remain aware that all people do not think like you, nor should they. We can celebrate differences since so many individuals have values and beliefs that differ. Be aware of your own beliefs and how they can be viewed in the organizational or community culture that surrounds you. Taking time to care for yourself can help you avoid feeling oppressed (Newcomb, Saxton, Lovric, et al., 2023). Support strategies for the client should always consider the culture of the client and client system.

Our community will be a better place because of people like you. We hope you are excited about the social work profession and what it has to offer people; this excitement can become an incredible source of energy that will strengthen and enhance your passion to work with and on behalf of others for years to come.

REFERENCES

Apgar, D. (2022). Social work license portability: A necessity in a post-COVID-19 world. *Social Work, 67*(4), 381–390.

Arden, J. B., & Linford, L. (2009). *Brain-based therapy with adults: Evidence-based treatment for everyday practice.* Hoboken, NJ: Wiley.

Association of Social Work Boards. (2022a). *Mission statement.* Retrieved December 28, 2022, from https://www.aswb.org/about-aswb/mission/

Association of Social Work Boards. (2022b). *Licenses.* Retrieved December 28, 2022, from https://www.aswb.org/licenses/

Association of Social Work Boards. (2022c). *2022 ASWB exam pass rate analysis: Final report.* Retrieved December 28, 2022, from https://www.aswb.org/wp-content/uploads/2022/07/2022-ASWB-Exam-Pass-Rate-Analysis.pdf

Blackwell, C. W., & Dziegielewski, S. F. (2005). The privatization of social services from public to sectarian: Negative consequences for America's gays and lesbians. *Journal of Human Behavior and the Social Environment, 11*(2), 25–43.

Bloom, M. (1990). *Introduction to the drama of social work.* Itasca, IL: Peacock.

Dziegielewski, S. F., Nelson-Gardell, D. & Colby, I. (2024). *Introduction to social work: The people's profession* (5th ed.). Chicago, IL: Lyceum Books.

Corcoran, K., & Vandiver, V. (1996). *Maneuvering the maze of managed care: Skills for mental health practitioners.* New York, NY: Free Press.

Council on Social Work Education. (2022a). *2022 EPAS—Educational Policy, and Accreditation Standards for baccalaureate and master's social work programs.* Alexandria, VA: Author. Retrieved from Retrieved from: https://www.cswe.org/getmedia/bb5d8afe-7680-42dc-a332-a6e6103f4998/2022-EPAS.pdf

Council of Social Work Education. (2022b). *Addressing licensing exam pass rate data.* Retrieved December 28. 2002, from https://www.cswe.org/news/news/addressing-licensing-exam-pass-rate-data/

Cox, L. E., Tice, C. J., & Lon, D. D. (2018). *Introduction to social work: An advocacy-based profession* (2nd ed.). Thousand Oaks, CA: Sage.

Day, P. J., & Schiele, J. H. (2013) *A new history of social welfare* (7th ed.). Boston, MA: Pearson.

Drisco, J. W., & Grady, M. D. (2019). *Evidence-based practice in clinical social work.* Cham, Switzerland: Springer Nature Switzerland.

Dziegielewski, S. F., & Holliman, D. (2020). *The changing face of health care social work: Opportunities and challenges for professional practice* (4th ed.). New York, NY: Springer.

Dziegielewski, S. F., & Jacinto, G. (2013). GLBT cultural sensitivity: Introduction. *Journal of Social Service Research, 39,* 1–2.

Eamon, M. K. (2008). *Empowering vulnerable populations.* Chicago, IL: Lyceum Books.

Ellis, R., Frantz, A., Karimi, F., & McLaughlin, E. C. (2016, June 13). *Orlando shooting: 49 killed, shooter pledged ISIS allegiance.* Retrieved from https://www.cnn.com/2016/06/12/us/orlando-nightclub-shooting

Estrine, S. A., Hettenbach, R. T., Arthur, H., & Messina, M. (Eds.). (2011). *Service delivery for vulnerable populations: New directions in behavioral health.* New York, NY: Springer.

Fitzsimons, N. M. (2009). *Combating violence & abuse of people with disabilities: A call to action.* Baltimore, MD: Brooks.

Forenza, B., & Eckert, C. (2018). Social worker identity: A profession in context. *Social Work, 63*(1), 17–26.

Foundation for Economic Education. (2022). *What is cancel culture? Getting beyond the talking partisan points.* Retrieved December 28, 2022, from http://bit.ly/3hVAEp8

Gelman, S. R. (2009). On being an accountable profession: The code of ethics, oversight by boards of directors, and whistle-blowers as a last resort. In A. R. Roberts (Ed.), *Social workers' desk reference* (2nd ed., pp. 156–162). New York, NY: Oxford University Press.

Gobman, L. M. (Ed.). (2019). *Days in the lives of social workers: 62 professionals tell "real-life" stories from social work practice* (5th ed.). Harrisburg, PA: New Social Worker Press.

Hall, H. R., & Roussel, L. A. (2022). *Evidence-based practice: An integrative approach to research, administration, and practice* (3rd ed.). Burlington, MA: Jones & Bartlett Learning.

Harris, M. B., & Franklin, C. (2008). *Taking charge: A school-based life skills program for adolescent mothers.* New York, NY: Oxford University Press.

Hoefer, R., & Watson, L. D. (2021) *Essentials of non-profit management and leadership: A skills-based approach*. San Diego, CA: Cognella Academic Publishing.

Howlett, B., Rogo, E., & Shelton, T. G. (2021). *Evidence-based practice for health professionals* (2nd ed.). Burlington, MA: Jones & Bartlett Learning.

Lepkowsky, C. M. (2020). Telehealth reimbursement allows access to mental health care during COVID-19. *The American Journal of Geriatric Psychiatry, 28*(8), 898–899.

Lepkowsky, C. M. (2023). Ageism, mentalism, and ableism shape telehealth policy. *American Journal of Geriatric Psychiatry, 31*(3), 235–236.

Lepkowsky, C. M., & Arndt, S. (2019). The internet barrier to healthcare for older adults? *Practice Innovation, 4*(2), 124–132.

Lubove, C. (1965). *The professional altruist*. Cambridge, MA: Harvard University Press.

Marks, A. T., & Knox, K. S. (2009). Social work regulation and licensing. In A. R. Roberts (Ed.), *Social workers' desk reference* (2nd ed., pp. 148–155). New York, NY: Oxford University Press.

Morales, A. T., Sheafor, B. W., & Scott, M. E. (2009). *Social work: A profession of many faces*. Boston, MA: Allyn & Bacon.

National Association of Social Workers. (2018). *Code of ethics of the National Association of Social Workers*. Washington, DC: Author. Retrieved December 28, 2022, from https://www.socialworkers.org/About/Ethics/Code-of-Ethics/Code-of-Ethics-English

National Association of Social Workers. (2022a, September). *NASW statement on ASWB exam pass rate report that confirms racial disparities concern*. Retrieved December 28, 2022, from https://www.socialworkers.org/News/News-Releases/ID/2531/ASWB-social-work-licensing-exam-pass-rate-data-confirm-concern-over-racial-disparities

National Association of Social Workers. (2022b). *Social workers interstate compact public comment*. Retrieved December 28, 2022, from https://www.socialworkers.org/LinkClick.aspx?fileticket=fSvAwJFwleg%3d&portalid=0

Newcomb, M., Saxton, K., Lovric, E., Harris, S., & D. Davidson. (2023). Creating safety: Group reflections on surviving as a female, social work early career academic in the neoliberal academy. *Qualitative Social Work, 22*(6), 1092–1107.

Niu, D., & Haugen, H. O. (2019). Social workers in China: Professional identity in the making. *The British Journal of Social Work, 49*(7), 1932–1949.

Prigoff, A. (2000). *Economics for social workers: Social outcomes of economic globalization with strategies for community action*. Belmont, CA: Wadsworth/Thomson Learning.

Reamer, F. G. (2020). *Ethics and risk management in online and distance behavioral health*. San Diego, CA: Cognella Academic Publishing.

Reamer, F. G. (2022). *The philosophical foundations of social work* (2nd ed.). New York, NY: Columbia University Press.

Rice, W. S., Narasimhan, S., Newton-Levinson, A., Pringle, J., Redd, S. K., & Evans, D. P. (2022). Post-Roe abortion policy context heightens the imperative for multilevel, comprehensive, integrated health education*Heath Education and Behavior, 49*, 913–918.

Richan, W., & Mendelsohn, A. R. (1973). *Social work, the unloved profession*. New York, NY: Franklin Watts.

Richan, W. C. (2006). *Lobbying for social change* (3rd ed.). New York, NY: Haworth Press.

Specht, H., & Courtney, M. (1994). *Unfaithful angels.* New York, NY: Free Press.

Wolfe, E., & Andone, D. (2022, November 22). *What we know about the suspect in the Colorado Springs LGBTQ nightclub shooting.* Retrieved from https://www.cnn.com/2022/11/21/us/anderson-lee-aldrich-colorado-springs-shooting-suspect

Wright, R. N., Faul, L., Graner, J. L., Stewart, G. W., & LaBar, K. S., (2022). Psychosocial determinants of anxiety about the COVID-19 pandemic. *Journal of Health Psychology, 27*(10), 2344–2360.

Appendix A

SELECTED NATIONAL AND INTERNATIONAL SOCIAL WORK ASSOCIATIONS AND RELATED WEB PAGES

Association for Community Organization and Social Action (ACOSA)

ACOSA promotes social justice through community practice, using collective work with community groups and agencies to solve community problems.

https://acosa.clubexpress.com/

Clinical Social Work Association (CSWA)

The CSWA dedicates itself to the voices of clinical social workers in the social work mission of a just society.

https://www.clinicalsocialworkassociation.org/

Council on Social Work Education (CSWE), Educational Policy and Accreditation Standards

The CSWE serves as the national organization representing social work education in the United States. Membership is made up of accredited social work education programs, along with individual social work educators. It also accredits social work education programs in the United States.

https://www.cswe.org/accreditation/standards/2022-epas

CSWE Accredited Social Work Programs in the United States (Fall 2022)

https://www.cswe.org/accreditation/directory/?

International Association of Social Workers (IASW)

IASW serves as the worldwide organization representing social work education programs and educators.

https://www.iassw-aiets.org/

International Federation of Social Workers (IFSW), Global Social Work Statement of Ethical Principles

The IFSW serves as a global body for the profession of social work.

https://www.ifsw.org/global-social-work-statement-of-ethical-principles/

Latino Social Workers Organization (LSWO)

A professional organization dedicated to Latinx social work professionals and advocating the La Familia Perspective.

https://lswo.org/

National Association of Black Social Workers (NABSW)

NABSW members are social workers of African ancestry with a mission of a world free of racial domination, exploitation, and oppression.

https://www.nabsw.org/

National Association of Social Workers (NASW), Code of Ethics

The NASW serves as U.S. social workers' primary and largest professional organization.

https://www.socialworkers.org/About/Ethics/Code-of-Ethics/Code-of-Ethics-English

North American Association of Christians in Social Work (NAACSW)

The NAACSW works to help members of its organization integrate Christian faith and social work practice.

https://www.nacsw.org/

School Social Work Association of America (SSWAA)

Empowers social workers and promotes the profession of social work in schools, with the vision of a social worker in every school.

https://www.sswaa.org/

Society for Social Work and Research (SSWR)

SSWR focuses on the promotion of social work research-focused efforts.

https://secure.sswr.org/

Glossary

absolute poverty: Qualitative measure of poverty that compares a person's situation with a numerical standard that usually reflects bare subsistence; cf. relative poverty.

abuse: Improper behavior that can result in physical, psychological, or financial harm to an individual, family, group, or community. In social work the term is most often related to acts against children, elderly people, those with mental impairment, or spouses, or used in relation to drug or other substance abuse.

accreditation: Professional recognition that a social work program meets explicit standards; voted on by the Council on Social Work Education's Commission on Accreditation after it reviews the program's self-study documents, the site visitors' written report, and the program's written response to the site visit.

advocacy: Professional activities aimed at educating, informing, or defending and representing the needs and wants of clients through direct intervention or empowerment.

Affordable Care Act (ACA): Also known as Obamacare, this health insurance law created important access to the health care system for many who, prior to its enactment, were unable to receive health services. Passed on March 23, 2010, during Barack Obama's tenure, the legislation is thus named after the ex-president.

ageism: Stereotyping or generalization based on a person's age. This is considered a form of discrimination that is commonly directed toward older individuals. *Unintentional ageism* differs in that it is discrimination against older adults that occurs when the age of an individual is known or suspected and societal expectations influence responses to that individual based on age rather than ability. Places this may occur are in employment, self-care, or other areas unfairly influencing perceptions of capability.

agency: An organization that provides social services and is typically staffed by social service professionals, including social workers. Public, private, and not-for-profit agencies provide an array of services, usually to a target population. Policy is set by a board of directors and is implemented by administrators.

agency-based: Occurring in an agency. Agency-based practice can include a few specific practice methodologies or span the continuum of social work practice, depending on the agency's size, mission, and purpose.

Aid to Families with Dependent Children: A means-tested program that provided financial aid to children in need because of parental disability, absence, or death. It was administered nationally through the Administration for Children and Families division of the U.S. Department of Health and Human Services; state and county departments of public welfare provided local administration. The program ended in 1996 with the creation of Temporary Assistance for Needy Families.

almshouse (aka poorhouse): A place of refuge for those who are poor, medically ill, or mentally ill of all ages; considered the forerunner of the hospital.

assessment: Process of determining the nature, cause, progression, and prognosis of a problem and identifying the personalities and situations involved; process of reasoning from facts to tentative conclusions about their meaning.

at-risk populations (aka vulnerable populations): Groups with increased exposure to potential harm as a result of specific characteristics. Examples are infants born to drug-using mothers, who are at risk for birth defects; minorities, who are at risk for oppression; and poor children, who are at risk for malnutrition.

biopsychosocial approach: A perspective to social work practice, especially in health care and mental health, that assesses and places appropriate emphasis on the biological, psychological, and social or environmental aspects of the client's situation.

Black Lives Matter: Also known as BLM, this advocacy group made its first appearance in 2013 and generally focuses on the violence suffered by people of color, specifically Black communities.

blended family: A term applied to a family unit when two previously separate families are joined and portray traditional family roles. Often referred to as a stepfamily.

block grant: A lump sum given to a state by the federal government. The state has authority over expenditure of block grants and may supplement them with state funds.

BSW (baccalaureate in social work): Also known as BSSW (bachelor of science and social work), this is the undergraduate degree in social work from a program accredited by the Council on Social Work Education; the entry-level social work qualification. The BSW and bachelor of arts (BA) or bachelor of science (BS) in social work are equivalent degrees.

candidacy preaccreditation: Status for a social work program, which generally lasts two years; signifies that an educational program meets general criteria to conduct a self-study for accreditation.

charity assistance: Aid given to the poor in the 1600s; viewed as a mechanism that reinforced dependent lifestyles.

charity organization society: A privately or philanthropically funded agency that delivered social services to the needy in the mid- to late-nineteenth century; considered the forerunner of the nonprofit social service agency.

Child Protective Services (CPS): This program is intended to protect children from abusive situations, thereby serving children affected by neglect, medical neglect, physical abuse, sexual abuse, and psychological maltreatment.

child welfare: A series of human service and social welfare programs designed specifically to promote the protection, care, and health development of children; found at the national, state, and local levels.

client: An individual, couple, family, group, or community that is the focus of intervention.

community organizing: A process of working within a community that shares a common problem of interest. In social work this requires empowering groups or communities to achieve common goals and objectives.

continuing education: Training acquired after the completion of a degree program. The National Association of Social Workers and state licensure boards require specified hours of continuing education to maintain a license or certification.

Council on Social Work Education (CSWE): The sole national accreditation board for schools of social work; founded in 1952 from the merger of the American Association of Schools of Social Work (founded 1919) and the National Association of Schools of Social Administration (founded 1942).

COVID-19: More formally, SARS-CoV-2 virus (CO = corona, VI = virus, D = disease, 19 = 2019). A contagious viral pandemic that affected people across the globe.

diagnosis: The process of identifying a problem—social, mental, or medical—and its underlying causes and formulating a solution.

disadvantaged: A term used to describe individuals, groups, communities, and the like that are unable to access the resources and services needed to maintain a minimal standard of living.

discharge planning: A service provided by health care social workers to assist clients in, for example, securing placement and services to support a timely transition from a health care facility to home or to another less restrictive environment.

discrimination: The prejudgment and negative treatment of someone or a group of people based on known characteristics. Common sources of discrimination include race, gender, ethnicity, religion, or sexual identity.

domestic violence: Violent acts toward another person perpetrated in a domestic situation.

DSM-5-TR (*Diagnostic and Statistical Manual*, 5th edition, Text Revision): Published in 2023, this version of the American Psychiatric Association's manual is designed to provide the standard classification system for documenting the criteria needed to place a diagnosis. This book is the text revision of the *Diagnostic and Statistical Manual of Mental Disorders* (*DSM-5*) published in 2013. Social workers are listed as one of the mental health professionals encouraged to use this book to support diagnostic activity.

DSW (doctor of social welfare or social work): One of the highest social work degrees, the DSW typically requires two years of full-time post-master's course work, successful completion of comprehensive examinations, and successful completion of a dissertation or some type of specialization paper. There is also a PhD in social work or social welfare that often has similar requirements.

dual diagnosis: Generally refers to a client with two diagnoses, most often referred to as a substance use disorder and a mental health disorder where both occur and require treatment at the same time.

Educational Policy and Accreditation Standards (EPAS): A written document that outlines the purpose and framework of social work education programs. The CSWE Commission on Accreditation is responsible for oversight of the EPAS.

entitlement programs: Governmental programs offered to all individuals who meet the predetermined criteria.

environmental justice: This concept holds that all people (no matter their income level, their race, and so on) are entitled to fair and meaningful participation, along with enjoying any benefits and bearing any risks when it comes to the process of decision-making and implementation of decisions related to environmental concerns.

evidence-based practice (EBP): In social work, this requires identifying the client's needs and providing care that is based on the most up-to-date data on effectiveness of the treatment(s) employed. Treatment provided is consistent with the social worker's knowledge and skills and data are based on the latest up-to-date research.

ethical practice in social work: Adhering to the standards and principles set forth in the profession and acting in a way that highlights the core values and expectations of the profession.

ethics: A system of moral principles used in decision-making to discern right from wrong or to choose between two or more seemingly equal alternatives.

Family Preservation Services (FPS): This program includes short-term, family-focused social services designed to stabilize troubled families while keeping children safe in their own homes and providing family-based intensive social services. The expectation is that providing services in the home may help to avoid the need for out-of-home placement.

field placement: Work in an agency during the BSW or MSW educational experience, supervised by a social worker. The agency and the educational institution jointly train and monitor the students during placement.

Food Stamp Program: A program that distributes stamps that can be used to purchase basic food items to people in need. It was implemented in 1964 and administered by the U.S. Department of Agriculture until 1996; it is now administered by states under the Personal Responsibility and Work Opportunity Reconciliation Act of 1996.

friendly visitor: A volunteer from a charity organization society who visited poor families to offer aid and to serve as a role model.

gaslighting: When an individual uses psychological methods to manipulate or "bait" another, causing the affected individual to question their own reasoning ability. Generally, when the term is used, one individual *gaslights* the other and causes the affected individual to question existing beliefs and reasoning.

generalist practice: Practice underpinned by knowledge and skills across a broad spectrum and by comprehensive assessment of problems and their solutions; includes coordination of activities of specialists.

globalization: Highlights the connection and interdependence of countries across the globe, especially linked to interconnections based in trade and subsequent social influences and connections with technology.

home care: In this type of health care, social work services are provided to individuals and families in their home or community and/or other home-like settings.

hospice care: This type of care involves providing services to individuals who are terminally ill and their family members. In this type of care, there is open acknowledgment that no cure is expected for the client's illness, and the goal is to support the process of dying in a dignified manner; physical, emotional, social, and spiritual care are provided.

hospital social worker: A social worker who practices in hospitals and health care facilities, focusing on assessments, discharge planning, preventive services, interdisciplinary coordination, and individual and family counseling.

human rights: Universal social rights all persons share without distinction as to race, gender, language, or religion. An example of this is civil rights.

indoor relief: Assistance provided during colonial times to *unworthy* poor people in poorhouses.

in kind: A benefit in the form of food, clothing, education, and so forth, in place of, or in addition to, cash.

immigrants: In this text it refers to individuals born in foreign countries who relocate to the United States.

institutional social welfare: Social programs available to all as a part of well-being in the modern state; cf. residual social welfare.

interdisciplinary team: A variety of health care professionals brought together to provide a client with effective, better coordinated, and improved quality of services.

International Association of Schools of Social Work (IASSW): An international association that, according to their website, reports that as of June 29, 2022, the "global census" of social work education member programs consisted of 416 entities worldwide.

International Federation of Social Workers (IFSW): An international association of social workers comprising members through their national organizations; founded in 1928 in Paris; promotes social work, establishes standards, and provides a forum for exchange among associations throughout the world.

intervention: Treatment, services, advocacy, mediation, or any other practice action, performed for or with clients, that is intended to ameliorate problems.

intimate partner violence (IPV): Also known as intimate partner domestic violence, IPV is a pattern of coercive control within intimate partnerships that is maintained through tactics such as physical, psychological, sexual, and/or economic abuse. This differs from domestic violence, where the abuse can occur between more than an intimate partner and can include siblings, parent and child, or others who live in the household, such as roommates.

label: In mental health it is generally referred to as a clinical diagnosis of a client that stays with the client indefinitely, possibly to the client's detriment.

LGBTQ+: An acronym used to identify a community of individuals who identify as lesbian, gay, bisexual, or transgender and queer. More inclusive acronyms used to identify this community collectively is LGBTQIA (lesbian, gay, bisexual, transgender, queer, intersex, and asexual people). The plus (+) symbol should be added at the end to denote all other identities not encompassed by the acronym, such as pansexual and two-spirited.

macro-social work practice (aka macro system level): Community, administrative, and environmental forces that affect the human condition. Political action, community organizing, and administration of large public welfare agencies are examples of macropractice.

managed care: A form of health care delivery within a specific framework with specific rules, requirements, and expectations for the delivery of service.

Meals on Wheels: Delivery of meals to the homes of people unable to meet their own nutritional needs, usually because of physical or mental impairment. The providers of service are usually community agencies, such as senior citizen councils, local human service departments, and private agencies.

means-tested program: A program for which eligibility is determined by the recipient's resources and whether the need is great enough within a predetermined criteria set.

Medicaid: A program established in 1965 that funds hospital and other medical services to people who meet means tests; administered by the federal Health Care Financing Administration.

Medicare: A national health insurance program established in 1965. Eligibility is universal, with attainment of age sixty-five as the criterion for most people; however, there are allied programs for those with disabilities, among others. Medicare is funded through employee and employer contributions and administered by the Social Security Administration and the Health Care Financing Administration.

mezzo social work practice (aka mezzo system level): A system that connects microsystems and macrosystems. This level of practice can consist of work with schools, communities, and neighborhoods, and in some cases professionals who work in administrative roles.

micro-level practice social work practice (aka micro system level): Individual, family, or small group. Direct intervention and casework are examples of micropractice.

MSW (master of social work): A degree requiring approximately sixty hours of postbaccalaureate education, including nine hundred hours of field placement, in a program accredited by the Council on Social Work Education. The master's of science and social work (MSSW) and master of arts (MA) or master of science (MS) in social work are equivalent degrees.

multidisciplinary team: A mix of health and social welfare professionals, with each discipline working, for the most part, on an independent or referral basis.

National Association of Social Workers (NASW): The world's largest social work membership association, with approximately 120,000 members in 2022; established in 1955 through the merger of five special interest organizations. Chapters exist in all fifty states and the District of Columbia, New York City, Puerto Rico, and the Virgin Islands, in addition to any international chapters.

New Deal: A set of social welfare programs and legislation implemented during President Franklin D. Roosevelt's administration in response to the Great Depression. Examples include the Economic Security Act of 1935, the Works Progress Administration, and the Federal Emergency Relief Act.

non-profit or non-governmental social service agencies (NGOs): These are two types of agencies where many social workers are employed. In non-profit agencies the organizations that administer programs are not designed to generate profit and income is distributed internally. Examples include public charities, public clinics and hospitals, churches and other charitable institutions. An NGO is harder to define but it is any non-governmental agency with a social mission that operates independently of governmental control.

outdoor relief: Minimal assistance provided during the colonial period to *worthy poor* people in their own homes.

overseer of the poor: An individual responsible during colonial times for identifying poor individuals, assessing their needs, and coordinating a community response by levying and collecting taxes; considered a colonial version of a social worker.

person-in-situation (also called person-in-environment): A casework concept that focuses on the interrelation among problem, situation, and the interaction between them.

PhD (doctorate in philosophy): The highest social work degree, emphasizing research, knowledge expansion, and advanced clinical practice. It is similar and often identical to the DSW. See DSW for requirements.

policy: The plan that an agency, organization, or governmental institution follows as a framework; includes formal written policies and unwritten (informal) policies.

political lens: The political context—often candidates for public office and their campaigns—that influences how society defines a term such as family.

poor laws: Codified in 1601; redefined welfare as no longer a private affair, but rather a public governmental responsibility.

poverty: A general term used to describe a state of deprivation. *See* absolute poverty and relative poverty.

poverty threshold: The level of income below which a person is living in poverty. This level is based on the cost of securing the necessities of living.

psychosocial history: Systematic compilation of information about a client; encompasses family, health, education, spirituality, legal position, interpersonal relations, social supports, economic status, environment, sexual orientation, and culture.

racism: Prejudice, discrimination or antagonism (either openly or covertly) against a person/people on the basis of their racial/racialized/Ethnoracial identity.

rapport: An important part of the therapeutic relationship that results in harmony, compatibility, and empathy, fostering mutual understanding and a working relationship between the client and social worker.

reaffirmation: Confirmation of CSWE accreditation, for which an accredited program must undergo the self-study and review process every seven years.

relative poverty: Subjective measure of poverty that compares a person's situation with a normative standard (cf. absolute poverty).

residual social welfare: Social programs activated only when normal structures of family and market are not sufficient (cf. institutional social welfare).

role: Culturally expected behavior associated with a person or status.

sanction: (1) Formal or informal authorization to perform services; (2) penalty imposed for noncompliance with policies and procedures. The National Association of Social Workers sanctions members who have violated the code of ethics with membership suspension or removal of certification.

selective eligibility (aka means-tested eligibility): Eligibility based on demonstrating need or inability to provide for one's needs (cf. universal eligibility).

site visit: Visit to a social work educational program by a site team composed of social work educators and, for graduate programs, an MSW practitioner. The site team makes a written report to the Council on Social Work Education's Commission on Accreditation that is considered during the commission's deliberations on the program's accreditation.

sexism: Prejudice, discrimination or antagonism (either openly or covertly) against a person/people on the basis of their gender (generally against females).

social justice: A core social work value that involves efforts to confront discrimination, oppression, and other social inequities.

social welfare: (1) Society's specific system of programs to help people to meet basic health, economic, and social needs; (2) general state of well-being in society.

specialist practice: Practice focused on approach and knowledge of a specific problem or goal or underpinned by highly developed expertise in specific activities.

stigma: Negative connotation attached to individuals, or groups of individuals, based on characteristics that may include economic status, health, appearance, education, sexual orientation, and mental health.

strengths-based assessment: This type of assessment relies on the social worker's ability to critically analyze the positive aspects, attributes, or strengths in a client or client system and to utilize these strengths in every aspect of the problem-solving process.

Temporary Assistance for Needy Families (TANF): A program established in 1996 to replace Aid for Families with Dependent Children. It is subject to strict eligibility requirements, which mandate employment, and to a lifetime limit on benefits of five years; funded through federal block grants to states, which administer the program.

undocumented immigrants: These are non–U.S. citizens who enter the United States without inspection or proper documentation. It can also include non–U.S. citizens who have entered the United States on a visa that has now expired. Using the label *illegal aliens* to refer to undocumented immigrants is offensive and highly discouraged.

unworthy poor: A category of people undeserving of public aid introduced by the 1601 Poor Laws. Unworthy poor people consisted of the vagrant or able-bodied who, although they were able to work, did not seek employment.

victim blaming: A philosophy or orientation that attributes blame and responsibility to the person who is harmed by a social circumstance. An example of this would be a female who is raped, but publicly is accused of dressing seductively and thereby seducing her attacker.

Violence against Women Act (VAWA): Passed in 1994, the VAWA is a comprehensive federal response to the problems of domestic violence that promotes preventive programs and victims' services.

worthy poor: A category of people deserving of public aid introduced by the 1601 Poor Laws; including people who were ill or disabled, orphans, and elderly individuals—people viewed as having no control over their life circumstances—as well as people who were involuntary unemployed.

Index

ableism, 12, 164
abortion, 337–38
Abramowitz, M., 51
absolute poverty, 42, 208
abuse, 27, 38, 59, 251, 398–99. *See also* intimate partner violence (IPV); sexual abuse and assault
academic advisors, 116
access, 320
accountability, 147, 531. *See also* regulation of social work field
accreditation of social workers
    Accreditation Standards (AS), 100
    and areas of practice in social work, 6–7
    and core competencies for social work, 3, 35, 103t
    and definitions of social work, 15–16
    and education of social workers, 91–95
    importance of, 97–112
    and process of becoming a social worker, 19, 23–24
action plans, 151
ACTION programs, 54b
activities of daily living, 38, 153
activity theory, 377–78, 379b, 380
acute care settings, 281, 310, 313, 349–54
acute health conditions, 298, 309–11, 313–14
Adams, Monica, 142
adaptive behaviors, 339–40, 360
adaptive equipment, 13
Addams, Jane, 66, 68, 70b, 76, 76f, 185, 444
addiction, 232
Administration for Children and Families, 40, 486
Administrative Simplification Compliance Act (ASCA), 355
administrative skills, 138, 182–83, 308–9, 361, 458t, 513
admissions process, 108
adoption, 255t
Adoption and Safe Families Act, 258
Adoption Assistance and Child Welfare Act, 257
adoption services, 261–64
Adult Protective Services, 53, 398

Advanced Standing (Educational Program), 111
advocacy role of social work
    and child welfare services, 243, 255, 266
    and definitions of social work, 17
    and diversity issues in social work, 175–76
    experiences of featured practitioners, 447–48, 522
    and future of social work field, 522, 523
    and global social welfare arena, 495
    and goals of text, 512
    and health care social work, 303, 307, 309, 316
    and intersectional perspective on poverty, 220
    and mental health social work, 329–30, 346, 349, 358
    and risk factors for intimate partner violence, 417t
    and role of professional social workers, 26–27
    and social work advocacy in political arena, 458t
    and social work targeting intimate partner violence, 420–23, 425–31
    and social work targeting older adults, 376, 384–85, 389, 399, 403–4
    See also political arena
affluent Americans, 51–52
Affordable Care Act (ACA), 284–86
    and coordinated care, 316
    and current health care environment, 299
    and federal social welfare programs, 54b
    and future of social work field, 527
    and historical background of social work, 81–82
    and inclusive health care access, 288
    patient's bill of rights, 285b
    and social work targeting older adults, 383–85
    and telemental health, 355
Africa, 479b
African Americans
    and child welfare services, 248

    and cultural context of social work, 133
    and diversity issues in social work, 170
    and intersectional perspective on poverty, 217
    and intimate partner violence, 421
    and poverty in social work settings, 206
    and programs to aid the poor, 227
    See also Black Americans
age
    age discrimination, 392
    ageism, 22, 39, 206, 400, 403–4
    aging defined, 390
    aging population, 370–71
    aging process, 368, 374–76
    and definitions of social work, 12
    and health care social work, 292
    and intersectional perspective on poverty, 213, 218–20, 218t
    and poverty in social work settings, 210
    and Social Security benefits, 393b
    See also older adults, social work aimed at
Agency for Persons with Disabilities, 372
agency-based practice
    agency consultation, 305
    agency liaisons, 305
    agency representation, 183
    and child welfare services, 256, 256b, 262–64, 268
    and definitions of social work, 11–12, 14
    and health care social work, 290, 307, 309, 315
    and mental health social work, 331, 361
    and social work advocacy in political arena, 441–42, 463–65
Aid to Families with Dependent Children (AFDC), 79, 80, 224, 225t, 229
Aid to the Blind, 232
Aid to the Totally and Permanently Disabled, 232
AIDS, 319, 455
Alabama, 92, 226
Alabama A&M University, 397
Alabama Partnership for Children, 397
Alabama State University, 397
Alaska, 88, 211, 226, 478

547

Index

Alaska Natives, 165, 170, 227
alcohol abuse and addiction
   and intimate partner violence, 416, 421
   and medical issues in mental health assessments, 347
   and mental health social work, 330
   and multidimensional psychosocial evaluation, 335
   and person-in-situation context, 178
   and suicide risk, 400
Aleuts, 165
Alignment Healthcare, 382
alimony, 419
allied health care providers, 301
allocation of social services, 43
almshouses, 72–74
ambulatory health care facilities, 281
American Assembly, 79
American Association of Group Workers, 28
American Association of Hospital Social Workers, 291
American Association of Medical Social Workers, 28
American Association of Psychiatric Social Workers, 28
American Association of Retired Persons (AARP), 369
American Association of Schools of Social Work, 97
American Association of Social Workers, 28
American Bar Association, 93
American Cancer Society, 386
American Civil Liberties Union, 84
American College of Surgeons, 292
American Enterprise Institute, 205
American Families Plan, 83
American Federation of State, City, and Municipal Employees, 451
American Indians, 165, 170, 422. *See also* Indigenous cultures; Native Americans
American Land Title Association, 42
American Medical Association, 93
American Psychiatric Association, 135, 169, 388
American Red Cross, 26
American Rescue Plan, 83
AmeriCorps, 221
Amnesty International, 489
Anadolu University, 270
Anglo-European histories, 248
Annie E. Casey Foundation, 252
anthropology, 91–92
anti-oppressive social work, 143–44
antipoverty efforts, 203–37

anti-racism
   and accreditation of social workers, 102
   Anti-Racism, Diversity, Equity, and Inclusion (ADEI), 104, 160, 411
   and Black Lives Matter movement, 446–47
   and core competencies for social work, 3, *103t*, 127, 139, 160, 241, 367, 471, 509
   and cultural context of social work, 134
   and diversity in social work settings, 131
   experiences of featured practitioners, 448
   and mental health social work, 339
   See also racial justice
apprenticeships, 69, 96
Arizona State University, 220, 499
Arndt, S., 403–4
Articles of Confederation, 88
ASCA, 355
Asian Americans, 42, 170, 206, *207t*, *214t*, 220, 248
Aslan, Harun, 270
Asperger's syndrome, 13
assessment
   biopsychosocial, 331
   and child welfare services, 270
   and core competencies for social work, 127, 160
   and cultural influences, 134–36
   and diversity issues in social work, 161, 192
   and ethical principles in social work, 335
   experiences of featured practitioners, 221, 244, 476, 497
   and health care social work, 302–3, 304, 310, 313
   and health care support services, 315
   and mental health social work, 330, 332, 335–50, *345t*, *350b*, 352–53, 358, *359t*, 360–61
   and multidimensional psychosocial evaluation, 332–40
   and risk factors for intimate partner violence, *417t*, 419
   and skills of social work, 138
   and social work targeting intimate partner violence, 412–13, 420–21, 424–25, 427, 429–30
   and social work targeting older adults, 368, 385–86, 390, 398–403
   and steps in professional helping, 150
Association canadienne des travailleuses et travailleurs sociaux, 7

Association for Community Organization & Social Action, 454
Association for the Study of Community Organization, 28
Association of Schools of Social Work, 23
Association of Social Work Boards (ASWB), 95, 116–17, 119, 533
Association of Work Boards, 16
asylums, 72–74
Atlanta School of Social Work, 78
at-risk populations, 11, 12, 305, 456. *See also* vulnerable populations
attention deficit hyperactivity disorder (ADHD), 13
Auburn University at Montgomery, 427
Austin, M., 247
autism spectrum disorder, 13

Babbie, E., 147
baby boomers, 242, 373, 395
Baccalaureate in Social Work (Educational Model), 108–9
bachelor of social work BSW
   and accreditation of social workers, *95t*, 98, 100, 101, 102, 108
   and areas of practice in social work, 6, 7
   and core competencies for social work, 128, 130
   and definitions of social work, 15
   and education of social workers, 91, 92–93
   and employment opportunities for social workers, 118–19
   featured social work practitioners, 84–85, 112, 142, 397, 427, 475
   and field placement requirement, 519
   and future of social work field, 524–26
   and health care social work, 301
   and health care support services, 306–7
   and job market for social workers, 91, 122
   and mental health social work, 330, 337
   and mezzopractice settings, 183
   and micropractice settings, *181b*
   number of students, *98t*
   and process of becoming a social worker, 22, 24–25
   and professional organization membership, 524–25
   and regulation of social work field, 532–33
   and state licensing requirements, 116
   states with social work programs, 94
   and structure of social work curriculum, 519, 526
balanced budget proposals, 54

Barker, R. L., 45, 130
Barofsky, J., 233
Barrows, A., 233
Barry University, 372
Bass, Karen, 446
Baylor College of Medicine, 520
Be Your Own Hero (Owens), 402–3
behavioral biopsychosocial approach, 341–43
behavioral disorders, 329
behavioral training, 304
Belarus, 243
Bellevue Hospital, 73
Bellhaven College, 372
Belonging: Intentional Inclusivity (Richardson-Melecio), 188
Bengston, V. L., 379b
Bergh, Henry, 256b
Berlin Wall, 473
biases, 134, 136
Biden, Joe, 83, 168f
Binghamton University, 84, 142
biopsychosocial approach
 and health care social work, 301, 303
 and medical issues in mental health assessments, 344, 345t
 and mental health social work, 331, 352
bipolar disorder, 333b, 354
birth rate, 242, 374
Black Americans
 and child welfare services, 247–48
 and cultural context of social work, 133
 and definitions of social welfare, 42
 and diversity issues in social work, 170
 and historical background of social work, 76–77
 and intersectional perspective on poverty, 214t, 215f, 216, 218t, 220
 and poverty in social work settings, 207t, 213
 and state licensing requirements, 116–17
 and traumatic stress response, 145
Black Lives Matter, 27, 83, 133, 162, 446–47
blame-the-victim mentality, 85
blended families, 131, 250
blindness, 70b, 73
block grants, 55, 224
block placements, 108–9
Bloom, M., 45
Boehm, W., 130
Boehner, John, 205
Boes, M., 312
Boone, Xan, 244–45
border security, 82
Bosnia and Herzegovina, 243

Boston, Massachusetts, 70b
Boys & Girls Clubs, 55
Brace, Charles Loring, 70b, 262
Bradshaw, T., 222
Brandt, B., 304
Brazil, 23
breadth of the social work profession, 112–15
Bristow, D., 313
British Association of Social Workers, 7
British Empire, 478
British poor laws, 72
Bronstein, L. R., 235
Brown, W. Gertrude, 76
Bruening, M., 222
Bryant, Montavious, 534
Brzuzy, S., 45
BSCorbett Consulting, LLC, 512
Buffalo, New York, 74
Buffalo Charity Organization Society Handbook, 74
Buffum, W., 454
Bullock, H., 214
burnout, 360, 425, 530
Bush, George W., 80–83, 204
Bywaters, P., 314

Cabot, Richard C., 293–94, 307, 319, 349
California, 24
Calvinism, 68
Campaign Reform Act, 451
Canada, 7, 371
Canadian Association of Social Workers, 7
cancel culture, 522
cancers, 386
candidacy (pre-accreditation) programs, 6
candidates, political, 452, 455–56
Cannon, Ida Maude, 293, 319, 320
capital gains, 52t
capitalism, 483
Career Center (of NASW), 91, 113
career decision process, 514–22
caregivers, 458t
Carlton, Tom, 288
Carnochan, S., 247
Carter Center, 204
Caruso, J. M., 423
case management, 303, 312, 390–91
Case Western Reserve University, 499
caseloads, 20
cash assistance, 47, 211. See also *specific program names*
Catholic Charities, 55
Caucasians, 169
census data, 167–69, 309. See also U.S. Census and Census Bureau

Center for Justice, 464
Center for Responsive Politics, 451, 460
Centers for Disease Control and Prevention, 42, 319, 386
Central Americans, 170
Central Asia, 479b
Cerra, F., 304
The Changing Face of Health Care Social Work (Dziegielewski and Holliman), 511
charity assistance, 204, 444
Charity Organization Society, 66
charity organization society (COS) movement, 74–75
Charleston, South Carolina, 70b
Chatterjee, P., 478, 481
Cherokee Nation, 448
Chicago, Illinois, 252–53
Child Protective Services (CPS)
 child welfare case study, 256b
 and design of American child welfare system, 254–57
 experiences of featured practitioners, 71, 84
 and foster care, 258, 259b
 and process of becoming a social worker, 19–20, 21
 and public social welfare, 53
child welfare, 241–73
 and 19th century reform efforts, 73
 and ACA patient's bill of rights, 285b
 and aging population of U.S., 370
 child abuse and neglect, 19, 40, 255t
 child care tax exemption, 51
 child health programs, 54b
 child labor laws, 183
 child tax credits, 52t
 and child welfare services, 273
 childhood malnutrition, 230
 and children with special needs, 264–67, 320
 and context of social work, 41b
 and definitions of social work, 12
 design of America's child welfare system, 254–64
 and diversity of America's children, 247–51
 experiences of featured practitioners, 244–45, 270–72, 397
 and future of social work field, 528
 and global social welfare arena, 484–87, 489, 501–2
 and health care social work, 311
 and intimate partner violence, 419
 and misconceptions about social welfare, 37
 and poverty in social work settings, 40–44, 45, 209

child welfare (*Cont.*)
  and process of becoming a social worker, 19–21
  and rights of children, 251–54
  and sexual abuse and trauma, 267–70
  and social work advocacy in political arena, 442, 455–56
  and social work targeting intimate partner violence, 421
  system defined, 245–47
Child Welfare Information Gateway, 261, 268
Children's Aid Society, 70b, 73, 262, 294
Children's Bureau, 70b, 245, 260
Children's Defense Fund, 41, 218, 220, 229, 257
Children's Medical Services, 372
children's poverty, 169
China, 7, 476, 480, 525
choosing social work as profession, 137
chronic illness
  and current health care environment, 300
  and depression, 387–88
  and health care social work, 314
  and health care support services, 311, 313
  and inclusive health care access, 287
  and social work targeting older adults, 375, 385–86
chronological age, 368–69
Chui, E., 476
Cincinnati, Ohio, 354
Citizens United v. Federal Election Commission, 451
citizenship rights and responsibilities, 43, 65
civil court, 255f
Civil War veterans, 293
Civilian Conservation Corps, 77
Clark, E., 309
class divisions and conflict, 56, 74, 213, 414
classification of social work providers, 56–58
Cleveland City Hospital, 293
client system
  client advocacy role, 329
  and diversity issues in social work, 161–63, 173–77, 179–80, 191, 194
  and evidence-based practices, 147
  and future of social work field, 535
  and health care social work, 291, 319
  and mental health social work, 359–60
  and role of professional social workers, 26
  and social work in social welfare system, 58–59

and social work targeting older adults, 391
climate change, 497
clinical social work, 22, 132, 288
Clinton, Bill, 80, 284
Clinton, Hillary, 284
codes of conduct, 178. *See also* ethical practice in social work
codification of laws, 67
cognitive behavioral therapy (CBT), 296
cognitive skills, 138, 350b, 385
Colby, I., 56, 454
collaboration role of social workers
  and diversity issues in social work, 161
  and future of social work field, 530
  and health care social work, 280, 290t, 295, 312, 319
  and health care support services, 306
  and mental health in criminal justice system, 357–58
  and mental health social work, 357–61
  and process of becoming a social worker, 22
  and professional organizations for social workers, 29
collective responsibility, 495
colonial America, 67, 68–71
Colorado, 226
Columbia University, 75, 79, 94
Columbus, Christopher, 88
Commission for Diversity and Social and Economic Justice, 99
Commission on Accreditation (COA), 6, 94–95, 99–101
Commission on Education Policy, 101
Commission on Global Social Work Education, 499
Committee on Health and Human Services, 442
Commonwealth Organisation for Social Work, 489
community activism, 183, 184b
community mental health centers, 286
community organizing
  and child welfare services, 246
  community care, 390–91
  community connection assistance, 303
  community consultation, 305
  community health centers, 295, 300
  community liaisons, 305
  community protection programs, 38, 55
  community supports, 384
  community-based social movements, 162
  experiences of featured practitioners, 84–85, 188, 317, 497

and historical background of social work, 76
  and macropractice settings, 183
  and process of becoming a social worker, 22
  and public perception of social work, 9
  and social work advocacy in political arena, 445, 463–64
Community Tool Box, 463
community-based care, 390–91
comparative methodology, 477–82, 481t, 482t, 483
compassion, 311
compassion fatigue, 353, 425
compassionate conservatism, 80–83, 527
competencies for social work. *See* Educational Policy and Accreditation Standards (EPAS); *specific competency areas*
complexity of social work, 129, 131, 189
compliance with treatments, 347
comprehensive benefits, 320
concentration practice, 24
concurrent placements, 109
Conference of Non-governmental Organizations, 489
conferences, 117
confidentiality, 141, 331, 355
congregate care, 260–61
Congress, E. P., 135
Congress of Industrial Organizations (CIO), 450–51
Congressional Budget Office, 226
Connolly, Mary, 256b
conservatism, 79, 80, 223
consultants, 458t
consultation, 305
consumer choice, 320
contextual practice, 162, 194
contingency plans, 151
continued care, 389–90
continuing education, 15, 273, 306, 525, 526, 530, 532, 534
continuity of care, 295, 303, 312, 320, 359
Contract with America, 80
contributions, 452
coordinated care, 316
coping skills and strategies, 192, 390
Corbett, Becky S., 512–14
corporate welfare, 51
cost containment, 59–60, 320
cost control measures, 383
cost of living, 113
cost-effective managed care, 154
Council for Higher Education Accreditation, 23
Council of Europe, 489
Council of Higher Education (Turkey), 271

Council on Disability and Persons with Disabilities, 99
Council on Racial, Ethnic, and Cultural Diversity, 99
Council on Social Work Education (CSWE)
  and accreditation of social workers, 94–95, 97–100, 109, 533
  and areas of practice in social work, 6
  Commission on Accreditation (COA), 94–95
  contact information, 348b
  and core competencies for social work, 3–4, 35, 64, 90, 127, 159, 203, 241, 279, 328, 367, 411, 471–72, 509
  Curriculum Policy Statement (CSWE), 171
  and definitions of social work, 15, 16, 17
  and diversity issues in social work, 162
  and education of social workers, 91–92
  and evidence-based practices, 148
  and global social welfare arena, 483, 487, 494, 499–500, 502
  and health care social work, 301
  and job market for social workers, 122
  and knowledge base for social work, 139
  and mental health social work, 349, 353, 357, 359
  and process of becoming a social worker, 19, 23, 24–25
  and regulation of social work field, 533
  and role of professional social workers, 27
  and social work advocacy in political arena, 439, 443, 447
  and social work major curriculum, 517, 518
  and social work targeting older adults, 373
Council on the Role and Status of Women in Social Work Education, 99
counseling, 303, 312, 401, 419, 427
COVID-19 pandemic
  and accreditation of social workers, 108
  and definitions of social welfare, 39–40, 42
  and diversity issues in social work, 162, 195
  experiences of featured practitioners, 371
  and global social welfare arena, 472–73, 496, 500–501
  and health care social work, 280–81, 295, 297–98, 312
  and historical background of social work, 83

impact on older adults, 386, 403
and intersectional perspective on poverty, 217, 220
and mental health social work, 330
and poverty in social work settings, 204
and programs to aid the poor, 229
and regulation of social work field, 533
and self-care, 120–21
and social work advocacy in political arena, 439, 465
and social work targeting older adults, 382
and telemental health, 354, 355
Cowdry, E., 375
Cowles, L. A., 314
credentialing standards, 531. *See also* accreditation of social workers
criminal justice system, 9, 204, 356–59
crisis management, 331
critical race theory, 83
Cross, T., 245–46
CSWE COVID-19 Member "Pulse" Survey, 108
CSWE-China Collaborative, 499
cultural awareness and sensitivity
  and challenges facing social workers, 131–32
  and child welfare services, 247, 248, 273
  and critical race theory, 83
  cultural complexity, 189–90
  cultural influences, 134–36
  and cultural influences in assessment process, 135
  cultural responsiveness, 189
  cultural universality and relativism, 167
  culturally sensitive practices, 192
  and diversity issues in social work, 160, 162–67, 190–92
  and evidence-based practice models, 186–87
  and health care social work, 295, 302
  and mental health social work, 338, 352
  and selection of practice methods, 179–85
Cultural Formulation Interview, 135
Culturally and Socially Responsive Assessment: Theory, Research and Practice (Taylor), 192
Cumming, W., 378
curriculum for social work majors, 517–20

Daley, D. C., 347
Dallas Morning News, 48b
Darby, M. R., 204, 222

data managers, 458t
Davies, J., 421
Days in the Lives of Social Workers (Gobman), 511
deafness, 70b, 73
death
  death penalty cases, 10, 283
  death rates, 371
  planning for, 399–403
  and social work targeting older adults, 380–81
decision to join social work profession, 514–22, 523–26
declassification, 21
defined benefit plans, 52t
defining social work and welfare, 8–9, 38–46, 523
deinstitutionalization, 356–58
Delaney, C., 304
Delaware, 94
Delegate Assembly, 329
dementia, 385, 388, 521
Democratic Party, 284f, 457
demographic trends and statistics
  and aging population, 370, 376
  and child welfare services, 242
  and diversity issues in social work, 168
  global population growth, 477, 500
  and historical perspective on social welfare, 67
  and poverty in social work settings, 206, 213, 213t
Department of Economic and Social Affairs, 485
Department of Labor, 112–13
Department of Veterans Affairs, 110, 294
dependent tax credits, 52t
depreciation, 52t
depression, 352, 387–89, 421
determinism, 66
developed world, 480
development theory, 377, 485
developmental disability, 13, 21, 71
diabetes, 174–76, 300
diagnosis
  diagnostic related groups (DRGs), 383
  experiences of featured practitioners, 354, 520–21
  and health care social work, 294, 301, 304, 314
  and mental health social work, 330, 339–41, 344, 352, 358, 360
  and multidimensional psychosocial evaluation, 332–40
  and social work targeting older adults, 383, 388
Diagnostic and Statistical Manual, 5th edition *(DSM-5),* 339–40

Diagnostic and Statistical Manual, 5th edition, Text Revision (*DSM-5-TR*), 135, 169, 339, 340, 360
dialectical behavioral therapy (DBT), 296
dietetic counseling, *174b*, 175–76
differing abilities, 172. *See also* disability
digital health technologies, 280, 291
digital literacy, 118
dignity of individuals, 38–39, 141, 179
DiNitto, D. M., 219
direct care provision, 302
direct interventions, 177
direct practice, 10, 301–4
direct service roles, *114t*
direct supervision, 305, 306–7
Directory of Accredited Programs, 115
disability
    and 19th century reform efforts, 72–74
    Agency for Persons with Disabilities, 372
    Aid to the Totally and Permanently Disabled, 232
    and core competencies for social work, 71
    Council on Disability and Persons with Disabilities, 99
    and definitions of social work, 13
    disablism, 164
    and diversity issues in social work, 172
    experiences of featured practitioners, 372
    and health care social work, 311
    and process of becoming a social worker, 21
disadvantaged populations, 79, 178, 498
disaster response, 26
discharge planning
    and diversity issues in social work, *174b*
    and health care social work, 280, 303, 310, 312–13
    and mental health social work, 330–32, 349, 350, 353, 357
    and role of medical social worker, 154
    and social work targeting older adults, 384, 389
discrimination
    and definitions of social welfare, 39
    and definitions of social work, 12
    and diversity issues in social work, 194
    experiences of featured practitioners, 189, 245
    and future of social work field, 526, 529
    and intersectional perspective on poverty, 217
    and intimate partner violence, 425
    and poverty in social work settings, 223
    and regulation of social work field, 533
disease eradication, 320
disengagement theory, 377–78, *378b*, 380
Disraeli, Benjamin, 72
District of Columbia, 231
diversity, 159–95
    and accreditation of social workers, 102
    and census data, 167–69
    and child welfare system, 247–51
    and core competencies for social work, 3, 7, 8–9, 31, *103t*, 127, 139, 367, 411, 471, 509
    and cultural awareness, 190–92
    and cultural complexity, 189–90
    and cultural context of social work, 133
    and definitions of social work, 13
    experiences of featured practitioners, 187–89
    and future of social work field, 524, 529, 535
    and generalist practice, 171–77
    and global social welfare arena, 495
    and health care social work, 295, 302
    and inclusive social work practices, 190–92
    and person-in-situation view of social work, 177–79
    and practice of social work, 162–67
    and process of becoming a social worker, 22
    and professional organizations for social workers, 29
    racial and ethnic, 169–71
    respecting in social work settings, 130–31
    and selection of practice method, 179–85
    and short-term evidence-based interventions, 185–89
    and social work in social welfare system, 60
    and specialist practice, 146–47
dividends, *52t*
Division of Tribal Management, 227
divorce, 9, 130, 249–50, 334, 423, 429
Dix, Dorothea Lynde, *70b*, 73
doctorate in philosophy (PhD)
    and accreditation of social workers, 111
    and areas of practice in social work, 6
    and education of social workers, 92
    featured social work practitioners, 96
    and job market for social workers, 91
    number of programs and students, *95t*, *98t*
    and specialist practice, 147
    and state licensing requirements, 116
    See also doctorate in social work (DSW)
doctorate in social work (DSW)
    and accreditation of social workers, *95t*, 111
    and areas of practice in social work, 6
    and education of social workers, 92
    featured social work practitioners, 271
    and job market for social workers, 91
    number of students, *98t*
    and specialist practice, 147
    and state licensing requirements, 116
documentation, 281
domestic violence
    and definitions of social welfare, 39
    experiences of featured practitioners, 354
    and health care support services, 312
    and homicide cases, 412
    risk factors for, 416
    and risk factors for intimate partner violence, *417t*
    and social work targeting intimate partner violence, 413, 420–27, 428–30
    and social work targeting older adults, 398–99
    See also intimate partner violence (IPV)
do-no-harm philosophy, 528
Douglass, Frederick, 66
Down syndrome, 13, 72
Dred Scott v. Sandford, 65, 88
Drifthnery, F., 398
drinking water, 483
drug abuse and addiction
    and definitions of social welfare, 39
    drug-free zones, *184b*
    experiences of featured practitioners, 245
    and intimate partner violence, 416, 421
    and medical issues in mental health assessments, 347
    and mental health in criminal justice system, 356
dual diagnosis, 332, 344–47
duty to warn, 331
dyslexia, 13
Dziegielewski, S. F., 298, 302, 352–53, 374, 389

earned income tax credit (EITC), *52t*, 210, 234
earnings of social workers, 113–15, 120
Earthrise (photograph), 500
East Asia, *479b*
East Carolina State University, 500
EBT cards, 228

ecological systems perspective, 161
Economic and Social Council, 485
economic conditions
 and core competencies for social work, 64, *103t*, 139, 279, 328, 437–38, 471, 509
 and definitions of social welfare, 40–44
 and definitions of social work, 12
 and diversity issues in social work, 160
 economic crises, 42, 465
 and health care social work, 316
 and historical background of social work, 76–80
 and intimate partner violence, *415t*, 416
 and mental health social work, 361
 and poverty in social work settings, 204
Economic Security Act (1935), 223, 232, 369, 371, 375, 382, 394
Economics for Social Workers (Prigoff), 511
Edda, Martha, 152–54
education
 and accreditation standards for social workers, 91–92
 and definitions of social work, 14–16
 and federal social welfare programs, *54b*
 and future of social work field, 530
 and global social welfare arena, *481t*
 and health care social work, 303, 308
 and misconceptions about social welfare, 38
 and poverty in social work settings, 204
 and public social welfare, 53
 social importance of, 65
 and social work targeting intimate partner violence, 430
education costs, 51–52
Education Legislative Network, 451–54
education policy, *103t*
Education Policy and Accreditation Standards Handbook, 24
Educational Policy (EP), 100–101
Educational Policy and Accreditation Standards (EPAS)
 and accreditation of social workers, 101–2, 111
 and core competencies for social work, 3–4, 35–36, 64, 127–28, 159–60, 203, 241, 279, 328, 367–68, 411–12, 437–38, 471–72, 509
 and diversity issues in social work, 162
 and global social welfare arena, 501
 and process of becoming a social worker, 23–24
 and social work advocacy in political arena, 443, 447
 and social work curriculum, 90, 517
EducationWeek, 253
elderly population
 abuse and neglect, 398–99
 and definitions of social work, 12
 eldercare services, 389–90
 and social welfare in colonial America, 68
 See also older adults, social work aimed at
electoral politics, 115, 440, 445–46, 449–63, 527
electronic benefit transfer (EBT) cards, 205
Electronic Benefits Transfer (EBT), 47
electronic communications, 354
eligibility for social welfare
 eligibility workers, 235
 and historical background of social work, 82, 85
 and mental health social work, 331
 and programs to aid the poor, 210, 227, 229, 235
 and residual vs. institutional social welfare, 47, 49
Elizabethan Poor Law of 1601, 67–68
Ellis Island, 65, *65f*, 88
email, 459, 460–62, 472
Emancipation Proclamation, 65, 88
EMDR therapy, 296, 297
emergency room social work, 25, 311–13
empathy, *138b*, 149
empirical techniques, 147
Employer Mandates responsibilities, 384
employer-defined contribution plans, *52t*
employment
 employment opportunities for social workers, 91, 115–21, 329
 and misconceptions about social welfare, 38
 of older adults, 391–96
Empowering Vulnerable Populations (Eamon), 511
empowerment objective, 92, 160, 171, 338–39, 523, 530
endogenous depression, 388
endorsements, 452, 453, 454
English Poor Law of 1601, 67–69, *70b*
ENSACT, 489
entitlement programs
 and food aid programs, 230–31
 and health care support services, 310
 and historical background of social work, 79
 and mental health assessments, *359t*
 and mental health social work, 353
 and poverty in social work settings, 223
 and programs to aid the poor, 224
 and residual vs. institutional social welfare, 50
 See also institutional social welfare
environmental factors, 146, 178, 352, 360
environmental hazards, 498
environmental justice
 and core competencies for social work, 64, *103t*, 130, 160, 203, 279, 328, 437–38, 471, 509
 and future of social work field, 526, 528
 and role of professional social workers, 26
 and social work advocacy in political arena, 443, 466
environmental triggers, 145
Eppard, L., 214
equifinal goal system, 379
Equity Dynamics, LLC, 187–88
Erikson, Erik, 377, 380
Erlich, J. L., 463–64
Estrine, S. A., 511
ethical practice in social work
 and core competencies for social work, 3, *17b*, 35, 64, 90, *103t*, 127, 129–30, 139, 159–60, 279, 328, 367, 411, 471, 509
 and cultural responsiveness, 131–34
 and definitions of social welfare, 43
 and definitions of social work, 12–16
 and diversity issues in social work, 162, 193, 194
 and future of social work field, 522, 529–30, 535
 and health care social work, 306, 307, 310–12, 317
 and historical background of social work, 77, 83
 and key skills of social work, 137–38, *138b*
 and knowledge base for social work, 139–40
 and language choices, 233
 and mental health social work, 331, 335, 338, 348, *348b*, 353, 355
 and person-in-situation context, 177–78
 and residual vs. institutional social welfare, 49
 and self-care, 121
 and skills of social work, 138
 and social work advocacy in political arena, 439, 443
 and social work in social welfare system, 57, 60
 and social work targeting older adults, 375

ethical practice in social work (*Cont.*)
  values and ethics standards in social work, 140–42
Ethical Principles of the National Association of Social Workers' Code of Ethics, 43
ethnicity
  and child welfare services, 247, 248
  and diversity issues in social work, 165–66, 170, 190
  ethnic minorities, 386
  ethnically sensitive practices, 191, 352
  ethnocentrism in social work, 525
  and intersectional perspective on poverty, 213, *218t*
  and professional organizations for social workers, 29
Ethnoracial Equity and Inclusion Task Force, 169
Europe, 133, 478, *479b*
European Union, 489
evaluation
  and core competencies for social work, *103t*, 128, 139
  and diversity issues in social work, 161
  process described, 152
  and steps in professional helping, 150
  See also assessment; diagnosis
evidence-based practices (EBP)
  and child welfare services, 273
  and cultural responsiveness, 132
  and definitions of social work, 19
  and diversity issues in social work, 185–89
  emergence of, 147–48
  and evaluation/follow-ups, 152
  and future of social work field, 522–23, 529, 530
  and inclusive health care access, 287
  and mental health social work, 351, 352
  and social work targeting older adults, 384
evolution of social work, 130, 139, 147–48, 154
exam performance, 533
expansion of social work mission, 442
expendable services, 59
exploitation, 398–99
extended care, 389–90
extreme poverty, 40, 204
extremism, 179

Facebook, *48b*, 459–60
face-to-face meetings, 117
facilitation, 177
faculty advisors, 119
failed interventions, 178
fairness standard, 43

faith-based programs, 53, 81
family adjustment, 191
Family Assistance Program, 79
family court system, 9
family planning, 315
Family Preservation Services, 257–58
Family Services, 55
family structure and support
  in acute care settings, 349–54
  and child welfare services, 249–51
  and core competencies for social work, 31
  and death planning, 400–402, *401b*
  and definitions of social work, 11
  and depression in older adults, 388
  and diversity in social work settings, 130–31
  family therapists, *57t*, 329
  family values, 134
  family-oriented approaches in health care social work, 319
  and health care social work, 315
  and intimate partner violence, 429–30
  and mental health social work, 360–61
  and social work targeting intimate partner violence, 425
  and social work targeting older adults, 371, 390
Federal Adoption Assistance and Child Welfare Act, 263
federal budget, 226
Federal Budget Challenge, 54
Federal Bureau of Investigation (FBI), 414
Federal Emergency Relief Act, 77
Federal Emergency Relief Administration, 66
Federal Interagency Forum on Aging-Related Statistics, 400
federal social welfare, 54, *54b*. See also *specific program names*
Federal Surplus Relief Corporation, 228
federal welfare, 53–54
feedback, 149
Feeding America, 229
fertility rate, 242
field placements
  and accreditation of social workers, 108–10
  and curriculum for social work majors, 517–18
  and diversity issues in social work, 160
  and employment opportunities for social workers, 117–18
  experiences of featured practitioners, 475
field practicum, 15
  and global social welfare arena, 500
  and social work targeting older adults, 373
50-50 model, 109

fight-or-flee behavior, 145
fill-the-gap measures, 55
films featuring social welfare themes, 86–87
financial counselors, 352
financial insecurity, 12, 309, 319, 332, 352, *359t*, *415t*
fire services, 53
First World nations, 478, *479b*, 481, *481t*, *482t*
fiscal welfare, 51
Fischer, J., 147–48
Fisher, J., 145, 146
529 savings accounts, 52
fixed incomes, 219
Fletcher, Samantha, 447–48
Florida, 227, 354, *532t*
Florida Board of Clinical Social Work, Marriage & Family Therapy and Mental Health Counseling, 21–22
Florida State University, 353, 475, 500, 534
Flowers, T., 217
Floyd, George, 448
follow-ups, 152
Food and Nutrition Service, 231
Food and Nutrition Service (USDA), 229
food insecurity and assistance, 36, 39, 82, 228–32, *255t*. *See also* Food Stamp Program; Supplemental Nutritional Assistance Program (SNAP)
Food Stamp Program, 36, *48b*, 228
Ford, Ariel Champaloux, 112
Fordham University, 499
foreign corporations, *52t*
forensic social work, 9, 110
for-profit agencies, 55, 180
foster care, 41, *255t*, 258–60, *259b*
Fourteenth Amendment, 76
Fourth World nations, 81
Frankel, Lee, 177
Franklin, Benjamin, 68, 69, 85
Freedmen's Bureau, *70b*
Friedlander, W., 45
Friedman, T. L., 472
friendly visitors, 74
Friends Program, 487
Frisch, L. A., 423
From Poor Law to Welfare State (Trattner), 67
Frost, Robert, 523
fulfillment from social work, 120
functional decline, 381–82
functional factors, *359t*
funding for social work, 195, 347, 465. *See also* lobbying; policy practice
fundraisers, 452, 458

Gallaudet School for the deaf, 70b
Gapminder Worldview Upgrader web page, 480
Gardellia, L. G., 98
gaslighting, 420, 516
Gates, Bill, 208
Gay and Lesbian Alliance against Defamation, 27
gay and lesbian parents, 131
gay rights, 82
Gaza war, 503
gender issues in social work
    and diversity issues in social work, 163–64
    experiences of featured practitioners, 354
    and future of social work field, 523
    gender discrimination, 39, 94
    and intersectional perspective on poverty, 213, 217–18
    and life expectancy, 371
    and mental health social work, 360
generalist practice
    and accreditation of social workers, 101
    described, 145–46
    and diversity issues in social work, 159–95
    and evidence-based practice models, 187
    and evolution of social work, 154–55
    and health care social work, 301
    and process of becoming a social worker, 24
    and regulation of social work field, 532
generation Z, 164
genetic testing, 132
Georgia, 24
Germany, 369
Gero-Ed center, 373–74
Gerontological Society, 376
gerontology, 373, 375–76
Gestalt therapy, 296, 297
Ghana, 475–76
Gilbert, N., 67
Ginsberg, L., 233
Girl Scouts, 55
GLAAD, 164
Global Agenda for Social Work and Social Development, 496
global relations, 42
global scope of social work profession, 5, 31
Global Social Policy, 496
global social welfare, 471–504
    comparative approach to, 477–82
    expansion of field, 476–77
    experiences of featured practitioners, 496–98

and future of social work field, 525
international initiatives of NASW, 498–500
international professional social welfare organizations, 487–96
international social welfare associations, 484–87
studying international social welfare, 482–84
globalization, 472, 477, 501–2
goal identification, 303
goal systems theory, 378–79
goal-setting, 150
gold stamp of approval., 14
Gonzalez, M. J., 135
Gonzalez-Ramos, G., 134
Gorbachev, Mikhail, 83
grading process, 519
graduate degrees, 15, 24–25, 92–93, 98t, 519. *See also* doctorate in social work (DSW); master of social work (MSW)
graduate-level education, 22
Grand Challenges for Social Work (2022), 31
grandparents, 131
Gray, John, 163
Gray, Lecia, 372–73
Great Depression, 55, 66, 78, 129, 223, 228, 375, 444, 473
Great Recession, 204
Great Society, 78, 79, 295
Greek origins of social welfare, 67
Grigorenko, E. L., 192
Group for the Advancement of Doctoral Education in Social Work, 6, 95
group practice, 76
group psychodrama, 296
group sessions, 182
growth of health care field, 281
growth of social work profession, 112–13, 129
Guam, 478
guest speakers, 462
Gurteen, Humphrey, 74, 75

Hacettepe University, 270, 271
Hadley, Massachusetts, 69
Hafford-Letchfield, T., 165, 373
Hamby, Sherry, 420
Hanks, J., 449
Hansan, J. E., 45–46
hard money, 452
Harrington, Michael, 78
Hartford, Connecticut, 70b
hate and hate crimes, 179, 527
Hawaii, 211, 478
Haynes, K. S., 449
Hayward, R., 375

Head Start program, 46t, 50, 78, 209
health benefit exchanges, 52t
Health Care and Social Assistance, 281
health care organizations, 186
health care social work, 279–320
    and current health care environment, 297–301
    direct practice, 301–4
    experiences of featured practitioners, 296–97, 317–18
    and future of social work field, 528
    and health care social work, 288–91
    health counseling, 307–8
    health education, 305, 307–8
    historical background of, 292–95
    inclusive health care access, 284–88
    motivations, 315–17
    practice of, 291–92
    and public social welfare, 53, 54
    roles and tasks of health care social worker, 301
    support services, 305–15
health departments, 46t
health insurance, 82, 186–87, 313
Health Insurance Portability and Accountability Act (HIPAA), 355, 403
Health Resource Service Administration, 304
HealthCare.gov website, 287
hearing loss, 386
heart disease, 319
Heart Gallery of America, Inc., 264
Help Me Grow program, 397
help-seeking behaviors, 424
Henry, E., 378
Henry, M. J., 265
hereditary conditions, 319
Herrick, C., 313
Hettenbach, R. T., 511
High Commissioner of Human Rights, 489
Hispanic Americans
    and child welfare services, 247–48
    and cultural context of social work, 133
    and definitions of social welfare, 42
    and diversity issues in social work, 170, 174b
    experiences of featured practitioners, 188
    and intersectional perspective on poverty, 213–14, 214t, 215f, 216–17, 218t, 220
    and poverty in social work settings, 206, 207t
    and programs to aid the poor, 227
historical background of social work, 65–86

HIV/AIDS, 84–85, 319, 343–44, 455, 501
Hmong people, 170
Hoeffer, R., 56, 512
Hokenstad, Terry, 501
Holliman, D., 298, 302, 352–53, 374, 389
Hollis-Taylor report, 173
home care
    and child welfare services, 246, 255t
    and health care social work, 310, 313–15
    home health care services, 153, 154
    and social work targeting older adults, 371
    and support services of social workers, 313–15
home mortgage crisis, 42
homelessness
    and definitions of social welfare, 41
    and definitions of social work, 18
    and diversity issues in social work, 168
    homeless shelters as residual social welfare, 46t
    and mental health in criminal justice system, 357
    and mental health social work, 333b
    and poverty measurements, 210
    and role of professional social workers, 26–27
homicide, 333b, 412, 414, 416, 418–19, 427
homophyly, 166
Hood, Thomas, 73
Hopkins, Harry, 66
hospice care
    experiences of featured practitioners, 283, 317–18
    and health care social work, 310
    and social work targeting older adults, 391, 402
    and support services of social workers, 314–15
Hospital Insurance Trust Fund, 383
hospital social workers, 25, 281, 291, 293f, 311–13
host setting, 294
housing, 18, 38, 53–54, 54b, 204, 481t. See also homelessness
Huang, C., 421
Hull House, 68, 70b, 76, 185
human development theory, 377, 377b
human rights
    and core competencies for social work, 64, 103t, 139, 160, 203, 241, 279, 328, 411, 437–38, 471, 509
    defined, 204
    and future of social work field, 524
    and global social welfare arena, 472, 483, 485, 490b, 492, 495, 504

    and goals of text, 512
    and social work advocacy in political arena, 439, 443
    and social work targeting intimate partner violence, 412
    and social work targeting older adults, 374

illiteracy, 482
immigrants
    and census data, 168
    and historical background of social work, 65, 76–77
    illegal aliens, 13, 233
    and intimate partner violence, 422
    and poverty in social work settings, 222
    and programs to aid the poor, 232–34
    and social work targeting older adults, 374
immorality associated with poverty, 72
immunizations, 528
implementation, 151
incarceration, 41
inclusiveness
    and accreditation of social workers, 102
    and core competencies for social work, 3, 9, 103t, 127, 139, 160, 367, 411, 471, 509
    and definitions of social work, 11, 13
    and diversity issues in social work, 164, 190–92
    inclusive health care access, 284–88, 320
    inclusive social work practices, 190–92
income
    eligibility requirements, 229 (see also (means testing)
    and global social welfare arena, 481t
    income maintenance, 203–37
    of social workers, 330
incumbents, 452
indentured servitude, 69
independence, 441
India, 23, 264
Indian Child Welfare Act (ICWA), 248
Indian Health Service, 286
Indian Tribal Organizations, 231
Indiana University, 317
Indigenous cultures, 165, 448
indigent people, 283
individualism, 161, 166
Individualized Education Program (IEP), 221
Industrial Society and Social Welfare (Wilensky and Lebeaux), 46
industrialization of U.S. economy, 394
infants, 264

inflation, 204
injury compensation systems, 300
in-kind benefits, 46, 211
in-service training, 384
insomnia, 387
institutional group quarters, 210
institutional racism, 134
institutional social welfare, 46t, 49–50, 484
insurance
    ACA reimbursement provisions, 384
    and current health care environment, 299
    experiences of featured practitioners, 354
    insurance industry, 298
    insurance providers, 186
    life insurance, 29
    malpractice insurance, 29
    and professional organizations for social workers, 29
    and scope of social welfare programs, 52t
    social insurance, 53, 54b
    uninsured and underinsured population, 313
intake process, 96–97, 330
integrated care, 319
interdisciplinary teams
    experiences of featured practitioners, 84–85
    and health care social work, 289, 290t, 292, 294, 307, 315
    and hospice care, 402
    and mental health social work, 330, 332
    and role of medical social worker, 154
    and social work advocacy in political arena, 442
internal family systems, 296, 297
internalized racism, 133–34
international accreditation associations, 23
International Activities Committee, 498
International Association of Schools of Social Work (IASSW), 6, 17, 17b, 95, 489, 494
International Classification of Diseases, 10th Edition, Clinical Modification (ICD-10-CM), 340
International Classification of Disorders, 11th edition (ICD-11), 340–41
International Conference of Schools of Social Work, 495
International Consortium for Social Development (IASSW), 7
International Council on Social Welfare, 489, 495–96

International Covenant on Economic, Social and Cultural Rights, 504
International Federation of Social Workers (IFSW)
  and areas of practice in social work, 5
  and definitions of human rights, 204
  and definitions of social work, 13, 17, *490b*
  and ethics standards, 233
  and global social welfare arena, 473, 486–94, *488b*, 489, *493b*, 495, 501
  and language choices in assessments, 335
  and values/ethics standards in social work, 142
International Federation of the Red Cross, 91
International Paralympic Committee, 13
international professional social welfare organizations, 487–96
international social welfare associations, 482–87
international social work, 110. *See also* global scope of social work profession
International Women's Day, 486
internet resources, 118–19, 516
internet technology, 12
interpersonal skills, 138
interprofessional approach, 304
intersectionality, 213–20
Interstate Compact for Social Work Licensure, 533
intervention
  behavioral biopsychosocial approach, 341–42
  and child welfare services, 243, 248, 260, 263, 267–68, 273
  and core competencies for social work, 4, *103t*, 128, 139, 160, 241, 279, 328
  and cultural context of social work, 134
  and definitions of social work, 12, 15, 18
  experiences of featured practitioners, 221, 448, 476
  and future of social work field, 529
  and health care social work, 289, 301, 308
  and mental health social work, 332, *333b*, 334, 337–39, 341–47, *348b*, 349–50, *350b*, 352, 360–61
  and process of becoming a social worker, 20–21, 31
  and risk factors for intimate partner violence, *417t*

  and role of professional social workers, 26–27
  and social welfare competencies, 36, 43, 45, 57
  and social work advocacy in political arena, 442, 457, 464
  and social work targeting intimate partner violence, 413, 415, 420–25, *425b*, 428, 430
  and social work targeting older adults, 375, 378–80, 388–89, 393, 395–96, 398–99, 401
intimate partner violence (IPV), 411–31
  barriers to escaping, 416–20
  and core competencies for social work, 411–12
  defined, 413–15
  and definitions of social welfare, 39–40
  experiences of featured practitioners, 427–28
  helping survivors, 420–27
  impact on children, 421
  and legal system, 422–23
  risk factors for, 415–16, *417t*
  and role of social workers, 423–27
  and sexual abuse, 267
  types of abuse, *415t*, 426–27
  and women's shelter social workers, 428–30
intradisciplinary teams, *290t*
Introduction to Social Work (Cox, Tice, and Long), 511
Introduction to the Drama of Social Work (Bloom), 511
Inuits, 165
Iraq War, 81
isolationism, 473
Israel, 503

Jackson, Julie, 220–21
Jackson, K., 121
Jackson, Mississippi, 84
Jaime, J., 329
Jane Addams Hull-House Museum, 68
January 6 2021 Capitol insurrection, 438, 439, 465
Jefferson County Committee for Economic Opportunity Head Start Program, 397
Jewish Community Centers, 55
Jews and Judaism, 135, 266
Jiang, H., 476
Jim Crow, 76
Job Corps, 78, 209
job fairs, 120
job notifications, 113

Job Opportunities and Basic Skills Training program, 224
job placement offices, 116
Job Training Partnership Act, 209
John A. Hartford Foundation, 373–74
Johnson, D. H., 219
Johnson, J., 249
Johnson, L. C., 223
Johnson, Lyndon B., 78, 224, 295
joint problem-solving, 357
Joint University Council for Social and Public Administration, 23
Jones, Mary Harris (Mother Jones), 183
Joubert, L., 308
Journal of Gerontology, 375–76
Jung, H., 329
juvenile court, 252, 253, 255

Kadushin, A., 246
Kang, Y., 375
Kansas, 205
Karger, H. J., 55–56, 67, 243
Karolinska Institutet, 296
Kastamonu University, 270
Katherine A. Kendall Institute for International Social Work Education, 499
Kayser, K., 249
Kearney, M., 242
Kelley, Florence, 444
Kendall, Katherine, 501
Kentucky, *70b*
Khoshnoodi, Jamshid, 296–97
Kim, S., 375
King, Martin Luther, Jr., 504
Klonoff, E. A., 217–18
knowledge base for social work, 137–39, *138b*
Korea, 264
Kosovo, 478
Kourgiantakis, T., 361
Kumar, Dinesh, 382

labels, 14, 341, 346, 350, 360
labor activism, 183
labor force participation, 222
labor market, 473
labor requirements, 73–74
labor shortages, 477
Lai Kwan (Denise), 96–97
Landrine, H., 217–18
Lane, S., 217
Laohmong people, 170
Latimer, T. R., 349
Latin America and the Caribbean region, 216, 248, 264, *479b*

Latinx people
    and child welfare services, 248
    and cultural influences in assessment process, 135
    and diversity issues in social work, 169, 170
    and intersectional perspective on poverty, 216
    and poverty in social work settings, 206
Laundrie, Brian, 412
law enforcement, 430. *See also* police
law practice requirements, 93
laziness stereotype, 68
Leadership Education in Neurodevelopmental Disabilities, 297
Leadership in Public Health Education, 304
learning moments, 189
Lebeaux, Charles, 46, 49–51, 484
Lee, S., 329
legal services, 209, 424, 429
legal system, 421–22, 425
legislative politics, 54, 449–50
Leipzig, R. M., 289
leisure time, 396
Lemon, B. L., *379b*
lending practices, 215, *216f*
Lepkowsky, C. M., 403–4
letter-writing campaigns, 460, *461b*
Levine, P., 242
LGBTQ+ people, 84, 131, 171, 414, 422, 529
liberal arts education, 20, 515
libraries, *46t*, 53, *57t*
licensed master's social worker (LMSW), 187–88, 455
licensing standards, 7, *70b*, 116–17, 119, 531, 533. *See also* accreditation of social workers
life changes, 393–96
life expectancy, 320, 369–71, 376, 391–93
life insurance, 29
life stage, *350b*
lifestyle behaviors, 300
lifetime limits on social aid, 80, 85, 227, 285, 528
Lincoln, Nebraska, 44–45
LinkedIn, 91, 118
literacy, 118, 482
lobbying
    and political life cycle, *450f*
    and social work advocacy in political arena, 449–52, 454, 457, 459–60, 462, 464, 466
local welfare, 55, 71
location, 215
long-term care settings, 309–11, 389

Los Angeles County, California, 356
low-income housing, 36
low-wage jobs, 222
Lutfiyya, M. N., 304
Lyon, E., 421

Mackelprang, R. W., 164
macro-level social work practice (macro system level)
    and anti-oppressive social work, 143
    and areas of practice in social work, 5–6
    and definitions of social work, 16–19
    and diversity issues in social work, 180–81, 183–85, 190–94
    and evidence-based practices, 523
    experiences of featured practitioners, 282–83, 447–48, 497
    and future of social work field, 523
    and health care social work, 316
    and job market for social workers, *91f*
    and mental health social work, 329, 351, 357
    and process of becoming a social worker, 20, 31
    and role of professional social workers, 26–27
    and social work advocacy in political arena, 464, 465
    and social work targeting intimate partner violence, 415
    and specialist practice, 146
Mahaffey, M., 449
Maine, 253
maintenance of services, 152
malnutrition, 230
malpractice, 29, 298–300
managed care, 154, 352
managed competition, 284
management duties, 183. *See also* administrative skills
mandatory arrest policies, 423
mandatory reporting, 256
Maneuvering the Maze of Managed Care (Corcoran and Vandiver), 511
manic depression, *333b*, 334. See also *bipolar disorder*
Marcus, S., 314, 347, 385
marriage
    and definitions of social work, 11
    and diversity in social work settings, 130
    and divorce, 9, 249–50, 334, 423, 429
    and child welfare services, 250
    marriage therapists, *57t*, 329
Martin, J. A., 246
Martin, Trayvon, 83, 446

Massachusetts, 69, *70b*, 261–62
Massachusetts General Hospital, *70b*, 294, 331, 349
master of social work (MSW)
    and accreditation of social workers, *95t*, 98, *98t*, 100, 102, 109–12
    and areas of practice in social work, 7
    and core competencies for social work, 64, 128, 130, 509
    and diversity issues in social work, 192
    and education of social workers, 91, 92
    and employment opportunities for social workers, 118, 119
    featured social work practitioners, 142, 187–88, 220–21, 244, 282, 317, 353–54, 372–73, 397, 427, 447, 475, 496, 512–13, 534
    and field placement requirement, 519
    and future of social work field, 524, 526
    and generalist practice, 145
    and health care social work, 301
    and health care support services, 306–7
    and job market for social workers, 91, 122
    and mental health social work, 330, 337
    and mezzopractice settings, 183
    and microprocess settings, *181b*, 182
    number of students, *98t*
    and process of becoming a social worker, 22, 24
    and professional organization membership, 524–25
    and regulation of social work field, 532–33
    and social work advocacy in political arena, 455
    and specialist practice, 146–47
    and state licensing requirements, 116
    states with social work programs, 94
    and structure of social work curriculum, 519, 526
maternal health programs, *54b*
Matos, E., 233
Maust, D., 314, 347, 385
McCain-Feingold Act, 451
McConnell, Mitch, 205
McCrea, S. M., 248
McLeod, E., 314
McPhee, D., 235
meal planning, *174b*, 175–76
Meals on Wheels, 25, 177, 229, 232
mean, statistical, 211
means testing
    and federal social welfare programs, *54b*
    and food aid programs, 229

Index

and poverty measurements, 212
and programs to aid the poor, 232
and residual vs. institutional social welfare, 47, 50
and social work in social welfare system, 58
and social work targeting older adults, 374
measurement of client outcomes, 132, 192
media depictions of social work, 19, 60
median, statistical, 211
Medicaid
  and adoption, 263
  and current health care environment, 299
  and EITC benefits, 234
  experiences of featured practitioners, 354
  and federal social welfare programs, *54b*
  and health care support services, 314
  and historical background of social work, 78, 82
  and inclusive health care access, 285–87
  and mental health social work, 354–55
  and multidimensional psychosocial evaluation, 332
  and poverty measurements, 212
  and public social welfare, 53
  as residual social welfare, *46t*
  and role of medical social worker, 153
  and social work advocacy in political arena, 455–56
  and social work targeting older adults, 383–85, 403
medical conditions and care
  advances in, 349
  and depression, 387
  and health care social work, 288
  medical facilities, *54b*
  medical outcome data, 298
  medical practice requirements, 93
  medical social work, 152–54, 293
  and mental health social work, 336, 339–40, 343–47, 349
  and process of becoming a social worker, 22
  research, *54b*
  and role of professional social workers, 25
  and social work targeting older adults, 380–90
Medicare
  and federal social welfare programs, *54b*
  and health care support services, 314, 315
  and historical background of social work, 78
  and hospice care, 402
  and inclusive health care access, 285–87
  as institutional social welfare, *46t*
  Medicare Act, 82
  and multidimensional psychosocial evaluation, 332
  and public social welfare, 53
  and social work targeting older adults, 382–85, 403
  and telemental health, 355
medications, 346–47, 385, 388, 400
meditation, 307
Melville, Herman, 31
membership organizations for social workers, 28–30, *30b*
Men Are from Mars, Women Are from Venus (Gray), 163
Mental Health Services, *333b*
mental health social work, 328–61
  and acute care settings, 349–54
  assessments, 345, *359t*
  behavioral biopsychosocial approach, 341–43
  and classification of social work providers, *57t*
  counselors, 329
  and criminal justice system, 356–59
  and diagnostic criteria, 340–41
  experiences of featured practitioners, 112, 245, 353–54, 534
  glossary entry on, 455
  and medical conditions, 343–47
  and medical health conditions, 343–48
  mental asylums, *70b*, 73
  mental function, *350b*
  mental illness, 39, 350, 400
  and mental impairment, 331, 389
  and multidimensional psychosocial evaluation, 332–40
  placing diagnoses, 340–41
  and social work targeting older adults, 380–90
  and telemental health resources, 354–56, 535
metropolitan ares, 215
Mettler, S., 52
Mexican-American War, 88
mezzo-level social work practice (mezzo system level)
  and anti-oppressive social work, 143
  and areas of practice in social work, 5–6
  and definitions of social work, 16–19
  and diversity issues in social work, 180–83, 185, 190, 192–94
  and evidence-based practices, 523
  and future of social work field, 523, 526
  and health care social work, 281, 282
  and job market for social workers, *91f*
  and mental health social work, 351
  and process of becoming a social worker, 20, 31
  and role of professional social workers, 26
  and social work targeting intimate partner violence, 415
  and specialist practice, 146
Michigan, *168f*
Mickelson, J. S., 449
micro-level practice social work practice (micro system level)
  and anti-oppressive social work, 143
  and areas of practice in social work, 5–6
  case study in, *181b*
  and definitions of social work, 16–19
  and diversity issues in social work, 180–82, 185, 190, 192–94
  and evidence-based practices, 523
  experiences of featured practitioners, 497
  and future of social work field, 523, 526
  and health care social work, 282
  and job market for social workers, *91f*
  and mental health social work, 351
  and process of becoming a social worker, 20, 31
  and role of professional social workers, 25–26
  and social work targeting intimate partner violence, 415
  and specialist practice, 146
Middle Ages, 67
Middle Alabama Area Agency on Aging, 397
Middle East and North Africa region, 248, *479b*
Midgley, J., 483–84
migrant workers, *168f*
Mikulski, Barbara, 446
military personnel, *57t*
military social work, 110
Miller, P. J., 288, 308
minimum income proposals, 79
minimum wage, 80, 204, 211–12, 236, 391, 444, 465, 528
Ministry of Civil Affairs (China), 7, 476, 499
Minneapolis, Minnesota, 76
minority populations, 169, 247. *See also* racism; *specific racial and ethnic groups*
mirror welfare state, 56

misconceptions about social work, 10, 36–38, 43–44, 47–49, *48b*, 51
mission creep, 442
Mississippi, 226, 261
mobile health (mmHealth), 355
mobilizers, *458t*
Moby Dick (Melville), 31
mode, statistical, 211
Modesto Bee, 48b
Mong people, 170
Montenegro, 243, 484
mood disorders, 341, 342
Morales, A. T., 511
Morrison, M., 394
mortality, 388. *See also* death
Mosher-Ashley, P. M., 381
Mother Jones, 183
motivational theory of life-span development, 379
Mr. Smith Goes to Washington (film), 438
Mullarkey, E., 424, 427
Multicultural Psychoeducational Assessment (Grigorenko), 192
multidimensional psychosocial assessment, 332–40
multidisciplinary teams, 289, *290t*, 307, 310
multifinal goal system, 379
multiple-heritage couples, 193
Murray Alzheimer Research and Education Program, 310
Muslim students, 166

National Alliance on Mental Illness, 358
National Anti-Hunger Coalition, 79
National Association of Black Social Workers (NABSW), 15–16, 266
National Association of Realtors, 451
National Association of Schools of Social Administration, 97–100
National Association of Schools of Social Work, 23, 28
National Association of Social Workers (NASW)
  Anti-Racism Statement, 131, 162, 171
  and areas of practice in social work, 5–6, 7
  Board Governance Committee, 171
  Career Center, 91, 113
  Code of Ethics, 16, 57–58, 130, 131, 140–42, 162, 185, 335, 355, 439, 443
  contact information, *348b*
  and cultural context of social work, 134
  decision to join social work profession, 514–15
  and definitions of social work, 12, 13, 15–17, *17b*
  Delegate Assembly, 329
  and diversity issues in social work, 162
  Education Legislative Network, 451–54
  and employment opportunities for social workers, 117, 118
  experiences of featured practitioners, 447–48, 513
  and future of social work field, 529
  and global social welfare arena, 473, 487, 501, 502
  headquarters, *498f*
  and health care social work, 301, 305, 311, 316
  and health care support services, 306
  and historical background of social work, 78
  importance of professional memberships, 27–30
  and inclusive health care access, 287
  international initiatives of NASW, 498–500
  and intersectional perspective on poverty, 217
  and mental health social work, 330–32, 352
  and political action for candidate election, *452b*
  and process of becoming a social worker, 31
  and regulation of social work field, 533
  revised policy statement, 329–30
  and social work advocacy in political arena, 445–46, 456
  and social work targeting intimate partner violence, 413
National Association of Social Workers in South Africa, 7
National Center for Children in Poverty, 40
National Child Traumatic Stress Network, 267
National Conference of Social Work, 291, 376
National Conference of State Legislatures, 205
National Domestic Violence Hotline, 414
National Football League (NFL), 520–21
National Guard, 82
National Hospice and Palliative Care Organization, 315, 402
National Immigration Law Center, 233
National Indian Child Welfare Association (NICWA), 248
National Institute of Mental Health, 354
National Institutes of Health (NIH), 354
National Intimate Partner and Sexual Violence Survey, 413
National Park Service, *48b*
National School Lunch and School Breakfast Programs, 209, 229–30
National Social Work Month, 502–3
National Urban League, 78
Native Americans, 42, 165, 227, 248, 260, 266, 273
Native Hawaiians, 170
Nebraska, 44–45
negative income tax, 79
neglect, 38, 59, *251b*, *255t*, 256, 398–99
networking, 117
New Deal, 65, 77, 80–81, 88, 444
New Hampshire, 24
New Orleans, Louisiana, 260
New York Charity Organization Society, 75, 94
New York City, 120, *256b*, 262
New York City Department of Charities, *256b*
New York Society for the Prevention of Cruelty to Animals, 256
New York State, 94
New York State legislature, 448
New York Times, 478
Nineteenth Amendment, 71
Nixon, Richard, 79
Nobel Peace Prize, 68, *76f*, 485
nonbinary gender, 164. *See also* LGBTQ+ people
nonevent fundraisers, 458
non-Hispanic White people, *215f*, 386
non-profit or non-governmental social service agencies (NGOs), 7, 14, 26, 56, 254, 450
non-social work majors, 515–16
nontraditional family, 131
nontraditional social work, 308
North America, 478
North Carolina, 69
Northern Ireland, 477–78
not-for-profit agencies, 55
nurses, *57t*, 93, 290
nursing homes, 153–54
nutrition programs, 79. *See also* Supplemental Nutritional Assistance Program (SNAP); Women, Infants, and Children

Obama, Barack, 81–82, 457, 459
Observatory on the Global South, 496
Occupational Outlook Handbook, 28, 91, 99, 329
Occupy Wall Street (OWS) movement, 446
Office of Economic Opportunity, 78, 79
Office of Management and Budget, 170
Office of Public Affairs, 486
Office of Refugee Resettlement, 487

Ohio Child Welfare Training Program, 244
Ohio Human Services Training System, 244
Okantey, Beth, 475–76
Old Age Assistance, 232
older adults, social work aimed at, 367–404
 abuse, neglect, and exploitation, 398–99
 and the aging process, 374–76
 community care and case management, 390–91
 and current health care environment, 298
 defining old adults, 373–74
 employment of older adults, 391–96
 experiences of featured practitioners, 397–98
 health and mental health considerations, 380–90
 and health care social work, 291
 and health care support services, 314
 and intersectional perspective on poverty, 219
 Older Americans Act, 219
 suicide risk and planning for death, 399–403
 theoretical framework, 377–80
O'Neill, Tip, 453
online environments, 118–19
on-the-job training, 523. *See also* field placements
open seats, 452
oppressed populations, 178
Oregon, 269
Orlando, Florida, 372
orphans and orphanages, 68, 73
Orphan's Train, 262
Orshansky, Mollie, 208–9, 210
Oslin, D. W., 314, 347, 385
The Other America: Poverty in the United States (Harrington), 78
outcomes-focused intervention, 15
outdoor relief, 69
out-of-area placements, 153
out-of-home services, 258–64
overmedicalization, 360
overseer of the poor, 69
Owens, C. L., 402–3

Pacific Islanders, 170, 207t
Pacific Lutheran University, 475
Pacific region, 479b
Palestine, 478, 484
Palm Beach Atlantic College, 372
Palm Institute, 475
Palmer, J., 79
pandisciplinary teams, 290t

panic attacks, 521
paraprofessionals, 59
Pardue, L., 242
parens patriae principle, 252
partisanship, 439, 452
paternalism, 141
patient bill of rights, 285b, 316
Patient Protection and Affordable Care Act (ACA), 81–82, 301, 355
"patient" term, 288
payday lending, 215, 216f
Paymar, M., 419
payments, 320
peace and social justice, 483
Peace Corps, 78–79, 445, 487, 503
peacekeeping missions, 484
Pechacek, J., 304
peer relations, 192
Pell grants, 465
Pence, E., 419
Pendleton, Helen B., 294
Penn, William, 73
Pennsylvania, 69, 94
Pennsylvania Hospital, 73
performance indicators, 288
Perkins, Frances, 66, 77, 440
Perkins, K., 401
personal information, 119, 190
Personal Responsibility and Work Opportunity Reconciliation Act, 80, 224
personality disorders, 333b
person-in-environment view of social work
 and areas of practice in social work, 5
 and cultural influences in assessment process, 135
 and diversity issues in social work, 161, 167
 experiences of featured practitioners, 513–14
 and goals of text, 512–13
 and health care social work, 304
 and trauma in social work settings, 145
person-in-situation view of social work
 and areas of practice in social work, 5
 and cultural influences in assessment process, 135
 and diversity issues, 177–79
 and future of social work field, 522
 and goals of text, 512–13
 and health care social work, 304
 and social work targeting older adults, 390–91
 and trauma in social work settings, 145
Peterson, J. A., 379b
Petito, Gabby, 412
PHI, 355
Philadelphia, Pennsylvania, 232
Philippines, 264

Phyllis Wheatley Settlement House, 76
physical abuse, 415t
physical health conditions, 385–87
physical therapy, 94, 153
physician-oriented care, 313
Pierce, Franklin, 70b
Pitcairn Islands, 480
placement services, 359t
planning, 303, 340, 458t
Plymouth Colony, 70b
police
 and classification of social work providers, 57, 57t
 experiences of featured practitioners, 428
 and intimate partner violence, 421, 423, 424, 428
 and mental health in criminal justice system, 357
 police reform, 446–47
 and public social welfare, 53
 and trauma in social work settings, 144
policy practice
 and core competencies for social work, 3–4, 35, 103t
 and definitions of social work, 18
 and evidence-based practice models, 187
 experiences of featured practitioners, 44–45
 and future of social work field, 524, 530
 and global social welfare arena, 472
 and health care social work, 282, 316
 and health care support services, 305
 and knowledge base for social work, 139
 and macropractice settings, 183, 184
 and mental health in criminal justice system, 357–58, 359
 and mental health social work, 351–52, 361
 policy papers, 494
 and process of becoming a social worker, 23–24
 and professional organizations for social workers, 29
 and role of professional social workers, 26–27
 and social welfare competencies, 42, 58
 and social work advocacy in political arena, 438
 and social work targeting intimate partner violence, 412
 and telemental health, 355
 See also political arena
political action committee, 450–51
Political Action for Candidate Election (PACE), 445, 452–57, 452b, 464

political arena, 437–66
    and child welfare services, 250
    and community organization, 463–64
    defining, 440–41
    election day work, 458–59
    experiences of featured practitioners, 447–48
    historical background of social work politics, 444–49
    importance to social work, 441–42
    Political Action for Candidate Election (PACE), 452–53, *452b*
    political ideology, 466
    and role of professional social workers, 27
    social works organizations and electoral politics, 450–63
    and values of social work, 443–44
    See also policy practice
Pollack, D., 265
poor laws, 67–69, *70b*, 72
popular culture, 243
population growth, 168, 485. *See also* demographic trends and statistics
portrayals of social workers, 60
postplacement services, 263
posttraumatic stress syndrome (PTSS), 145–46, 503
poverty, 203–37
    and 19th century reform efforts, 72–74
    causes of, 222–23
    and child welfare services, 249, 257, 264
    defined, 208–13, *213t*
    and definitions of social welfare, 39–43, 45
    and definitions of social work, *17b*
    and diversity issues in social work, 169
    and evolution of social work, 154
    experiences of featured practitioners, 220–21, 245, 271–72
    and future of social work field, 526
    and global social welfare arena, 483, 495, 502
    and health care social work, 295, 311
    and history of social reform in U.S., 78, 79
    intersectional perspective on, 213–20
    and intersectional perspective on poverty, *219t*
    and intimate partner violence, 415
    measuring, 208–13
    and mental health social work, 360
    and origins of social work, 57
    poverty threshold, 208–9, *209t*, 211–12
    and process of becoming a social worker, 22
    programs to aid the poor, 223–34
    rate of, 212–13, *213t*
    and role of professional social workers, 27
    and scope of social work profession, 57–58
    and settlement house movement, 75–76
    and social work targeting older adults, 375, 382
    and stereotypes of social welfare recipients, 72
    War on Poverty, 78, 81, 224, 235, 444
Poverty USA, 42
power structures, 163
practice areas of social workers, *114t*
practice of social work, 127–55
    basics of practice, 136
    and core competencies for social work, 127–28
    and cultural influences, 134–36
    and cultural responsiveness, 131–32
    and diversity, 130–31
    and diversity issues, 162–67
    and evidence-based social work practice, 147–48
    generalist vs. specialist practice, 145–47
    importance of anti-oppressive social work, 143–44
    key concepts, 137–43
    medical social workers, 152–54
    steps in professional helping, 148–52
    and technological challenges, 132–34
    and trauma and recovery, 144–45
practice-informed research, *103t*, 139, 279, 328, 367
preexisting conditions, *285b*
pregnancy, 337–38, 419
prejudice, 194
preplacement training, 265
preretirement counseling, 396
preservice or preadmission planning, 302
preventative services, 50, 320
"Preventing Child Abuse and Neglect" (factsheet), 257
prison, 356. *See also* criminal justice system
privacy, 355, 403
private practice, 14, 180
Private Voluntary Bodies, 487
privatization of social welfare, 53, 55–56, 80–81
privileged communication, 141
problem identification, 149–50
problem-focused education, 175–76
Problems of Aging (Cowdry), 375
productivity statistics, 40
professionalism
    and core competencies for social work, 3, 5–7, 64, *103t*, 140–42, 279
    and definitions of social work, 11–12
    and process of becoming a social worker, 19
    professional contact information, *348b*
    professional organizations for social workers, 27–30
    and social work in social welfare system, 59
    See also Educational Policy and Accreditation Standards (EPAS)
profit motive, 483
program development, 183, 305
Progressive Era, 444
protected health information (PHI), 355
protective orders, *417t*, 422, 429
psychiatric hospitals, 328, 329
psychiatrists, *57t*
psychological conditions and history, 192
    and health care social work, 303
    and historical background of social work, 66
    and mental health social work, 349, 360
    and multidimensional psychosocial evaluation, 332–40, *333b*
    and psychiatric disorders, 385
    and psychoeducation, 308
    psychological abuse, *415t*
    and psychological services, 424
    and psychological testing, 336
    and psychosocial needs, 384
    and psychotherapy, 317, 521
    and psychotic disorders, 347
    and psychsocial care, 319
    and social work targeting older adults, 390
    and trauma, 40
psychologists, 12, *57t*
public aid, 53, *54b*
public perception of social work, 8–9, 47–49, 51
public sanitation programs, 293
public schools, 51
Public Services International, 489
public social welfare, 51, 53–55
public testimony, 463
public/private balance in social welfare provision, 85
Puerto Rico, *70b*, 478
Pulse Night Club shooting, 527
punitive element of social welfare programs, 69
Puritanism, 68

quality care management teams, 175
quality improvement, 305
quality of social welfare provision, 59–60

race issues in social work
    and accreditation of social workers, 94
    and child welfare services, 260, 266
    and core competencies for social work, 3–4
    and cultural context of social work, 133
    and cultural influences in assessment process, 135
    and definitions of social work, 12
    and diversity awareness, 169–71
    and historical background of social work, 76
    and intersectional perspective on poverty, 213, *214t*, *215f*, 216, *218t*
    and intimate partner violence, 423
    and mental health social work, 338–39, 352
    and poverty in social work settings, 206
    and process of becoming a social worker, 22
    and professional organizations for social workers, 29
    racial categories, 170
    racial discrimination, 39, 76
    racialization, 169
    and social work profession, 7, 31
    See also anti-racism; racial justice; racism
racial justice
    and core competencies for social work, 64, *103t*, 160, 203, 279, 328, 437–38, 471, 509
    experiences of featured practitioners, 448
    and historical background of social work, 79, 83
    and regulation of social work field, 533
racism
    and Black Lives Matter movement, 446
    and diversity issues in social work, 194
    experiences of featured practitioners, 189, 245
    institutional racism, 134
    and intimate partner violence, 414
    and mental health assessments, 339
    and mental health social work, 360
    and process of becoming a social worker, 22
    and social work advocacy in political arena, 441
    and technological challenges, 133–34
    See also race issues in social work; racial justice
Rank, M., 214, 222
Rankin, Jeanette Pickering, 71, *440f*, 441
rape, 181–82. *See also* sexual abuse and assault

rapport, 149, 267, 430–31
Readdy, T., 248
reaffirmation, 100
Reagan, Ronald, 79, 81–83, 438
Reamer, F. G., 140–42, 177, 306
reapportionment, *452b*
recidivism, 357–58
reciprocity, 194
recreation specialists, *57t*
recruiting, 120
Red Cross, 43, 55
redistribution, 85
redistricting, *452b*
re-enablement, 310
referrals, 151, 175, 303, 336, 357
reform efforts of 19th century, 72–76
Reformation, 67
regulation of social work field, 531–33, *532t*
rehabilitation, 50, 178, 356, 389
Reid, P. N., 45
relative poverty, 42, 208
reporting standards, 256, 268–70
reproductive coercion, 419, 429
reproductive health, 419
Republican National Committee, 459
Republican Party, 81, 455, 457
research-informed practice, 279, 328, 367
residency requirements, 69–71
residential care, 260–61
residual social welfare, *46t*, 47–49, 60, 484
respect, 38–39, 141, 160, 172
resumes, 116
retirement, 369, 371, 375, 381, 391, 393–96, *393b*, 403
Reynolds, P., 165, 373
Rhode Island School of Design, 220
Rice, Ray, 412
Richan, W. C., 524
Richardson-Melecio, Jacqueline, 187–89
Richman, W., 449
Richmond, Mary, 66, *70b*, 75, 464
Ricks, Jan, 71–72
Ride for Five initiative, 44
risk assessment, 341
risk-taking behavior, 400
Risser, H., 245–46
road crews, *57t*
Rodriguez, D., 233
roles, 5, 354
Roman origins of social welfare, 67
Rome, S. H., 444–45, 464
Roosevelt, Franklin D., 66, 77, 88, 444
Rossi, P., 314
Rothman, D., 73
Rothman, J., 463–64
Rubin, A., 147
Rugy, V. D., 282

rural settings, 42, 67, 134, *207t*, 215, 320
Russia and Russian Federation, 465, 473, 478
Ryan, J., 385
Ryff, C. D., 377, 380

Safe Homes Act, 422
safety net programs, 49, 233. See also *specific program names*
Safety Planning with Battered Women: Complex Lives/Difficult Choices (Davies and Monti-Catania), 416–17
safety plans, *401b*
salaries of social workers, 102, 120, *121t*, 217
Salem, Massachusetts, 65, 88
Salsgiver, R. O., 164
Salvation Army, 55, *70b*
same-sex relationships, 11, 82, 234
Samples, M., 247
sanctions, 14, 243, 262, 264
sanitation programs, *57t*, 293, 307–8
Satcher, David, 41
Sawhill, I., 79
schema therapy, 296
S-CHIP, 286
schizophrenia, 335–36, 343–44
School Breakfast Program, 230
school health programs, *54b*
school meal programs, 51, 53, 209, 229–30
Schwartz, C. L., 223
scope of social work profession, 5–6, 57–58, 60, 130
Scotland, 477–78
Scots Charitable Society, *70b*
Scott, M. E., 511
Scott, W. D., 248
Second World nations, 478, *479b*, 481, *481t*, *482t*
Section 8, housing, 85, 210–11
Segal, E., 45
Segal, W., 45
segregation, 76. *See also* racism
selection, optimization, and compensation model, 379
self-awareness, *350b*
self-care, 120–21
self-determination and self-sufficiency, 141, 177, 191, 338–39, 361, 441, 527–28
Seneca Falls Conference, 65, 88
senescence, 390
September 11 2001 terrorist attacks, 501
Serbia, 484
service access assistance, 303
service advocacy, 305
service outreach, 305

Setting It Straight w/Ms. Gray, 372
settlement house movement, 75–76, 185
Seward, William, 88
Seward's Folly, 65, 88
sexism, 22, 414
sexual abuse and assault, 181–82, 257, 267–70, 412–13, 415–16, 422
sexuality, 39, 164, 213, 373. *See also* LGBTQ+ people
sexually-transmitted disease, 343–44
shadow welfare state, 51
Sheafor, B. W., 511
shelter services
    and diversity issues in social work, 168
    homeless shelters, *46t*
    and intimate partner violence, 422–23, 428–30
    and role of professional social workers, 27
    women's shelter social workers, 428–30
Shing Nam Hung, 97
short-term evidence-based interventions, 185–89
Sills, Faith, 282–83
Simmons College, 293
Simpson, P., 165, 373
Sinema, Kyrsten, 446
single-parent families, 131, 221, 222, 242, 250
single-payer systems, 284
site visits, 100
situational depression, 388
situational factors, *359t*
Sixth Amendment, 427
skills of social work, 137–39, *138b*
Skype, 118–19
slavery, 88
sleep quality, 387
social action activities, *184b*
Social Diagnosis (Richmond), *70b*
social distancing, 298, 472
social entrepreneurship, 482–83, 504
social environments, 12, 316
social factors and mental health assessment, *345t*
social insurance, 53, *54b*. *See also* Social Security system
social isolation, 425, 429
social justice
    and challenges facing social work field, 31
    and core competencies for social work, 64, *103t*, 130, 139, 140, 160, 203, 279, 328, 437–38, 471, 509
    and definitions of social welfare, 40–44
    experiences of featured practitioners, 448

and future of social work field, 522, 526
and global social welfare arena, 472, 483, *490b*, 495
and historical background of social work, 82, 85–86
and poverty in social work settings, 223
and role of professional social workers, 26, 27
and social work advocacy in political arena, 443–44
social media
    and critics of social welfare, *48b*
    and electoral politics, 459–60
    and employment opportunities for social workers, 117, 118–19
    and global social welfare arena, 472, 503
    and health care social work, 280
    and historical background of social work, 82, 83
    and intimate partner violence awareness, 412
    and job market for social workers, 91
    and residual vs. institutional social welfare, 49
Social Security Act, 77, 82, 440
Social Security Administration, 56, 208–9, 232, 381, 487
Social Security Income (SSI), 48, 210, 211, 229, 232, 234
Social Security system
    and critics of social welfare, *48b*
    and historical background of social work, 82
    as institutional social welfare, 46
    and intersectional perspective on poverty, 219
    and poverty measurements, 211
    and public social welfare, 53
    and residual vs. institutional social welfare, 50
    and retirement benefits, 392, *393b*, 394–95
    and social work targeting older adults, 369–70
Social Services Block Grant, 210
social supports, 178, 371
Social Threats to Aging Well in America, 382
social welfare, 35–61
    defining, 38–46
    and definitions of social work, 14
    experiences of featured practitioners, 44–45
    and global social welfare arena, 483, 494, 504
    misconceptions about, 36
    private social welfare, 55–56
    public social welfare, 53–55
    quiz on, 36–38

residual and institutional, 46–50
role of social work in, 56–60
scope of services, 51–52
and social work advocacy in political arena, 441
Social Welfare History Project, 67
Social Work (journal), 185, 517
Social Work, the Unloved Profession (Richan and Mendelsohn), 511
Social Work Day, 486
The Social Work Dictionary, 146, 208, 258, 289, 301
social work legislation, 459–60
social work organizations, 450–63
social work profession, 3–32
    current state of profession, 5–7
    definitions of, 8–19
    experiences of featured practitioners, 9–10, 96–97, 112, 142–43
    importance of professional memberships, 27–30
    and process of becoming a social worker, 19–25
    and role of professional social workers, 25–27
Social Work Research Group, 28
Social Work Today, 91
Social Work Yearbook, 376
"Social Worker Burnout: 8 Self-Care Tips," 353
societal lag, 132–34
sociology, 91–92
South America, 170, 478
South Asia, *479b*
Southern Poverty Law Center, 179, 439
Spade, J. Z., 164
Specht, H., 67
special consultative status, 489
special needs, 264–67, 320
Special Supplemental Nutrition Program for Women, Infants, and Children (WIC), 209, 229, 230, 233
special-interest groups, 29
specialist practice
    and accreditation of social workers, 101–2, 109–11
    and curriculum for social work majors, 519
    described, 146–47
    and employment opportunities for social workers, 119
    and evolution of social work, 155
    models of, *109b*
    and process of becoming a social worker, 24
    and regulation of social work field, 532
spiritual abuse, *415t*
stalking, *415t*
Stalking Resource Center, 414

standardized testing, 192
Stanton, Elizabeth Cady, 88
Starr, Ellen Gates, 70b, 76
start where the client is approach, 193
state boards of health, 70b
State Children's Health Insurance Program, 299
state departments of labor, 113
state licensing requirements, 16, 116–17
"State of America's Children 2021," 220
The State of America's Children (Children's Defense Fund), 2021, 40
state-level social welfare, 21, 55, 79, 81, 224t
status offenses, 251–52
Stein, Dodie M., 317–18
steps in professional helping, 148–52
stereotypes of social welfare recipients
    and aging, 403
    and child welfare services, 249
    and cultural influences in assessment process, 135
    experiences of featured practitioners, 85
    and historical background of social work, 68
    and mental health social work, 333b
    and misconceptions about social welfare, 48b
    and reform efforts of 19th century, 72
    and residual vs. institutional social welfare, 47–49
    and social reform of the early 20th century, 77
    and social work targeting older adults, 381
stereotypes of social workers, 57, 524
Stewart, Jimmy, 438
stigma associated with social welfare
    and children with special needs, 265
    and definitions of social work, 14
    experiences of featured practitioners, 297, 534
    and future of social work field, 527–28
    and health care support services, 313
    and intimate partner violence, 414
    and mental health in criminal justice system, 356, 357
    and mental health social work, 330, 339
    and poverty in social work settings, 205
    and residual vs. institutional social welfare, 47–49
    and social work targeting older adults, 380–81
Stoesz, D., 55–56, 67, 243
strengths-based assessment, 148, 339–40
strikes, 183
strokes, 153, 385

Strom-Gottfried, K., 308
student associations, 120
Sualp, Kenan, 496–98
subsidies, 51–52, 52t
substance abuse
    and definitions of social welfare, 39
    and global social welfare arena, 501
    and growth of social work field, 113
    and intimate partner violence, 416
    and macropractice settings, 184, 184b
    and mental health in criminal justice system, 358
    and mental health social work, 329, 330, 341–42
    and programs to aid the poor, 232
Substance Abuse and Mental Health Services Administration, 39
Sue, D, 166
Sue, D. W., 166
suffragists, 440f
suicide risk
    and intimate partner violence, 412, 429
    and medical issues in mental health assessments, 347
    and mental health assessments, 342–43
    and mental health social work, 352
    and retirement, 396
    and social work in social welfare system, 59
    and social work targeting older adults, 387, 399–403
Super, N., 385
supervised living arrangements, 152–53
supervision roles, 114t
Supplemental Nutritional Assistance Program (SNAP), 36f, 85
    and federal social welfare programs, 54b
    and immigrant populations, 233
    and poverty measurements, 209, 211, 212
    program described, 227, 228–29
    and public social welfare, 53, 54
    and residual vs. institutional social welfare, 46t, 49
    and role of social workers, 235
    and scope of social welfare programs, 51
Supplemental Poverty Measure, 169
Supplemental Security Act, 219
Supplemental Security Income (SSI), 210–11, 232
support groups, 384
support services, 305–15
supportive supervision, 306–7, 312
surplus food programs, 228
Sustainable Development Goals, 236, 485

Sutton, Amber, 427–28
Swedish University of Agricultural Sciences, 296
sympathy, 138b
Syracuse University, 84, 317
systemic racism, 447
systems-oriented approaches, 173–77, 319

Tan, J., 382
tax deductions, 52t
tax loopholes, 52t
Taylor, Breonna, 446–47
Tea Party Nation, 223
teachers, 458t
technology
    and definitions of social work, 12
    and evidence-based practices, 147
    and future of social work field, 528, 534–35
    and global social welfare arena, 472–73, 477
    and intimate partner violence, 415t
    and mental health social work, 349–50
    and social work targeting older adults, 382
    telemedicine and teletherapy, 180, 292, 320, 330, 354–55, 535
telephone call campaigns, 462
telephone-based reassurance programs, 330
Temporary Assistance to Needy Families (TANF)
    and EITC benefits, 234
    and federal social welfare programs, 54b
    and future of social work field, 527, 528
    and historical background of social work, 77, 80, 81
    and misconceptions about social welfare, 37
    and poverty measurements, 210
    program described, 224, 229
    as residual social welfare, 46t
    and residual vs. institutional social welfare, 46t
    and role of social workers, 235
    state-level programs, 205, 224t
terminal illness, 314–15
termination of services, 152
terminology issues in social work, 13–14, 148
Terrell, Joanne, 9–10
Texas, 94, 261, 455
texting, 472
theoretical foundations of social work, 161
Third World nations, 81, 479b, 481, 481t, 482t
third-party payers, 186, 309

Tice, C., 401
title protection, 19
Title XVIII, 382–83
Titmus, Richard, 45, 51
top-down professionalization, 476
Tourette's syndrome, 13
traditional family structure, 130–31, 222, 242
training programs, 85
Training School for Jewish Social Work, 177
transdisciplinary teams, *290t*
transience, 168
transitional care, 310
transplants, 318, 320
transportation services
    experiences of featured practitioners, 142, 318
    and future of social work field, 528
    and health care social work, 282, 292
    and impact of poverty, 210
    and mental health assessments, *359t*
    and risk factors for intimate partner violence, *417t*
    and role of professional social workers, 25, 40
    and social work advocacy in political arena, 459
    and social work targeting intimate partner violence, 430
    and social work targeting older adults, 382, 391, 398
transracial adoptions, 266
Trattner, W., 67, 292–93
trauma
    and mental health social work, 347
    posttraumatic stress syndrome (PTSS), 145–46
    psychological trauma, 40
    and social work targeting older adults, 387
    trauma-informed care, 144–45, 182
    traumatic stress response, 145
    See also intimate partner violence (IPV); sexual abuse and assault
Tribal Boundary and Annexation Survey, 165
Tropman, J. E., 464
Troubled Asset Relief Program, 204
Trump, Donald, 82, 83, 233, 439
trust, 172
tuition fees, 51
Turkey, 270–72
Twitter, 118, 459
typologies of welfare states, 483–84
Tyser, J., 248

Ukraine, 7, 465, 473–74, 478
undeveloped world, 480
undocumented immigrants, 168, 233–34
unemployment
    and child welfare, *255t*
    and child welfare services, 250
    and definitions of social welfare, 41
    and definitions of social work, 12
    and historical perspective on social welfare, 67, 81
    and intimate partner violence, 416
    and poverty in social work settings, 204
    and social welfare in colonial America, 69
Unfaithful Angels (Specht and Courtney), 511
unhoused people, 168. *See also* homelessness
Union of Soviet Socialist Republics, 478
United Kingdom, 7, 23, 477–78
United Nations (UN)
    and definitions of social work, 11
    and global social welfare arena, 473, 477–78, 484–87
    and job market for social workers, 91
    Millennium Declaration, 204
    Sustainable Development Goals, 236
    UN Children's Fund (UNICEF), 485, 489, 503
    UN Convention on the Rights of the Child, 253–54
    UN Department of Economic and Social Affairs, 489
    UN Developmental Programme, 485
    UN Educational, Scientific and Cultural Organization (UNESCO), 482
    UN High Commissioner for Refugees, 485, 489
    UN Office of the High Commissioner Human Rights, 504
    UN Population Fund, 485
    UN Sustainable Development Goals, 496
United Way, 14, 53, 55
universal health care coverage, 284. *See also* Affordable Care Act (ACA)
University at Albany, 187, 447
University Consortium for Child and Adult Services, 244
University of Alabama, 9, 96, 427, 499, 500, 512, 513
University of California at Santa Cruz, 220
University of Central Florida, 71, 112, 496, 500
University of Chicago, 499
University of Cincinnati, 71, 244, 353
University of Florida, 353
University of Houston, 499, 500, 504, 520
University of Iowa, 317
University of Kansas, 463
University of Louisville, 142
University of Michigan, 84
University of Montevallo, 427
University of Nebraska, 44
University of New Mexico, 520
University of New York, 447
University of North Carolina, 500
University of South Carolina, 500
University of Southern California, 317, 499
University of Tennessee, 296
University of Tulsa, 447
unworthy poor, 68–69, 79
Uppsala University, 296
urban settings, 42, 134, *207t*, 320
Ursuline nuns, 260
U.S. and World Population Clock, 242
U.S. Attorney's Office, 465
U.S. Bureau of Labor Statistics, 113, 281, 289, 329
U.S. Bureau of Statistics, 330
U.S. Census and Census Bureau
    and aging population data, 373, 376
    American Community Survey, 280
    and birth rates, 242
    and changing family structure, 11
    County Business Patterns, 281
    data on aging population, 374
    and definitions of social welfare, 42
    and diversity issues in social work, 165, 170, 173, 194
    and diversity measures, 167–69
    and health care support services, 309
    and "Hispanic" term, 133, 216, 248
    and intersectional perspective on poverty, 217–18
    and poverty in social work settings, *207t*
    and poverty measures, 39
    race and ethnicity data, 190
U.S. Centers for Medicare & Medicaid Services, 287
U.S. Congress
    and comparative approach to global social welfare, 478
    and food aid programs, 230
    and historical background of social work, 71, 78, 80
    and Hospital Insurance Trust Fund, 383
    and inclusive health care access, 285
    and issues of aging population, 392
    and programs to aid the poor, 227
    and social work advocacy in political arena, 441, 446, 460, 465
U.S. Constitution, 65, 76

U.S. Council on Social Work Education Kendall Institute, 91
U.S. Department of Agriculture, *48b*, 228, 229, 230–31
U.S. Department of Health and Human Services (HHS), 209–10, *209t*, 226–27, 257, 260, 286
U.S. Department of Homeland Security, 233
U.S. Department of Justice, 257
U.S. Department of Labor, 5, 28, 91, 99
U.S. House of Representatives, 54, 81, 115, 205, 442, 446, 453, 455, 460
U.S. International Development Finance Corporation, 487
U.S. Public Health Department, *70b*
U.S. Public Health Services, 313
U.S. Senate, 54, 115, 205, 442, 446, 453
U.S. Social Security Administration, *53f*
U.S. Supreme Court, 81–82, 234, 253, 451
U.S. Veterans' Bureau, 294

vagrancy laws, 69
Valentine, C. G., 164
values and beliefs
    and core competencies for social work, 140–42
    and diversity issues in social work, 160
    and mental health social work, 337–38
    and politics of social work, 443–44
    and practice of social work, 136
    and skills of social work, 138, *138b*
Van Hook, M. P., 374
Van Wormer, K., 312
Vanderbilt Medical Center, 296
Vanderbilt University, 296, 297
Vargas, A., 233
vascular dementia, 152–53
Vatican City, 478, 484
Veterans Health Administration, 286
veteran's programs and benefits, *46t*, 52–53, *54b*, 68–69, 71
veterinary social work, 110
Vietnam, 264
VIGOR (Victim Inventory of Goals, Options, and Risks), 420, 429
violence, 181–82, 184, *184b*, 245. *See also* intimate partner violence (IPV); trauma
Violence Against Women Act (VAWA), 422–23
Violent Crime Control and Law Enforcement Act, 422
Virginia Commonwealth University, 67, 142

virtual networks, 180
virtual services, 474
vision conditions, 386
VISTA, 445
volunteers and volunteer organizations
    and compassionate conservatism, 80–81
    experiences of featured practitioners, 84, 372, 497
    and friendly visitors, 74–75
    and micropractice settings, *181b*
    and role of professional social workers, 26
    and social reform of the 1960s, 78–79
    and social work in social welfare system, 58
    and social work targeting older adults, 378
Volunteers in Service to America, 79
Voter Challenge, 459
voting rights, 71
vulnerable populations
    and child welfare, *255t*
    and child welfare services, 251, 267
    and food aid programs, 229
    and global social welfare arena, 473
    and health care social work, 312–14
    and intersectional perspective on poverty, 215
    and regulation of social work field, 531
    and scope of social work profession, 57–58
    and social reform of the 1980s-1990s, 79
    and social work targeting older adults, 398–99
    undocumented immigrants, 234

wages, 204, 391
Wales, 477–78
Walker, Lenore, 418
Walla Walla University, 475
Wang, Y., 476
War on Poverty, 78, 81, 224, 235, 444
wars, 465
Washington University in St. Louis, 427
waste management services, 53. *See also* sanitation programs
water accessibility, 483
Watson, L. D., 512
WebMD, 516
Weismiller, T., 309, 444–45, 464
Welfare Reform Act of 1996, 80, 232
welfare state variables, *482t*
wellness training, 303
Werner, Terry, 44
West Side, Chicago, 76
West Virginia, 92

West Virginia University, 142
Western cultural hegemony, 525
Western Reserve University, *70b*
Wheeler, Etta Angell, *256b*
Whitaker, T., 309
White supremacists, 76–77, 83
widowhood, 68–69, 400–401
Wilensky, Harold, 46, 49–51, 484
Williamsburg, Virginia, *70b*
Williamson, Sharon, 353–54
Wilson, M., 309
Wilson, Mary Ellen, *256b*
Winston, Karen, 520–22
Wisconsin, 227
Wolk, J., 449
Women, Infants, and Children, 54, 78–79
Women against Abuse, 414
women as social workers, 354, 428–30. *See also* gender issues in social work
women's rights, 82, 88, 503
work ethic ideology, 79–80, 441
work requirements, 79, 81, 227
work roles of social workers, *114t*
workfare, 85
work-life balance, 96–97, 319
workplace participation, 172
Works Progress Administration, 77
World Bank, 39–40, 369, *479b*, 482
World Health Organization (WHO), 473, 485, 501
The World Is Flat (Friedman), 472
World Social Report, 473
World War I, 375
World War II, 374, 484
World Water Day, 486
worthy poor, 68, 69, 527
wraparound services, 292
Wren, Brianna, 397–98
Wyoming, 94, 253

xenophobia, 76, 179
Xu, Y., 476

Yeager, K. R., 342, 349
YMCA, 55, *70b*, 266, 487
Yoo, J. A., 421
Young, Sarah, 84
Young, Whitney M., Jr., 78
youth at risk, 252
youth programs, 266–67
YWCA, 55, 72, 266, 487

Zarit, J. M., 400
Zarit, S. H., 400
Zimmerman, George, 83
Zoom, 118–19
Zuckoff, A., 347